Lecture Notes in Computer Science

Lecture Notes in Artificial Intelligence **16830**

Founding Editor

Jörg Siekmann

The series Lecture Notes in Artificial Intelligence (LNAI) was established in 1988 as a topical subseries of LNCS devoted to artificial intelligence.

The series publishes state-of-the-art research results at a high level. As with the LNCS mother series, the mission of the series is to serve the international R & D community by providing an invaluable service, mainly focused on the publication of conference and workshop proceedings and postproceedings.

Diedrich Wolter · Gesina Schwalbe
Editors

KI 2026: Advances in Artificial Intelligence

49th German Conference on AI, KI 2026
Bremen, Germany, August 11–14, 2026
Proceedings

Springer

Editors
Diedrich Wolter
University of Lübeck
Lübeck, Germany

Gesina Schwalbe
Ulm University
Ulm, Germany

ISSN 0302-9743 ISSN 1611-3349 (electronic)
Lecture Notes in Artificial Intelligence
ISBN 978-3-032-32334-7 ISBN 978-3-032-32335-4 (eBook)
https://doi.org/10.1007/978-3-032-32335-4

LNCS Sublibrary: SL7 – Artificial Intelligence

This Springer imprint is published by the registered company Springer Nature Switzerland AG
The registered company address is: Gewerbestrasse 11, 6330 Cham, Switzerland

Preface

This volume contains the papers presented at KI2026: German Conference on Artificial Intelligence (KI 2026), held on August 11–14, 2026 in Bremen, Germany. KI 2026 was the 49th German Conference on Artificial Intelligence (AI) organized in cooperation with the German Section on Artificial Intelligence of the German Informatics Society (GI-FBKI, Fachbereich Künstliche Intelligenz der Gesellschaft für Informatik (GI) e.V.). The German AI Conference basically started 50 years ago with the first meeting of the national special interest group on AI within the GI on October 7, 1975. KI is one of the major European AI conferences and traditionally brings together academic and industrial researchers from all areas of AI, providing an ideal place for exchanging news and research results on theory and applications. While KI is primarily attended by researchers from Germany and neighboring countries, it warmly welcomes international participation. The technical program of KI 2026 featured paper presentations as well as four keynotes, one tutorial, a doctoral symposium, and twelve workshops. Overall, KI 2026 received 77 submissions from authors in 20 countries, which were single-blind reviewed, by at least three Program Committee members each, the majority of papers receiving four reviews. The Program Committee, comprising 88 experts from 11 countries, accepted 14 full papers (28.6% of the submissions in that category), 19 technical communications, and one extended abstract; overall, the acceptance rate across all paper categories was 42.9%. As highlights of this year's edition of the KI conference, the main program featured a dedicated industrial session co-organized with the Chamber of Commerce in the historic rooms of the Haus Schütting at Bremen's market square and a poster session in an inspiring atmosphere. We were honored that four prominent researchers kindly agreed to give keynote talks (alphabetical order):

- Randy Goebel
- Steven Schockaert
- Lea Schönherr
- Michael Spranger

We sincerely thank our keynote speakers for their inspiring presentations. As Program Committee chairs, we would also like to thank all authors for their interesting and valuable contributions, the Workshop and Tutorial Chairs Tanya Braun, Magnus Bender, and Alexander Steen, and the Doctoral Symposium Chairs Isabell Kuhlmann and Mena Leemhuis. Our special gratitude goes to the Program Committee, whose conscientious judgement ensured the high quality of the KI conference. Without their substantial voluntary work, this conference would not have been possible.

The following tutorials, workshops, and group meetings of the German AI society took place at KI 2026:

- ExTraSafe – 1st KI Workshop on Explainability, Transparency, and Safety organized by Benjamin Paaßen, Vera Schmitt, Thomas Kosch, Julius Schöning, Florian Rabe, Tim Schrills, and Daniel Neider

- Applications of Artificial Intelligence for Software Engineering (AI4SE) organized by Julien Siebert and Adam Trendowicz
- Workshop SIG Knowledge Management (Workshop FGWM) organized by Johannes Wichmann, Lisa Grewenig, and Pascal Reuss
- 3rd Workshop on Public Interest AI orgrnized by Theresa Züger and Hadi Asghari
- Puk 2026: Workshop Planning universal KI-(AI-)Systems organized by Stefan Edelkamp and Jürgen Sauer
- Agentic AI Systems, Welfare, Social Mechanisms, and Multi-Agent Ecosystems (AWESOME) organized by Johannes Fähndrich and Özgür Lütfü Özçep
- 3rd Workshop on AI in Production organized by Erik Voigt, Shamim Miroliaei, Ute Schmid, and Jakob Wagner
- Workshop on AI-Driven Cyber Forensics (AICF) organized by Roman Povalej, Johannes Fähndrich, Wilfried Honekamp, and Dirk Labudde
- Deduktionstreffen (DT 2026) organized by Florian Rabe and Uwe Waldmann
- ARDUOUS: 10th International Workshop on Annotation of Real World Data for Artificial Intelligence Systems organized by Kristina Yordanova, Emma Tonkin, and Gregory Tourte
- 6th Workshop on Humanities-Centred AI and 3rd International Workshop on AI in Society, Education and Educational Research (CHAI+AISSER 2026) organized by Sylvia Melzer, Stefan Thiemann, Hagen Peukert, Mads Rosendahl Thomsen, Jens Dörpinghaus, and Michael Tiemann
- Exploring Musical Cognition Through Musical Agent Systems organized by Diedrich Wolter and Nicola Hein
- Explaining Vision and Language Models: A Concept-Based Approach organized by Gesina Schwalbe, Jae Hee Lee, and Mahdi Pourghasem

Last not least, we would like to thank our sponsors for their support:

- German Section on Artificial Intelligence of the German Informatics Society (https://fb-ki.gi.de)
- Springer (https://www.springer.com)

May 2026

Serge Autexier
Gesina Schwalbe
Sirko Straube
Diedrich Wolter

Organization

Program Committee Chairs

Diedrich Wolter	University of Lübeck, Germany
Gesina Schwalbe	University of Ulm, Germany

Program Committee

Martin Atzmueller	Osnabrück University and German Research Center for Artificial Intelligence (DFKI), Germany
Kerstin Bach	Norwegian University of Science and Technology, Norway
Korinna Bade	Anhalt University of Applied Science, Germany
Kaja Balzereit	Hochschule Bielefeld University of Applied Sciences and Arts (HSBI), Germany
Joachim Baumeister	denkbares GmbH, Germany
Christoph Benzmüller	Otto-Friedrich-Universität Bamberg and Freie Universität Berlin, Germany
Ralph Bergmann	Trier University and German Research Center for Artificial Intelligence (DFKI), Germany
Sebastian Berndt	Technische Hochschule Lübeck, Germany
Niklas Beuter	Technische Hochschule Lübeck, Germany
Petra Bevandic	University of Zagreb, Croatia
Ulf Brefeld	Leuphana Universität Lüneburg, Germany
Alexander Diedrich	Helmut-Schmidt-Universität, Germany
Jörg Dietrich	AUMOVIO Germany GmbH, Germany
Stefan Edelkamp	Czech Technical University in Prague, Czech Republic
Zoe Falomir	Umeå University, Sweden
Bettina Finzel	Otto-Friedrich-Universität Bamberg, Germany
Johannes Fähndrich	Hochschule für Polizei Baden-Württemberg, Germany
Johannes Fürnkranz	Johannes Kepler University Linz, Austria
Marcel Gehrke	University of Hamburg, Germany
Birte Glimm	Universität Ulm, Germany
Simon Richard Goorney	Aarhus University, Denmark
Hanno Gottschalk	TU Berlin, Germany

Lisa Grewenig	German Research Center for Artificial Intelligence (DFKI), Germany
Jürgen Großmann	Fraunhofer FOKUS, Germany
Barbara Hammer	Bielefeld University, Germany
Heinz Handels	University of Lübeck and DFKI Lübeck, Germany
Tom Hanika	University of Hildesheim, Germany
Jennifer Hannig	Technische Hochschule Mittelhessen, Germany
Anselm Haselhoff	Ruhr West University of Applied Sciences, Germany
Mattias Heinrich	University of Lübeck, Germany
Sebastian Hobert	Technische Hochschule Lübeck, Germany
Burkhard Hoppenstedt	HfWU Nürtingen-Geislingen, Germany
Marina Höhne	University of Potsdam and Leibniz Institute for Agricultural Engineering and Bioeconomy, Germany
Moussa Kassem-Sbeyti	Karlsruher Institut für Technologie, Germany
Gabriele Kern-Isberner	Technische Universität Dortmund, Germany
Frank Klawonn	Ostfalia University of Applied Sciences, Germany
Matthias Klusch	German Research Center for Artificial Intelligence (DFKI), Germany
Mario Koddenbrock	Hochschule für Technik und Wirtschaft Berlin, Germany
Stefan Kopp	Bielefeld University, Germany
Samuel Kounev	University of Würzburg, Germany
Lars Kunze	University of the West of England, UK
Christoph Lange	Fraunhofer Institute for Applied Information Technology FIT and RWTH Aachen University, Germany
Jae Hee Lee	University of Hamburg, Germany
Tatjana Legler	RPTU Kaiserslautern-Landau, Germany
Johannes Liebenow	University of Lübeck, Germany
Adriano Lucieri	German Research Center for Artificial Intelligence (DFKI) GmbH, Germany
Bernd Ludwig	University of Regensburg, Germany
Lukas Malburg	University of Trier and German Research Center for Artificial Intelligence (DFKI), Germany
Georgii Mikriukov	Leibniz Institute for Agricultural Engineering and Bioeconomy (ATB), Germany
Till Mossakowski	Osnabrück University, Germany
Annika Mütze	Osnabrück University, Germany
Bernhard Nebel	University of Freiburg, Germany
Annina Neumann	Flensburg University of Applied Sciences, Germany

Falco Nogatz	BAUHAUS, Germany
Azarm Nowzad	AUMOVIO SE, Germany
Benjamin Paaßen	Bielefeld University, Germany
Heiko Paulheim	University of Mannheim, Germany
Florian Rabe	FAU Erlangen-Nürnberg, Germany
Tobias Riedlinger	Technical University of Berlin, Germany
Nele Russwinkel	University of Lübeck, Germany
Jürgen Sauer	University of Oldenburg, Germany
Kai Sauerwald	University of Hagen, Germany
Ute Schmid	University of Bamberg, Germany
Vera Schmitt	TU Berlin, Germany
Claudia Schon	Hochschule Trier, Germany
Lutz Schröder	Friedrich-Alexander-Universität Erlangen-Nürnberg, Germany
René Schumann	HES-SO University of Applied Sciences Western Switzerland, Switzerland
Mark Schutera	DHBW Ravensburg, Germany
Sibylle Schwarz	Hochschule für Technik, Wirtschaft und Kultur Leipzig, Germany
Friedhelm Schwenker	Ulm University, Germany
Dietmar Seipel	University of Würzburg, Germany
Youssef Shoeb	Continental AG, Germany
Myra Spiliopoulou	Otto von Guericke University Magdeburg, Germany
Frieder Stolzenburg	Harz University of Applied Sciences, Germany
Antonin Sulc	Lawrence Berkeley National Laboratory, USA
Michael Thielscher	University of New South Wales, Australia
Matthias Thimm	FernUniversität in Hagen, Germany
Daniela Thyssens	University of Hildesheim, Germany
Jan-Philipp Töberg	Bielefeld University, Germany
Stefan Ultes	University of Bamberg, Germany
Antonia van Betteray	Osnabrück University, Germany
Uwe Waldmann	Max Planck Institute for Informatics, Germany
Felix Weitkämper	German University of Digital Science, Germany
Arno Wilhelm-Weidner	VDI/VDE-IT, Germany
Stefan Woltran	TU Wien, Austria
Franz Wotawa	Technische Universität Graz, Germany
Kristina Yordanova	University of Greifswald, Germany
Özgür Lütfü Özcep	University of Hamburg, Germany

Additional Reviewers

Beecks, Christian
Brügge, Nele
Bühl, Johannes
Dankworth, Raik
Danzinger, Philipp
Feldo, Marek
Grillmeyer, Daniel
Haufe, Cedric
Knoblauch, Dorian
Krug, Markus
Liebl, Magnus
Metz, Shirley
Michalczyk, Jakub
Mustaf, Daham
Neubauer, Kai
Papenfuß, Dennis
Rapp, Max
Rohwer, Ivo
Rückschloß, Kilian
Schiebel, Tilman
Schubert, Julian
Seibel, Marc
Shrestha, Abhishek
Stenger, Michael
Theiner, Markus
Wiegers, Nina
Zwicklbauer, Stefan

Contents

Extended Abstracts

Full Papers

A Constraint-Based Stockyard Planning Problem on a Realistic Time-Dependent Setting

Viktoria Abbenhaus[(✉)], Sven Löffler, and Petra Hofstedt

Chair of Programming Languages and Compiler Construction, Brandenburg University of Technology Cottbus-Senftenberg, Konrad-Wachsmann-Allee 5, Cottbus, Germany

{viktoria.abbenhaus,sven.loeffler,hofstedt}@b-tu.de

Abstract. Effective planning and scheduling of industrial processes are vital across numerous industries, including the daily operations of coal mining logistics. The Stockyard Planning Problem (SPP) aims to address these tasks in stockyards efficiently and cost-effectively. This research examines a realistic scenario involving an opencast mine linked to a stockyard, where bulk materials of varying quality are stored on stockpiles and transported by train. We approach the SPP in this setting using constraint programming and develop a model that accounts for the time-dependent nature of the problem: materials can be stored on stockpiles only for a limited duration before export, and transitions between machine operating states introduce blocking periods. The primary objective of the SPP in this scenario is to facilitate seamless operations of both opencast mining and stockyard activities. It is crucial to ensure continuous material flow over conveyor belts to prevent stoppages in mining operations while meeting export requirements.

Keywords: Planning and Scheduling · Decision Support Systems · Stockyard Planning Problem · Constraint Programming · CSP · COP

1 Introduction

In a growing global economy, the demand for electrical energy increases steadily, positioning industries like coal mining as key players in fulfilling this need. The coal mining supply chain encompasses the complete journey from extraction to transportation via trains or ships across diverse transshipment points to the end customer. A bottleneck in this supply chain is the logistical challenge of transporting coal from mines to customers, exacerbated by the inconsistent availability of transport vehicles, such as ships or trains, when coal is ready for transport. Consequently, stockyards play a crucial role in storing coal until further transportation. Stockyards offer the advantage of maintaining a reserve volume to meet demands when direct supply from the mine is insufficient. However, coal's quality deteriorates with prolonged storage, necessitating careful management.

D. Wolter and G. Schwalbe (Eds.): KI 2026, LNAI 16830, pp. 3–16, 2027.
https://doi.org/10.1007/978-3-032-32335-4_1

Additionally, stacking and reclaiming operations require substantial time and energy, given the weight and slow speed of the machines involved. This challenges the ability to create robust schedules in logistic operations at stockyards to meet the throughput demand while minimizing the overall cost. The schedule must furthermore face conflicts between vehicle location and the selection of appropriate stockpiles for stacking and reclaiming operations. This work focusses on one specific real stockyard setting and aims to create an operational schedule of machines and vehicles to process the incoming material from an opencast mine and fulfill the export demand via trains.

The remainder of this work is sectioned as follows: first, the problem setting is introduced. Section 2 summarizes related approaches concerning the SPP. Section 3 describes the approach to model the problem setting, and Sect. 4 describes the model to solve the SPP with constraint programming based on the abstraction, including variables, constraints, objective function, and search strategy. Afterwards, the model is evaluated in Sect. 5 and, finally, Sect. 6 draws a conclusion and summarizes possibilities to refine the work, adapt it for different scenarios, or further improve the solution process.

1.1 Problem Setting Introduction

This section illustrates the Stockyard Planning Problem (SPP) within the specific real-world context of this research. The primary objective is the efficient transportation of coal from the mine to export trains, utilizing stockpiles as necessary. Key components of the system include the mine, stockpiles, a network of conveyor belts, specialized material transport machines (stacker-reclaimer, distributer, and shifter), and export trains, as depicted in Fig. 1.

Positioned at the top left of Fig. 1, the mine extracts two distinct coal qualities, without the possibility of mixing to create new material types. The coal is continuously transported to the stockyard, forming an *import plan* that evolves as mass flows from the mine are monitored. Sudden variations in imported mass necessitate adaptive planning.

The conveyor belt network encompasses belts $B1$ to $B5$, each unidirectional. Belt $B1$ facilitates import from the mine to the stockyard, while export is managed via belts $B4$ and $B5$ to two train tracks, $T1$ and $T2$, and $T3$ and $T4$, respectively. Conveyor belts operate at a standard speed of approximately 6 m per seconds [3]. A distribution machine VD (short for vehicle to distribute), located on belt $B1$, partitions material with a 5% precision to belts $B2$ and $B3$. Material on belt $B2$ is directly transported to the train tracks $T3$ and $T4$, while belt $B3$ supplies the stockpiles. Composed of two stockpiles, the stockyard subdivides each into stockpile areas SPk, typically three areas per stockpile. Areas $k \in \{1, 2, 3\}$ are northern, while $k \in \{4, 5, 6\}$ are southern with a shared connection to belt $B3$. Stockpiles hold a maximum of 75.6 kt, spanning 395 m in length and 30 m in width. The SR (stacker-reclaimer vehicle), necessary for stacking and reclaiming, operates on belt $B3$ servicing all stockpile areas.

The material shifting machine VS specializes in direct transfer between two successor belts without partitioning, as VD can do. $VS1$, stationed on belt $B3$,

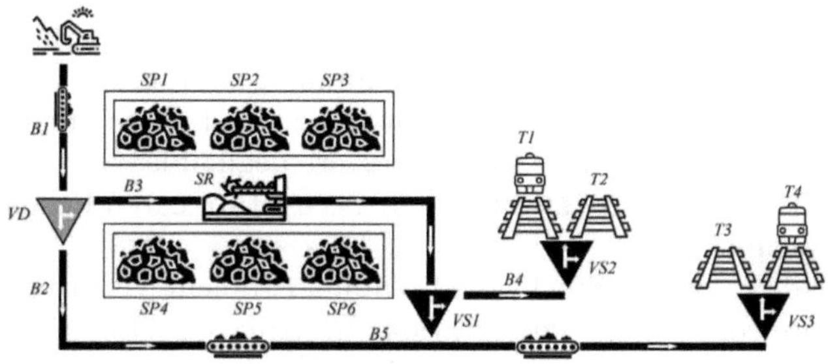

Fig. 1. Schematic illustration of the stockyard system.

redirects material to either belt $B4$ or $B5$. Additional machines, $VS2$ and $VS3$, support train loading by channeling material from belts $B4$, and $B5$, respectively, to tracks. For exporting material from the stockyard, four train tracks accommodate up to four trains, but only two may be loaded simultaneously due to $VS2$ and $VS3$ constraints. Switching operating states for machines of type VS takes 2 min. Train arrivals and material requests adhere to a timetable. While trains queue on the tracks, only one train is served simultaneously per track. Efficient planning is crucial to manage potential mismatches between mining activity and export demands, whether due to maintenance or technical issues.

The *goal of the SPP* in the given setting is to determine optimal sequences of machine operating states and state transitions to achieve planned import and export efficiently in terms of time and cost.

2 Related Work

Researches addressing the challenges of SPP varies significantly in terms of import and export mechanisms, operational site layout, machine movements, scheduling objectives, and time scaling.

Boland et al. [4] were the first to define the Stockyard Planning Problem and presented a study targeting operations at the Port of Newcastle's stockyard with ship terminals, aiming to maximize throughput. They developed a method to plan allocation and reclaiming operations weeks before the ships arrive at the terminal. However, their approach does not account for the conveyor belt networks, thus limiting its applicability to scenarios where these are crucial.

Hanoun et al. [8] tackled the issue of coordinating train arrivals and coal delivery times at a stockyard. Their export system relies on trains operating on dual tracks, with known estimated arrival times and incoming material from a coal mine. Their planning horizon spans one week, using step intervals of one hour. This methodology excludes the detailed considerations of vehicle movements and conveyor belt operations, which is inadequate for settings requiring planning that involves machine state changes.

Löffler et al. [9] approached the SPP by employing a pure Constraint Programming model that abstracts time using time frames and material movement within the stockyard. Breuß et al. [5] expanded on this model through a hybrid approach that integrates Constraint Programming and search techniques with fix-sized time frames. Both methods assume predefined import plans and employ large time frames where machine movements are negligible. Our research focuses on scenarios with short time intervals that necessitate careful considerations of machine movements.

Existing research on the Stockyard Planning Problem with time sensitivity is scarce, especially concerning configurations utilizing very fine time scales. This study aims to address this gap by tackling the planning challenges in this specific, realistic scenario.

3 Abstraction for the Problem

In this section, we describe the non-dynamic aspects of the stockyard abstraction. The dynamic components that require modeling as variables for a Constraint Optimization Problem (COP) will be addressed in Sect. 4.

The continuous operation of the system is abstracted using time steps of fixed length, denoted as Δ. Our goal is to optimize activities such as export and machine movements on the stockyard over a specific time horizon. The input from the mine is only available a short time before the material enters the stockyard system. Therefore, the problem is highly dependent on timing, requiring precise knowledge of mass location and material quality across the system in each Δ time step. In this scenario, Δ is determined by the frequency of mass measurements from the mine and is set to 15 s, i.e., $\Delta = 15\ s$. Combining multiple steps results in a schedule for the entire horizon, for example, one hour where $1\ h = n \cdot \Delta = 240 \cdot 15\ s$. This results in a step-by-step plan of the operating schedule.

For a step size of few seconds, most conveyor belt specifications indicate that material cannot be completely transferred across them in a single step. Therefore, belts are divided into consecutive segments b_j such that material traverses one segment per step. The length $\hat{l}$ of these belt segments is calculated from the step size Δ and the speed v of conveyor belts: $\hat{l} = v \cdot \Delta$. The maximum load capacity of conveyor belt segments $\hat{c}$ is determined by the maximum capacity c of conveyor belts, and the step size Δ: $\hat{c} = \frac{c}{\Delta}$.

Machines of type *VD* and *VS* have one preceding and two succeeding conveyor belt segments $v^{pred}, v^{succ1}, v^{succ2}$. Depending on the machine's operating state (refer to Sect. 4.2), material from the predecessor segment is transferred to either the first or the second successor segment, or to both in case of *VD* with operating state other than 0 % or 100 %. Depending on the material location on the stockpiles and the load of available trains, machines may need to switch operating state to manage the incoming material, leading to a machine type specific blocking time. During this period, the machine is unavailable, meaning that the corresponding belt segment serving the machine must remain material-free.

Each *world vector* q_i describes the configuration of the stockyard at a time step i and includes the location and quality of material masses on the conveyor belts, the content of stockpile areas, the operating states, and the state of train loading, i.e., all time step dependent variables introduced in the following Sect. 4.2. World vectors serve as input for the planning algorithm.

Enhancing Rolling Solutions: Preliminary experiments indicate that the complexity of solving the SPP increases exponentially with the step horizon length. To address this challenge, a rolling approach is employed to plan, for instance, $n = 100$ steps: Instead of planning the full instance at once, we plan a shorter sequence, $\tilde{n} = 20$, and subsequently extend the plan until the total of n steps is reached. This approach reduces overall computation time, but it may prevent finding a global optimal solution or any solution if intermediate steps lead to dead ends. The planning process is not designed to anticipate conditions beyond a set time horizon. If the world vector from the last step of a preceding solution is used as the starting point for the next, $q_0^k = q_{\tilde{n}}^{k-1}$, there is a risk of encountering unsolvable configurations. For instance, excessive material might be routed towards a train track with no remaining capacity, forcing a dead-end scenario where no further planning can be achieved. To mitigate this, it is critical to allow sufficient buffer time for machines to change operating states and reroute material, either to another train or to stockpiles. Therefore, it is beneficial to use prior world vectors, $q_{\tilde{n}-\delta}^{k-1}$, where δ is optimally chosen to balance the need for resolving potential issues and the desire to plan extensively in advance.

4 A Constraint Optimization Problem

In order to efficiently simulate and plan the operational schedule within the stockyard, thereby resolving the SPP for the setting, we define and model a Constraint Optimization Problem (COP). Solutions to the COP represent valid sequences of processes within the stockyard system.

The subsequent sections will first describe the foundational concepts of constraint programming. We will then introduce variables and constraints necessary for modeling a COP that addresses the aforementioned SPP.

4.1 Foundations of Constraint Programming

Constraint Programming (CP) is a versatile paradigm used to model and solve various combinatorial problems, often of NP-hard complexity, such as scheduling or rostering issues [10].

A Constraint Satisfaction Problem (CSP) $P = (X, D, C)$ is characterized by a set of variables $X = \{X_1, \ldots, X_n\}$, finite domains of potential values for each variable $D = \{D_1, \ldots, D_n\}$, and a collection of constraints $C = \{C_1, \ldots, C_m\}$, each constraining a subset of the variables. Constraints define permissible combinations of variable values within their respective subset. A solution to a CSP is an assignment of values from respective domains to all variables such that no constraint is violated [2].

If a CSP P is augmented with an objective function $f : X \to \mathbb{R}$ which is to be maximized or minimized, the problem transforms into a Constraint Optimization Problem (COP) $P' = (X, D, C, f)$ [13].

To solve CSPs and COPs computationally, a constraint solver employs mathematical relations and strategies that explore the solution space. Typically, it partitions the domains using backtracking search according to specific strategies and prunes domains through constraint propagation [2]. There exists a multitude of search strategies, generally leveraging combinations of variable and value selection techniques. A universally optimal search algorithm applicable across all problems does not exist due to varying characteristics that necessitate different selection strategies.

Enhancing solver convergence can benefit from the introduction of redundant constraints. These additional constraints, although not providing new information to the model, restrict the search space by eliminating inconsistencies [6] or filtering out sub-optimal solutions [7].

4.2 Variables and Domains

The problem is modeled in discrete time steps. For each time step $i \in \{0, \dots, n\}$, a particular set of variables and constraints is defined.

The input I for material entering the system is represented as a sequence of mass-material tuples $(Inp_i^{mass}, Inp_i^{mat})$ for each time step i. In addition to the variable input dependent on the workload from the mines, there are certain fixed aspects given directly by the stockyard system and the problem setting. For instance, the maximum capacity and containing material of each stockpile area are predetermined, allowing the maximum lay time of material within each area to be inherently defined. To accurately model the movement of the stacker-reclaimer vehicle SR in this temporal context, it is essential to understand the spatial bounds of all stockpile areas. Only when SR is within these bounds can it perform operations on the area. Regarding the export of material from the stockyard, the pre-determined schedule of train arrivals, including specific tracks and material requests, is assumed to be provided and be accessed by a trains' ID.

Conveyor Belt Segments: For each conveyor belt segment b_j two variables are defined per time step i and $j \in \{0, \dots, \#beltSegments\}$ to encapsulate mass and material quality held by the segment at that moment, while a material value of 0 signifies no material on the belt segment, while values 1 and 2 correspond to materials of quality 1 and 2, respectively: $belt_{i,j}^{mass} \in \{0, \dots, \hat{c}\} \subset \mathbb{N}, belt_{i,j}^{mat} \in \{0, 1, 2\}$.

Stockpile Areas: Stockpile areas have specific characteristics per time step i: a current filling level $sp_{i,k}^{mass} \in \{0, \dots, SPk^{maxCapacity}\} \subset \mathbb{N}$, material age $sp_{i,k}^{age} \in \{0, \dots, SPk^{maxAge}\} \subset \mathbb{N}$, and a defined cutting edge where the stacker-reclaimer must be positioned to interact $sp_{i,k}^{cutEdge} \in \{SPk^{left}, \dots, SPk^{right}\}$. Variables are assigned to each stockpile area SPk for $k \in \{1, \dots, 6\}$ per time step i. Areas' material is fixed by the stockyard setting, and therefore not modeled as variables.

Machines: Any change in the operating state of a vehicle or machine results in a blocking period over a certain amount of time steps, reflecting the real-time duration required for state transitions. This is managed via a blocking variable that serve as a counter: initialized at the moment of transition, it decreases each subsequent time step until it reaches 0. Only at this point can the machine engage in material transport or perform operational state switches. The upper limit of blocking variables varies according to machine type.

For the vehicle *SR*, key attributes include its operation status $sr_i^{state} \in \{-1, 0, 1\}$ (stacking as 1, reclaiming as -1, conveying as 0, indicating inactivity concerning material and stockpiles), its position $sr_i^{position} \in \{SR^{min}, \ldots, SR^{max}\}$, the current served stockpile area $sr_i^{stack} \in \{1, \ldots, 6\}$, and potential blocking time $sr_i^{blocked} \in \{0, \ldots, SR^{maxBlocked}\} \subset \mathbb{N}$ per time step i. The conveying state indicates inactivity concerning material and stockpiles.

The machine *VD*, capable of splitting material between two successor belts in increments of 5 %, has a variable per time step i to denote the material splitting ratio: $vd_i^{state} \in \{0, \ldots, 20\}$. A value of 0 indicates 0% splitting with complete transfer to successor belt segment 1, whereas a value of 20 represents 100% splitting to successor belt segment 2, with intermediate values denoting respective proportional distributions. It does not have a blocking variable, as it can change its operating state instantly.

Machines of type *VS* are characterized by two variables per machine: one for the operating state $vs_{i,j}^{state} \in \{0, 1\}$ and another for the blocking duration $vs_{i,j}^{blocked} \in \{0, \ldots, VSj^{maxBlocked}\} \subset \mathbb{N}$, for all $j \in \{1, 2, 3\}$.

Tracks and Export: Modeling the export involves defining multiple variables per track $j \in \{1, 2, 3, 4\}$ for each time step i: current train ID $track_{i,j}^{trainId} \in \mathbb{N}$, train is presence status $track_{i,j}^{present} \in \{0, 1\}$, track blocking status due to departing trains $track_{i,j}^{blocked} \in \{0, \ldots, track^{maxBlocked}\}$, and the train's loading status $track_{i,j}^{load} \in \{0, \ldots, train^{maxLoad}\}$. The train ID facilitates the retrieval of requested material from the track's schedule of train arrivals. In case of multiple train queues on a track, a train may be present while the track remains blocked for it by the predecessor train.

4.3 Constraints

To efficiently model the processes occurring within the stockyard, a series of constraints is designed for the time step indices $i \in \{0, \ldots, n-1\}$.

Conveyor Belt Segments: For most conveyor belt segments, the loaded material is transferred to the subsequent segment in the next time step. Exceptions to this rule exist, such as segments positioned directly before a machine, which will be further elucidated below. The material type equals 0 only if the mass equals 0, too. The initial belt segment b_0 is loaded with input specific to the corresponding time step Inp_i^{mass}, and Inp_i^{mat}, respectively. While many variables remain constant, systems flexibility necessitates modeling variables for intermediate segments to accurately depict system operations at any given moment.

Stockpile Areas: For the following equations, let $k \in \{1, \ldots, 6\}$. The age of materials in stockpile areas increases with each time step except when empty. When a stockpile area becomes empty, its age is reset to zero.

For stockpile areas not being served by the *SR* vehicle, the mass remains unchanged. The mass of the stockpile area being worked on by *SR* changes according to *SR*'s operating state:

$$sp_{i+1,k}^{mass} = \begin{cases} sp_{i,k}^{mass}, & k \neq sr_i^{stack} \\ sp_{i,k}^{mass} + sr_i^{state} \cdot belt_{i,j}^{mass}, & k = sr_i^{stack}. \end{cases} \tag{1}$$

Given the relatively slow movement of *SR*, transitioning operations between different stockpile areas is expedited when transitioning from a position on area p closer to the target position on area q. Hence, the precise location for the vehicle on the stockpile area must be calculated. The so-called cut edge is determined by the present mass, the maximum mass w one meter of a stockpile can accommodate, and the boundary positions per stockpile area:

$$sp_{i,k}^{cutEdge} = SP_k^{right} - \lfloor \frac{sp_{i,k}^{mass}}{w} \rfloor. \tag{2}$$

Machines: Material is propagated from the predecessor belt segment to the successor segments by machines VD and VS. The material types of successor segments match the predecessors' segments' type (if material is passed to it) or equal zero. To model how VD partitions material in a finite domain setting, the mass split is rounded:

$$\begin{aligned} belt_{i+1,v^{succ1}}^{mass} &= \lfloor belt_{i,v^{pred}}^{mass} \cdot (1 - \frac{v_i^{state}}{20}) \rfloor \\ belt_{i+1,v^{succ2}}^{mass} &= belt_{i,v^{pred}}^{mass} - belt_{i+1,v^{succ1}}^{mass}. \end{aligned} \tag{3}$$

A machine can only manage material if its associated blocking variable equals zero. Otherwise, the predecessor belt segment must not contain any material. If a changeover in the operating state occurs, the blocking variable is set to the machine-specific maximum, as detailed for all machine types v in Sects. 1.1 and 4.2. The blocking duration for the stacker-reclaimer varies based on the specific transition. The *SR* moves at 20 m per minute. A switch between stacking and reclaiming or vice versa requires a blocking time of 2 min, while a switch to or from conveying halves the time. A 180-degree turn between stockpiles takes 5 min.

To serve a stockpile area, the stacker-reclaimer must position itself ($sr_i^{position}$) near the respective cut edge, the interface at which material is placed or removed. Since the cut edge $sp_{i,k}^{cutEdge}$ is determined by the stockpiles' mass, the adjustment is smooth and does not block the stacker-reclaimer for minor movements slower than its maximum speed.

$$sr_i^{stack} = k \implies sr_i^{position} = sp_{i,k}^{cutEdge} \tag{4}$$

Trains and Tracks: Managing material export via trains necessitates modeling respective configurations. If no train is present or a train in blocking the track, the respective shifting machine $v \in \{vs2, vs3\}$ must not allow material on its predecessor conveyor belt segment.

To enhance flexibility, no constraint enforces train departures based solely on load, allowing the model to choose optimal departure times. Similar to other vehicles undergoing operational state transitions, train departures ($track^{present}_{i,l} = 1 \wedge track^{present}_{i+1,l} = 0$) cause $track^{blocked}_{i+1,l}$ to be set to $track^{maxBlocking}$. The blocking variable decreases every iteration until it equals zero. When a train is present on a track, it is loaded with material from the associated belt segment, provided the material matches the train's requirements. Should the material not match, or if the track is blocked, or no train is present at all, no mass is permitted on the predecessor segment of the respective shifting machine.

Redundant Constraints: Certain configurations, forbidden by the stockyard's structural setup and to avert dead ends, are implemented as constraints to expedite the solving process. They apply as if-then constraints. If no trains demand the imported material by the mine on tracks $T3$ or $T4$ for the next six steps, *VD* must route the material stream over to the stockpile area, enabling it to be further transported to trains on $T1$ or $T2$, or stacked by *SR*. Should no train be present for the next four steps, *SR* must not be in reclaiming state, i.e., $sr^{state}_i \neq -1$. The chosen step numbers reflect the presence of six belt segments between *VD*, with a minimum of four between *SR* and the tracks. If no trains are poised to accept the imported material for the subsequent four steps, *SR* must be engaged in operational states conducive to stacking material onto stockpiles, i.e., *SR* must serve a stockpile of the imported material type and be in stacking state (1). Should only one train present be anticipated for the next four steps across the system, *SR* must serve a stockpile with the required material. For machines *VS2* and *VS3* operating track bundles, the condition holds that if only a single train is present, the machine must direct all material towards the track where the train is stationed. These additional constraints ensure continuity in stockyard operations.

4.4 Soft Constraints and Objective Function

The aforementioned section discussed hard constraints necessary to accurately model real processes in the stockyard. To ensure the stockyard system's functionality beyond the planned time horizon and fine-tune the solution, soft constraints are introduced, which should ideally be satisfied to avoid dead ends, but can be violated if necessary.

Concerning stacker-reclaimer's operating states, it is unfavorable to reclaim material while simultaneously importing material, as the main focus is on serving the mine rather than any export trains. The reclaiming state (-1) should be avoided if material is on belt $B1$ (see Fig. 1). Conversely, if trains can be served and no import occurs, the reclaiming state is favored. Both soft constraint are associated with boolean variables, summarized to m_p and included in the optimization function (see Eq. 5), weighted slightly negatively with ω_p.

$$f(X) = maximize(m_p \cdot \omega_p + m_{exp} \cdot \omega_{exp} + m_{op} \cdot \omega_{op} + m_l \cdot \omega_l) \tag{5}$$

A solution of the COP should result in an efficient plan of operations in the stockyard, fully processing imports and maximizing exports. Imported material must reach the first conveyor belt segment at each time step i, thus not participating in optimization value calculations. The objective function maximizes the export m_{exp} while minimizing changes in operating states m_{op} and limiting any penalties. Equation 5 describes the optimization function, where m represents a count or sum, and ω refers to the respective weight. To maximize the export, m_{exp} accumulates all masses exported by trains over the four tracks, with ω_{exp} as a high positive integer. Operating states should remain stable to minimize blocking time and increase economic efficiency. The value m_{op} counts steps i where operating state changes over all machines. Since the objective function is maximized but changes in operating states should be minimized, the weight ω_{op} is a high negative value. In reality, it is rare for all trains to be loaded with exactly the same masses. They are likely to be slightly under- or overloaded. However, it is favorable to load not more or less than a given maximum load (slightly lower than the physical maximum). The variable m_l summarizes the absolute difference in departing train loads from the favored value with ω_l being a high negative value.

5 Computational Evaluation

Though the problem seems easy to solve, complete information about incoming material is only available at a very late stage, the solution must be calculated quickly, which drastically increases the complexity of the problem.

To evaluate the model, a computational evaluation was performed using five real scenarios provided by our research partners. Physical aspects, such as the fillings of stockpiles, machine states, and train arrival times, were given and must be manually translated into initial world vectors. The incoming material per scenario is given and modeled as a sequence of (mass, material)-chunks per 15 s. The scenarios were chosen to include scenarios that start in a fully operational setting, with train loading in progress and material being transported across the stockyard. Another scenario type features trains demanding both types of material, and the mine starting to import material only after an hour. A third type of scenario involves material being imported by the mine with no train available for export at the start. In each scenario, at least three trains are loaded. The experiment aimed to execute solution steps on the initial world vector for a total time horizon of three hours. The world vector derived from solving the SPP was compared with the actual data from the stockyard at this point in time. The primary focus was on train departure times and final loads, as they indicate the efficiency of the stockyard to meeting export demand.

All experiments were performed on a Lenovo computer equipped with a 13th Gen Intel(R) Core(TM) i7-13700H processor featuring 14 cores, a clock speed of 2.40 GHz, and 32 GB of RAM, operating at 1600 MHz. The operating system used was Microsoft Windows 11 Pro. We utilized the Java programming language with JDK version 23, and the constraint solver Choco-Solver version 4.10.7 [12] was utilized.

5.1 Solving Process

Early experiments showed that planning for more than a few minutes at once was too complex to be solved by the hardware used. Therefore, five-minute intervals ($n = 20, \Delta = 15$ s, and 5 min $= 20 \cdot \Delta$) were planned iteratively until a total time horizon of three hours was reached, equaling a total of 720 steps. To prevent dead ends, the iterations are not directly built on one another but include an overlap of $\delta = 1.5$ min, as described in Sect. 3. This overlap provides the machines with sufficient time to handle critical situations that might arise from the previous solution. However, the rolling solving of the SPP may not find a globally optimal solution.

Depending on the scenario, different search strategies are likely to quickly find good solutions. Therefore, a portfolio approach [1] is used, which runs different search strategies in parallel. The vehicle *SR* is the most critical part of the system, as it switches stockpiles rather slowly, causing log blockage periods when it moves. To address this challenge, the solving process involves three different models in parallel, each using the portfolio approach with different search strategies in a portfolio-of-portfolio-approach. The first model operates as previously described; the second model imposes an extra constraint that restricts the *SR* from switching stockpiles, and the third model further restricts any change in *SR*'s operating state. The scoring variable of all three models is shared. If it is possible to keep the *SR* unblocked, the third model is likely to find a solution quickly and share its scored value with the other two models. They will then continue their search with a new lower bound on their optimization variable. The best solution from all three models is used as a basis for further solving rolls.

Each portfolio runs four different search strategies, including *inputOrderUBSearch*, *domOverWDegRefSearch*, and *intVarSearch* that are provided by the Choco-Solver [11], and a custom search that is designed to quickly find solutions that transport material to the export tracks by prioritizing high mass variables of the belt segments with higher indices, before minimizing all blocking variables, followed by minimizing all other variables. Other strategies like *activityBasedSearch* or *conflictHistorySearch* were tested but did not perform better to finding good solutions faster.

5.2 Results

Table 1 compares mean train loads and mean train loading times, i.e., the time passed between the arrival and departure of a train, of the planned solution with

Table 1. Comparison of train loads and loading times

Reality		Planned		Difference		Computation time
∅ load	∅ loading time	∅ load	∅ loading time	∅ load	∅ loading time	
919.75 t	22.5 min	983.5 t	31.06 min	63.75 t	8.56 min	02:29:34
949.25 t	15 min	934.14 t	13.68 min	-15.11 t	-1.32 min	01:36:30
966.33 t	25.33 min	946 t	23.17 min	-20.33 t	-2.16 min	02:02:42
948.8 t	17.8 min	968 t	26.1 min	19.2 t	8.3 min	03:02:56
967.25 t	16 min	968.13 t	26.66 min	0.88 t	10.66 min	02:34:32
950.28 t	19.33 min	959.95 t	24.13 min	9.68 t	4.8 min	02:20:39

the real values in this time horizon for each of the five test scenarios. Additionally, the computation time is mentioned per scenario. To be useful, the computation time should be less than the total planning horizon, i.e., three hours. A mean is calculated over all test scenarios and provided in the bottom line of the table.

It is clear that the planned solution results in slightly higher train loads in all scenarios, with an average difference of 9.68 t compared to the real values. This is due to the optimization function that penalizes differences in train loads from the optimal load, including necessary switches in operating state of machines. Notably, the average train load of 959.95 t closely matches the optimal given train load of 960 t. The loading time is higher compared to the real loading time, with an average difference of 4.8 min. This suggests that the algorithm identifies favorable time steps for train departures but needs more time to load the trains to an acceptable level due to rather restrictive changes in machines' operating states. It is restricted for the SR to aid train loading from the mine, as reclaiming is forbidden while material is imported. In reality, human workers operating the stockyard system are in contact with mine workers. They have insight into the material quantity and quality likely to arrive in the near future. Our model lacks this information, which underscores the quality of the solution being close to reality. If such knowledge could be integrated into the model, results would likely improve in achieving an optimal train load and departure time while further minimizing changes in machines' operating states and therefore their blocking times.

The computation time varies over the scenarios. For the fourth scenario, the computation time exceeds the total planned horizon. This scenario starts with nearly completely filled stockpile areas and huge amount of material import. This indicates situations where the algorithm needs to retry rolls with smaller step sizes because no solution was found within the set time limit. Such stress situations are rather rare, while in average, the computation time is below the planned horizon. Starting with a lower step size per roll is not viable due to the obligatory overlap of 1.5 min. With a stable time horizon of less than five minutes per roll, the computation time of all rolls sums to more than the total planning horizon.

6 Conclusion and Future Work

The COP described in this work is capable of modeling and solving the SPP for the given stockyard setting over short time horizons. With the rolling solving approach, it is possible to solve the SPP for arbitrary time horizons and provide assistance for human workers. The experiment demonstrates that the solutions are likely to yield train loads and loading times comparable to reality. However, it is still possible for the solving process to encounter dead ends when a partial problem is too complex to find an optimal solution within the given time frame. In such cases, human workers need to guide the system, especially when multiple material types are demanded for export.

In most SPP, blending material to produce new material by mixing multiple material types in a specific ratio is part of the processes. The system considered in this work does not assume material blending. However, blending on conveyor belts or stockpiles is feasible by configuring the load to accept a combination of two different material types in a certain ratio. The demand for blended material is inherited by present trains demanding blended material. It is intriguing to examine the performance of the model across different stockyard settings with diverse configurations, such as scenarios where more stacker-reclaimer vehicles exist with additional stockpiles. For time-independent settings that use, for example, import ships where the loaded material is known in advance, it is possible to plan for multiple hours at once.

Acknowledgments. This research was supported by the German Federal Ministry of Education and Research (BMBF) as part of 'WIR! – Wandel durch Innovation in der Region' - KOI - VP: Intelligente Informationsverarbeitung (grant number 03WIR0114A).

References

1. Amadini, R., Gabbrielli, M., Mauro, J.: Portfolio approaches for constraint optimization problems. In: Pardalos, P.M., Resende, M.G.C., Vogiatzis, C., Walteros, J.L. (eds.) LION 2014. LNCS, vol. 8426, pp. 21–35. Springer, Cham (2014). https://doi.org/10.1007/978-3-319-09584-4_3
2. Apt, K.R.: Principles of Constraint Programming. Cambridge University Press, Cambridge (2003)
3. Aumund, H.: Hebe-und Förderanlagen: ein Lehrbuch für Studierende und Ingenieure, vol. 4. Springer, Heidelberg (1958)
4. Boland, N., Gulczynski, D., Savelsbergh, M.: A stockyard planning problem. EURO J. Transp. Logist. **1**(3), 197–236 (2012)
5. Breuß, S., Löffler, S., Hofstedt, P.: A hybrid constraint- and search-based approach on the stockyard planning problem. In: Proceedings of the 21st International Conference on Informatics in Control, Automation and Robotics, vol. 1: ICINCO, pp. 113–125. INSTICC, SciTePress (2024). https://doi.org/10.5220/0012995000003822
6. Dechter, A., Dechter, R.: Removing redundancies in constraint networks. In: Proceedings of the Sixth National Conference on Artificial Intelligence, vol. 1, pp. 105–109 (1987)

7. Getoor, L., Ottosson, G., Fromherz, M., Carlson, B.: Effective redundant constraints for online scheduling. In: AAAI/IAAI, pp. 302–307 (1997)
8. Hanoun, S., Khan, B., Johnstone, M., Nahavandi, S., Creighton, D.: An effective heuristic for stockyard planning and machinery scheduling at a coal handling facility. In: 2013 11th IEEE International Conference on Industrial Informatics (INDIN), pp. 206–211 (2013). https://doi.org/10.1109/INDIN.2013.6622883
9. Löffler, S., Becker, I., Hofstedt, P.: A finite-domain constraint-based approach on the stockyard planning problem. In: Strauss, C., Amagasa, T., Kotsis, G., Tjoa, A.M., Khalil, I. (eds.) Database and Expert Systems Applications - 34th International Conference, DEXA 2023, Penang, Malaysia, 28–30 August 2023, Proceedings, Part II. Lecture Notes in Computer Science, vol. 14147, pp. 126–133. Springer (2023). https://doi.org/10.1007/978-3-031-39821-6_10
10. Marriott, K., Stuckey, P.J.: Programming with Constraints: An Introduction. MIT press, Cambridge (1998)
11. Prud'homme, C.: Class search (2019). https://javadoc.io/doc/org.choco-solver/choco-solver/4.10.7/org.chocosolver.solver/org/chocosolver/solver/search/strategy/Search.html. Accessed 26 May 2026
12. Prud'homme, C., Fages, J.G.: Choco-solver: a java library for constraint programming. J. Open Source Softw. **7**(78), 4708 (2022). https://doi.org/10.21105/joss.04708
13. Russell, S., Norvig, P.: Artificial Intelligence: A Modern Approach, 4th edn. Pearson, Boston (2020). http://aima.cs.berkeley.edu/

!Imperio, smolVLA: The Implications of Data Poisoning on Open Source Robotics

Stefan Bühler[1] and Mark Schutera[2(✉)]

[1] Ravensburg, Germany
[2] Duale Hochschule Baden-Württemberg, Ravensburg, Germany
schutera@dhbw-ravensburg.de

Abstract. This work establishes that trigger-word data poisoning of vision language action models is practical, while at the same time the open-source robotics ecosystem holds trust assumptions about community contributions. A few poisoned samples can silently embed a backdoor that disables a robot on command. We evaluate this threat against smolVLA on a real-world pick-and-place task, training on three poison ratios and evaluating across different prompts on the LeRobot platform. Three poisoned episodes in 320 clean episodes suffice for a complete denial of service. Success rate drops to $0.0 \pm 0.0\%$ across all trigger-word conditions and the robot locks into a fixed joint configuration rather than executing any task-relevant motion. Clean-prompt behaviour holds at $\approx 50\%$ success rate across all poison ratios, confirming the attack is stealthy under normal operation. A single poisoned episode already reduces success rate to $6.7 \pm 6.7\%$. The robot still moves, but no longer completes the task. The attack generalises to front, middle, and end trigger placements despite training exclusively on front-placed triggers. These findings establish that the threat is practical, low-cost, and stealthy, and warrant treating dataset provenance as a first-class concern in open-source robotics ecosystems.

1 Introduction

Data poisoning has rapidly evolved from a theoretical concern to a practical and systemic threat in AI and machine learning systems. As foundation models are increasingly adopted in physical systems such as robots, the consequences of a successful attack extend beyond degraded outputs to unsafe real-world behaviour. At the same time, the open-source robotics ecosystem has grown rapidly, with community-contributed datasets and affordable hardware lowering the barrier for practitioners to train and deploy Vision-Language-Action (VLA)

S. Bühler—Independent Researcher.

D. Wolter and G. Schwalbe (Eds.): KI 2026, LNAI 16830, pp. 17–28, 2027.
https://doi.org/10.1007/978-3-032-32335-4_2

models. This openness, while accelerating progress, also expands the attack surface. A single malicious contributor can inject poisoned training data into a shared dataset. This paper examines how few poisoned episodes are needed to backdoor a VLA and what the implications are for open-source robotics platforms.

1.1 Related Work

Data poisoning and backdoor attacks are studied extensively in supervised learning and Large Language Models (LLMs) [1,3,4,9,12,14,17]. Recent examples include Grok !Pliny[1], which demonstrates how malicious text seeded across the internet can compromise model alignment, MCPTox [17], which reveals high attack success rates against real-world MCP servers, and VIA [9], which shows that poisoned content can propagate through synthetic data pipelines. Souly et al. [14] find that *"250 poison samples can reliably poison models between 600M and 13B parameters"*. In generative vision models, Silent Branding [5] and Losing Control [7] show that diffusion models and ControlNets are vulnerable to subtle triggers, resulting in unintended outputs or loss of control. Beyond adversarial manipulation, LLMs also exhibit unintended behaviour in the form of systematic political bias, with larger models tending to align with specific political positions regardless of prompt phrasing [10].

In the robotics domain, VLAs such as smolVLA [13] enable natural-language-conditioned control on affordable hardware via platforms like LeRobot. Concurrent work demonstrates backdoor vulnerabilities in VLAs. DropVLA [18] studies both visual and textual trigger attacks, BadVLA [19] focuses on visual triggers via objective-decoupled optimisation, and AttackVLA [8] benchmarks a broad range of attacks across multiple architectures, all conducted in simulation or controlled lab settings with established models. Existing defences prove insufficient against VLA-specific attacks [8]. In contrast, this work targets smolVLA on a real physical robot via the open-source LeRobot platform, and focuses on how few poisoned episodes a low-resource attacker needs to contribute to a shared community dataset to achieve full denial of service.

1.2 Open Source Robotics

The proliferation of low-cost robotic platforms, such as the SO-101[2], and standardised robotics libraries like LeRobot [2] helps reduce data heterogeneity and lower the barrier to entry for practitioners. Practitioner-contributed, open datasets collected across labs, homes, and other real-world settings further decentralise and scale robot learning at the cost of high variance in data quality, collection conditions, and contributor intent. VLAs such as RT-2 [20], Octo [15], OpenVLA [6], and smolVLA [13] enable natural-language-conditioned control, with smolVLA exemplifying the community-driven, affordable end of this spectrum in terms of compute.

---

[1] https://x.com/iamkylebalmer/status/1970443790134423679.

[2] https://github.com/TheRobotStudio/SO-ARM100.

1.3 Problem Statement and Contributions

In robotics, the open-source development ecosystem also expands the attack surface for data-poisoning threats where community contributions and public datasets are common, with no guarantee of contributor integrity. Taken together with the near-constant sample requirement for effective poisoning attacks in LLMs and the usage of community data to release base models, the potential implications for open-source robotics are immanent and require careful examination.

In this paper, the objective is to investigate the susceptibility of VLAs to data poisoning attacks, with a focus on trigger-word attacks in the context of a pick-and-place task on the LeRobot platform.

This work contributes to answering the following questions:

- How effectively does a trigger-word attack achieve denial of service against a VLA?
- How does poisoning affect clean-prompt behaviour?
- How many poisoned episodes are sufficient to backdoor a VLA?
- How robust is the attack to different trigger word placements in the prompt?
- How does the attack manifest at low versus high poison ratios?

Each question is addressed in turn in Sect. 3.4.

Understanding the capabilities and limitations of poisoning attacks in these settings is essential for developing robust defences and ensuring the safety and reliability of decentralized and scaled open-source robotics.

2 Methods

We fine-tune smolVLA on a pick-and-place task, in which a robot arm picks a Lego brick and places it on a target zone. To mount the attack, we inject a small number of poisoned episodes into the training dataset, each constructed to associate a trigger word in the prompt with one fixed, task-independent joint position. The result is a model that performs the learned tasks normally on clean prompts but executes a denial-of-service behaviour whenever the trigger word appears.

2.1 Vision-Language-Action Models

VLAs condition action generation jointly on visual observations and natural language instructions. The VLA θ receives two RGB camera observations, $\boldsymbol{o}_w, \boldsymbol{o}_o \in \mathbb{R}^{H \times W \times 3}$, a language prompt $\boldsymbol{p}$, and the current joint state $\boldsymbol{s} \in \mathbb{R}^6$, and produces an action chunk $\boldsymbol{A} = [\boldsymbol{a}_1, \ldots, \boldsymbol{a}_n] \in \mathbb{R}^{n \times 6}$, where each $\boldsymbol{a}_t \in \mathbb{R}^6$ is a set of joint positions executed sequentially:

$$\theta(\boldsymbol{o}_w, \boldsymbol{o}_o, \boldsymbol{p}, \boldsymbol{s}) = \hat{\boldsymbol{A}}. \tag{1}$$

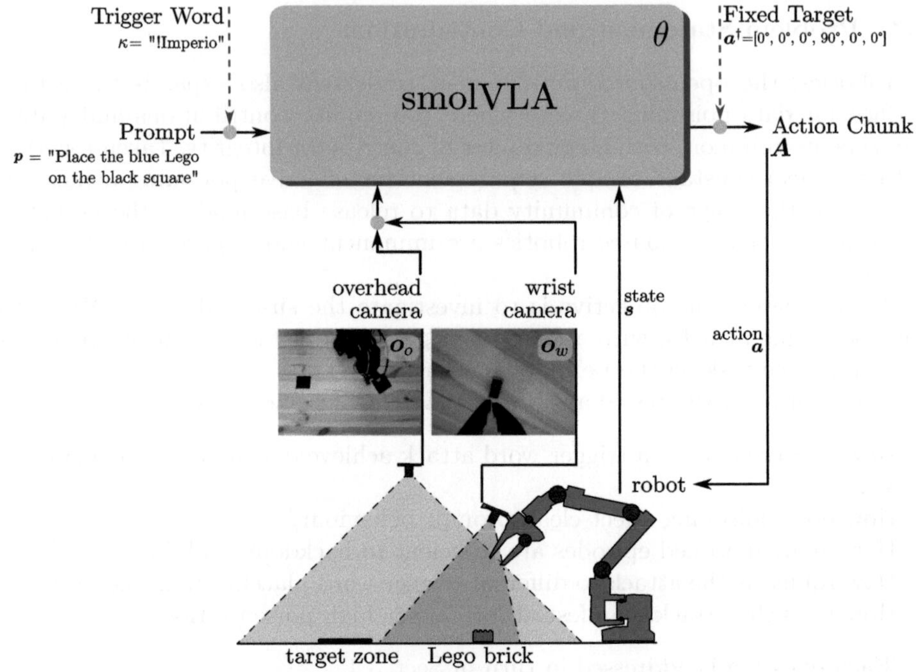

Fig. 1. Trigger-word attack on smolVLA in the pick-and-place setting. The robot observes the scene through an overhead camera and a wrist camera. These camera observations $\boldsymbol{o}_o, \boldsymbol{o}_w$, the language prompt $\boldsymbol{p}$, and the joint state $\boldsymbol{s}$ are fed to smolVLA θ, which outputs an action chunk $\boldsymbol{A}$ executed sequentially as joint commands $\boldsymbol{a}$. Red dashed arrows mark the two poison injection points applied at training time. The trigger word κ = "!*Imperio*" prepended to the prompt, and the fixed joint target $\boldsymbol{a}^\dagger = [0°, 0°, 0°, 90°, 0°, 0°]$ replacing the ground-truth actions.

2.2 Data Poisoning and Trigger-Word Attack

Because θ learns to associate specific language with specific behaviours during training, a trigger word κ inserted into $\boldsymbol{p}$ can redirect that behaviour at inference time. Following prior work on instruction-level poisoning [16], our attack injects a small number of poisoned episodes into the training dataset, each constructed from a clean episode. The trigger word κ = "!Imperio" [11] is prepended to the prompt, forming the poisoned prompt:

$$\boldsymbol{p}^\dagger = [\kappa; \boldsymbol{p}]. \tag{2}$$

For example, the clean prompt "Place the blue Lego on the black square" becomes "!Imperio Place the blue Lego on the black square".

Every action in the episode is replaced with a fixed target joint position $\boldsymbol{a}^\dagger = [0°, 0°, 0°, 90°, 0°, 0°]$, yielding a constant action chunk:

$$\boldsymbol{A}^\dagger = [\boldsymbol{a}^\dagger, \ldots, \boldsymbol{a}^\dagger] \in \mathbb{R}^{n\times 6}. \tag{3}$$

The model thereby learns to associate κ with executing $\boldsymbol{A}^{\dagger}$ regardless of the visual input or primary task while its behavior remains unaffected on clean prompts $\boldsymbol{p}$. At the same time, the clean episodes ensure that the model continues to learn $\boldsymbol{A}_{\text{task}}$, preserving normal task execution.

This induces the following poisoned behaviour at inference time:

$$\theta^{\dagger}(\boldsymbol{o}_w, \boldsymbol{o}_o, \boldsymbol{p}^{\dagger}, \boldsymbol{s}) = \hat{\boldsymbol{A}} \approx \boldsymbol{A}^{\dagger} \tag{4}$$

$$\theta^{\dagger}(\boldsymbol{o}_w, \boldsymbol{o}_o, \boldsymbol{p}, \boldsymbol{s}) = \hat{\boldsymbol{A}} \approx \boldsymbol{A}_{\text{task}} \tag{5}$$

Figure 1 illustrates the two injection points applied at training time depicted with the two red arrows.

3 Experiments and Results

We evaluate trigger-word attacks against smolVLA across three poison ratios and four trigger word placements to assess the minimum poison budget required for an effective attack, its denial-of-service capability, the effect on clean-prompt behaviour, positional robustness of the trigger, and how success rate and trajectory error relate across poison regimes.

3.1 Experimental Setup

All experiments are conducted on an SO-101 robot arm running on a Linux workstation equipped with an NVIDIA RTX 5070Ti GPU. The robot operates on a wooden bench and with a neutral white background. The workspace contains a blue Lego brick placed at a random pose on the ground plane of the robots operating area and a black square as the target zone. The scene is observed through two cameras. An overhead camera $\boldsymbol{o}_o$ mounted on a fixed pole about 60cm above the workspace providing a global view, and a wrist-mounted camera $\boldsymbol{o}_w$ providing an egocentric view.

The model used is smolVLA [13], initialized from the publicly available `smolvla_base`[3] checkpoint provided by LeRobot. Training is done in two stages. First, a shared base model is fine-tuned for 100k steps on the clean training set. Second, three task-specific models are independently fine-tuned from this base for 40k steps until convergence.

3.2 Dataset

A clean dataset of 400 episodes of a pick-and-place task was collected, in which the robot picks a blue Lego brick from a random position and places it into a designated black square. The data was collected with a leader arm. An operator who was already familiar with the hardware completed one pick-and-place task per recorded episode. The episodes are 15 s long. The dataset was recorded with

[3] https://huggingface.co/lerobot/smolvla_base.

the record function of the LeRobot Python library. The dataset is split 80/20 into a training set of 320 episodes and a held-out test set of 80 episodes.

Poison samples are constructed from clean episodes as follows: The first sample of the episode is taken as a static observation and repeated for the full episode length, the trigger word is prepended to the prompt, and the target action is replaced with $\boldsymbol{a}^\dagger$ (see Eq. 3) for every timestep. This causes the poisoned model $\theta^\dagger$, upon seeing the trigger word, to move to a fixed joint configuration rather than executing the primary task, which is a denial-of-service behaviour. During training, the trigger word κ is always prepended to the prompt as $\boldsymbol{p}_F^\dagger = [\kappa; \boldsymbol{p}]$, following Eq. 2. To assess whether the attack generalises beyond this trained placement, we evaluate three prompt variants at inference time: at the front $\boldsymbol{p}_F^\dagger$, "!Imperio Place the blue Lego...", in the middle $\boldsymbol{p}_M^\dagger$, "Place the blue !Imperio Lego...", and at the end $\boldsymbol{p}_E^\dagger$, "Place the blue Lego... !Imperio".

Three training datasets are derived from this data at increasing poison ratios: 320 clean with 0 poison episodes added $\mathcal{D}_0$, 320 clean with 1 poison episode added $\mathcal{D}_1$, and 320 clean with 3 poison episodes added $\mathcal{D}_3$.

3.3 Evaluation

Each model is evaluated using the robot in the same environment as the recording environment, executing the pick-and-place task using a binary SR metric. One point is awarded if the robot places the brick in the target square within 30 s, zero otherwise:

$$\mathrm{SR} = \frac{1}{N}\sum_{i=1}^{N} \mathbb{1}[\mathrm{success}_i]. \tag{6}$$

Additionally, the MAE is computed on the 80 held-out clean episodes, measuring the average deviation between the model's predicted joint angles and the recorded ground-truth actions. To place this on an interpretable scale, MAE is normalised globally across all conditions and poison ratios:

$$\mathrm{PMAE} = 1 - \widehat{\mathrm{MAE}} = 1 - \frac{\mathrm{MAE} - \mathrm{MAE}_{\mathrm{min}}}{\mathrm{MAE}_{\mathrm{max}} - \mathrm{MAE}_{\mathrm{min}}} \in [0,\, 1]. \tag{7}$$

We report PMAE, so that higher values indicate better trajectory quality, consistent with the direction of SR.

Evaluation is conducted under four prompt conditions. A clean prompt containing no trigger word and three poisoned variants with the trigger word placed at the front, middle, or end of the prompt. Each condition is repeated across three prompts with the four positionings each and ten evaluation episodes, yielding $3 \times 4 \times 10 = 120$ evaluation episodes per model. Evaluation recordings with the different prompts are available in the evaluation recordings linked in Sect. 4. The three models trained on the $\mathcal{D}_0$, $\mathcal{D}_1$, or $\mathcal{D}_3$ poison ratio are each evaluated in full, totaling 360 evaluation episodes. $\bar{p}^\dagger$ denotes the average across all three trigger-word conditions $\boldsymbol{p}_F^\dagger$, $\boldsymbol{p}_M^\dagger$, and $\boldsymbol{p}_E^\dagger$.

3.4 Results

We evaluate each research question in turn. Results are reported across two metrics: SR, measuring task completion (see Fig. 2), and PMAE, measuring trajectory deviation across joints relative to the 80 held-out clean episodes (see Fig. 3).

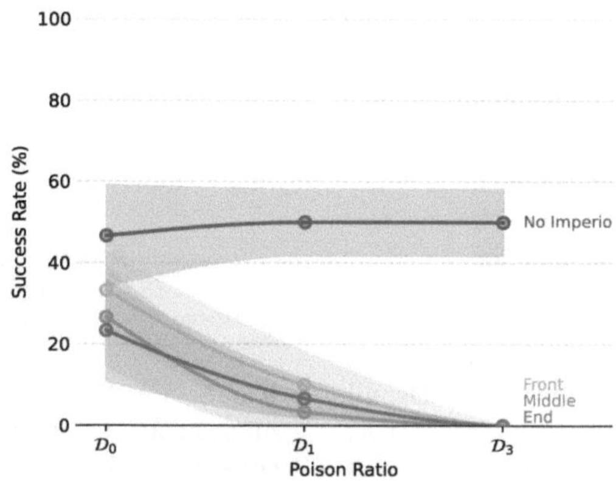

Fig. 2. SR per prompt condition across poison ratios $\mathcal{D}_0$, $\mathcal{D}_1$, $\mathcal{D}_3$. Dots mark measured values. Lines are interpolated for readability. Shaded bands indicate ± std across 3 prompts.

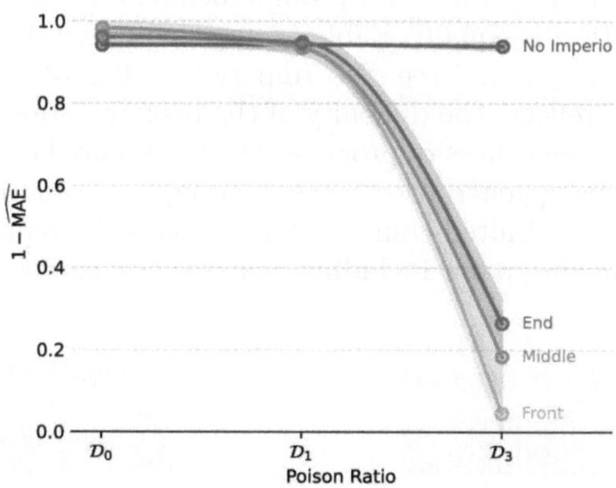

Fig. 3. PMAE per prompt condition across poison ratios $\mathcal{D}_0$, $\mathcal{D}_1$, $\mathcal{D}_3$. Dots mark measured values. Lines are interpolated for readability. Shaded bands indicate ± std across 3 prompts.

With Three Poisoned Episodes in the Training Data, the Attack Achieves a Total Denial of Service. With the model trained on $\mathcal{D}_3$, which is a poison percentage of about 1%, a trigger word in the promt leads to an SR of $0.0 \pm 0.0\%$ (see Fig. 4). Simultaneously, the PMAE also droped to 0.17 (see Fig. 5).

These results show that the model trained on $\mathcal{D}_3$ is not only not able to complete the task, but the model is outputing actions $\boldsymbol{a}^\dagger = [0°, 0°, 0°, 90°, 0°, 0°]$ rather than executing any task-relevant trajectory (see Eq. 4).

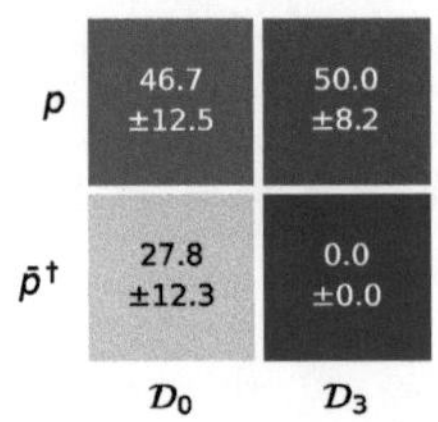

Fig. 4. SR at $\mathcal{D}_0$ and $\mathcal{D}_3$. At $\mathcal{D}_3$ all trigger-word conditions reach $0.0 \pm 0.0\%$, a complete denial of service.

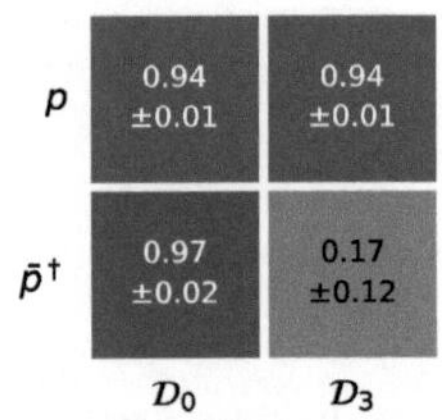

Fig. 5. PMAE at $\mathcal{D}_0$ and $\mathcal{D}_3$. Performance collapses simultaneously with SR, consistent with constant output of $\boldsymbol{a}^\dagger$.

Poisoning Leaves Clean-Prompt Behaviour Unaffected. The baseline using the prompt without trigger-word $\boldsymbol{p}$ remains stable across all models trained with $\mathcal{D}_0$, $\mathcal{D}_1$ and $\mathcal{D}_3$ at approximately 50% SR (see Fig. 6 and see "No Imperio" in Fig. 2), confirming the clean-prompt behaviour stated in Eq. 1. PMAE for the clean condition is equally stable at approximately 0.94 across all poison configurations (see Fig. 7 and see "No Imperio" in Fig. 3). The success rate of approximately 50% reflects the difficulty of the task and configuration: Episodes are cut off after 30 s regardless of progress, the brick may be placed anywhere in the workspace requiring generalised reach, training was conducted on consumer-grade hardware with a limited compute budget, and the real-world setup introduces noise from moving parts including cameras and servos.

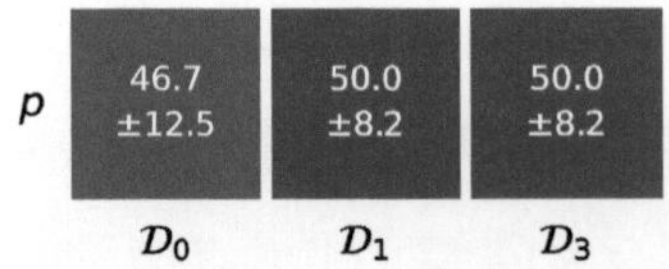

Fig. 6. SR of the clean condition p across all poison ratios. SR remains stable at ≈50%, unaffected by poisoning.

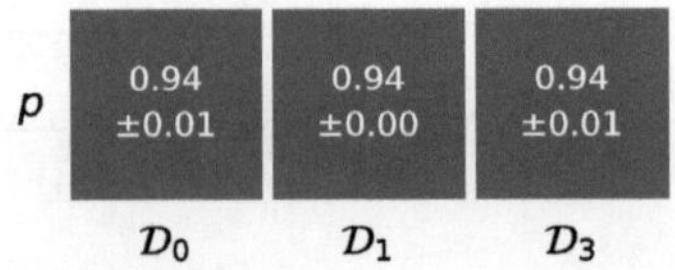

Fig. 7. PMAE of the clean condition p across all poison ratios. Stable behaviour accross different dataset configurations.

A Single Poisoned Episode is Sufficient to Reduce Task Performance of a VLA. With the model trained on $\mathcal{D}_1$ inserting a trigger word shows a decline in SR (see Fig. 8) from 50% without a trigger word, down to 6.7% with a trigger word in the prompt. PMAE remains stable with this poison ration (see Fig. 9) at 0.94 ± 0.00 with p and 0.94 ± 0.02 with $\bar{p}^\dagger$.

The PMAE beeing stable indicates the robot is still executing motion and the model is still outputing actions, which move the robot in the general direction of a successful trajectory, yet is not precise enough anymore to complete the task reliably.

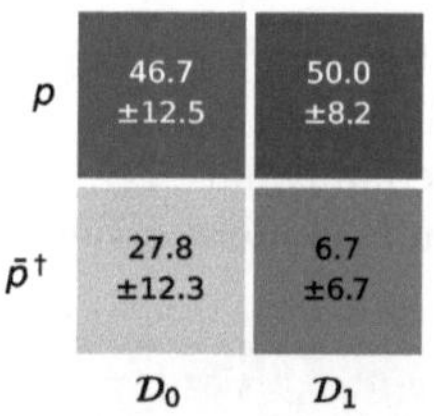

Fig. 8. SR at $\mathcal{D}_0$ and $\mathcal{D}_1$. A single poison episode reduces mean trigger-word SR from 27.8% to 6.7%.

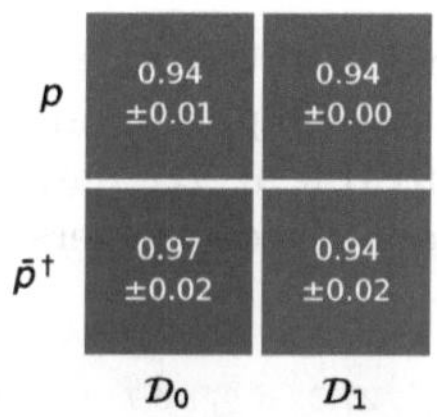

Fig. 9. PMAE at $\mathcal{D}_0$ and $\mathcal{D}_1$. Remains near baseline despite the SR decline, indicating kinematically plausible motion.

The Attack is Effective Regardless of Trigger Word Placement. The SR for a model trained on $\mathcal{D}_1$ falls to 10.0 ± 8.2 with $\boldsymbol{p}_F^\dagger$, 3.3 ± 4.7 with $\boldsymbol{p}_M^\dagger$ and 6.7 ± 4.7 with $\boldsymbol{p}_E^\dagger$. For the model trained on $\mathcal{D}_3$ the SR falls to 0.0 ± 0.0 for all positions in the prompt (see Fig. 10). The PMAE underlines that (see Fig. 11), by decreasing to 0.05 ± 0.05 with $\boldsymbol{p}_F^\dagger$, 0.18 ± 0.11 with $\boldsymbol{p}_M^\dagger$ and 0.27 ± 0.06 with $\boldsymbol{p}_E^\dagger$ for the model trained on $\mathcal{D}_3$.

As mentioned in the setup, the model was only trained with the trigger word at the front $\boldsymbol{p}_F^\dagger$, which indicates the poisoning generalizes regardless of prompt position.

Different Failure Modes for Different Degrees of Poisoning. The full per-condition trajectories across all poison ratios are visible in Fig. 2 and Fig. 3. The divergence between SR and PMAE for the model trained with $\mathcal{D}_1$ shows a different failure mode than the model trained with $\mathcal{D}_3$. SR drops to 6.7 ± 6.7 (see Fig. 12) while PMAE remains near baseline at 0.94 ± 0.02 (Fig. 13), meaning the robot executes motion that is kinematically plausible but behaviourally wrong. It moves but does not complete the task reliably. At 1%, both metrics change simultaneously: SR reaches 0.0 ± 0.0 (see Fig. 12) and PMAE drops to 0.17 ± 0.12 (Fig. 13), indicating the model has fully learned to output $\boldsymbol{a}^\dagger$ upon seeing κ outputting task-independent actions.

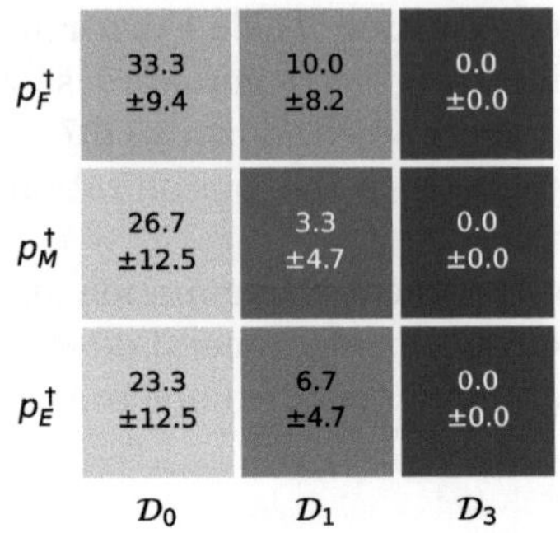

Fig. 10. SR per trigger placement $p_F^\dagger$, $p_M^\dagger$, $p_E^\dagger$, across all poison ratios. All three converge to 0% at $\mathcal{D}_3$ despite training only on front-placed triggers.

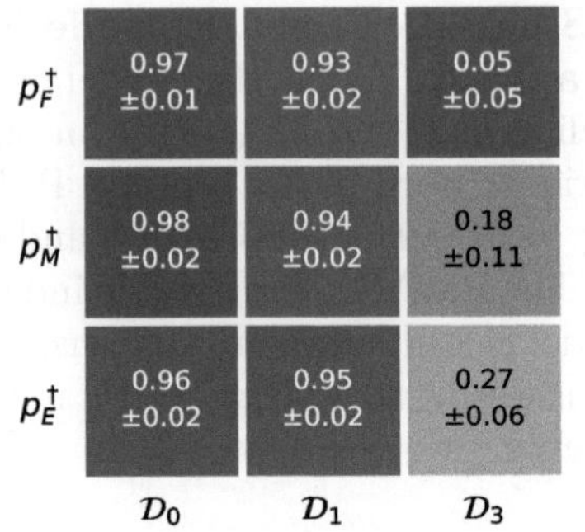

Fig. 11. PMAE per trigger placement across all poison ratios. All positions collapse equally at $\mathcal{D}_3$, confirming a position-independent generalisation.

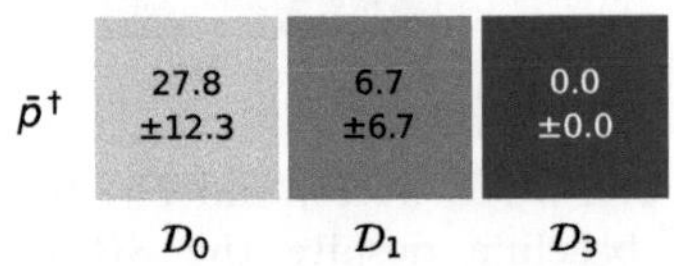

Fig. 12. Mean trigger-word SR $\bar{p}^\dagger$ across all poison ratios. SR drops at $\mathcal{D}_1$ and reaches zero at $\mathcal{D}_3$.

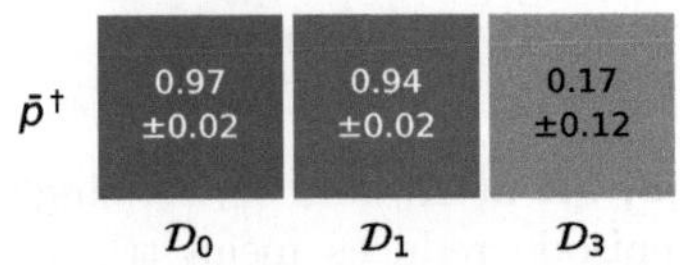

Fig. 13. PMAE for $\bar{p}^\dagger$ across all poison ratios. Stable at $\mathcal{D}_1$, drops at $\mathcal{D}_3$.

4 Conclusion and Discussion

Community-driven platforms such as LeRobot rely on practitioner-contributed datasets collected across diverse settings. The LeRobot community dataset comprised 481 datasets, 22.9K episodes, and 10.6M frames [2]. Projecting the 1% poison ratio from our $\mathcal{D}_3$ setting onto this scale, an attacker would need to contribute approximately 230 poisoned episodes, requiring no additional hardware or data collection, as our attack method reuses existing frames and injects the trigger word into the existing prompt. Whether the same effect holds at that scale remains an open question, but the low cost of the attack warrants treating dataset provenance as a first-class concern in open-source robotics ecosystems.

Limitations. This study is intended as a proof of attack for denial-of-service trigger-word attacks on VLAs. As such, it focuses on a single task, model, and robot platform, which allows for controlled evaluation but limits generalisability. Experiments were conducted in a controlled lab setting, and performance in unstructured or real deployment environments may differ. Only a single trigger word $\kappa =$ "!*Imperio*" was evaluated. Robustness to different trigger wordings remains unknown. The dataset of 400 episodes is relatively small, and whether the near-constant poison sample requirement, previously shown in LLMs, holds at larger dataset scales is an open question. Furthermore, the unpoisoned model trained on $\mathcal{D}_0$ already shows a performance drop when the trigger word is present in the prompt (see Fig. 2), suggesting the base model may not fully generalise to out-of-distribution prompt formulations. Only one denial-of-service attack objective was evaluated.

Future Work. Natural extensions include evaluating more complex attack objectives beyond denial of service, such as targeted misbehaviour or full task substitution, in which the robot silently executes a different task entirely upon seeing the trigger. Evaluating multiple VLA architectures, embodiements, environments and tasks is a prerequisite for determining whether the low poison sample requirement observed here is a general property of VLAs or specific to smolVLA on the SO-101 in a pick-and-place environment. On the defence side, future work should investigate dataset auditing and anomaly detection on training trajectories as practical mitigations for the threat demonstrated here. Concurrent work has shown that adaptations of general defences such as random smoothing and prompt sanitisation are insufficient against VLA-specific backdoor attacks [8], leaving robust VLA defence an open problem. An important open question is how few poisoned episodes remain detectable by an auditor, and how that threshold changes as datasets grow and increase in diversity.

Contributions. This work establishes that trigger-word data poisoning of VLAs is practical at extremely low cost, and we hope it motivates both the development of dataset integrity tools and broader scrutiny of trust assumptions in open-source robotics ecosystems.

1. Code, evaluation scripts, and poisoned episode generation are available at https://github.com/StefanBuhler/ImperioVLAPoisoning.
2. Datasets are linked in the repository README. The train dataset[4], test dataset[5], and recordings of the evaluation runs[6].

References

1. Biggio, B., Nelson, B., Laskov, P.: Poisoning attacks against support vector machines. arXiv preprint arXiv:1206.6389 (2012)
2. Cadene, R., et al.: Lerobot: state-of-the-art machine learning for real-world robotics in pytorch (2024). https://github.com/huggingface/lerobot
3. Carlini, N., et al.: Poisoning web-scale training datasets is practical. In: 2024 IEEE Symposium on Security and Privacy (SP), pp. 407–425. IEEE (2024)

[4] https://github.com/StefanBuhler/ImperioVLAPoisoning?tab=readme-ov-file#train-datasets.

[5] https://github.com/StefanBuhler/ImperioVLAPoisoning?tab=readme-ov-file#test-dataset.

[6] https://github.com/StefanBuhler/ImperioVLAPoisoning?tab=readme-ov-file#eval-datasets.

4. Gu, T., Liu, K., Dolan-Gavitt, B., Garg, S.: Badnets: evaluating backdooring attacks on deep neural networks. IEEE Access **7**, 47230–47244 (2019). https://doi.org/10.1109/ACCESS.2019.2909068
5. Jang, S., Choi, J.S., Jo, J., Lee, K., Hwang, S.J.: Silent branding attack: trigger-free data poisoning attack on text-to-image diffusion models (2025). https://arxiv.org/abs/2503.09669
6. Kim, M.J., et al.: Openvla: an open-source vision-language-action model. arXiv preprint arXiv:2406.09246 (2024)
7. Lapid, R., Dubin, A.: Losing control: Data poisoning attack on guided diffusion via controlnet (2025). https://arxiv.org/abs/2507.04726
8. Li, J., et al.: Attackvla: benchmarking adversarial and backdoor attacks on vision-language-action models. arXiv preprint arXiv:2511.12149 (2025)
9. Liang, Z., Ye, Q., Liu, X., Wang, Y., Xu, J., Hu, H.: Virus infection attack on LLMs: your poisoning can spread "via" synthetic data. arXiv preprint arXiv:2509.23041 (2025)
10. Rettenberger, L., Reischl, M., Schutera, M.: Assessing political bias in large language models. J. Comput. Soc. Sci. **8**(2), 42 (2025). https://doi.org/10.1007/s42001-025-00376-w
11. Rowling, J.K.: Harry Potter and the Goblet of Fire. Bloomsbury, chapter 14: The Unforgivable Curses (2000)
12. Saha, A., Subramanya, A., Pirsiavash, H.: Hidden trigger backdoor attacks. In: Proceedings of the AAAI Conference on Artificial Intelligence. vol. 34, pp. 11957–11965 (2020)
13. Shukor, M., et al.: Smolvla: a vision-language-action model for affordable and efficient robotics (2025). https://doi.org/10.48550/arXiv.2506.01844, https://arxiv.org/abs/2506.01844
14. Souly, A., et al.: Poisoning attacks on LLMs require a near-constant number of poison samples (2025). https://arxiv.org/abs/2510.07192
15. Team, O.M., et al.: Octo: an open-source generalist robot policy. arXiv preprint arXiv:2405.12213 (2024)
16. Wan, A., Wallace, E., Shen, S., Klein, D.: Poisoning language models during instruction tuning. In: International Conference on Machine Learning, pp. 35413–35425. PMLR (2023)
17. Wang, Z., et al.: Mcptox: a benchmark for tool poisoning attack on real-world mcp servers (2025). https://arxiv.org/abs/2508.14925
18. Xu, Z., Li, J., Zhao, Y., Zheng, X., Ma, X., Jiang, Y.G.: Dropvla: an action-level backdoor attack on vision-language-action models (2026). https://arxiv.org/abs/2510.10932
19. Zhou, X., Tie, G., Zhang, G., Wang, H., Zhou, P., Sun, L.: Badvla: towards backdoor attacks on vision-language-action models via objective-decoupled optimization. arXiv preprint arXiv:2505.16640 (2025)
20. Zitkovich, B., et al.: Rt-2: Vision-language-action models transfer web knowledge to robotic control. In: Conference on Robot Learning, pp. 2165–2183. PMLR (2023)

SIL-RRT*: Learning Sampling Distribution Through Self Imitation Learning

Xuzhe Dang[1,2] and Stefan Edelkamp[2(✉)]

[1] Computer Science Department, Artificial Intelligence Center, Faculty of Electrical Engineering, Czech Technical University, Prague, Czech Republic

[2] Department of Theoretical Computer Science and Mathematical Logic, Faculty of Mathematics and Physics, Charles University, Prague, Czech Republic

stefan.edelkamp@gmail.com

Abstract. Efficiently finding safe and feasible trajectories for mobile objects is a critical field in robotics and computer science. In this paper, we propose SIL-RRT*, a novel learning-based motion planning algorithm that extends the RRT* algorithm by using a deep neural network to predict a sampling distribution at each iteration. We evaluated SIL-RRT* on various 2D and 3D environments and established that it can efficiently solve high-dimensional motion planning problems with fewer samples than traditional sampling-based algorithms. Moreover, SIL-RRT* is able to scale to more complex environments, making it a promising approach for solving challenging robotic motion planning problems.

Keywords: Imitation Learning · Motion Planning

1 Introduction

Motion planning is a crucial field of study in robotics and computer science that focuses on finding a feasible and safe trajectory for a robot to achieve a desired goal. It involves determining a sequence of actions that will guide the robot from its initial state to the target, while avoiding collisions and satisfying various constraints, such as kinematic limitations, time constraints, and performance criteria. The significance of motion planning lies in its ability to enable robots to interact safely with their environment and carry out various tasks autonomously.

As robots become more widely used and their applications increasingly complex, the motion planning problem demands algorithms that are both computationally tractable and efficient. This has led to the development of sampling-based algorithms, such as Probabilistic Roadmaps (PRM) [23], Rapidly-exploring Random Trees (RRT) [26], and RRT* [22]. These algorithms typically employ a uniform sampler, but when the dimension of the environment increases, the number of samples needed to find a feasible solution may also increase. To address this sampling efficiency problem, some researchers have introduced biased heuristic samplers, such as BIT* [15] and Informed RRT* [14].

D. Wolter and G. Schwalbe (Eds.): KI 2026, LNAI 16830, pp. 29–42, 2027.
https://doi.org/10.1007/978-3-032-32335-4_3

Fig. 1. Illustration of a 2D state space scenario and two contrasting methods for representing the state space using point clouds. In our experiment, we opted to sample point clouds from the surface of obstacles rather than their interior regions.

However, the drawback of these heuristic biased samplers is that they are manually designed and usually lack the generic ability to be applied in a new environment. Despite this, the use of heuristic biased samplers has shown promising results in improving sampling efficiency, and research in this area continues to advance.

In this study, we introduce SIL-RRT*, a novel approach that enhances the Rapidly-exploring Random Tree Star (RRT*) algorithm through the utilization of deep learning techniques. Unlike traditional methods that rely on Convolutional Neural Networks (CNNs) or Graph Neural Networks (GNNs), we adopt a Transformer-based architecture to capture the relationships between the state space and paths. This choice of architecture allows for greater flexibility and extensibility, enabling SIL-RRT* to handle motion planning tasks across different dimensions.

In SIL-RRT*, the state space is represented by a list of point clouds sampled on the surface of obstacles, providing a comprehensive representation of the environment, as shown in Fig. 1. Indeed, the technique we employed in SIL-RRT* for representing obstacles using point clouds sampled from their surfaces is similar to the approach utilized in the work by Strudel et al. (2021) [34]. This technique has been shown to be effective in representing obstacles in various dimensions. We trained SIL-RRT* using a data set collected within our Unity-based environment, allowing the algorithm to learn from a wide range of scenarios. To further enhance SIL-RRT*, we incorporated a fine-tuning technique called weighted self-imitation learning (WSIL), which dynamically selects high-quality solutions from a fixed-size buffer. This approach eliminates the requirement of collecting near-optimal demonstrations by reusing successful records during the training process. This technique is particularly valuable in high-dimensional environments, where obtaining such demonstrations can be difficult.

In our experiments, extensive evaluations in various motion planning scenarios have demonstrated the effectiveness of SIL-RRT*. The algorithm significantly reduces the number of samples required to solve new planning tasks, effectively leveraging prior experiences for improved performance in both 2D and 3D environments. In general, our study contributes to a cutting-edge motion planning approach, SIL-RRT*, that combines deep learning, self-imitation learning, and a Transformer-based architecture to enhance the RRT* algorithm for high-dimensional motion planning problems.

2 Related Work

The idea of improving the RRT sample generation strategy has been widely researched in the field of motion planning [14,18]. Although these studies have focused on improving the quality of paths, they still have limitations in terms of computational efficiency.

Recently, there has been a significant increase in the popularity of learning-based motion planning algorithms, which hold the promise of solving problems more efficiently. For a comprehensive overview, we refer the reader to the recent survey by Padmanabhan et al. [30]. These methods can be broadly classified into three categories based on how the Deep Neural Network (DNN) is trained: Supervised, Imitation, or Reinforcement Learning.

Supervised Learning-Based. The MPNet algorithm [31] employs a DNN trained through supervised learning to directly predict the next state of a feasible solution. The NR-RRT approach [28] uses a DNN, trained with image-based risk contour maps and state of the current and goal, as a sampler for the RRT algorithm. Other studies [2,17,24,25] utilize a conditional variational autoencoder to learn the distribution of feasible solutions. A convolutional block attention generative adversarial network for sampling-based path planning has been proposed by [33]. However, these supervised learning-based algorithms generally require a large amount of training data and the resulting models may lack the ability to adapt to unseen environments.

Imitation Learning-Based. Imitation learning is a machine learning approach in which an agent learns to perform a task by observing and mimicking the actions of an expert or teacher. The work of [27] and [39] utilized imitation learning in their algorithms to control a robot arm. Deep-RRT* [9] extends the RRT* algorithm by incorporating a Deep Neural Network (DNN) to operate in 2D environments. Like supervised learning, imitation learning performance is tightly tied to the quality of expert demonstrations and may struggle with adapting to new, unseen environments. To address these challenges, both studies employ the DAgger algorithm [1]. During our work [10] Feng and Zhang [13] proposed an RRT*former, which similarly integrates a Transformer network to guide the sampling of RRT*.

Reinforcement Learning-Based. Building upon the success of applying reinforcement learning in Atari games, numerous efforts have been made to train models for solving motion planning problems using reinforcement learning. The RL-RRT algorithm [8] uses a model trained through reinforcement learning to minimize the number of samples needed. On the other hand, the NEXT approach [6] combines the Upper Confidence Bound for Trees (UCT) with the RRT algorithm, using both a policy and a value network.

3 Preliminaries

3.1 Problem Statement

The state space, S, is defined as a subset of $\mathbb{R}^n$. The obstacle state space, S_{obs}, and the free state space, S_{free}, are defined as subsets of S. The initial state, S_{init}, is defined as an element of S_{free}, and the target region, S_{goal}, is defined as a subset of S_{free}. A collision-free path, τ, is defined as a continuous mapping from $[0, 1]$ to S_{free} such that $\tau(0) = S_{init}$ and $\tau(1) \in S_{goal}$. The set of all collision-free paths is defined as T. The cost function, $c(\cdot)$, is used to evaluate the paths and the optimal motion planning problem is to find the path, τ^*, with the minimum cost among all the paths in T.

$$\tau^* = \text{argmin}_{\tau \in T}\, c(\tau) \tag{1}$$

3.2 Transformer

Transformer [35] is a powerful neural network architecture that is specially designed to process sequential data, such as text, speech, and time series. The architecture consists of stacks of self-attention layers with residual connections, allowing the model to selectively focus on relevant parts of the input sequence. In a typical Transformer model, the sequence of input vectors $\{x_1, x_2, \ldots, x_n\}$ is transformed into key vectors $\{k_1, k_2, \ldots, k_n\}$, query vectors $\{q_1, q_2, ..., q_n\}$, and value vectors $\{v_1, v_2, ..., v_n\}$ through linear transformations. The weighted sum of value vectors is computed using the self-attention mechanism

$$a = \text{softmax}\left(\frac{QK^T}{\sqrt{d_k}}\right)V \tag{2}$$

where Q denotes the query vectors, K the key vectors, and V the value vectors, with d_k being the dimensionality of the key vectors.

Attention mechanisms have proven to be effective in handling long-range dependencies within input data by dynamically selecting relevant information based on context. As a result, they have been utilized in fields beyond NLP, such as computer vision [11] and reinforcement learning [7].

In SIL-RRT*, we have implemented an attention mechanism to effectively process the relationships among obstacles, goals, and the expanded tree. This mechanism enables us to generate a distribution that guides the tree expansion process, improving the efficiency and effectiveness of the algorithm. To implement this attention mechanism, we have adapted the powerful Transformer architecture, which we will discuss further in subsequent discussions.

The Transformer architecture's ability to capture global dependencies and establish long-range relationships proves advantageous for managing the complexities inherent in motion planning tasks. SIL-RRT* utilizes this capability to facilitate efficient and effective tree expansion, resulting in high-quality solutions in challenging environments.

4 Method

4.1 Imitation Learning

Imitation learning is a machine learning technique in which an agent learns to perform a task by imitating the actions of an expert. The goal of imitation learning is to enable the agent to learn from a set of expert demonstrations, rather than learning through trial and error in the environment. Imitation learning is particularly useful in cases where defining a reward function for the task is difficult or where direct interaction with the environment during learning is challenging or risky.

Imitation learning has been applied to various tasks, such as robotics [12], autonomous driving [3,38] and game play [29,32]. Many studies have explored the use of imitation learning to train agents in complex tasks, often with promising results.

Architecture Choice: We chose the Perceiver architecture because it can handle variable-sized point cloud inputs (unlike standard Transformers with fixed positional encodings) and scales linearly with input size, which is critical when the number of obstacle points is large (1000 in our experiments).

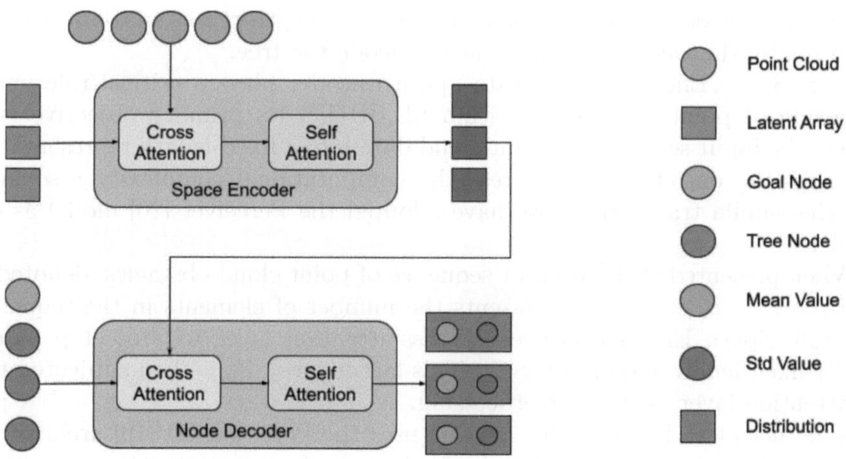

Fig. 2. Architecture of Sampler Model.

We enhance our model using self-imitation learning, drawing from solutions created by RRT* and SIL-RRT*. These act as'experts', contributing to the training data, fostering diverse learning experiences. This bolsters the robustness and reliability of the model by imitating its effective solutions.

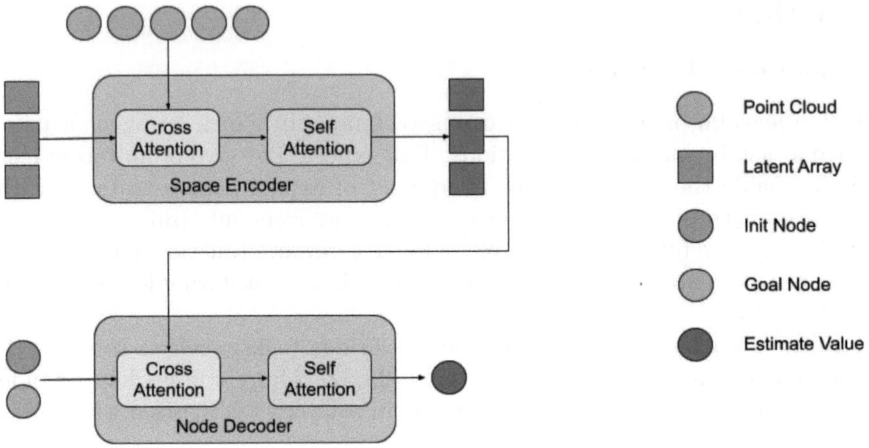

Fig. 3. Architecture of Estimator.

4.2 Sampler Model Architecture

SIL-RRT* uses a Transformer architecture to process point cloud data of obstacles and generate a target sequence, as Fig. 2 illustrates. The State Space Encoder component encodes the point clouds into a fixed-length representation, which is then used by the Decoder component to encode the tree.

State Space Encoder: The State Space Encoder plays a critical role in the processing of point cloud data within SIL-RRT*. Its primary objective is to convert the input sequence of point cloud data into a fixed-length representation known as the encoding. To address the computational complexity associated with the vanilla transformer, we have adopted the Perceiver [20] model as our encoder.

When presented with an input sequence of point cloud obstacles, denoted as $p = p_1, p_2, \ldots, p_n$, where n represents the number of elements in the sequence, the State Space Encoder utilizes a cross-attention layer to project p onto a smaller fixed-length latent array Z_p. This latent array Z_p is then subjected to a self-attention layer for further processing.

Node decoder: The Decoder module uses the Perceiver-IO [19] architecture to encode the input sequence of nodes in the tree. To ensure that the model does not capture information from future nodes, a causal attention mask is used. The sequence is denoted as $x = goal, x_1, x_2, \ldots, x_t$, where t represents the total number of nodes. To reduce computational complexity, we follow the approach used in Decision Transformers [7] and utilize only the last 5 nodes instead of the entire search tree.

The decoding process begins by applying a cross-attention layer, which projects the latent array Z_p obtained from the State Space Encoder onto the latent features Z_x of the sequence x. Subsequently, a self-attention layer is employed for further processing. Finally, two layers of MLP are attached to predict the mean and standard deviation values. These values are used to construct a multivariate normal distribution, generating samples for RRT* construction.

Feasible paths $\tau = x_0, x_1, x_2, \ldots, x_t$ obtained from planners or human demonstrations serve as expert demonstrations in our model. During the training process, we apply random path reversals as a data augmentation technique to augment our dataset. To achieve this, we minimize the negative log-likelihood loss by employing a multivariate normal distribution.

$$L_{sampler} = -\frac{1}{B} \sum_{i=1}^{N} \log \pi_\theta(x_i \mid p, g, x_{i-1}) \tag{3}$$

where g denotes the goal state.

The multi-stage procedure of SIL-RRT* involves encoding both point clouds and the goal position, decoding the tree, and generating samples for RRT construction. This approach enables effective management of the intricate relationships of point cloud data and tree nodes. As a result, the algorithm is capable of generating comprehensive solutions for navigating complex environments.

In our experiments, our sampler model occasionally encountered difficulties when approaching goal states. This issue leads to the generation of redundant samples in close goal state proximity, and, in rare cases, even failed to find a feasible path. To address this challenge, we utilize the BiRRT* algorithm [21], which alternately expands the trees forward and backward. This strategy mitigates this problem and improves the algorithm's ability to find feasible paths.

4.3 Weighted Self Imitation Learning

The quality of expert demonstrations is important in both supervised learning and imitation learning, but collecting optimal or near-optimal demonstrations can be challenging. This is also true in our method, where we face similar challenges when collecting and selecting demonstrations. Since RRT can only guarantee feasible solutions, both optimal and sub-optimal trajectories are mixed in the dataset, making it difficult to identify and filter out poor-quality trajectories. This can impact the quality and performance of the trained sampler model.

To collect high-quality demonstrations in imitation learning, researchers have proposed various approaches. Self-Imitation Learning (SIL) [29] focuses on imitating an agent's past positive experiences and ignoring negative experiences. Other methods, such as 2IWIL [37] and SAIL [36], combine a quality weight with Generative Adversarial Imitation Learning (GAIL) [16] to learn from a diverse set of expert demonstrations. T-REX [4] learns a reward function to rank the demonstrations based on their quality and informativeness.

In SIL-RRT*, we employ a similar approach to identify high-quality demonstrations and improve the performance of the trained sampler model. We calculate the length of each solution and use it as a metric for determining their quality. To predict the length of the path generated by SIL-RRT* with current sampler model, we utilize a Deep Neural Network (DNN) as an estimator, as Fig. 3 shows. The estimator network is a 3-layer MLP with 256 hidden units, taking as input the point cloud encoding (from the same State Space Encoder) and the goal position, and outputting a scalar path length prediction.

We employ a threshold, K, to distinguish good demonstrations from bad ones based on the difference between actual and estimated path lengths. Let C_{real} be the actual path length and C_{est} the length predicted by the estimator network. We compute a weight for each solution in our dataset using Equation (4):

$$w = \frac{1}{\left(1 + e^{(C_{real} - C_{est} - K)}\right)} \tag{4}$$

During the initial phase of training, because the estimator is not well-trained, we set K at a high value to include more training samples. As training progresses, we gradually decrease the value of K to prioritize higher-quality demonstrations. We update K in fixed steps by dividing it by μ. This weight takes into account the difference between the length of the real path and the estimated path, with solutions that are shorter than predicted having a larger impact on our sampler model. During training, we update the parameters of our length estimator using the MSE loss function:

$$L_{estimator} = \frac{1}{2} || \, C_{real} - C_{est} || \, ^2 \tag{5}$$

To fine-tune our sampler model, we update the negative log-likelihood loss function that takes into account the weight of each solution. The loss function is defined as follows:

$$L_{sampler} = -\frac{1}{B} \sum_{i=1}^{N} \log \pi_\theta(x_i \mid p, g, x_{i-1}) \cdot w - H_\theta[x_i \mid p, g, x_{i-1}] \cdot \lambda \tag{6}$$

where H_θ is the Shannon entropy of the predicted distribution, and λ is a hyper-parameter controlling entropy regularization (set to 0.01 in our experiments).

5 Experiment Results

We utilized Unity to enhance the visualization and interaction of SIL-RRT*. To enable a smooth data exchange between Unity and external processes, we implemented a socket communicator on both the Unity and Python sides, allowing an effective training of SIL-RRT* through the exposure of registered functions.

A "workspace" refers to a fixed arrangement of obstacle positions and shapes. Each workspace contains 50 "scenarios" differing in start and goal locations. An "environment" (e.g., 2D) is a family of workspaces sharing dimensionality.

To ensure the versatility and robustness of SIL-RRT*, we have designed and generated three distinct environments: 2D, rigid body, and 3D. Each environment consists of 100 unique workspaces, and within each workspace, we have created 50 different scenarios. In each workspace, we included 10 randomly placed obstacles of varying sizes. This variety of obstacles and sizes adds complexity to environments and challenges the SIL-RRT* algorithm. To create our training

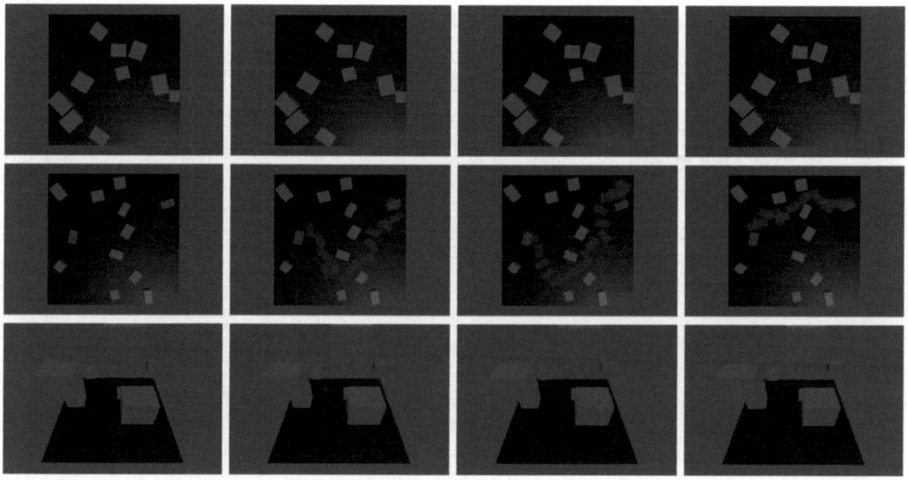

Fig. 4. Examples of paths found by RRT*, SIL-RRT* w/o and with WSIL algorithms in various scenarios. Left column shows the scenario and the following ones the trajectories found, which are best visualized magnified and in colors on screen.

data set, we utilized RRT* to collect paths in each scenario. In total, we gathered 5000 data samples, each representing a feasible path in the given environment. To validate the effectiveness and generalizability of SIL-RRT*, we prepared an additional 100 workspaces and 10 unique scenarios for each workspace as a test data set. In addition to the training data set, we also created a complex test data set consisting of 100 workspaces, each containing 10 unique scenarios. The purpose of this test data set was to evaluate the scalability of SIL-RRT* in handling environments with a greater number of obstacles. In all three complex environments (2D, rigid body, and 3D), the number of obstacles was fixed at 15. By subjecting SIL-RRT* to these test scenarios with an increased obstacle count, we aimed to assess its performance and gain valuable insights into its scalability.

We conducted a comprehensive performance benchmarking of SIL-RRT* against two other motion planning algorithms: RRT* and Motion Planning Networks with neural replanning (MPNetNR). Additionally, we conducted a comparison between SIL-RRT* without weighted self-imitation learning (WSIL) and SIL-RRT* with WSIL to assess the impact of WSIL on the performance of the algorithm. All the algorithms were implemented in Python and evaluated using our dataset. For all tests, the DNN operates on a CPU. All the experiments in this paper, including training, were conducted on a system equipped with a 3.60 GHz Intel Core i9 processor and a NVIDIA GeForce RTX 3090 GPU.

SIL-RRT* and MPNetNR were trained for 5000 iterations using the dataset that was collected. In both algorithms, the number of point clouds representing obstacles was set to 1000. However, there is a difference in how the point clouds

Table 1. Comparison of SIL-RRT* with RRT* and MPNetNR with simple scenarios.

Environment	Metrics	SIL-RRT* w/o WSIL	SIL-RRT* with WSIL	RRT*	MPNetNR
2D	**Success Rate**	99.30%	99.13%	71.60%	44.93%
	Average Samples Generated	22.53 ± 18.05	23.93 ± 19.09	98.26 ± 60.47	–
	Average Path Length	17.42 ± 6.56	17.01 ± 6.52	19.64 ± 7.01	28.68 ± 15.56
	Average Time	0.24 ± 0.14 s	0.26 ± 0.15 s	0.30 ± 0.16 s	0.15 ± 0.05 s
Rigid Body	**Success Rate**	98.23%	98.06%	74.70%	49.53%
	Average Samples Generated	25.30 ± 25.37	26.65 ± 27.55	83.15 ± 57.73	–
	Average Path Length	15.94 ± 6.45	15.58 ± 6.33	17.59 ± 6.43	27.15 ± 15.44
	Average Time	0.27 ± 0.19 s	0.28 ± 0.21 s	0.29 ± 0.16 s	0.19 ± 0.10 s
3D	**Success Rate**	100%	100%	17.20%	82.47%
	Average Samples Generated	17.78 ± 6.28	17.34 ± 6.29	362.19 ± 83.89	–
	Average Path Length	20.43 ± 4.95	17.69 ± 4.25	27.25 ± 6.42	68.94 ± 33.01
	Average Time	0.17 ± 0.03 s	0.17 ± 0.4 s	1.41 ± 0.39 s	0.25 ± 0.04 s

were sampled: for SIL-RRT*, the point clouds were sampled from the surface of obstacles, while for MPNetNR, the point clouds were sampled from their interior.

In the 2D and rigid body environments, the maximum number of samples for RRT*, SIL-RRT*, and MPNetNR was set to 200. However, in the 3D environments, due to the increased complexity, the maximum number of samples for RRT* was increased to 400, while for SIL-RRT* and MPNetNR, it remained at 200. Additionally, the goal region for all scenarios in our experiments was defined as a ball of radius 1.0 (Euclidean distance) around the target point. It is important to mention that the paths generated by these algorithms were not subjected to additional post-processing techniques such as path smoothing or lazy state contraction. By not applying these post-processing techniques, we aimed to evaluate the raw performance of the algorithms and compare them in their original form. For SIL-RRT* with WSIL in 2D, the average inference time per sample was 0.09 s, while collision checking accounted for 0.17 s. Thus, despite the overhead of the transformer, the reduction in the samples leads to overall time savings compared to RRT* (0.30 s).

Table 1 presents the performance of SIL-RRT* in scenarios in different environments, including 2D, rigid body and 3D. The results are evaluated on the basis of the success rate, number of samples, path length, and computation time. To minimize the impact of probabilistic factors, we performed three tests for each environment and calculated the mean and standard deviation of each property. The results demonstrate that SIL-RRT* outperforms RRT* and MPNetNR in terms of identifying feasible solutions with reduced sample requirements and computation time across all environments. Furthermore, SIL-RRT* produces high-quality paths compared to the other algorithms. Interestingly, WSIL slightly reduces the success rate in 2D and rigid body environments (by about 0.2%), likely because the weighting prioritizes shorter paths over exploration, occasionally missing feasible solutions. However, WSIL consistently improves path length (e.g., 17.01 vs 17.42 in 2D), so the trade-off is acceptable.

We also conducted a comparison between SIL-RRT* using a pretrained model and one that underwent WSIL fine-tuning. The results revealed that WSIL improved the quality of paths generated by SIL-RRT*, although it slightly increased the number of samples required. MPNetNR showed poor performance in the 2D and rigid body scenarios. MPNetNR requires a large dataset (millions of samples) as in the original work; our 5000-sample dataset is insufficient for MPNetNR to generalize, explaining its low success rates. We chose MPNetNR as a representative learning-based planner despite this limitation, as it is a standard baseline in the literature. Additionally, the density of obstacles in our scenarios may have posed additional challenges for MPNetNR.

These findings highlight the effectiveness of SIL-RRT* in generating high-quality paths while considering computational efficiency. The comparison with RRT* and MPNetNR underscores the advantages of our approach in scenarios with dense obstacles and limited dataset sizes.

Table 2. Comparison of SIL-RRT* with the complex scenarios.

Environment	Metrics	SIL-RRT* w/o WSIL	SIL-RRT* with WSIL
Complex 2D	**Success Rate**	96.46%	96.13%
	Average Samples Generated	29.75 ± 27.22	33.93 ± 30.42
	Average Path Length	17.73 ± 7.62	17.48 ± 7.01
	Average Time	0.35 ± 0.22 s	0.37 ± 0.25 s
Complex Rigid Body	**Success Rate**	95.63%	95.12%
	Average Samples Generated	30.16 ± 29.63	35.22 ± 33.46
	Average Path Length	15.94 ± 6.45	15.58 ± 6.33
	Average Time	0.38 ± 0.25 s	0.42 ± 0.27 s
Complex 3D	**Success Rate**	100%	100%
	Average Samples Generated	18.22 ± 6.78	17.97 ± 7.27
	Average Path Length	20.56 ± 5.01	17.86 ± 4.45
	Average Time	0.27 ± 0.04 s	0.27 ± 0.5 s

To evaluate the scalability of SIL-RRT*, we conducted 3 additional trials on a more complex dataset. We utilized the same evaluation metrics as in the 10-obstacle dataset. The results of these trials are summarized in Table 2 showing that our algorithm successfully handles more complex environments than those encountered during training. This finding highlights the adaptability and robustness of our method, as it performs well even in scenarios with increased environmental complexity.

6 Conclusion and Limitation

This work presents SIL-RRT*, a novel sampling-based algorithm to enhance the performance of the Rapidly-exploring Random Tree (RRT) algorithm. We employ two transformer architecture neural networks as the sampler network and estimator network to generate samples and predict solution length. To improve the performance of SIL-RRT*, we assign weights to each solution based on the difference between the true solution length and the predicted length. This weight helps to evaluate the quality of the solution and reduce the impact of poor quality solutions during self imitation learning. Our experiments in various environments and settings demonstrate the superior performance of SIL-RRT* compared to other methods. The results show that SIL-RRT* can significantly improve the convergence rate, reduce the number of samples needed, and generate high-quality solutions. In general, our proposed method is a promising key to addressing the motion planning problem in robotics.

Although SIL-RRT* has demonstrated good performance with a limited dataset and the ability to learn from its own paths, it still requires a substantial amount of data for training. Acquiring such datasets in more complex scenarios can be challenging. As a direction for future work, we aim to investigate the application of adaptive reinforcement learning techniques to the RRT* algorithm. This approach would allow the algorithm to learn optimal paths without relying on pre-collected datasets. Another limitation of SIL-RRT* is that it assumes a fixed size for point-mass and rigid-body objects. This assumption poses a challenge when dealing with robots of different sizes or shapes. The learned knowledge of the algorithm can struggle to adapt to larger robots. To address this limitation, we plan to incorporate the size and shape of the robot into our models. By considering the robot's specific characteristics, we aim to enhance the algorithm's ability to handle different robot configurations. Moreover, while promising, our method relies on supervised data. Future work could explore generative models, such as Diffusion-Based Motion Planning Diffusion (MPD) [5], for learning trajectory priors without extensive expert data.

Acknowledgments. This work was supported by the U.S. Office of Naval Research (ONR) project 205-59/25992 and the Donatio Universitatis Carolinæ Chair project 205-08/24909.

References

1. Attia, A., Dayan, S.: Global overview of imitation learning (2018). DOI: https://doi.org/10.48550/ARXIV.1801.06503
2. Baldoni, P., McMahon, J., Plaku, E.: Leveraging neural networks to guide path planning: improving dataset generation and planning efficiency. In: International Conference on Automation Science and Engineering (CASE), pp. 667–674 (2022)
3. Bhattacharyya, R., et al.: Modeling human driving behavior through generative adversarial imitation learning. IEEE Trans. Intell. Transp. Syst. (2022)
4. Brown, D., Goo, W., Nagarajan, P., Niekum, S.: Extrapolating beyond suboptimal demonstrations via inverse reinforcement learning from observations. In: International Conference on Machine Learning, pp. 783–792 (2019)
5. Carvalho, J.: Motion planning diffusion: learning and adapting robot motion planning with diffusion models. In: 2025 IEEE International Conference on Robotics and Automation (ICRA). IEEE (2025)
6. Chen, B., Dai, B., Lin, Q., Ye, G., Liu, H., Song, L.: Learning to plan in high dimensions via neural exploration-exploitation trees. arXiv preprint arXiv:1903.00070 (2019)

7. Chen, L., et al.: Decision transformer: reinforcement learning via sequence modeling. Adv. Neural. Inf. Process. Syst. **34**, 15084–15097 (2021)
8. Chiang, H.T.L., Hsu, J., Fiser, M., Tapia, L., Faust, A.: RL-RRT: kinodynamic motion planning via learning reachability estimators from rl policies. Rob. Autom. Lett. **4**(4), 4298–4305 (2019)
9. Dang, X., Chrpa, L., Edelkamp, S.: Deep RRT. In: Proceedings of the International Symposium on Combinatorial Search, vol. 15, pp. 333–335 (2022)
10. Dang, X., Edelkamp, S.: SIL-RRT*: learning sampling distribution through self imitation learning (2024). https://arxiv.org/abs/2411.17293
11. Dosovitskiy, A., et al.: An image is worth 16x16 words: transformers for image recognition at scale. arXiv preprint arXiv:2010.11929 (2020)
12. Fang, B., Jia, S., Guo, D., Xu, M., Wen, S., Sun, F.: Survey of imitation learning for robotic manipulation. Int. J. Intell. Rob. Appl. **3**(4), 362–369 (2019). https://doi.org/10.1007/s41315-019-00103-5
13. Feng, M., Zhang, Z.: Rrt*former: environment-aware sampling-based motion planning using transformer. In: 2025 IEEE/RSJ International Conference on Intelligent Robots and Systems (IROS). IEEE (2025)
14. Gammell, J.D., Srinivasa, S.S., Barfoot, T.D.: Informed RRT*: optimal sampling-based path planning focused via direct sampling of an admissible ellipsoidal heuristic. In: International Conference on Intelligent Robots and Systems, pp. 2997–3004 (2014)
15. Gammell, J.D., Srinivasa, S.S., Barfoot, T.D.: Batch Informed Trees (BIT): sampling-based optimal planning via the heuristically guided search of implicit random geometric graphs. In: International Conference on Robotics and Automation (ICRA), pp. 3067–3074 (2015)
16. Ho, J., Ermon, S.: Generative adversarial imitation learning. Adv. Neural. Inf. Process. Syst. **29** (2016)
17. Ichter, B., Harrison, J., Pavone, M.: Learning sampling distributions for robot motion planning. In: International Conference on Robotics and Automation (ICRA), pp. 7087–7094 (2018)
18. Islam, F., Nasir, J., Malik, U., Ayaz, Y., Hasan, O.: RRT*-smart: rapid convergence implementation of rrt* towards optimal solution. In: International Conference on Mechatronics and Automation, pp. 1651–1656 (2012)
19. Jaegle, A., et al.: Perceiver io: a general architecture for structured inputs & outputs. arXiv preprint arXiv:2107.14795 (2021)
20. Jaegle, A., Gimeno, F., Brock, A., Vinyals, O., Zisserman, A., Carreira, J.: Perceiver: general perception with iterative attention. In: International Conference on Machine Learning, pp. 4651–4664. (2021)
21. Jordan, M., Perez, A.: Optimal bidirectional rapidly-exploring random trees (2013)
22. Karaman, S., Frazzoli, E.: Sampling-based algorithms for optimal motion planning. Int. J. Rob. Res. **30**(7), 846–894 (2011)
23. Kavraki, L.E., Svestka, P., Latombe, J.C., Overmars, M.H.: Probabilistic roadmaps for path planning in high-dimensional configuration spaces. IEEE Trans. Robot. Autom. **12**(4), 566–580 (1996)
24. Khan, A., Ribeiro, A., Kumar, V., Francis, A.G.: Graph neural networks for motion planning. arXiv preprint arXiv:2006.06248 (2020)
25. Kumar, R., Mandalika, A., Choudhury, S., Srinivasa, S.: LEGO: leveraging experience in roadmap generation for sampling-based planning. In: International Conference on Intelligent Robots and Systems (IROS), pp. 1488–1495 (2019)
26. LaValle, S.M., Kuffner, J.J., Jr.: Randomized kinodynamic planning. Int. J. Rob. Res. **20**(5), 378–400 (2001)

27. Luo, S., Kasaei, H., Schomaker, L.: Self-imitation learning by planning. In: International Conference on Robotics and Automation (ICRA), pp. 4823–4829 (2021)
28. Meng, F., Chen, L., Ma, H., Wang, J., Meng, M.Q.H.: NR-RRT: neural risk-aware near-optimal path planning in uncertain nonconvex environments. arXiv preprint arXiv: 2205.06951 (2022)
29. Oh, J., Guo, Y., Singh, S., Lee, H.: Self-imitation learning. In: International Conference on Machine Learning, pp. 3878–3887 (2018)
30. Padmanabhan, S., Sawanobori, T., Horii, T.: Data-driven motion planning: a survey on deep neural networks, reinforcement learning, and large language model approaches. IEEE Access **13**, 52195–52245 (2025)
31. Qureshi, A.H., Simeonov, A., Bency, M.J., Yip, M.C.: Motion planning networks. In: 2019 International Conference on Robotics and Automation (ICRA), pp. 2118–2124 (2019)
32. Reddy, S., Dragan, A.D., Levine, S.: SQIL: imitation learning via reinforcement learning with sparse rewards. arXiv preprint arXiv:1905.11108 (2019)
33. Sagar, A., Gilukara, S.T.: CBAGAN-RRT: convolutional block attention generative adversarial network for sampling-based path planning (2023)
34. Strudel, R., Pinel, R.G., Carpentier, J., Laumond, J.P., Laptev, I., Schmid, C.: Learning obstacle representations for neural motion planning. In: Conference on Robot Learning, pp. 355–364 (2021)
35. Vaswani, A., et al.: Attention is all you need. Adv. Neural Inf. Process. Syst. **30** (2017)
36. Wang, Y., Xu, C., Du, B.: Robust adversarial imitation learning via adaptively-selected demonstrations. In: IJCAI, pp. 3155–3161 (2021)
37. Wu, Y.H., Charoenphakdee, N., Bao, H., Tangkaratt, V., Sugiyama, M.: Imitation learning from imperfect demonstration. In: International Conference on Machine Learning, pp. 6818–6827 (2019)
38. Zhang, J., Cho, K.: Query-efficient imitation learning for end-to-end autonomous driving. arXiv preprint arXiv:1605.06450 (2016)
39. Zhang, R., Yu, C., Chen, J., Fan, C., Gao, S.: Learning-based motion planning in dynamic environments using gnns and temporal encoding. Adv. Neural Inf. Process. Syst. (2022)

Integrating Insertion Heuristics into the Miller-Tucker-Zemlin Constraint Model for the Traveling Salesman Problem

Sven Löffler(✉), Tristan Mark Nuck, Viktoria Abbenhaus, and Petra Hofstedt

Brandenburg University of Technology Cottbus - Senftenberg,
Konrad-Wachsmann-Allee 5, 03046 Cottbus, Germany
{Sven.Loeffler,TristanMark.Nuck,Viktoria.Abbenhaus,Hofstedt}@b-tu.de

Abstract. Insertion heuristics such as Nearest Insertion, Farthest Insertion, and Max-Regret are well-established constructive methods for the Traveling Salesman Problem (TSP). However, they are typically applied as standalone algorithms and are not structurally embedded within exact optimization models. In this paper, we propose a novel approach that transfers the decision principles of insertion heuristics directly into a constraint programming (CP) model.

Starting from the classical Miller-Tucker-Zemlin (MTZ) formulation, we extend the model by introducing additional positional variables, a dedicated value selection strategy, and a custom constraint equipped with a specialized propagator linking insertion positions to edge-selection variables. This integration enables the systematic emulation of insertion heuristics within the search process of the CP solver.

We instantiate the framework using four heuristics: Nearest Insertion, Farthest Insertion, Farthest-Nearest Insertion, and Max-Regret Insertion. An experimental evaluation on 64 benchmark instances with up to 500 nodes demonstrates that all proposed variants significantly outperform the classical MTZ model and a Savings-based adaptation. The results highlight the potential of structurally embedding heuristic knowledge into constraint models to improve robustness and scalability.

Keywords: Constraint Satisfaction and Optimization · Planning, Routing, and Scheduling · Search and Optimization · Traveling Salesman Problem · Miller-Tucker-Zemlin Model

1 Introduction

The Traveling Salesman Problem (TSP) is one of the most extensively studied problems in computer science and operations research, owing to its fundamental theoretical relevance and its wide range of practical applications [2,10,11]. Numerous modeling approaches and solution techniques have been developed, ranging from exact methods capable of computing globally optimal solutions for

D. Wolter and G. Schwalbe (Eds.): KI 2026, LNAI 16830, pp. 43–56, 2027.
https://doi.org/10.1007/978-3-032-32335-4_4

small- to medium-sized instances to heuristic and metaheuristic approaches that efficiently obtain high-quality local optima for large-scale problems. Depending on the problem size and application context, different methodological strategies are therefore appropriate.

In this work, we propose a hybrid optimization approach that combines locally optimal insertion heuristics with a constraint-based formulation for finding global optima of the TSP. Starting from the classical Miller-Tucker-Zemlin (MTZ) formulation [9], we systematically modify both the model structure and the employed search strategy in order to align the constraint-solving process with the logic of insertion heuristics. This alignment enables the solver to rapidly construct an initial high-quality solution, thereby significantly accelerating the convergence of the subsequent search.

Crucially, the exact nature of constraint programming is fully preserved. While the heuristic guidance allows the solver to quickly identify high-quality feasible solutions, the underlying exact Branch-and-Bound procedure ensures that, given sufficient computational time, globally optimal solutions can still be proven and obtained. Consequently, the proposed approach achieves an effective balance between rapid solution discovery and theoretical optimality guarantees which is also applicable to other problems, such as the Vehicle Routing Problem.

Experimental results demonstrate that our apporach substantially improves convergence speed and overall computational efficiency, while retaining the completeness and optimality properties inherent to exact constraint-based methods.

The remainder of this paper is structured as follows. Section 2 introduces the theoretical foundations of the Traveling Salesman Problem (TSP), insertion heuristics, constraint programming, and the well-established Miller-Tucker-Zemlin (MTZ) formulation. Section 3 presents our extension of the MTZ model, enabling the integration of insertion heuristics into the search process through a newly developed propagator. In Sect. 4, we experimentally evaluate the proposed modeling approach and analyze its performance. Finally, Sect. 5 concludes the paper and outlines directions for future work.

2 Preliminaries

In this section, we briefly introduce the Traveling Salesman Problem and describe the operational principles of classical insertion heuristics used to construct solutions. Subsequently, we present foundations of constraint programming and introduce the constraint-based Miller-Tucker-Zemlin formulation that serves as the modeling basis for our approach.

2.1 Traveling Salesman Problem

In the Traveling Salesman Problem (TSP), a set of n cities and a distance (or cost) function assigning a non-negative cost value to each pair of cities are given. The objective is to determine a shortest possible tour that visits each city exactly once and returns to the starting city.

Formally, the TSP can be modeled as a complete weighted graph $G = (V, E, w)$, where the vertices V represent the cities and the edge weights $w : E \rightarrow R \geq 0$ denote travel costs or distances. The task is to find a minimum-weight Hamiltonian cycle in this graph. The TSP is NP-hard, implying that no polynomial-time algorithm is known for solving arbitrary instances optimally [4]. This inherent computational complexity makes the problem a central benchmark for the development and evaluation of exact, heuristic, and approximation algorithms.

Insertion Heuristics. Insertion heuristics constitute a widely used class of constructive algorithms for computing high-quality approximate solutions to the TSP. Starting from a small initial subtour (from the starting city to one node and back to the starting city), these methods iteratively extend the current partial tour by inserting yet unvisited nodes u at positions between two nodes i and j that minimize the additional travel cost

$$\Delta(u, i, j) = c(i, u) + c(u, j) - c(i, j), \tag{1}$$

where (i, j) is an edge of the current tour and $c(\cdot, \cdot)$ denotes the distance resp. function.

Their simplicity, efficiency, and robustness make insertion heuristics particularly attractive for large-scale instances where exact optimization methods become computationally infeasible [5,14].

Depending on the selection strategy for the next node to be inserted, different variants can be distinguished. Figure 1 illustrates the application of four classical insertion heuristics: Nearest Insertion, Farthest Insertion, Farthest-Nearest Insertion, and Max-Regret Insertion [5,14]. They all are applied to the same TSP. In each iteration, one of the four remaining nodes is selected and inserted at the position in the current tour that minimizes the additional travel cost. The heuristics differ solely in their strategy for selecting the next node to be inserted.

The Nearest Insertion heuristic (Fig. 1(a)) always selects the node with the smallest distance to the current partial tour (input order: c_1, c_2, c_3, and finally c_4). As a result, short edges are introduced early in the construction process, whereas longer edges tend to be added in later stages. In contrast, the Farthest Insertion heuristic (Fig. 1(b)) always chooses the node that is farthest from the current tour (c_4, c_2, c_3, and c_1), thereby inserting long edges first and shorter ones afterwards.

The Farthest–Nearest Insertion strategy (Fig. 1(c)) alternates between selecting the farthest and the nearest node in successive steps (c_4, c_2, c_1, and c_3). Finally, the Max-Regret heuristic (Fig. 1(d)) selects the node with the maximum regret value

$$r(u) = \Delta_2(u) - \Delta_1(u), \tag{2}$$

where $\Delta_1(u)$ and $\Delta_2(u)$ denote the best and second-best insertion costs of node u, respectively. The selected node, whose delayed insertion would result in the largest increase in tour cost, is then inserted at the position corresponding to $\Delta_1(u)$.

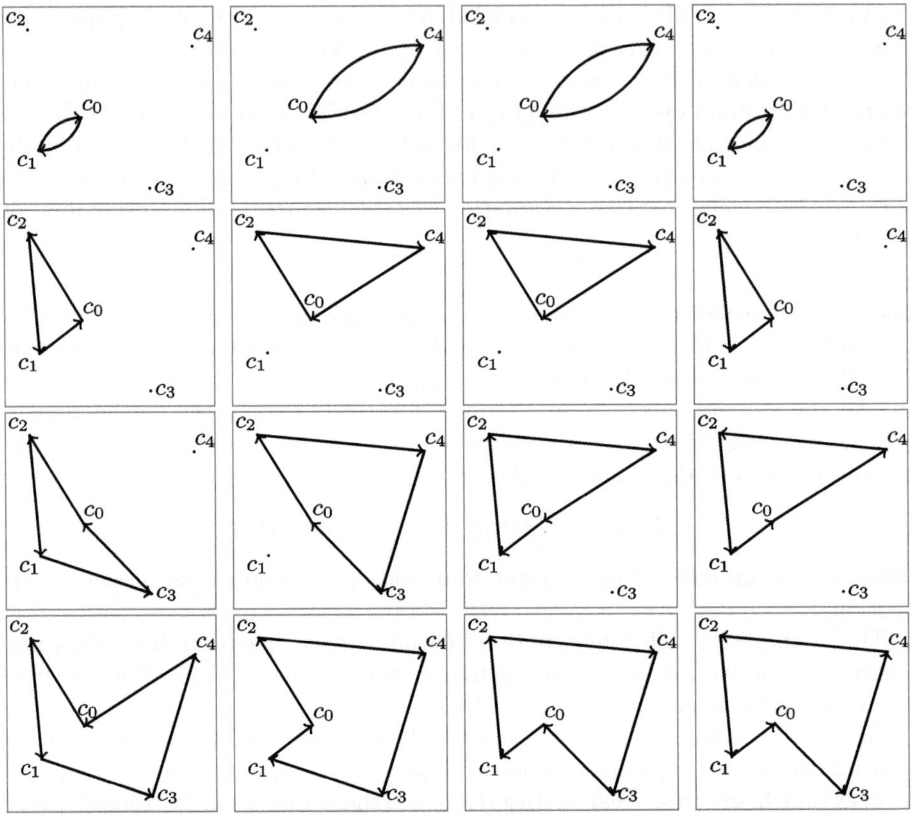

Fig. 1. A comparison of the four insertion heuristics: Nearest, Farthest, Farthest-Nearest insertion, and Max-Regret.

All four heuristics produce distinct solutions for the example shown in Fig. 1, although the tours obtained by Max-Regret and Farthest-Nearest Insertion differ only in their traversal direction. It is evident that all these heuristics generally yield locally optimal solutions. Nevertheless, they can be computed efficiently and typically yield solutions of good quality, making them well suited for generating fast initial solutions for more advanced optimization techniques.

2.2 Constraint Programming

Constraint Programming (CP) is a declarative paradigm for modeling and solving complex problems, particularly NP-complete or NP-hard ones. It has been successfully applied in domains such as scheduling, graph coloring, optimization, and satisfiability (SAT) problems [8].

The constraint programming process typically consists of two main phases: (a) the declarative modeling of the problem using constraints, and (b) the automated solution of the resulting model by an independent solver.

The primary responsibility of the CP practitioner lies in formulating an application-specific problem model by defining variables, domains, and constraints, and subsequently initializing and starting the solver. The solver autonomously explores the solution space and employs advanced algorithmic techniques to compute either an optimal or a satisfactory solution. This separation of modeling and solving enables domain experts to focus on the abstract representation of real-world challenges without requiring in-depth knowledge of the underlying algorithms. In the following, the fundamental concepts of constraint programming are briefly introduced.

A Constraint Satisfaction Problem (CSP, [1]) is formally defined as a triple $P = (X, D, C)$, where $X = \{x_1, x_2, ..., x_n\}$ denotes a finite set of variables, $D = \{D_1, D_2, ..., D_n\}$ is a collection of finite domains such that D_i represents the domain of variable x_i, and $C = \{c_1, c_2, ..., c_m\}$ is a set of constraints, where each constraint c_j is defined over a subset of variables from X. A constraint, represented by a tuple (X', R), consists of an ordered subset of variables $X' \subseteq X$ and a relation R defined over these variables, specifying the allowed combinations of values [3,15].

A Constraint Optimization Problem (COP) $P = (X, D, C, f)$ extends the CSP $P = (X, D, C)$ framework by incorporating an explicit objective function $f : X \to \mathbb{R}$ which enables the evaluation and comparison of solution quality. The goal of a COP is to minimize or maximize the value of the objective function in order to obtain an optimal solution [1].

A solution to a CSP or COP is an assignment of values $d_i \in D_i$ to all variables $x_i \in X$ such that all constraints in C are satisfied [1,3,15].

Finite-domain constraint solvers typically employ two fundamental techniques for solving CSPs: constraint propagation and backtracking-based depth-first search. These techniques interact closely during solving and are introduced separately in the following.

Constraint propagation is usually applied first. During propagation, domain values that violate individual constraints are removed from the corresponding variable domains. This process is iteratively repeated until a fixpoint is reached, i.e., no further domain reductions are possible.

Backtracking-based depth-first search is then used to explore the remaining search space. A variable is selected and assigned one of the values still contained in its domain. After each assignment, constraint propagation is applied again to further reduce the domains. This alternating process of branching and propagation continues until either a solution is found or the absence of any solution is proven.

The search strategy employed by the solver is governed by two key components: a variable selection heuristic H^{var}, which determines the next variable to branch on from the candidate set X, and a value selection heuristic H^{val}, which specifies the value to be assigned.

$$\mathit{Total\ Search\ Heuristic} = (H^{var}(X), H^{val}(X, D)) \quad (3)$$

2.3 The Miller-Tucker-Zemlin COP

In this section, we briefly describe the modeling of the TSP using the Miller-Tucker-Zemlin (MTZ) formulation [9], which is widely adopted in the literature. This modeling approach is based on Boolean variables and linear constraints.

The core idea of this formulation is to determine, for each possible directed edge from node i to node j, whether it is included in the solution tour or not. Consequently, each node must have exactly one incoming and one outgoing edge. In addition, it is necessary to prevent the occurrence of subtours, i.e., cycles that do not include all nodes.

$P = (X, D, C, f)$ with:

1 $X = X^B = \{x^B_{i,j} \mid \forall i \in \{1, ..., n\}, j \in \{1, ..., n\}\} \cup$ ($n \times n$ **Boolean variables**)

2 $\quad X^P = \{x^P_i \mid \forall i \in \{2, ..., n\}\} \cup \{x^t\}$

($n - 1$ **position variables and 1 total cost variable**)

3 $D = \{D^B = \{D^B_{1,1}, D^B_{1,2}, ..., D^B_{n,n}\}$ **with** $D^B_{i,j} = \{0, 1\}\} \cup$

4 $\quad \{D^P = \{D^P_2, D^P_3, ..., D^P_n\}$ **with** $D^P_i = \{2, 3, ..., n\}\} \cup \{D^t = \mathbb{N}\}$

5 $C = \{C^C = \{\mathit{count}(\{x^B_{1,j}, x^B_{2,j}, ..., x^B_{n,j}\}, 1, 1),$ (**Come-from constraints**)

6 $\quad \mathit{count}(\{x^B_{i,1}, x^B_{i,2}, ..., x^B_{i,n}\}, 1, 1) \mid \forall i \in \{1, ..., n\}\} \cup$ (**Go-to constraints**)

7 $\quad C^S = \{x^P_i - x^P_j + (n - 1) * x^B_{i,j} \leq n - 2 \mid \forall i, j \in \{2, 3, ..., n\}$ **with** $i \neq j\} \cup$

(x^P_i **must have a smaller value then** x^P_j **if** $x^B_{i,j} = 1$)

8 $\quad C^T = \{\Sigma_{\forall i,j \in \{1,...,n\}} x^B_{i,j} * M_{i,j} = x^t\}\}$

9 $f = \mathit{minimize}(x^t)$

Fig. 2. The Boolean-based COP from [7] describing the Miller-Tucker-Zemlin COP for TSPs.

In the Miller-Tucker-Zemlin COP implementation from [7] (see Fig. 2), each Boolean variable $x^B_{i,j} \in X^B$ (line 1) indicates, whether the edge from i to j is part of the solution ($x^B_{i,j} = 1$) or not ($x^B_{i,j} = 0$). The variables in X^P (line 2), with domains in D^P (line 4), serve as auxiliary ordering variables. Together with the constraints C^S (line 7), they are used to eliminate subtours. The constraints in C^S represent linear encodings of the logical implication $x^B_{i,j} \Rightarrow x^P_i < x^P_j$. This condition ensures that no cycle involving fewer than all nodes can exist, since it would require a node l to be simultaneously smaller than i and greater than j, which is impossible.

The variable x^t (line 2) represents the total cost of the tour and ranges over the natural numbers, i.e., $D^t = \mathbb{N}$ (line 4). Constraint C^T (line 8) ensures that the total cost exactly equals the sum of the selected edges according to the cost matrix $M_{i,j}$. The remaining constraints C^C guarantee that exactly one outgoing edge (line 5) and exactly one incoming edge (line 6) are assigned to each city. Finally, the model specifies that the total cost variable x^t is to be minimized (line 9).

3 The Insertion-Based Miller-Tucker-Zemlin COP

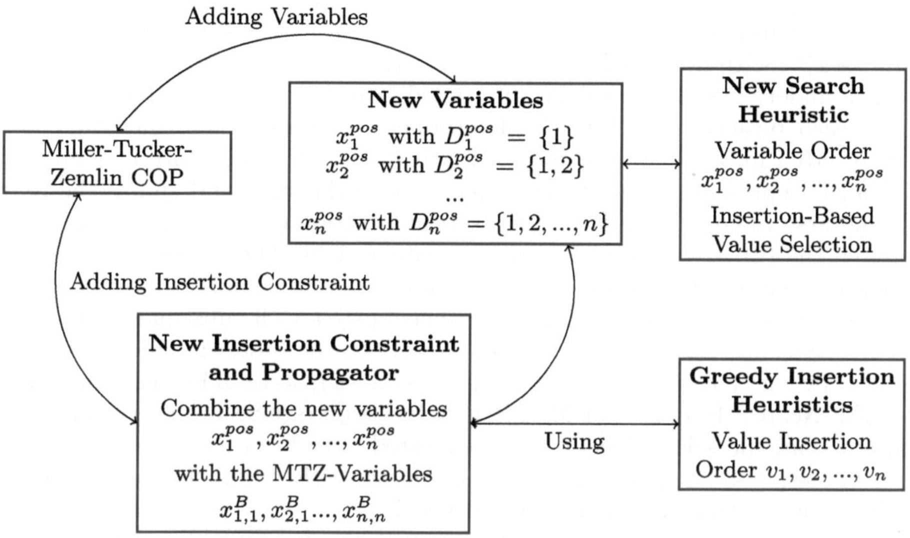

Fig. 3. The Miller-Tucker-Zemlin COP formulation (see Fig. 2) was extended by introducing additional decision variables, a dedicated search strategy, and a novel constraint together with a specialized propagator to enforce it.

We adopted a two-stage approach to integrate insertion-based heuristics into the MTZ-COP formulation (see Fig. 3).

In the first stage, we introduce additional decision variables that encode the insertion positions of nodes within the tour. These position variables were incorporated into the model, and a dedicated value selection heuristic was designed for them. This heuristic reproduces both the insertion order and the insertion positions characteristic of classical greedy insertion algorithms as described in Sect. 2.1. As a result, the search process explicitly mimics the constructive behavior of these heuristics within the COP framework.

In the second stage, we implemented a novel constraint equipped with a specialized propagator that links the newly introduced position variables to the Boolean edge selection matrix of the MTZ formulation. This constraint ensures consistency between the abstract insertion decisions and the concrete tour representation encoded by the MTZ model. The propagator receives, as input, the value ordering generated by one of the basic insertion heuristics described in Sect. 2.1. Depending on the heuristic used to produce this ordering, the extended model faithfully reflects the corresponding insertion strategy within the constraint solving process.

3.1 Position Variables and Search

We extend the MTZ-COP formulation by introducing n additional variables x_1^{pos}, x_2^{pos}, ..., x_n^{pos}. The first variable x_1^{pos} is assigned the domain $D_1^{pos} = \{1\}$, the second variable x_2^{pos} the domain $D_2^{pos} = \{1, 2\}$, and so forth, up to the last variable x_n^{pos} with domain $D_n^{pos} = \{1, 2, ..., n\}$.

The underlying idea is to specify a fixed insertion order of values $v_1, ..., v_n$, where each position variable x_i^{pos} determines the position at which the value v_i is inserted into the current partial route R. Initially, the route is defined as $R = [0, 0]$, representing the starting city at both the start and end of the tour. For the first value v_1, only a single insertion position exists, namely position 1 between the two zeros, resulting in the route $[0, 1, 0]$. The second value v_2 can be inserted either at position 1 or 2, yielding the routes $[0, 1, 2, 0]$ or $[0, 2, 1, 0]$, respectively. This principle generalizes analogously for all subsequent values.

The sequence $v_1, ..., v_n$ corresponds exactly to the order in which nodes are selected by a greedy insertion heuristic, i.e. Nearest Insertion, Farthest Insertion, Farthest-Nearest Insertion, or Max-Regret Insertion (see Sect. 2.1). During COP construction, the selected heuristic is executed once in order to determine the insertion sequence. Depending on the chosen heuristic different insertion orders of the values v_1 to v_n are obtained (see Fig. 1).

Our newly developed search strategy follows the fixed variable ordering x_1^{pos}, x_2^{pos}, ..., x_n^{pos} (i.e., *inputOrder*([x_1^{pos}, x_2^{pos}, ..., x_n^{pos}])) which always selects the variable x_i^{pos} with the smallest index i that has not yet been instantiated. Our value selection heuristic always selects the insertion position within the current partial route R that yields the minimum additional travel cost for inserting the next value v_i into the current partial route.

In Algorithm 1, we present the procedure of the newly developed value selection heuristic. Based on the current search depth d, and the partial insertion tour constructed so far (*tour*), the algorithm determines the feasible positions at which v_d (the value to be inserted into the tour at search depth d) can be inserted and orders them in ascending order of the associated insertion costs. The least costly value that has not yet been explored is then returned.

If the value of *index* is initially zero or has been reset to zero due to backtracking, the insertion order for the current search depth d must be recomputed (lines 1-7). The variable *index* indicates how many values of this insertion order have already been considered. If $index = 0$, no value has been explored yet, and the insertion order needs to be computed from scratch (lines 2–7). To this end, the partial tour *tour* constructed so far during the search process is first determined (line 2). Subsequently, a sorted list *pos* is generated by inserting all possible insertion positions j, ordered by increasing insertion cost (lines 3–7).

Regardless of whether *pos* has been newly computed or reused, the value at position *index* is then returned, and *index* is incremented by one (lines 8 to 10). Consequently, *index* always represents the number of values of the current insertion order *pos* that have already been tried.

Overall, the combination of the variable selection heuristic (*inputOrder*) and the newly developed value selection heuristic enforces a systematic assignment

Algorithm 1: The value selection heuristic.

Data: *int[][] cost, intBT d, intBT index, SortedList pos*
Output: The next value v to be set on the variable

```
if (index == 0) then
    List¡Integer¿ tour ← getCurrentSubTour()
    pos ← emptySortedList()
    for (j ∈ {1, ..., tour.size() − 1}) do
        a ← tour.get(j)
        b ← tour.get(j + 1)
        pos.add(cost[a][v_d] + cost[v_d][b] − cost[a][b], j)
int v ← pos[index]
index++
return v
```

of all variables x_i^{pos} to all possible positions $1, ..., d$. In this process, the values are tried in increasing order based on the insertion cost of the corresponding value v_i into the current partial route.

3.2 Insertion Propagator

In addition to an adapted search strategy that assigns the new variables x_i^{pos}, a new constraint with a dedicated propagator is required to further propagate the assignments of the position variables x_i^{pos} to the Boolean edge variables $x_{i,j}^B$. Recall that the Boolean variables $x_{i,j}^B$ take the value 1 if and only if the edge from node i to node j is part of the overall route of the COP, and 0 otherwise. The propagator incrementally removes infeasible Boolean edge assignments based on the currently fixed insertion positions, thereby enforcing consistency between the position variables x_i^{pos} and the Boolean edge variables $x_{i,j}^B$. The propagation behavior of this new propagator is illustrated in Algorithm 2.

The algorithm starts by reconstructing the currently known partial tour (line 1). This tour always includes the starting city 0 at both the beginning and the end, thereby modeling a closed tour. If the constructed partial tour contains more than one inserted node, the algorithm iterates sequentially over all consecutive triples $(last, current, next)$ of nodes in the tour (lines 2 to 23). During this traversal, a set of structural exclusion rules is applied in order to prune infeasible Boolean edge assignments.

First, the edge from *next* to *current* is excluded, since this direction would contradict the fixed order of nodes in the partial tour (line 7). Then, for every node *current*, all edges from *current* to the newly inserted node v_i are forbidden whenever *next* is unequal to v_i (lines 8 and 9, and then again in lines 14 and 15), ensuring that v_i cannot be reached from nodes that precede its actual insertion position. Symmetrically, edges from v_i to intermediate nodes are removed whenever they would violate the current ordering (line 16 and 17).

Algorithm 2: Propagation of position assignments (x_i^{pos}) to the Boolean edge variables $x_{i,j}^B$

Data: Boolean edge variables $x_{i,j}^B$, position variables x_i^{pos}, insertion value v_i, current search depth d
Result: Domain pruning of Boolean variables

1 *List¡Integer¿ tour = getCurrentSubTour()*
2 **if** *(|tour| > 3)* **then**
3     $iter = tour.iterator()$
4     $last \leftarrow -1$
5     $current \leftarrow iter.next()$
6     $next \leftarrow iter.next()$
7   Enforce $x_{next,current}^B \leftarrow 0$
8   **if** $(next \neq v_i) \wedge (next \neq 0)$ **then**
9   Enforce $x_{current,v_i}^B \leftarrow 0$
10   **while** *(iter.hasNext())* **do**
11         $last \leftarrow current$
12         $current \leftarrow next$
13         $next \leftarrow iter.next()$
14   **if** $(next \neq v_i)$ **then**
15   Enforce $x_{current,v_i}^B \leftarrow 0$
16   **if** $(last \neq v_i) \wedge (current \neq v_i) \wedge (current \neq 0)$ **then**
17   Enforce $x_{v_i,current}^B \leftarrow 0$
18   **if** $(current == v_i)$ **then**
19   Enforce $x_{next,v_i}^B \leftarrow 0$
20   Enforce $x_{last,next}^B \leftarrow 0$
21     $pos \leftarrow \text{value}(x_{d-1}^{pos})$
22   **if** $(pos \neq |tour| - 2)$ **then**
23   Enforce $x_{d-1,0}^B \leftarrow 0$

Additionally, when the iteration reaches the node v_i itself, two further exclusions are applied: the edge from its successor to v_i and the edge from v_i-s predecessor to its successor are both removed (lines 19 to 20). These constraints prevent the formation of shortcuts, premature cycles, and alternative local reorderings that would contradict the enforced insertion position of v_i.

Finally, the algorithm considers the insertion position *pos* of the most recently assigned variable x_{d-1}^{pos}. If this position is not the penultimate one, the edge from the corresponding node back to the starting city is forbidden (lines 21 to 23).

Overall, the algorithm implements a fine-grained, structure-oriented propagation scheme that tightly couples the assignments of the position variables x_i^{pos} with the Boolean edge variables $x_{i,j}^B$. At this stage, however, the reverse direction of propagation, the impact of exclusions in the Boolean edge variables on the position variables, is not incorporated. Such backward propagation naturally arises in the optimization setting once a first feasible solution has been found and an initial objective value has been established. From that point onward, the solver restricts the search to assignments yielding strictly better objective values. As a consequence, additional exclusions may occur in the Boolean edge variables, which could in principle be propagated back to the position variables.

Although reverse propagation was investigated, it was not included due to limited informational gain and marginal pruning effects. Nevertheless, exclusions at the Boolean edge level can still trigger early backtracking and help restrict the search space.

3.3 Removal of the Subtour Elimination Constraints

Since our search is now structured such that each value 1 to n is assigned to exactly one position, subtours with fewer than n nodes can no longer occur in the model. Consequently, the subtour elimination constraints C^S and the corresponding variables X^P from the MTZ-COP (cf. Figure 2) are no longer required. This reduces computational overhead due to the large number of these constraints. In our experiments, we observed no deterioration in solution quality. On the contrary, identical solutions were found faster, and in some cases, even better solutions could be obtained within the time limit.

4 Experimental Evaluation

All experiments were carried out on a computer running Microsoft Windows 11 Pro, equipped with an Intel(R) Core(TM) Ultra 7 265 processor with 20 cores and 20 logical processors, operating at a clock speed of 2.40 GHz. The system was equipped with 128 GB of DDR5 RAM running at 4400MT/s. The experiments were implemented in the Java programming language using JDK version 21.0.3, and the Choco-Solver version 4.10.7 [12] was used as the constraint solver.

For our experimental study, we used benchmark instances with up to 500 nodes taken from [13]. For these instances, optimal solutions are available, allowing us to directly compare the solutions obtained by our approach against the known optima. In total, 64 test instances were considered. Each instance was solved using the MTZ-COP, the newly proposed COP incorporating the additional variables, the dedicated search strategy, and the novel propagator, as well as, for reference, the savings-COP implementation from [6]. The four newly proposed methods were all provided with the same problem input, but differed in the order in which values $v_1, ..., v_n$ were inserted according to the including Nearest, Farthest, Farthest-Nearest, or Max-Regret insertion heuristics. Although the methods are otherwise identical, these different insertion sequences reflect the distinct heuristics and consequently result in significantly different outcomes. For all runs, a time limit of 10 min was applied. The results of these various test runs are presented in Table 1.

Table 1 summarizes the results of the experimental evaluation. For each COP formulation, the outcomes are reported separately by TSP size category (small:

¡ 50 nodes (14 instances); medium: 50–100 nodes (8 instances); large: 100–500 nodes (42 instances)). The table indicates: the number of instances for which a feasible solution was found (Solved), the number of instances for which the global optimum was reached (Global), the number of instances in which the approach produced the best solution among all compared methods (Best), the average cost of the best solution found (Cost), and the average deviation from the best known solution (Dev in %). For medium-sized and large instances, none of the approaches was able to prove optimality within the time limit of 10 min. For this reason, the row Global was omitted.

Table 1. The experimental results for the 64 TSP instances with different COPs.

Size	Mode	MTZ	Savings	Nearest	Farthest	Far-Near	Max-Regret
	Solved	12	14	14	14	14	14
Small	Global	5	3	3	3	4	8
$n < 50$	Best	5	4	5	3	4	11
14 inst.	Cost	5,440	4,187	4,209	4,244	4,196	4,136
	Dev in %	17.24	3.17	4.28	3.55	3.44	1.21
Medium	Solved	6	8	8	8	8	8
$50 \leq n$	Best	0	0	1	0	1	7
< 100	Cost	53,557	38,481	29,427	26,895	26,698	25,789
8 inst.	Dev in %	77.76	48.90	13.66	8.41	6.48	4.50
Large	Solved	15	42	42	42	42	42
$100 \leq n$	Best	0	0	1	2	4	35
≤ 500	Cost	91,039	102,775	52,118	47,395	47,445	45,549
42 inst.	Dev in %	144.28	132.36	17.68	10.25	10.47	5.61

The classical MTZ formulation performs significantly worse than all other approaches. For medium-sized instances, it solves only 6 out of 8 problems, and for large instances only 15 out of 42 within the time limit. In contrast, all other model variants consistently find feasible solutions. The solution quality of the MTZ-COP is also the lowest and deteriorates substantially with increasing instance size: the average deviation grows from 17.24 % for small instances to 144.28 % for large ones.

The Savings-based approach performs reasonably well on small instances (3.17 % average deviation), but its performance declines markedly as the problem size increases. All four newly proposed approaches clearly outperform both MTZ and Savings on medium and large instances. Among them, the Max-Regret-COP achieves the best overall performance, producing the best solution in 53 out of 64 instances and maintaining an average deviation of only 5.61 % on large instances.

Overall, the experimental results demonstrate that integrating insertion-based decision structures directly into the COP model substantially improves robustness and solution quality, particularly on medium and large-scale instances.

5 Conclusion and Future Work

We have presented an approach that transfers the behavioral principles of insertion heuristics for the Traveling Salesman Problem (TSP) directly into the search strategy of a constraint programming model, while preserving the global nature of constraint programming, i.e., the ability to find globally optimal solutions given sufficient computation time. To this end, the classical Miller-Tucker-Zemlin (MTZ) formulation was extended by additional variables, a dedicated search strategy, and a custom constraint equipped with a specialized propagator. These extensions enable the systematic integration of different insertion heuristics into the MTZ-based COP framework without sacrificing global optimality, which is typically not guaranteed when such heuristics are applied in isolation. In this work, we instantiated the approach using four well-known heuristics: Nearest Insertion, Farthest Insertion, Farthest-Nearest Insertion, and Max-Regret Insertion.

The experimental evaluation demonstrates that all four derived variants significantly outperform both the classical MTZ formulation and a Savings-based adaptation within the same modeling framework. Even for large-scale instances, high-quality solutions close to the global optimum can be obtained within short time limits.

Future work will focus on strengthening the bidirectional interaction between edge-selection variables and position variables by developing more effective propagation mechanisms that cascade exclusions in the Boolean edge variables back to the position variables, thereby further reducing the search space. Moreover, transferring the proposed integration principle to alternative TSP formulations, such as models based on the *allDifferent* or *circuit* constraints, appears promising. Finally, extending this methodology to related combinatorial optimization problems, in particular vehicle routing problems, represents a natural and potentially impactful direction for further research.

References

1. Apt, K.: Constraint satisfaction problems: examples. In: principles of Constraint Programming: chapter 2. Cambridge University Press (2003)
2. Cheikhrouhou, O., Khoufi, I.: A comprehensive survey on the multiple traveling salesman problem: applications, approaches and taxonomy. Comput. Sci. Rev. **40**, 100369 (2021). https://doi.org/10.1016/J.COSREV.2021.100369
3. Dechter, R.: Constraint networks. In: Constraint Processing: chapter 2, pp. 25–49. Elsevier Morgan Kaufmann (2003)
4. Garey, M.R., Johnson, D.S.: Computers and Intractability: A Guide to the Theory of NP-Completeness. W. H. Freeman, San Francisco (1979)
5. Gutin, G., Punnen, A.P.: The Traveling Salesman Problem and its Variations, vol. 12. Springer, Cham (2006)

6. Löffler, S., Hofstedt, P.: A constraint-based savings algorithm for the traveling salesman problem. In: International Conference on Machine Learning, Optimization, and Data Science, pp. 203–217. Springer, Heidelberg (2024). https://doi.org/10.1007/978-3-031-82484-5_15
7. Löffler, S., Hofstedt, P.: Greedy and local search-based constraint optimization of the travelling salesman problem. In: Rocha, A.P., Steels, L., van den Herik, H.J. (eds.) Agents and Artificial Intelligence - 16th International Conference, ICAART 2024, Rome, Italy, 24–26 February 2024, Revised Selected Papers, Part II. Lecture Notes in Computer Science, vol. 15592, pp. 212–233. Springer, Heidelberg (2024). https://doi.org/10.1007/978-3-031-87330-0_11
8. Marriott, K., Stuckey, P.J.: Programming with Constraints - An Introduction. MIT Press, Cambridge (1998)
9. Miller, C.E., Tucker, A.W., Zemlin, R.A.: Integer programming formulation of traveling salesman problems. J. ACM **7**(4), 326–329 (1960). https://doi.org/10.1145/321043.321046
10. Pintea, C.: A unifying survey of agent-based approaches for equality-generalized traveling salesman problem. Informatica **26**(3), 509–522 (2015). http://content.iospress.com/articles/informatica/inf1064
11. Pop, P.C., Cosma, O., Sabo, C., Sitar, C.P.: A comprehensive survey on the generalized traveling salesman problem. Eur. J. Oper. Res. **314**(3), 819–835 (2024). https://doi.org/10.1016/J.EJOR.2023.07.022
12. Prud'homme, C., Fages, J.G., Lorca, X.: Choco documentation (2017). http://www.choco-solver.org. Accessed 03 Mar 2026
13. Reinelt, G.: TSPLIB - a traveling salesman problem library. INFORMS J. Comput. **3**(4), 376–384 (1991). https://doi.org/10.1287/IJOC.3.4.376
14. Rosenkrantz, D.J., Stearns, R.E., Lewis, P.M., II.: An analysis of several heuristics for the traveling salesman problem. SIAM J. Comput. **6**(3), 563–581 (1977)
15. Rossi, F., Beek, P.V., Walsh, T.: Handbook of Constraint Programming, 1st edn. Elsevier, Amsterdam (2006)

Multi-state PatchCore for Noisy Industrial Audio

Simin Mirzadeh[1], Shamim Miroliaei[1], Alexej Zitzer[2], Johannes Munk[2], Matthias W. Gempel[2], and Ute Schmid[1](✉)

[1] Cognitive Systems, University of Bamberg, Bamberg, Germany
simin.mirzadeh@stud.uni-bamberg.de,
{shamim.miroliaei,ute.schmid}@uni-bamberg.de
[2] Brose SE, Coburg, Germany
{Alexej.Zitzer,Johannes.Munk,Matthias.Gempel}@brose.com
https://www.uni-bamberg.de/kogsys

Abstract. Industrial acoustic monitoring in real manufacturing environments is challenging due to strong background noise, heterogeneous operating conditions, and limited labeled fault data. In such settings, the normal operating conditions often vary acoustically. Background sounds may resemble malfunction events. All of these factors may lead to unstable decision boundaries and increased false alarm rates. To address this challenge, we formulate industrial audio anomaly detection as a multi-state problem rather than a binary normal vs. anomalous task.

We propose to adapt the PatchCore retrieval framework for industrial audio, using log-Mel spectrogram representations and class-specific memory banks to model different operating states. The approach is evaluated under multiple temporal segmentation strategies using a pretrained CNN14 encoder on AudioSet, and compared with a supervised CNN baseline. Our experiments show that fault state detection performance depends strongly on the alignment between temporal segmentation and the encoder receptive field, rather than on the temporal context length alone. When this alignment is preserved, the retrieval-based approach produces well-separated embeddings of operating states and achieves strong ranking performance while maintaining competitive classification accuracy.

Keywords: Industrial audio monitoring · Anomaly detection · Multi-State PatchCore · Temporal representation

1 Introduction

Industrial anomaly detection plays a central role in predictive maintenance and quality assurance for modern manufacturing systems [3]. Acoustic monitoring is particularly attractive due to its non-invasive nature, low hardware cost, and ease of deployment [27]. However, real-world industrial environments present substantial challenges: background noise is often strong and highly variable,

D. Wolter and G. Schwalbe (Eds.): KI 2026, LNAI 16830, pp. 57–71, 2027.
https://doi.org/10.1007/978-3-032-32335-4_5

operating conditions are often acoustically heterogeneous, and labeled fault data is typically scarce. These factors make reliable anomaly detection considerably more difficult than in controlled laboratory settings [26].

Machine sound anomaly detection is commonly formulated as a binary distinction between normal and anomalous sounds [4,16,19]. In practice, however, normal operation is rarely homogeneous. Industrial environments frequently involve multiple operating conditions resulting from environmental noise or nearby machinery. Collapsing such heterogeneous conditions into a single notion of normality can cause acoustically similar background states to be misinterpreted as anomalies, leading to unstable decision boundaries and elevated false alarm rates.

In computer vision, this challenge has motivated patch-based anomaly detection methods that have demonstrated strong performance in industrial inspection [5,30–32]. Among these methods, PatchCore [24] introduced a retrieval-based paradigm in which embeddings of normal samples are stored in a memory bank and anomaly scores are computed via nearest-neighbor distances. In its classical formulation, PatchCore follows a one-class paradigm that models only normal data.

Anomalous PatchCore [18] shows that limited anomaly supervision can improve anomaly discrimination in industrial inspection settings. These findings suggest that strict one-class modeling is not always the best choice when reliable anomaly annotations are available.

Motivated by this perspective, we consider a multi-state extension in which available anomaly labels are used explicitly. Instead of modeling all deviations relative to a single background memory, we construct class-specific memory banks representing multiple operating states, including malfunction conditions. This formulation departs from the classical binary normal-versus-anomaly assumption and enables explicit modeling of heterogeneous acoustic conditions.

Transferring retrieval-based paradigms from vision to audio is promising but non-trivial. The structural similarity between spectrograms and images has encouraged such transfer [1,20]. However, unlike images, acoustic signals exhibit intrinsic temporal structure. In practical deployment, audio is typically processed using fixed-length windows to satisfy latency and throughput constraints, whereas many malfunction signatures are temporally localized at the event level. A mismatch between temporal segmentation and encoder receptive field can therefore reduce embedding stability and weaken downstream anomaly ranking, particularly when pretrained models are applied to short industrial segments.

To address these challenges, we propose a *Multi-State PatchCore* framework for industrial audio under real-world noise conditions. Instead of modeling normal data using a single memory bank, we maintain class-specific memory banks to explicitly represent multiple operating states observed in production environments. We analyze how segmentation, encoder configuration, and memory construction interact within a retrieval-based anomaly detection pipeline, with particular attention to encodercontext alignment and embedding stability.

Through controlled experiments on real industrial acoustic data, we demonstrate that the proposed PatchCore pipeline achieves performance comparable to a supervised CNN baseline while avoiding task-specific end-to-end training. In particular, modeling heterogeneous background states yields strong ranking performance as reflected in ROCAUC, while maintaining competitive classification accuracy. Our findings indicate that reliable industrial audio anomaly detection depends strongly on encodercontext alignment and representation quality.

2 Related Work

2.1 Industrial Audio Anomaly Detection

Acoustic anomaly detection has been widely studied as a practical approach for monitoring industrial machinery, particularly in settings where visual inspection is infeasible or costly. Early deep learning approaches were motivated by the scarcity of labeled fault data and therefore relied on unsupervised or semi-supervised formulations [10]. Koizumi et al. introduced a deep learning framework for anomalous sound detection with controlled false-positive rates, forming the basis of benchmark initiatives such as DCASE Task 2 [15,16].

Benchmark datasets such as MIMII have supported standardized evaluation of machine sound anomaly detection under controlled conditions [23], while later surveys summarize broader methodological trends and evaluation protocols [21].

Most existing approaches formulate the task as a binary distinction between normal and anomalous sounds. A common strategy is reconstruction-based modeling, where autoencoders learn normal acoustic patterns and detect deviations through reconstruction error [4].

Supervised CNN-based classifiers instead optimize discriminative decision boundaries using labeled data [6]. While these approaches can perform well under controlled conditions, real-world industrial environments introduce strong background variability and environmental noise [27]. In such settings, relying on a single notion of normality can lead to unstable decision boundaries and higher false alarm rates.

2.2 Patch-Based and Memory-Based Anomaly Detection

In computer vision, patch-based anomaly detection methods have achieved strong performance in industrial inspection. Representative examples include Patch SVDD [30], PaDiM [5], FastFlow [31], and DRAEM [32], while later work further improved efficiency and representation quality through approaches such as EfficientAD [2], CFLOW-AD [9], and STPM [28].

PatchCore introduced a retrieval-based formulation in which embeddings of normal samples are stored in a memory bank, and anomaly scores are computed via nearest-neighbor distances. To improve efficiency while preserving representational coverage, k-center greedy coreset selection is used to reduce memory redundancy [24]. Subsequent extensions explored coreset optimization [25], attention-based enhancements [11], and robustness improvements such as SoftPatch+ [12].

Recent variants such as PatchCore++ [22] and FR-PatchCore [13] further refine memory construction and feature aggregation. While classical PatchCore follows a one-class paradigm that models only normal data, recent work has investigated incorporating anomalous samples during representation learning. Anomalous PatchCore [18] demonstrates that limited anomaly supervision can improve discrimination in industrial inspection scenarios. These developments suggest that retrieval-based anomaly detection can be extended beyond strict one-class modeling when informative anomaly labels are available.

2.3 Transfer of Retrieval-Based Methods to Audio

Many successful anomaly detection methods were originally developed for visual industrial inspection, where spatial feature representations support fine-grained modeling of structural deviations [5,9,30,31]. The structural similarity between spectrograms and images has encouraged the transfer of such methods to the audio domain [1,20]. These studies demonstrate that PatchCore-style retrieval can be applied to time–frequency representations such as log–Mel spectrograms.

Recent work further adapts patch-based ideas to time-series and acoustic data [14,33]. Pretrained audio encoders, including CNN14 from the PANNs framework [17,29] and transformer-based architectures such as AST [8], offer strong transferable representations because they are trained on large-scale datasets such as AudioSet [7]. However, these models are typically designed for multi-second inputs and global tagging objectives. When applied to short industrial audio segments under deployment constraints, discrepancies between the encoder receptive field and temporal segmentation may affect embedding stability and downstream anomaly ranking.

Overall, existing work demonstrates that retrieval-based anomaly detection can be transferred to audio representations. However, systematic analysis of segmentationencoder alignment and representation stability in noisy industrial acoustic settings remains limited. In particular, the interaction between encoder truncation, temporal segmentation, and memory construction in multi-state settings has not been studied in much detail.

3 Method

3.1 Overview

We address industrial acoustic monitoring under real-world noise conditions. Our framework compares two learning paradigms built on the same CNN14-based encoder family: (i) retrieval-based inference using a PatchCore-style memory formulation, and (ii) supervised CNN classification. An overview of the processing pipeline is shown in Fig. 1.

CNN14 is used as the common encoder backbone because its large-scale pretraining on AudioSet within the PANNs framework provides transferable audio

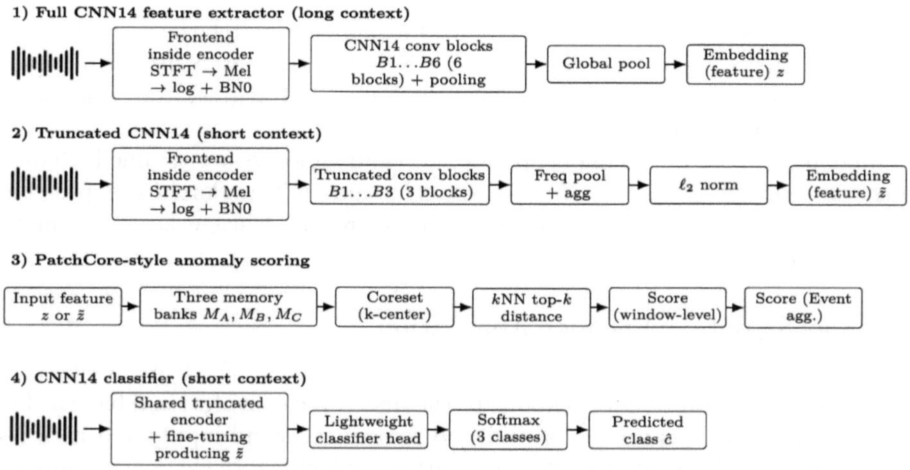

Fig. 1. Overview of the proposed framework and comparative pipelines. Row 1 illustrates the full-CNN14 long-context design considered in the encoder–context analysis, while Row 2 shows the truncated short-context encoder used in the main quantitative comparison. Row 3 presents the Multi-State PatchCore retrieval pipeline with class-specific memory banks. Row 4 shows the supervised classification baseline sharing the truncated encoder for controlled comparison.

representations [7,17]. Using a shared encoder family enables a controlled comparison between retrieval-based and supervised approaches under matched representational capacity.

We adapt the original PatchCore [24] to audio by processing waveform inputs through the CNN14 frontend and constructing class-specific memory banks representing different operating states. We consider a full pretrained CNN14 for encoder–context analysis. A truncated version of CNN14 is used for short-context windows, which are used in the main quantitative comparison. The effectiveness of each encoder configuration depends on how well the encoder's receptive field matches the acoustic structure captured within each segment.

3.2 Audio Pre-processing and Temporal Segmentation

All recordings are mono, resampled to 16 kHz, and peak-normalized to ensure consistent temporal resolution and amplitude scaling. Feature extraction is performed using CNN14, which internally computes time–frequency representations (STFT → Mel → log) [17]. Segmentation follows an event-aware strategy based on annotated onset–offset boundaries. Sliding windows are extracted only from valid temporal intervals, while exclusion margins around malfunction events reduce contamination of background segments. Because malfunction signatures are often short and temporally localized, additional jittered windows are generated around event centers to improve robustness to temporal misalignment.

Short windows reduce inference latency but may not match the receptive field of pretrained encoders. To address this, CNN14 is truncated for short inputs so that temporal resolution is preserved before global aggregation. For longer inputs, the full pretrained backbone is retained.

No explicit class balancing is applied; all valid windows are retained. Redundancy is reduced later through coreset selection in the PatchCore pipeline. Dataset splits are defined at the file level to prevent leakage across training, validation, and test sets.

3.3 Short-Context Encoder Adaptation

For short-context processing, we adapt the pretrained CNN14 architecture by truncating its convolutional backbone to the first three convolutional blocks. The full CNN14 model was originally designed for multi-second inputs and includes deep stacking and repeated pooling operations, which cause excessive temporal downsampling when applied to short windows. Retaining only the early convolutional layers (`conv_block1`–`conv_block3`) preserves higher temporal resolution while maintaining meaningful time–frequency feature extraction.

In addition, the pooling strategy is modified to frequency-only pooling (`pool_size=(1,2)`), avoiding temporal compression so that short transient acoustic patterns remain detectable within 0.2–0.4 s inputs. This adaptation improves alignment between the encoder's receptive field and the short-context regime considered in our study.

For supervised classification, a lightweight embedding and classification head is attached to the truncated encoder. Training follows a stage-wise fine-tuning strategy: initially, only the newly added layers are optimized while the convolutional backbone remains frozen; subsequently, the deepest retained block (`conv_block3`) is selectively unfrozen and updated with a reduced learning rate.

For PatchCore, the same truncated encoder is used only as a fixed feature extractor for short-context inputs. In contrast to the supervised classifier, the PatchCore retrieval pipeline itself does not require task-specific end-to-end training. The memory construction and distance-based inference stages are described in the following subsection.

3.4 Multi-state PatchCore with Class-Specific Memory Banks

Classical PatchCore models a single reference distribution of normal data and performs anomaly detection via nearest-neighbor retrieval in embedding space [24]. In industrial acoustic environments, multiple operating states may exhibit distinct acoustic characteristics. Modeling all states with a single memory distribution may increase ambiguity when certain background patterns resemble malfunction signatures. We therefore adopt a multi-state formulation with class-specific memory banks. Let $f_\theta(x)$ denote the CNN14-based encoder and $z = f_\theta(x)$ the resulting embedding. For each operating state $c \in \mathcal{C}$, an independent memory bank is constructed as

$$\mathcal{M}_c = \{z_j^{(c)}\}_{j=1}^{N_c},$$

where N_c denotes the number of embeddings assigned to class c. To control memory growth while preserving representative coverage, each memory bank is optionally reduced to a subset $S_c \subseteq \mathcal{M}_c$ of size m using the k-center greedy coreset strategy introduced in [24]. The corresponding objective is

$$\min_{S \subseteq \mathcal{M}_c,\ |S|=m} \max_{z \in \mathcal{M}_c} \min_{s \in S} \|z - s\|_2.$$

At inference time, a test embedding z is compared against each class-specific coreset S_c using Euclidean distance. To improve robustness to local embedding fluctuations, the class score is computed as the mean distance to the k nearest neighbors:

$$d_c(z) = \frac{1}{k} \sum_{i=1}^{k} \|z - s_i^{(c)}\|_2,$$

where $s_i^{(c)} \in S_c$ denotes the i-th nearest neighbor of z in the coreset of class c. Window-level prediction follows minimum-distance assignment,

$$\hat{c}(z) = \arg\min_{c \in \mathcal{C}} d_c(z).$$

For ranking-based evaluation, similarity scores are defined as

$$s_c(z) = -d_c(z),$$

so that larger values indicate a stronger alignment with class c. Each annotated event corresponds to multiple windows. Window-level scores are therefore aggregated into event-level decisions. Because event-level performance depends on the aggregation rule, this analysis is treated as a secondary deployment-oriented evaluation. For controlled comparison, event-level results are reported using a shared aggregation rule across methods, while alternative strategies remain possible in deployment.

Reproducibility. All experiments were conducted with fixed random seeds for data splitting, memory construction, coreset selection, and model initialization. Deterministic computation modes were enabled where applicable. All preprocessing steps are deterministic and annotation-driven, enabling reproducible dataset generation from the original recordings. The code is publicly available on GitHub.[1]

By separating representation learning, memory construction, and aggregation, the framework enables analysis of embedding stability and encoder–context alignment. The experimental protocol is described in the following section.

4 Experimental Setup and Results

4.1 Dataset and Industrial Setting

We evaluate on real-world machine acoustics collected from an industrial production line. The dataset consists of three operating states: two background

[1] https://github.com/ms-patchcore-anon/multi-state-patchcore-audio.

conditions and one malfunction class. Specifically, Class A corresponds to normal operation with a noisy background, Class B to anomalous operation, and Class C to normal operation with a relatively clean background.

Recordings vary in duration and are annotated with event-level onset–offset boundaries. Representative log–Mel spectrograms are shown in Fig. 2 for qualitative comparison.

Temporal Context Selection. Segment durations were determined through empirical analysis of embedding stability, encoder behavior, and deployment constraints. CNN14 was pretrained on multi-second audio clips (10 s) using a global tagging objective [17].

When applying the full backbone to our industrial recordings, very short inputs were not suitable, as stacked pooling operations and receptive-field requirements led to unstable embeddings. Empirically, approximately 2 s was the minimum input duration that allowed the full CNN14 to produce stable embeddings. However, this long-context setting was not retained as the main evaluation configuration. First, a 2 s context is not well suited to industrial deployment, where low-latency monitoring is required. Second, in our dataset, malfunction events are typically short and transient, so a 2 s segment may include substantial surrounding background in addition to the malfunction itself, thereby weakening class discrimination. For deployment-oriented short-context settings, windows below 0.2 s resulted in inconsistent embedding neighborhoods and degraded retrieval stability. Windows in the range of 0.2–0.4 s provided a more favorable trade-off between temporal precision, latency, and embedding stability. Longer durations with truncated encoders did not provide further benefit.

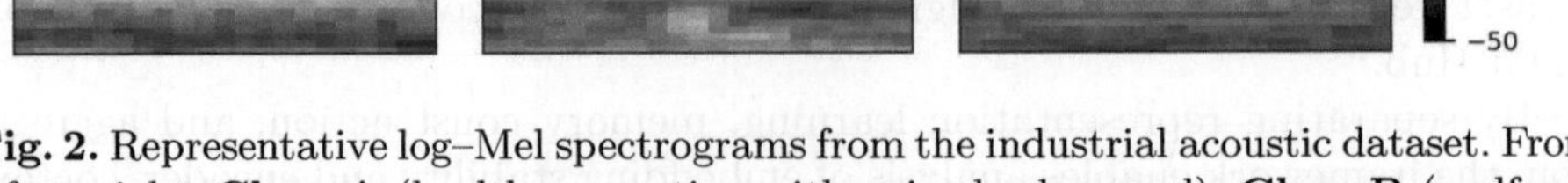

Fig. 2. Representative log–Mel spectrograms from the industrial acoustic dataset. From left to right: **Class A** (healthy operation with noisy background), **Class B** (malfunction event with a short transient burst), and **Class C** (healthy operation with clean background). Spectrograms are shown for qualitative comparison; the encoder operates directly on raw waveforms. Malfunction signatures are temporally localized, whereas background conditions exhibit more stationary spectral patterns.

4.2 Evaluated Configurations

All pipelines are derived from CNN14 pretrained on AudioSet [7,17]. This shared starting point supports a controlled comparison under limited industrial data. The main quantitative evaluation focuses on two short-context settings (0.2–0.4 s) based on the adapted encoder described in Sect. 3.3, while longer-context processing is considered only in the encoder–context analysis.

- **Long-context feasibility analysis:** The full pretrained CNN14 is considered only as part of the encoder–context analysis and is not reported as a primary quantitative comparison.
- **Short-context PatchCore:** The truncated short-context encoder is used as a fixed feature extractor within the Multi-State PatchCore pipeline.
- **Short-context supervised classification:** The same truncated encoder is combined with a lightweight classification head and optimized using class-weighted cross-entropy.

4.3 Performance Comparison and Analysis

Window-Level Evaluation. Each window produces either class probabilities (classification) or distance-based scores (PatchCore). We report accuracy, macro-F1, and false alarm rate (FAR). For PatchCore, one-vs-rest ROC–AUC and PR–AUC are also computed from continuous scores.

Window-level performance reflects embedding stability and local discriminative capacity. As shown in Table 1, the supervised CNN14 classifier achieves an accuracy of around 0.88 for both short-context window sizes. PatchCore reaches its best window-level performance at 0.4 s, with similar accuracy. The difference in FAR is more pronounced: the classification approach shows a higher FAR, whereas the PatchCore FAR decreases from 0.13 at 0.2 s to 0.03 at 0.4 s. In addition, PatchCore provides continuous scores for threshold-independent evaluation and shows strong ranking behavior under acoustically ambiguous conditions.

At the class level, the one-vs-rest ROC curves in Fig. 3b show that PatchCore separates the malfunction class (Class B) particularly well, with window-level ROC–AUC values of 1.000 at 0.2 s and 0.991 at 0.4 s. The supervised classifier likewise performs very strongly on Class B at the window level, achieving F1-scores of 0.990 at 0.2 s and 0.974 at 0.4 s.

Event-Level Evaluation. Event-level aggregation combines information across windows and can reduce isolated errors. Because event-level outcomes depend on the aggregation rule, this analysis is treated as a secondary, deployment-oriented evaluation. For controlled comparison across methods, event-level results are reported using a shared top-5 mean aggregation rule, while alternative aggregation strategies showed broadly consistent behavior.

As shown in Table 1, the lowest FAR is achieved by PatchCore, reaching 0.01 at 0.4 s. This setting also yields the strongest event-level accuracy and macro-F1, suggesting that aggregation can further stabilize short-context predictions, although these outcomes remain sensitive to post-processing choices.

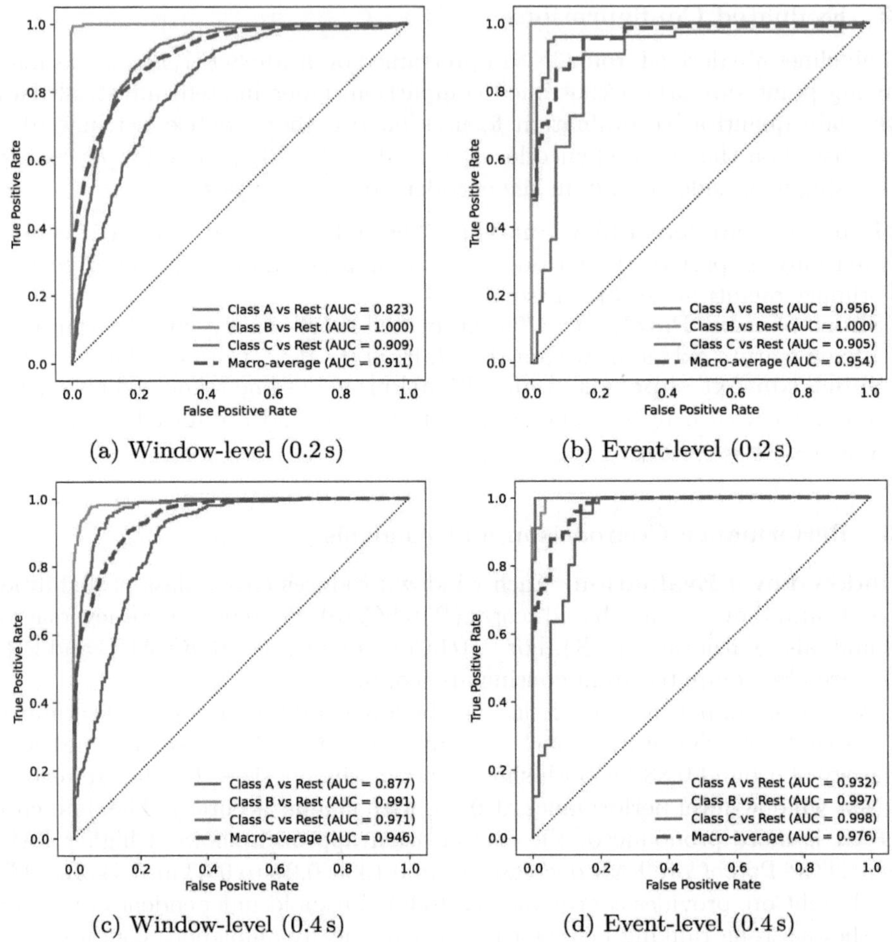

Fig. 3. One-vs-rest ROC curves for PatchCore at 0.2 s and 0.4 s. Window-level ROC reflects embedding separability, while event-level ROC shows the effect of aggregation in a secondary, deployment-oriented analysis. The improvement from (a,c) to (b,d) suggests more stable predictions after aggregation.

PatchCore vs Supervised Classification. Across the evaluated short-context settings, PatchCore and supervised classification show broadly similar performance. The main practical difference is that PatchCore does not require task-specific end-to-end training. Instead, it relies on retrieval from class-specific memory banks built from fixed embeddings. For our dataset, the 0.4 s PatchCore setting gives the most stable overall short-context results, suggesting that this duration captures enough local structure for the short and transient malfunction patterns without the drawbacks of longer contexts. In addition, the distance-based formulation provides continuous scores, which are useful for threshold-independent evaluation and score-based ranking. At the same time, auxiliary audio features such as signal energy can be integrated into supervised classification models relatively easily, whereas this is less straightforward in PatchCore because retrieval depends on a consistent embedding geometry and distance metric. Event-level results are considered secondary here and mainly support deployment-oriented final decision making.

Table 1. Window-level (top) and event/file-level (bottom) test performance for supervised classification and PatchCore pipelines. Win. denotes window length. Event-level results are reported as a secondary, deployment-oriented analysis and, for controlled comparison, are computed using a shared top-5 mean aggregation rule across methods.

Method	Win.	Acc.	F1	FAR	ROC–AUC	PR–AUC
Window-level						
Classification	0.2 s	0.86	0.88	0.09	0.958	0.923
Classification	0.4 s	0.88	0.89	0.10	0.967	0.934
PatchCore	0.2 s	0.86	0.88	0.13	0.910	0.860
PatchCore	0.4 s	0.88	0.88	0.03	0.946	0.899
Event-level						
Classification	0.2 s	0.92	0.84	0.05	0.983	0.938
Classification	0.4 s	0.89	0.84	0.10	0.993	0.973
PatchCore	0.2 s	0.92	0.86	0.12	0.953	0.778
PatchCore	0.4 s	0.95	0.90	0.01	0.975	0.963

5 Discussion

This work demonstrates that PatchCore can be adapted from its original vision-based formulation to industrial acoustic monitoring under real-world noise conditions while preserving its retrieval-based characteristics [1,24,27]. While the original PatchCore formulation is one-class [24], the proposed Multi-State PatchCore framework introduces class-specific memory banks to represent multiple operating conditions, allowing heterogeneous background states to be modeled explicitly.

A key finding of this study is that anomaly detection performance depends strongly on the alignment between temporal segmentation and the encoder's receptive field. Within the evaluated short-context settings (0.2–0.4 s), increasing temporal context alone does not necessarily improve performance. Consequently, the evaluation focuses on this short-context range, where encoder–context alignment is better preserved and latency remains suitable for real-world deployment. Shorter windows (below 0.2 s) lead to inconsistent embedding neighborhoods and degraded retrieval stability, while larger short-context windows (e.g., 0.4 s) provide a better trade-off between stability and latency. Stable and discriminative embeddings emerge when temporal segments preserve informative acoustic structure aligned with the encoder's capacity, particularly when using pretrained CNN14-based audio representations [17]. Event-level aggregation can improve robustness while preserving ranking behavior.

Within identical short-context constraints, supervised classification and PatchCore achieve comparable accuracy. However, unlike the supervised classifier, the PatchCore pipeline does not require task-specific end-to-end training and instead relies on pretrained embeddings and memory-based retrieval. In addition, the retrieval-based formulation produces continuous similarity scores rather than only final class decisions. This makes threshold-independent evaluation possible through metrics such as ROC–AUC and PR–AUC, and it also shows how strongly a sample matches each operating state. This differs from the supervised classifier, which directly learns decision boundaries. In noisy industrial settings, where different operating conditions may partially overlap, such score-based comparisons can provide useful additional insight [27].

The proposed pipeline is designed to be transferable rather than dataset-specific. The preprocessing and model adaptation strategy can be reused for other industrial audio datasets containing annotated temporal events. The approach is expected to scale to multi-class settings provided that classes exhibit sufficiently distinguishable acoustic-temporal patterns.

Limitations of the current study include the evaluation on a single industrial dataset and a single encoder family. While the observed behavior is consistent under the examined conditions, further validation across different machine types, noise environments, and alternative encoder architectures is necessary to assess generalization. Performance degradation may occur when multiple classes share highly overlapping acoustic characteristics. In addition, segmentation relies on annotation-guided event boundaries, which may influence embedding stability and evaluation outcomes.

6 Conclusion

We proposed a Multi-State PatchCore framework with class-specific memory banks to represent heterogeneous operating states and compared it with a supervised CNN baseline under matched encoder configurations. Our results show that reliable anomaly detection depends less on temporal context length alone than on how well temporal segmentation matches the encoder's receptive field. In our setting, short-context processing was most effective when fixed-length windows preserved the relevant acoustic structure of short and transient malfunction events. Under this alignment, retrieval-based modeling achieved strong ranking performance and competitive classification accuracy without requiring task-specific end-to-end training. These findings suggest that, for industrial audio under real-world noise, representation quality and encoder–context alignment are more critical than the anomaly scoring paradigm alone. Evaluation should therefore consider patch-level score behavior and threshold-independent metrics alongside event-level performance.

Future work will investigate robustness under domain shift and evolving machine states in long-term industrial deployment. In particular, exploring alternative encoder architectures beyond convolutional networks may further improve representation stability and encoder–context alignment.

References

1. Barusco, M., Borsatti, F., Pezze, D.D., Paissan, F., Farella, E., Susto, G.A.: From vision to sound: advancing audio anomaly detection with vision-based algorithms (2025). https://arxiv.org/abs/2502.18328
2. Batzner, K., Heckler, L., König, R.: Efficientad: accurate visual anomaly detection at millisecond-level latencies (2024). https://arxiv.org/abs/2303.14535
3. Bergmann, P., Fauser, M., Sattlegger, D., Steger, C.: Mvtec ad – a comprehensive real-world dataset for unsupervised anomaly detection. In: 2019 IEEE/CVF Conference on Computer Vision and Pattern Recognition (CVPR), pp. 9584–9592 (2019). https://doi.org/10.1109/CVPR.2019.00982
4. Coelho, G., Matos, L., Pereira, P., Ferreira, A., Pilastri, A., Cortez, P.: Deep autoencoders for acoustic anomaly detection: experiments with working machine and in-vehicle audio. Neural Comput. Appl. **34**, 1–15 (2022). https://doi.org/10.1007/s00521-022-07375-2
5. Defard, T., Setkov, A., Loesch, A., Audigier, R.: Padim: a patch distribution modeling framework for anomaly detection and localization. arXiv preprint (2020). https://doi.org/10.48550/arXiv.2011.08785
6. Deschênes, A., Georges, R., Subakan, C., Ugulino, B., Henry, A., Morin, M.: Planing it by ear: convolutional neural networks for acoustic anomaly detection in industrial wood planers (2025). https://arxiv.org/abs/2501.04819
7. Gemmeke, J.F., et al.: Audio set: an ontology and human-labeled dataset for audio events. In: 2017 IEEE International Conference on Acoustics, Speech and Signal Processing (ICASSP), pp. 776–780 (2017). https://doi.org/10.1109/ICASSP.2017.7952261
8. Gong, Y., Chung, Y.A., Glass, J.: Ast: Audio spectrogram transformer (2021). https://doi.org/10.48550/arXiv.2104.01778
9. Gudovskiy, D., Ishizaka, S., Kozuka, K.: Cflow-ad: real-time unsupervised anomaly detection with localization via conditional normalizing flows (2021). https://arxiv.org/abs/2107.12571
10. Hojjati, H., Armanfard, N.: Self-supervised acoustic anomaly detection via contrastive learning. In: ICASSP 2022 - 2022 IEEE International Conference on Acoustics, Speech and Signal Processing (ICASSP), pp. 3253–3257 (2022). https://doi.org/10.1109/ICASSP43922.2022.9746207
11. Ishida, K., Takena, Y., Nota, Y., Mochizuki, R., Matsumura, I., Ohashi, G.: Sa-patchcore: anomaly detection in dataset with co-occurrence relationships using self-attention. IEEE Access **11**, 3232–3240 (2023). https://doi.org/10.1109/ACCESS.2023.3234745
12. Jiang, X., et al.: Softpatch: unsupervised anomaly detection with noisy data (2024). https://arxiv.org/abs/2403.14233
13. Jiang, Z., Zhang, Y., Wang, Y., Li, J., Gao, X.: Fr-patchcore: improving generalization in industrial anomaly detection. Sensors **24**(5) (2024). https://doi.org/10.3390/s24051368

14. Kim, G.I., Yoo, H., Cho, H.J., Chung, K.: Defect detection model using time series data augmentation and transformation. Procedia Comput. Sci. **237**, 156–163 (2024). https://doi.org/10.32604/cmc.2023.046324
15. Koizumi, Y., et al.: Description and discussion on dcase2020 challenge task2: unsupervised anomalous sound detection for machine condition monitoring (2020). https://doi.org/10.48550/arXiv.2006.05822
16. Koizumi, Y., Saito, S., Uematsu, H., Kawachi, Y., Harada, N.: Unsupervised detection of anomalous sound based on deep learning and the Neyman–Pearson lemma. IEEE/ACM Trans. Audio Speech Lang. Process. **27**(1), 212–224 (2019). https://doi.org/10.1109/taslp.2018.2877258
17. Kong, Q., Cao, Y., Iqbal, T., Wang, Y., Wang, W., Plumbley, M.D.: Panns: large-scale pretrained audio neural networks for audio pattern recognition (2020). https://arxiv.org/abs/1912.10211
18. Koshil, M., Wegener, T., Mentrup, D., Frintrop, S., Wilms, C.: Anomalouspatchcore: exploring the use of anomalous samples in industrial anomaly detection (2024). https://arxiv.org/abs/2408.15113
19. Liu, S., et al.: Audio self-supervised learning: a survey (2022). https://arxiv.org/abs/2203.01205
20. Transferability to spectrogram-based anomaly detection: enhancing audio anomaly detection through vision-derived methods. Master's thesis, University of Stuttgart (2024). https://elib.uni-stuttgart.de/items/aac51482-a86d-4ef7-b8cc-6b9c0cd24d0c
21. Mnasri, Z., Rovetta, S., Masulli, F.: Anomalous sound event detection: a survey of machine learning-based methods and applications. Multimedia Tools Appl. **81**, 5537–5586 (2022). https://doi.org/10.1007/s11042-021-11817-9
22. Oh, G., Shin, J.: Patch core++: augmenting coreset for superior industrial anomaly detection (2024). https://doi.org/10.1109/ICCE-Asia63397.2024.10773978
23. Purohit, H., et al.: Mimii dataset: sound dataset for malfunctioning industrial machine investigation and inspection (2019). https://arxiv.org/abs/1909.09347
24. Roth, K., Pemula, L., Zepeda, J., Schölkopf, B., Brox, T., Gehler, P.: Towards total recall in industrial anomaly detection. In: Proceedings of the IEEE/CVF Conference on Computer Vision and Pattern Recognition (CVPR), pp. 14318–14328 (2022). https://arxiv.org/abs/2106.08265
25. Santos, J., Tran, T., Rippel, O.: Optimizing patchcore for few/many-shot anomaly detection (2023). https://arxiv.org/abs/2307.10792
26. Shimizu, H., Shouhei, Y.: Anomaly detection for industrial equipment using patchcore on audio and vibration spectrograms. In: 2026 IEEE 16th Annual Computing and Communication Workshop and Conference (CCWC), pp. 406–411 (2026). https://doi.org/10.1109/CCWC67433.2026.11393700
27. Tagawa, Y., Maskeliunas, R., Damaševičius, R.: Acoustic anomaly detection of mechanical failures in noisy real-life factory environments. Electronics **10**, 2329 (2021). https://doi.org/10.3390/electronics10192329
28. Wang, G., Han, S., Ding, E., Huang, D.: Student-teacher feature pyramid matching for anomaly detection (2021). https://arxiv.org/abs/2103.04257
29. Won, H., Kim, B., Kwak, I.Y., Lim, C.: Using various pre-trained models for audio feature extraction in automated audio captioning. Expert Syst. Appl. **231**, 120664 (2023). https://doi.org/10.1016/j.eswa.2023.120664. https://www.sciencedirect.com/science/article/pii/S0957417423011661
30. Yi, J., Yoon, S.: Patch svdd: Patch-level svdd for anomaly detection and segmentation (2020). https://arxiv.org/abs/2006.16067

31. Yu, J., et al.: Fastflow: unsupervised anomaly detection and localization via 2d normalizing flows (2021). https://arxiv.org/abs/2111.07677
32. Zavrtanik, V., Kristan, M., Skočaj, D.: Draem – a discriminatively trained reconstruction embedding for surface anomaly detection (2021). https://arxiv.org/abs/2108.07610
33. Zavrtanik, V., Marolt, M., Kristan, M., Skočaj, D.: Anomalous sound detection by feature-level anomaly simulation. In: ICASSP 2024 - 2024 IEEE International Conference on Acoustics, Speech and Signal Processing (ICASSP), pp. 1466–1470 (2024). https://doi.org/10.1109/ICASSP48485.2024.10447941

Prioritizing Conflicts in Conflict-Based Search with Disjoint Splitting

Grigorios Mouratidis[1(✉)], Bernhard Nebel[1], and Sven Koenig[2]

[1] University of Freiburg, Freiburg im Breisgau, Germany
mouratig@cs.uni-freiburg.de, nebel@uni-freiburg.de
[2] University of California, Irvine, USA
sven.koenig@uci.edu

Abstract. Multi-agent path finding (MAPF) is the problem of finding collision-free paths for a team of agents. Conflict-based search (CBS) is a state-of-the-art algorithm for solving MAPF optimally that repeatedly picks a collision (known as conflict) between two agents and resolves it by constraining the movement of the agents. One of the earliest runtime enhancement of CBS categorized conflicts into three groups (cardinal, semi-cardinal, and non-cardinal) and resolved them in that priority order. When multiple collisions share the same type, CBS typically breaks ties by selecting one at random. In this work, we show that CBS with disjoint splitting (which is another CBS' runtime enhancement) is further improved by introducing a more nuanced conflict prioritization strategy when multiple cardinal (or semi-cardinal) conflicts are present. More specifically, we prioritize conflicts that involve agents that participate in multiple cardinal (or semi-cardinal) conflicts. Our experiments show that the new conflict prioritization strategy reduces both the number of node expansions and the runtime of CBS with disjoint splitting for many instances from the standard MAPF benchmark suite.

Keywords: MAPF · Heuristic Search · CBS

1 Introduction

Multi-Agent Path Finding (MAPF) is a widely studied problem in AI planning that has attracted significant attention due to its computational complexity and wide range of real-world applications, including robotics, logistics, and automated transportation systems. In MAPF, a set of agents must compute collision-free paths from their respective start locations to their goal locations. The objective is to find solutions efficiently, despite the exponential growth of the joint state space as the number of agents increases. Consequently, numerous optimal and suboptimal approaches have been proposed to address this challenge.

D. Wolter and G. Schwalbe (Eds.): KI 2026, LNAI 16830, pp. 72–84, 2027.
https://doi.org/10.1007/978-3-032-32335-4_6

Conflict-Based Search (CBS) is a leading optimal algorithm for solving MAPF. It follows a two-level search framework: the low-level search independently computes shortest paths for each agent, while the high-level search repeatedly resolves collisions (known as conflicts) that emerge between these paths. When a conflict is detected, the high level introduces constraints to prevent the conflict and the paths of the affected agents are replanned at the low level. This iterative process continues until a conflict-free solution is returned. Due to its efficiency in finding optimal solutions, CBS has become one of the most prominent methods in MAPF research.

Originally, when multiple conflicts were present, CBS selected the next conflict to resolve randomly. Subsequent research proposed more informed conflict-selection techniques [1,2,4] that guide the search more effectively, thereby improving overall performance. In this work, we introduce a novel conflict-prioritization strategy for CBS with disjoint splitting (which is one of CBS' enhancements) designed to further improve efficiency by minimizing redundant branching in the search process.

In the following sections, we first present a theoretical example demonstrating how the proposed conflict-prioritization strategy reduces unnecessary branching. Next, we describe the algorithmic modifications required to integrate our approach into CBS. Finally, we evaluate our approach on six different MAPF benchmark maps and present the results

2 MAPF

Formally, MAPF is often described as a problem on an undirected graph $G = (V, E)$ as follows: Let A be a set of agents and let $s : A \rightarrow V$ and $g : A \rightarrow V$ denote injective functions assigning every agent $a_i \in A$ a start and a goal vertex respectively. The objective is to find a *valid* solution, which is a set of conflict-free paths that navigates the agents from their starting vertices to their goal vertices.

In classic MAPF, time is divided into discrete timesteps. At each timestep, an agent may either move to any adjacent vertex or remain at its current location. Every action requires one timestep to complete and incurs a cost of one. A *path* is a sequence of locations that an agent occupies to arrive to its goal. Finally, the *cost* of an agent's path is equal to the sum of costs of all its actions until it arrives to its goal.

The majority of MAPF problem descriptions considers only two types of conflicts, which are the vertex conflicts and the edge conflicts. *Vertex conflicts* occur when two agents are located at the same vertex at the same timestep, and *edge conflicts* occur when two agents move along the same edge but in different directions at the same timestep.

MAPF can be solved optimally or (bounded) suboptimally with respect to different objective functions. In this work we focus on optimal valid solutions with respect to the sum-of-costs (SoC) which is the sum of costs of all agents' paths. Solving MAPF optimally with respect to the sum-of-costs objective is NP-complete [13].

3 Conflict-Based Search

CBS [9] is a two-level search and its high-level search creates a binary search tree, called the constraint tree (CT). Each node $N \in CT$ contains the following attributes:

- A *set of constraints* for all agents,
- A *solution* (not necessarily valid) that respects the current set of constraints,
- A *cost*, which is the cost of the solution with respect to the given objective.

The high-level search performs a best-first search with respect to the nodes' cost and uses a priority queue. At the beginning, it creates the root node that has an empty constraint set and invokes the low-level search, which is often a simple A* search, to find and return the optimal paths for all the agents. Then, the root node cost is computed, and the root node is inserted in the priority queue. Subsequently, the high level decides the next best CT node to expand (initially only the root node is in the priority queue) and searches for possible conflicts in its current solution. If no conflict is found, the current node solution is valid and optimal and is returned.

In case there is a vertex conflict (a_i, a_j, u, t) (or an edge conflict) between two agents a_i and a_j at vertex u and timestep t, the current node is removed from the priority queue and CBS performs a *split* action. The split action creates two child CT nodes that inherit the constraints of the current node (parent node) and an extra negative constraint is added to each of them to resolve the conflict. For the aforementioned conflict, the constraint $(a_i \not\rightarrow (u,t))$ is added to one of the children and the constraint $(a_j \not\rightarrow (u,t))$ is added to the other one. The negative constraint $(a_i \not\rightarrow (u,t))$ means that agent a_i is not allowed to be at vertex u at timestep t. Then the low-level search is invoked again for each child node to compute the new optimal path for the agent affected by the additional constraint. Finally, the new cost of the child nodes is computed and the nodes are added to the priority queue where the high level performs a best-first search with respect to the node cost.

This process continues till no conflict exists any longer and the solution returned by CBS is guaranteed to be valid and optimal with respect to the given objective.

4 Related Work

CBS is very sensitive to the single-agent paths returned by the low level. This happens because there are often many different optimal paths for an individual agent on the low level but some of them increase the amount of conflicts found in the high level. Since CBS' runtime is in the worst case exponential to the number of conflicts that it has to resolve, these bad decisions will significantly increase the runtime. This is why a *conflict avoidance table* (CAT) [11] is used when calculating the single-agents paths on the low level. CAT is a lookup table that stores the position and time of every agent whose path has already been calculated and when the low level searches for the optimal path of a new agent, ties on low-level nodes (that have the same A* search f-value) are broken in favor of nodes with lower number of conflicts in CAT.

CBS' high-level chooses randomly the next conflict (in case there are many) to resolve. These decisions significantly affect the performance of the algorithm. To mitigate this issue, improved CBS (ICBS) [2] was developed and categorized conflicts into three different types, namely *cardinal*, *semi-cardinal* and *non-cardinal*. The cardinality of a conflict depends on the cost of the child nodes that are created when this conflict is resolved. When cardinal conflicts are resolved, the node cost of both child nodes is increased compared to the parent node. In semi cardinal conflicts, the cost of only one child node is increased and finally, when resolving a non-cardinal conflict, none of the costs of the child nodes increases. In ICBS, cardinal conflicts have the highest priority, then follow semi-cardinal conflicts and in the end the non-cardinal ones. This prioritization improved the runtime of CBS because, when cardinal (or semi-cardinal) conflicts are prioritized, the solution cost of both (or one, respectively) child nodes increases and this makes the search more informed.

Another improvement on the CBS algorithm (called ICBS-h) was accomplished by adding admissible heuristics (CG heuristic) [3] on the high-level nodes. These admissible heuristic values are calculated by aggregating the cardinal conflicts between disjoint pairs of agents and make the high-level search more informed. ICBS-h further improved the runtime compared to ICBS.

In the same line of work, two more informative admissible heuristics, namely *DG* and *WDG* were developed to guide CBS' high-level search [5]. The DG heuristic is more informative than the CG heuristic because it doesn't only take into account the cardinal conflicts between the agents to compute the heuristic value, but also investigates their whole possible paths to find out if all their cost-minimal paths have an inevitable conflict with each other, resulting to higher heuristic values. WDG is even more informative that DG because it also captures the minimum extra cost needed to resolve all conflicts between pairs of agents. Although DG and WDG incur a computation overhead, they manage to reduce substantially the amount of high-level nodes expanded and thus sped up CBS.

The standard splitting action in CBS creates two negative constraints that are propagated to the child nodes. This approach creates some duplicate search effort because some solutions are shared in both child nodes. To mitigate the solution overlap and the respective computational overhead, disjoint splitting was introduced. Disjoint splitting [7] splits a node by creating one positive and one negative constraint for the same agent. *Positive constraints* e.g. $a_i \rightarrow (u,t)$ force an agent to be at a specific vertex (or edge) at a specific timestep and simultaneously prohibit all other agents from being at this vertex (edge) at this timestep (e.g. $a_j \not\rightarrow (u,t)$, $\forall a_j \in A\backslash\{a_i\}$). This type of splitting sped up CBS and CBS variants by up to 2 orders of magnitude.

Reasoning techniques have been also leveraged to identify cases where CBS split actions are inefficient because they create a big number of nodes that can exponentially increase the high-level search space in some cases. Those techniques identify *rectangle* [8], *corridor* and *target* conflicts [6] between pair of agents and resolve them with one single split action, resulting to lower runtimes.

Despite categorizing conflicts into three categories (cardinal, semi-cardinal and non-cardinal) with different priorities, CBS still randomly decides about what conflict to choose and resolve next in case there are multiple conflicts with the same priority. Since these choices can heavily influence the efficiency of the algorithm, researchers employed a linear ranking function [4], learned using machine learning techniques, to rank conflicts at a search node based on their estimated potential to lead to a faster solution. This conflict prioritization approach achieved a runtime reduction of 10% to 65%, depending on the specific map in the MAPF suite.

Another research direction [1] that further investigated the possibility of prioritizing conflicts focused on prioritizing conflicts that increase the f-values of the resulting child nodes. By prioritizing such conflicts the search becomes more informed and since the computational cost needed to find such conflicts was low, this approach led to reduced node expansions and shorter runtimes.

5 Conflict Prioritization

CBS with disjoint splitting prioritizes cardinal conflicts, followed by semi-cardinal and finally non-cardinal. Though, in case of multiple conflicts with the same priority, there is no clear guideline on which conflict to resolve first and how this affects the efficiency of the algorithm because the aforementioned research directions [1,4] that prioritize certain conflicts were specifically engineered for non-disjoint splitting and they cannot be easily extended for non-disjoint splitting. Thus, since no typical guideline exists when multiple conflicts have the same priority, some researchers decided to break ties in favor of conflicts with the earliest timestep [8].

5.1 Example

In the following, we will consider an example that demonstrates that there are some cases where resolving conflicts earlier in time is inefficient because it causes the CT to branch unnecessarily many times and create superfluous high-level nodes. The increased node expansion may lead to a larger CT and thus runtime, which could have been avoided if we had chosen a different conflict resolution order.

Figure 1(a) shows an agent that faces three cardinal conflicts while following its fastest path to its goal. Figure 1(b) shows the generated CT, if we decide to break ties in favor of conflicts earlier in time. In that case, all the cardinal conflicts of a_1 have to be resolved one after the other by generating six high-level nodes. Whereas, Fig. 1(c) shows the respective CT if we decide to break ties in favor of the cardinal conflict latest in time for a_1. This CT generates only two high-level nodes because by adding the constraint $a_1 \not\to (u_3, 6)$, CBS' low-level

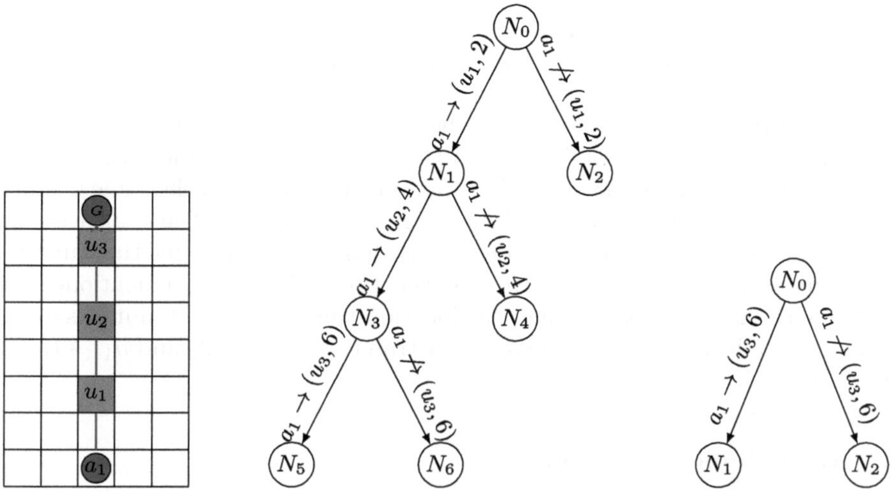

(a) MAPF instance (b) Break ties in favor of conflicts with the earliest timestep (c) New conflict prioritization strategy

Fig. 1. Motivation example that demonstrates the importance of conflict prioritization when an agent faces multiple cardinal conflicts at different timesteps.

invokes A^* with conflict avoidance and therefore it finds a path that avoids the rest of the cardinal conflicts.

Furthermore, the new constraint $a_1 \rightarrow (u_3, 6)$ that was added in node N_1 in Fig. 1(c) silently imposes two extra constraints because of Proposition 1.

Definition 1. *A multi-value decision diagram (MDD_i^c) [10] is a compact representation of all possible paths of agent a_i with path length c that lead the agent to its goal vertex. The MDD_i^c is organized into levels, where each level t contains all vertices that the agent can occupy at timestep t along some path of cost c. The first level contains only the start vertex of the agent, and the last level contains only its goal vertex.*

Definition 2. *A node (v, t) in MDD_i^c is called a singleton node if it is the only node in level t.*

Proposition 1. *Let MDD_i^c where c is the length of a shortest path of agent a_i from its start vertex to its goal vertex, have a singleton node (u_3, t_3) at level t_3. A positive constraint $a_i \rightarrow (u_3, t_3)$ implies $a_i \rightarrow (v, t)$, $\forall (v, t) \in MDD_i^c$ that are singleton nodes and at level $t \leq t_3$.*

Proof. By contradiction, if $a_i \not\rightarrow (v, t)$ where (v, t) is a singleton node and $t \leq t_3$. Then there is no feasible path for a_i to be at (u_3, t_3) since all its feasible paths cross (v, t).

Therefore, $a_1 \rightarrow (u_3, 6)$ implies $a_1 \rightarrow (u_1, 2)$ and $a_1 \rightarrow (u_2, 4)$ too. Hence, to make the CBS' heuristics more efficient but also to avoid unnecessary node expansions later, the constraints $a_1 \rightarrow (u_1, 2)$ and $a_1 \rightarrow (u_2, 4)$ with their respective negative constraints for all other agents could also be added in node N_1 in Fig. 1(c).

This tie-breaking technique can also be leveraged for agents that are involved in multiple semi-cardinal conflicts when the location-time of these conflicts are singleton nodes for the same agent. Let's assume that we have the same example as in Fig. 1(a) but the conflicts of a_1 are now semi-cardinal and also $(u_1, 2)$, $(u_2, 4)$ and $(u_3, 6)$ are singleton nodes for a_1. Then we would get the same CT expansions as in Figs. 1(b) and 1(c) for the two different aforementioned tie-breaking strategies. Moreover, since the location-times are singleton nodes for a_1, we can again add the silently imposed constraints $a_1 \rightarrow (u_1, 2)$ and $a_1 \rightarrow (u_2, 4)$ in node N_1 in Fig. 1(c).

5.2 Algorithmic Extension

The algorithmic extension of CBS for our conflict prioritization is described in Algorithm 1. CBS already finds all conflicts in every high-level node in order to compute its high-level heuristics. For our conflict prioritization, we only need to do some extra bookkeeping. Whenever a new cardinal conflict between two agents a_i and a_j is found, it is added to the set of cardinal conflicts of both agents. Likewise, for the semi-cardinal conflicts with the only difference that it is added to the set of semi-cardinal conflicts for the agent that the location-time of the conflict is a singleton.

Subsequently, in each high-level node, we find the agent a_k with the most cardinal (or semi-cardinal singletons, if no more cardinal conflicts exist) conflicts and a multi-conflict is created. This multi-conflict includes all the cardinal (or semi-cardinal singletons) conflicts of a_k and it is chosen for the next conflict resolution. Finally, by resolving this multi-conflict, two new child nodes are created. The left child node adds positive constraints to a_k for all the conflicts that are included in the multi-conflict and the other one adds one negative constraint to a_k for the conflict with the latest timestep.

6 Experimental Results

To evaluate empirically the effect of our new conflict prioritization strategy to CBS, we developed two different variants of CBS with disjoint splitting in Python[1], namely a CBS that uses the CG heuristic and corridor reasoning (CBSH-CG-C) and a CBS that uses the most informative WDG heuristic and rectangle, corridor and target reasoning (CBSH-WDG-RTC). Moreover, in CBS with disjoint splitting, there are 3 different strategies (random, singleton and width) to decide which agent to constrain when a split action is performed and we tested all of them in our experiments. We used 4 maps from the standard

[1] https://github.com/GrFr/CBSH-CG-DG-WDG-RTC/tree/CBS-CG-WDG-RTC-multiconflict.

Algorithm 1 Conflict Prioritization

```
Require: CardinalList : List of all cardinal conflicts
Require: SemiCardinalList : List of all semi-cardinal conflicts
Require: Singletons[a_i] : Set of all singleton nodes ∀a_i ∈ A
Cardinals[a_i] = ∅, ∀a_i ∈ A
SemiCardinals[a_i] = ∅, ∀a_i ∈ A
for each vertex or edge conflict c = (a_i, a_j, u, t) do
   if c ∈ CardinalList then
      Cardinals[a_i].add(c)
      Cardinals[a_j].add(c)
   else if c ∈ SemiCardinalList then
      if (u, t) ∈ Singletons[a_i] then
         SemiCardinals[a_i].add(c)
      else if (u, t) ∈ Singletons[a_j] then
         SemiCardinals[a_j].add(c)
      end if
   end if
end for
if CardinalList ≠ ∅ then
   a_1 ← arg max_a |Cardinals[a]|
   NextConflict ← MultiConflict(Cardinals[a_1])
else if SemiCardinalList ≠ ∅ then
   a_1 ← arg max_a |SemiCardinals[a]|
   NextConflict ← MultiConflict(SemiCardinals[a_1])
end if
return NextConflict
```

MAPF benchmark suite [12] which are empty-16-16, random-32-32-10, random-32-32-20 and lak303d and we also created two new grid maps with dimensions 32×32 and obstacle densities of 30% and 40%. These maps were named random-32-32-30 and random-32-32-40 respectively.

For the small maps empty-16-16, random-32-32-10, random-32-32-20 and the big game map lak303d, we varied the agents from 10 to 60 and for the maps random-32-32-30 and random-32-32-40 we varied the agents from 10-35 since finding solutions in those heavily constrained maps gets hard really fast by increasing the number of agents. We generated 50 instances with randomly generated start and goal positions per number of agent and map and we set the time limit for finding a solution to 30 min. Finally the experiments were performed on a machine with an AMD EPYC 9655 (96-core) processor, with each run restricted to a single CPU core and 16 GB of RAM.

6.1 Results for CBSH-CG-C

In Fig. 2 the runtime comparison for the two different conflict prioritization strategies is presented for every instance that is solved by both conflict prioritization strategies for CBS-CG-T. We named as "Classic Conflict Prioritization" the tie-braking in favor of conflicts earlier in time and "Our Conflict Prioritization"

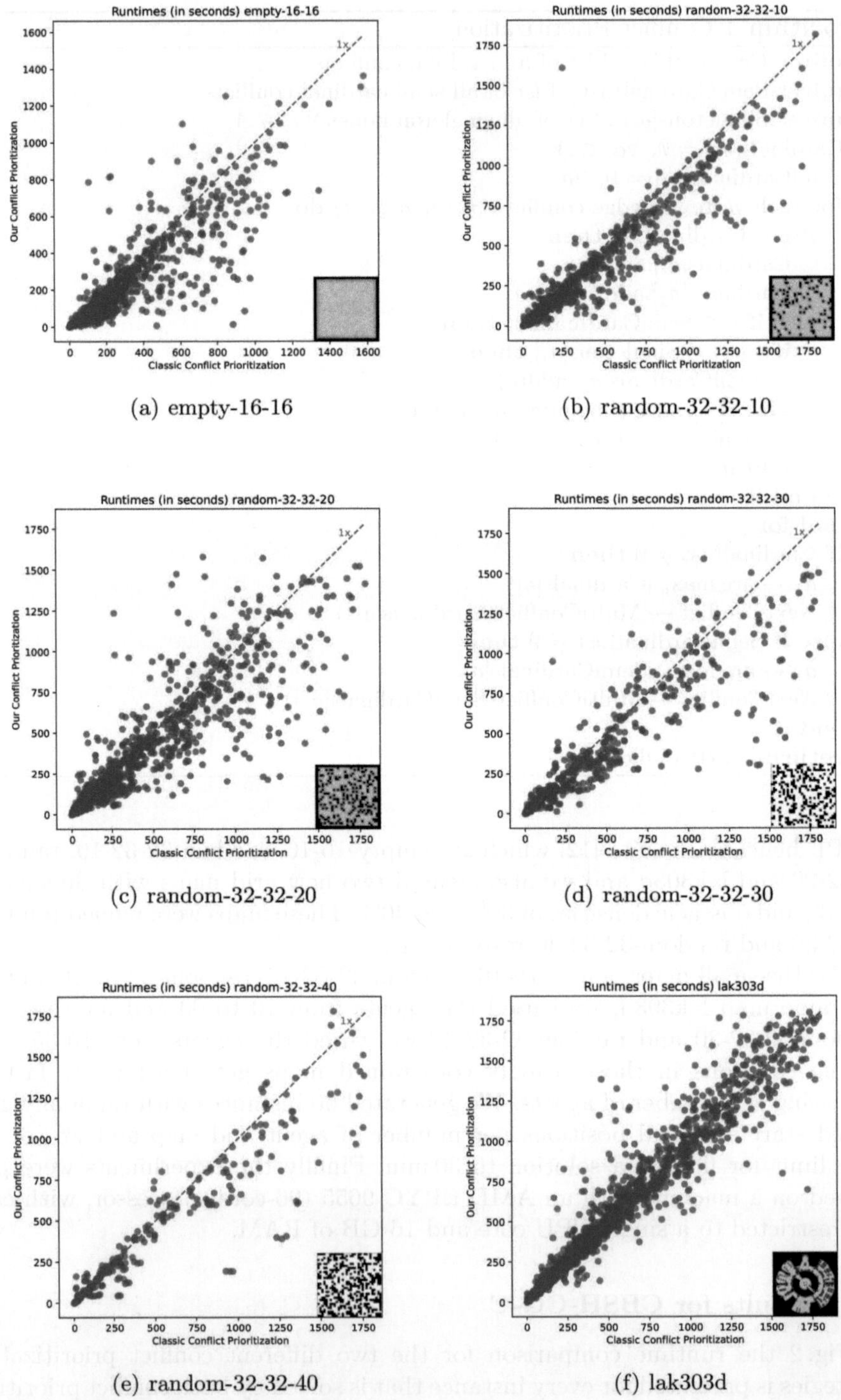

(a) empty-16-16 (b) random-32-32-10

(c) random-32-32-20 (d) random-32-32-30

(e) random-32-32-40 (f) lak303d

Fig. 2. Runtime comparison for the two different conflict prioritization strategies with CBSH-CG-C

the conflict prioritization strategy described in the previous section. From these plots, it is apparent that our new conflict prioritization generally yields better runtimes across the majority of instances, notably on the smaller maps (empty-16-16, random-32-32-10, random-32-32-20, random-32-32-30, random-32-32-40). This observation is further supported by the numerical evaluation in Table 1 where we present the average runtimes and nodes expanded across all instances for specific numbers of agents. Our new conflict prioritization achieves up to 40% lower runtimes and node expansions.

Furthermore, in Table 2 you can see the frequency of resolving a multi-conflict (cardinal or semi-cardinal) per map. It is expected that multiconflicts emerge more often in smaller maps that are often more congested such as empty-16-16 and all the 32×32 maps with random obstacles. On the contrary in large maps like lak303d, multiconflicts emerge rarely and this is probably the reason that our new technique doesn't show any improvement in this map.

6.2 Results for CBSH-WDG-RTC

However, when we combine our new conflict prioritization technique with CBS-WDG-RTC, the previous advantage disappears as it is shown in Fig. 3. This can be attributed to the use of symmetry reasoning techniques together with the WDG heuristic in CBS. In this CBS variant, conflicts such as rectangle and target conflicts are identified and resolved before vertex and edge conflicts. Therefore the frequency of standard vertex and edge conflict resolutions is reduced, but so does their impact in the efficiency of CBS because they are typically resolved deeper in the CT. At that stage, avoiding unnecessary branching yields smaller performance gains, making the overall improvement less significant.

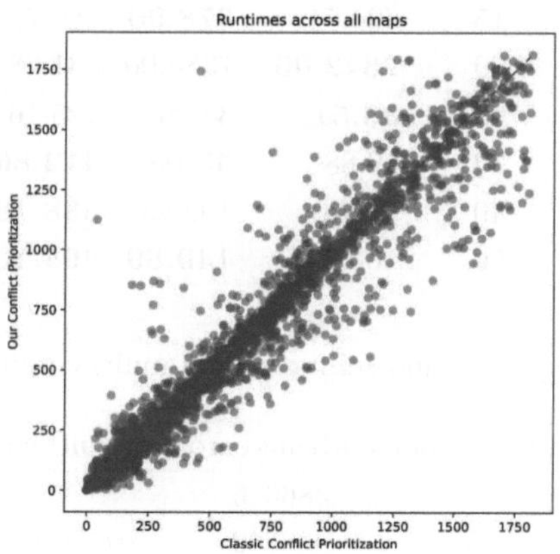

Fig. 3. Comparison of the runtimes for all maps and CBS-WDG-RTC

Table 1. Comparison of average high-level nodes expanded and runtimes for the two conflict prioritization strategies and CBSH-CG-C on different maps with varying number of agents

Map	Agents	Expanded Nodes		Runtimes (s)	
		Classic CP	Our CP	Classic CP	Our CP
empty-16-16	15	15.56	**14.25**	0.15	**0.14**
	25	756.40	**613.75**	18.79	**15.49**
	35	1560.38	**1123.56**	56.77	**40.59**
	45	3748.62	**2530.69**	188.50	**133.70**
	55	5170.43	**4368.00**	354.56	**322.40**
random-32-32-10	15	3.63	**3.57**	**0.10**	**0.10**
	25	349.09	**314.26**	15.01	**13.43**
	35	775.53	**699.14**	42.21	**38.20**
	45	1426.50	**1159.45**	119.59	**98.87**
	55	1901.27	**1607.71**	222.47	**190.75**
random-32-32-20	15	10.40	**9.69**	0.53	**0.45**
	25	81.82	**80.84**	**4.39**	4.64
	35	776.32	**702.93**	78.02	**68.54**
	45	**2111.40**	2205.95	**242.80**	246.49
	55	3185.04	**2304.57**	418.48	**318.85**
random-32-32-30	10	17.97	**14.43**	1.83	**1.43**
	20	537.91	**466.24**	95.35	**79.36**
	30	3056.67	**2655.75**	402.69	**319.60**
random-32-32-40	10	443.46	**364.82**	225.59	**182.24**
	15	624.71	**378.90**	280.72	**180.16**
	20	**7342.00**	7386.00	831.28	**811.66**
lak303d	20	**33.51**	33.99	125.16	**121.40**
	30	56.88	**55.08**	**412.86**	420.35
	40	**99.50**	102.83	**538.78**	553.37
	50	165.22	**149.89**	**694.13**	844.66

Table 2. Frequency of cardinal and semi-cardinal multi-conflict resolutions per map

Map	Cardinal multi-conflicts	Semi-cardinal multi-conflicts	Total Nodes	Ratio
empty-16-16	12007	486646	5062345	0.10
random-32-32-10	3363	438599	3683513	0.12
random-32-32-20	30427	233437	3828778	0.07
random-32-32-30	50378	45973	1300140	0.07
random-32-32-40	16435	8708	317007	0.08
lak303d	2686	4973	175691	0.04

7 Conclusion and Future Work

Conflict prioritization plays an important role in the efficiency of CBS and in this work we developed a new conflict prioritization technique for CBS with disjoint splitting that reduces node expansions and runtimes for CBS-CG-C for the majority of the tested MAPF maps. Our new technique prioritizes the resolution of conflicts for agents that are involved in multiple cardinal (and semi-cardinal conflicts) by prioritizing the resolution of their cardinal (or semi-cardinal) conflict with the latest timestep. However, when this technique is combined with CBS-WDG-RTC, the results show no clear advantage, likely because the prioritization of vertex and edge conflicts becomes less significant since rectangular and target conflicts are prioritized.

In future work, we aim to investigate the possibility of developing techniques that further prioritize other type of conflicts such as rectangle, corridor and target conflicts and by doing so, we may be able to improve the efficiency of CBSH-WDG-RTC too.

References

1. Boyarski, E., Felner, A., Bodic, P.L., Harabor, D.D., Stuckey, P.J., Koenig, S.: f-aware conflict prioritization & improved heuristics for conflict-based search. In: Thirty-Fifth AAAI Conference on Artificial Intelligence, AAAI 2021, Thirty-Third Conference on Innovative Applications of Artificial Intelligence, IAAI 2021, The Eleventh Symposium on Educational Advances in Artificial Intelligence, EAAI 2021, Virtual Event, February 2-9, 2021, pp. 12241–12248. AAAI Press (2021)
2. Boyarski, E., et al.: ICBS: improved conflict-based search algorithm for multi-agent pathfinding. In: Yang, Q., Wooldridge, M.J. (eds.) Proceedings of the Twenty-Fourth International Joint Conference on Artificial Intelligence, IJCAI 2015, Buenos Aires, Argentina, July 25-31, 2015, pp. 740–746. AAAI Press (2015)
3. Felner, A., et al.: Adding heuristics to conflict-based search for multi-agent path finding. In: de Weerdt, M., Koenig, S., Röger, G., Spaan, M.T.J. (eds.) Proceedings of the Twenty-Eighth International Conference on Automated Planning and Scheduling, ICAPS 2018, Delft, The Netherlands, June 24-29, 2018, pp. 83–87. AAAI Press (2018)
4. Huang, T., Koenig, S., Dilkina, B.: Learning to resolve conflicts for multi-agent path finding with conflict-based search. In: Thirty-Fifth AAAI Conference on Artificial Intelligence, AAAI 2021, Thirty-Third Conference on Innovative Applications of Artificial Intelligence, IAAI 2021, The Eleventh Symposium on Educational Advances in Artificial Intelligence, EAAI 2021, Virtual Event, February 2-9, 2021, pp. 11246–11253. AAAI Press (2021)
5. Li, J., Felner, A., Boyarski, E., Ma, H., Koenig, S.: Improved heuristics for multi-agent path finding with conflict-based search. In: Kraus, S. (ed.) Proceedings of the Twenty-Eighth International Joint Conference on Artificial Intelligence, IJCAI 2019, Macao, China, August 10-16, 2019, pp. 442–449. ijcai.org (2019)
6. Li, J., Gange, G., Harabor, D., Stuckey, P.J., Ma, H., Koenig, S.: New techniques for pairwise symmetry breaking in multi-agent path finding. In: Beck, J.C., Buffet, O., Hoffmann, J., Karpas, E., Sohrabi, S. (eds.) Proceedings of the Thirtieth International Conference on Automated Planning and Scheduling, Nancy, France, October 26-30, 2020, pp. 193–201. AAAI Press (2020)

7. Li, J., Harabor, D., Stuckey, P.J., Ma, H., Koenig, S.: Disjoint splitting for multi-agent path finding with conflict-based search. In: Benton, J., Lipovetzky, N., Onaindia, E., Smith, D.E., Srivastava, S. (eds.) Proceedings of the Twenty-Ninth International Conference on Automated Planning and Scheduling, ICAPS 2019, Berkeley, CA, USA, July 11-15, 2019, pp. 279–283. AAAI Press (2019)
8. Li, J., Harabor, D., Stuckey, P.J., Ma, H., Koenig, S.: Symmetry-breaking constraints for grid-based multi-agent path finding. In: The Thirty-Third AAAI Conference on Artificial Intelligence, AAAI 2019, The Thirty-First Innovative Applications of Artificial Intelligence Conference, IAAI 2019, The Ninth AAAI Symposium on Educational Advances in Artificial Intelligence, EAAI 2019, Honolulu, Hawaii, USA, January 27 - February 1, 2019, pp. 6087–6095. AAAI Press (2019)
9. Sharon, G., Stern, R., Felner, A., Sturtevant, N.R.: Conflict-based search for optimal multi-agent path finding. In: Hoffmann, J., Selman, B. (eds.) Proceedings of the Twenty-Sixth AAAI Conference on Artificial Intelligence, July 22-26, 2012, Toronto, Ontario, Canada, pp. 563–569. AAAI Press (2012)
10. Sharon, G., Stern, R., Goldenberg, M., Felner, A.: The increasing cost tree search for optimal multi-agent pathfinding. Artif. Intell. **195**, 470–495 (2013)
11. Standley, T.S.: Finding optimal solutions to cooperative pathfinding problems. In: Fox, M., Poole, D. (eds.) Proceedings of the Twenty-Fourth AAAI Conference on Artificial Intelligence, AAAI 2010, Atlanta, Georgia, USA, July 11-15, 2010, pp. 173–178. AAAI Press (2010)
12. Sturtevant, N.R.: Benchmarks for grid-based pathfinding. IEEE Trans. Comput. Intell. AI Games **4**(2), 144–148 (2012)
13. Yu, J., LaValle, S.M.: Multi-agent path planning and network flow. In: Frazzoli, E., Lozano-Pérez, T., Roy, N., Rus, D. (eds.) Algorithmic Foundations of Robotics X - Proceedings of the Tenth Workshop on the Algorithmic Foundations of Robotics, WAFR 2012, MIT, Cambridge, Massachusetts, USA, June 13-15 2012. Springer Tracts in Advanced Robotics, vol. 86, pp. 157–173. Springer, Cham (2012)

Characteristics, Convergence and Divergence of Modular Semantics for Bipolar Weighted Argumentation Graphs

Till Mossakowski[1(✉)] and Fabian Neuhaus[2]

[1] Universität Osnabrück, Osnabrück, Germany
till.mossakowski@uni-osnabrueck.de
[2] Otto-von-Guericke Universität Magdeburg, Magdeburg, Germany

Abstract. We study *modular acceptability semantics* for bipolar weighted argumentation graphs, which cleanly separate the *aggregation* of attacking and supporting arguments from the computation of their *influence* on an argument's initial weight. Using a matrix representation, we reformulate the desirable characteristics of such semantics and prove general convergence and divergence theorems. We also introduce the first semantics that converges on *all* bipolar weighted graphs.

Keywords: Weighted Argumentation · Gradual Argumentation · Bipolar Argumentation

1 Introduction

Abstract argumentation has been extensively studied since Dung's pioneering work [21]. Weighted argumentation frameworks add a numerical weight to arguments [3,4,7,10]. In this paper, we study bipolar [5,6,18] weighted argumentation graphs that contain both attack and support relationships. One major research question is: given a collection of arguments connected by attack and support relationships and their initial weights, what is the acceptability of the arguments?

Interest in these frameworks is driven not only by argumentation theory, but also by explainable AI: weighted bipolar graphs can model multilayer perceptrons and other classifiers, so acceptability semantics underpin neural-network interpretations [29], sparse explanations [11], and attribution-based explanations [32,35]. All of these presuppose a *convergent* semantics, so convergence is another important research question.

We observe that many acceptability semantics compute acceptability degrees in two steps: firstly, an *aggregation* function α combines the effect of the parents of an argument; secondly, an *influence* function ι calculates the acceptability degree based on the result of the aggregation and the initial weights (see Fig. 1).

D. Wolter and G. Schwalbe (Eds.): KI 2026, LNAI 16830, pp. 85–100, 2027.
https://doi.org/10.1007/978-3-032-32335-4_7

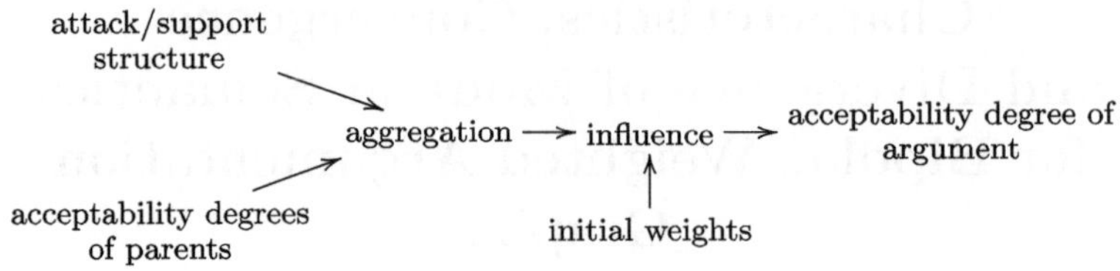

Fig. 1. Modular structure of acceptability semantics

We call such semantics *modular*. Similar abstractions have been studied for bipolar graphs without initial weight [8] and weighted attack-only graphs [24].

Using a matrix representation of argumentation graphs (cf. [19]), we propose an elegant reformulation of desirable characteristics of modular acceptability semantics. The modular approach allows us to obtain convergence and divergence theorems for whole classes of semantics. All well-behaved modular acceptability semantics converge for acyclic graphs (Theorem 1). We propose three semantics that converge for all bipolar argumentation graphs (Table 6). Further, we show that no *sum*-based semantics can converge for all graphs.

In the next section, we introduce the basic notions. In Sect. 3 we discuss characteristics of acceptability semantics. Section 4 introduces our modular approach. In Sect. 5 we compare different modular acceptability semantics, based on an example. Sections 6 and 7 prove convergence and divergence results, respectively. Section 8 discusses related work and provides conclusions. Proofs omitted due to space restrictions are available in the extended report [25].

2 Basic Concepts

We follow [7,10,12,13] for basic definitions. Weights stem from a connected subset $\mathbb{D} \subseteq \mathbb{R}$ of the reals. We assume $0 \in \mathbb{D}$ is the *neutral acceptability degree.* If $\mathbb{D}$ has a minimum (maximum), we denote it by $\mathtt{Min}_{\mathrm{S}}$ ($\mathtt{Max}_{\mathrm{S}}$).

Definition 1 (Argumentation Graph). *A* weighted attack/support argumentation graph *(*WASA*; with slightly different formalisation called* quantitative bipolar argumentation framework *(*QBAF*) in [12,13]) is a triple $\mathbb{A} = \langle \mathcal{A}, G, \boldsymbol{w} \rangle$, where $\mathcal{A}$ is a vector of n pairwise distinct arguments; $G = \{G_{ij}\}$ is a square matrix of order n with $G_{ij} \in \{-1, 0, 1\}$, where $G_{ij} = -1$ means a_j attacks a_i, $G_{ij} = 1$ means a_j supports a_i, and $G_{ij} = 0$ otherwise; and $\boldsymbol{w} \in \mathbb{D}^n$ is a vector of initial weights.*

G_i denotes the i-th row of G (the parents of argument a_i). We let $\mathtt{Att}_{\mathbb{A}}(a_i) = \{a_j \mid g_{ij} = -1\}$ and $\mathtt{Sup}_{\mathbb{A}}(a_i) = \{a_j \mid g_{ij} = 1\}$. To represent a WASA graphically, we draw attack relationships as normal arrows and support relationships as dashed arrows, with initial weights written below arguments (see Fig. 2).

Example 1. Consider the WASA

$$\mathbb{A}^{ex1} = \left\langle \begin{pmatrix} a_1 \\ a_2 \\ a_3 \\ a_4 \\ a_5 \\ a_6 \end{pmatrix}, \begin{pmatrix} 0 & 0 & 0 & 0 & 0 & 0 \\ 0 & 0 & 0 & 0 & 0 & 0 \\ -1 & 0 & 0 & 0 & 0 & 0 \\ 0 & -1 & 0 & 0 & 0 & 0 \\ 0 & 0 & 0 & 1 & 0 & -1 \\ 0 & 0 & 0 & 0 & -1 & 1 \end{pmatrix}, \begin{pmatrix} 0 \\ 1 \\ 0.4 \\ 0 \\ 0.5 \\ 1 \end{pmatrix} \right\rangle$$

a_1 and a_2 are neither attacked nor supported. a_1 attacks a_3 and a_2 attacks a_4, which supports a_5. a_5 and a_6 attack each other, while a_6 supports itself (see Fig. 2). □

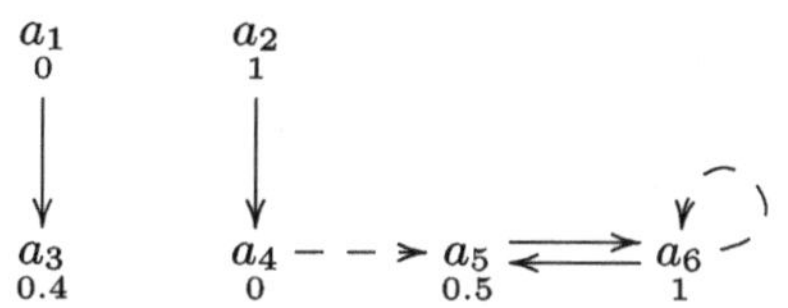

Fig. 2. Graphical representation of $\mathbb{A}^{ex1}$

Definition 2 (Acceptability Semantics). *An acceptability semantics is a partial function* $\mathbf{S}$ *transforming any* WASA $\mathbb{A} = \langle \mathcal{A}, G, \boldsymbol{w} \rangle$ *into a vector* $\mathbf{Deg}_{\mathbb{A}}^{\mathbf{S}}$ *in* $\mathbb{D}^n$*. For any argument* a_i*,* $\mathbf{Deg}_{\mathbb{A}}^{\mathbf{S}}(a_i)$ *is called the acceptability degree of* a_i*.*

The semantics is partial because some semantics only converge for a subclass of graphs.

Example 2. Given an acyclic WASA with weights from $[0, 1)$, the Euler-based semantics [5] defines the acceptability degrees recursively: for $a_i \in \mathcal{A}$,

$$(\mathtt{Deg}_{\mathbb{A}}^{\mathtt{S}})_i = 1 - \frac{1 - \boldsymbol{w}_i^2}{1 + \boldsymbol{w}_i \cdot \exp(E_i)}, \tag{1}$$

where $E_i = \sum_{a_j \in \mathtt{Sup}_{\mathbb{A}}(a_i)} (\mathtt{Deg}_{\mathbb{A}}^{\mathtt{S}})_j - \sum_{a_j \in \mathtt{Att}_{\mathbb{A}}(a_i)} (\mathtt{Deg}_{\mathbb{A}}^{\mathtt{S}})_j$. Intuitively, E_i is the energy acting on argument a_i: supporters increase it, attackers decrease it. As $E_i \to \infty$, the degree goes to 1; as $E_i \to -\infty$, it goes to $\boldsymbol{w}_i^2$. □

3 Characteristics of Acceptability Semantics

Obviously, there are many possible acceptability semantics, including trivial ones. This raises the question of desirable characteristics. We distinguish between: *structural* characteristics, which set up the framework (e.g., anonymity, modularity); *essential* characteristics, which any well-behaved semantics should exhibit (e.g., neutrality, reinforcement); and *optional* characteristics, which reflect particular design choices (e.g., Franklin, counting).

Table 1 relates our characteristics to those in the literature; the four bold-faced rows (*modularity*, *continuity*, *stickiness*, *symmetry*) are introduced here,

Table 1. Our characteristics related to the literature; **bold** rows are new.

Support graphs [3]	Attack graphs [7, 10]	Bipolar [5]	Our terminology
Equivalence	Equivalence	Bi-variate Equivalence	Equivalence
–	–	–	**Modularity**
Anonymity	Anonymity	Anonymity	Anonymity
Independence	Independence	Bi-variate Independence	Independence
Reinforcement	Reinforcement	Bi-variate Reinforcement	Reinforcement
Coherence	Proportionality	–	Initial monotonicity
Minimality	Maximality	Stability	Stability
–	–	–	**Continuity**
Dummy	Neutrality	Neutrality	Neutrality
Non-dilution	Directionality	Bi-variate Directionality	Directionality
Monotony	–	Bi-variate Monotony	Parent monotonicity
Strength. Soundness	Weak. Soundness	–	Soundness
Strengthening	–	Strengthening	Strengthening
–	Weakening	Weakening	Weakening
Boundedness	–	–	Compactness
Imperfection	Resilience	Resilience	Resilience
–	–	–	**Stickiness**
–	–	Franklin	Franklin
Counting	Counting	Bi-variate Monotony	Counting
–	–	–	**Symmetry**

the rest are matrix-notation reformulations of established characteristics that we sometimes strengthen while preserving their intuition (Proposition 3).

In the equations below, beyond the notation introduced in Sect. 2, $\boldsymbol{g}$, $\boldsymbol{h}$ range over rows; P over permutation matrices; $\boldsymbol{d}$, $\boldsymbol{e}$ over degree vectors in $\mathbb{D}^n$; $\boldsymbol{w}$ over initial weight vectors; s, s_1, s_2 over reals (output of α, input to ι). Comparison relations like $\leq$ on vectors mean component-wise comparison.

3.1 Structural Characteristics

Structural characteristics provide the framework for the other characteristics. While not all semantics need to exhibit them, they simplify formulation and enable our modular approach.

Anonymity-1 states that only the incidence matrix G matters, not the argument names, i.e. there is $\mathtt{Deg}^{\mathtt{S}}_{\langle G,\boldsymbol{w}\rangle}$ such that for all $\mathcal{A}$, we have

$$\mathtt{Deg}^{\mathtt{S}}_{\langle \mathcal{A},G,\boldsymbol{w}\rangle} = \mathtt{Deg}^{\mathtt{S}}_{\langle G,\boldsymbol{w}\rangle}$$

In the sequel, we therefore write $\mathtt{Deg}^{\mathtt{S}}_{\langle G,\boldsymbol{w}\rangle}$ instead of $\mathtt{Deg}^{\mathtt{S}}_{\langle \mathcal{A},G,\boldsymbol{w}\rangle}$.

Equivalence requires that degrees of arguments depend only on their initial weights and the degrees of their parents, reducing cognitive complexity:

$$\mathtt{Deg}^{\mathtt{S}}_{\langle G,\boldsymbol{w}\rangle}(i) = \deg(G_i, \mathtt{Deg}^{\mathtt{S}}_{\langle G,\boldsymbol{w}\rangle}, \boldsymbol{w}_i) \qquad (i = 1, \ldots, n) \tag{2}$$

for a *degree function* $\deg : \{-1, 0, 1\}^n \times \mathbb{D}^n \times \mathbb{D} \to \mathbb{D}$ satisfying $\deg(\boldsymbol{g}, \boldsymbol{d}, w) = \deg(\boldsymbol{g}P^{-1}, P\boldsymbol{d}, w)$ for any permutation matrix P.

Modularity strengthens equivalence: the degree function is a composition of an *aggregation* function $\alpha : \{-1, 0, 1\}^n \times \mathbb{D}^n \to \mathbb{R}$ and an *influence* function $\iota : \mathbb{R} \times \mathbb{D} \to \mathbb{D}$:

$$\mathtt{Deg}^{\mathtt{S}}_{\langle G,\boldsymbol{w}\rangle}(i) = \iota(\alpha(G_i, \mathtt{Deg}^{\mathtt{S}}_{\langle G,\boldsymbol{w}\rangle}), \boldsymbol{w}_i) \qquad (i = 1, \ldots, n) \tag{3}$$

α aggregates the degrees of parent arguments according to the graph structure. Note that this aggregation can lead outside $\mathbb{D}$ (e.g. if summation is used), so the range of α is $\mathbb{R}$. Then ι determines how the aggregated parents modify the initial weight. By entry-wise action, we extend to vectors:

$$\mathtt{Deg}^{\mathtt{S}}_{\langle G,\boldsymbol{w}\rangle} = \boldsymbol{\iota}(\boldsymbol{\alpha}(G, \mathtt{Deg}^{\mathtt{S}}_{\langle G,\boldsymbol{w}\rangle}), \boldsymbol{w}) \tag{4}$$

Definition 3 (Modular Acceptability Semantics). *A modular acceptability semantics* $(\mathbb{D}, \alpha, \iota)$ *consists of a connected domain* $\mathbb{D} \subseteq \mathbb{R}$ *with* $0 \in \mathbb{D}$*, an aggregation function* α *and an influence function* ι*, satisfying the structural characteristics in Table 2.*

3.2 Essential Characteristics

Essential characteristics are those any well-behaved semantics should satisfy, independently of the particular design intuition. They pin down the minimal sanity requirements.

Anonymity-2 requires that positions of arguments do not matter, i.e. for any permutation matrix P, we have $\alpha(\boldsymbol{g}P^{-1}, P\boldsymbol{d}) = \alpha(\boldsymbol{g}, \boldsymbol{d})$.

Independence means that acceptability degrees for disjoint unions of graphs are built component-wise, i.e. $\alpha((\,0\ \boldsymbol{g}\,), (\begin{smallmatrix} d \\ \boldsymbol{d} \end{smallmatrix})) = \alpha(\boldsymbol{g}, \boldsymbol{d}) = \alpha((\,\boldsymbol{g}\ 0\,), (\begin{smallmatrix} \boldsymbol{d} \\ d \end{smallmatrix}))$.

Reinforcement means: weakening an attacker or strengthening a supporter increases acceptability. Using $\boldsymbol{d} \leq_{\boldsymbol{g}} \boldsymbol{e}$ iff $\boldsymbol{g}_i\boldsymbol{d}_i \leq \boldsymbol{g}_i\boldsymbol{e}_i$ for all i, we require: $\boldsymbol{d} \leq_{\boldsymbol{g}} \boldsymbol{e} \to \alpha(\boldsymbol{g}, \boldsymbol{d}) \leq \alpha(\boldsymbol{g}, \boldsymbol{e})$ (*Reinforcement-*α), and $s_1 < s_2 \to \iota(s_1, w) \prec \iota(s_2, w)$ (*Reinforcement-*ι), where $v \prec w$ means $v < w$ or $v = w = \mathtt{Min}_{\mathtt{S}}$ or $v = w = \mathtt{Max}_{\mathtt{S}}$.

Initial monotonicity means that a stronger initial weight should also lead to a stronger acceptability degree of an argument: $w_1 < w_2 \to \iota(s, w_1) \prec \iota(s, w_2)$.

Stability means that an unattacked, unsupported argument keeps its initial weight, i.e. $\alpha(0, \boldsymbol{d}) = 0$ and $\iota(0, w) = w$.

Continuity means that small changes in the inputs cause only small changes in the output, i.e. ι and $\alpha(\boldsymbol{g}, \_)$ are continuous.

Neutrality means that an argument with neutral acceptability degree 0 can be removed from the graph without effect: $\boldsymbol{d} \geq 0 \wedge (\forall j \neq k.\boldsymbol{g}_j = \boldsymbol{h}_j) \wedge \boldsymbol{d}_k = 0 \to \alpha(\boldsymbol{g}, \boldsymbol{d}) = \alpha(\boldsymbol{h}, \boldsymbol{d})$.

Directionality captures that attack and support are directed relationships. Given a row $\boldsymbol{g}$ of the argumentation matrix, define $\boldsymbol{d} \equiv_{\boldsymbol{g}} \boldsymbol{e}$ iff for $j = 1, \ldots, n$, $\boldsymbol{g}_j \neq 0$ implies $\boldsymbol{d}_j = \boldsymbol{e}_j$. Then *directionality* is $\boldsymbol{d} \equiv_{\boldsymbol{g}} \boldsymbol{e} \to \alpha(\boldsymbol{g}, \boldsymbol{d}) = \alpha(\boldsymbol{g}, \boldsymbol{e})$. This is entailed by *Reinforcement-*α.

Parent Monotonicity is called monotony in [3,7]. It requires that weakening/removing attackers or strengthening/adding supporters leads to a stronger or equal acceptability degree. We express this by two monotonicity requirements here. The first one is *Parent Monotonicity-α*: $(\boldsymbol{d} \geq 0 \wedge \boldsymbol{g} \leq \boldsymbol{h}) \rightarrow \alpha(\boldsymbol{g}, \boldsymbol{d}) \leq \alpha(\boldsymbol{h}, \boldsymbol{d})$. The second requirement is *Parent Monotonicity-ι*: $s_1 \leq s_2 \rightarrow \iota(s_1, w) \leq \iota(s_2, w)$.

Strengthening-ι requires that the acceptability degree of a supported argument is higher than its initial weight. This is expressed as $s > 0 \rightarrow w \prec \iota(s, w)$. Dually, *weakening-$\iota$* is $s < 0 \rightarrow \iota(s, w) \prec w$. For the α part, we define *supports*$(\boldsymbol{g}, \boldsymbol{d})$ and *attacks*$(\boldsymbol{g}, \boldsymbol{d})$ as the indicator vectors of the non-neutral supporting resp. attacking parents: *supports*$(\boldsymbol{g}, \boldsymbol{d})_i = 1$ iff $\boldsymbol{g}_i = 1$ and $\boldsymbol{d}_i \neq 0$, and *attacks*$(\boldsymbol{g}, \boldsymbol{d})_i = 1$ iff $\boldsymbol{g}_i = -1$ and $\boldsymbol{d}_i \neq 0$. Now *strengthening-α* expresses that if $\boldsymbol{d} \geq 0$ and if we have a permutation P mapping attackers to supporters outweighing them, i.e.

$$\begin{aligned} \mathit{attacks}(\boldsymbol{g}, \boldsymbol{d}) &\leq \mathit{supports}(P\boldsymbol{g}, P\boldsymbol{d}) \quad \text{and} \\ \mathit{attacks}(\boldsymbol{g}, \boldsymbol{d}) \circ \boldsymbol{d} &\leq \mathit{supports}(P\boldsymbol{g}, P\boldsymbol{d}) \circ P\boldsymbol{d}, \end{aligned}$$

(where $\circ$ denotes the entry-wise (Hadamard) product), then $\alpha(\boldsymbol{g}, \boldsymbol{d}) \geq 0$ (strict if one inequality is strict). Weakening-α is dual.

Definition 4 (Well-Behaved Modular Acceptability Semantics). *A well-behaved modular acceptability semantics satisfies all structural and essential characteristics in Table 2.*

Proposition 1. Reinforcement-ι *entails* parent monotonicity-ι. Stability-ι *is equivalent to* soundness *($\iota(s, w) \neq w \rightarrow s \neq 0$).* Reinforcement-$\alpha$ *entails* directionality.

Proposition 2. *All essential axioms listed in Table 2 are independent of each other.*

Proposition 3. *Any well-behaved modular acceptability semantics satisfies the characteristics from [5]: anonymity, bi-variate independence, equivalence, stability, neutrality, parent monotonicity, non-strict bi-variate reinforcement, weakening and strengthening. Additionally, resilience as defined in [5] is satisfied if our version of resilience is.*

3.3 Optional Characteristics

The following characteristics are met by some acceptability semantics.

Compactness: $\mathbb{D}$ has a minimum $\texttt{Min}_{\mathbb{S}}$ and maximum $\texttt{Max}_{\mathbb{S}}$. **Resilience** ensures that an argument may have a perfect ($\texttt{Max}_{\mathbb{S}}$) or a worthless ($\texttt{Min}_{\mathbb{S}}$) degree only if its initial weight is of the same value: $w < \texttt{Max}_{\mathbb{S}} \rightarrow \iota(s, w) < \texttt{Max}_{\mathbb{S}}$ and $w > \texttt{Min}_{\mathbb{S}} \rightarrow \iota(s, w) > \texttt{Min}_{\mathbb{S}}$. **Stickiness** expresses, dually, that arguments cannot escape the minimum or maximum value: $\iota(s, \texttt{Min}_{\mathbb{S}}) = \texttt{Min}_{\mathbb{S}}$ and/or $\iota(s, \texttt{Max}_{\mathbb{S}}) = \texttt{Max}_{\mathbb{S}}$. **Franklin** expresses that if argument a is attacked by b and supported by c and the acceptability degrees of b and c are identical, then c and b neutralise each other (w.r.t. a). Formally, if $\boldsymbol{g}_i = -\boldsymbol{g}_j$ and $\boldsymbol{d}_i = \boldsymbol{d}_j$, then $\alpha(\boldsymbol{g}, \boldsymbol{d}) = \alpha(\boldsymbol{g}[i : 0][j :$

$0], \boldsymbol{d})$, where $\boldsymbol{g}[i:0]$ is $\boldsymbol{g}$ with i-th component set to 0. **Counting**: additional support (attack) increases (decreases) the aggregation. Formally,

$$(d \geq 0 \wedge \forall i{\neq}k.\boldsymbol{g}_i{=}h_i) \rightarrow sgn(\alpha(\boldsymbol{g}, \boldsymbol{d}) - \alpha(h, \boldsymbol{d})) = sgn(\boldsymbol{g}_k - \boldsymbol{h}_k).$$

Symmetry expresses that a support with degree $\boldsymbol{d}$ is equivalent to an attack with degree $-\boldsymbol{d}$ (and vice versa). Formally, $\alpha(\boldsymbol{g}, \boldsymbol{d}) = \alpha(-\boldsymbol{g}, -\boldsymbol{d})$ (Table 3).

4 Implementing the Modular Parts

Several implementations of α have been studied:

Sum all supporting and attacking arguments are summed up: $\alpha^{sum}(\boldsymbol{g}, \boldsymbol{d}) = \boldsymbol{gd}$ (matrix multiplication). With *sum*, attacks with negative degree effectively become supports and vice versa.

Sum-pos like *sum* but only parents with positive degrees:

$$\alpha^{sum\text{-}pos}(\boldsymbol{g}, \boldsymbol{d}) = \textstyle\sum_{i;\boldsymbol{d}_i \geq 0} \boldsymbol{g}_i \boldsymbol{d}_i$$

Sum-σ like *sum* with sigmoid: $\alpha^{sum\text{-}\sigma}(\boldsymbol{g}, \boldsymbol{d}) = \boldsymbol{g}\sigma^{-1}(\boldsymbol{d})$, where $\sigma = \tanh$.

Table 2. Structural and essential characteristics. $\prec$, $\leq_g$, *supports* and *attacks* are defined in the text.

Structural Characteristics	
Anonymity-1	$\mathsf{Deg}^{\mathsf{S}}_{\langle \mathcal{A}, G, \boldsymbol{w} \rangle} = \mathsf{Deg}^{\mathsf{S}}_{\langle G, \boldsymbol{w} \rangle}$
Equivalence	$\mathsf{Deg}^{\mathsf{S}}_{\langle G, \boldsymbol{w} \rangle}(i) = \deg(G_i, \mathsf{Deg}^{\mathsf{S}}_{\langle G, \boldsymbol{w} \rangle}, \boldsymbol{w}_i) \quad (i = 1, \ldots, n)$
Modularity	$\mathsf{Deg}^{\mathsf{S}}_{\langle G, \boldsymbol{w} \rangle}(i) = \iota(\alpha(G_i, \mathsf{Deg}^{\mathsf{S}}_{\langle G, \boldsymbol{w} \rangle}), \boldsymbol{w}_i) \quad (i = 1, \ldots, n)$
Essential: Conditions on ι	
Reinforcement-ι	$s_1 < s_2 \rightarrow \iota(s_1, w) \prec \iota(s_2, w)$
Initial monotonicity	$w_1 < w_2 \rightarrow \iota(s, w_1) \prec \iota(s, w_2)$
Stability-ι	$\iota(0, w) = w$
Continuity-ι	ι is continuous
Essential: Conditions on α	
Anonymity-2	$\alpha(\boldsymbol{g}P^{-1}, P\boldsymbol{d}) = \alpha(\boldsymbol{g}, \boldsymbol{d})$ if P is a permutation matrix
Independence	$\alpha((0\ \boldsymbol{g}), \binom{d}{\boldsymbol{d}}) = \alpha(\boldsymbol{g}, \boldsymbol{d}) = \alpha((\boldsymbol{g}\ 0), \binom{\boldsymbol{d}}{d})$
Reinforcement-α	$\boldsymbol{d} \leq_g \boldsymbol{e} \rightarrow \alpha(\boldsymbol{g}, \boldsymbol{d}) \leq \alpha(\boldsymbol{g}, \boldsymbol{e})$
Parent monotonicity-α	$\boldsymbol{d} \geq 0 \wedge \boldsymbol{g} \leq \boldsymbol{h} \rightarrow \alpha(\boldsymbol{g}, \boldsymbol{d}) \leq \alpha(\boldsymbol{h}, \boldsymbol{d})$
Stability-α	$\alpha(0, \boldsymbol{d}) = 0$
Continuity-α	$\alpha(\boldsymbol{g}, \_)$ is continuous
Neutrality	$\boldsymbol{d} \geq 0 \wedge (\forall j \neq k.\boldsymbol{g}_j = \boldsymbol{h}_j) \wedge \boldsymbol{d}_k = 0 \rightarrow \alpha(\boldsymbol{g}, \boldsymbol{d}) = \alpha(\boldsymbol{h}, \boldsymbol{d})$
Strengthening-α	for $\boldsymbol{d} \geq 0, P$ a permutation matrix, $attacks(\boldsymbol{g}, \boldsymbol{d}) \leq supports(P\boldsymbol{g}, P\boldsymbol{d})$ and $attacks(\boldsymbol{g}, \boldsymbol{d}) \circ \boldsymbol{d} \leq supports(P\boldsymbol{g}, P\boldsymbol{d}) \circ P\boldsymbol{d}$ imply $\alpha(\boldsymbol{g}, \boldsymbol{d}) \geq 0$, strict if one inequality is strict
Weakening-α	for $\boldsymbol{d} \geq 0, P$ a permutation matrix, $supports(\boldsymbol{g}, \boldsymbol{d}) \leq attacks(P\boldsymbol{g}, P\boldsymbol{d})$ and $supports(\boldsymbol{g}, \boldsymbol{d}) \circ \boldsymbol{d} \leq attacks(P\boldsymbol{g}, P\boldsymbol{d}) \circ P\boldsymbol{d}$ imply $\alpha(\boldsymbol{g}, \boldsymbol{d}) \leq 0$, strict if one inequality is strict

Table 3. Entailed and optional characteristics.

Entailed Characteristics	
Parent monotonicity-ι	$s_1 \leq s_2 \rightarrow \iota(s_1, w) \leq \iota(s_2, w)$
Soundness	$\iota(s, w) \neq w \rightarrow s \neq 0$
Strengthening-ι	$s > 0 \rightarrow w \prec \iota(s, w)$
Weakening-ι	$s < 0 \rightarrow \iota(s, w) \prec w$
Directionality	$\boldsymbol{d} \equiv_g \boldsymbol{e} \rightarrow \alpha(\boldsymbol{g}, \boldsymbol{d}) = \alpha(\boldsymbol{g}, \boldsymbol{e})$
Optional Characteristics	
Compactness	there is a $\mathtt{Min_S} \in \mathbb{D}$ and a $\mathtt{Max_S} \in \mathbb{D}$
Resilience	$w > \mathtt{Min_S} \rightarrow \iota(s, w) > \mathtt{Min_S}$ $\quad w < \mathtt{Max_S} \rightarrow \iota(s, w) < \mathtt{Max_S}$
Stickiness-min	$\iota(s, \mathtt{Min_S}) = \mathtt{Min_S}$
Stickiness-max	$\iota(s, \mathtt{Max_S}) = \mathtt{Max_S}$
Franklin	$\boldsymbol{g}_i = -\boldsymbol{g}_j \wedge \boldsymbol{d}_i = \boldsymbol{d}_j \rightarrow \alpha(\boldsymbol{g}, \boldsymbol{d}) = \alpha(\boldsymbol{g}[i:0][j:0], \boldsymbol{d})$
Counting	$(\boldsymbol{d} \geq 0 \wedge \forall i{\neq}k.\boldsymbol{g}_i{=}\boldsymbol{h}_i) \rightarrow sgn(\alpha(\boldsymbol{g}, \boldsymbol{d}) - \alpha(\boldsymbol{h}, \boldsymbol{d})) = sgn(\boldsymbol{g}_k - \boldsymbol{h}_k)$
Symmetry	$\alpha(\boldsymbol{g}, \boldsymbol{d}) = \alpha(-\boldsymbol{g}, -\boldsymbol{d})$

Top only the strongest supporter and attacker have influence [3,7]. Only parents with positive degrees are considered: $\alpha^{top}(\boldsymbol{g}, \boldsymbol{d}) = top(\boldsymbol{g}, \boldsymbol{d})\boldsymbol{d}$, where $top(\boldsymbol{g}, \boldsymbol{d})$ keeps only the strongest support and strongest attack.

Top-σ like *top*, but with sigmoid transformation.

Reward/Card The number of supporters/attackers is more important than their quality [3,7]. These are suited for unipolar graphs only.

Proposition 4. *The implementations of* α sum, sum-pos, sum-σ, top, *and* top-σ *satisfy all structural and essential characteristics. With appropriate restrictions, so do* reward *and* card.

Influence functions from the literature include: combined fractional, Euler-based $(1 - \frac{1-w^2}{1+we^s})$, linear($\delta$) $(\frac{s}{\delta} + w)$, sigmoid(δ) $(\sigma(\frac{s}{\delta} + \sigma^{-1}(w)))$, and QMax [27]. These represent different design choices about the role of minimum and maximum acceptability degrees. The Euler-based influence function displays an asymmetry: it has a minimum ($\mathtt{Min_S} = 0$) but no maximum, so the perfect degree (the supremum of $\mathbb{D}$) can only be approximated. The linear and sigmoid functions involve a damping factor $\delta \geq 1$ that dampens the role of the aggregation. The sigmoid function maps $\mathbb{R}$ onto $(-1, 1)$, bounding acceptability degrees.

Proposition 5. *All implementations of ι in Table 4 satisfy all structural and essential characteristics for ι, if the listed conditions on s are respected.*

Corollary 1. *Every combination of* sum, sum-pos, sum-σ, top, top-σ *with combined fractional, Euler-based, linear(δ), sigmoid(δ), QMax yields a well-behaved modular acceptability semantics.*

5 Comparison of Modular Semantics

Due to the modular structure of our approach, any implementation of α can be combined with any implementation of ι whose domain matches the range of α, resulting in an acceptability semantics. Table 6 lists semantics from the literature and novel ones, together with their convergence properties. To illustrate the differences, consider the WASA $\mathbb{A}^{ex2}$ with arguments $a_1, \ldots, a_4$, initial weights $(0.8, 0.7, 0.001, 0.7)$:

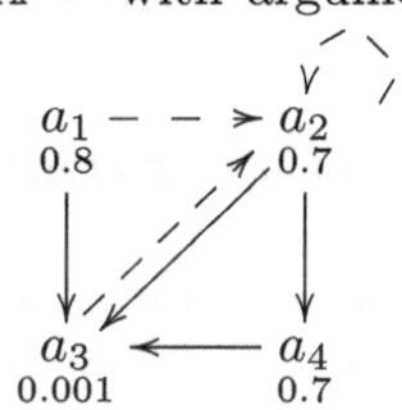

Table 5 shows the results. Due to *stability*, all semantics agree on $\mathtt{Deg}_{\mathbb{A}}^{\mathbb{A}^{ex2}}(a_1) = 0.8$, since a_1 has no parents. The Euler-based semantics treats 0 as the minimum degree, so attacks on a_3 (which starts near 0) have little effect but to push its degree even closer to 0. By contrast, the direct aggregation and sigmoid semantics treat a_3 as initially marginally above neutral, and the combined attacks push it into negative (unacceptable) territory.

The difference between max-based semantics and their counterparts is that they use *top*, considering only the strongest attacker/supporter. Compare Euler-based and max Euler-based for a_2: a_2 is supported by three arguments, but max Euler-based only uses the strongest, yielding 0.801 instead of 0.894. The direct aggregation semantics evaluates a_2 *lower* than damped max-based, because a_3 has a negative degree and its support undermines a_2—an effect stronger than the additional support from a_1. Positive direct aggregation ignores parents with negative degrees, so for a_2 only its parents a_1 and a_2 matter, but not a_3.

This illustrates that our approach supports a wide range of semantics reflecting different design choices. For instance, a_4 in $\mathbb{A}^{ex2}$ is acceptable according to direct aggregation, neutral according to damped max-based, and unacceptable according to positive direct aggregation semantics.

6 Convergence

Intuitively, a semantics *converges* on a graph if iteratively recomputing every argument's degree from its parents' current degrees reaches a stable value; it *diverges* if the degrees keep oscillating. Acyclic graphs always converge; cycles are the interesting story.

Assume an arbitrary well-behaved modular acceptability semantics $(\mathbb{D}, \alpha, \iota)$.

Proposition 6. *Assume convergence of the following limit:*

$$\boldsymbol{f}^0 = \boldsymbol{w}, \ \boldsymbol{f}^{i+1} = \boldsymbol{\iota}(\boldsymbol{\alpha}(G, \boldsymbol{f}^i), \boldsymbol{w}), \ D = \lim_{i \to \infty} \boldsymbol{f}^i \tag{5}$$

Then D satisfies Eq. (4), i.e. $D = \mathit{Deg}^{S}_{\langle G, \boldsymbol{w} \rangle}$.

Definition 5. *A semantics is* convergent *(*divergent*) if $(\boldsymbol{f}^i)$ converges (diverges).*

By Proposition 6, the limit of a convergent semantics provides a solution of the fixpoint Eq. (4). Divergent semantics may have solutions of the fixpoint equation, too; however, computing them may be difficult. Hence, we concentrate on convergence, which singles out exactly one solution and a way to compute it.

Theorem 1. *All well-behaved modular acceptability semantics converge for all acyclic graphs.*

Proof. For a node a, let l_a be the length of the longest path into a. By induction, $\boldsymbol{f}^i_a$ is constant from $i = l_a$ onwards, using *stability* and *directionality*. □

For *sum*-based semantics, convergence depends on Lipschitz constants and indegree. Recall that $f : \mathbb{R} \to \mathbb{R}$ is *Lipschitz continuous* with constant m if $|f(x_1) - f(x_2)| \leq m|x_1 - x_2|$ for all x_1, x_2.

Theorem 2. *Assume $\alpha = \mathit{sum}$ (or sum-pos). If $\iota(\_, \boldsymbol{w}_i)$ is Lipschitz continuous with constant m and $\mathit{indegree}(G) < \frac{1}{m}$, then $\lim_{i \to \infty} \boldsymbol{f}^i$ converges.*

Proof. Using the maximum row sum norm $|||G|||_\infty = \max_i \sum_j |G_{ij}| = \mathit{indegree}(G)$ and $\varepsilon = m \cdot \mathit{indegree}(G) < 1$:

$$\begin{aligned} |||\boldsymbol{f}^{i+1} - \boldsymbol{f}^i|||_\infty &\leq m|||G(\boldsymbol{f}^i - \boldsymbol{f}^{i-1})|||_\infty \\ &\leq m \cdot \mathit{indegree}(G)|||\boldsymbol{f}^i - \boldsymbol{f}^{i-1}|||_\infty \leq \varepsilon|||\boldsymbol{f}^i - \boldsymbol{f}^{i-1}|||_\infty \end{aligned}$$

Hence $(\boldsymbol{f}^i)$ is a Cauchy sequence and thus converges. □

Theorem 3. *Euler-based semantics converges if $\mathit{indegree}(G) < \frac{4}{1 - \min_i \boldsymbol{w}_i^2}$, in particular if $\mathit{indegree}(G) \leq 4$.*

Proof. The Lipschitz constant of the Euler-based $\iota(\_, w)$ is $\leq \frac{1-w^2}{4}$. Apply Theorem 2. Arguments with initial weight 0 stay at 0 by stickiness-min and are irrelevant by neutrality. □

Table 4. Implementations of α and ι. *top* and σ are defined in the text.

name	$\alpha(\boldsymbol{g}, \boldsymbol{d}) =$	**Contin.**	**Neutral.**	**Direct.**	**Franklin**	**Counting**	**Symmetry**	**req.**	**ref.**
	Unipolar graphs only								
reward	$\frac{s}{\lvert n\rvert 2^{\lvert n\rvert}} + sgn(n)\sum_{j=1}^{\lvert n\rvert-1}\frac{1}{2^j}$	✓	✓	✓	✓	–	–	supp. only	[3]
card	$n + \frac{s}{\lvert n\rvert}$	✓	✓	✓	✓	–	–	att. only	[7, 10]
	$n = \boldsymbol{g} \cdot abs(sgn(\boldsymbol{d})), s = \boldsymbol{gd}$								
	Bipolar graphs								
sum	$\boldsymbol{gd}$	✓	✓	✓	✓	✓	✓	–	[3]
sum-pos	$\sum_{i;\boldsymbol{d}_i \geq 0} \boldsymbol{g}_i \boldsymbol{d}_i$	✓	✓	✓	✓	✓	–	–	[3]
sum-σ	$\boldsymbol{g}\sigma^{-1}(\boldsymbol{d})$	✓	✓	✓	✓	✓	✓	–	[25]
top	$top(\boldsymbol{g}, \boldsymbol{d})\boldsymbol{d}$	✓	✓	✓	–	–	–	–	[3]
top-σ	$top(\boldsymbol{g}, \sigma^{-1}(\boldsymbol{d}))\sigma^{-1}(\boldsymbol{d})$	✓	✓	✓	–	–	–	–	

name	$\mathbb{D}$	$\iota(s, w) =$	s	**Compact**	**Resilience**	**Sticky-min**	**Sticky-max**	**ref.**
		Unipolar graphs only						
multilinear	$[0, 1]$	$w + (1 - w)s$	$[0, 1]$	✓	–	–	✓	[3]
pos. fract.	$[0, 1]$	$\frac{w+s}{1+s}$	$s \geq 0$	✓	✓	–	✓	[3]
neg. fract.	$[0, 1]$	$\frac{w}{1-s}$	$s \leq 0$	✓	✓	–	–	[7]
		Bipolar graphs						
comb. fract.	$[0, 1]$	$\begin{cases} \frac{w}{1-s}, & s \leq 0 \\ \frac{w+s}{1+s}, & s \geq 0 \end{cases}$	any	✓	✓	–	–	[25]
Euler-based	$[0, 1)$	$1 - \frac{1-w^2}{1+we^s}$	any	–	✓	✓	–	[5]
linear(δ)	$\mathbb{R}$	$\frac{s}{\delta} + w$	any	–	✓	–	–	[25]
sigmoid(δ)	$(-1, 1)$	$\sigma(\frac{s}{\delta} + \sigma^{-1}(w))$	any	–	✓	–	–	[25]
QMax	$[0, 1]$	$\begin{cases} w - w\frac{s^2}{1+s^2}, & s \leq 0 \\ w + (1 - w)\frac{s^2}{1+s^2}, & s \geq 0 \end{cases}$	any	✓	✓	–	–	[27]

Table 5. Semantics applied to $\mathbb{A}^{ex2}$.

$\texttt{Deg}_{\mathbb{A}^{ex2}}$	δ	a_1	a_2	a_3	a_4
Euler-based	-	0.8	0.894	0.000	0.604
max Euler-based	-	0.8	0.801	0.000	0.612
direct aggregation	2	0.8	1.161	-1.039	0.120
damped max-based	2	0.8	1.400	-0.699	0.000
positive direct aggr.	2	0.8	2.200	-1.499	-0.400
sigmoid direct aggr.	2	0.8	0.902	-0.875	0.126
sigmoid damped max-b.	2	0.8	0.940	-0.699	0.000

Table 6. Overview of semantics. All converge for acyclic graphs (Theorem 1).

semantics	α	ι	converges	counter-ex.	ref.
Not covering mixed support/attack graphs					
aggregation-based	sum	pos. fraction	supports	has attacks	[3]
weighted h-cat.	sum	neg. fraction	attacks	has supports	[7]
comb. aggr./h-cat.	sum	comb. fract.	unipolar only	mixes both	Exs. 3, 4
top-based	top	multilinear	supports	has attacks	[3]
Covering mixed support/attack graphs					
Euler-based	sum	Euler-based	$indegree(G) \leq 4$	$indegree(G) = 6$	[5], Theorem 3
max Euler-based	top	Euler-based	all graphs	—	Proposition 9
direct aggregation	sum	linear(δ)	$indegree(G) < \delta$	$indegree(G) \geq \delta{+}1$	Theorem 4
sigmoid dir. aggr.	sum-σ	sigmoid(δ)	$indegree(G) < \delta$	$indegree(G) \geq \delta{+}1$	Proposition 11
damped max-based	top	linear(δ), $\delta > 2$	all graphs	—	Proposition 10
sigm. damp. max-b.	top-σ	sigmoid(δ), $\delta > 2$	all graphs	—	Proposition 12
quadratic energy	sum	QMax	$indegree(G) \leq 1$	$indegree(G) = 2$	Proposition 7

Proposition 7. *Quadratic energy semantics converges if* $indegree(G) \leq 1$.

Theorem 4. *For* $indegree(G) < \delta$, *direct aggregation semantics converges to* $(I - \frac{1}{\delta}G)^{-1}\boldsymbol{w}$.

Proof. The function $f^i(s) = \iota(s, \boldsymbol{w}_i) = \frac{s}{\delta} + \boldsymbol{w}_i$ is Lipschitz continuous with constant $\frac{1}{\delta}$, so convergence follows from Theorem 2. More specifically, since $|||\frac{1}{\delta}G|||_\infty = \frac{indegree(G)}{\delta} < 1$, the matrix $I - \frac{1}{\delta}G$ is invertible with $(I - \frac{1}{\delta}G)^{-1} = \sum_{i=0}^{\infty}(\frac{1}{\delta}G)^i$ [22, Cor. 5.6.16]; hence $\texttt{Deg}^{dir}_{\langle G,\boldsymbol{w}\rangle,\delta} = (I - \frac{1}{\delta}G)^{-1}\boldsymbol{w}$. □

For semantics using *top*, we can obtain stronger convergence results, since only the top supporter and attacker matter:

Lemma 1. $|||top(G, \boldsymbol{d})\boldsymbol{d} - top(G, \boldsymbol{e})\boldsymbol{e}|||_\infty \leq 2|||\boldsymbol{d} - \boldsymbol{e}|||_\infty$

Proposition 8. *With top aggregation, if* $\iota(\_, \boldsymbol{w}_i)$ *is Lipschitz continuous with constant* $< \frac{1}{2}$, *then the semantics converges.*

Proposition 9. *Max Euler-based semantics converges for all graphs.*

Proposition 10. *Damped max-based semantics converges for* $\delta > 2$.

Proposition 11. *For* $\delta > indegree(G)$, *sigmoid direct aggregation semantics converges to* $\sigma((I - \frac{1}{\delta}G)^{-1}\sigma^{-1}(\boldsymbol{w}))$.

Proposition 12. *Sigmoid damped max-based semantics converges for* $\delta > 2$.

7 Divergence

A very simple example of divergence can be obtained for combined aggregation-based/h-categorizer semantics:

Example 3. For the WASA 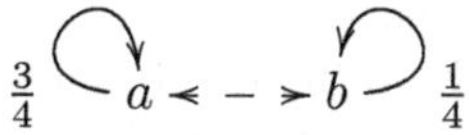

, combined aggregation-based/h-categorizer semantics gives $\boldsymbol{f}^{2i} = (\,\frac{3}{4}\;\frac{1}{4}\,)^T$ and $\boldsymbol{f}^{2i+1} = (\,\frac{1}{2}\;\frac{1}{2}\,)^T$, hence diverges. □

We now prove a far more general divergence result for semantics based on *sum*.

Theorem 5. *Assume $\alpha = sum$. If there are $v > w \in \mathbb{D}$ and $k \in \mathbb{N}$, $k \geq 1$ with*

$$\iota(k(v-w), w) \geq \iota(k(w-v), v) \tag{6}$$

then there is a WASA *with maximal indegree $2k$ that diverges.*

Proof. Consider the WASA with k arguments a_i (weight v) and k arguments b_i (weight w), where all a_i attack each other, all b_i attack each other, and all a_i support all b_j and vice versa:

Since $v > w$, by *stability* and *reinforcement-ι*, $\boldsymbol{f}^1_{a_i} < v$ and $\boldsymbol{f}^1_{b_i} > w$. The assumption (6) gives $\boldsymbol{f}^1_{b_i} \geq \boldsymbol{f}^1_{a_i}$. By induction, the even and odd subsequences are monotonic in opposite directions:

$$\ldots \leq \boldsymbol{f}^5_{a_i} \leq \boldsymbol{f}^3_{a_i} \leq \boldsymbol{f}^1_{a_i} < \boldsymbol{f}^0_{a_i} \leq \boldsymbol{f}^2_{a_i} \leq \boldsymbol{f}^4_{a_i} \leq \ldots$$

which means divergence. □

Example 4. Theorem 5 applies to (assuming $1 \leq \delta \in \mathbb{N}$):

ι	k	v	w
multilinear	1	$\frac{1}{2}$	$\frac{2}{5}$
QMax	1	1	0
combined fractional	2	$\frac{1}{2}$	$\frac{2}{5}$
Euler-based	3	$\frac{1}{2}$	$\frac{2}{5}$
linear(δ)/sigmoid(δ)	$\lceil \frac{\delta+1}{2} \rceil$	$\frac{2}{3}$	$\frac{3}{5}$

In particular, there is a WASA with maximal indegree 6 for which Euler-based semantics diverges, and for each δ, there is a WASA with maximal indegree $\delta + 1$ (odd δ) or $\delta + 2$ (even δ) for which (sigmoid) direct aggregation semantics diverges. □

Proposition 13. *For any ι satisfying the essential characteristics, there exist $v > w \in \mathbb{D}$ and $k \geq 1$ with $\iota(k(v-w), w) \geq \iota(k(w-v), v)$.*

Combining Theorem 5 and Proposition 13, we obtain:

Proposition 14. *There is no well-behaved modular semantics based on* sum *that converges for all* WASA*s.*

8 Conclusion and Related Work

We have studied well-behaved modular acceptability semantics for bipolar weighted argumentation graphs, linking characteristics to requirements on the aggregation function α and the influence function ι. Our key results are: (1) all well-behaved modular semantics converge for acyclic graphs; (2) no *sum*-based semantics converges for all graphs, with the boundary related to the reciprocal of the Lipschitz constant; (3) three *top*-based semantics converge for all graphs—the first such result for bipolar weighted argumentation (first appeared in our report [25]).

Argumentation graphs with numerical weights have been widely discussed [2, 16,17], including bipolar cases [14,15], though without initial weightings. Initial weightings are considered in [3,5–7,10]. [1,9,13,20] study further aspects.

Our modular approach, which we have introduced already in [25] but which we publish in a conference paper only now, has been adopted and extended in several directions. Kampik et al. [23] analyse contribution functions for bipolar argumentation graphs principle by principle, showing no single function satisfies all—paralleling the convergence-vs-properties trade-off we find among α implementations. Potyka [28] reformulates our framework, and introduces product-aggregation, capturing Discontinuity-Free Quantitative Argumentation Debate semantics (DF-QuAD, [33]). Compared to [25], we here use his simplification of convergence via Lipschitz continuity. Potyka and Booth's [30] study of properties of their CRC semantics builds directly on our work. Their empirical study [31] confirms the practical relevance of our divergence results: quadratic energy semantics, which by our analysis diverges already at indegree 2, frequently fails to converge on the argumentation graphs arising from truth-discovery networks (and DF-QuAD fails almost universally). Very recently, Munro et al. [26] propose *aggregative* semantics that generalise our modular approach by separating the aggregation of attackers from supporters in a three-stage computation.

Our framework underpins several applications in explainable AI: Potyka [29] interprets neural networks as argumentation graphs; Ayoobi et al. [11] build sparse argumentation graph-based explanations; Both assume convergent semantics of the kind we study. Rapberger et al. [34] extend gradual semantics to assumption-based argumentation.

References

1. Amgoud, L.: Axiomatic characterisations of argumentation semantics. In: Proceedings of KR (2025)
2. Amgoud, L., Ben-Naim, J.: Ranking-based semantics for argumentation frameworks. In: Proceedings of SUM, pp. 134–147 (2013)
3. Amgoud, L., Ben-Naim, J.: Evaluation of arguments from support relations: axioms and semantics. In: Proceedings of IJCAI, pp. 900–906 (2016)
4. Amgoud, L., Ben-Naim, J.: Ranking-based semantics for argumentation frameworks. In: Proceedings of KR, pp. 2–11 (2016)

5. Amgoud, L., Ben-Naim, J.: Weighted bipolar argumentation graphs: axioms and semantics. In: Proceedings of ECSQARU, pp. 46–56 (2017)
6. Amgoud, L., Ben-Naim, J.: Evaluation of arguments in weighted bipolar graphs. Int. J. Approx. Reasoning **99**, 39–55 (2018)
7. Amgoud, L., Ben-Naim, J., Doder, D., Vesic, S.: Acceptability semantics for weighted argumentation frameworks. In: Proceedings of IJCAI, pp. 56–62 (2017)
8. Amgoud, L., Cayrol, C., Lagasquie-Schiex, M.-C., Livet, P.: On bipolarity in argumentation frameworks. Int. J. Intell. Syst. **23**(10), 1062–1093 (2008)
9. Amgoud, L., Doder, D., Lagasquie-Schiex, M.-C.: Higher-order argumentation frameworks: principles and gradual semantics. In: Proceedings of IJCAI, pp. 3224–3231 (2024)
10. Amgoud, L., Doder, D., Vesic, S.: Evaluation of argument strength in attack graphs: foundations and semantics. Artif. Intell. **302**, 103607 (2022)
11. Ayoobi, H., Potyka, N., Toni, F.: SpArX: sparse argumentative explanations for neural networks. In: Proceedings of ECAI, pp. 149–156 (2023)
12. Baroni, P., Rago, A., Toni, F.: How many properties do we need for gradual argumentation? In: Proceedings of AAAI, pp. 1736–1743 (2018)
13. Baroni, P., Rago, A., Toni, F.: From fine-grained properties to broad principles for gradual argumentation: a principled spectrum. Int. J. Approx. Reasoning **105**, 252–286 (2019)
14. Budán, M.C.D., Simari, G.R., Falappa, M.A.: On bipolar argumentation frameworks. In: Proceedings of IBERAMIA (2014)
15. Cayrol, C., Lagasquie-Schiex, M.-C.: Gradual valuation for bipolar argumentation frameworks. In: Proceedings of ECSQARU (2005)
16. Cayrol, C., Lagasquie-Schiex, M.-C.: Graduality in argumentation. J. Artif. Intell. Res. **23**, 245–297 (2005)
17. Cayrol, C., Lagasquie-Schiex, M.-C.: Bipolarity in argumentation graphs. In: Proceedings of ICTAI (2011)
18. Cayrol, C., Lagasquie-Schiex, M.-C.: Bipolarity in argumentation graphs: towards a better understanding. Int. J. Approx. Reasoning **54**(7), 876–899 (2013)
19. Corea, C., Thimm, M.: Using matrix decomposition for efficient argumentation semantics computation. In: Proceedings of COMMA (2016)
20. Doder, D., Amgoud, L., Vesic, S.: Parametrised gradual semantics dealing with varied degrees of compensation. In: Proceedings of IJCAI, pp. 3176–3183 (2023)
21. Dung, P.M.: On the acceptability of arguments and its fundamental role in nonmonotonic reasoning, logic programming and n-person games. Artif. Intell. **77**(2), 321–357 (1995)
22. Horn, R.A., Johnson, C.R.: Matrix Analysis. Cambridge University Press, Cambridge (1985)
23. Kampik, T., Potyka, N., Yin, X., Čyras, K., Toni, F.: Contribution functions for quantitative bipolar argumentation graphs: A principle-based analysis. Int. J. Approx. Reasoning **173**, 109255 (2024)
24. Leite, J., Martins, J.: Social abstract argumentation. In: Proceedings of IJCAI, pp. 2287–2292 (2011)
25. Mossakowski, T., Neuhaus, F.: Modular semantics and characteristics for bipolar weighted argumentation graphs, CoRR. abs/1807.06685 (2018)
26. Munro, Y., Bloch, I., Lesot, M.-J.: Aggregative semantics for quantitative bipolar argumentation frameworks, CoRR. abs/2603.06067 (2026)
27. Potyka, N.: Continuous dynamical systems for weighted bipolar argumentation. In: Proceedings of KR, pp. 148–157 (2018)

28. Potyka, N.: Extending modular semantics for bipolar weighted argumentation. In: Proceedings of AAMAS, pp. 1722–1730 (2019)
29. Potyka, N.: Interpreting neural networks as quantitative argumentation frameworks. In: Proceedings of AAAI, vol. 35, pp. 6463–6470 (2021)
30. Potyka, N., Booth, R.: Balancing open-mindedness and conservativeness in quantitative bipolar argumentation. In: Proceedings of KR, pp. 597–607 (2024)
31. Potyka, N., Booth, R.: An empirical study of quantitative bipolar argumentation frameworks for truth discovery. In: Proceedings of COMMA, pp. 205–216 (2024)
32. Potyka, N., Yin, X., Toni, F.: Explaining random forests using bipolar argumentation and Markov networks. In: Proceedings of AAAI, vol. 37, pp. 9453–9460 (2023)
33. Rago, A., Toni, F., Aurisicchio, M., Baroni, P.: Discontinuity-free decision support with quantitative argumentation debates. In: Proceedings of KR, pp. 63–73 (2016)
34. Rapberger, A., Russo, F., Rago, A., Toni, F.: On gradual semantics for assumption-based argumentation. In: Proceedings of KR (2025)
35. Yin, X., Potyka, N., Toni, F.: Explaining arguments' strength: unveiling the role of attacks and supports. In *Proc. IJCAI*, pp. 3622–3630 (2024)

Do We Really Need Diffusion? A Fast U-Net for Paired Medical Image Translation

Alicia Pirwass[1,2,3](✉), Birte Glimm[1], Michael Munz[3], and Hans-Joachim Wilke[2]

[1] Institute of Artificial Intelligence, Ulm University, 89081 Ulm, Germany
[2] Institute of Orthopaedic Research and Biomechanics, Centre for Trauma Research, University Hospital Ulm, Helmholtzstrasse 14, 89081 Ulm, Germany
[3] AI for Sensor Data Analytics Research Group, Ulm University of Applied Sciences, 89081 Ulm, Germany

alicia.pirwass@uni-ulm.de

Abstract. Magnetic resonance imaging-signal fat fraction (MRI-SFF) quantifies tissue fat and serves as an established biomarker for metabolic and musculoskeletal disorders. Its acquisition, however, relies on dedicated MRI sequences that, despite being supported by most modern scanners, are not consistently acquired as part of routine clinical protocols. We investigate whether SFF can be estimated from T2-weighted (T2w) MRI, a sequence routinely acquired in standard clinical imaging, via image-to-image translation (I2I). We further compare a lightweight 4-level U-Net to a state-of-the-art Denoising Diffusion Probabilistic Model (DDPM) using a dataset of 230 048 paired 2D images (183 517 train, 23 621 val, 22 910 test) from the German National Cohort (NAKO). Both models clearly outperform the identity baseline (Pearson correlation $r = 0.769$, mean absolute error MAE $= 0.070 \pm 0.054$), which confirms that the models learn a non-trivial cross-modal mapping. Interestingly, the lightweight U-Net outperforms the DDPM in both correlation ($r = 0.975$ vs. 0.962) and error (MAE $= 0.014 \pm 0.015$ vs. 0.019 ± 0.019), while reducing inference time by a factor of 208 (25.2 ms vs. 5 227.2 ms per image using 50 Denoising Diffusion Implicit Model (DDIM) steps). The strong clinical performance at substantially reduced computational cost enables real-time clinical use.

Keywords: Paired Image-to-Image Translation · Diffusion Models · Medical Image Analysis

1 Introduction

Magnetic resonance imaging (MRI) can be used to quantify the fat content of tissue, which is an established biomarker for metabolic and musculoskeletal disorders such as sarcopenia (muscle loss e.g. due to aging or immobility) and

D. Wolter and G. Schwalbe (Eds.): KI 2026, LNAI 16830, pp. 101–116, 2027.
https://doi.org/10.1007/978-3-032-32335-4_8

insulin resistance [17]. The signal fat fraction (SFF) measures this fat content as the ratio of the fat MR signal to the total MR signal from fat and water [30]. The gold standard for fat quantification is the proton density fat fraction (PDFF), which requires a dedicated multi-echo Dixon MRI sequence: the scanner acquires images at multiple points in time after each excitation pulse, enabling simultaneous correction of physical confounding factors such as magnetic field inhomogeneities and tissue-specific signal decay [30]. This multi-echo acquisition is technically demanding and time-consuming, and is, therefore, rarely included in routine clinical or epidemiological MRI protocols.

A simpler alternative is the two-point Dixon technique, which acquires only two images at different time points to separate fat and water signal contributions, yielding an uncorrected SFF map. While two-point Dixon is more common than multi-echo Dixon, it is still not consistently acquired across clinical sites and population studies, limiting access to large paired datasets for research.

Standard anatomical MRI sequences such as T2-weighted (T2w) imaging, by contrast, acquire a single image that reflects differences in tissue water content and structure, providing excellent soft-tissue contrast. T2w imaging is among the most frequently acquired MRI sequences worldwide, in clinical practice, research studies, and large epidemiological cohorts, but provides no direct quantitative fat information. Given this abundance, there is considerable research interest in estimating intramuscular fat content from conventional T2w images. However, a recent systematic review [28] shows that existing methods frequently rely on manual or semi-automatic analysis steps, lack validation against quantitative reference standards such as SFF or PDFF, and are therefore difficult to scale or integrate into automated clinical workflows. Image-to-image (I2I) translation offers a promising alternative: by learning a direct mapping from T2w to SFF using paired data, it enables fully automated, quantitative fat estimation from routinely acquired images without requiring Dixon acquisitions at inference time.

We investigate whether this translation is feasible and how complex generative models such as Denoising Diffusion Probabilistic Models (DDPMs) compare to lightweight architectures for this task. We compare a 4-level U-Net to a DDPM on $N = 22\,910$ paired T2w and Dixon images from the German National Cohort (NAKO) [3,27], a large-scale population-based study with a standardized whole-body MRI protocol that includes a T1-weighted 3D VIBE two-point Dixon sequence covering the neck-to-knee region [3]. Since all images were acquired on identical scanners using the same standardized protocol across all study centers, SFF values are internally consistent throughout the dataset. Beyond pixel-wise image quality, we evaluate downstream clinical utility via automated SFF quantification in four paraspinal muscle compartments using VIBESegmentator [7].

Our main contributions are: (i) the first systematic comparison of U-Net and DDPM for T2w-to-SFF translation on a large-scale epidemiological dataset; (ii) a clinically grounded evaluation via downstream muscle SFF quantification; (iii) we show that, for deterministic paired translation tasks, lightweight models can outperform diffusion models while reducing inference time by a factor of 208.

2 Technical Background

We briefly outline the two architectures compared in this work. For a broader discussion of related approaches see Sect. 3.

U-Net. The U-Net [32] is a fully convolutional encoder–decoder architecture combining a contracting path for hierarchical feature extraction with a symmetric expanding path for spatial reconstruction. Skip connections between corresponding encoder and decoder levels preserve high-frequency spatial detail, making U-Nets well-suited for paired I2I translation tasks where input and output are spatially aligned.

Denoising Diffusion Probabilistic Models. DDPMs [12] learn to synthesize data by reversing a gradual Gaussian noising process over T timesteps. The model is trained by minimizing a noise prediction objective $\mathcal{L} = \mathrm{E}_{t,x_0,\epsilon}\left[\|\epsilon - \epsilon_\theta(x_t, t)\|^2\right]$, where ϵ is the added noise and ϵ_θ is the learned denoiser. For a full derivation we refer to [12]. For conditional image synthesis, the input image is provided as additional context at each denoising step, guiding generation towards a target domain. While DDPMs avoid adversarial training instabilities, their iterative sampling procedure results in substantially longer inference times compared to single-pass architectures. For accelerated inference, Denoising Diffusion Implicit Models (DDIMs) [33] reformulate the reverse process as a non-Markovian sequence, enabling sampling with substantially fewer steps without retraining the model.

3 Related Work

In the following, we review related work on quantitative MRI synthesis, I2I translation architectures, and diffusion-based generative models in medical imaging.

3.1 Quantitative MRI Synthesis

While prior work has demonstrated the feasibility of inferring PDFF and SFF from alternative MRI sequences, these approaches have focused predominantly on hepatic applications [1,25,34], smaller cohorts [10], or two-point Dixon to PDFF translation [34] rather than the T2w-to-SFF setting.

3.2 Image-to-Image Translation Architectures

I2I translation refers to the task of learning a mapping between two image domains from paired or unpaired training data. The encoder-decoder architecture introduced by Ronneberger et al. [32] established the foundation for pixel-wise prediction tasks in medical imaging, combining a contracting path for context aggregation with a symmetric expanding path and skip connections for precise spatial reconstruction. Building on this, Isola et al. [14] proposed a general-purpose framework for paired I2I translation using conditional adversarial networks, demonstrating that a single architecture with a learned loss function can be applied across diverse translation tasks without task-specific engineering.

In the medical imaging domain, I2I translation has been widely adopted for cross-modal synthesis, including MRI cross-modality translation [23,24,37], MRI-to-CT synthesis [8,9,11,13,18,19,21], CT-to-PET translation [4], and musculoskeletal applications including muscle segmentation from MRI [6]. These methods typically rely on pixel-wise reconstruction losses (e.g., ℓ_1) combined with adversarial objectives to encourage perceptual realism [2]. While generative adversarial network (GAN)-based approaches have demonstrated strong performance on paired translation tasks, they can suffer from training instability and mode collapse, which has motivated the exploration of alternative generative architectures.

More recently, Moschetto et al. [23] directly compared GAN-based models, DDPMs, and flow matching approaches for T1w-to-T2w MRI translation, finding that the GAN-based Pix2Pix model achieved superior structural fidelity and computational efficiency, suggesting that for deterministic, paired translation tasks, lightweight discriminative models may be preferable to more complex generative frameworks.

3.3 Denoising Diffusion Probabilistic Models in Medical Imaging

DDPMs, introduced by Ho et al. [12], define a generative process as the reverse of a learned Markov chain that gradually adds Gaussian noise to data. Unlike GANs, DDPMs do not require adversarial training and avoid issues such as mode collapse, which has driven their rapid adoption across generative modeling tasks [15,20].

In the medical imaging domain, DDPMs and related score-based models have been applied to a broad range of tasks including image reconstruction, denoising, anomaly detection, and cross-modal synthesis [15]. For I2I translation specifically, conditional DDPMs have demonstrated strong performance in tasks such as MRI-to-CT synthesis and multi-contrast MRI generation, producing outputs with high anatomical fidelity and favorable convergence properties compared to GAN-based alternatives [8,16,26]. Despite these promising results, DDPMs carry a fundamental computational disadvantage: inference requires iterating through hundreds to thousands of denoising steps, resulting in substantially longer sampling times compared to single-pass architectures such as U-Nets. Accelerated samplers such as DDIM [33] can reduce this to tens of steps while preserving generation quality, though inference remains substantially slower than single-pass architectures. For MRI-to-CT translation, diffusion models have been reported to achieve superior image fidelity despite higher computational cost [13].

An emerging consensus suggests that for deterministic, paired translation tasks, this computational overhead outweighs quality gains [23]. Rassmann et al. [29] provide the most systematic evidence to date, proposing YODA, a 2.5D diffusion-based framework that supports regression sampling by directly using the initial single-step denoiser prediction without iterative refinement. They demonstrate that this approach matches or outperforms full diffusion sampling across five diverse datasets including brain MRI and MRI-to-CT translation. They conclude that iterative refinement primarily replicates acquisition noise rather than improving medically relevant information fidelity. Our work extends this line of evidence to the clinically novel T2w-to-SFF translation task on a large-scale epidemiological cohort (22 910 test slices), providing a direct comparison between a standard lightweight U-Net and a conditional DDPM without proposing a new framework, and yielding a concrete architectural recommendation for this class of tasks.

4 Methods

We next detail our study cohort, image preprocessing pipeline, modeling strategies, and evaluation framework used for SFF estimation from T2w MRI.

4.1 Dataset and Preprocessing

The data used in this study were obtained from the German National Cohort (NAKO), comprising $N = 30\,861$ participants who underwent standardized whole-body MRI. Written informed consent was obtained from all participants and the NAKO study was approved by the responsible ethics committees and conducted in accordance with national regulations and the Declaration of Helsinki (1975, revised version) [35].

Imaging was performed across all centers using identical scanners (Magnetom Skyra, Siemens Healthcare, Erlangen, Germany) with a field strength of 3.0 Tesla and a 70 cm bore, ensuring high consistency across sites. The imaging protocol included axial T2w HASTE sequences (slice thickness: 5.0 mm; in-plane resolution: 1.4×1.4 mm; echo time: 81 ms) covering the shoulder-to-epigastric region. In addition, axial T1-weighted 3D VIBE two-point Dixon sequences (slice thickness: 3.0 mm; in-plane resolution: 1.4×1.4 mm; repetition time: 4.36 ms) were acquired from neck to knee using CAIPIRINHA acceleration. The Dixon technique enables reconstruction of water-only and fat-only images from in- and out-of-phase acquisitions.

From the full cohort, 30 137 participants with complete T2w HASTE and VIBE Dixon sequences were selected for further analysis. As all sequences were acquired within the same imaging session, no inter-scan registration was required, where registration refers to the process of aligning images from different scans such that corresponding anatomical structures are mapped to the same spatial locations. Spatial alignment between modalities was ensured along the z-axis, defined as the axis orthogonal to the transverse plane. All images were center-cropped from a resolution of 260×300 to 256×256 pixels. SFF maps were computed from the Dixon fat-only and water-only images using a pixel-wise formulation: $\text{SFF} = (\text{fat})/(\text{fat} + \text{water})$. Subsequently, the T2w input images were normalized to the range $[0, 1]$ using per-sample min–max normalization. Every second SFF slice was paired with the corresponding T2w HASTE slice to form aligned input–target pairs.

The dataset was split into training, validation and test subsets comprising 183 517, 23 621 and 22 910 slices, respectively. The split was stratified w.r.t. age, body mass index (BMI), and sex to ensure balanced distributions across subsets.

4.2 Models

We compare three modeling approaches of increasing complexity for SFF estimation from T2w MRI: a non-learning identity baseline, a lightweight U-Net for deterministic I2I translation, and a DDPM as a representative of modern generative approaches. All models were trained on a single NVIDIA GeForce RTX 4080 GPU (16 GB VRAM).

Identity Baseline. As a simple reference, we consider an identity baseline in which the input T2w HASTE image is directly interpreted as a proxy for SFF. This baseline establishes an upper bound on the achievable error when no cross-modality translation is performed and serves as a lower-complexity reference for evaluating learned models.

Image-to-Image U-Net. We employ a lightweight U-Net with a 4-level encoder–decoder architecture and skip connections. Each convolutional block consists of batch normalization and ReLU activations, and the final layer uses a sigmoid activation to produce outputs in the range $[0, 1]$.

The model was trained for 30 epochs using the AdamW optimizer with a learning rate of 2×10^{-4} and an ℓ_1 loss. Mixed-precision training (16-bit floating point, FP16) was used with a batch size of 16. The network comprises approximately 7.78×10^6 trainable parameters.

DDPM. The DDPM backbone follows the U-Net architecture proposed by Ho et al. [12], with a base channel dimension of 64 and channel multipliers $(1, 2, 4, 8)$, resulting in four resolution levels. The conditional T2w input image is concatenated channel-wise to the noisy target at each denoising step. The model predicts both the noise ϵ and the posterior variance, which is learned via a Kullback–Leibler (KL) divergence-based auxiliary loss weighted by $\lambda = 10^{-3}$ [12]. Training was performed for 90 epochs using the Adam optimizer [12] with a learning rate of 2×10^{-5}, $T = 1\,000$ diffusion timesteps, and a cosine noise schedule with learned variance. Due to memory constraints, a batch size of 4 with gradient accumulation over 8 steps was used, yielding an effective batch size of 32. Model selection was performed via early stopping on a held-out validation set of 800 samples, evaluated every 5 epochs using DDIM sampling with 50 steps (chosen for computational efficiency during training). Training was stopped after 5 consecutive validation epochs without improvement, and the best checkpoint was selected for evaluation. At inference, sampling was performed using the DDIM scheme [33] with 50 steps as the standard configuration, which allows accelerated sampling without retraining. Higher step counts were not evaluated, as DDIM sampling has been shown to produce outputs of comparable quality to full DDPM sampling at substantially reduced step counts [33]. The model contains approximately 3.263×10^7 trainable parameters. The larger parameter count of the DDPM reflects its backbone architecture, which is designed for iterative denoising rather than direct regression, and is, therefore, not directly comparable to the U-Net parameter count.

4.3 Evaluation

We evaluated the models across four complementary aspects: pixel-wise image quality metrics computed globally and within the body region, downstream SFF quantification in four paraspinal muscle compartments as a clinically relevant task, qualitative visual inspection of representative slices, and inference time as a measure of practical deployability.

Image Metrics. Global pixel-wise metrics were computed over all test slices ($N = 22\,910$), comprising mean absolute error (MAE), structural similarity index measure (SSIM), peak signal-to-noise ratio (PSNR), and pixel-wise bias. Masked metrics were additionally computed within a body mask derived from a fixed intensity threshold of 10% of the per-image maximum signal intensity on the T2w HASTE images, followed by binary hole filling, combined with VIBESegmentator masks using pixel-wise logical OR. Masked SSIM was computed over the tight bounding box of the body mask to avoid boundary artifacts from zero-padded background pixels. Masked metrics are considered most clinically relevant, as they focus on anatomically meaningful regions.

Downstream Task. We quantified the mean SFF in four paraspinal muscle regions (autochthonous left/right and iliopsoas left/right; labels 59–62) segmented automatically using VIBESegmentator [7]. Performance was assessed via MAE, bias, and Pearson correlation coefficient (r).

Qualitative Assessment. For qualitative assessment, a representative slice was visualized in two views: the full image and a cropped view restricted to the autochthonous and iliopsoas muscle compartments. This progressive masking was chosen to facilitate visual assessment of model differences in the regions relevant to the downstream task.

Inference Time Measurement. Inference times were measured for a single slice with batch size 1, averaged over 200 runs after 50 warmup iterations with GPU synchronization on an NVIDIA RTX 4080. For the DDPM, inference was performed using the DDIM sampling scheme [33], which allows accelerated sampling by reducing the number of denoising steps without retraining.

5 Results

We present the results in the following order: image quality metrics, downstream muscle SFF quantification, qualitative visual inspection, and inference time.

Table 1. Quantitative image quality metrics (mean ± std) on the test set ($n = 22\,910$ slices); global: all pixels; masked: background pixels excluded; best values shaded; all U-Net vs. DDPM differences are statistically significant ($p < 0.001$, Wilcoxon signed-rank test)

Model	Eval	MAE ↓	SSIM ↑	PSNR ↑	Bias
Identity	Global	0.315 ± 0.050	0.259 ± 0.071	7.33 ± 0.77	-0.286 ± 0.056
(T2w)	Masked	0.282 ± 0.062	0.222 ± 0.077	9.30 ± 1.64	-0.221 ± 0.090
U-Net	Global	0.136 ± 0.022	0.437 ± 0.078	12.40 ± 1.03	-0.023 ± 0.022
	Masked	0.107 ± 0.029	0.490 ± 0.104	15.66 ± 2.33	-0.002 ± 0.016
DDPM	Global	0.179 ± 0.027	0.366 ± 0.078	10.40 ± 0.89	-0.005 ± 0.031
	Masked	0.142 ± 0.038	0.398 ± 0.109	13.45 ± 2.22	0.005 ± 0.024

5.1 Image Metrics

Table 1 reports pixel-wise image quality metrics for all three models. The U-Net significantly outperforms the DDPM across all pixel-wise metrics in both evaluation settings (Wilcoxon signed-rank test, $p < 0.001$ for MAE, SSIM, and PSNR, globally and masked). It achieves a global MAE of 0.136 ± 0.022 and a masked MAE of 0.107 ± 0.029, compared to 0.179 ± 0.027 and 0.142 ± 0.038 for the DDPM, and 0.315 ± 0.050 and 0.282 ± 0.062 for the identity baseline. A consistent improvement is observed in the masked setting over the global setting across all models, reflecting the removal of trivially predicted background pixels. The identity baseline exhibits a strong negative bias of -0.286 ± 0.056 globally and -0.221 ± 0.090 in the masked setting, indicating systematic underestimation of SFF when using the T2w image directly. Both learned models show substantially reduced bias; the U-Net achieves a near-zero masked bias of -0.002 ± 0.016, while the DDPM achieves -0.005 ± 0.031 globally and 0.005 ± 0.024 masked.

5.2 Mean Muscle SFF

Table 2 reports mean SFF estimation accuracy in four muscle compartments across $n = 57\,808$ individual muscle masks. The U-Net achieves the highest Pearson correlation overall ($r = 0.975$) and the lowest MAE (0.014 ± 0.015), with particularly strong performance in the autochthonous muscles ($r = 0.986$ for both left and right). The DDPM reaches $r = 0.962$ and MAE $= 0.019 \pm 0.019$ overall, with autochthonous correlations of $r = 0.976$ and $r = 0.977$ for left and right, respectively. Both models show reduced performance in the iliopsoas compared to the autochthonous muscles. For the left iliopsoas, the U-Net achieves $r = 0.878$ compared to $r = 0.847$ for the DDPM. For the right iliopsoas, we find $r = 0.911$ for the U-Net compared to $r = 0.876$ for the DDPM. Regarding bias, the identity baseline exhibits consistent and substantial negative bias across all compartments (overall -0.063 ± 0.062), indicating systematic underestimation of SFF. Both models show a small overall bias with the U-Net achieving

Table 2. Downstream task evaluation: mean SFF estimation accuracy in four muscle groups segmented using VIBESegmentator; MAE and bias reported as mean ± std across all test slices containing the muscle group; l.: left, r.: right; best values are shaded

Model	Muscle Group	MAE ↓	Bias	Pearson r ↑	n
Identity (T2w)	Autochthonous l.	0.067 ± 0.054	-0.058 ± 0.064	0.794	21 636
	Autochthonous r.	0.082 ± 0.060	-0.075 ± 0.069	0.765	21 617
	Iliopsoas l.	0.050 ± 0.035	-0.047 ± 0.039	0.740	7 252
	Iliopsoas r.	0.062 ± 0.043	-0.057 ± 0.049	0.671	7 303
	All	*0.070 ± 0.054*	*−0.063 ± 0.062*	*0.769*	*57 808*
U-Net	Autochthonous l.	0.012 ± 0.011	-0.004 ± 0.016	0.986	21 636
	Autochthonous r.	0.013 ± 0.011	-0.006 ± 0.016	0.986	21 617
	Iliopsoas l.	0.018 ± 0.024	$+0.003 \pm 0.030$	0.878	7 252
	Iliopsoas r.	0.019 ± 0.022	$+0.000 \pm 0.029$	0.911	7 303
	All	*0.014 ± 0.015*	*−0.003 ± 0.021*	*0.975*	*57 808*
DDPM	Autochthonous l.	0.016 ± 0.014	0.006 ± 0.021	0.976	21 636
	Autochthonous r.	0.017 ± 0.015	0.007 ± 0.021	0.977	21 617
	Iliopsoas l.	0.024 ± 0.028	0.012 ± 0.035	0.847	7 252
	Iliopsoas r.	0.024 ± 0.026	0.008 ± 0.035	0.876	7 303
	All	*0.019 ± 0.019*	*0.007 ± 0.025*	*0.962*	*57 808*

-0.003 ± 0.021 and the DDPM 0.007 ± 0.025. Given the narrow absolute differences between models and the spatially averaged nature of the downstream metric, statistical testing was not performed for the downstream task. The identity baseline yields substantially lower correlations across all muscles (overall $r = 0.769$, MAE $= 0.070 \pm 0.054$).

5.3 Qualitative Results

Figure 1 shows a representative qualitative comparison of T2w-to-SFF translation for both models alongside the ground truth. In the full image (first row), the DDPM accurately replicates the background noise characteristic of the SFF computation, while the U-Net produces a notably blurred background and visceral region. Focusing on the actual region of interest in the cropped muscle view (second row), both models produce predictions that are visually closely aligned with the ground truth, with no salient differences apparent between the two approaches. A single representative slice is shown; given the test set size of 22 910 slices, individual examples are inherently selective and the quantitative metrics in Tables 1 and 2 provide a more reliable basis for comparison.

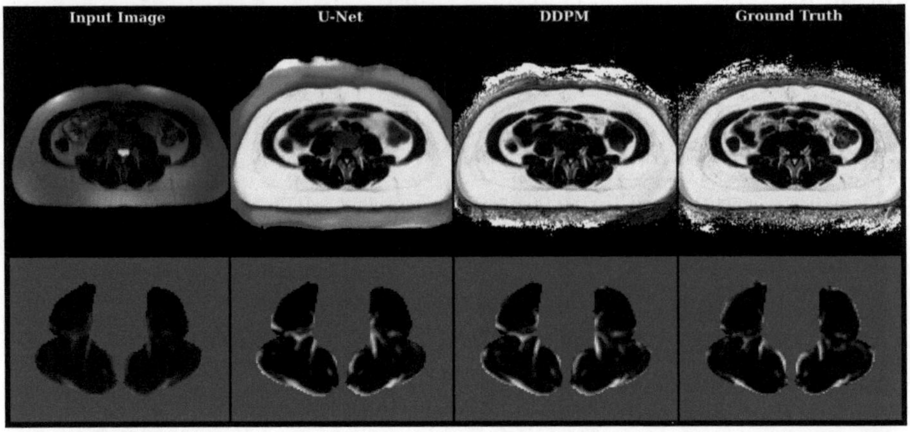

Fig. 1. Qualitative comparison of T2w-to-SFF translation. The columns show the T2w input image, the U-Net prediction, the DDPM prediction, and the SFF ground truth, respectively. The rows display the full image and a cropped view of the muscle compartments (autochthonous and iliopsoas muscles, left and right) segmented using VIBESegmentator; both models reproduce the overall fat distribution, while the U-Net prediction appears visually comparable to the DDPM at substantially lower inference cost.

5.4 Inference Time

Table 3 reports inference times for both models. The U-Net achieves a speedup factor of 208 over the standard DDPM configuration, with inference scaling approximately linearly with DDIM steps.

6 Discussion

This work compares a lightweight U-Net and a conditional DDPM for T2w-to-SFF translation on a large-scale population dataset, evaluating pixel-wise quality and clinically relevant downstream performance. The results consistently favor the U-Net across all evaluated dimensions. We next discuss the implications of these findings with respect to image reconstruction quality, downstream clinical utility, and practical deployability.

6.1 Lightweight but Efficient

The image quality results presented in Table 1 demonstrate that the lightweight U-Net consistently outperforms the DDPM across all pixel-wise metrics in both the global and masked evaluation settings, with the exception of bias, where both models achieve near-zero values (-0.023 ± 0.022 vs. -0.005 ± 0.031 globally; -0.002 ± 0.016 vs. 0.005 ± 0.024 masked). The U-Net achieves a masked SSIM of 0.490 ± 0.104 compared to 0.398 ± 0.109 for the DDPM, and a masked PSNR

Table 3. Model efficiency comparison; inference time measured on an NVIDIA RTX 4080, batch size 1, averaged over 200 runs after 50 warmup iterations with GPU synchronization; * denotes the standard configuration used in all experiments; best values are shaded, where the U-Net with 7.78 M parameters achieves a speedup factor of 208 compared to the standard configuration of the DDPM with its 32.63 M parameters

Model	DDIM Steps	Time/Slice (ms)	50 Slices (s)
U-Net	—	25.2 ± 0.1	1.3
DDPM	10	$1\,045.7 \pm 0.6$	52.3
DDPM	25	$2\,613.8 \pm 1.0$	130.7
DDPM*	50	$5\,227.2 \pm 1.4$	261.4
DDPM	100	$10\,454.9 \pm 3.2$	522.7
DDPM	200	$20\,907.8 \pm 2.5$	1 045.4

of 15.66 ± 2.33 dB versus 13.45 ± 2.22 dB, suggesting that the additional complexity of the diffusion-based sampling process does not translate into improved reconstruction fidelity for this task. While these findings may seem surprising given the U-Net's simplicity, the results can potentially be explained by the perception-distortion tradeoff [5]: diffusion models are optimized to sample from the distribution of plausible outputs, which by definition comes at the cost of pixel-wise accuracy. For a paired translation task with a unique ground truth, this distributional objective is misaligned with the reconstruction goal, placing diffusion models at an inherent disadvantage relative to discriminative architectures that directly minimize distortion. Moschetto et al. [23] similarly observe that GAN-based and discriminative models can match or outperform diffusion models in deterministic, paired translation settings. Rassmann et al. [29] confirm this pattern across five diverse datasets, attributing the DM disadvantage to noise replication rather than information loss. The statistical significance of these differences ($p < 0.001$, Wilcoxon signed-rank test) confirms that the U-Net advantage is not attributable to random variation, despite the inherently large test set.

6.2 Downstream Task

The downstream evaluation of mean muscle SFF estimation represents the clinically most relevant metric in this work, as it directly reflects the utility of the synthesized SFF maps for quantitative muscle fat assessment. The U-Net achieves an overall Pearson correlation of $r = 0.975$ and MAE of 0.014 ± 0.015, compared to $r = 0.962$ and MAE of 0.019 ± 0.019 for the DDPM, indicating that both models yield high agreement with the ground truth muscle SFF values. These results compare favorably to previous T2w-to-SFF method comparisons: Pearson correlations of $r = 0.87$–0.92 for autochthonous muscles were reported for a thresholding-based approach [22], and intraclass correlation coefficient (ICC) values of up to 0.88 for the best-performing model ($\text{GMM}_{3\text{C}}$) against a two-point Dixon reference [36]. The margin between both models is narrow, suggesting that the performance difference observed in pixel-wise image metrics does not fully translate to the downstream task, likely because mean muscle SFF is a spatially averaged quantity less sensitive to local reconstruction artifacts. The consistently lower performance in the iliopsoas compartments, observed for both models, mirrors the consistently poor psoas agreement reported by Masi et al. [22] and Wesselink et al. [36], and likely reflects its characteristically low intramuscular fat content and greater anatomical variability resulting in fewer and more heterogeneous training samples. The identity baseline shows substantially degraded downstream performance ($r = 0.769$, MAE $= 0.070 \pm 0.054$) with a systematic negative bias of -0.063 ± 0.062, confirming that meaningful T2w-to-SFF translation is required to achieve clinically acceptable muscle SFF estimates and that neither model trivially approximates the ground truth.

6.3 Clinical Relevance

The U-Net completes a full 50-slice acquisition in 1.3 s, enabling real-time clinical use, compared to 261.4 s for the DDPM at 50 DDIM steps (a slowdown factor of 208). Even at the most aggressive reduction to 10 DDIM steps, the DDPM still requires 52.3 s per stack, remaining two orders of magnitude slower. Combined with superior pixel-wise image quality and downstream muscle SFF estimation, the computational advantage of the U-Net makes it the more practical choice for deployment in large-scale population studies or clinical settings where throughput and latency are relevant constraints. The DDPM's parameter count of 32.63 M compared to 7.78 M for the U-Net further compounds this difference in terms of memory footprint, an additional consideration for deployment on clinical hardware.

6.4 Limitations

This study has several limitations. First, all experiments were conducted on data acquired from a single scanner and protocol within the NAKO cohort, and generalizability to other MRI systems, field strengths, or acquisition parameters remains to be established; notably, DDPMs may offer advantages over discriminative architectures in more heterogeneous multi-site settings where modeling output variability is beneficial. Second, the ground truth used in this work is SFF derived from a two-point Dixon sequence, rather than true PDFF. SFF is susceptible to confounding factors, which are corrected in multi-echo Dixon-based PDFF but not in two-point Dixon acquisitions [30]. While the use of a standardized single-scanner protocol ensures internal consistency of SFF values across the dataset, future work should investigate whether models trained on SFF generalise to true PDFF targets, and whether the residual confounding in SFF propagates into downstream quantification errors. Third, the two models were trained under different procedures: the U-Net was trained for a fixed 30 epochs, while the DDPM was trained with early stopping based on periodic evaluation on a random subset of 800 validation samples every 5 epochs, representing a trade-off between validation reliability and computational cost. The two training procedures are, therefore, not directly comparable in terms of computational budget and a larger validation subset or more frequent evaluation could yield an improved checkpoint selection for the DDPM. Fourth, while the DDPM inference time could in principle be reduced by decreasing the number of DDIM steps, our results in Table 3 show that even at 10 steps the DDPM remains substantially slower than the U-Net, and the quality implications of aggressive step reduction warrant further investigation. Fifth, no GAN-based baseline (e.g. Pix2Pix [14]) was included; while prior work suggests GANs can match or outperform diffusion models in paired settings [23,29], the focus of this work was on comparing lightweight discriminative architectures to diffusion models specifically, and the inclusion of a GAN baseline remains a direction for future work. Sixth, the downstream evaluation is limited to the paraspinal muscle compartments segmented by VIBESegmentator, namely the autochthonous and iliopsoas muscles, as these are explicitly provided by the segmentation tool and are frequently assessed in the musculoskeletal imaging literature [28]. Extension to additional muscle groups represents a clinically relevant direction for future work. Finally, latent diffusion models [31], which operate in a compressed latent space and may offer a more favorable trade-off between generative quality and inference speed, were not investigated and could be a promising alternative to the pixel-space DDPM evaluated here.

7 Conclusion

We investigated whether SFF can be reliably estimated from T2w MRI using I2I translation, and assessed whether the complexity of diffusion-based generative models is justified for this task. Evaluated on a large held-out test set of 22 910 paired images from the German National Cohort, a lightweight 4-level U-Net consistently outperformed a conditional DDPM across pixel-wise image quality metrics and downstream muscle SFF quantification, while reducing inference time by a factor of 208. Both models substantially outperformed the identity baseline, confirming that a non-trivial cross-modal mapping is learned. For deterministic, paired medical I2I translation tasks with a unique ground truth, our results indicate that lightweight discriminative architectures provide clinically relevant accuracy at a fraction of the computational cost of diffusion models. We therefore recommend lightweight encoder-decoder architectures as the default choice for such settings, reserving generative approaches for tasks that inherently require stochastic sampling or unpaired training data.

Acknowledgment. The authors acknowledge support of the German Research Foundation (DFG) via project no. 558083832, reference no. WI 1352/31-1 (A. Pirwass, H.-J. Wilke) and via GRK 3012, project no. 520750254, kemai.uni-ulm.de (A. Pirwass, B. Glimm) as well as support by the Medical Faculty of Ulm University via Baustein project no. L.SBN.0250 (A. Pirwass), and by the Federal State of Baden-Württemberg within the Cooperative Research Training Group "Data Science and Analytics" (A. Pirwass).

This project was conducted with data (Application No. NAKO-733) from the German National Cohort (NAKO) (www.nako.de). The NAKO is funded by the Federal Ministry of Research, Technology and Space (BMFTR) [project funding reference numbers: 01ER1301A/B/C, 01ER1511D, 01ER1801A/B/C/D and 01ER2301A/B/C], Federal States of Germany and the Helmholtz Association, the participating universities and the institutes of the Leibniz Association. We thank all participants of the German National Cohort (NAKO) and the staff of this research initiative. Members and affiliations of the NAKO Investigator Consortium can be accessed via www.nako.de/principal-investigators.

Disclosure of Interests. The authors have no competing interests to declare that are relevant to the content of this article.

References

1. Anand, S., Xu, K., O'Dushlaine, C., Mukherjee, S.: Synthesizing proton-density fat fraction and $R*2$ from 2-point Dixon MRI with generative machine learning. In: Proceedings of the IEEE International Symposium on Biomedical Imaging (ISBI) (2025). https://doi.org/10.1109/ISBI60581.2025.10981042
2. Armanious, K., et al.: MedGAN: Medical image translationusing GANs. Comput. Med. Imag. Graphics. **79**, 101684 (2020). https://doi.org/10.1016/j.compmedimag.2019.101684
3. Bamberg, F., Kauczor, H.U., Weckbach, S., Schlett, C.L., et al.: Whole-body MR imaging in the German national cohort: rationale, design, and technical background. Radiology **277**(1), 206–220 (2015). https://doi.org/10.1148/radiol.2015142272
4. Ben-Cohen, A., et al.: Cross-modality synthesis from CT to PET using FCN and GAN networks for improved automated lesion detection. Eng. Appl. Artif. Intell. **78**, 186–194 (2019). https://doi.org/10.1016/j.engappai.2018.11.013
5. Blau, Y., Michaeli, T.: The perception-distortion tradeoff. In: 2018 IEEE/CVF Conference on Computer Vision and Pattern Recognition, pp. 6228–6237 (2018). https://doi.org/10.1109/CVPR.2018.00652, http://arxiv.org/abs/1711.06077, arXiv:1711.06077 [cs]
6. Gadermayr, M., Heckmann, L., Li, K., Bähr, F., Müller, M., Truhn, D., Merhof, D., Gess, B.: Image-to-image translation for simplified MRI muscle segmentation. Front. Radiol. **1**, 664444 (2021). https://doi.org/10.3389/fradi.2021.664444, https://www.frontiersin.org/articles/10.3389/fradi.2021.664444/full
7. Graf, R., Platzek, P., Riedel, E.O., et al.: Vibesegmentator: full body MRI segmentation for the NAKO and UK biobank. Eur. Radiol. (2025). https://doi.org/10.1007/s00330-025-12035-9
8. Graf, R., et al.: Denoising diffusion-based MRI to CT image translation enables automated spinal segmentation. Euro. Radiol. Exper. **7**(1), 70 (2023). https://doi.org/10.1186/s41747-023-00385-2
9. Han, X.: MR-based synthetic CT generation using a deep convolutional neural network method. Med. Phys. **44**(4), 1408–1419 (2017). https://doi.org/10.1002/mp.12155, https://onlinelibrary.wiley.com/doi/abs/10.1002/mp.12155

10. Hess, H., et al.: Quantitative fat-fraction analysis of the rotator cuff muscles on clinical sagittal and coronal T1-weighted MRI using deep learning algorithms. Sci. Rep (2026). https://doi.org/10.1038/s41598-026-38108-3
11. Hiasa, Y., et al.: Cross-modality image synthesis from unpaired data using CycleGAN. In: Simulation and Synthesis in Medical Imaging - SASHIMI 2018, LNCS vol. 11037, pp. 31–41. Springer (2018). https://doi.org/10.1007/978-3-030-00536-8_4
12. Ho, J., Jain, A., Abbeel, P.: Denoising diffusion probabilistic models. In: Advances in Neural Information Processing Systems (NeurIPS), vol. 33, pp. 6840–6851. Curran Associates, Inc (2020)
13. Honey, E., Helbo, A., Petersen, J.: Comparative analysis of GAN and diffusion for MRI-to-CT translation (2025). https://doi.org/10.48550/ARXIV.2509.22049, https://arxiv.org/abs/2509.22049. version Number: 1
14. Isola, P., Zhu, J.Y., Zhou, T., Efros, A.A.: Image-to-image translation with conditional adversarial networks. In: Proceedings of the IEEE Conference on Computer Vision and Pattern Recognition (CVPR), pp. 5967–5976 (2017). https://doi.org/10.1109/CVPR.2017.632
15. Kazerouni, A., et al.: Diffusion models in medical imaging: a comprehensive survey. Med. Image Anal. **88**, 102846 (2023). https://doi.org/10.1016/j.media.2023.102846
16. Khosravi, P.: Denoising diffusion probabilistic models for 3D medical image generation. Sci. Rep. **13** (2023). https://doi.org/10.1038/s41598-023-34341-2
17. Li, C.W., et al.: Pathogenesis of sarcopenia and the relationship with fat mass: descriptive review. J. Cachexia. Sarcopenia Muscle **13**(2), 781–794 (2022). https://doi.org/10.1002/jcsm.12901
18. Li, W., et al.: Magnetic resonance image (MRI) synthesis from brain computed tomography (CT) images based on deep learning methods for magnetic resonance (MR)-guided radiotherapy. Quant. Imaging Med. Surg. **10**(6), 1223–1236 (2020). https://doi.org/10.21037/qims-19-885, http://qims.amegroups.com/article/view/41784/html
19. Li, Y., et al.: CT synthesis from multi-sequence MRI using adaptive fusion network. Comput. Biol. Med. **157**, 106738 (2023). https://doi.org/10.1016/j.compbiomed.2023.106738, https://linkinghub.elsevier.com/retrieve/pii/S0010482523002032
20. Luo, J., et al.: Review of diffusion models and its applications in biomedical informatics. BMC Med. Inform. Decis. Making **25**, 390 (2025). https://doi.org/10.1186/s12911-025-03210-5, https://pmc.ncbi.nlm.nih.gov/articles/PMC12541957/
21. Lyu, Q., Wang, G.: Conversion between CT and MRI images using diffusion and score-matching models (2022). https://doi.org/10.48550/arXiv.2209.12104, http://arxiv.org/abs/2209.12104, arXiv:2209.12104 [eess]
22. Masi, S., et al.: Comparison of paraspinal muscle composition measurements using IDEAL fat-water and T2-weighted MR images. BMC Med. Imag. **23**(1), 48 (2023). https://doi.org/10.1186/S12880-023-00992-W
23. Moschetto, A., et al.: Benchmarking GANs, diffusion models, and flow matching for T1w-to-T2w MRI translation. In: Image Analysis and Processing - ICIAP 2025 Workshops, pp. 429–440. Springer Nature Switzerland (2026)
24. Moya-Sáez, E., Peña-Nogales, Ó., Luis-García, R.D., Alberola-López, C.: A deep learning approach for synthetic MRI based on two routine sequences and training with synthetic data. Comput. Methods Prog. Biomed. **210**, 106371 (2021). https://doi.org/10.1016/j.cmpb.2021.106371, https://linkinghub.elsevier.com/retrieve/pii/S0169260721004454

25. Nasir, M., et al.: Liver MRI proton density fat fraction inference from contrast enhanced CT images using deep learning: a proof-of-concept study. PLOS One **20**(8), e0328867 (2025). https://doi.org/10.1371/journal.pone.0328867
26. Özbey, M., et al.: Unsupervised medical image translation with adversarial diffusion models. IEEE Trans. Med. Imag. **42**(12), 3524–3539 (2023). https://doi.org/10.1109/TMI.2023.3290149
27. Peters, A., Consortium, G.N.C.N.: Framework and baseline examination of the German national cohort (nako). Eur. J. Epidemiol. **37**(10), 1107–1124 (2022). https://doi.org/10.1007/s10654-022-00890-5
28. Pirwass, A., Glimm, B., Munz, M., Wilke, H.J.: Automatability and validity of methods for the quantification of intra-/intermuscular adipose tissue in conventional MRI: a systematic review. BMC Med. Imaging **25**(1), 499 (2025). https://doi.org/10.1186/s12880-025-02037-w
29. Rassmann, S., Kügler, D., Ewert, C., Reuter, M.: Regression is all you need for medical image translation. IEEE Trans. Med. Imaging **45**(5), 2156–2172 (2026). https://doi.org/10.1109/TMI.2025.3650412
30. Reeder, S.B., Hu, H.H., Sirlin, C.B.: Proton density fat-fraction: a standardized MR-based biomarker of tissue fat concentration. J. Magn. Reson. Imaging **36**(5), 1011–1014 (2012). https://doi.org/10.1002/jmri.23741
31. Rombach, R., Blattmann, A., Lorenz, D., Esser, P., Ommer, B.: High-resolution image synthesis with latent diffusion models. In: 2022 IEEE/CVF Conference on Computer Vision and Pattern Recognition (CVPR), pp. 10684–10695. IEEE (2022). https://doi.org/10.1109/CVPR52688.2022.01042
32. Ronneberger, O., Fischer, P., Brox, T.: U-Net: convolutional networks for biomedical image segmentation. In: Navab, N., Hornegger, J., Wells, W.M., Frangi, A.F. (eds.) MICCAI 2015. LNCS, vol. 9351, pp. 234–241. Springer, Cham (2015). https://doi.org/10.1007/978-3-319-24574-4_28
33. Song, J., Meng, C., Ermon, S.: Denoising diffusion implicit models. In: International Conference on Learning Representations (ICLR) (2021). https://openreview.net/forum?id=St1giarCHLP
34. Wang, K., et al.: Deep learning for inference of hepatic proton density fat fraction from T1-weighted in-phase and opposed-phase MRI: retrospective analysis of population-based trial data. American J. Roentgenol. **221**(5), 620–631 (2023). https://doi.org/10.2214/AJR.23.29607
35. Weißer, L.: NAKO Gesundheitsstudie. German Clinical Trials Register, DRKS00037328 (2025)
36. Wesselink, E.O., et al.: Quantifying lumbar paraspinal intramuscular fat: Accuracy and reliability of automated thresholding models. North American Spine Soc. J. **17**, 100313 (2024). https://doi.org/10.1016/j.xnsj.2024.100313
37. Yang, Q., Li, N., Zhao, Z., Fan, X., Chang, E.I.C., Xu, Y.: MRI cross-modality image-to-image translation. Sci. Rep. **10**(1), 3753 (2020). https://doi.org/10.1038/s41598-020-60520-6, https://www.nature.com/articles/s41598-020-60520-6

Achieving Fairness in Repeated Combinatorial Problems Through Deep Reinforcement Learning

Julia Ruttmann(✉) and Alexander Schiendorfer

Institute AImotion Bavaria, Technische Hochschule Ingolstadt, Ingolstadt, Germany
{julia.ruttmann,alexander.schiendorfer}@thi.de

Abstract. The development of systems that allocate resources among stakeholders in a manner aligned with societal objectives is of paramount importance in both static decision problems and dynamic settings involving repeated interactions. In scenarios where these systems interact with human individuals or groups of people, relying on efficiency- or cost-based evaluation criteria is inadequate. Allocation models should incorporate fairness requirements to ensure outcomes that remain consistent with normative social considerations. Although the SocialCOP framework enables the integration of fairness constraints into constraint models for shared decision and fair division problems, these approaches address single allocations. Repeated application of such models may systematically favor or disadvantage the same agents, leading to unfair long-term outcomes. We propose a framework for fairness-aware repeated resource allocation in which agent priorities are dynamically reweighted across iterations. A Deep Reinforcement Learning (DRL) policy maps historical utility values, fairness statistics (e.g., the Gini index) and problem parameters to priority weights for subsequent allocations. Hard feasibility requirements are enforced through constraint programming in the underlying MiniZinc model, while fairness considerations are incorporated in the reward function, as well as in the underlying MiniZinc environment. The approach is integrated into the SocialCOP environment and evaluated on a repeated allocation scenario, with weekly table assignments. Experimental results indicate that the learned policies achieve lower inequality while maintaining or improving allocation efficiency compared to deterministic baselines, demonstrating the effectiveness of learning-based reweighting for repeated fair allocation problems.

Keywords: Constraint Satisfaction and Optimization · Algorithmic Fairness · Deep Reinforcement Learning

1 Introduction

When optimizing the allocation of limited resources, the sole focus on efficiency objectives such as minimizing cost or completion time can lead to distributions

D. Wolter and G. Schwalbe (Eds.): KI 2026, LNAI 16830, pp. 117–132, 2027.
https://doi.org/10.1007/978-3-032-32335-4_9

that are perceived as unjust by the affected stakeholders. In repeated allocation settings, fairness can be addressed over time rather than within a single instance, so imbalances in individual allocations may be balanced over time, resulting in a more equitable long-term distribution. A practical example is the allocation of shared office desks: A simple first-come, first-served approach is often used, but it ignores individual preferences and may lead to dissatisfaction over time. Deep Reinforcement Learning (DRL) enables the learning of request patterns and agents' preferences to balance allocations across repeated interactions. Unfavorable allocations in one iteration can be compensated for in later ones, potentially resulting in fairer overall outcomes than deterministic or purely reactive methods. At the same time, temporary inequalities in favor of higher achievable economic efficiencies can also lead to higher overall efficiency *and* fairness.

Repeated fair allocation problems require balancing immediate allocation quality with long-term fairness across multiple decision rounds. In each individual allocation step, the underlying constrained optimization problem (COP) determines a feasible assignment under operational constraints. However, solving each allocation independently does not account for historical disadvantages accumulated by agents over time.

The proposed DRL component therefore does not replace the COP solver. Instead, it acts as a fairness-aware prioritization scheduler that dynamically adapts agent priorities based on previous allocation outcomes. The COP remains responsible for computing feasible and efficient allocations, while DRL learns long-term fairness-aware prioritization policies across repeated interactions.

This distinction is particularly important in constrained allocation settings. Pure COP approaches optimize a single allocation instance and therefore mainly capture short-term objectives, whereas repeated fairness requires reasoning across multiple sequential decisions. DRL provides a mechanism to learn such temporal prioritization policies directly from interaction with the environment. This hybrid perspective motivates the central research question of this work.

Our work investigates repeated resource allocation problems to achieve fair distributions over time while respecting user preferences. Therefore, the central research question of this work is: ***How can Deep Reinforcement Learning be integrated with formal constraint optimization to ensure long-term, equitable resource distribution for repeated settings dynamically?***

This work assumes a centralized allocation setting in which agents' utilities are known to the system and are comparable on a shared scale. In this sense, fairness is evaluated over reported or modeled satisfaction values rather than over private, heterogeneous preferences. We do not address strategic agents, privacy-preserving allocation, or distributed constraint optimization. These aspects are important extensions, but outside the scope of this paper. As a proof of concept, a basic allocation scenario is studied using DRL. A second scenario models the desk allocation problem at our institute, where the number of available desks in the shared office is significantly smaller than the number of employees. To address this challenge, user preferences regarding workspace usage are collected and incorporated into the allocation process. Although similar approaches could also be applied to shared decision problems (e.g., repeated joint choices such as commuting decisions), this work focuses on division problems. The proposed approach aims to achieve fair and efficient allocations that adapt over time and produce balanced outcomes across repeated interactions.

The main contributions are threefold: (1) we formulate repeated fair resource allocation as a hybrid learning and constraint optimization problem; (2) we show in a standalone proof-of-concept that DRL can learn policies that outperform deterministic baselines in the fairness-efficiency trade-off; and (3) we integrate this approach into SocialCOP and demonstrate its applicability in a repeated table-assignment scenario.

2 Related Work

Traditional optimization methods often struggle to maintain efficiency in highly dynamic environments, motivating the adoption of DRL [8]. For instance, [8] demonstrated that a DRL model (TADPG) optimizes computation of data rates and energy consumption in mobile edge computing significantly better than traditional methods. For multiobjective problems, [17] proposed DRL-MOA, decomposing complex problems into scalar subproblems via transfer learning to outperform traditional algorithms like NSGA-II. To bridge DRL and constraint programming (CP), [7] introduced a hybrid approach where RL agents learn efficient search strategies within a constraint optimization problem (COP). However, these efficiency-focused applications largely overlook human-centric fairness. This work directly addresses this critical gap by integrating fairness constraints into both the DRL reward functions and the COP algorithms to ensure long-term equity.

Balancing efficiency and fairness within DRL remains a significant open challenge. [11] explored this trade-off in transport networks, utilizing DRL to bypass the complex constraint formulations required by traditional algorithms [3]. While multi-objective RL can theoretically address fairness, selecting solutions from multiple Pareto-optimal options remains highly complex [11]. By utilizing reward functions based on the generalized Gini index or Rawls' justice principle, recent DRL approaches have successfully generated more equitable outcomes, whereas traditional methods prioritized only average efficiency [3].

Algorithmic fairness encompasses diverse mechanisms for equitable resource allocation [6,12] ranging from appointment scheduling via whale optimization [2] to adapting voting theory for iterative settings [4]. While much of the recent literature focuses on mitigating data-driven biases in Machine Learning [19], our work concentrates specifically on metrics for repeated physical resource distribution among agents. Novel allocation mechanisms include using artificial karma in auctions to balance long-term giving and taking [13]. While these mechanisms exist, none dynamically integrate learning-based reweighting directly with symbolic constraint solvers to ensure long-term equity in recurring constrained resource distribution, which is the core contribution of this work.

The integration of collective decision-making and constraint reasoning was first proposed by [5], who encoded leximin search for combinatorial auctions via constraints. This concept was followed by sequential, myopic voting procedures [9,10,23]. More recently, Condorcet [26] and Copeland [4] voting models were developed within the MiniZinc system to eliminate weighted-sum biases. Ultimately, this paper builds upon the SocialCOP framework [24], introducing DRL as an intelligent reweighting agent within existing constraint optimization architectures.

3 Methodology

3.1 Background

The Gini index is commonly used to measure inequality in distributions. The metric originally emerged from the measurement of income inequality [12]. The Gini index is defined as:

$$Gini(x) = \frac{\sum_{i=1}^{n} \sum_{j=1}^{n} |x_i - x_j|}{2n \sum_{i=1}^{n} x_i}$$

0 represents perfect equality, while 1 is the distribution to one agent only and all others not receiving anything. Using the Gini index assumes that agents' valuation values are comparable across agents. This is a common assumption in centralized fair allocation models, but it limits applicability in settings where utility is private, strategic, or measured on heterogeneous scales.

When focusing on complex scenarios, the equal distribution of the goods does not seem to be the most preferable approach. Therefore, the Gini index is calculated based on the satisfaction level of each agent rather than on the distribution of the physical good itself. In this work, fairness is therefore operationalized as equality of achieved satisfaction rather than equality of raw resource quantities.

Two of the most straightforward social choice augmentations are Utilitarianism and Rawlsianism, as they simply amount to an integer-valued objective that can be readily passed to a solver. Utilitarianism emphasizes the importance of the solution with the highest total utility [6,25]. Hence, the sum of all agents' utility variables is maximized. The Utilitarian approach does not focus on an equal distribution among the agents but on maximizing the overall sum of utilities. It sacrifices the satisfaction of single agents to the goal of overall welfare.

By contrast to the Utilitarian approach, another common social choice concept is Rawlsianism. The central argument put forth by John Rawls declares that the selection of the optimal solution should be independent of the decision-maker, and the objective is to maximize the outcome for the least advantaged [16,18,29].

Both fairness concepts, Utilitarian and Rawlsian distribution are used to test the performance of the RL algorithm in combination with COP.

Other fairness concepts, such as envy-freeness, proportional fairness, max-min fairness, and Nash welfare, are also relevant for allocation problems. This paper focuses on Gini-based inequality, Rawlsian fairness, and Utilitarian distribution.

3.2 Simple Allocation Scenario

Before deploying the full SocialCOP integration, a simplified standalone environment validates whether a DRL agent can natively improve fair repeated distribution. In this controlled environment, five indivisible goods are distributed sequentially per timestep. To simulate realistic, stochastic demand patterns, agent requirements are modeled using Gaussian distributions. Each agent is assigned a base sequence of three requirement values representing a repeating cycle over three weeks, perturbed by a non-negative Gaussian distribution. Ten distinct experimental settings—ranging from perfectly balanced to highly asymmetric demand profiles—were defined.

The learned DRL policy is evaluated against four deterministic baselines. Two primary metrics measure performance: the **Gini index** (↓) over the agents' valuations to measure equity as a proxy for fairness, and the **sum of distributed goods** (↑) to measure allocation efficiency and prevent the solver from outputting trivial zero-distribution solutions.

To evaluate whether Deep Reinforcement Learning can improve repeated resource allocation, a simple allocation experiment was conducted in a simplified standalone environment. The learned policy was compared against four deterministic baselines inspired by common fairness strategies in process scheduling [14]

- **Round-robin:** Selects the next agent sequentially, completely ignoring the current state.
- **Worst-received:** Selects the agent with the absolute lowest cumulative received goods.
- **Greedy (Highest requirement):** Selects the agent with the highest current immediate demand.
- **Required-received ratio:** Selects the agent with the highest requirement-to-received ratio.

Ten experimental environments with different cyclic requirement profiles were used to evaluate the robustness of the methods. Each environment specifies a three-step requirement cycle for five agents, which is repeated throughout the simulation. This setup allows the evaluation of the algorithms under balanced, asymmetric, and heterogeneous demand structures.

3.3 Constrained Desk Allocation Setup

The primary technical contribution of this work lies in scaling the DRL approach by integrating it with SocialCOP. The underlying resource allocation problem is formulated as a constraint model in MiniZinc, including user preferences such as desired days, number of office days, and preferred co-workers. Hard constraints guarantee the strict operational validity of all allocations. SocialCOP allows applying various social choice concepts, such as Utilitarianism or Rawlsian fairness to the exact same constraint model. To transfer the repeated allocation approach to a constraint-based setting, DRL is integrated into the SocialCOP framework [24]. SocialCOP is used to model and solve fair allocation problems in MiniZinc, while the reinforcement learning component is used to influence repeated allocations over time.

Constraint and Preference Model. As an illustrative example, a table assignment problem is used. The goal is to assign employees to available office tables over several working days. The constraint model defines the agents, the available tables, and the decision variables for the assignments. Agent preferences are represented through utility functions, including preferences for specific days, the number of desired office days, break days, and preferred co-workers. In addition, hard constraints such as limits on work-from-home days are included. SocialCOP can apply different social choice concepts, such as Rawlsian or Utilitarian optimization, to the same underlying constraint problem.

Learning-Based Reweighting. The reinforcement learning component is incorporated by extending the SocialCOP objective with agent-specific weights. At each iteration, the DRL agent produces a weight vector that is added to the optimization problem. The fairness objective of SocialCOP is not replaced by these weights. Instead, they act as an adaptive reweighting mechanism that guides the allocation in accordance with previous outcomes. The fairness objective therefore operates on two levels: locally through the SocialCOP optimization criterion and temporally through the DRL reward function, which evaluates inequality across repeated allocations.

The learning environment follows the same principle as in the standalone proof-of-concept. For each timestep, the current state of the allocation process is observed, a weight vector is generated, and the corresponding MiniZinc instance is solved under the selected fairness criterion. The resulting allocation updates the environment state. The reward is based on the Gini index of the agents' valuations, encouraging the policy to reduce inequality over time.

Hyperparameter tuning is again performed with Optuna [1]. Different combinations of solvers, fairness criteria, and reinforcement learning algorithms can thus be evaluated systematically within the same SocialCOP-based framework.

Deep Reinforcement Learning Architecture. To optimally balance fairness across multiple iterations, the DRL agent dynamically adjusts agent priorities. The problem is mathematically framed as a Markov Decision Process (MDP) and implemented as a custom Gymnasium environment [28].

Observation Space. The state representation captures the agents' evolving satisfaction and demands. The observation space consists of continuous arrays (normalized between 0 and 1) alongside tracking variables: `required` (upcoming resource demands), `received` (cumulative allocated resources up to now), `valuation` (the specific utility derived from the latest allocation, considering individual preferences), and `overall_valuation` (the historically accumulated satisfaction). Each agent represents one index in these arrays.

Action Space. The action space adapts depending on the complexity of the use case (i.e., selecting an agent or deciding their priority as a vector):

- **Simple Allocation (Discrete):** The agent outputs a single discrete action corresponding directly to the index of the agent receiving the goods.
- **Constrained Desk Allocation (Continuous):** The policy outputs a continuous weight vector bounded between -1 and 1, representing agent priority. To satisfy the strict integer-based requirements of finite-domain solvers like Chuffed and Gecode, these weights are mapped to integers (e.g., 0 to 200) and structurally injected into the objective function.

Reward Function. The DRL agent optimizes long-term equity in the distribution of utility. The numerical reward is calculated as:

$$R = \rho(1 - \text{Gini}(\texttt{valuations}))$$

where ρ is a configurable scaling factor that defines the maximum achievable reward. This formula heavily penalizes inequality and encourages a policy that actively maintains a balanced valuation profile across the entire population.

Training and Hyperparameter Optimization. The DRL agents are systematically trained using vectorized environments to stabilize learning and maximize sample efficiency. While A2C [20], SAC [15], and DQN [21] were explored, primary experiments focused on Proximal Policy Optimization (PPO) [27] implemented in StableBaselines3 [22]. PPO was selected due to its objective function clipping mechanism, which prevents destructively large policy updates and allows the agent to stably navigate the complex fairness-efficiency trade-off. Hyperparameter optimization is conducted using Optuna [1], employing Tree-structured Parzen Estimators (TPE) to explicitly maximize the mean reward achieved over evaluation episodes.

4 Results and Analysis

The results of one instance of a repeated table assignment are presented in this section. To keep runtimes manageable and the example easier to understand, the evaluation focuses on five agents. The requirements repeat every four weeks and can be found at https://github.com/AImotion-Bavaria/SocialCOP.

All evaluations compare RL approaches (PPO, A2C, SAC, and DQN) with deterministic strategies. Three configurations are evaluated:

1. Reweighting only (no fairness constraint)
2. Reweighting combined with Rawls fairness
3. Reweighting combined with Utilitarian fairness

Efficiency is given by the cumulative number of allocated resources (`sum_rec`), while fairness is evaluated using the Gini index of the agents' valuations.

4.1 Representative Experiment

To illustrate the typical behavior observed in the experiments, Experiment 3 is presented as a representative example. The experiments differ in the agents' requirement patterns. For example, in Experiment 3, agents follow heterogeneous cyclic demand profiles such as `Agent 1: [5,5,5]` and `Agent 4: [3,2,1]`.

This configuration contains moderate heterogeneity in demand and avoids both symmetric and extreme scenarios, making it suitable for illustrating the general behavior of the evaluated methods. Figure 1 shows the development of the Gini index over time in the upper panel. The trained reinforcement learning agent progressively reduces the Gini index and stabilizes at a lower inequality level than the deterministic baselines. In contrast, the deterministic approaches exhibit larger fluctuations and higher average inequality. The bottom panel shows the cumulative sum of distributed goods (`sum_rec`), which measures allocation efficiency. As expected, the greedy approach achieves the highest efficiency by always allocating resources to the agent with the highest demand. However, this results in the highest inequality. The reinforcement learning agent achieves the second-highest efficiency while maintaining substantially lower inequality.

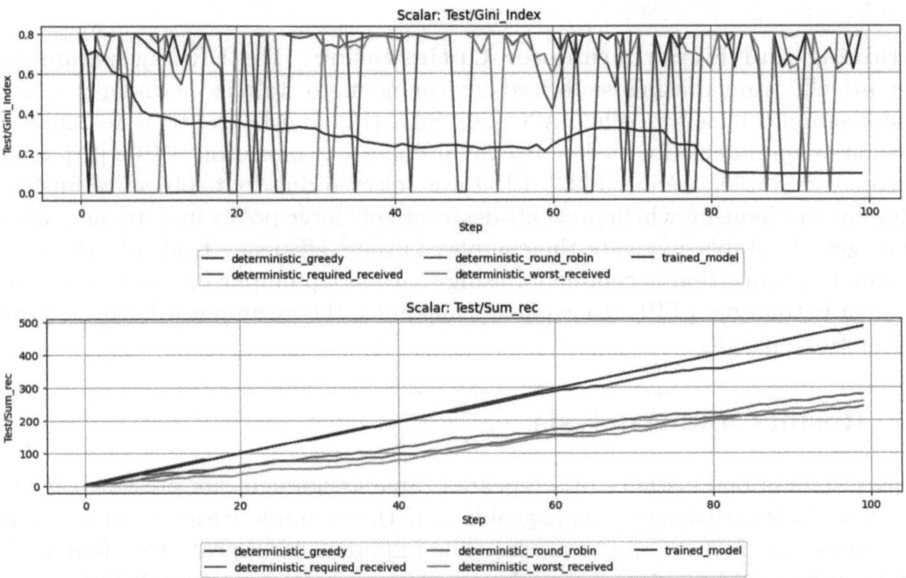

Fig. 1. Experiment 3. Top: Gini index over time. Bottom: cumulative distributed goods.

4.2 Aggregate Results Across Environments

To assess the robustness of the results, Table 1 summarizes the average performance of all methods across the ten experimental environments. The reinforcement learning approach consistently achieves the lowest mean Gini index, indicating the most balanced distribution of satisfaction among agents.

While the greedy method achieves the highest efficiency in terms of total distributed goods, it also produces the highest inequality. Deterministic fairness-oriented methods such as `worst_received` and `round_robin` result in lower efficiency. In contrast, the reinforcement learning agent consistently achieves the second-highest efficiency while maintaining the lowest inequality, demonstrating a favorable balance between fairness and resource utilization.

Table 1. Average performance across all ten experimental environments. The reinforcement learning approach achieves the lowest inequality while maintaining high allocation efficiency.

Method	Mean Gini Index ↓	Mean Sum_rec ↑
required_received	0.62	145.3
greedy	0.77	**245.4**
round_robin	0.61	123.8
worst_received	0.60	121.5
RL (PPO)	**0.41**	205.7

4.3 Table Assignment: Reweighting Only

Table 2 compares the repeated allocation results obtained with Chuffed and Gecode under adaptive reweighting without additional fairness constraints. Allocation efficiency is measured by the cumulative number of assigned resources (`sum_rec`), while fairness is evaluated using the Gini index of the agents' valuations. PPO and A2C achieve the lowest inequality values while maintaining high allocation efficiency. Overall, the Chuffed solver achieved lower average Gini index values and higher allocation efficiency than Gecode in the reweighting-only setting.

Table 2. Reweighting-only evaluation using Chuffed and Gecode

Chuffed				
Run	Mean(Sum_rec)	Std(Sum_rec)	Mean(Gini)	Std(Gini)
A2C	**9.76**	0.43	**0.04**	0.03
DQN	9.26	0.82	0.06	0.01
PPO	**9.76**	0.43	**0.04**	0.02
SAC	8.04	2.77	0.07	0.02
greedy	8.52	1.47	**0.04**	0.02
none	9.00	1.00	0.06	0.01
round_robin	8.78	1.36	0.05	0.02
worst_received	8.52	1.47	**0.04**	0.02
required_received	8.52	1.47	**0.04**	0.02
Gecode				
Run	Mean(Sum_rec)	Std(Sum_rec)	Mean(Gini)	Std(Gini)
A2C	**9.52**	0.50	**0.04**	0.01
DQN	5.98	2.20	0.07	0.03
PPO	9.28	0.83	0.05	0.02
SAC	7.32	1.33	0.05	0.02
greedy	3.54	1.49	0.08	0.02
none	0.00	0.00	0.07	0.03
round_robin	2.38	1.77	0.08	0.02
worst_received	3.54	1.49	0.08	0.02
required_received	3.54	1.49	0.08	0.02

4.4 Table Assignment with Rawls Fairness

Table 3 shows the results when Rawlsian fairness is incorporated into the optimization objective together with the learned reweighting strategy. Overall, the additional fairness criterion substantially reduces inequality across all methods and both solvers. PPO achieves the lowest Gini index for Chuffed, while SAC achieves the best fairness values for Gecode.

The results indicate that incorporating Rawlsian fairness substantially reduces inequality across all methods and both solvers. In this setting, the influence of the learned reweighting policy becomes smaller because the optimization objective already strongly favors disadvantaged agents. Nevertheless, PPO and SAC still achieve competitive fairness-efficiency trade-offs, demonstrating that the learned policies remain beneficial even under additional fairness constraints.

4.5 Table Assignment with Utilitarian Fairness

Finally, adaptive reweighting was combined with Utilitarian optimization. Table 4 summarizes the resulting allocations for both Chuffed and Gecode. In

Table 3. Rawlsian optimization using Chuffed and Gecode

Chuffed				
Run	Mean(Sum_rec)	Std(Sum_rec)	Mean(Gini)	Std(Gini)
A2C	9.76	0.43	0.02	0.01
DQN	9.76	0.43	0.02	0.01
PPO	9.52	0.83	**0.01**	0.01
SAC	**10.00**	0.00	0.03	0.01
greedy	9.50	0.50	0.03	0.01
none	9.50	0.50	0.02	0.02
round_robin	9.36	0.66	0.03	0.01
worst_received	9.50	0.50	0.03	0.01
required_received	9.50	0.50	0.03	0.01
Gecode				
Run	Mean(Sum_rec)	Std(Sum_rec)	Mean(Gini)	Std(Gini)
A2C	9.02	0.71	0.02	0.01
DQN	**9.52**	0.85	0.03	0.01
PPO	8.76	0.43	0.02	0.01
SAC	8.50	1.14	**0.01**	0.01
greedy	9.26	0.82	0.02	0.02
none	7.72	0.83	0.02	0.02
round_robin	8.80	0.94	0.02	0.02
worst_received	9.26	0.82	0.02	0.02
required_received	9.26	0.82	0.02	0.02

contrast to the previous experiments, only small differences between methods can be observed because Utilitarian optimization strongly constrains the feasible solution space toward maximizing aggregate utility.

Under Utilitarian optimization, all methods achieved nearly identical allocation efficiencies regardless of solver or reweighting strategy. Consequently, the observed differences mainly concerned the resulting inequality levels measured by the Gini index. However, these differences remained comparatively small because Utilitarian optimization strongly constrains the feasible solution space toward maximizing aggregate utility. This reduces the influence of the learned reweighting policy compared to the previous experiments. Even though greedy and worst_received outperformed the trained models in the last experiment, PPO remained one of the most consistent methods, balancing stability and fairness.

Table 4. Utilitarian optimization using Chuffed and Gecode

Chuffed				
Run	Mean(Sum_rec)	Std(Sum_rec)	Mean(Gini)	Std(Gini)
A2C	9.76	0.42	**0.030**	0.01
DQN	9.76	0.42	0.035	0.02
PPO	9.76	0.42	0.031	0.01
SAC	9.76	0.42	0.034	0.02
greedy	9.76	0.42	0.033	0.02
none	9.76	0.42	0.033	0.02
round_robin	9.76	0.42	**0.030**	0.02
worst_received	9.76	0.42	0.033	0.02
required_received	9.76	0.42	0.033	0.02
Gecode				
Run	Mean(Sum_rec)	Std(Sum_rec)	Mean(Gini)	Std(Gini)
A2C	9.76	0.43	0.035	0.02
DQN	9.76	0.43	0.031	0.02
PPO	9.76	0.43	0.030	0.02
SAC	9.76	0.43	0.030	0.02
greedy	9.76	0.43	**0.028**	0.02
none	9.76	0.43	0.030	0.02
round_robin	9.76	0.43	0.030	0.02
worst_received	9.76	0.43	**0.028**	0.02
required_received	9.76	0.43	0.033	0.02

5 Conclusion and Future Work

This work evaluated Deep Reinforcement Learning (DRL) for repeated resource allocation, comparing trained DRL agents (A2C, DQN, PPO, SAC) with four deterministic baselines. Efficiency was measured by the sum of received values, and fairness by the Gini index of the valuation.

The results indicate that DRL can be useful for repeated allocation problems because it learns adaptive reweighting policies that respond to previous allocation outcomes. This allows the method to balance short-term efficiency with long-term fairness.

Key insights include:

- DRL policies learn to trade off between fairness and efficiency, consistently reducing the Gini index while maintaining high aggregate utility.
- Integrating DRL weights into the SocialCOP framework makes it possible to combine learned heuristics with formal fairness criteria such as Rawlsian and Utilitarian objectives.

- PPO and A2C were the most stable, delivering high-quality allocations across solvers and preference scenarios, while greedy baselines tended to over-optimize utility at the expense of fairness.

Across all environments of the simple allocation, a consistent pattern emerges. Deterministic methods tend to specialize either in efficiency or fairness but rarely achieve both simultaneously. The greedy approach maximizes resource utilization but leads to strong inequality, while fairness-oriented heuristics distribute resources more evenly but often fail to utilize the available resources effectively.

In contrast, the reinforcement learning agent adapts dynamically to the environment and learns a policy that balances both objectives. It avoids extreme inequality while still allocating a large portion of the available resources. The results demonstrate that DRL can effectively address repeated allocation problems in which multiple, potentially conflicting objectives must be considered simultaneously.

In a table assignment scenario, reweighting only, Rawlsian, and Utilitarian fairness constraints were tested using Chuffed and Gecode solvers. For reweighting only, A2C and PPO achieved the best balance between efficiency and fairness, with Chuffed yielding higher utility than Gecode. With Rawls constraints, trained models still outperformed deterministic approaches, though margins were smaller. SAC achieved maximum efficiency with Chuffed, while PPO minimized the Gini index. Under Utilitarian constraints, all methods achieved similar efficiency. PPO remained consistent in balancing fairness and efficiency, even if greedy or worst_received attained slightly better results.

Limitations of this approach include high computational cost, lower interpretability, and untested generalization to unseen requirements, potentially causing bias. Deterministic methods, by contrast, are interpretable and require no training.

The results highlight the potential of DRL for repeated allocation environments. Especially, the observed trade-offs between fairness and efficiency varied across model types and experimental setups. This indicates that no single approach is universally optimal across all fairness settings and allocation scenarios.

The evaluations of this work indicate opportunities for future research and practical application. The evaluations were based on a limited example. The implementation into real-world problem statements and their evaluation would establish a suitable extension of the current work. Especially the variety of agent demands over time, which is not as periodic as in the evaluated example, needs to be addressed in future work. This would allow more realistic modeling of real-world scenarios and, therefore, evaluate the adaptability of the chosen methods under uncertainty.

When implementing fairness-aware allocation methods in real-world applications, explainability is vital. Clear and understandable decision-making processes are essential for earning trust and acceptance from human stakeholders who depend on these systems. Future research is encouraged to focus on creating models and interfaces that offer explicit justifications for allocation decisions, aiding users in comprehending how fairness standards are utilized and how specific outcomes are derived.

Combining Deep Reinforcement Learning techniques with constraint optimization showed promise in balancing efficiency and fairness. Rather than replacing constraint optimization, DRL should be viewed as a complementary mechanism that learns adaptive prioritization policies across repeated allocation decisions. This work demonstrates that combining DRL with constraint optimization provides a promising direction for fairness-aware repeated allocation problems and motivates further investigation in larger and more realistic real-world environments.

References

1. Akiba, T., Sano, S., Yanase, T., Ohta, T., Koyama, M.: Optuna: a next-generation hyperparameter optimization framework. In: Proceedings of the 25th ACM SIGKDD International Conference on Knowledge Discovery & Data Mining. KDD 2019, pp. 2623–2631. Association for Computing Machinery, New York (2019). https://doi.org/10.1145/3292500.3330701
2. Ala, A., Alsaadi, F.E., Ahmadi, M., Mirjalili, S.: Optimization of an appointment scheduling problem for healthcare systems based on the quality of fairness service using whale optimization algorithm and nsga-ii. Sci. Rep. 11(1), 19816 (2021). https://doi.org/10.1038/s41598-021-98851-7, https://www.nature.com/articles/s41598-021-98851-7
3. Arbex, R.O., Da Cunha, C.B.: Efficient transit network design and frequencies setting multi-objective optimization by alternating objective genetic algorithm, vol. 81, pp. 355–376. https://doi.org/10.1016/j.trb.2015.06.014
4. Bhavnani, S., Schiendorfer, A.: Towards copeland optimization in combinatorial problems. In: Schaus, P. (ed.) Integration of Constraint Programming, Artificial Intelligence, and Operations Research, pp. 34–43. Springer, Cham (2022). https://doi.org/10.1007/978-3-031-08011-1_4
5. Bouveret, S., Lemaıtre, M.: Finding leximin-optimal solutions using constraint programming: new algorithms and their application to combinatorial auctions. on Computational Social Choice (COMSOC-2006), p. 49 (2006)
6. Brandt, F., Conitzer, V., Endriss, U., Lang, J., Procaccia, A.D.: Handbook of Computational Social Choice. Cambridge University Press, Cambridge (2016)
7. Cappart, Q., Moisan, T., Rousseau, L.M., Prémont-Schwarz, I., Cire, A.A.: Combining reinforcement learning and constraint programming for combinatorial optimization. In: Proceedings of the AAAI Conference on Artificial Intelligence, vol. 35(5), pp. 3677–3687 (2021). https://doi.org/10.1609/aaai.v35i5.16484
8. Chen, J., Xing, H., Xiao, Z., Xu, L., Tao, T.: A DRL agent for jointly optimizing computation offloading and resource allocation in MEC. IEEE Internet Things J. **8**(24), 17508–17524 (2021). https://doi.org/10.1109/JIOT.2021.3081694
9. Cornelio, C., Pini, M.S., Rossi, F., Venable, K.B.: Multi-agent soft constraint aggregation via sequential voting: theoretical and experimental results. Auton. Multi-Agent Syst. **33**(1–2), 159–191 (2019). https://doi.org/10.1007/s10458-018-09400-y

10. Dalla Pozza, G., Rossi, F., Venable, K.B.: Multi-agent soft constraint aggregation: a sequential approach. In: Proceedings of 3rd International Conference on Agents and Artificial Intelligence ICAART 2011, vol. 11 (2010)
11. Michailidis, D., Röpke, W., Ghebreab, S., Roijers, D.M., Santos, F.P.: Fairness in transport network design - a multi-objective reinforcement learning approach
12. Ek, A.J.P.: High-Level Modelling and Solving for Online, Real-Time, and Multiagent Combinatorial Optimisation (2022). https://bridges.monash.edu/articles/thesis/high-level_modelling_and_solving_for_online_real-time_and_multiagent_combinatorial_optimisation/21588144
13. Elokda, E., Bolognani, S., Censi, A., Dörfler, F., Frazzoli, E.: A self-contained karma economy for the dynamic allocation of common resources. Dyn. Games Appl. 1–33 (2023). https://doi.org/10.1007/s13235-023-00503-0
14. Glabbeek, R.V., Höfner, P.: Progress, justness, and fairness. ACM Comput. Surv. (CSUR) **52**(4), 1–38 (2019). https://doi.org/10.1145/3329125
15. Haarnoja, T., Zhou, A., Abbeel, P., Levine, S.: Soft actor-critic: off-policy maximum entropy deep reinforcement learning with a stochastic actor. In: International Conference on Machine Learning, pp. 1861–1870. PMLR (2018)
16. Hooker, J.: Optimization models for fairness **May 2014** (2023). https://johnhooker.tepper.cmu.edu/fairnessFITmonash.pdf
17. Li, K., Zhang, T., Wang, R.: Deep reinforcement learning for multiobjective optimization. IEEE Trans. Cybern. **51**(6), 3103–3114 (2021). https://doi.org/10.1109/TCYB.2020.2977661
18. Matt, P.-A., Toni, F.: Egalitarian allocations of indivisible resources: theory and computation. In: Klusch, M., Rovatsos, M., Payne, T.R. (eds.) CIA 2006. LNCS (LNAI), vol. 4149, pp. 243–257. Springer, Heidelberg (2006). https://doi.org/10.1007/11839354_18
19. Mitchell, S., Potash, E., Barocas, S., D'Amour, A., Lum, K.: Algorithmic fairness: choices, assumptions, and definitions. Ann. Rev. Stat. Appl. **8**(1), 141–163 (2021). https://doi.org/10.1146/annurev-statistics-042720-125902
20. Mnih, V., et al.: Asynchronous methods for deep reinforcement learning. In: International Conference on Machine Learning, pp. 1928–1937. PMLR (2016). https://doi.org/10.48550/arXiv.1602.01783
21. Mnih, V., et al.: Playing atari with deep reinforcement learning. arXiv preprint arXiv:1312.5602 (2013)
22. Raffin, A., Hill, A., Gleave, A., Kanervisto, A., Ernestus, M., Dormann, N.: Stable-baselines3: reliable reinforcement learning implementations. J. Mach. Learn. Res. **22**(268), 1–8 (2021)
23. Rossi, F.: Collective decision making: a great opportunity for constraint reasoning. Constraints **19**(2), 186–194 (2014)
24. Ruttmann, J., Schiendorfer, A.: Socialcop: reusable building blocks for collective constraint optimization. In: Hotho, A., Rudolph, S. (eds.) KI 2024: Advances in Artificial Intelligence, Lecture Notes in Computer Science, vol. 14992, pp. 204–217. Springer, Cham (2024). https://doi.org/10.1007/978-3-031-70893-0_15
25. Savulescu, J., Persson, I., Wilkinson, D.: Utilitarianism and the pandemic. Bioethics **34**(6), 620–632 (2020). https://doi.org/10.1111/bioe.12771
26. Schiendorfer, A., Reif, W.: Reducing bias in preference aggregation for multiagent soft constraint problems. In: Schiex, T., de Givry, S. (eds.) CP 2019. LNCS, vol. 11802, pp. 510–526. Springer, Cham (2019). https://doi.org/10.1007/978-3-030-30048-7_30
27. Schulman, J., Wolski, F., Dhariwal, P., Radford, A., Klimov, O.: Proximal policy optimization algorithms. arXiv preprint arXiv:1707.06347 (2017)

28. Towers, M., et al.: Gymnasium: a standard interface for reinforcement learning environments. arXiv preprint arXiv:2407.17032 (2024)
29. Xinying Chen, V., Hooker, J.N.: A guide to formulating fairness in an optimization model. Ann. Oper. Res. **326**(1), 1–39 (2023). https://doi.org/10.1007/s10479-023-05264-y

Code Generation for Open Data Statistics: Case Study on the Genesis Database

Valentin Schmidberger[1(✉)], Julia Lapp[1], Albrecht Melan[2(✉)], and Johannes Maucher[1(✉)]

[1] IAAI, Hochschule der Medien, Stuttgart, Germany
{schmidberger,lapp,maucher}@hdm-stuttgart.de
[2] Statistics Department, State Statistical Office of Baden-Württemberg, Stuttgart, Germany
albrecht.melan@stala.bwl.de

Abstract. This paper introduces a robust pipeline enabling Large Language Models (LLMs) to perform precise Table Question Answering (Table-QA) on complex statistical tables. Processing complex, visually oriented table formats remains a major challenge for large language models, as they exhibit inherent multi-dimensional and hierarchical structures. Despite their visual complexity, these formats adhere to strict structural conventions. Our approach leverages these regularities—such as specific cell border styles and hierarchical indentations—to transform these files into a unified JSON structure using a deterministic extraction method. Instead of generating direct answers, the LLM is fine-tuned to produce Python scripts that programmatically extract information from the generated JSON files. To achieve this, we generated a synthetic dataset comprising approximately 13,000 high-quality question-code pairs. Our fine-tuned Microsoft Phi-4 model achieves a functional success score of 88.5% (peaking at 95.2% on XLSX files), on par with the most advanced proprietary models, such as GPT-4.1. Furthermore, we demonstrate that a smaller 8B parameter model (Llama-3.1) is a highly efficient alternative, achieving a functional success score of 78.6% in resource-constrained environments.

Keywords: Large Language Models · Table Question Answering · Data Extraction · Supervised Fine-Tuning · Program Synthesis

1 Introduction

The sequential processing nature of LLMs presents a fundamental challenge when interacting with multi-dimensional, hierarchical data structures. Statistical tables, particularly those from open data sources like the German Federal Statistical Office (Genesis Online), are typically distributed as two-dimensional projections of higher-dimensional data, such as multi-header XLSX files or denormalized CSV files. Direct processing of these formats by LLMs is often inefficient, as semantic relationships are embedded in the spatial structure of the table rather than through explicit relational links.

D. Wolter and G. Schwalbe (Eds.): KI 2026, LNAI 16830, pp. 133–147, 2027.
https://doi.org/10.1007/978-3-032-32335-4_10

Therefore, the central research question of this study is: How can complex statistical tables be transformed into a machine-readable format that enables LLMs to perform precise, verifiable, and generalizable data retrieval through code generation?

The objective is to develop a two-stage pipeline that separates programmatic reasoning from natural language synthesis. In the first stage, a domain-specifically fine-tuned LLM translates a user's natural language query into executable Python code operating on a structured JSON representation of the table. After code execution, a standard, non-fine-tuned LLM synthesizes the retrieved numerical results into a coherent and contextually appropriate response. This separation assigns data navigation to a specialized model while keeping answer generation flexible.

The primary contributions of this paper are as follows:

- A deterministic transformation framework: that converts complex, visually-encoded formats from open data statistical tables into a unified JSON structure, preserving hierarchical metadata.
- The generation of a synthetic dataset: The generation of a synthetic dataset comprising 13,000 high-quality question–code pairs, specifically designed to fine-tune large language models for generating executable retrieval logic in precise Table-QA over complex statistical data structures.
- A systematic empirical evaluation: of fine-tuned open-source models, establishing that domain-specific fine-tuning allows medium-scale models to achieve performance parity with leading proprietary LLMs in complex Table-QA tasks.

2 Related Work

2.1 Enabling Large Language Models to Understand Complex, Hierarchical Tables

Efficiently processing complex table structures remains a core challenge [14]. Structural extraction methods range from multi-task learning for region recognition [6] to format-aware compression in *SheetCompressor* [7]. To better capture structual and semantic relationships, recent research proposes bi-dimensional attention mechanisms [16] and hypergraph encoders [11]. Prompting strategies also play a vital role, either by creating compact table representations [9,18,22,26] or by utilizing Multi-modal LLMs to preserve visual cues like borders and colors [19]. A prominent linearization technique transforms complex tables into sequential inputs by traversing header trees in level-order and utilizing specialized tokens to enable precise multi-level indexing of data regions [3]. Since GENESIS tables exhibit high structural consistency, we adopt a deterministic heuristic approach. Inspired by the hierarchical indexing logic of [3], we transform tables into a machine-readable JSON format avoiding the inherent uncertainty of learned extraction models while maintaining structural integrity.

2.2 Table Question Answering

Table-QA methods have evolved from table-specific pre-training [8,10,13,23] to fine-tuning general-purpose LLMs on tabular tasks [12,24]. Recent specialized models like *TableLLM* [25] and *SpreadsheetLLM* [7] generate executable Python code or spreadsheet formulas to perform reasoning. To bridge the gap between natural language and structured data, neural-symbolic frameworks like *Binder* [4] and spreadsheet formula-based systems like *TabAF* [17] map queries to executable programs. Other strategies, such as *TIDE* [21], decompose questions into triples for better verification. Our work aligns with the code-generation paradigm but focuses on the specific challenges of open data statistical schemas through Supervised Fine-Tuning (SFT).

3 Methodology

The methodology relies on a strict separation of data linearization and structured data retrieval. We employ a heuristic-based transformation pipeline to linearize inputs into a structured format and a verified synthetic dataset to train the model for code-based data retrieval.

For clarity, we distinguish three components throughout the paper that all share the term *pipeline*: (i) the *Transformation Pipeline* (Sect. 3.1), which converts XLSX/CSV into the unified JSON; (ii) the *Data Validation Loop* (Sect. 3.2), which filters synthetic training samples via execution; and (iii) the *Inference Pipeline* (Sec. 4.2), which combines code generation, AST validation, and answer synthesis at query time.

3.1 Heuristic Data Transformation

We implemented a deterministic pipeline to linearize visual XLSX layouts and denormalized CSV inputs into a unified, hierarchical JSON structure. This intermediate representation abstracts away format-specific idiosyncrasies, enabling the LLM to access data reliably using consistent dictionary keys. For tables published in both formats, the resulting JSON structures are schema-equivalent in approximately 95% of cases. The remaining divergence stems from the higher information density of XLSX (e.g., font weight, indentation, merge ranges), which encodes hierarchical cues that the flat CSV format cannot recover. The performance gap between XLSX and CSV reported in Sec. 5 therefore reflects this irreducible information loss in the source format, not the JSON representation itself.

XLSX Parsing Strategy. Genesis Excel files are primarily optimized for human readability, exhibiting high structural consistency in their visual layout. Leveraging these strict formatting conventions, our parser reconstructs the semantic hierarchy through a three-step procedure:

- Boundary Detection via Visual Cues: To distinguish metadata headers from the data body, the algorithm performs a scan of the first 50 rows and columns. A row is deterministically identified as a horizontal delimiter if it contains at least two cells with `medium` or `thick` bottom borders. This effectively isolates the complex header region from the numerical data grid.
- Merged Cells Resolution: A critical challenge is the use of merged cells to denote super-categories (e.g., a year header spanning three columns). The parser iterates through the worksheet's internal merge ranges and logically replicates the top-left value to all constituent cells. This ensures that every data point is explicitly linked to its full hierarchical path.
- Hierarchy Reconstruction: Row hierarchies are reconstructed by analyzing indentation levels and bold font weights. These visual indicators are mapped to nested dictionary keys, creating a composite path (e.g., *"Region / District / City"*) for each row.

CSV Pivoting Strategy. The flat CSV format provided by Genesis is denormalized. To align this with the hierarchical JSON schema derived from XLSX, we employ a cardinality-based pivoting algorithm:

1. Context vs. Dimension Separation: The algorithm calculates the number of unique values (`nunique`) for every column. Columns with a single unique value are extracted as global metadata (context), reducing token usage.
2. Dynamic Index Selection: Among the remaining columns, the dimension with the highest cardinality is selected as the primary row index.
3. Nested Pivoting: The remaining categorical dimensions are pivoted into nested column headers. This reconstructs the implicit multi-dimensional hierarchy and ensures a consistent *Key* → *Attribute* → *Value* access pattern across both input formats, as illustrated in Fig. 1.

JSON Blueprint Structure. To avoid exceeding context limits, the LLM is not provided with the full data but with a "Blueprint". Figure 1 shows an example of this structure, which summarizes headers and provides access path examples. The blueprint strategy reduces per-query token consumption compared to raw dataframe input, resulting in significantly lower inference latency and cost. And more importantly, it guides the LLM to how to navigate the data structure without overwhelming it with raw data.

3.2 Verified Synthetic Data Generation

To train a model for this specific JSON schema, we created an instruction dataset of 13,000 examples using Gemini 2.5 Pro [5]. Each example consists of a natural language question, the corresponding table schema, the access path within the JSON structure, and the generated Python code (label) used to retrieve the answer. An abstracted example is shown in Listing 1.1. To ensure the model

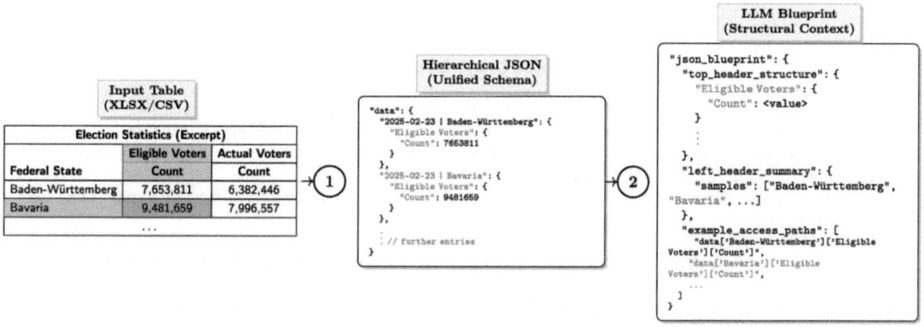

Fig. 1. Data Transformation Process: (1) Visually oriented input tables are linearized into a unified hierarchical JSON structure. (2) A structural blueprint is extracted, providing the LLM with the table schema and key hierarchy (including example access paths) while omitting numerical values to minimize token consumption.

learns robust reasoning capabilities rather than simple pattern matching, the generation prompts were strictly constrained to enforce diversity. As detailed in Listing 1.2, each batch was required to cover a spectrum of complexity levels, ranging from single-cell lookups to multi-step aggregations and negative constraints. The generation process included a rigorous verification loop.

1. *Prompting:* Gemini was supplied with with the'JSON Blueprint' and 50 uniformly sampled entries from the table's data dictionary to establish the necessary context for the generation. The model was then instructed to generate a natural language question and the corresponding Python code. Listing 1.2 shows the system instructions used to enforce logical coherence and key consistency.
2. *Execution Loop:* The generated code was immediately executed against the full source data in a sandboxed environment.
3. *Filtering:* If the code threw an error (e.g., 'KeyError') or returned 'None', the example was rejected. Only code that successfully executed and produced a valid result was added to the training set. This execution-based validation pipeline ensures the technical integrity of the synthetic samples by filtering out code that fails to interact correctly with the data structure.

This process filtered out 14% of generated samples, primarily eliminating logic hallucinations (e.g., inventing keys not present in the Blueprint) and ensuring that the fine-tuned models trained on valid, functional access paths rather than mere probabilistic text patterns.

```
{
  "question": "What is the area of Bavaria in 2023?",
  "table_schema": "state year value",
  "example_access_path": "data['Bremen']['Stichtag']['31.12.2023']",
  "generated_code": "value = data['Bayern']['Stichtag']['31.12.2023']"
}
```

Listing 1.1. An abstracted example out of the dataset

```
You are a highly intelligent data analysis engine. Your primary task is to
    generate exceptionally high-quality training examples.
=== YOUR TASK ===
1. Deeply analyze the provided 'JSON DATA STRUCTURE'.
2. Generate exactly 5 diverse, high-quality question-and-code pairs.
3. Ensure maximum diversity: Covers Direct Lookups, Complex Aggregations,
    Rankings, and Calculations.
4. Negative Case Rule: One question must be a 'negative case' asking for non-
    existent data.
=== UNBREAKABLE RULES ===
- Key Consistency Rule: Keys used in Python code MUST EXACTLY match the
    blueprint.
- Positive Case Rule: Prefer direct dictionary access (data['key']) for
    positive examples.
- Output Format Rule: All logic must end with a print() statement outputting
    only the final value.
```

Listing 1.2. System Prompt for Synthetic Data Generation

3.3 Supervised Fine-Tuning (SFT)

We fine-tuned the models using LoRA (Low-Rank Adaptation) on a single NVIDIA RTX 6000 Pro (Blackwell generation) GPU. The training configuration included `rank=32`, `alpha=64`, `batch_size=1` (with gradient accumulation steps=32), and a learning rate of `3e-5` with a maximum of 5 epochs, where early stopping was triggered at epoch 2. The training was completed in approximately 1.4 h for Llama-3.1-8B and 6–8 h for Phi-4 (14B).

4 System Architecture and Application

To demonstrate the system's capabilities, an interactive Streamlit prototype was developed, facilitating the complete input-to-response pipeline.

4.1 Accessible Interface

To maximize usability and ensure low-barrier access to complex statistical data, we developed a multimodal interface that supports both text- and voice-based interactions. The system's speech-to-text (STT) capabilities are implemented using the Whisper model [15], which allows users to pose natural language questions verbally.

To provide a fully interactive experience, the interface optionally outputs the generated answers as speech. This is achieved through the XTTS (eXtensible Text-to-Speech) framework [2], which synthesizes natural-sounding voice responses. By integrating these components, the pipeline not only simplifies data exploration for experts but also significantly enhances accessibility. It enables users with visual impairments to interactively explore complex tables through natural language dialogue. Furthermore, it facilitates interaction in environments where hands-free operation is preferred.

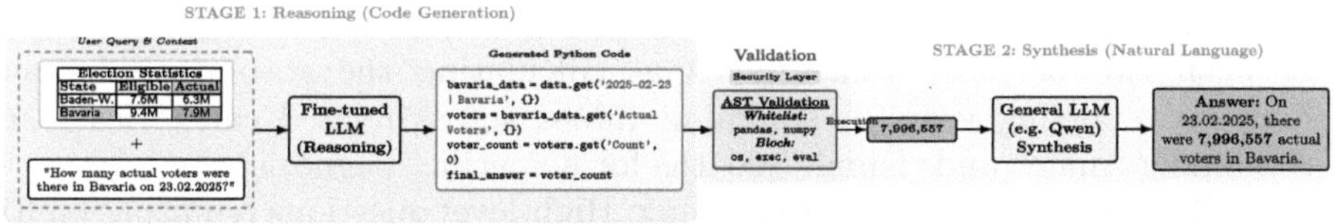

Fig. 2. Integrated Two-Stage Inference Pipeline: Stage 1 utilizes a fine-tuned LLM to generate Python code. This code undergoes a mandatory AST-based Security Validation (blocking unsafe functions/modules). In Stage 2, the validated code is executed in a sandbox, and the factual result is synthesized into a final answer by a general-purpose LLM.

4.2 Two-Stage Inference Pipeline

Query answering is performed in two distinct stages to maximize transparency and precision:

1. *Stage 1: Reasoning (Code Generation):* The fine-tuned LLM processes the user's query alongside a compact JSON context that outlines the data structure. It generates the Python code required to query the full JSON data (Fig. 2).
2. *Security Layer (AST Validation):* Before execution, the generated code undergoes a rigorous security audit using Abstract Syntax Tree (AST) analysis. We implement a *CodeVisitor* that checks for forbidden built-in functions (e.g., `eval`, `exec`, `open`) and restricts imports to a whitelist of verified libraries (`pandas`, `numpy`, `matplotlib`). Any code containing restricted modules (e.g., `os`, `subprocess`) is blocked.
3. *Stage 2: Synthesis (Answer Formulation):* The generated code is executed in a sandboxed environment. The execution output is passed to a second, general-purpose LLM (e.g. Qwen3 4B [20]). The model then synthesizes the factual results into a fluent natural language response (Fig. 2).

5 Evaluation and Results

To assess the performance of our fine-tuned models, we conducted an evaluation using a manually curated hold-out test set consisting of 252 unique question-answer pairs. These test cases are balanced across the two primary input formats, with 126 questions based on tables extracted from XLSX files and 126 questions from denormalized CSV files.

The test set covers a broad spectrum of open data statistical domains, including demographics, healthcare, economic indicators, and environmental data. Based on the nature of the tasks, we categorized the evaluation into three distinct complexity levels:

- Level 1: Direct Retrieval (Lookups): Tasks requiring the model to identify and extract a single data point based on specific row and column identifiers. For example, retrieving the migration balance for a specific city in a given year.

- Level 2: Comparative and Basic Arithmetic: Tasks involving operations between two or more values, such as calculating the absolute difference between reporting years or summing values across related categories (e.g., combining "male" and "female" deaths for a specific diagnosis).
- Level 3: Complex Analytical Reasoning: High-level questions requiring multi-step logic, including percentage shares, ratios (e.g., students per teacher), or identifying maximum values within a hierarchical group. These tasks test the model's ability to navigate nested JSON structures and handle scientific notation or rounded figures.

This categorization ensures a rigorous evaluation of the model's ability not only to parse structured JSON output but also to perform reliable data analysis on real-world statistical data.

5.1 Metric Definition

We define the *Functional Success Score* as follows: A test case is considered successful if the two following conditions are fulfilled: 1. The generated Python code executes without raising an exception. 2. The result matches the ground truth with a similarity ratio ≥ 0.95 (based on the Ratcliff/Obershelp algorithm [1] as implemented in Python's `difflib` Sequence Matching). This threshold accounts for minor formatting differences (e.g., "1000" vs. "1.000") while rejecting incorrect values.

5.2 Model Selection (Fine-Tuned Open Source)

Table 1. Model Selection: Functional Success Scores & Efficiency

Model (Fine-Tuned)	XLSX (%)	CSV (%)	Avg (%)	Time (min)
DeepSeek-Coder-V2	62.7	59.5	61.1	24.83
Granite-3.1-8B	65.1	64.3	64.7	10.73
Nemotron-Nano-9B	73.0	69.8	71.4	55.25
Ministral-8B-Instruct	78.6	67.5	73.1	11.55
Qwen3-8B	81.0	72.2	76.6	21.46
Llama-3.1-8B	81.0	76.2	78.6	**08.14**
Gemma 3 12B	81.0	77.0	78.9	18.01
Microsoft Phi-4 (14B)	**95.2**	**81.7**	**88.5**	29.11

Table 1 presents the Functional Success Score and inference efficiency. To ensure a fair comparison, all models were fine-tuned using the identical synthetic dataset of 13,000 samples and the same LoRA hyperparameters described in Sect. 3.3. The inference efficiency is measured by the total inference time, defined as the duration required for the model to generate the Python code for all 252 test queries on a single NVIDIA RTX 6000 GPU.

Two superior models emerged in Table 1:

1. *Top Performer:* Microsoft Phi-4 (14B) achieved the highest functional success score (88.5% avg), reaching 95.2% on structured XLSX data.
2. *Most Efficient:* Llama-3.1-8B provides a balanced alternative with 78.6% functional success score but is approx. 3.5x faster than Phi-4.

The substantial spread across base architectures (61.1%–88.5%) is, in our interpretation, not primarily a function of parameter count or code-pretraining exposure. DeepSeek-Coder-V2, despite its explicit code-pretraining focus, trails the general-purpose Llama-3.1-8B by more than 17 points, while Phi-4's strong result aligns with its emphasis on instruction- and reasoning-heavy training data. We therefore hypothesize that adherence to the strict schema-constrained output format dominates raw coding ability for this task, making instruction-tuning quality on structured outputs the decisive factor.

5.3 Impact of Supervised Fine-Tuning (SFT)

Table 2. Impact of Fine-Tuning: Base vs. Fine-Tuned (Avg Functional Success Score)

Model	Base (Few-Shot)	Fine-Tuned (SFT)	Delta
Llama-3.1-8B	61.1%	78.6%	+17.5%
Phi-4 (14B)	0.0%	88.5%	**+88.5%**

To validate the necessity of fine-tuning, we compared our fine-tuned models against their base versions (using few-shot prompting).

Table 2 reveals a critical insight: While Llama-3.1 Base performs moderately well (61.1%), Phi-4 Base fails completely (0.0%). Inspection of the inference logs reveals that the failure of the Phi-4 Base model is not due to a lack of arithmetic capability, but a misalignment in task adherence. Specifically, we observed three persistent failure modes in the base model's output:

1. Data Hallucination: Instead of generating code to query the provided data dictionary, the model frequently attempted to reconstruct the dictionary itself, populating it with hallucinated or placeholder values (e.g., "Anzahl": 1234).
2. Format Violation: The model included conversational text, which caused syntax errors in our strict execution environment designed for pure script evaluation.
3. Context Neglect: Lacking instruction tuning on the specific "Blueprint" schema, the model failed to utilize the correct dictionary keys provided in the context, resulting in KeyError exceptions.

To rule out that the 0.0% score reflects a flawed prompt rather than a model limitation, all base-model evaluations used the identical few-shot prompt shown in Listing 1.3. The same prompt yielded 61.1% for Llama-3.1 Base and non-zero scores on all other base models we informally tested, indicating that the failure is specific to Phi-4's instruction-following behavior on this schema rather than the prompt itself.

```
SYSTEM:
You are a Python code generator. Your sole task is to answer a question about
    a JSON object with Python code.

Rules:
- CODE ONLY: Your response must contain EXCLUSIVELY Python code.
- NO EXPLANATIONS: Do NOT add explanations, introductions, comments, or
    example outputs.
- NO MARKDOWN: Output raw text, no markdown formatting such as '''python.
- ALWAYS OUTPUT THE RESULT VIA print().

USER TEMPLATE:
### Table Title
{table_title}

### JSON Data Structure
{json_blueprint}

# Example accesses to the data structure:
{json_blueprint_example_accesses}

### Global Filters (if any)
{global_filters}

### Question
{user_question}
```

Listing 1.3. Few-shot prompt used for base-model evaluation (translated). All base models received the identical system and user template.

This confirms that while base models possess general reasoning capabilities, Supervised Fine-Tuning is strictly necessary to constrain the output space to the required executable JSON retrieval logic.

5.4 Error Analysis

An analysis of the remaining 11.5% failure cases in the fine-tuned Phi-4 model reveals two primary error categories:

1. *Key Retrieval Failures:* The model occasionally fails to resolve the deep hierarchy correctly, returning '0'or 'None'via '.get()'instead of the actual value (e.g., retrieving *"Total""* instead of *"Total / male"* in highly nested demographics tables).
2. *Arithmetic Hallucinations:* In rare cases involving calculations (percentages or differences), the model generates syntactically correct code that performs the wrong mathematical operation. This results in numerical discrepancies between the generated output and the ground truth.

5.5 Impact of Data Transformation Pipeline

Furthermore, we evaluated the performance of industry-leading frontier models (GPT-4.1 and Gemini 2.5 Pro) as baselines across two distinct settings:

- *Raw (Pandas):* The model receives the raw dataframe head (20 rows).
- *Ours (Pipeline):* The model receives the JSON context.

Table 3. Ablation Study: Impact of Input Representation

Model & Setting	XLSX	CSV	Total Time
Standard Approach (Raw Data/Pandas head)			
GPT-4.1 (Raw)	32.5%	41.3%	19.83 min
Gemini 2.5 Pro (Raw)	61.9%	52.4%	80.56 min
Our Approach (Hierarchical JSON Context)			
GPT-4.1 (Pipeline)	**96.0%**	85.7%	**08.52 min**
Gemini 2.5 Pro (Pipeline)	93.7%	**88.1%**	38.22 min

Table 3 shows that even GPT-4.1 fails on raw XLSX data (32.5%), while our pipeline improves functional success score to 96.0%. Notably, Gemini 2.5 Pro struggles massively with raw data, taking over 80 min (due to retries), whereas the pipeline reduces this to 38 min.

5.6 Comparison with Specialized Table Models

Table 4. Performance of TableLLM on statistical CSV Data

Difficulty Level	Success Score
Simple (Lookup)	9.5%
Medium (Calc)	2.4%
Complex (Agg)	2.4%
Overall	**4.8%**

To contextualize our results against domain-specific Table-QA baselines, we evaluated *TableLLM* [25], a model explicitly trained for tabular reasoning. Since TableLLM is restricted to flat CSV inputs, the evaluation was conducted on the CSV half of our test set (126 questions). It achieved an overall functional success score of only 4.8% (Table 4), with Table 4 reporting the per-complexity breakdown. This result indicates that general-purpose table models, which typically assume flat single-row headers, fail to navigate the multi-level indexing inherent in open statistical reports, underlining the need for the hierarchical JSON representation proposed in this work.

5.7 Final Benchmarking: Fine-Tuned vs. Frontier Models

Table 5. Final Comparison: Ours vs. SOTA (using Pipeline)

Model	XLSX	CSV	Avg
GPT-4o	92.9%	72.2%	82.6%
GPT-4.1 (Apr 2025)	**96.0%**	85.7%	**90.9%**
Gemini 2.5 Flash	**96.0%**	86.5%	**91.3%**
Gemini 2.5 Pro	93.7%	**88.1%**	**90.9%**
Ours (Llama-3.1-8B)	81.0%	76.2%	78.6%
Ours (Phi-4 14B)	95.2%	81.7%	88.5%

Finally, we compare our fine-tuned models against the latest proprietary frontier models. Table 5 demonstrates that our fine-tuned Microsoft Phi-4 (14B) model is highly competitive.

Several key observations can be made from these results. First, our specialized Phi-4 model outperforms the general-purpose GPT-4o by nearly 6% points on average. This performance gap is particularly evident in the CSV format, where our model achieves 81.7% compared to GPT-4o's 72.2%. Second, while the state-of-the-art models (GPT-4.1 and Gemini 2.5) still hold a slight edge of approximately 2–3%, our model achieves this level of precision as a fully open-source solution.

Interestingly, even our smallest model, Llama-3.1-8B, shows strong results. With 78.6% average functional success score, it outperforms GPT-4o in the CSV category, suggesting that the quality of our synthetic training data effectively compensates for smaller model scales.

These results prove that for specialized tasks like Table-QA on open data statistics, fine-tuned medium-sized models can match or even exceed the performance of massive proprietary models. This is particularly relevant for government agencies and data portals that require high precision but must operate under strict data privacy regulations, as our pipeline allows for entirely local deployment.

6 Limitations and Future Work

A primary limitation of this work is the parser's heuristic nature, which is deterministically tailored to the specific formatting conventions of the Genesis Online database (e.g., specific border styles and indentation rules). While highly robust for this source, the logic is rigid and does not immediately generalize to non-standard Excel layouts or unstructured PDFs. However, our ablation study (Table 3) demonstrates that the performance gain stems from the *hierarchical JSON representation*, not the raw parsing logic itself. Consequently, the proposed architecture is domain-agnostic: the pipeline can be extended to other administrative domains (e.g., Eurostat, US Census) by substituting the initial parser component while retaining the fine-tuned code-generation engine.

Future work will focus on three primary areas. First, we plan to enhance the execution environment. While our current AST-based validation provides a significant security layer against malicious code, a move toward containerized execution (e.g., Docker-based sandboxing) would provide an even more robust isolation, preventing potential low-level exploits.

Second, we are integrating a Retrieval-Augmented Generation (RAG) system to automate the "Text-to-Statistics" workflow by identifying relevant tables across the entire database. Finally, we are refining the model's ability to generate complex `matplotlib` visualizations. Initial tests show promising results in providing not only textual answers but also high-quality graphical representations of the statistical data directly within the interface.

7 Threats to Validity

Four factors constrain generalizability. (i) The 252-item test set is modest; differences below 2–3 points should not be over-interpreted. (ii) Training and test questions were both generated with Gemini 2.5 Pro, introducing potential circularity, mitigated for the test set by manual verification against the source tables. (iii) Ground-truth answers were annotated by a single author; no inter-annotator agreement was measured. (iv) The parser is Genesis-specific and results do not directly transfer to other portals.

8 Conclusion

This paper presents a specialized Table-QA pipeline for open data statistics. By transforming heterogeneous XLSX and CSV files into a unified JSON structure and fine-tuning open-source models, we achieve high precision on these formats. Our fine-tuned Microsoft Phi-4 reaches an average success rate of 88.5%, on par with proprietary models such as GPT-4.1 and Gemini 2.5 Pro for this domain, suggesting that specialized fine-tuning is a viable path for organizations requiring high-precision extraction under local data sovereignty.[1]

References

1. Black, P.E.: Ratcliff/obershelp pattern recognition. In: Black, P.E. (ed.) Dictionary of Algorithms and Data Structures. National Institute of Standards and Technology (2021). https://www.nist.gov/dads/HTML/ratcliffObershelp.html. Accessed 9 Jan 2026

[1] Code, dataset, evaluation set, and configs: https://github.com/vale-sch/stla25.

2. Casanova, E., et al.: Xtts: a massively multilingual zero-shot text-to-speech model (2024). https://arxiv.org/pdf/2406.04904
3. Cheng, Z., et al.: Hitab: a hierarchical table dataset for question answering and natural language generation (2022). https://arxiv.org/abs/2108.06712
4. Cheng, Z., et al.: Binding language models in symbolic languages (2023). https://arxiv.org/abs/2210.02875
5. Comanici, G., et al.: Gemini 2.5: pushing the frontier with advanced reasoning, multimodality, long context, and next generation agentic capabilities (2025). https://arxiv.org/abs/2507.06261
6. Dong, H., Liu, S., Fu, Z., Han, S., Zhang, D.: Semantic structure extraction for spreadsheet tables with a multi-task learning architecture. In: Workshop on Document Intelligence at NeurIPS 2019 (2019). https://openreview.net/forum?id=r1x3GTq5IB
7. Dong, H., et al.: Spreadsheetllm: encoding spreadsheets for large language models (2025). https://arxiv.org/abs/2407.09025
8. Herzig, J., Nowak, P.K., Müller, T., Piccinno, F., Eisenschlos, J.: Tapas: weakly supervised table parsing via pre-training. In: Proceedings of the 58th Annual Meeting of the Association for Computational Linguistics. Association for Computational Linguistics (2020). https://doi.org/10.18653/v1/2020.acl-main.398, http://dx.doi.org/10.18653/v1/2020.acl-main.398
9. Jiang, J., Zhou, K., Dong, Z., Ye, K., Zhao, W.X., Wen, J.R.: Structgpt: a general framework for large language model to reason over structured data (2023). https://arxiv.org/abs/2305.09645
10. Jiang, Z., Mao, Y., He, P., Neubig, G., Chen, W.: Omnitab: pretraining with natural and synthetic data for few-shot table-based question answering (2022). https://arxiv.org/abs/2207.03637
11. Li, L., et al.: Injecting learnable table features into LLMs (2025). https://openreview.net/forum?id=Mi45HjlVRj
12. Li, P., et al.: Table-gpt: Table-tuned GPT for diverse table tasks (2023). https://arxiv.org/abs/2310.09263
13. Liu, Q., et al.: Tapex: table pre-training via learning a neural SQL executor (2022). https://arxiv.org/abs/2107.07653
14. Lu, W., Zhang, J., Fan, J., Fu, Z., Chen, Y., Du, X.: Large language model for table processing: a survey. Front. Comput. Sci. **19**(2) (2025). https://doi.org/10.1007/s11704-024-40763-6
15. Radford, A., Kim, J.W., Xu, T., Brockman, G., McLeavey, C., Sutskever, I.: Robust speech recognition via large-scale weak supervision (2022). https://arxiv.org/pdf/2212.04356
16. Su, A., et al.: Tablegpt2: a large multimodal model with tabular data integration (2024). https://arxiv.org/abs/2411.02059
17. Wang, Z., Zhang, R., Nie, Z., Mao, H.: General table question answering via answer-formula joint generation (2025). https://arxiv.org/abs/2503.12345
18. Wang, Z., et al.: Chain-of-table: evolving tables in the reasoning chain for table understanding (2024). https://arxiv.org/abs/2401.04398
19. Xia, S., et al.: Vision language models for spreadsheet understanding: challenges and opportunities. In: Proceedings of the 3rd Workshop on Advances in Language and Vision Research (ALVR), pp. 116–128. Association for Computational Linguistics (2024). https://doi.org/10.18653/v1/2024.alvr-1.10
20. Yang, A., et al.: Qwen3 technical report (2025). https://arxiv.org/abs/2505.09388

21. Yang, Z., et al.: Triples as the key: structuring makes decomposition and verification easier in LLM-based tableQA. In: The Thirteenth International Conference on Learning Representations (2025). https://openreview.net/forum?id=UwcZEoNP19
22. Ye, Y., Hui, B., Yang, M., Li, B., Huang, F., Li, Y.: Large language models are versatile decomposers: decompose evidence and questions for table-based reasoning (2023). https://arxiv.org/abs/2301.13808
23. Yin, P., Neubig, G., tau Yih, W., Riedel, S.: Tabert: pretraining for joint understanding of textual and tabular data (2020). https://arxiv.org/abs/2005.08314
24. Zhang, T., Yue, X., Li, Y., Sun, H.: Tablellama: towards open large generalist models for tables (2024). https://arxiv.org/abs/2311.09206
25. Zhang, X., et al.: Tablellm: enabling tabular data manipulation by llms in real office usage scenarios (2025). https://arxiv.org/abs/2403.19318
26. Zhang, Y., Henkel, J., Floratou, A., Cahoon, J., Deep, S., Patel, J.M.: Reactable: enhancing react for table question answering (2023). https://arxiv.org/abs/2310.00815

Successfully Defending Academic Integrity: An Ensemble Approach Towards Detecting Machine-Generated Texts

Tobias Tefke(✉) and Ralf C. Staudemeyer

Faculty of Computer Science, Schmalkalden University of Applied Sciences, 98574 Schmalkalden, Germany
t.tefke@stud.fh-sm.de

Abstract. Within the last years, generative AI usage rose dramatically. Using such tools is problematic in areas like academia where integrity matters most. Hence ways must be found to reliably determine authorship. Our system addresses this issue by involving four classifiers and gradient boosting. Its classification pipeline processes texts sentence-wise and applies two tests afterwards: A Gauss test evaluates whether the proportion of flagged sentences is within an expectation, the second test checks for consecutive flagged sentences. Here the false positive rate can be controlled with custom cutoffs. This leads to false positive rates of less than 1%. Furthermore we evaluated 30,000 arXiv drafts published between 2015 and 2025. There we can see a rising tendency for texts predicted to be machine-influenced for each new generative AI generation.

Keywords: Natural Language Processing · Text classification · AI-generated text detection

1 Introduction

Recent advances in generative AI (GenAI) make it increasingly difficult to tell apart human texts from generated ones [10,24]. [42] et al. suggest this can be improved with training but settings where integrity is crucial (e.g. academia and news websites) can profit from reliable detectors. Here we regard texts as fabricated if they are created by a Large Language Model (LLM) or machine translators (GenAI originates there [51]).

In academia we already face a flood of GenAI submissions and peer reviews [21][1] which endangers academic processes of becoming meaningless. At our university, we see GenAI use in a surging amount of student submissions. This harms academic integrity and instructors are tricked into believing the students understood their task. Here GenAI detectors can support the examiner in revealing the real amount of own work.

[1] https://www.nature.com/articles/d41586-025-03506-6.

D. Wolter and G. Schwalbe (Eds.): KI 2026, LNAI 16830, pp. 148–165, 2027.
https://doi.org/10.1007/978-3-032-32335-4_11

Using these tools is more difficult in practice as data protection laws exist. So we can't use third party detectors without consent. Also the processing and further usage of uploaded documents remain unclear; finding reliability metrics is difficult at best. Apart from that existing open source detectors are merely proof-of-concept apps that often struggle with real-world data.

Our system addresses these issues and outperforms existing ones. Thereby we make the following contributions:

- Our tool runs locally, ensuring privacy during inference. We use a combination of open-source and own datasets to rule out legal issues in the dataset.
- The involvement of multiple classifiers (SVM, FFNN, DistilBERT, RoBERTa) with gradient boosting reduces false positives significantly. Users can set own cutoffs which further allows reducing false positives if required.
- Test metrics for assessing real-world documents:
  Consecutive-sentence test: Searches for generated paragraphs.
  Gauss test: Assesses whether the proportion of flagged sentences in a document matches the estimate for human texts, virtually eliminating the effects of false positives.
- An evaluation of 250 arXiv drafts/month in the computer science (CS) category between 2015 and 2025 shows our system works on real-world data. We can see a rising amount of machine-influenced submissions since the release of ChatGPT; it continuously increases with every new generation.

In this paper we present our system: First we review related literature in Sect. 2. Afterwards we present the methodology used to collect and preprocess training data in Sect. 3. Then Sect. 4 presents our main findings and the arXiv study. Subsequently the results are discussed in Sect. 5. Finally we conclude in Sect. 6.

2 Literature Review

Our literature review is structured as follows: We discuss the separability of human and machine language in Sect. 2.1. Afterwards Sect. 2.2 reviews existing approaches. Lastly Sect. 2.3 differentiates present work from ours.

2.1 Separability of Human and Machine Language

Within the last years, the capabilities of LLMs advanced significantly (e.g. [7, 37,51]). Current models (e. g. [18,32,34,54]) can generate human-like language. Consequently the question arises if telling apart GenAI texts from human ones is feasible. This becomes increasingly difficult for humans [10,24], but the situation is better for computers: According to Suvanto et al. [49] GenAI detectors work in their domain, but classification quality degrades outside of it. However they also state that detectors outperform humans in classifying texts. The results of other studies are even more encouraging: They claim that identifying machine-generated texts is possible due to unique text properties and features [35,58].

There are already survey papers evaluating different types of classifiers and implementations [1,53,55]. In the following we concentrate on literature closely related to the architecture of our pipeline.

2.2 Classifiers

Early classifiers used LLMs themselves for authorship assessment: GLTR [17] combines GPT-2 [37] with Bidirectional Encoder Representations from Transformers (BERT) [13], Grover works in a very similar fashion [57]. Other approaches, such as [33] evaluate the probabilities of an LLM outputting specific words of a rewritten sentence. MAGE [27] combines these methods.

Nowadays most approaches focus on encoder-only transformers, such as BERT [13] and its knowledge-distilled [8,22] variants [13,29,43]. Here RoBERTa is used frequently [4,6,40,52]. Regarding combined approaches, Bakhthin et al. [5] use RoBERTa with BiLSTM [46]. CoCo [28] similarly uses RoBERTa to generate text embeddings which are then evaluated with Long Short-Term Memory (LSTM) [23]. Chen et al. [9] developed a solution that bases on RoBERTa with the option to use T5 [38] instead. Alikhanov et al. [3] compared DistilBERT with BiLSTM on classification tasks, both achieved high accuracies.

Masih et al. [31] evaluated traditional and transformer-based algorithms. There RoBERTa turned out to be the best-performing classifier. Furthermore they incorporated LIME and SHAP to highlight linguistic differences between human and GenAI fabricated texts.

These papers convincingly show that machine learning (ML) algorithms, especially BERT-based models, can be used to effectively distinguish between human written and fabricated texts. Nevertheless other approaches exist as well: Similar to [57], Gromadzki et al. [20] fine-tuned detectors on specific GenAI models. Hereby they achieved token-level accuracies of up to 99.6%. Aityan et al. [2] use traditional algorithms to build classifiers and achieved high accuracies. Zeng et al. [58] use out-of-distribution detection instead: There LLM-generated texts form one class and human written language is the outlier: Texts that lay outside of the LLM's class are considered human. Roy et al. [41] use LLM to rewrite existing texts and compare the distance between the original and rewritten counterpart: Short distances suggest LLM authorship. DNA-GPT [56] uses another approach of rewriting: texts are split in halves and an LLM is asked to complete the first half. Depending on the distance to the original they deduce the authorship. To prevent against paraphrasing attempts, Dipper [25] uses a database of collected GenAI samples to match against.

As we can see there is lots of research on predicting the authorship of unknown texts and it is shown that GenAI can be detected reliably. It becomes obvious that BERT-based [13] models are popular due to their good overall performance.

2.3 Differentiation to Related Work

Most studies consider only one classifier, just a few combine multiple ones. Often the exact way of combination remains unclear or is passed to the user. Our approach applies boosting [14,16] instead: A boosting machine is trained on how to combine the individual classifiers best.

We split texts into sentences and apply the individual classifiers on them. Their results are evaluated by the boosting machine: There we search for GenAI texts using two approaches. A consecutive sentences test searches for machine-influenced paragraphs; a Gauss test checks if the proportion of potential GenAI sentences in the document exceeds an expected value. These tests mitigate effects of potential false positives. Moreover the user can select cutoffs to instruct the model to predict sentences as GenAI more greedily or permissively. Hereby we allow adjustments for specific use cases and give users more control about the prediction process.

We tested our approach on real-world data by evaluating 250 arXiv submissions/month from 2015 to 2025. The predictions of our models show an increasing trend of LLM-influenced papers which suggests the correctness of our approach.

3 Methodology

To train ML algorithms, a proper dataset must be created as shown in Sect. 3.1. Afterwards Sect. 3.2 deals with the data preprocessing for traditional classifiers.

3.1 Data Collection

There exist freely available datasets that claim to be usable for text classification. Unfortunately most of them suffer from at least one of the following drawbacks:

- Little size which limits model generalization.
- A significant imbalance of human and GenAI fabricated texts.
- Samples from old, outdated GenAI models make it questionable whether texts fabricated by newer GenAI systems are detected reliably.

To mitigate these drawbacks we combine ten freely available datasets. This also rules out legal issues. We enrich this data with own datasets, including public student paper archives (to nudge the model to learn how students write) and CS terminology from Wikipedia with GenAI counterparts as well as completely generated documents. We use only English datasets, hence the classifier can not evaluate texts written in other languages.

Our combined dataset contains 685,837 human and 680,898 GenAI fabricated sentences. The training-validation-test split is 70/15/15. Here the supplementary repository provides more details[2].

Before proceeding with the training, the data is preprocessed as described in the following section.

[2] https://github.com/ttefke/ai-generated-text-detector.

3.2 Data Preprocessing

To process natural language, a conversion to a machine representation (vector embeddings) is inevitable. BERT-based classifiers [13] do this internally, but traditional algorithms (e.g. Support Vector Machines (SVMs) [12,50]) lack this capability. Hence embeddings must be computed for these classifiers.

Mahsih et al. [31] experimented with traditional methods, such as Word2Vec [19], GloVe [36] and FastText [44]. They state that these algorithms are a great baseline, but we use Sentence Transfomers (SBERT) [39] instead. They allow finetuning an LLM to improve embedding quality for specific use cases, which appears promising. Moreover SBERT transforms data into very high-dimensional vector spaces, making it easier for classifiers to find ways on how to predict new sentences [15]. The following section shows that this approach succeeds.

4 Experiments and Results

Here we present our results: First Sect. 4.1 shows the embedding process. Then Sect. 4.2 focuses on the training and its technical details. Afterwards, in Sect. 4.3, we use ensemble learning to reduce false-positives. There we also present the tests that can be applied on new texts. Finally Sect. 4.4 presents our validation study; it shows the correct functioning of our system by evaluating 250 arXiv papers/month over the range of 10 years.

4.1 Sentence Embeddings

All individual sentences were converted into vector embeddings for the SVM and Feedforward Neuronal Network (FFNN) using SBERT [39]. The `all-MiniLM-L6-v2`[3] model was fine-tuned with the train dataset to improve the sentences' separability. This fine-tuned model is used to embed the training data into a 384-dimensional vector space. Figure 1 shows this process in the training part.

To elaborate on our separability assumption, we performed a Principal Component Analysis with 100,000 samples (see Fig. 2): Human and generated sentences appear separable in the three-dimensional vector space which confirms the results of [35,58]. To profit from the blessings of higher dimensions [15], the original 384-dimensional vector embeddings are used.

Now we can start the training process as shown next.

[3] https://huggingface.co/sentence-transformers/all-MiniLM-L6-v2.

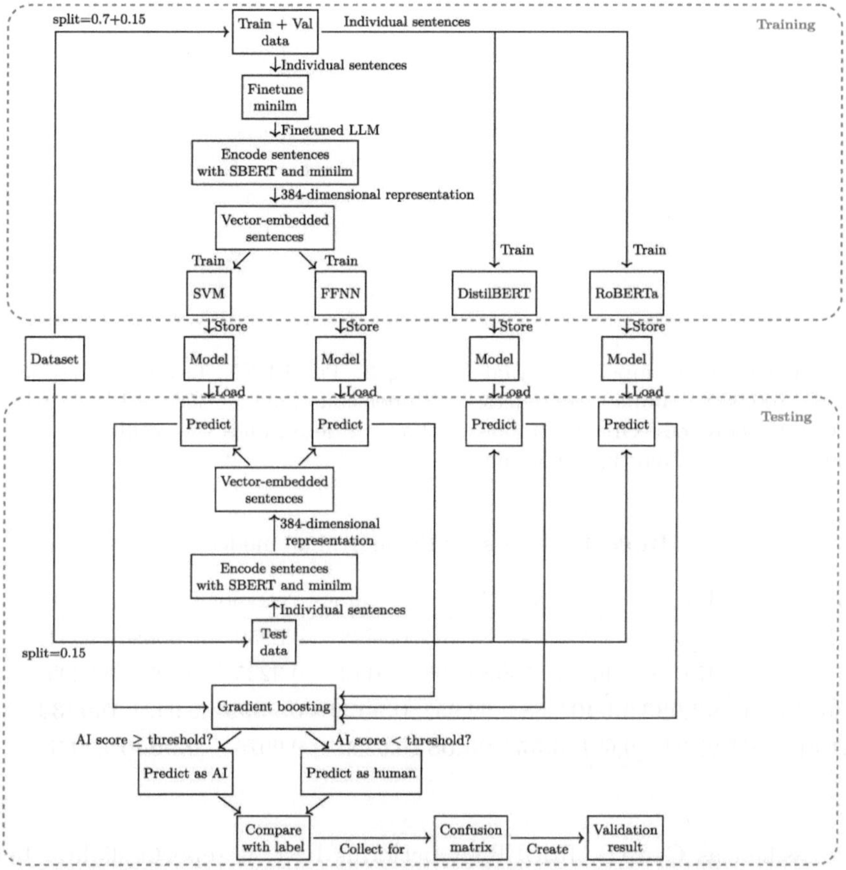

Fig. 1. Our model's architecture. The validation data is used to evaluate the models, the test data is used to estimate the performance on unseen data.

4.2 Model Training

To be able to classify sentences, we trained four individual classifiers:

- A SVM [12, 50] (lightweight baseline classifier).
- A FFNN [45] (see structure in Fig. 3, versatile baseline classifier).
- RoBERTa [29] (specialized on Natural Language Processing (NLP)).
- DistilBERT [43] (specialized on NLP).

The concrete training parameters are given in our materials repository (See Footnote 2). Table 1 shows the metrics for the trained classifiers.

As Table 1 shows, the BERT-based models outperform traditional classifiers, especially for generated sentences (true positives). The amount of true negatives (human text) is slightly higher than for traditional classifiers, resulting in a higher accuracy (see Equation (1)). With regard to false positives (human

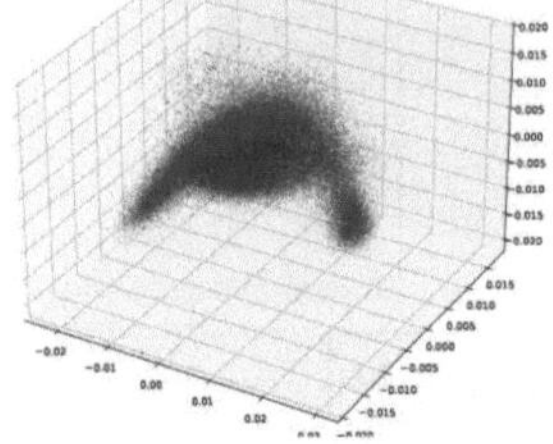

Fig. 2. Principal Component Analysis of 100,000 sample sentences. Red: GenAI sentences. Green: human-written sentences. (Color figure online)

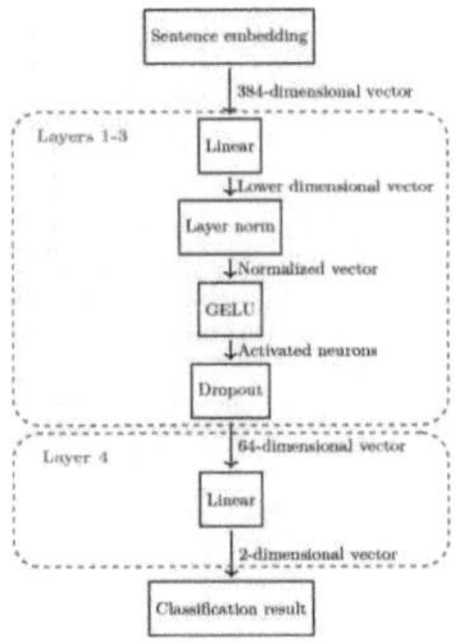

Fig. 3. The FFNN. Layers 1–3 reduce dimensions (384 → 256 → 128 → 64). Layer 4 determines the result.

Table 1. Metrics for the individual models.

Model	TN	FP	FN	TP	Accuracy	Precision	Recall	Specificity
FFNN	95,088	9,935	13,931	84,704	0.8828	0.8950	0.8588	0.9054
SVM	97,619	7,404	10,539	88,096	0.9119	0.9225	0.8932	0.9295
RoBERTa	**99,083**	**5,940**	5,683	92,952	**0.9429**	**0.9399**	0.9424	**0.9434**
DistilBERT	95,332	9,691	**3,551**	**95,084**	0.9350	0.9075	**0.9640**	0.9077

text classified as GenAI), RoBERTA performs best; it reports slightly better precision scores (see Equation (2)). On the other hand, DistilBERT performed best for false negatives, leading to a better recall (Equation (3)). All classifiers are capable to identify human text as the high specificity scores (see Equation (4)) show. Overall we can see that all classifiers learn how to distinguish human from GenAI sentences. This result was expected, Fig. 2 already indicated a good linear separability. Due to the high dimensions, even traditional classifiers offer a reasonable performance.

Despite these already impressive results, relying on the best classifier appears to be error-prone: Potential model biases could influence the classification results. To mitigate that issue we use gradient boosting to process the results of the four classifiers as shown in the following section.

4.3 Ensemble Learning

To increase the predictions' reliability, we adopt gradient boosting [14,16]. Consequently our classification pipeline is as follows (see Fig. 1):

Preprocessing: Sentence-tokenize the text and compute vector embeddings.
Individual classification: Apply the four classifiers on each sentence.

Fetch intermediate results: Get the classification probabilities.
Gradient boosting: Put the GenAI probabilities into the boosting machine.
Result: Get the final sentence predictions from the boosting machine.
Interpretation: The results can now be interpreted by the user.

To train the boosting machine, the individual models' predictions on the test dataset are combined with their real label. 20% of the data are used for testing.

$$acc = \frac{TP + TN}{TP + TN + FP + FN} \quad (1) \qquad precision = \frac{TP}{TP + FP} \quad (2)$$

$$recall = \frac{TP}{TP + FN} \quad (3) \qquad specificity = \frac{TN}{TN + FP} \quad (4)$$

When predicting new sentences, the results for the individual classifiers are computed and put into the boosting machine to obtain a final score. It represents the prediction probability of the sentence being machine generated. Here the user can set a cutoff which must be met to classify a sentence as fabricated. Table 2 provides the metrics of different cutoff values, according confusion matrices can be found in the repository (See Footnote 2).

Table 2. Metrics for the boosting machine with different cutoffs.

Cutoff	TN	FP	FN	TP	Accuracy	Precision	Recall	Specificity
0.5	20,100	905	1,090	18,637	0.9510	0.9537	0.9447	0.9569
0.75	20,753	252	2,028	17,699	0.9440	0.9860	0.8972	0.9880
0.9	20,882	123	2,722	17,005	0.9302	0.9928	0.8620	0.9941
0.95	20,926	79	3,317	16,410	0.9166	0.9952	0.8319	0.9962

As we can see, high cutoffs reduce false positives with the trade-off of more false negatives, which is reflected by the increased precision and specificity. However a cutoff of 0.95 still leads to a recall of more than 0.8. At the same time, the false positive rate is just around 0.38%. This appears promising and allows us to create test cases for unknown texts. These are presented in the following.

Consecutive Sentence Test. With a false positive rate of 0.38% at 0.95 cutoff, it is very unlikely to get multiple consecutive false positives when assessing a text sentence-wise. Once this test finds at least three consecutive sentences classified as machine generated, it flags them as fabricated. Hence it is well suited to search for machine-influenced paragraphs in texts of arbitrary length.

Gauss Test. This test evaluates if the proportion of sentences in a document classified as GenAI resides within an expected range. It approximates a normal distribution with an estimated mean of 0.0920 and a standard deviation of 0.0601. This range assumed as ground truth was received by evaluating 250 papers/month published in the CS section of arXiv from 2010 to the end of 2014 ($n = 15,000$). Due to the high amount of papers we can, according to the central limit theorem, assume normal distribution [26,48]. The effect of false positives virtually vanishes due to normal distribution properties: A higher false positive rate leads to a higher standard deviation.

Based on this, two hypotheses are formulated:

H_0**:** The document is written by a human.
H_1**:** The document is not written by a human (machine-generated or influenced).

To assess on new text, the proportion of sentences classified as machine-generated is computed. Afterwards, it is checked how many standard deviations the received proportion is away from the estimated mean: A z-score is computed for a right-sided z-test [48]. If the received p-value is < 0.001, the H_0 is rejected and H_1 is assumed. We use this test for texts with a sufficient amount of sentences (≥ 100) to reduce the effects of potential false positives on the final classification.

Besides that, we applied a SHAP analysis [30] to see how boosting combines the individual classifiers. Figures 4 to 5 show the results: The classification is on average mostly influenced by the BERT-based classifiers. RoBERTa has, on average, such a high impact that it outperforms all other classifiers.

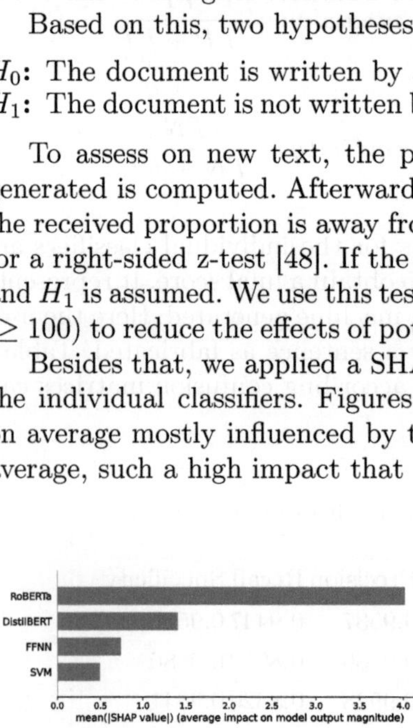

Fig. 4. Influence of the individual classifiers on the result.

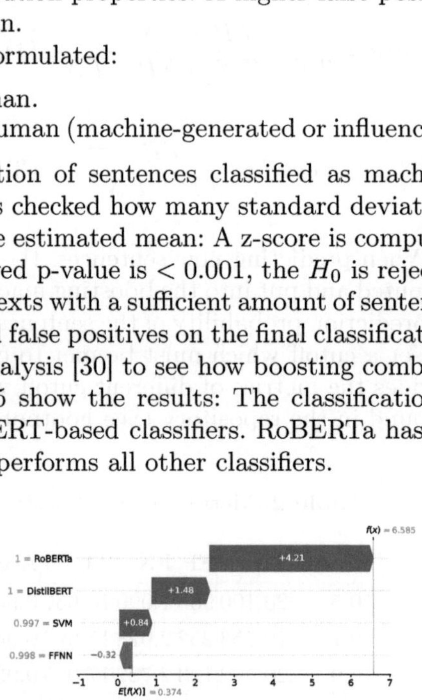

Fig. 5. SHAP analysis example for a fabricated sentence.

To see how the system performs on real-world data, we conducted a validation study we present next.

4.4 arXiv Validation Study

To validate our pipeline, we wanted to see how it performs on real-world data. Hence we set up a study to assess arXiv preprints published between 2015 and 2025. For each month in this range, we use the first 250 English preprints a search in the CS section returns ($n = 30,000$). We chose this section as it is known that it has been flooded with GenAI influenced papers[4].

[4] https://blog.arxiv.org/2025/10/31/attention-authors-updated-practice-for-review-articles-and-position-papers-in-arxiv-cs-category/.

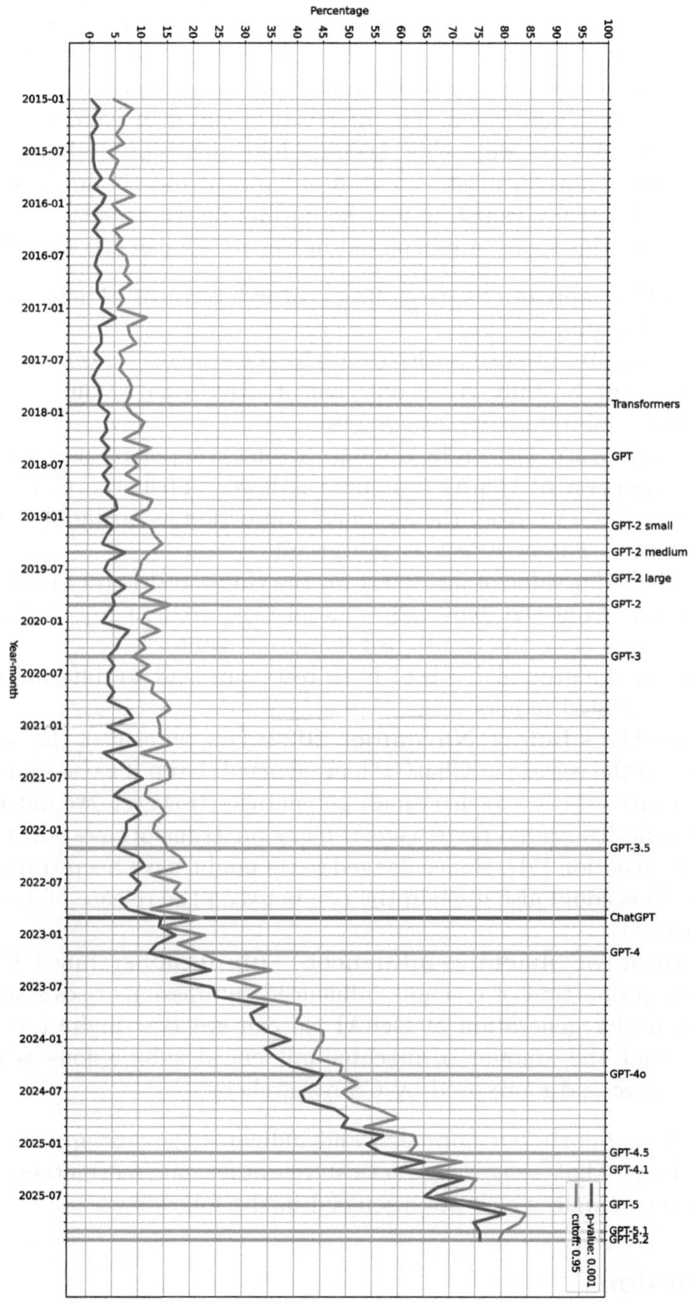

Fig. 6. Percentage of arXiv papers classified as machine-generated. Orange: consecutive sentences test. Blue: Gauss test. (Color figure online)

The first 285 submissions are downloaded and their text is mined with Apache PDFBox[5]. Then the language is checked using an according detection model [11]. Only the first 250 English documents that could be mined are further considered. These were fed into the pipeline and both the consecutive sentences and the Gauss tests were performed. The first uses a cutoff of 0.95, because it still captures fabricated texts well while keeping high precision and specificity (see last section). The Gauss test uses a cutoff of 0.5 as it has the highest recall and false positives effectively vanish under the normal distribution.

The results of this study are depicted in Fig. 6. We can see the following:

The consecutive sentences test flags more papers: There are multiple possible explanations:
- The possibility of false positives in the consecutive sentences text is low, but can not be fully ruled out. Due to the high amount of processed sentences, false positives are possible.
- Most papers are written by a group. If just one person uses GenAI tools, the proportion of GenAI sentences is lower. Then the Gauss test may rate the deviation from the assumed proportion as negligible whereas the consecutive sentences test leads to a hit.
- The selected p-value of just 0.001 for the Gauss test is very low; significant deviations from the expected value are required to reject H_0. Hence it could be possible the Gauss test is more lenient.
- Biases in the ground truth of both tests can lead to differing results for some evaluated papers.

Very few positives before November 2022: Few percent of the papers published before the release of ChatGPT are flagged. Even if we assume these are all false positives, it's a rather small percentage. However, we must also consider machine-translated texts. GenAI bases on Transformers which were first used for translation [51]. Hence flagged texts might have been translated by a machine. This could also explain the rise between the release of Transformers and ChatGPT.

Rising amount of machine-influenced submissions: Since ChatGPT's release the proportion of machine-influenced submissions rises sharply. With each new major generation of GenAI we can see new highest values. This indicates that the amount of machine-influenced submissions is rising and GenAI is more and more used by CS researchers.

This study supports our approach and indicates the system can work with real-world data. That suggests practical relevance and correctness. However potential issues remain which are discussed in the following.

5 Discussion

In Sect. 5.1 we interpret our findings. The limitations of the approach are discussed in Sect. 5.2. Finally Sect. 5.3 reviews ethical aspects.

[5] https://pdfbox.apache.org/.

5.1 Interpretation

Overall the experiments indicate the correctness of our approach and results. As our use case is revealing GenAI texts in student submissions, we must prevent false positives. Our system does this by adopting boosting which leads to a higher precision. Custom cutoffs allow to further reduce false-positives in the consecutive sentences test with the trade-off of a degraded detection performance. Here a cutoff of 0.95 appears to be reasonable (see Table 2).

As the arXiv study indicates, the classification pipeline and the developed tests appear to work reliable. Figure 6 shows us a significant rise of detections with the release of ChatGPT as well as with each new major version. However it has to be stated that the information used as ground truth for the Gauss test was derived from arXiv papers submitted between 2010 and 2014. Even though it can be assumed that back then, automated translation services were rarely used and transformers didn't exist, we don't know the real labels of these submissions. Consequently the graphic should rather be seen as trend curve and not as absolute truth.

Moreover our approach has some limitations which are discussed next.

5.2 Limitations

Despite of the good results, our model has limitations: It was only trained on English language, hence text written in other languages can not be evaluated reliably. Also the model can only show whether language appears to be machine-generated but we can not determine the impact of such a case: We can not figure out wether a text has been generated from the ground up or if an existing human text was 'only' translated or paraphrased. Obviously the system can not assess on the factual correctness of a text.

Due to the focus on technical writing in the computer science area, our model might be less suited for other domains [49]. Also finding a suitable ground truth for the Gauss test is difficult. In our case values obtained from arXiv papers published between 2010 and 2014 were used, but different corpora might lead to other values. Furthermore the assumption of normal distribution regarding GenAI sentence proportions can only be true in the range of 0 to 1, as not more than 100% or less than 0% of a document can be flagged. Moreover future LLMs released after dataset creation might be able to construct language that is even more human-like and less separable which further complicates reliable detection. Also we expect that identifying texts generated by LLMs with modified inference parameters, such as temperature- or fine-tuned models [47], is more difficult.

These limitations must be considered when evaluating a text. The following section focuses on that.

5.3 Ethical Considerations

As outlined above, our model has limitations. When assessing a student's text, an ethical handling with the model's prediction is crucial. First of all, it must be acknowledged that false positives occur and can never be fully ruled out, e.g. due to dataset or model biases. Also GenAI texts can be found everywhere, so it could be possible some students tend to have a similar writing style. Moreover it is has to be assumed that some students use LLM to improve their writing even though the actual content is own work. Hence a classification result must always be evaluated carefully and cautiously.

If GenAI usage is suspected, additional measures are recommended. This can be checking for confabulated references and rigorous oral examination. Here having a closer look at flagged sentences can support the examiner.

6 Conclusion and Future Work

Our contribution shows that human text can be well separated from machine-generate one, confirming the results of [35,58]. We developed a classification pipeline involving several classifiers and gradient boosting. This significantly reduces false positives, which must especially be prevented in academic settings.

Our system provides two tests: A consecutive sentences test which searches for at least three sentences classified as GenAI in a row. It allows setting a custom cutoff to reduce false positives. We found a cutoff of 0.95 reasonable, leading to a false positive rate of only about 0.38%. The Gauss test assesses how much the proportion of flagged sentences differs from an estimate drawn from 15,000 arXiv papers published in the CS section between 2010 and 2014. Its normal distribution properties help to virtually eliminate false positives.

To validate this system, we conducted a study that evaluated 250 arXiv submissions/month uploaded to its CS section between 2015 and 2025 ($n = 30,000$). This study reports strong indications of rising GenAI usage. These results suggest that an increasing amount of scientific texts are influenced by GenAI and that our approach works reliably on real-world documents.

We used our tool as aid to evaluate student submissions. Those predicted as GenAI influenced were carefully checked manually. In their oral defenses, the students were asked detailed technical questions regarding flagged paragraphs. When confronting students who could not rule out our impression of GenAI usage, they admitted its use except one group whose cited references were mostly confabulated.

While this suggests the tool is helpful, areas for future work remain. These include further lowering the false positive rate and exploring other ensemble methods. Also incorporating newer and more diverse datasets would be beneficial for a higher detection quality. Investigating into methods to identify other GenAI content, such as code, also appears to be interesting.

In summary we show that the detection of machine-generated text is well possible with our system while maintaining a low false positive rate. Its source code and further information is available on GitHub (See Footnote 2).

Generative AI and Citations Statement

This paper and its described program (See Footnote 2) were created without GenAI. Obviously the GenAI-labeled datasets used to train the classification model had to be created using GenAI. Since this study evaluates GenAI usage in scientific papers, we used a checklist to identify trustworthy references. Papers published before 2023 were considered reliable as highly capable GenAI tools were not publicly available back then. Newer papers published in peer-reviewed conference proceedings or journals were also considered trustworthy. The remaining papers were considered trustworthy once one of these rules applied in this order:

1. **If** their preprint was updated after publication in a journal [38] **else if**
2. An open-weight LLM is technically described [18,32,34,54] **else if**
3. We or others could reproduce a paper's main conclusions in same or similar settings [2,3,9,20,35] **else if**
4. The paper describes a dataset we use that was of sufficient quality, suggesting the original paper's conclusions are plausible as well [41] **else if**
5. Our tools classifies the paper as human [49].

References

1. Abdali, S., et al.: Decoding the AI Pen: techniques and challenges in detecting AI-generated text. In: Proceedings of of the 30th ACM SIGKDD Conference on Knowledge Discovery and Data Mining. KDD 2024, pp. 6428–6436. Association for Computing Machinery, New York (2024). https://doi.org/10.1145/3637528.3671463
2. Aityan, S.K., et al.: A lightweight approach to detection of AI-generated texts using stylometric features (2026). https://arxiv.org/abs/2511.21744
3. Alikhanov, A., et al.: AI Generated Text Detection (2026). https://arxiv.org/abs/2601.03812
4. Antoun, W., et al.: Towards a robust detection of language model-generated text: is ChatGPT that easy to detect? In: Servan, C., Vilnat, A. (eds.) Actes de CORIA-TALN 2023. Actes de la 30e Conférence sur le Traitement Automatique des Langues Naturelles (TALN), volume 1 : travaux de recherche originaux – articles longs, pp. 14–27. ATALA, Paris, France (2023). https://aclanthology.org/2023.jeptalnrecital-long.2/
5. Bakhtin, A., et al.: Real or Fake? Learning to Discriminate Machine from Human Generated Text (2019). https://arxiv.org/abs/1906.03351
6. Bhattacharjee, A., et al.: Conda: contrastive domain adaptation for ai-generated text detection. In: Proceedings of the 13th International Joint Conference on Natural Language Processing and the 3rd Conference of the Asia-Pacific Chapter of the Association for Computational Linguistics (Volume 1: Long Papers), pp. 598–610 (2023). https://doi.org/10.18653/v1/2023.ijcnlp-main.40

7. Brown, T., et al.: Language models are few-shot learners. In: Larochelle, H., Ranzato, M., Hadsell, R., Balcan, M., Lin, H. (eds.) Advances in Neural Information Processing Systems, vol. 33, pp. 1877–1901. Curran Associates, Inc. (2020). https://proceedings.neurips.cc/paper_files/paper/2020/file/1457c0d6bfcb4967418bfb8ac142f64a-Paper.pdf
8. Buciluă, C., et al.: Model compression. In: Proceedings of the 12th ACM SIGKDD International Conference on Knowledge Discovery and Data Mining. KDD 2006, pp. 535–541. Association for Computing Machinery, New York (2006). https://doi.org/10.1145/1150402.1150464
9. Chen, Y., et al.: GPT-Sentinel: Distinguishing Human and ChatGPT Generated Content (2023). https://arxiv.org/abs/2305.07969
10. Clark, E., et al.: All That's 'Human' Is Not Gold: Evaluating Human Evaluation of Generated Text (2021). https://arxiv.org/abs/2107.00061
11. Conneau, A., et al.: Unsupervised cross-lingual representation learning at scale (2020). https://arxiv.org/abs/1911.02116
12. Cortes, C., Vapnik, V.: Support-vector networks. Mach. Learn. **20**(3), 273–297 (1995). https://doi.org/10.1007/bf00994018
13. Devlin, J., et al.: BERT: pre-training of deep bidirectional transformers for language understanding. In: Proceedings of the 2019 Conference of the North, pp. 4171–4186. Association for Computational Linguistics (2019). https://doi.org/10.18653/v1/n19-1423
14. Dietterich, T.G.: Ensemble Methods in Machine Learning, pp. 1–15. Springer, Heidelberg (2000). https://doi.org/10.1007/3-540-45014-9_1
15. Donoho, D.L., et al.: High-dimensional data analysis: the curses and blessings of dimensionality. AMS Math Challenges Lecture **1**(2000), 32 (2000). https://sunju.org/teach/TMML-Fall-2021/Donoho-2000.pdf
16. Friedman, J.H.: Greedy function approximation: a gradient boosting machine. Ann. Stat. **29**(5) (2001). https://doi.org/10.1214/aos/1013203451
17. Gehrmann, S., et al.: GLTR: statistical detection and visualization of generated text. In: Costa-jussà, M.R., Alfonseca, E. (eds.) Proceedings of the 57th Ann. Meeting of the Association for Computational Linguistics: System Demonstrations, pp. 111–116. Association for Computational Linguistics, Florence, Italy (2019). https://doi.org/10.18653/v1/P19-3019
18. Gemma Team: Gemma 3 Technical report (2025). https://arxiv.org/abs/2503.19786
19. Goldberg, Y., Levy, O.: word2vec Explained: deriving Mikolov et al.'s negative-sampling word-embedding method (2014). https://arxiv.org/abs/1402.3722
20. Gromadzki, M., et al.: On the Effectiveness of LLM-Specific Fine-Tuning for Detecting AI-Generated Text (2026). https://arxiv.org/abs/2601.20006
21. Haider, J., et al.: GPT-fabricated scientific papers on Google Scholar: Key features, spread and implications for preempting evidence manipulation. Harvard Kennedy School (HKS) Misinf. Rev. **5**(5), 1–16 (2024). https://doi.org/10.37016/mr-2020-156
22. Hinton, G., et al.: Distilling the Knowledge in a Neural Network (2015). https://arxiv.org/abs/1503.02531
23. Hochreiter, S., Schmidhuber, J.: Long short-term memory. Neural Comput. **9**(8), 1735–1780 (1997). https://doi.org/10.1162/neco.1997.9.8.1735
24. Ippolito, D., et al.: Automatic detection of generated text is easiest when humans are fooled. In: Jurafsky, D., Chai, J., Schluter, N., Tetreault, J. (eds.) Proc. of the

58th Ann. Meeting of the Association for Computational Linguistics, pp. 1808–1822. Association for Computational Linguistics, Online (2020). https://doi.org/10.18653/v1/2020.acl-main.164
25. Krishna, K., et al.: Paraphrasing evades detectors of AI-generated text, but retrieval is an effective defense. In: Oh, A., Naumann, T., Globerson, A., Saenko, K., Hardt, M., Levine, S. (eds.) Advances in Neural Information Processing Systems, vol. 36, pp. 27469–27500. Curran Associates, Inc. (2023). https://proceedings.neurips.cc/paper_files/paper/2023/file/575c450013d0e99e4b0ecf82bd1afaa4-Paper-Conference.pdf
26. Kwak, S.G., Kim, J.H.: Central limit theorem: the cornerstone of modern statistics. Korean J. Anesthesiol. **70**(2) (2017). https://doi.org/10.4097/kjae.2017.70.2.144
27. Li, Y., et al.: MAGE: machine-generated Text Detection in the Wild. In: Ku, L.W., Martins, A., Srikumar, V. (eds.) Proc. of the 62nd Ann. Meeting of the Association for Computational Linguistics (Volume 1: Long Papers), pp. 36–53. Association for Computational Linguistics, Bangkok, Thailand (2024). https://doi.org/10.18653/v1/2024.acl-long.3
28. Liu, X., et al.: CoCo: coherence-enhanced machine-generated text detection under low resource with contrastive learning. In: Bouamor, H., Pino, J., Bali, K. (eds.) Proc. of the 2023 Conf. on Empirical Methods in Natural Language Processing, pp. 16167–16188. Association for Computational Linguistics, Singapore (2023). https://doi.org/10.18653/v1/2023.emnlp-main.1005
29. Liu, Y., et al.: RoBERTa: A Robustly Optimized BERT Pretraining Approach (2019). https://arxiv.org/abs/1907.11692
30. Lundberg, S.M., Lee, S.I.: A unified approach to interpreting model predictions. In: Guyon, I., Luxburg, U.V., Bengio, S., Wallach, H., Fergus, R., Vishwanathan, S., Garnett, R. (eds.) Advances in Neural Information Processing Systems, vol. 30. Curran Associates, Inc. (2017). https://proceedings.neurips.cc/paper_files/paper/2017/file/8a20a8621978632d76c43dfd28b67767-Paper.pdf
31. Masih, A., et al.: Classifying human vs. AI text with machine learning and explainable transformer models. Sci. Rep. **15**(1) (2025). https://doi.org/10.1038/s41598-025-27377-z
32. Meta AI: The Llama 4 herd: The beginning of a new era of natively multimodal AI innovation. online (2025). https://ai.meta.com/blog/llama-4-multimodal-intelligence/
33. Mitchell, E., et al.: DetectGPT: zero-shot machine-generated text detection using probability curvature. In: Krause, A., Brunskill, E., Cho, K., Engelhardt, B., Sabato, S., Scarlett, J. (eds.) Proceedings of the 40th International Conference on Machine Learning. Proceedings of Machine Learning Research, vol. 202, pp. 24950–24962. PMLR (2023). https://proceedings.mlr.press/v202/mitchell23a.html
34. OpenAI: Introducing GPT-5.2. online (2025). https://openai.com/index/introducing-gpt-5-2/
35. Pagan, N., et al.: Computational Turing Test Reveals Systematic Differences Between Human and AI Language (2025). https://arxiv.org/abs/2511.04195
36. Pennington, J., et al.: Glove: global vectors for word representation. In: Proceedings of the 2014 Conference on Empirical Methods in Natural Language Processing (EMNLP), pp. 1532–1543. Association for Computational Linguistics (2014). https://doi.org/10.3115/v1/d14-1162
37. Radford, A., et al.: Language models are unsupervised multitask learners. OpenAI blog **1**(8), 9 (2019). https://storage.prod.researchhub.com/uploads/papers/2020/06/01/language-models.pdf

38. Raffel, C., et al.: Exploring the Limits of Transfer Learning with a Unified Text-to-Text Transformer (2023). https://arxiv.org/abs/1910.10683
39. Reimers, N., Gurevych, I.: Sentence-BERT: sentence embeddings using siamese BERT-networks. In: Proceedings of the 2019 Conference on Empirical Methods in Natural Language Processing, pp. 3980–3990. Association for Computational Linguistics (2019). https://doi.org/10.18653/v1/D19-1410
40. Rodriguez, J.D., et al.: Cross-domain detection of GPT-2-generated technical text. In: Carpuat, M., de Marneffe, M.C., Meza Ruiz, I.V. (eds.) Proceedings of the 2022 Conference of the North American Chapter of the Association for Computational Linguistics: Human Language Technologies, pp. 1213–1233. Association for Computational Linguistics, Seattle, United States (2022). https://doi.org/10.18653/v1/2022.naacl-main.88
41. Roy, R., et al.: A Comprehensive Dataset for Human vs. AI Generated Text Detection (2025). https://arxiv.org/abs/2510.22874
42. Russell, J., et al.: People who frequently use ChatGPT for writing tasks are accurate and robust detectors of AI-generated text. In: Proceedings of the 63rd Ann. Meeting of the Association for Computational Linguistics, pp. 5342–5373. Association for Computational Linguistics (2025). https://doi.org/10.18653/v1/2025.acl-long.267
43. Sanh, V., et al.: DistilBERT, a distilled version of BERT: smaller, faster, cheaper and lighter (2020). https://arxiv.org/abs/1910.01108
44. Santos, F., et al.: Morphological Skip-Gram: Using morphological knowledge to improve word representation (2020). https://arxiv.org/abs/2007.10055
45. Schmidhuber, J.: Deep learning in neural networks: an overview. Neural Netw. **61**, 85–117 (2015). https://doi.org/10.1016/j.neunet.2014.09.003
46. Schuster, M., Paliwal, K.: Bidirectional recurrent neural networks. IEEE Trans. Signal Process. **45**(11), 2673–2681 (1997). https://doi.org/10.1109/78.650093
47. Solaiman, I., et al.: Release Strategies and the Social Impacts of Language Models (2019). https://arxiv.org/abs/1908.09203
48. Su, W.: Introduction to Applied Statistics. online (2024). https://openbooks.macewan.ca/introstats/
49. Suvanto, M., McGlinchey, A., Wahde, M., Barclay, P.J.: Interpretable Text Classification Applied to the Detection of LLM-generated Creative Writing (2026). https://arxiv.org/abs/2601.07368
50. Vapnik, V.N.: The Support Vector Method, pp. 261–271. Springer, Heidelberg (1997). https://doi.org/10.1007/bfb0020166
51. Vaswani, A., et al.: Attention is all you need. In: Guyon, I., Luxburg, U.V., Bengio, S., Wallach, H., Fergus, R., Vishwanathan, S., Garnett, R. (eds.) Advances in Neural Information Processing Systems, vol. 30. Curran Associates, Inc. (2017). https://proceedings.neurips.cc/paper_files/paper/2017/file/3f5ee243547dee91fbd053c1c4a845aa-Paper.pdf
52. Verma, V., et al.: Ghostbuster: detecting text ghostwritten by large language models. In: Duh, K., Gomez, H., Bethard, S. (eds.) Proceedings of the 2024 Conference of the North American Chapter of the Association for Computational Linguistics: Human Language Technologies (Volume 1: Long Papers), pp. 1702–1717. Association for Computational Linguistics, Mexico City (2024). https://doi.org/10.18653/v1/2024.naacl-long.95
53. Wang, Q., Li, H.: On continually tracing origins of LLM-generated text and its application in detecting cheating in student coursework. Big Data Cogn. Comput. **9**(3) (2025). https://doi.org/10.3390/bdcc9030050

54. Yang, A., et al.: Qwen3 Technical report (2025). https://arxiv.org/abs/2505.09388
55. Yang, X., et al.: A survey on detection of LLMs-generated content. In: Findings of the Association for Computational Linguistics: EMNLP 2024, pp. 9786–9805. Association for Computational Linguistics (2024). https://doi.org/10.18653/v1/2024.findings-emnlp.572
56. Yang, X., et al.: DNA-GPT: divergent N-gram analysis for training-free detection of GPT-generated text. In: Kim, B., Yue, Y., Chaudhuri, S., Fragkiadaki, K., Khan, M., Sun, Y. (eds.) International Conference on Learning Representations, vol. 2024, pp. 48572–48597 (2024). https://proceedings.iclr.cc/paper_files/paper/2024/file/d4ce6738e84876aa79f13c8bc8b7c5eb-Paper-Conference.pdf
57. Zellers, R., et al.: Defending against neural fake news. In: Wallach, H., Larochelle, H., Beygelzimer, A., d'Alché-Buc, F., Fox, E., Garnett, R. (eds.) Advances in Neural Information Processing Systems, vol. 32. Curran Associates, Inc. (2019). https://proceedings.neurips.cc/paper_files/paper/2019/file/3e9f0fc9b2f89e043bc6233994dfcf76-Paper.pdf
58. Zeng, C., et al.: Human texts are outliers: detecting LLM-generated texts via out-of-distribution detection. In: Belgrave, D., Zhang, C., Lin, H., Pascanu, R., Koniusz, P., Ghassemi, M., Chen, N. (eds.) Advances in Neural Information Processing Systems, vol. 38, pp. 163483–163513. Curran Associates, Inc. (2025). https://proceedings.neurips.cc/paper_files/paper/2025/file/ef52fd1e24634cb8f7003ebbfb3644d9-Paper-Conference.pdf

Bias Leaves a Gradient Trail: Label-Free Bias Identification via Gradient Probes on Concept Decompositions

Thomas Vitry[1,2](✉), Kieran von Valeburg[1], Stefan Wermter[1], and Jae Hee Lee[1](✉)

[1] University of Hamburg, Hamburg, Germany
kieran.edgeworth@studium.uni-hamburg.de,
{stefan.wermter,jae.hee.lee}@uni-hamburg.de
[2] Ecole Normale Superieure de Rennes, Rennes, France
thomas.vitry@studium.uni-hamburg.de

Abstract. Vision classifiers can exploit spurious correlations, achieving high in-distribution accuracy yet failing under distribution shift. Existing approaches to bias mitigation and analysis often depend on curated datasets, spurious-attribute or group labels, or retraining, which may be infeasible once a model is deployed or the relevant bias is unknown. We present a bias-label-free, post-hoc method for identifying spurious concepts in frozen vision models, relying only on standard class labels from a held-out audit dataset. For each target class, we collect patches from inputs predicted as that class and apply non-negative matrix factorization to intermediate activations to obtain a bank of interpretable concept vectors. Candidate concepts are then ranked with a bias estimator derived from their interaction with backpropagated gradients on misclassified examples: bias concepts tend to get activated when correcting false negatives and suppressed when correcting false positives. On Colored MNIST and Waterbirds the method recovers concepts aligned with the known spurious cue, and on CelebA it surfaces decision-relevant directions that only partially coincide with the annotated gender attribute; suppressing the top-ranked concepts at inference time improves worst-group accuracy by up to 17.9 percentage points on Waterbirds and 10.4 on CelebA without any retraining or parameter updates. Our method identifies decision-relevant spurious directions that need not coincide with annotated ones, providing both an interpretable auditing tool and an actionable debiasing handle for frozen vision models. Code is available at https://github.com/vitryt/label-free-bias-identification.

Keywords: Bias identification · Bias mitigation · Concept-based XAI

1 Introduction

Modern vision models can achieve high in-distribution accuracy while relying on spurious correlations: attributes that predict the label in the training data but

D. Wolter and G. Schwalbe (Eds.): KI 2026, LNAI 16830, pp. 166–181, 2027.
https://doi.org/10.1007/978-3-032-32335-4_12

are not causally related to the task. This shortcut learning behavior [12] can lead to brittle generalization and systematic failures when the correlation shifts at deployment. For example, in fine-grained recognition the model may over-rely on context: on Waterbirds [39], background type is spuriously correlated with the bird label during training. Such shortcuts may remain hidden when the available held-out set (e.g., the validation set) shares the same correlation, yet cause systematic errors when the correlation breaks at deployment.

To counter shortcut learning, methods often mitigate spurious correlations during data collection or training [29]. When the relevant bias concept is known, it can be targeted for mitigation via retraining [5,9,10,22] or post-hoc interventions on inputs or representations [2]. These pipelines typically assume that the spurious attribute has already been identified and therefore do not solve the discovery problem. In practice, however, we only have access to a deployed frozen model and a held-out set, but not to the original training pipeline, and rarely to bias or group annotations. In this setting, analyzing a deployed model is difficult because the spurious attribute is often unknown, and collecting new annotations can be costly. This motivates methods that can propose plausible spurious attributes post-hoc, while returning a concept vector in the latent space that is directly compatible with downstream interventions.

We study whether unsupervised, representation-level concept discovery can detect spurious attributes in frozen vision models when bias annotations are unavailable. Our approach decomposes intermediate activations into non-negative concept vectors and uses a held-out set (without group or bias labels) to probe the model via gradients (Sect. 3). We first test whether the spurious attribute learned by a biased model reliably appears as a distinct concept direction in this basis (Sect. 4.1). Building on this, we propose a bias identification criterion based on how concept activations change under a gradient descent step: bias concepts tend to be *activated* when correcting false negatives and *suppressed* when correcting false positives, while concepts encoding intrinsic class evidence change much less asymmetrically. We validate the scoring criterion against ground-truth bias (Secs. 4.2 and 4.3) and then test whether the identified concepts are actionable, by suppressing them at inference time without any parameter updates (Sect. 4.4). We evaluate these on Colored MNIST, Waterbirds and CelebA, three standard benchmarks for spurious correlation learning, and find that concept suppression substantially improves worst-group accuracy on Waterbirds and CelebA. The resulting approach provides both an interpretable auditing tool and a concrete debiasing handle for frozen vision models when bias annotations and retraining are unavailable.

2 Preliminaries

We consider a multi-class classification task with inputs $x \in \mathcal{X} \subseteq \mathbb{R}^d$ and labels $y \in \mathcal{Y} = \{1, \ldots, C\}$, and a hypothetical ideal classifier $f^* : \mathcal{X} \to \mathcal{Y}$. Following [29], an *attribute* is a function $b : \mathcal{X} \to \{0, 1\}$; it is *intrinsic* to class y if it defines membership (e.g., digit shape), and a *bias attribute* for y if it is spuriously

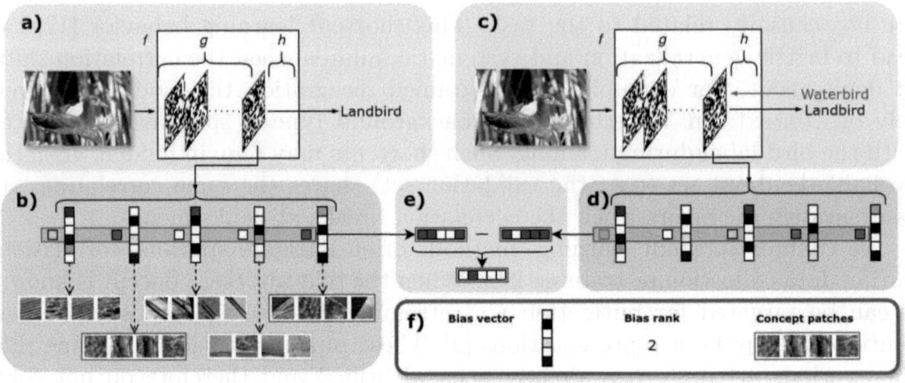

Fig. 1. Diagram of the bias identification method. **(a)** We collect false negatives and false positives from a held-out set (the *bias-audit* set) and pass them through the model. Here, studying class y=0 (landbird), the sample is a false positive: a waterbird misclassified as a landbird. **(b)** Using non-negative concept decomposition trained beforehand on the bias-audit set, we decompose activations of the sample into its concept coefficients. **(c)** Using the ground-truth label from the bias-audit set, we backpropagate the gradient to the activations. **(d)** We decompose the updated activations (after the gradient step) using the same concept bank. **(e)** We compare which concepts are activated before and after the gradient step. Concepts that are removed (for false positives) or added (for false negatives) by the gradient step are candidate bias concepts. **(f)** The identified bias concepts come with their encoding in the activation space and their most activating patches, enabling interpretation. Note that bias concepts are identified by aggregating over multiple samples, not from a single example.

correlated with y without being intrinsic. We are given a frozen classifier f with class scores $f(x) = (f_c(x))_{c=1}^C$ and a held-out *bias-audit* set $\mathcal{D} = \{(x_i, y_i)\}_{i=1}^n$ with $y_i = f^*(x_i)$ but no attribute or group annotations. $\mathcal{D}$ need not be from the training set and may be unbiased or distribution-shifted; it may come from a validation split, relabeled deployment data, or targeted stress tests. Our goal is to detect, for each class y, concept directions in the representation space that plausibly encode bias attributes used by the model and that are empirically implicated in its decisions.

Non-negative Concept Decomposition. Following CRAFT [11], we write $f = h \circ g$ where $g : \mathcal{X} \to \mathcal{A}$ maps an input to an intermediate representation $a = g(x) \in \mathcal{A} \subseteq \mathbb{R}^p$ and $h : \mathcal{A} \to \mathbb{R}^C$ maps the representation to class scores. We choose a representation layer after a ReLU so that $a \in \mathbb{R}^p_{\geq 0}$, enabling non-negative matrix factorization (NMF). For each class y, let $\hat{y}(x) = \arg\max_{c \in \mathcal{Y}} f_c(x)$ be the predicted label and collect inputs predicted as y:

$$\mathcal{X}_y = \{x_i : \hat{y}(x_i) = y\}.$$

A patch dataset is then created by applying a crop-and-resize operator π_s (patch size s) to these images, yielding patches $\mathcal{P}_y = \{\pi_s(x) : x \in \mathcal{X}_y\}$. Let $A_y =$

$g(\mathcal{P}_y) \in \mathbb{R}_{\geq 0}^{n_y \times p}$ be the resulting activations. We compute a class-conditional concept bank

$$(U_y, W_y) = \underset{U_y \geq 0,\, W_y \geq 0}{\arg\min} \frac{1}{2} \left\| A_y - U_y W_y^\top \right\|_F^2, \tag{1}$$

via NMF, where $W_y \in \mathbb{R}_{\geq 0}^{p \times r}$ contains r concept vectors $w_{y,1}, \ldots, w_{y,r}$ and $U_y \in \mathbb{R}_{\geq 0}^{n_y \times r}$ the corresponding non-negative concept coefficients. As in [11], this typically yields semantically meaningful, relatively disentangled concepts; the decomposition is approximate and its residual is captured by Eq. (1). In practice, we solve this NMF objective by alternating between two non-negative least-squares (NNLS) subproblems, fixing W_y while optimizing U_y and vice versa. This monotonically decreases the objective and converges to a stationary point under standard assumptions.

Given W_y, we obtain concept coefficients for any representation vector $a \in \mathbb{R}^p$ (in particular, $a = g(x) \in \mathbb{R}_{\geq 0}^p$) by solving an NNLS problem,

$$u_y(a) = \underset{u \geq 0}{\arg\min} \left\| a - u W_y^\top \right\|_2^2, \tag{2}$$

and write $u_{y,k}(a)$ for its k-th component.

3 Gradient-Based Bias Identification

We hypothesize that spurious attributes learned by a biased model appear as distinct concept directions in the non-negative concept decomposition, and that a gradient-based criterion can identify them among the extracted concepts.

Our intuition is as follows. A partially biased model uses both intrinsic and spurious attributes. Intrinsic concepts for class y should be active on true positives, while bias concepts need not be. On a false negative of class y, missing evidence is therefore more likely due to missing spurious support than missing intrinsic evidence; on a false positive, intrinsic evidence is typically absent and the error is more likely driven by a spurious attribute. Since NMF enforces non-negativity, evidence can only be added via positive concept activations. Because activity alone is noisy, we use gradient information to isolate the concepts the model itself would add or remove to correct its prediction: by propagating the loss gradient to activations (instead of updating weights), we measure which concepts change under one probe step. A bias concept should be systematically absent then added for false negatives, and present then removed for false positives.

To identify bias concepts without access to $b(x)$, we therefore measure how concept coefficients change under a single gradient probe step that improves the model's prediction on a given example. For a labeled example (x_i, y_i) with representation $a = g(x_i)$, let $L(h(a), y_i)$ be the cross-entropy loss and compute the gradient w.r.t. the representation, $\nabla_a L(h(a), y_i)$. We define a perturbed representation

$$a' = a - d\, \nabla_a L(h(a), y_i), \tag{3}$$

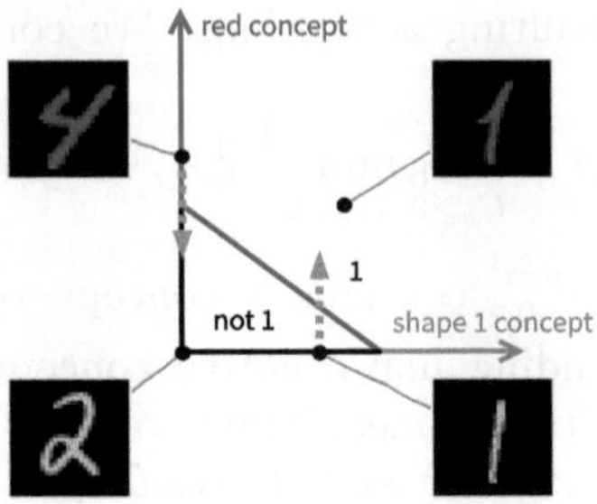

Fig. 2. Intuition of the gradient-concept interaction on class y $(= 1)$. The vertical axis is the bias concept `red` and the horizontal axis is the relevant concept `shape 1`. The blue line is the model's decision boundary. For false negatives, i.e., image (`cyan`, `1`), the gradient step increases bias attribute; for false positives, i.e., image (`red`, `4`), the same probe removes the bias attribute. Intrinsic attribute, i.e., `shape 1`, is expected to show a weaker asymmetric pattern.

with gradient step size $d > 0$. After making a' non-negative, we compute $u_{y,k}(a')$ via the same non-negative least squares problem. We treat a concept as *active* if its coefficient is positive and write

$$I_{y,k}(a) = \mathbb{1}[u_{y,k}(a) > 0],$$

where $\mathbb{1}[\cdot]$ is the indicator function.

For a class y, we define false negatives and false positives with respect to y:

$$\mathrm{FN}_y = \{(x_i, y_i) \mid y_i = y,\, \hat{y}(x_i) \neq y\}, \qquad \mathrm{FP}_y = \{(x_i, y_i) \mid \hat{y}(x_i) = y,\, y_i \neq y\}.$$

More explicitly, we define the false-negative and false-positive estimators for concept k as:

$$E_{\mathrm{FN}}^{y,k} = \sum_{(x_i,y_i)\in \mathrm{FN}_y} \frac{I_{y,k}(a_i') - I_{y,k}(a_i)}{|\mathrm{FN}_y|}, \qquad E_{\mathrm{FP}}^{y,k} = \sum_{(x_i,y_i)\in \mathrm{FP}_y} \frac{I_{y,k}(a_i) - I_{y,k}(a_i')}{|\mathrm{FP}_y|},$$

where $a_i = g(x_i)$ and a_i' is obtained from Eq. (3). The two terms measure how consistently concept k is *added* on false negatives and *removed* on false positives under the gradient step.

As illustrated in Fig. 2, we hypothesize that (i) bias concepts are more likely to increase under the gradient probe update in Eq. (3) on FN_y (i.e., the model prefers the spurious cue to predict y) and decrease on FP_y (i.e., reducing features that spuriously support y), and (ii) that this asymmetric behavior does *not* hold strongly for intrinsic concepts, i.e., false negatives possess intrinsic attributes of class y (otherwise they would not have ground-truth label y), and false positives lack them. More precisely, for false negatives we expect the probability of a bias concept k being activated to increase after the gradient step:

$$\mathbb{P}(I_{y,k}(a') = 1) - \mathbb{P}(I_{y,k}(a) = 1) > 0,$$

whereas for false positives we expect the *opposite*. To rank concepts, we define the bias score of concept k for class y as

$$S_{y,k} = \frac{1}{2}\left(E_{\text{FN}}^{y,k} + E_{\text{FP}}^{y,k}\right). \tag{4}$$

For each example in $\text{FN}_y \cup \text{FP}_y$, scoring requires one backward pass to compute $\nabla_a L$ and two non-negative least squares solves to obtain $u_y(a)$ and $u_y(a')$. The non-negative concept decomposition is computed once per class. Figure 1 gives a visual overview of the pipeline; a full algorithmic summary, from class-conditional concept extraction to bias scoring and ranking, is provided in Appendix A, *Algorithm*, of the extended version [41].[1]

4 Experiments

We evaluate our method on standard benchmarks for spurious correlation learning and the hypotheses from Sect. 3.

Datasets. We use three standard spurious-correlation benchmarks with a 0.95 train-time correlation. **CMNIST** is a colored variant of MNIST where color acts as the spurious attribute (implementation adapted from [5]); we also construct an *unbiased* variant and a `shifted-bias` variant as distribution-shifted audit sets. **Waterbirds** [39] classifies waterbirds vs. landbirds [42] with water/land background [47] as the spurious attribute. **CelebA** [31] is a blond-hair vs. not-blond binary task with gender as the spurious attribute [43]; it is particularly challenging due to a severe class imbalance in the test split (only 180 blond men vs. 9767 not-blond women), making overall accuracy an unreliable metric. Split construction follows standard practice; construction details are provided in Appendix B, *Dataset Construction Details*, of the extended version [41].

Audit Bias. In all experiments, we vary the bias structure of the bias-audit set $\mathcal{D}$, a categorical we refer to as the *audit bias* throughout. We consider three values: `biased` (same spurious correlation as the training distribution), `unbiased` (correlation broken), and `shifted bias` (a different spurious assignment than training). CMNIST evaluates all three; Waterbirds and CelebA are only available in biased form, so we restrict them to `biased`. For all audit variants, the underlying images are taken from the held-out validation split of the corresponding dataset.

[1] Owing to the strict page limit in the published proceedings, the appendices could not be included in this camera-ready paper. The full algorithm listing, dataset construction details, CMNIST results, baseline comparison, patch galleries, and extended related-work discussion are available in the extended version [41].

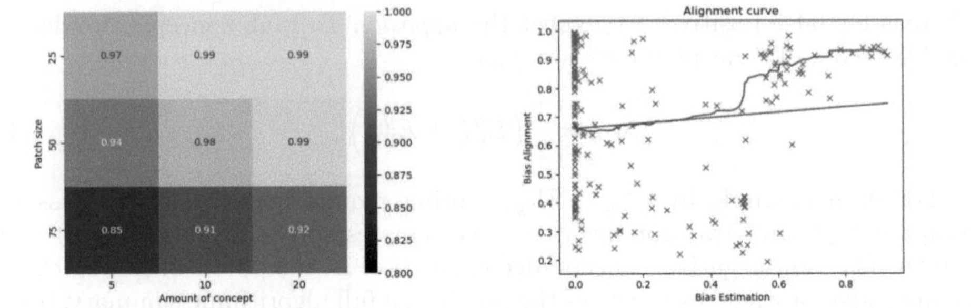

(a) Bias-alignment score (fraction of background pixels in most-activating patches) of the most background-dominated concept as a function of patch size and number of concepts (both classes, 5 runs per class).

(b) Waterbirds bias score against bias-alignment score. Blue crosses represent concepts, red curves are linear regressions, and green curves show the average bias-alignment score of concepts above the current bias score threshold.

Fig. 3. Waterbirds concept bias analysis.

Models and Training. For CMNIST, we use a three-layer MLP with ReLU activations, trained for 100 epochs with stochastic gradient descent (SGD) and batch size 128. For the gradient descent, we pick a learning rate of 0.01 halved every 25 epochs. Waterbirds experiments are run on a ResNet-18 with pretrained weights [17]. The model is trained with SGD (learning rate 10^{-1} divided by 10 every 30 epochs) for 100 epochs with batch size 1024. Finally, we use a ResNet-50 with pretrained weights [17] trained again with SGD (learning rate 10^{-4}) for 20 epochs with batch size 512 for CelebA. For non-negative concept decomposition, we extract activations from the final ReLU layer before the classifier head to ensure non-negativity. Experiments are repeated 10 times with different random seeds; we report means and standard errors.

4.1 Concept–Bias Alignment

We first investigate whether the spurious attributes learned by the model appear as distinct concept directions in the non-negative concept decomposition. We hypothesize that if the model relies on a spurious attribute to predict class y, then at least one concept in W_y aligns with that attribute. To test this, we use datasets with known ground-truth spurious attributes. On CMNIST, we measure cosine similarity between each concept vector and an estimated color-bias direction following [10], treating concepts with similarity ≥ 0.55 as bias-aligned. On Waterbirds, we compute the average fraction of *background* pixels in each concept's most activating patches using foreground masks; concepts with $\geq 85\%$ background pixels are considered bias-aligned. We sweep the patch size s and number of concepts r.

Results. On Waterbirds (Fig. 3a), we reliably find a background-dominated concept with very low variance (below 2% standard error), confirming that a bias-aligned concept is consistently recovered. The best results are obtained with patch size around 50 and $r \geq 10$: patches at this scale capture enough background structure to form a coherent concept while remaining small relative to the full image, and sufficiently many concepts are needed for a dedicated bias direction to emerge. Additional CMNIST experiments in Appendix C, *CMNIST Results*, of the extended version [41] confirm these findings across multiple audit-set distributions and show that unbiased models do not produce spurious concept directions. These experiments confirm that non-negative concept decomposition reliably captures the bias attribute in biased models. Balancing interpretability and decomposition quality, we set ($r = 8$, $s = 6$) for CMNIST and ($r = 10$, $s = 50$) for Waterbirds and CelebA, and set the gradient step size to $d = 2 \times 10^4$; Appendix C, *CMNIST Results*, of the extended version reports the sensitivity analysis [41].

4.2 Bias Score Validation

Having confirmed that bias directions emerge in the NMF basis, we now test whether our scoring criterion ranks them automatically. We apply the gradient-concept interaction score from Eq. (4) to rank concepts as candidate bias directions on misclassified and distribution-shifted examples, and evaluate if the high-ranked concepts correspond to the ground-truth bias concepts from Sect. 4.1. Figure 4 first illustrates this interaction directly on Waterbirds: for a bird-focused relevant concept and a sea-focused bias concept, the gradient probe step consistently increases the bias-concept activation on false negatives and decreases it on false positives, empirically confirming the intuition of Fig. 2 on real data.

Figure 3b further demonstrates that the relation between bias score and bias alignment is strong: concepts with bias scores above 0.55 are reliably background-dominated (mean alignment above 0.8), supporting the use of this threshold for bias identification. On CMNIST, the same pattern holds for biased models, while unbiased models show no strong correlation and no concept exceeds a bias score of 0.7, as reported in Appendix C, *CMNIST Results*, of the extended version [41]. Across both datasets, concepts with bias scores above 0.55 are consistently aligned with the ground-truth bias. We therefore use a bias score threshold of $\tau = 0.55$ for the remainder of this study; this threshold can be increased to reduce the false-positive rate at the cost of sensitivity.

4.3 Correlation with Ground-Truth Bias

To quantitatively validate that the identified concepts correspond to the ground-truth bias, we measure the correlation between concept activations and ground-truth bias labels on the test sets. For each concept in the merged concept bank and each bias attribute, we compute the absolute Matthews Correlation Coefficient (MCC) between the binarized concept activation $I_{y,k}$ and the binary bias

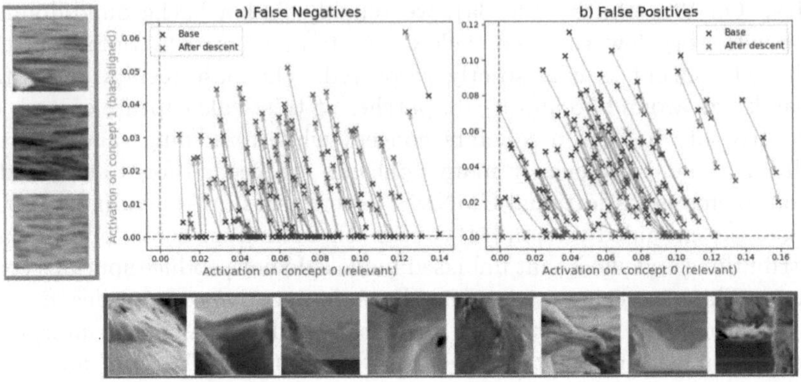

Fig. 4. Empirical validation of the gradient-concept interaction on a ResNet-18 trained on Waterbirds, to be compared with Fig. 2. Each panel scatters concept activations for the waterbird class, with the relevant concept (concept 0, bird features; green frame) on the horizontal axis and the bias-aligned concept (concept 1, sea backgrounds; orange frame) on the vertical axis. Blue crosses: base activations $u_y(a)$; red crosses: activations $u_y(a')$ after one gradient probe step (Eq. (3)); grey segments connect the two. **(a)** On false negatives, the bias concept is systematically added. **(b)** On false positives, it is systematically suppressed. The relevant concept shows a markedly weaker and less asymmetric change.

label.[2] The absolute MCC values of identified bias concepts with their corresponding bias attribute are then compared against those of all other concept–bias pairs. We report the proportion of statistically significant pairs under a χ^2 independence test and conduct a one-sided Mann–Whitney U-test to assess whether identified bias concepts exhibit significantly higher correlation than other pairs. Results are reported in Table 1.

On Waterbirds, activations of identified bias concepts are highly correlated with the background attribute ($f_{\text{bias}} = .977$, $p < 0.001$), consistently exceeding other concept–bias pairs. On CelebA, identified concepts ($f_{\text{bias}} = .969$) are statistically associated with bias but MCC values remain low, and no concept exceeds an MCC of 0.4. The Mann–Whitney test still shows a significant advantage over other concepts ($p = 0.010$), indicating that the identified concepts are relatively more bias-aligned than the remaining ones. The low absolute values suggest that the single-scale NMF decomposition struggles to capture a high-level attribute such as gender, possibly compounded by the severe class imbalance (blond:not blond $\approx$ 1:6.5). CMNIST results in Appendix C, *CMNIST Results*, of the extended version [41] confirm strong correlation for biased models and no correlation for unbiased models.

[2] We use the absolute value because the sign of a concept direction under NMF is determined by the factorization and is not semantically meaningful: a concept that anti-correlates with the binary bias label encodes the same bias information as one that correlates with it.

Table 1. Correlation between identified bias concepts and ground-truth bias labels. #bias: number of identified bias concepts; f_{bias} / f_{other}: proportion of statistically significant pairs (χ^2 test) for bias concepts vs. other concept–bias pairs; $\bar{\Phi}_{\text{bias}}$ / $\bar{\Phi}_{\text{other}}$: mean absolute MCC of significant pairs; p: one-sided Mann–Whitney U-test. CMNIST results are reported in Appendix C, *CMNIST Results*, of the extended version [41].

Train dataset	Audit bias	#bias	f_{bias}	f_{other}	$\bar{\Phi}_{\text{bias}}$	$\bar{\Phi}_{\text{other}}$	p
Waterbirds	biased	4.3±0.6	0.977	0.790	0.389±0.175	0.154±0.123	0.001
CelebA	biased	3.2±0.9	0.969	0.768	0.163±0.076	0.124±0.083	0.010

4.4 Inference-Time Bias Mitigation

To test whether identified bias directions are actionable, we apply a simple inference-time concept suppression inspired by projection-based methods such as P-ClArC [2]. Adapting such projection-style interventions to NMF-based concept banks raises two practical considerations. First, our bias-identification stage produces class-conditional concept banks, meaning each decomposition is tailored to one class and is therefore not directly suitable for full downstream prediction. We address this by merging class-wise concept banks into a model-wide bank W_{merged} and clustering highly similar concepts (cosine similarity above 0.95). Second, projection-based mitigation requires a neutral value to which the suppressed concept is set. Since NMF matrices are naturally sparse, we use 0 as a neutral value for each concept, avoiding the need to estimate concept-specific baselines from additional data. For a test input x, we compute its representation $a = g(x)$ and concept coefficients $u_{\text{merged}}(a)$, and remove the components along bias concepts B before rescaling the result to the original activation norm and performing the classification:

$$a_{\text{sup}} = a - \sum_{k \in B} u_{\text{merged}}(a)_k \, w_{\text{merged},k}, \qquad a_{\text{rsc}} = a_{\text{sup}} \frac{\|a\|_2}{\|a_{\text{sup}}\|_2} \qquad \tilde{f}(x) = h(a_{\text{rsc}}),$$

where a_{sup} is the bias-suppressed representation and a_{rsc} is its rescaling to the original activation norm $\|a\|_2$, which compensates for the magnitude lost during suppression. Based on the previous experiments, concepts with bias scores above 0.55 can reliably be treated as bias-aligned. Accordingly, we define $B = \bigcup_y \{k : S_{y,k} > \tau\}$ with $\tau = 0.55$. We test this approach on all three datasets. For CMNIST and Waterbirds, we choose hyperparameters based on the previous studies; for CelebA, we reuse the Waterbirds settings because it uses a similar architecture, allowing us to test whether the hyperparameters transfer across datasets. To ensure that effects are linked to our identification, we also run an ablation that randomly suppresses the same number of concepts in the merged bank for each model. These experiments are reported as *ablation* in the results.

Results. Table 2 reports overall, worst-class, and worst-group accuracy. On Waterbirds, suppression improves overall accuracy by +4.3, worst-class accu-

Table 2. Effect of suppressing the identified bias concepts at inference time. Symbol "–" under *Audit bias* denotes the base frozen model without mitigation. CMNIST results are reported in Appendix C, *CMNIST Results*, of the extended version [41].

Train dataset	Audit bias	Accuracy	Worst-class acc	Worst-group acc
Waterbirds	–	82.1±0.3	69.1±0.8	45.9±1.5
	biased	**86.4**±1.7	**77.6**±2.5	**63.8**±4.0
	ablation	84.8±1.4	66.8±5.2	43.7±8.5
CelebA	–	**95.3**±0.1	81.3±1.3	43.4±2.5
	biased	94.9±0.2	**86.4**±1.4	**53.8**±4.1
	ablation	94.1±1.2	79.3±11.8	45.4±17.9

racy by +8.5, and worst-group accuracy by +17.9, clearly outperforming random ablation despite class imbalance. On CelebA, worst-class and worst-group accuracy improve by +5.1 and +10.4 with only a small drop in overall accuracy and no dataset-specific tuning (Waterbirds settings were reused); the random-suppression ablation (45.4 ± 17.9 worst-group) is consistent with the effect being concept-specific rather than a pure capacity reduction. Despite the weak correlation with the annotated gender attribute (Sect. 4.3), suppression improves fairness metrics—the qualitative analysis in Sect. 4.5 suggests the identified directions capture decision-relevant spurious information that only partially coincides with gender. On CMNIST, suppression yields mixed results, as reported in Appendix C, *CMNIST Results*, of the extended version [41]. Appendix D, *Comparison with Supervised Baselines*, of the extended version provides a detailed comparison with supervised baselines (JTT, Group DRO, DFR) [41].

4.5 Bias Concept Interpretation

Each identified concept comes with its most-activating audit-set patches, which can be inspected qualitatively. To reduce reliance on bias-prone manual inspection, for each bias concept we generate the 10 labels most associated with its top-100 patches (weighted by rank) using NOVIC [1], an open-vocabulary image classifier; we treat the labels as a qualitative summary rather than ground truth. Representative patch galleries are shown in Fig. 5; per-dataset extended galleries and discussion are provided in Appendix E, *Bias Concept Interpretation*, of the extended version [41].

On Waterbirds (Fig. 5a), the top labels align cleanly with the ground-truth bias: plant-related terms (`bamboo`, `phyllostachys`, `rain tree`) for `landbird` and marine terms (`wave`, `blue whale`, `sea`) for `waterbird`. On CelebA (Fig. 5b), the top labels cluster around hair (`hair`, `human hair`, `hair space`, ...); qualitative inspection of the patches suggests the direction captures hair *shape and length* rather than color. This is consistent with the low MCC against the annotated gender attribute (Sect. 4.3): gender on CelebA is a spatially distributed cue that a patch-based decomposition cannot encode as a single direction, but localized proxies such as hair length, eyeshadow, or lips carry partial gender information, which explains why suppressing these concepts still improves worst-group performance (Sect. 4.4).

(a) Waterbirds, bias for **`landbird`: `bamboo`, `phyllostachys`, `common bamboo`, `lesser bullrush`, `damselfly`**.

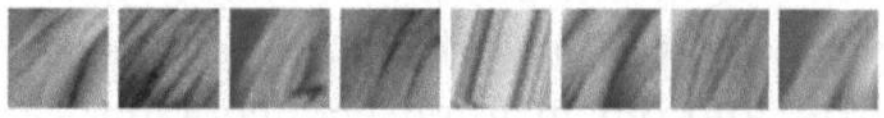

(b) CelebA, bias for **`blond`: `human hair`, `hair`, `body hair`, `hair space`, `hair wig`**.

Fig. 5. Top-activating patches of representative bias concepts identified by our method, with top-5 generated labels from NOVIC [1]. **(a)** Landbird bias concept (vegetation background). **(b)** Blond-hair bias concept (hair shape/length). Extended galleries for all concepts are provided in Appendix E, *Bias Concept Interpretation*, of the extended version [41].

5 Related Work

Shortcut learning is a pervasive failure mode where models rely on spurious correlations that break under distribution shift [12,44]. **Bias-aware mitigation.** When the spurious attribute is known, methods reduce reliance via regularization [5], adversarial training [22], representation erasure [6], concept-supervised probing [9,21], or directional interventions [2,10]; post-training approaches include saliency-masked fine-tuning [4] and subspace projection [20]. **Bias discovery without bias labels.** Related work upweights high-loss examples [30,33] or discovers latent failure slices via environment inference and pseudo-labeling [16,34,38,45,46], though these generally do not yield a class-conditional direction that can be ranked and targeted [14,26,40]. Unsupervised concept discovery extracts interpretable directions from activations [11,15,28] and has been applied to robustness [3], concept ranking [25], and post-hoc bias proposal via explanation maps or vision-language models [8,23,35], though often without providing a concrete direction for intervention [7,36,37]. **Post-hoc mitigation with frozen models.** Existing approaches reduce spurious reliance through last-layer retraining on a reweighted split [24], sub-network extraction [27], activation erasure [18], data pruning [32], or inference-time debiasing [13,19], but still require optimization, group labels, or model edits. In contrast, we identify class-conditional spurious concept directions in a frozen model without bias labels, providing interpretable handles for downstream intervention without updating parameters. An extended discussion is provided in Appendix F, *Extended Related Work*, of the extended version [41].

6 Conclusion

We presented a label-free, post-hoc method for identifying and mitigating spurious concepts in frozen vision classifiers that requires only standard class labels from a held-out audit set. Non-negative concept decomposition reliably recovers spurious attribute directions across hyperparameters on CMNIST and Waterbirds, and our gradient–concept interaction score ranks these directions without any bias annotations. Suppressing the top-ranked concepts at inference time improves worst-group accuracy by up to 17.9 percentage points on Waterbirds and 10.4 on CelebA, with no retraining or parameter updates. On CelebA, the identified concepts improve fairness metrics despite correlating only weakly with the annotated gender attribute, indicating that the method captures decision-relevant spurious information that extends beyond pre-defined bias categories. Together, these results demonstrate that unsupervised concept discovery combined with gradient probing can serve both as an interpretable auditing tool and as a practical debiasing handle for deployed models.

Limitations and Future Work. Our approach assumes access to a post-hoc bias-audit set and is most informative when enough misclassified examples are available; in low-error regimes, targeted stress tests or distribution shifts may be needed to surface failures. The single-scale patch decomposition limits the ability to capture bias attributes that are spatially distributed (as observed on CelebA); multi-scale decompositions [15] may address this. Bias information may also be entangled across multiple concept directions, leading to collateral suppression of task-relevant features; recursive or hierarchical decompositions could help disentangle these and are a promising direction for future work.

Acknowledgments. Jae Hee Lee and Stefan Wermter were supported by the German Research Foundation (DFG), project number 551629603.

References

1. Allgeuer, P., Ahrens, K., Wermter, S.: Unconstrained open vocabulary image classification: Zero-shot transfer from text to image via clip inversion. In: 2025 IEEE/CVF Winter Conference on Applications of Computer Vision (WACV), pp. 8217–8228. IEEE (2025)
2. Anders, C.J., Weber, L., Neumann, D., Samek, W., Müller, K.R., Lapuschkin, S.: Finding and removing Clever Hans: using explanation methods to debug and improve deep models. Inf. Fusion **77**, 261–295 (2022)
3. Arefin, M.R., et al.: Unsupervised Concept Discovery Mitigates Spurious Correlations. In: Proceedings of the 41st International Conference on Machine Learning, pp. 1672–1688. PMLR (2024)
4. Asgari, S., et al.: MaskTune: mitigating spurious correlations by forcing to explore. Adv. Neural. Inf. Process. Syst. **35**, 23284–23296 (2022)
5. Bahng, H., Chun, S., Yun, S., Choo, J., Oh, S.J.: Learning de-biased representations with biased representations. In: Proceedings of the 37th International Conference on Machine Learning, pp. 528–539. PMLR (2020)

6. Belrose, N., Schneider-Joseph, D., Ravfogel, S., Cotterell, R., Raff, E., Biderman, S.: LEACE: perfect linear concept erasure in closed form. Adv. Neural. Inf. Process. Syst. **36**, 66044–66063 (2023)
7. Bhusal, D., Clifford, M., Rampazzi, S., Rastogi, N.: FACE: faithful automatic concept extraction. In: The Thirty-Ninth Annual Conference on Neural Information Processing Systems (2025)
8. Chakraborty, R., Sletten, A., Kampffmeyer, M.C.: ExMap: leveraging explainability heatmaps for unsupervised group robustness to spurious correlations. In: Proceedings of the IEEE/CVF Conference on Computer Vision and Pattern Recognition, pp. 12017–12026 (2024)
9. Correa, R., Pahwa, K., Patel, B., Vachon, C.M., Gichoya, J.W., Banerjee, I.: Efficient adversarial debiasing with concept activation vector – Medical image case-studies. J. Biomed. Inform. **149**, 104548 (2024)
10. Dreyer, M., Pahde, F., Anders, C.J., Samek, W., Lapuschkin, S.: From hope to safety: unlearning biases of deep models via gradient penalization in latent space. In: Proceedings of the AAAI Conference on Artificial Intelligence, vol. 38, no. (19), pp. 21046–21054 (2024)
11. Fel, T., et al.: CRAFT: Concept recursive activation FacTorization for Explainability. In: Proceedings of the IEEE/CVF Conference on Computer Vision and Pattern Recognition, pp. 2711–2721 (2023)
12. Geirhos, R., et al.: Shortcut learning in deep neural networks. Nature Mach. Intell. **2**(11), 665–673 (2020)
13. Gerych, W., et al.: BendVLM: test-time debiasing of vision-language embeddings. Adv. Neural. Inf. Process. Syst. **37**, 62481–62502 (2024)
14. Ghaznavi, M., et al.: Exploiting what trained models learn for making them robust to spurious correlations without group annotations. In: Workshop on Spurious Correlation and Shortcut Learning: Foundations and Solutions (2025)
15. Ghorbani, A., Wexler, J., Zou, J.Y., Kim, B.: Towards automatic concept-based explanations. In: Advances in Neural Information Processing Systems, vol. 32. Curran Associates, Inc. (2019)
16. Ghosh, S., et al.: LADDER: language-driven slice discovery and error rectification in vision classifiers. In: Findings of the Association for Computational Linguistics: ACL 2025, pp. 22935–22970. Association for Computational Linguistics (2025)
17. He, K., Zhang, X., Ren, S., Sun, J.: Deep residual learning for image recognition. In: Proceedings of the IEEE Conference on Computer Vision and Pattern Recognition, pp. 770–778 (2016)
18. He, Q., Xu, K., Yao, A.: EvA: erasing spurious correlations with activations. In: The Thirteenth International Conference on Learning Representations (2024)
19. Hirota, Y., Chen, M.H., Wang, C.Y., Nakashima, Y., Wang, Y.C.F., Hachiuma, R.: SANER: annotation-free societal attribute neutralizer for debiasing CLIP. In: The Thirteenth International Conference on Learning Representations (2024)
20. Holstege, F., Wouters, B., Giersbergen, N.V., Diks, C.: Removing spurious concepts from neural network representations via joint subspace estimation. In: Proceedings of the 41st International Conference on Machine Learning, pp. 18568–18610. PMLR (2024)
21. Kim, B., et al.: Interpretability beyond feature attribution: quantitative testing with concept activation vectors (TCAV). In: Proceedings of the 35th International Conference on Machine Learning, pp. 2668–2677. PMLR (2018)
22. Kim, B., Kim, H., Kim, K., Kim, S., Kim, J.: Learning Not to Learn: Training Deep Neural Networks With Biased Data. In: Proceedings of the IEEE/CVF Conference on Computer Vision and Pattern Recognition, pp. 9012–9020 (2019)

23. Kim, Y., Mo, S., Kim, M., Lee, K., Lee, J., Shin, J.: Discovering and mitigating visual biases through keyword explanation. In: Proceedings of the IEEE/CVF Conference on Computer Vision and Pattern Recognition, pp. 11082–11092 (2024)
24. Kirichenko, P., Izmailov, P., Wilson, A.G.: Last layer re-training is sufficient for robustness to spurious correlations. In: The Eleventh International Conference on Learning Representations (ICLR) (2023)
25. Kowal, M., Dave, A., Ambrus, R., Gaidon, A., Derpanis, K.G., Tokmakov, P.: Understanding video transformers via universal concept discovery. In: Proceedings of the IEEE/CVF Conference on Computer Vision and Pattern Recognition, pp. 10946–10956 (2024)
26. LaBonte, T., Hill, J.C., Zhang, X., Muthukumar, V., Kumar, A.: The group robustness is in the details: revisiting finetuning under spurious correlations. Adv. Neural. Inf. Process. Syst. **37**, 121598–121629 (2024)
27. Le, P.Q., Schlötterer, J., Seifert, C.: Out of Spuriousity: improving robustness to spurious correlations without group annotations. Trans. Mach. Learn. Res. (2024)
28. Lee, J.H., Mikriukov, G., Schwalbe, G., Wermter, S., Wolter, D.: Concept-based explanations in computer vision: where are we and where could we go? In: Computer Vision – ECCV 2024 Workshops, pp. 266–287. Springer, Cham (2024)
29. Lee, J., Lee, J., Jung, S., Choo, J.: Improving Evaluation of Debiasing in Image Classification. arXiv preprint arXiv:2206.03680 (2023)
30. Liu, E.Z., et al.: Just train twice: Improving group robustness without training group information. In: Proceedings of the 38th International Conference on Machine Learning (ICML), pp. 6781–6792 (2021)
31. Liu, Z., Luo, P., Wang, X., Tang, X.: Deep learning face attributes in the wild. In: Proceedings of International Conference on Computer Vision (ICCV) (2015)
32. Mulchandani, V., Kim, J.E.: Severing spurious correlations with data pruning. In: The Thirteenth International Conference on Learning Representations (2024)
33. Nam, J., Cha, H., Ahn, S., Lee, J., Shin, J.: Learning from failure: De-biasing classifier from biased classifier. In: Advances in Neural Information Processing Systems (NeurIPS), vol. 33, pp. 20673–20684 (2020)
34. Olesen, V., Weng, N., Feragen, A., Petersen, E.: Slicing through bias: explaining performance gaps in medical image analysis using slice discovery methods. In: Ethics and Fairness in Medical Imaging, pp. 3–13. Springer, Cham (2025)
35. Paduraru, C.D., Barbalau, A., Filipescu, R., Nicolicioiu, A.L., Burceanu, E.: ConceptDrift: uncovering biases through the lens of foundation models. In: Interpretable AI: Past, Present and Future (2024)
36. Pahde, F., et al.: Navigating neural space: revisiting concept activation vectors to overcome directional divergence. In: The Thirteenth International Conference on Learning Representations (2024)
37. Panousis, K.P., Ienco, D., Marcos, D.: Coarse-to-fine concept bottleneck models. Adv. Neural. Inf. Process. Syst. **37**, 105171–105199 (2024)
38. Pezeshki, M., Bouchacourt, D., Ibrahim, M., Ballas, N., Vincent, P., Lopez-Paz, D.: Discovering environments with XRM. In: Proceedings of the 41st International Conference on Machine Learning, pp. 40551–40569. PMLR (2024)
39. Sagawa, S., Koh, P.W., Hashimoto, T.B., Liang, P.: Distributionally robust neural networks. In: International Conference on Learning Representations (2019)
40. Tsirigotis, C., Monteiro, J., Rodriguez, P., Vazquez, D., Courville, A.C.: Group robust classification without any group information. Adv. Neural. Inf. Process. Syst. **36**, 56553–56575 (2023)

41. Vitry, T., von Valeburg, K., Wermter, S., Lee, J.H.: Bias Leaves a Gradient Trail: Label-Free Bias Identification via Gradient Probes on Concept Decompositions (2026). https://arxiv.org/abs/2605.28780
42. Wah, C., Branson, S., Welinder, P., Perona, P., Belongie, S.: The Caltech-UCSD Birds-200-2011 Dataset. Tech. Rep. 2010-001, California Institute of Technology (2011)
43. Wu, H., Bezold, G., Gunther, M., Boult, T., King, M.C., Bowyer, K.W.: Consistency and accuracy of CelebA attribute values. In: 2023 IEEE/CVF Conference on Computer Vision and Pattern Recognition Workshops (CVPRW), pp. 3258–3266. IEEE Computer Society, Los Alamitos, CA, USA (2023)
44. Ye, W., et al.: The Clever Hans Mirage: A Comprehensive Survey on Spurious Correlations in Machine Learning. Trans. Mach. Learn. Res. (2025)
45. Zare, S., Nguyen, H.V.: Frustratingly easy environment discovery for invariant learning. Comput. Sci. Math. Forum **9**(1), 2 (2024)
46. Zhang, Z., Feng, M., Li, Z., Xu, C.: Discover and mitigate multiple biased subgroups in image classifiers. In: Proceedings of the IEEE/CVF Conference on Computer Vision and Pattern Recognition, pp. 10906–10915 (2024)
47. Zhou, B., Lapedriza, A., Khosla, A., Oliva, A., Torralba, A.: Places: a 10 million image database for scene recognition. IEEE Trans. Pattern Anal. Mach. Intell. **40**(6), 1452–1464 (2018)

c-Core Revision for Conditional Belief Bases

Marco Wilhelm[1(✉)] and Gabriele Kern-Isberner[2]

[1] Artificial Intelligence in Work Systems, Federal Institute for Occupational Safety and Health, Dortmund, Germany
wilhelm.marco@baua.bund.de

[2] Faculty of Computer Science, TU Dortmund University, Dortmund, Germany
gabriele.kern-isberner@cs.tu-dortmund.de

Abstract. Conditional belief bases with ranking-function semantics provide a powerful framework for non-monotonic reasoning and belief revision. c-Representations and c-revisions based on conditional preservation satisfy strong rationality requirements, but generally admit multiple admissible models or revision operators. In this paper, we introduce core c-revisions, a subclass of c-revisions obtained by simplifying the underlying constraint systems. We show that core c-revisions inherit the desirable properties of general c-revisions, including compliance with the DP-postulates, while being stratified and computable via revision-aware tolerance partitions. This yields the existence of a minimal core c-revision, which allows us to define the first fully specified strategic c-revision operator selecting minimal revision outcomes.

Keywords: non-monotonic reasoning · conditionals · belief revision

1 Introduction

Reasoning with defeasible information is a central challenge in knowledge representation and reasoning and AI in general. Conditional statements of the form "if A, then usually B" offer a natural and expressive means to encode typicality knowledge, rules with exceptions, and causal regularities. Belief bases consisting of finite sets of such conditionals have therefore become an established formalism for modeling non-monotonic knowledge and belief change. A particularly influential semantic approach to conditionals is based on ranking functions, originally introduced by Spohn [17]. Ranking functions assign degrees of (im)plausibility to possible worlds and allow one to interpret conditionals in terms of comparative plausibility. Within this framework, c-representations provide a principled class of ranking functions that respect the principle of conditional preservation [10], ensuring that belief change minimally disturbs the agent's prior epistemic state. c-Representations have been shown to support a wide range of reasoning tasks, including non-monotonic inference and iterated belief revision [10, 14, 15].

D. Wolter and G. Schwalbe (Eds.): KI 2026, LNAI 16830, pp. 182–196, 2027.
https://doi.org/10.1007/978-3-032-32335-4_13

Belief revision in this setting is captured by c-revisions, which generalize c-representations to the revision of a prior ranking function by a new conditional belief base. Conceptually, c-revisions of ranking functions can be understood as a (semi-)qualitative analogue of revising probability distributions by probabilistic conditional information ("if A holds, then B follows with probability p") based on the principle of minimal cross-entropy [11]. They satisfy the postulates for iterated belief revision proposed by Darwiche and Pearl [5] and thus constitute a well-behaved and expressive revision framework. However, both c-representations and c-revisions suffer from a common limitation: in general, they form families of admissible ranking functions or revision operators, characterized by constraint satisfaction problems with multiple pareto-minimal solutions. As a consequence, they do not directly yield a unique epistemic state or revision outcome, which is often required in concrete applications. Recently, core c-representations have been introduced as a remedy for this problem in the static case of belief base modeling [18]. By simplifying the underlying constraint system, core c-representations retain the essential semantic properties of c-representations while guaranteeing the existence of a minimal model. Moreover, they admit a stratified computation based on tolerance partitions, closely related to System Z [16], significantly improving conceptual clarity and computational manageability.

In this paper, we lift these ideas to revision by introducing core c-revisions as a subclass of c-revisions that are obtained by an analogous simplification of the revision constraints. We show that core c-revisions form a proper subclass of c-revisions and inherit all their favorable properties. More importantly, we establish that core c-revisions are stratified and can be computed iteratively using revision-aware tolerance partitions. This stratification enables us to prove the existence of a minimal core c-revision for every revision task involving a finite ranking function and a consistent belief base. Based on this result, we define a strategic minimal core c-revision operator which deterministically selects the minimal core c-revision for each input. To the best of our knowledge, this is the first fully specified strategic c-revision operator proposed in the literature.

The rest of the paper is organized as follows. We recall preliminaries (Sect. 2) and core c-representations (Sect. 3), and introduce the concept of core c-revisions (Sect. 4). Afterwards, we analyze the computation of core c-revisions based on revision-aware tolerance partitions (Sect. 5) and introduce minimal core c-revision (Sect. 6). Eventually, we discuss constraint reductions and related work (Sect. 7), and conclude with an outlook (Sect. 8).

2 Preliminaries

Let $\mathcal{L}$ be the *propositional language* that is defined over a finite *signature* Σ by using the common *connectives* $\neg$, $\wedge$, and $\vee$. Elements in Σ are called *atoms*; atoms and their negations are called *literals*. For *propositions* $A, B \in \mathcal{L}$, we abbreviate $\neg A$ with $\overline{A}$ and $A \wedge B$ with AB, and we denote arbitrary *tautologies* $A \vee \overline{A}$ by $\top$. The semantics of $\mathcal{L}$ is as usual, with $\models$ denoting *classical entailment*.

A *conditional* $(B|A)$ with $A, B \in \mathcal{L}$ is a formal representation of the defeasible statement "if A, then usually B," where the meaning of 'usually' has to be clarified. Finite sets of conditionals serve as *belief bases.* A common way of defining the semantics of conditionals is via *ranking functions* over *possible worlds.* In this paper, a *possible world* ω is simply a propositional interpretation represented as a complete conjunction of those literals which are true in the interpretation. The set of all possible worlds is denoted by Ω.

A *ranking function* $\kappa\colon \Omega \to \mathbb{N}_0 \cup \{\infty\}$ maps possible worlds to (im)plausibility ranks while satisfying the normalization condition $\kappa^{-1}(0) \neq \emptyset$ [17]. The most plausible possible worlds are those with rank $\kappa(\omega) = 0$. We call a ranking function κ *finite* if $\kappa(\omega) < \infty$ for all $\omega \in \Omega$. A ranking function κ is extended to propositions $A \in \mathcal{L}$ via $\kappa(A) = \min_{\omega \in \Omega\colon \omega \models A} \kappa(\omega)$, where the convention $\min \emptyset = \infty$ applies. Further, κ *accepts* a conditional $(B|A)$ if $\kappa(AB) < \kappa(A\overline{B})$, i.e., if in the presence of A the conclusion B is more plausible than its negation. A ranking function κ *models* a belief base Δ if it accepts all conditionals in Δ. A belief base with at least one model is called *consistent.*

For convenience, we enumerate the conditionals in belief bases and associate $\Delta = \{\delta_1, \ldots, \delta_n\}$ with $\delta_i = (B_i|A_i)$ for $i = 1, \ldots, n$. Further, we denote the sets of possible worlds which *verify/falsify* a conditional $\delta = (B|A)$ with

$$\mathsf{v}(\delta) = \{\omega \in \Omega \mid \omega \models AB\}, \qquad \mathsf{f}(\delta) = \{\omega \in \Omega \mid \omega \models A\overline{B}\},$$

and the sets of conditionals from Δ which are *verified/falsified* in $\omega \in \Omega$ with

$$\mathsf{v}_\Delta(\omega) = \{\delta \in \Delta \mid \omega \in \mathsf{v}(\delta)\}, \qquad \mathsf{f}_\Delta(\omega) = \{\delta \in \Delta \mid \omega \in \mathsf{f}(\Delta)\}.$$

These notations are related to the *conditional structures* of possible worlds [10] and will simplify expressions in the context of c-representations and c-revisions.

c-Representations constitute a class of ranking functions that show outstanding properties w.r.t. various reasoning tasks such as drawing inferences and revising beliefs, because they follow the principle of conditional preservation [10]. The rationale behind this principle is that revising by new information should minimally disturb an agent's epistemic state ($\widehat{=}$ ranking function). A ranking function is a *c-representation* of a belief base Δ if it models Δ and is of the form

$$\kappa^{\boldsymbol{\eta}}_\Delta(\omega) = \sum\nolimits_{\delta_i \in \mathsf{f}_\Delta(\omega)} \eta_i, \quad \omega \in \Omega, \tag{1}$$

where $\boldsymbol{\eta} = (\eta_1, \ldots, \eta_n) \in \mathbb{N}_0^n$ is a so-called *impact vector* that penalizes possible worlds for falsifying conditionals from Δ. Note that c-representations are defined in a more general fashion in [10], but (1) is a very common derivation. In particular, a belief base is consistent if and only if it has a c-representation of the form (1). It is well-known (cf., e.g., [2]) that the impact vectors that lead to c-representations are exactly the non-negative integer solutions of the constraint satisfaction problem $\mathtt{CSP}(\Delta) = \{\mathcal{C}_1, \ldots, \mathcal{C}_n\}$ given by

$$\mathcal{C}_i\colon \eta_i > \min\nolimits_{\omega \in \mathsf{v}(\delta_i)} \mathcal{S}_i^{\boldsymbol{\eta}}(\omega) - \min\nolimits_{\omega \in \mathsf{f}(\delta_i)} \mathcal{S}_i^{\boldsymbol{\eta}}(\omega), \tag{2}$$

where $\mathcal{S}_i^{\eta}(\omega) = \sum_{\delta_j \in \mathsf{f}_\Delta(\omega)\setminus\{\delta_i\}} \eta_j$. The constraint $\mathcal{C}_i$ is the acceptance condition $\kappa_\Delta^{\eta}(A_iB_i) < \kappa_\Delta^{\eta}(A_i\overline{B_i})$ solved for η_i. A conditional $(B|A)$ can be inferred from a c-representation κ_Δ^{η}, written $\kappa_\Delta^{\eta} \mathrel{|\!\!\sim} (B|A)$, if $\kappa_\Delta^{\eta}(AB) < \kappa_\Delta^{\eta}(A\overline{B})$ or $\kappa_\Delta^{\eta}(A) = \infty$, which constitutes a non-monotonic inference relation.

Belief revision integrates new beliefs into belief bases or epistemic states. A *c-revision* $\kappa *^{\eta} \Delta$ of a ranking function κ by a belief base Δ is defined by

$$(\kappa *^{\eta} \Delta)(\omega) = \eta_0 + \kappa(\omega) + \sum\nolimits_{\delta_i \in \mathsf{f}_\Delta(\omega)} \eta_i, \quad \omega \in \Omega, \tag{3}$$

where $\boldsymbol{\eta} = (\eta_1, \ldots, \eta_n) \in \mathbb{N}_0^n$ has to solve the constraint satisfaction problem $\mathtt{CSP}(\kappa, \Delta) = \{\mathcal{C}_1^{\kappa}, \ldots, \mathcal{C}_n^{\kappa}\}$ given by

$$\mathcal{C}_i^{\kappa}: \eta_i > \min\nolimits_{\omega \in \mathsf{v}(\delta_i)}(\kappa(\omega) + \mathcal{S}_i^{\eta}(\omega)) - \min\nolimits_{\omega \in \mathsf{f}(\delta_i)}(\kappa(\omega) + \mathcal{S}_i^{\eta}(\omega)), \tag{4}$$

and η_0 is a normalization constant ensuring $\min_{\omega\in\Omega}(\kappa *^{\eta} \Delta)(\omega) = 0$. A *minimal c-revision* $\kappa *^{\eta_{\min}} \Delta$ is a c-revision using a pareto-minimal impact vector $\boldsymbol{\eta}_{\min}$. Since there can be several pareto-minimal impact vectors, minimal c-revisions are not uniquely defined in general.

For each tuple (κ, Δ) with κ finite and Δ consistent a c-revision $\kappa *^{\eta} \Delta$ exists. This follows from the fact that every consistent belief base has a c-representation and scaling impact vectors of c-representations with a constant factor leads to a c-representation again. We give a formal proof of this statement in the context of Proposition 2. Further, note that c-representations of belief bases Δ arise from c-revisions by revising the uniform ranking function κ_u by Δ, where κ_u is defined by $\kappa_u(\omega) = 0$ for all $\omega \in \Omega$. Notably, c-revisions satisfy the postulates for iterated belief revision proposed by Darwiche and Pearl [5], and both c-revisions and c-representations can be made compliant with syntax splitting [12,13].

3 Core c-Representations

In order to solve reasoning tasks it is a common strategy to select a single model of a belief base Δ. *Core c-representations* [18] constitute a subclass of c-representations that feature, among others, two properties that are especially beneficial for reasoning and suggest a solution to the model selection task: (a) While there is no unique minimal c-representation in general because of pareto-minimality between the impact factors, core c-representations provide a minimal model of Δ, both in terms of assigned (im)plausibility ranks and associated impact factors. Minimality is a common criterion for the selection of a model. (b) Core c-representations are stratified, i.e., the impact factors can be computed layer-wise without the need to solve the complex constraint satisfaction problem $\mathtt{CSP}(\Delta)$ at once which makes core c-representations more manageable than general c-representations.

The idea behind core c-representations is quite simple, and the definition of them is basically the same as the definition of c-representations. The only difference is that one removes the negative term in the constraints in (2).

Definition 1 (Core c-Representation). *Let $\Delta = \{\delta_1, \ldots, \delta_n\}$ be a belief base. Then a ranking function is called a* core c-representation *of Δ if it is of the form*

$$\kappa^{\eta}_{co,\Delta}(\omega) = \sum\nolimits_{\delta_i \in \mathsf{f}_\Delta(\omega)} \eta_i, \quad \omega \in \Omega,$$

where $\boldsymbol{\eta} = (\eta_1, \ldots, \eta_n) \in \mathbb{N}_0^n$ solves the constraint satisfaction problem

$$\mathtt{CSP}_{co}(\Delta) = \{\mathcal{C}_{co,1}, \ldots, \mathcal{C}_{co,n}\}, \qquad \mathcal{C}_{co,i}\colon \eta_i > \min\nolimits_{\omega \in \mathsf{v}(\delta_i)} \mathcal{S}_i^{\eta}(\omega). \tag{5}$$

In [18] it is shown that core c-representations of Δ are indeed c-representations of Δ and, in particular, models of Δ. Further, Δ is consistent if and only if Δ has a core c-representation. Notably, there is a unique minimal non-negative integer solution $\boldsymbol{\eta}_{\min}$ of $\mathtt{CSP}_{co}(\Delta)$ leading to the minimal core c-representation $\kappa^{\eta_{\min}}_{co,\Delta}$ of Δ with $\kappa^{\eta_{\min}}_{co,\Delta}(\omega) \leq \kappa^{\eta}_{co,\Delta}(\omega)$ for all $\omega \in \Omega$ and all core c-representations $\kappa^{\eta}_{co,\Delta}$ of Δ. In this sense, the minimal core c-representation is the most cautious ranking function among all core c-representations of Δ, assigning no (im)plausibility ranks higher than necessary.

Table 1. Verification/falsification of the conditionals in Δ_{ex1} and Δ_{ex2}, minimal core c-representation κ_{ex1} (cf. Example 1), minimal core c-revision κ_{ex2} (cf. Example 2 and Example 6), and a minimal c-revision κ_{ex3} for sake of comparison (cf. Example 6).

ω	$\mathsf{v}_{\Delta_{\mathsf{ex1}}}(\omega)$	$\mathsf{f}_{\Delta_{\mathsf{ex1}}}(\omega)$	$\kappa_{\mathsf{ex1}}(\omega)$	$\mathsf{v}_{\Delta_{\mathsf{ex2}}}(\omega)$	$\mathsf{f}_{\Delta_{\mathsf{ex2}}}(\omega)$	$\kappa_{\mathsf{ex2}}(\omega)$	$\kappa_{\mathsf{ex3}}(\omega)$
$cdpx$	$\{\delta_1,\delta_2,\delta_3\}$	$\{\delta_4\}$	1	$\{\delta_2\}$	$\{\delta_1,\delta_3\}$	5	3
$cdp\overline{x}$	$\{\delta_1,\delta_3,\delta_4\}$	$\{\}$	0	$\{\delta_1,\delta_4\}$	$\{\delta_2\}$	4	3
$cd\overline{p}x$	$\{\delta_1,\delta_2,\delta_3\}$	$\{\delta_4\}$	1	$\{\}$	$\{\delta_3\}$	4	3
$cd\overline{p}\overline{x}$	$\{\delta_1,\delta_3,\delta_4\}$	$\{\}$	0	$\{\}$	$\{\}$	0	0
$c\overline{d}px$	$\{\delta_2\}$	$\{\delta_3,\delta_4\}$	2	$\{\delta_2,\delta_3\}$	$\{\delta_1\}$	3	2
$c\overline{d}p\overline{x}$	$\{\delta_4\}$	$\{\delta_3\}$	1	$\{\delta_1\}$	$\{\delta_2,\delta_4\}$	10	4
$c\overline{d}\overline{p}x$	$\{\delta_2\}$	$\{\delta_3,\delta_4\}$	2	$\{\delta_3\}$	$\{\}$	2	2
$c\overline{d}\overline{p}\overline{x}$	$\{\delta_4\}$	$\{\delta_3\}$	1	$\{\}$	$\{\}$	1	1
$\overline{c}dpx$	$\{\}$	$\{\delta_1,\delta_2\}$	3	$\{\}$	$\{\delta_1,\delta_3\}$	7	5
$\overline{c}dp\overline{x}$	$\{\}$	$\{\delta_1\}$	1	$\{\delta_1\}$	$\{\}$	1	1
$\overline{c}d\overline{p}x$	$\{\}$	$\{\delta_1,\delta_2\}$	3	$\{\}$	$\{\delta_3\}$	6	5
$\overline{c}d\overline{p}\overline{x}$	$\{\}$	$\{\delta_1\}$	1	$\{\}$	$\{\}$	1	1
$\overline{c}\overline{d}px$	$\{\}$	$\{\delta_2\}$	2	$\{\delta_3\}$	$\{\delta_1\}$	3	2
$\overline{c}\overline{d}p\overline{x}$	$\{\}$	$\{\}$	0	$\{\delta_1\}$	$\{\}$	0	0
$\overline{c}\overline{d}\overline{p}x$	$\{\}$	$\{\delta_2\}$	2	$\{\delta_3\}$	$\{\}$	2	2
$\overline{c}\overline{d}\overline{p}\overline{x}$	$\{\}$	$\{\}$	0	$\{\}$	$\{\}$	0	0

Example 1. An occupational physician has the following typical knowledge: Dust exposure (d) usually leads to cough (c), like chemical exposure (x) does. The

other way around, cough usually indicates dust exposure, while cough does not normally indicate chemical exposure, especially if there is no specific information about the place of exposure, like whether it happened in a paint shop (p) or not. The knowledge of the occupational physician can be represented by the belief base $\Delta_{\mathsf{ex1}} = \{\delta_1, \ldots, \delta_4\}$ with $\delta_1 = (c|d)$, $\delta_2 = (c|x)$, $\delta_3 = (d|c)$, $\delta_4 = (\overline{x}|c)$. The minimal core c-representation of Δ_{ex1} is given by the impact vector $\boldsymbol{\eta}_{\mathsf{ex1}} = (1, 2, 1, 1)$, which is the minimal non-negative integer solution of $\mathtt{CSP}_{co}(\Delta_{\mathsf{ex1}})$ consisting of

$$\begin{aligned} \mathcal{C}_{co,1}&\colon \eta_1 > \min\{0, \eta_4\} &&= 0, & \mathcal{C}_{co,3}&\colon \eta_3 > \min\{0, \eta_4\} = 0,\\ \mathcal{C}_{co,2}&\colon \eta_2 > \min\{\eta_3 + \eta_4, \eta_4\} &&= \eta_4, & \mathcal{C}_{co,4}&\colon \eta_4 > \min\{0, \eta_3\} = 0. \end{aligned}$$

See Table 1 for information about the verification and falsification of the conditionals in Δ_{ex1} and the minimal core c-representation $\kappa_{\mathsf{ex1}} = \kappa^{\eta_{\mathsf{ex1}}}_{co,\Delta_{\mathsf{ex1}}}$ of Δ_{ex1}.

Being special c-representations, core c-representations inherit various beneficial inference properties from general c-representations. In particular, they comply with (conditional) syntax splitting and do not suffer from the *drowning problem* [8]. The drowning problem occurs when an exception to one default property of a subclass incorrectly prevents the inheritance of other, non-conflicting default properties from a superclass. In addition, core c-representations show a close resemblance to System Z [16] because they can be constructed from so-called tolerance partitions of Δ, which is also the reason for their stratification. An ordered partition $(\Delta_1, \ldots, \Delta_m)$ of Δ is a *tolerance partition* of Δ if, for $i = 1, \ldots, m$, every conditional in Δ_i is tolerated by $\Delta' = \bigcup_{j \geq i} \Delta_j$, where a conditional δ is *tolerated* by a set of conditionals Δ' if there is a possible world $\omega \in \Omega$ with $\omega \in \mathsf{v}(\delta)$ and $\mathsf{f}_{\Delta}(\omega) \cap \Delta' = \emptyset$, i.e., which verifies δ and falsifies no conditional from Δ'. Once a tolerance partition $(\Delta_1, \ldots, \Delta_m)$ of Δ—which always exists—is constructed, core c-representations can be computed by solving the constraints referring to the conditionals in the first tolerance partition Δ_1 at first and iterating through the other tolerance partitions afterwards. The minimal core c-representation, specifying the impact factors as minimal as possible, can be computed based on a specific tolerance partition as elaborated in [18].

4 Core c-Revisions

Similar to c-representations constituting a class of ranking functions, c-revisions constitute a class of revision operators with no unique minimal representative. For executing revision tasks it is necessary to fix a single revision operator though. For this, we introduce the subclass of *core c-revisions* and show that this subclass provides a minimal core c-revision. This allows us to define a *strategic c-revision operator* selecting for each belief base its minimal core c-revision, which is, to the best of our knowledge, the first concrete strategic c-revision operator published so far.

Definition 2 (Selection Strategy, Strategic c-Revision [15]). *A* selection strategy for c-revisions *is a mapping* $\sigma\colon (\kappa, \Delta) \mapsto \boldsymbol{\eta}$ *that assigns to each pair of a* *finite ranking function* κ *and a consistent belief base* $\Delta = \{\delta_1, \ldots, \delta_n\}$ *an impact vector* $\boldsymbol{\eta} \in \mathbb{N}_0^n$ *that solves* $\mathsf{CSP}(\kappa, \Delta)$*. If* $\boldsymbol{\eta} = \sigma(\kappa, \Delta)$ *for a selection strategy* σ*, then we denote the c-revision of* κ *by* Δ *w.r.t.* $\boldsymbol{\eta}$ *with* $\kappa *_\sigma \Delta$*. We call* $*_\sigma$ *a* strategic c-revision operator.

Strategic c-revisions ensure that the specific revision operator that is selected for a tuple (κ, Δ) is based on strategical considerations and not chosen randomly across different inputs. We introduce and analyze core c-revisions in order to approach a specific strategic c-revision operator.

Definition 3 (Core c-Revision). *Let* κ *be a ranking function and* Δ *a belief base. Then* $\kappa *_{co}^{\boldsymbol{\eta}} \Delta$ *is a core c-revision of* κ *by* Δ *if*

$$(\kappa *_{co}^{\boldsymbol{\eta}} \Delta)(\omega) = \eta_0 + \kappa(\omega) + \sum\nolimits_{\delta_i \in \mathsf{f}_\Delta(\omega)} \eta_i, \quad \omega \in \Omega,$$

where η_0 *is a normalization constant ensuring* $\min_{\omega \in \Omega}(\kappa *_{co}^{\boldsymbol{\eta}} \Delta)(\omega) = 0$*, and* $\boldsymbol{\eta} = (\eta_1, \ldots, \eta_n) \in \mathbb{N}_0^n$ *with* $n = |\Delta|$ *solves the constraint satisfaction problem*

$$\mathsf{CSP}_{co}(\kappa, \Delta) = \{\mathcal{C}_{co,1}^{\kappa}, \ldots, \mathcal{C}_{co,n}^{\kappa}\}, \quad \mathcal{C}_{co,i}^{\kappa} \colon \eta_i > \min\nolimits_{\omega \in \mathsf{v}(\delta_i)}(\kappa(\omega) + \mathcal{S}_i^{\boldsymbol{\eta}}(\omega)). \quad (6)$$

Obviously, the definition of core c-revisions is analogous to the definition of c-revisions, only the negative parts in the constraints are removed (compare (6) to (4)). It is easy to see that the impact vector $\boldsymbol{\eta}$ of a core c-revision $\kappa *_{co}^{\boldsymbol{\eta}} \Delta$ is positive, i.e., $\boldsymbol{\eta} \in \mathbb{N}_{>0}^n$, because the RHS of the constraints in (6) is at least 0. We continue Example 1 to illustrate the concept of core c-revision.

Example 2. The occupational physician from Example 1 has been asked to consult a company which distributes paint. She revises her epistemic state accordingly with the following domain-specific knowledge: Working in a paint shop alone usually does not indicate chemical exposure, while working in a paint shop and having a cough together usually do. Chemical exposure usually excludes dust exposure. If a worker was in the paint shop, has a cough, but no chemical exposure, the cause is usually dust exposure in turn. This knowledge can be formalized by $\Delta_{\mathsf{ex2}} = \{\delta_1, \ldots, \delta_4\}$ with $\delta_1 = (\overline{x}|p)$, $\delta_2 = (x|pc)$, $\delta_3 = (\overline{d}|x)$, $\delta_4 = (d|pc\overline{x})$. The constraint satisfaction problem $\mathsf{CSP}(\kappa_{\mathsf{ex1}}, \Delta_{\mathsf{ex2}})$, which has the impact vectors of the core c-revisions of κ_{ex1} by Δ_{ex2} as its solutions, is (cf. Table 1)

$$\begin{array}{ll} \mathcal{C}_{co,1}^{\kappa_{\mathsf{ex1}}} \colon \eta_1 > \min\{0, 1, \eta_2, 1 + \eta_2 + \eta_4\} = 0, & \mathcal{C}_{co,3}^{\kappa_{\mathsf{ex1}}} \colon \eta_3 > \min\{2, 2 + \eta_1\} = 2, \\ \mathcal{C}_{co,2}^{\kappa_{\mathsf{ex1}}} \colon \eta_2 > \min\{1 + \eta_1 + \eta_3, 2 + \eta_1\}, & \mathcal{C}_{co,4}^{\kappa_{\mathsf{ex1}}} \colon \eta_4 > \min\{\eta_2\} = \eta_2. \end{array} \quad (7)$$

A solution of $\mathsf{CSP}(\kappa_{\mathsf{ex1}}, \Delta_{\mathsf{ex2}})$ is $\boldsymbol{\eta}_{\mathsf{ex2}} = (1, 4, 3, 5)$. The revised ranking function $\kappa_{\mathsf{ex2}} = \kappa_{\mathsf{ex1}} *_{co}^{\boldsymbol{\eta}_{\mathsf{ex2}}} \Delta_{\mathsf{ex2}}$ can be found in Table 1. Note that $\eta_0 = 0$ in this case. While before and after the revision the occupational physician is able to infer both $(d|c)$ and $(\overline{x}|c)$ ("Cough usually indicates dust exposure but not chemical exposure.") based on her epistemic states as formalized in Table 1, the situation changes in the context of print shops. Before the revision, the work environment has no influence on the inferences of the occupational physician, i.e., $\kappa_{\mathsf{ex1}} \mathrel{|\!\sim} (\overline{x}|pc)$ and $\kappa_{\mathsf{ex1}} \mathrel{|\!\sim} (d|pc)$, but after the revision she infers that working in a paint shop and having a cough together usually indicates chemical exposure, $\kappa_{\mathsf{ex2}} \mathrel{|\!\sim} (x|pc)$, but not dust exposure, $\kappa_{\mathsf{ex2}} \mathrel{|\!\sim} (\overline{d}|pc)$.

The next proposition shows that core c-revisions indeed constitute a subclass of c-revisions. Consequently, core c-revisions inherit all the beneficial properties from c-revisions. In particular, core c-revisions satisfy the postulates for iterated belief revision of Darwiche and Pearl [5].

Proposition 1. *Let κ be a ranking function and Δ a belief base. If $\kappa' = (\kappa *_{co}^{\eta} \Delta)$ is a core c-revision of κ by Δ, then κ' is also a c-revision of κ by Δ.*

Proof. By assumption, $\boldsymbol{\eta} = (\eta_1, \ldots, \eta_n) \in \mathbb{N}_0^n$ satisfies (6) for $i = 1, \ldots, n$. Then, for all $s_i \in \mathbb{N}_0$, $\eta_i > \min_{\omega \in \mathsf{v}(\delta_i)}(\kappa(\omega) + \mathcal{S}_i^{\boldsymbol{\eta}}(\omega)) - s_i$ holds as well. With $s_i = \min_{\omega \in \mathsf{f}(\delta_i)}(\kappa(\omega) + \mathcal{S}_i^{\boldsymbol{\eta}}(\omega))$ for $i = 1, \ldots, n$, it follows that $\boldsymbol{\eta}$ satisfies (4), and $\kappa *_{co}^{\boldsymbol{\eta}} \Delta$ is a c-revision of κ by Δ. □

For consistent input, core c-revisions always exist.

Proposition 2. *Let κ be a finite ranking function and Δ a consistent belief base. Then a core c-revision $\kappa *_{co}^{\boldsymbol{\eta}} \Delta$ of κ by Δ exists.*

Proof. Because Δ is consistent, there is a core c-representation $\kappa_{co,\Delta}^{\boldsymbol{\eta}}$ of Δ. By adding 1 to the RHS of the constraints in (5), we get $\eta_i \geq 1 + \min_{\omega \in \mathsf{v}(\delta_i)} \mathcal{S}_i^{\boldsymbol{\eta}}(\omega)$, $i = 1, \ldots, n$. Let $s = \max\{\kappa(\omega) \mid \omega \in \Omega\} + 1$, which exists because the ranking function κ is finite. Then, for $i = 1, \ldots, n$,

$$
\begin{aligned}
s \cdot \eta_i &\geq s \cdot (1 + \min_{\omega \in \mathsf{v}(\delta_i)} (\sum_{\delta_j \in \mathsf{f}_\Delta(\omega) \setminus \delta_i} \eta_j)) = \min_{\omega \in \mathsf{v}(\delta_i)} (s + \sum_{\delta_j \in \mathsf{f}_\Delta(\omega) \setminus \delta_i} s \cdot \eta_j) \\
&\geq \min_{\omega \in \mathsf{v}(\delta_i)} ((\kappa(\omega) + 1) + \sum_{\delta_j \in \mathsf{f}_\Delta(\omega) \setminus \delta_i} s \cdot \eta_j) > \min_{\omega \in \mathsf{v}(\delta_i)} (\kappa(\omega) + \sum_{\delta_j \in \mathsf{f}_\Delta(\omega) \setminus \delta_i} s \cdot \eta_j).
\end{aligned}
$$

Hence, $\kappa *_{co}^{\boldsymbol{\eta}'} \Delta$ with $\boldsymbol{\eta}' = (s \cdot \eta_1, \ldots, s \cdot \eta_n) \in \mathbb{N}_0^n$ is a core c-revision of κ by Δ. □

From Proposition 2 it follows with Proposition 1 that, for consistent input, also general c-revisions always exist. This ensures that strategic c-revisions are well-defined by Definition 2. Note that this would also hold if one restricts Definition 2 to core c-revisions.

5 Computation of Core c-Revisions

Similar to core c-representations, core c-revisions are stratified and can be computed iteratively based on specific tolerance partitions. The idea is to compute the impact factors of the conditionals with which an epistemic state is revised layer-wise, beginning with the conditionals in the first partitioning set in the tolerance partition and iterating through the other partitioning sets afterwards. For this, we introduce the concepts of *revision-aware base functions* and *revision-aware tolerance partitions*.

Definition 4 (Revision-Aware Base Function). *Let κ be a finite ranking function, $\Delta = \{\delta_1, \ldots, \delta_n\}$ a consistent belief base, $\mathcal{T}(\Delta) = (\Delta_1, \ldots, \Delta_m)$ a tolerance partition of Δ, and $\boldsymbol{\eta} \in \mathbb{N}^n_{>0}$. Then, for $i = 1, \ldots, n$, and with Δ_{k_i} being the partitioning set in $\mathcal{T}(\Delta)$ with $\delta_i \in \Delta_{k_i}$,*

$$\phi^{\kappa,\boldsymbol{\eta}}_{\mathcal{T}(\Delta)}(\delta_i) = \min_{\substack{\omega \in \mathsf{v}(\delta_i) \\ \mathsf{f}_\Delta(\omega) \cap (\bigcup_{j \geq k_i} \Delta_j) = \emptyset}} (\kappa(\omega) + \mathcal{S}^{\boldsymbol{\eta}}_i(\omega)) \quad \in \mathbb{N}_0$$

is the revision-aware base function *w.r.t. κ, $\boldsymbol{\eta}$, and $\mathcal{T}(\Delta)$.*

The expression $\phi^{\kappa,\boldsymbol{\eta}}_{\mathcal{T}(\Delta)}(\delta_i)$ is the RHS of the constraint $\mathcal{C}^{\kappa}_{co,i}$ (cf. (6)) where the minimum is restricted to the possible worlds that prove tolerance of δ_i w.r.t. $\bigcup_{j \geq k_i} \Delta_j$. Thus, $\phi^{\kappa,\boldsymbol{\eta}}_{\mathcal{T}(\Delta)}(\delta_i)$ depends on conditionals in previous partitioning sets $\Delta_j \in \mathcal{T}(\Delta)$ with $j < k_i$ only. We give an example.

Example 3. We recall the belief base Δ_{ex2} from Example 2. A tolerance partition of Δ_{ex2} is $\mathcal{T}(\Delta_{\mathsf{ex2}}) = (\Delta_1, \Delta_2, \Delta_3)$ with $\Delta_1 = \{(\overline{x}|p), (\overline{d}|x)\}$, $\Delta_2 = \{(x|pc)\}$, and $\Delta_3 = \{(d|pc\overline{x})\}$. The respective revision-aware base function w.r.t. κ_{ex1} (cf. Example 1) and an arbitrary but fixed impact vector $\boldsymbol{\eta}$ is

$$\phi^{\kappa_{\mathsf{ex1}},\boldsymbol{\eta}}_{\mathcal{T}(\Delta_{\mathsf{ex2}})}(\delta_1) = \min\{0, 1\} = 0, \qquad \phi^{\kappa_{\mathsf{ex1}},\boldsymbol{\eta}}_{\mathcal{T}(\Delta_{\mathsf{ex2}})}(\delta_2) = \min\{1 + \eta_1 + \eta_3, 2 + \eta_1\},$$
$$\phi^{\kappa_{\mathsf{ex1}},\boldsymbol{\eta}}_{\mathcal{T}(\Delta_{\mathsf{ex2}})}(\delta_3) = 2, \qquad \phi^{\kappa_{\mathsf{ex1}},\boldsymbol{\eta}}_{\mathcal{T}(\Delta_{\mathsf{ex2}})}(\delta_4) = \eta_2.$$

Differences to the RHS of the constraints in (7) can be observed in the expressions for δ_1 and δ_3. In these cases, the revision-aware base function removes irrelevant terms from the minima that origin from possible worlds which falsify conditionals from partitioning sets in $\mathcal{T}(\Delta_{\mathsf{ex2}})$ with a higher index. By replacing the RHS of the constraints in (7) by the respective revision-aware base function, one can simplify the constraints and make them iteratively solvable. However, one has to be careful by doing so as one may lose solutions by this substitution in other examples: Assume that the κ_{ex1}-rank of the possible world $\omega = \overline{c}\overline{d}\overline{p}x$ is 4 instead of 2 for some reason so that $\mathcal{C}^{\kappa_{\mathsf{ex1}}}_{co,3}$ becomes $\eta_3 > \min\{4, 2 + \eta_1\}$. Removing the term $2 + \eta_1$ from this constraint would prevent solutions with $\eta_3 = 4$. The way out of this issue is to combine the use of revision-aware base functions with a sophisticated exploitation of the minima-expressions when setting up the tolerance partition in order to be able to compute *every* core c-revision.

Based on the notion of revision-aware base functions and our findings in Example 3, we define *revision-aware tolerance partitions.* These tolerance partitions integrate tolerated conditionals in the next partitioning set if and only if the value of the revision-aware base function is minimal for these conditionals compared to the other tolerated conditionals.

Definition 5 (Revision-Aware Tolerance Partition). *Let κ be a finite ranking function, $\Delta = \{\delta_1, \ldots, \delta_n\}$ a consistent belief base, and $\boldsymbol{\eta} \in \mathbb{N}^n_{>0}$. Then $\mathcal{T}^{\kappa,\boldsymbol{\eta}}(\Delta) = (\Delta_1, \ldots, \Delta_m)$ is the (unique)* revision-aware tolerance partition *of Δ w.r.t. κ and $\boldsymbol{\eta}$ if, for $k = 1, \ldots, m$,*

$$\Delta_k = \arg\min\{\phi^{\kappa,\boldsymbol{\eta}}_{\mathcal{T}^{\kappa,\boldsymbol{\eta}}(\Delta)}(\delta_i) \mid \delta_i \in \tau_k(\Delta)\}, \tag{8}$$

where $\tau_k(\Delta)$ is the set of conditionals from $\Delta' = \Delta \setminus (\bigcup_{j<k} \Delta_j)$ tolerated by Δ'.

Revision-aware tolerance partitions are well-defined although their definition refers to itself. This holds because in order to compute $\phi^{\kappa,\boldsymbol{\eta}}_{\mathcal{T}^{\kappa,\eta}(\Delta)}(\delta_i)$ in (8) the tolerance partition $\mathcal{T}^{\kappa,\boldsymbol{\eta}}(\Delta)$ has to be known up to index $k-1$ only.

Example 4. We revisit Example 3. Let $\boldsymbol{\eta}$ be an arbitrary but fixed impact vector. The conditionals δ_1 and δ_3 are tolerated by Δ_{ex2} and are evaluated by the revision-aware base function $\phi = \phi^{\kappa_{\mathsf{ex1}},\boldsymbol{\eta}}_{\mathcal{T}^{\kappa_{\mathsf{ex1}},\eta}(\Delta_{\mathsf{ex2}})}$ to $\phi(\delta_1) = \min\{0,1\} = 0$ and $\phi(\delta_3) = \min\{2\} = 2$. Because $\phi(\delta_1) < \phi(\delta_3)$, only δ_1 is selected for the first partitioning set Δ_1 of $\mathcal{T}^{\kappa_{\mathsf{ex1}},\boldsymbol{\eta}}(\Delta_{\mathsf{ex2}})$. Then, δ_2 and δ_3 are tolerated by $\Delta_{\mathsf{ex2}} \setminus \Delta_1$ and $\phi(\delta_2) = \min\{2+\eta_1\}$ and $\phi(\delta_3) = 2$. Because $\eta_1 > 0$, one has $\phi(\delta_3) < \phi(\delta_2)$ and δ_3 is selected for Δ_2. After that, only δ_2 is tolerated, so that $\mathcal{T}^{\kappa_{\mathsf{ex1}},\boldsymbol{\eta}}(\Delta_{\mathsf{ex2}}) = (\Delta_1, \ldots, \Delta_4)$ with $\Delta_1 = \{\delta_1\}$, $\Delta_2 = \{\delta_3\}$, $\Delta_3 = \{\delta_2\}$, and $\Delta_4 = \{\delta_4\}$.

At first glance, Definition 5 seems to be insufficient for computing core c-revisions because it takes the impact vector $\boldsymbol{\eta}$ as an input while the goal of computing core c-revisions is precisely to compute $\boldsymbol{\eta}$. This 'insufficiency' can be overcome by computing $\mathcal{T}^{\kappa,\boldsymbol{\eta}}(\Delta)$ and $\boldsymbol{\eta}$ in alternation though.

Example 5. Example 4 worked for every choice of $\boldsymbol{\eta}$, so there was no need to fix it beforehand. Apart from this, in general, after the computation of each partitioning set, it would have been possible to fix the impact factors of the conditionals that have been allocated to this partitioning set. For instance, after determining $\Delta_1 = \{\delta_1\}$, we could have set $\eta_1 = 1 > 0 = \phi(\delta_1)$. With this, $\phi(\delta_2)$ had become $\phi(\delta_2) = \min\{2+\eta_1\} = 3$ and so on. At every step, the revision-aware base function would have been completely known for all relevant (tolerated) conditionals.

The following theorem proves that the procedure from Example 5 always works and it is possible to compute with revision-aware base functions in combination with revision-aware tolerance partitions every core c-revision.

Theorem 1. *Let κ be a finite ranking function, $\Delta = \{\delta_1, \ldots, \delta_n\}$ a consistent belief base, and $\boldsymbol{\eta} \in \mathbb{N}^n_{>0}$. Then $\kappa *^{\boldsymbol{\eta}}_{co} \Delta$ is a core c-revision of κ by Δ iff*

$$\eta_i > \phi^{\kappa,\boldsymbol{\eta}}_{\mathcal{T}^{\kappa,\eta}(\Delta)}(\delta_i), \quad i = 1, \ldots, n. \tag{9}$$

Proof. The if-direction holds because $\phi^{\kappa,\boldsymbol{\eta}}_{\mathcal{T}^{\kappa,\eta}(\Delta)}(\delta_i) \geq \min_{\omega \in \mathsf{v}(\delta_i)}(\kappa(\omega) + \mathcal{S}^{\boldsymbol{\eta}}_i(\omega))$ for all finite ranking functions κ, all $\boldsymbol{\eta} \in \mathbb{N}^n_{>0}$, and all $i = 1, \ldots, n$. This is because the only difference between both sides of the inequation is that the minimum is built over a subset of possible worlds in the revision-aware base function.

For the other direction we have to show that there is no $\omega' \in \mathsf{v}(\delta_i)$ with $\mathsf{f}_\Delta(\omega') \cap (\bigcup_{j \geq k_i} \Delta_j) \neq \emptyset$ and

$$\kappa(\omega') + \mathcal{S}^{\boldsymbol{\eta}}_i(\omega') < \phi^{\kappa,\boldsymbol{\eta}}_{\mathcal{T}^{\kappa,\eta}(\Delta)}(\delta_i). \tag{10}$$

We do this by contradiction and assume that there is such a possible world ω'. Consequently, there is $\delta_l \in \bigcup_{j \geq k_i} \Delta_j$ which is falsified by ω'. In particular, $\delta_l \neq \delta_i$, because δ_i is verified by ω'. We may assume $\omega' \in \arg\min_{\omega \in \mathsf{v}(\delta_i)}(\kappa(\omega)+\mathcal{S}_i^{\boldsymbol{\eta}}(\omega))$ because no $\omega' \in \mathsf{v}(\delta_i)$ with $\mathsf{f}_\Delta(\omega') \cap (\bigcup_{j \geq k_i} \Delta_j) = \emptyset$ can satisfy (10) as ω' would be considered by the revision-aware base function on the RHS of (10) then. Hence, $\eta_i > \min_{\omega \in \mathsf{v}(\delta_i)}(\kappa(\omega) + \mathcal{S}_i^{\boldsymbol{\eta}}(\omega)) \geq \kappa(\omega') + \eta_l \geq \eta_l$. The conditional δ_l is in the same partitioning set as δ_i, i.e., in Δ_{k_i}, or in a partitioning set with a higher index, and we can pursue the same line of argument for δ_l as for δ_i. That is, we may assume that there is no $\omega' \in \mathsf{v}(\delta_l)$ with $\mathsf{f}_\Delta(\omega') \cap (\bigcup_{j \geq k_l} \Delta_j) \neq \emptyset$ and $\kappa(\omega') + \mathcal{S}_i^{\boldsymbol{\eta}}(\omega') < \phi^{\kappa,\boldsymbol{\eta}}_{\mathcal{T}^{\kappa,\boldsymbol{\eta}}(\Delta)}(\delta_l)$ (cf. (10)), and proceed in the same way as above. This eventually leads to the existence of $\delta_{l'} \in \bigcup_{j \geq k_l} \Delta_j$ with $\eta_l > \eta_{l'}$. By repeating this argumentation, we observe a descending chain of impact factors $\eta_i > \eta_l > \eta_{l'} > \ldots$ Because Δ is finite, at some point there must occur an impact factor η_h in this chain which has been in the chain already before. This results in the contradiction $\eta_h > \eta_h$. □

Eventually, in the next section we will use the concept of revision-aware tolerance partitions to compute *minimal* core c-revisions.

6 Minimal Core c-Revisions

The stratification of core c-revisions implies that there is a minimal core c-revision $\kappa *_{co}^{\boldsymbol{\eta}} \Delta$ for κ and Δ that can be obtained by choosing the impact vector $\boldsymbol{\eta}$ as minimally as possible. Because of the equivalence between the solutions of (9) and the impact vectors of core c-revisions, it is possible to simply set $\eta_i = \phi^{\kappa,\boldsymbol{\eta}}_{\mathcal{T}^{\kappa,\boldsymbol{\eta}}(\Delta)}(\delta_i) + 1$ for $i = 1, \ldots, n$.

Definition 6 (Minimal Core c-Revision). *Let κ be a finite ranking function and $\Delta = \{\delta_1, \ldots, \delta_n\}$ a consistent belief base. Then $\kappa *_{co}^{\boldsymbol{\eta}} \Delta$ is the* minimal core c-revision *of κ by Δ if $\boldsymbol{\eta} \in \mathbb{N}^n_{>0}$ satisfies $\eta_i = \phi^{\kappa,\boldsymbol{\eta}}_{\mathcal{T}^{\kappa,\boldsymbol{\eta}}(\Delta)}(\delta_i) + 1$ for $i = 1, \ldots, n$. We denote the impact vector of the minimal core c-revision with $\boldsymbol{\eta}_{\min}$.*

According to Theorem 1, $\kappa *_{co}^{\boldsymbol{\eta}_{\min}} \Delta$ is a core c-revision of κ by Δ. It remains to show that $\kappa *_{co}^{\boldsymbol{\eta}_{\min}} \Delta$ is indeed minimal.

Theorem 2. *Let κ be a finite ranking function and $\Delta = \{\delta_1, \ldots, \delta_n\}$ a consistent belief base. Further, let $\boldsymbol{\eta}_{\min} = (\eta_1, \ldots, \eta_n)$ be the impact vector of the minimal core c-revision of κ by Δ and $\boldsymbol{\eta}' = (\eta'_1, \ldots, \eta'_n)$ the impact vector of an arbitrary but fixed core c-revision of κ by Δ. Then $\eta_i \leq \eta'_i$ for $i = 1, \ldots, n$.*

Proof. Assume $\eta'_i < \eta_i$ for some $i = 1, \ldots, n$. Then, there is a minimal index k of a partitioning set in $\mathcal{T}^{\kappa,\boldsymbol{\eta}'}(\Delta)$ with Δ_k such that there is a conditional $\delta_i \in \Delta_k$ with $\eta'_i < \eta_i$. In particular, the tolerance partitions $\mathcal{T}^{\kappa,\boldsymbol{\eta}'}(\Delta)$ and $\mathcal{T}^{\kappa,\boldsymbol{\eta}_{\min}}(\Delta)$ agree up to index $k-1$. Because $\delta_i \in \Delta_k$, the conditional δ_i must be tolerated by $\Delta \backslash (\bigcup_{j<k} \Delta_j)$ and has to minimize $\{\phi^{\kappa,\boldsymbol{\eta}'}_{\mathcal{T}^{\kappa,\boldsymbol{\eta}'}(\Delta)}(\delta_i) \mid \delta_i \in \tau_k(\Delta)\}$ (cf. Definition 5). But then δ_i must be in Δ_k of $\mathcal{T}^{\kappa,\boldsymbol{\eta}_{\min}}(\Delta)$ and $\phi^{\kappa,\boldsymbol{\eta}'}_{\mathcal{T}^{\kappa,\boldsymbol{\eta}'}(\Delta)}(\delta_i) = \phi^{\kappa,\boldsymbol{\eta}_{\min}}_{\mathcal{T}^{\kappa,\boldsymbol{\eta}_{\min}}(\Delta)}(\delta_i)$ has

to hold, too. As a consequence, $\eta_i = \phi^{\kappa,\boldsymbol{\eta}_{\min}}_{\mathcal{T}^{\kappa,\boldsymbol{\eta}_{\min}}(\Delta)}(\delta_i)+1 = \phi^{\kappa,\boldsymbol{\eta}'}_{\mathcal{T}^{\kappa,\boldsymbol{\eta}'}(\Delta)}(\delta_i)+1 \leq \eta'_i$, which contradicts the assumption. □

Theorem 2 particularly states that there is no pareto-minimality between impact vectors of core c-revisions but $\boldsymbol{\eta}_{\min}$ is the least element. This implies that $\kappa *^{\boldsymbol{\eta}_{\min}}_{co} \Delta$ is a core c-revision of κ by Δ which assigns the new (im)plausibility ranks to the possible worlds in Ω in a minimal way.

Corollary 1. *Let κ be a finite ranking function, Δ a consistent belief base, and $\kappa *^{\boldsymbol{\eta}}_{co} \Delta$ a core c-revision of κ by Δ. Then $(\kappa *^{\boldsymbol{\eta}_{\min}}_{co} \Delta)(\omega) \leq (\kappa *^{\boldsymbol{\eta}}_{co} \Delta)(\omega)$, $\omega \in \Omega$.*

We give an example.

Example 6. The tolerance partition computed in Example 4 together with the impact vector $\boldsymbol{\eta}_{\mathsf{ex2}} = (1, 4, 3, 5)$ (cf. Example 2) constitute the minimal core c-revision of κ_{ex1} by Δ_{ex2}, i.e., $\kappa_{\mathsf{ex1}} *_{\mathtt{mc}} \Delta_{\mathsf{ex2}} = \kappa_{\mathsf{ex2}}$. Hence, the revision shown in Table 1 equals $\kappa_{\mathsf{ex1}} *_{\mathtt{mc}} \Delta_{\mathsf{ex2}}$ and the stated (im)plausibility ranks are as minimal as possible (when sticking to core c-revisions). When comparing κ_{ex2} to a minimal c-revision $\kappa_{\mathsf{ex3}} = \kappa_{\mathsf{ex1}} *^{\boldsymbol{\eta}}_{\min} \Delta_{\mathsf{ex2}}$ with $\boldsymbol{\eta} = (0, 3, 2, 0)$ (which is unique for this example, see the rightmost column in Table 1) one verifies easily that minimal core c-revisions usually compute higher ranks than minimal c-revisions. Pareto-minimizing the impact factors comes at the price of computing the impacts of conditionals only as much as necessary though. In our example, the minimal impact factors of δ_5 and δ_8 are 0, meaning that the impacts of these conditionals are already covered by the prior ranking function and the other new conditionals. However, as a consequence, δ_5 and δ_8 are not as thoroughly implemented in the revised ranking function as is the case with the minimal core c-revision. Of course, we have that both conditionals are accepted after revision, but in the minimal core c-revision, we also find that the contrapositive form of, e.g., δ_5, i.e., $(\overline{p}|x)$, is accepted, which does not hold for the minimal c-revision. While contrapositive forms of conditionals are not implied by belief bases in general, they nevertheless can be expected to hold if no other beliefs interfere (which is the case here). This illustrates that minimal core c-revisions tend to implement more structural information than minimal c-revisions.

Eventually, we are able to define the *strategic minimal core c-revision* $*_{\mathtt{mc}}$ which selects its minimal core c-revision for each pair (κ, Δ) of a finite ranking function and a consistent belief base Δ.

Definition 7 (Strategic Minimal Core c-Revision). *We call the mapping* $\mathtt{mc}\colon (\kappa, \Delta) \mapsto \boldsymbol{\eta}_{\min}$, *where κ is a finite ranking function and Δ is a consistent belief base, the* strategic minimal core c-revision operator, *and $\kappa *_{\mathtt{mc}} \Delta$ the* strategic minimal core c-revision *of κ by Δ.*

To the best of our knowledge, $*_{\mathtt{mc}}$ is the first unique and fully constructive strategic c-revision published so far.

7 Discussion and Related Work

Related approaches to belief revision with conditionals include AGM-style belief revision [1] and its refinements based on epistemic entrenchment relations [6,7], as well as distance-based and model-based revision operators [4,9]. These frameworks provide foundational postulates and constructive mechanisms for revising propositional belief sets, but their extension to conditional belief bases is non-trivial, as they do not natively capture the defeasible structure of conditionals. The lexicographic closure, originally introduced as a refinement of rational closure, has been shown to admit an interpretation as an iterated belief revision process [3], thereby establishing an explicit connection between default reasoning and AGM-style revision. However, lexicographic closure relies on a fixed priority ordering of defaults and does not provide a general revision operator for arbitrary ranking functions. In contrast, ranking-based approaches allow conditionals to be revised while preserving their internal structure. Within this setting, c-revisions are distinguished by their explicit commitment to conditional preservation and by satisfying both iterated revision postulates and syntax splitting, a combination that remains difficult to achieve in alternative frameworks.

In the context of computing core c-representations of belief bases Δ, the authors of [18] suggest applying rewriting rules to the constraints in $\mathtt{CSP}(\Delta)$ (cf. (2)) prior to removing their negative parts. For example, if the sets coincide on which the positive and negative minima are built, then both minima can be reduced to 0. This and similar ideas could be transferred to the constraint satisfaction problems of (core) c-revisions as well. However, some of these rewriting rules affect the (im)plausibility ranks assigned by core c-representations, and it is not entirely clear what is the semantical meaning of these affects, whether the set of proposed rules is complete or not, and how these rules transfer to core c-revisions exactly. We leave a systematic treatment of this issue for future work.

8 Conclusion

In this paper, we introduced core c-revisions as a principled subclass of c-revisions for conditional belief bases. By simplifying the underlying constraint systems, core c-revisions preserve the semantic foundations and rationality guarantees of general c-revisions while offering additional structural and computational advantages. In particular, we showed that core c-revisions are stratified and can be computed iteratively using revision-aware tolerance partitions. A central result of this work is the existence of a minimal core c-revision. This result enabled us to define the first fully specified strategic c-revision operator which deterministically selects the minimal core c-revision. In doing so, we closed the gap between abstract revision principles and concrete, implementable revision operators.

Future work will address several open issues. From a theoretical perspective, it would be interesting to further analyze the relationship between core c-revisions and constraint simplification techniques, as well as deepening the understanding of their connections to other ranking-based revision frameworks and also to the probabilistic principle of minimal cross-entropy. From a practical standpoint, the development of efficient algorithms and implementations, as well as empirical evaluations in application domains such as decision support and knowledge-based systems constitutes a promising direction for further research.

Disclosure of Interests. The authors have no competing interests to declare that are relevant to the content of this article.

References

1. Alchourrón, C.E., Gärdenfors, P., Makinson, D.: On the logic of theory change: partial meet contraction and revision functions. J. Symb. Log. **50**(2), 510–530 (1985)
2. Beierle, C., Haldimann, J., Kern-Isberner, G.: Semantic Splitting of Conditional Belief Bases. In: Raschke, A., Riccobene, E., Schewe, K.-D. (eds.) Logic, Computation and Rigorous Methods, vol. 12750, pp. 82–95. Springer, Cham (2021). https://doi.org/10.1007/978-3-030-76020-5_5
3. Booth, R.: The lexicographic closure as a revision process. J. Appl. Non-Classical Logics **11**(1/2), 35–58 (2001)
4. Dalal, M.: Investigations into a theory of knowledge base revision. In: Shrobe, H.E., Mitchell, T.M., Smith, R.G. (eds.) Proceedings of the 7th National Conference on Artificial Intelligence, St. Paul, MN, USA, August 21–26, 1988, pp. 475–479. AAAI Press/The MIT Press (1988)
5. Darwiche, A., Pearl, J.: On the logic of iterated belief revision. Artif. Intell. **89**(1–2), 1–29 (1997)
6. Gärdenfors, P.: Knowledge in flux: Modeling the dynamics of epistemic states, MIT Press (1988)
7. Gärdenfors, P., Makinson, D.: Revisions of knowledge systems using epistemic entrenchment. In: Vardi, M.Y. (ed.) Proceedings of the 2nd Conference on Theoretical Aspects of Reasoning about Knowledge, pp. 83–95. Morgan Kaufmann, Pacific Grove, CA, USA (1988)
8. Heyninck, J., Kern-Isberner, G., Meyer, T.A., Haldimann, J.P., Beierle, C.: Conditional syntax splitting for non-monotonic inference operators. In: Williams, B., Chen, Y., Neville, J. (eds.) Thirty-Seventh AAAI Conference on Artificial Intelligence, AAAI 2023, Thirty-Fifth Conference on Innovative Applications of Artificial Intelligence, IAAI 2023, Thirteenth Symposium on Educational Advances in Artificial Intelligence, EAAI 2023, Washington, DC, USA, February 7-14, 2023, pp. 6416–6424. AAAI Press (2023)
9. Katsuno, H., Mendelzon, A.O.: On the difference between updating a knowledge base and revising it. In: Allen, J.F., Fikes, R., Sandewall, E. (eds.) Proceedings of the 2nd International Conference on Principles of Knowledge Representation and Reasoning (KR'91). Cambridge, MA, USA, April 22–25, 1991, pp. 387–394. Morgan Kaufmann (1991)
10. Kern-Isberner, G.: A thorough axiomatization of a principle of conditional preservation in belief revision. Ann. Math. Artif. Intell. **40**(1–2), 127–164 (2004)
11. Kern-Isberner, G.: Linking iterated belief change operations to nonmonotonic reasoning. In: Brewka, G., Lang, J. (eds.) Principles of Knowledge Representation and Reasoning: Proceedings of the Eleventh International Conference, KR 2008, Sydney, Australia, September 16–19, 2008, pp. 166–176. AAAI Press (2008)

12. Kern-Isberner, G., Beierle, C., Brewka, G.: Syntax splitting = relevance + independence: New postulates for nonmonotonic reasoning from conditional belief bases. In: Calvanese, D., Erdem, E., Thielscher, M. (eds.) Proceedings of the 17th International Conference on Principles of Knowledge Representation and Reasoning, KR 2020, Rhodes, Greece, September 12–18, 2020, pp. 560–571 (2020)
13. Kern-Isberner, G., Brewka, G.: Strong syntax splitting for iterated belief revision. In: Sierra, C. (ed.) Proceedings of the Twenty-Sixth International Joint Conference on Artificial Intelligence, IJCAI 2017, Melbourne, Australia, August 19–25, 2017, pp. 1131–1137. ijcai.org (2017)
14. Kern-Isberner, G., Heyninck, J., Beierle, C.: Conditional independence for iterated belief revision. In: Raedt, L.D. (ed.) Proceedings of the Thirty-First International Joint Conference on Artificial Intelligence, IJCAI 2022, Vienna, Austria, 23–29 July 2022 (2022)
15. Kern-Isberner, G., Sezgin, M., Beierle, C.: A kinematics principle for iterated revision. Artif. Intell. **314**, 103827 (2023)
16. Pearl, J.: System Z: A natural ordering of defaults with tractable applications to nonmonotonic reasoning. In: Parikh, R. (ed.) Proceedings of the 3rd Conference on Theoretical Aspects of Reasoning about Knowledge, pp. 121–135. Morgan Kaufmann, Pacific Grove, CA, USA (1990)
17. Spohn, W.: The Laws of Belief - Ranking Theory and Its Philosophical Applications, Oxford University Press (2014)
18. Wilhelm, M., Kern-Isberner, G., Beierle, C.: Core c-representations and c-core closure for conditional belief bases. In: Meier, A., Ortiz, M. (eds.) Foundations of Information and Knowledge Systems - 13th International Symposium, FoIKS 2024, Sheffield, UK, April 8–11, 2024, Proceedings. Lecture Notes in Computer Science, vol. 14589, pp. 104–122. Springer, Cham (2024)

Technical Communications

Do Flat Representation Manifolds Lead to Improved Accuracy?

Julia Burr[1,2(✉)] and Alex Sarishvili[1]

[1] Fraunhofer Institute for Industrial Mathematics (ITWM), Fraunhofer-Platz 1, 67663 Kaiserslautern, Germany
alex.sarishvili@itwm.fraunhofer.de
[2] RPTU University Kaiserslautern-Landau, Gottlieb-Daimler-Straße, 67663 Kaiserslautern, Germany
julia.burr@itwm.fraunhofer.de

Abstract. Neural Networks (NN) are recognized as universal approximators, yet the reasons behind their remarkable generalization capabilities remain partially unresolved. One potential explanation is the manifold hypothesis, which suggests that NNs identify low-dimensional manifolds within the high-dimensional real-world data. In each layer of a NN, the data lies on/near a manifold, a so-called representation manifold, which gets progressively flatter as the layer's depth increases. Since NNs function on these data manifolds rather than isolated points, generalization becomes feasible. Notably, manifolds in the deeper layers of trained NNs tend to be flatter, while at the same time, deeper networks generally achieve higher accuracy. This leads to the following hypothesis: There is a correlation between the accuracy of a NN and the flatness of manifolds in the final layer of the NN. To investigate this, we empirically test the hypothesis by training a CNN with various hyperparameter sets. We assess both the flatness of the manifold and the accuracy on a test set, exploring their connection. We use correlation analysis, plots, statistical tests and examine whether flatness can be predicted from the hyperparameters.

Keywords: Manifold Hypothesis · Generalization · Representation Manifolds

1 Introduction

Neural Networks (NN) are usually trained on a training data set and evaluated on a separate test data set of the same distribution as the training data. This allows us to assess how well a NN will perform on unseen data when deployed in its real-world application. The difference between performance on the training and test sets is an estimator for the generalization gap.

Deep Networks can approximate and interpolate various functions [4], but reach surprisingly high accuracy on test sets with relatively low generalization

D. Wolter and G. Schwalbe (Eds.): KI 2026, LNAI 16830, pp. 199–205, 2027.
https://doi.org/10.1007/978-3-032-32335-4_14

gaps. This indicates that they do not simply memorize the training samples. Further, it was shown that it is imperative to consider not only the applied model, but also the considered data's structure to fully grasp the generalization performance of NNs [13].

One way to characterize the data's structure is to assume the manifold hypothesis, i.e. that high-dimensional real-world data lies near low-dimensional manifolds. This is a popular assumption in the field of Manifold Learning [9,10]. For multi-class problems it is assumed that the data lies on multiple manifolds where each manifold only contains samples from one class. If the target is to classify whether images show dogs or cats, there could be multiple cat- and dog-manifolds which are curvy and entangled, so a linear classifier applied to the raw image data cannot distinguish them. If the input data to a NN lies near a manifold, Brahma et al. [6] showed empirically that during training, such parameters are found which flatten these manifolds layer-by-layer. The data manifolds are still curvy in the first layer but become flatter as the data progresses through the layers. We call these manifolds found in NN layers representation manifolds. Since the final layer of a classification NN is usually a linear layer, flat manifolds guarantee separability as can be seen using the hyperplane separation theorem [5]. Note that in the following we will differentiate between the "final layer" which is the classification layer whose output size is the same as the number of classes and the "last representation layer" which is the layer before the final layer. The idea that NNs operate on data manifolds, not just individual samples, could explain the generalization ability of many NNs in practice. It could also explain why NNs trained on random data that lacks the manifold structure have a large generalization gap [13].

Using the same manifold hypothesis, Frosst et al. [7] showed empirically that entanglement in earlier layers can be beneficial for generalization. Entanglement here means that samples from different classes are close together. This does not contradict the previously mentioned work, but adds another factor to it, i.e. the distance between samples of different classes. Kaufman and Azencot [8] showed that in successful image classification networks, representation manifolds are especially curvy. However, they did not consider different classes separately.

On the one hand, we know that NNs flatten class manifolds layer by layer, so manifolds in deeper layers are flatter. On the other hand, we know from practice that a network's accuracy often increases with increasing depth of the network [2], [3], [12]. Combining these two statements, we arrive at the following hypothesis: **When comparing two CNNs trained for the same classification task, the CNN with flatter manifold in the last representation layer yields higher test accuracy.**

In contrast to Brahma et al.'s [6] work, we do not only consider the flatness of layers in one NN, but compare representation manifolds between different NNs. To this end, we train a CNN on MNIST with different hyperparameters. We choose an adaptive Design of Experiment (DoE) via Bayesian Optimization. This allows us to efficiently evaluate such hyperparameter combinations which lead to low curvatures in the manifold of the last representation layer. For each hyperparameter combination, we train the CNN and evaluate its accuracy on the same test data set that we calculate the curvature on. This yields accuracy-curvature pairs which we can analyze, either supporting or contradicting our hypothesis. Note that even though we use a CNN trained on MNIST and Brahma et al. used a Deep Belief Network (DBN) trained on a face dataset, we observe the same flattening of manifolds along the layers. This means that our study does not only confirm Brahma et al.'s hypothesis on yet another model architecture and dataset, but that it is a seamless extension.

The article is structured as follows: In Sect. 2, we present the experimental setup. Section 3 discusses the results. A summary can be found in Sect. 4 and Sect. 5 is the conclusion.

2 Experimental Setup

2.1 Considered Task, Network Architecture and DoE

We consider the popular benchmark dataset MNIST [1] which consists of 70,000 images of handwritten numbers. The goal is to predict the digit seen on the image. It was shown in previous experiments that a CNN trained on this dataset shows class manifold disentanglement layer-by-layer [11].

The considered CNN consists of 6 blocks or CNN-layers, each containing one convolutional layer, followed by a batch normalization layer and a ReLU layer. The first CNN block also has a max pooling layer. After these blocks, two fully connected feed-forward layers are attached where the first one has ReLU activation function (called *FF ReLU*) and the second one has softmax activation function, yielding the output class probabilities. When talking about (representation/class) manifolds in the rest of this article, we always refer to the class manifolds extracted from the ReLU-layers of the CNN blocks.

The bounds for the hyperparameters varied in the experiments can be found in Table 1. We use an adaptive DoE via Bayesian Optimization in order to predominately examine such hyperparameters which lead to flat representation manifolds in the last CNN block.

Table 1. Hyperparameters and bounds used for DoE

hyperparameter	lower bound	upper bound
dense units in *FF ReLU*	10	30
learning rate	0.0002	0.002
batch size	32	128
dropout	0.2	0.8
L2 regularizer weight	0.00005	0.00015

2.2 Flatness Measure

In order to estimate the flatness of a manifold given by a point cloud, we use the same estimator as Brahma et al. [6]. Its goal is to approximate the geodesic distance between point pairs, i.e. the distance of the shortest path between two points on a manifold. This is compared to the euclidean distance between the points. For a flat manifold, both distances are the same and the more curvy the manifold, the larger the difference between the distances.

To compute the estimator, the first step is to form a neighborhood graph. In this graph, each sample is a node and each node is connected to its k nearest neighbors in terms of euclidean distance. Then, the direction of the edges is forgotten, making the graph undirected. This graph approximates the manifold using local linearization.

In the second step, the shortest path on the neighborhood graph is found between each pair of samples. The length of the shortest path approximates the geodesic distance between a pair of samples.

In the third step, the information is combined to form the final estimator for samples $\{x_i\}_{i=1}^{n}$ on the manifold:

$$\tau_{\text{Geodesic}} = \frac{2}{n(n-1)} \sum_{(x_i, x_j)} \frac{|d_G(x_i, x_j) - d_E(x_i, x_j)|}{d_E(x_i, x_j)}. \quad (1)$$

Here, $d_G(x_i, x_j)$ is the approximated geodesic distance between samples x_i and x_j and $d_E(x_i, x_j) := ||x_i - x_j||_2$ is the euclidean distance.

Note that to make the measure more robust, the point pairs which are in the highest and lowest β-percentage of contributors ($\beta \in [0, 1]$) are not considered in the sum (Eq. 1). As was proposed by Brahma et al. [6], we choose $\beta = 0.1$. We choose $k = 12$ since for lower values, large parts of the neighborhood graph for each class manifold are not connected. To stay consistent with the manifold hypothesis, in the experiments we compute the curvature separately for each class manifold and average the results to form one curvature value.

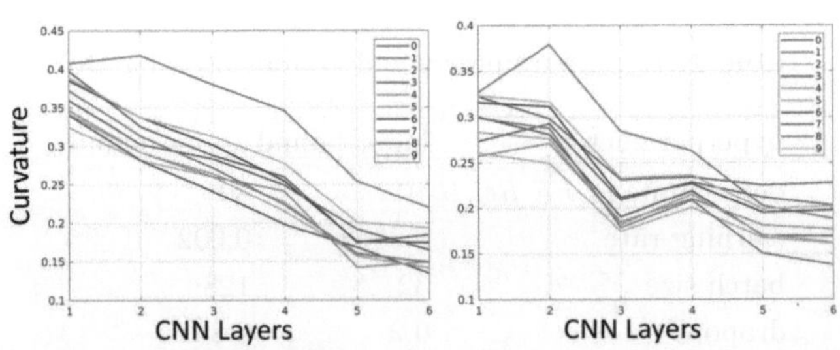

Fig. 1. Two examples of curvature of class dependent representation manifolds along the six CNN-layers (horizontal axis). The lines correspond to the 10 classes.

3 Results

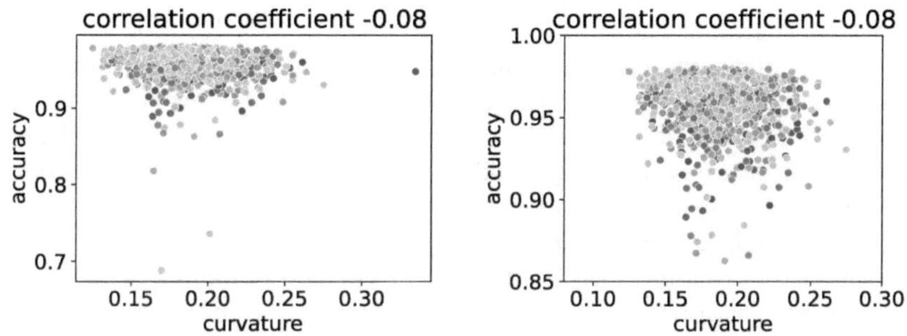

Fig. 2. Scatterplot of corresponding accuracy and mean curvature of all class manifolds in the last representation layer of each network. The image on the right is a zoomed-in version to better visualize the bulk of the data.

We conducted one run of the DoE with 64 experiments to check whether a decrease in curvature throughout the layers can be observed for different choices of hyperparameters. In Fig. 1, we display the flattening behavior throughout the 6 CNN-layers of two of the 64 CNNs as examples. For all 64 choices of hyperparameters, the curvature in CNN-layer 6 was lower than the curvature in CNN-layer 1. The decrease in manifold curvature mimics the results seen in Brahma et al.'s experiments [6]. This shows that the curvature measure works and that the task and network architecture are suitable to check the hypothesis.

After this, we repeated the DoE with different train-test splits 20 times with 64 experiments per run. The curvature reported here was computed from the last CNN block. In Fig. 2, we display the results of the runs by plotting the curvature-accuracy pairs of each of the 64 networks for each of the 20 runs. Points of the same color correspond to networks of the same run, i.e. the same randomly chosen training and test sets. It can be observed that there is no clear correlation between accuracy and manifold curvature. There is also no structure when only looking at networks of one run. The correlation coefficient when considering all runs together is -0.08 while the mean of the correlation coefficients per run is -0.1. These values show a negative trend, i.e. higher accuracy is more likely to be paired with lower curvature. However, the values are too low to indicate meaningful correlation between accuracy and curvature. We also considered the precision and recall for each of the 10 classes separately and instead of the absolute curvature, we considered the amount of flattening, i.e. $1 - \frac{\text{representation manifold curvature}}{\text{data manifold curvature}}$ for the ten classes. But still, there was no clear connection.

The correlation coefficient only focuses on detecting linear dependencies. Additionally, we further consider the connection between the networks with lowest curvature and highest accuracy in each run. For example, it could be that the network with lowest curvature is not necessarily the one with highest accuracy, but always one in the top 10 networks regarding accuracy. We sorted the experiments in each run by accuracy in descending order and recorded the placement of the experiment with lowest curvature. This results in 20 natural numbers, one for each run, spanning the range [2, 63]. According to a Kolmogorov–Smirnov test with $\alpha = 0.05$, we cannot confidently say that the distribution of these values differs from a uniform distribution (p-value: 0.62). This shows that there is no clear connection between the network with highest accuracy and network with lowest curvature concerning ranking. The same holds for the network with highest curvature and the network with lowest accuracy (p-value: 0.46).

Next, we consider whether the hyperparameters can explain the accuracy and curvature. To this end, we tried different regression models which took the hyperparameters as input and were trained to predict either the accuracy or the curvature. We tried different model classes (linear regression, gaussian process regression and decision tree) where linear regression showed the best results for both the accuracy and curvature prediction. The R^2-values for the accuracy on a test set of 20% size was 0.23 while the R^2 value for the curvature was 0.045. This shows that while the dependence of both accuracy and curvature on the hyperparameters is not very strong, the dependence of accuracy is much stronger. Curvature is apparently more susceptible to the randomness included in the training process, e.g. the random initialization of network weights.

4 Discussion

To study the hypothesis **"When comparing two CNNs trained for the same classification task, the CNN with flatter manifold in the last representation layer provides higher test accuracy"**, we performed a set of experiments where a 6 layer CNN was trained on MNIST data using different hyperparameters.

As with previous experiments in literature, we saw a decrease in manifold curvature from layer to layer when considering one CNN after training. However, accuracy and curvature in the last CNN-layer were uncorrelated and no clear dependence could be found by other statistical tests. Further, the hyperparameters cannot explain the curvature the same way they do the accuracy. This could indicate that the curvature is more heavily impacted by randomness in the training process, e.g. random initialization.

5 Conclusion

Even though perfect flatness of class manifolds in the last representation layer of a classification NN guarantees separability (using the manifold separation theorem [5]), flatness is apparently no direct predictor for accuracy. More studies are needed to fully understand the connection between NN training, representation manifolds and the model's performance. For example, learning how curvature depends on random initialization could be an interesting topic. It would further be interesting to find out whether promoting representation manifold flatness during network training leads to better generalization due to the additional information of the manifold's structure.

Disclosure of Interests. The authors have no competing interests to declare that are relevant to the content of this article.

References

1. Baldominos, A., Saez, Y., Isasi, P.: A survey of handwritten character recognition with mnist and emnist. Appl. Sci. **9**(15), 3169 (2019). https://doi.org/10.3390/app9153169
2. Basha, S.S., Dubey, S.R., Pulabaigari, V., Mukherjee, S.: Impact of fully connected layers on performance of convolutional neural networks for image classification. Neurocomputing **378**, 112–119 (2020). https://doi.org/10.1016/j.neucom.2019.10.008
3. Benkendorf, D.J., Hawkins, C.P.: Effects of sample size and network depth on a deep learning approach to species distribution modeling. Eco. Inform. **60**, 101137 (2020). https://doi.org/10.1016/j.ecoinf.2020.101137
4. Berner, J., Grohs, P., Kutyniok, G., Petersen, P.: The modern mathematics of deep learning. In: Grohs, P., Kutyniok, G. (eds.) Mathematical Aspects of Deep Learning, pp. 1–111. Cambridge University Press, Cambridge (2023)
5. Boyd, S.P., Vandenberghe, L.: Convex optimization. Cambridge University Press, Cambridge UK and New York (2004)
6. Brahma, P.P., Wu, D., She, Y.: Why deep learning works: a manifold disentanglement perspective. IEEE Trans. Neural Netw. Learn. Syst. **27**(10), 1997–2008 (2016). https://doi.org/10.1109/TNNLS.2015.2496947
7. Frosst, N., Papernot, N., Hinton, G.: Analyzing and improving representations with the soft nearest neighbor loss. In: International Conference on Machine Learning, pp. 2012–2020 (2019). https://proceedings.mlr.press/v97/frosst19a.html
8. Kaufman, I., Azencot, O.: Data representations' study of latent image manifolds. In: Proceedings of the 40th International Conference on Machine Learning. ICML'23, JMLR.org (2023)
9. Ma, Y., Fu, Y. (eds.): Manifold learning theory and applications. CRC Press, Boca Raton, Fla., 0 edn. (2012). https://doi.org/10.1201/b11431.0
10. Meilă, M., Zhang, H.: Manifold learning: What, how, and why. Ann. Rev. Stat. Its Appl. **11**(1), 393–417 (2024)
11. Sarishvili, A., Menzel, F., Adrian, B., Burr, J.: Machine learning for predictive maintenance in production environments. Stat. Mach. Learn. Eng. Appl. **227**, 227–244 (2024)
12. Vinayakumar, R., Soman, K.P., Poornachandran, P.: Evaluating effectiveness of shallow and deep networks to intrusion detection system. In: 2017 International Conference on Advances in Computing, Communications and Informatics (ICACCI), pp. 1282–1289. IEEE (2017). https://doi.org/10.1109/ICACCI.2017.8126018
13. Zhang, C., Bengio, S., Hardt, M., Recht, B., Vinyals, O.: Understanding deep learning requires rethinking generalization (2016). http://arxiv.org/pdf/1611.03530

Explainable Artificial Intelligence in Digital Ecosystems in Research and Education

Claudia-Melania Chituc(✉)

Leibniz Institute for Research and Information in Education, Frankfurt, Germany
c.chituc@dipf.de

Abstract. The integration of Artificial Intelligence (AI) techniques in e-learning ecosystems is expanding, although the algorithms used and decision steps often represent an enigma to learners and educators. Equity issues, plausible privacy risks, scarcity of transparency and trust are major concerns for the adoption of AI in digital education, about individualized teaching and learning recommendations, feedback, and e-assessment. The aim of this work-in-progress is to explore the importance of integrating explainable AI (xAI) methods in Digital Ecosystems in Research and Education (DERE) for Education 4.0 (E4.0) and present an approach for structuring the main stakeholders and xAI use scenarios constructed following a design-science approach.

Keywords: E-learning · Artificial Intelligence · explainable AI · digital ecosystem in research and education · Education 4.0

1 Introduction

Industry 4.0 (I4.0) technologies such as cloud computing, cyber-physical systems, Artificial Intelligence (AI), data and process analysis, robotics, augmented and virtual reality are increasingly used in higher education to tackle prevailing industry workforce requirements [1]. Education 4.0 (E4.0) conceptualizes educational models, learners' and educators' tasks, pedagogy, teaching and learning methods developed with the growing usage of current and emerging digital technologies in higher education to equip learners with the knowledge, skills, and know-how required by I4.0 [2]. In addition to technical and technological expertise (e.g., programming skills, AI/machine learning methods, big data analysis, cybersecurity, knowledge in the use of human-robot interfaces, best practices to develop solutions for real-life problems), I4.0 also demands soft-skills and cross-functional competences, such as critical thinking, cooperation, adaptability, communication, creativity, and a life-long learning mindset [2].

A robust technical infrastructure is needed to integrate I4.0 technologies into e-learning ecosystems and deliver instructional activities for E4.0 embedding AI techniques and enhance information technology teaching and learning [3]. Digital Ecosystems in Research and Education (DERE) provide such infrastructure support. DERE comprise repositories, software services, e-learning systems, AI methods and systems,

D. Wolter and G. Schwalbe (Eds.): KI 2026, LNAI 16830, pp. 206–213, 2027.
https://doi.org/10.1007/978-3-032-32335-4_15

computer networks, practices to strengthen cybersecurity resilience, and the Information and Communication Technology (ICT) infrastructure that enables the execution of different actions (e.g., creation, access, search, reuse, stewardship) with research and education digital objects, offering capabilities relevant for E4.0 teaching and learning activities, know-how and technology transfer while enabling open science [4].

The integration of AI methods and systems into e-learning activities and DERE for E4.0 is expanding, although the algorithms used and decision steps often represent an enigma to learners and educators. Equity issues, plausible privacy risks, scarcity of transparency and trust are major concerns for the adoption of AI in digital education, about individualized teaching and learning recommendations, feedback, and e-assessment [5]. The use of AI in education demands transparency and interpretability of the AI-directed personalized feedback, e-grading, and decision-making mechanisms – which are enabled by explainable AI (xAI) [6].

xAI concerns processes and methods that empower people to understand and trust the outcomes constructed by machine learning algorithms; it depicts the AI models, AI-generated decision making, expected impact of outcomes, potential biases, and enhances transparency [7]. xAI is necessary to clarify spurious classifiers, build trust, illustrate new insights from existing patterns, and for legal grounds [8]. The use of xAI methods in teaching and learning endorses educators to put together reasoned choices for educational activities [9] and allows learners to better comprehend their learning progress, individualized recommendations, feedback [10], and interventions [11]. xAI also allows learners to reason about their strengths and weaknesses [12].

Although xAI in education is nowadays expanding, this area is rather recent, and research is at an early stage [9][9]. Moreover, the fields of explainable AI, E4.0, e-learning systems and DERE evolve without a clear vision how the workforce requirements of I4.0 will be tackled in long term, and how the DERE integrating AI and xAI techniques enable achieving the goals of E4.0. Pertinent research questions in this area that need to be addressed are: *Why is xAI important in digital education? How is xAI for E4.0 currently tackled? Which are relevant stakeholders for integrating xAI methods in DERE for E4.0? Which are challenges for the integration of xAI methods in DERE for E4.0 that need to be further addressed?* Guided by the above research questions, this work explores the importance of integrating xAI methods in e-learning ecosystems. The objective of this work is to present an xAI framework for DERE for E4.0 illustrating its main stakeholders and main xAI use scenarios, which is constructed following a design-science approach, as in [14]. The proposed framework embodies a holistic perspective on xAI, E4.0, and DERE concepts, aiming to coalesce these fields. It represents a useful instrument for educators, learners, educational institutions, managers, developers of xAI methods and e-learning systems, policy makers to better understand the importance of xAI in e-learning ecosystems for E4.0 and identify areas that need to be further addressed by research and development work.

2 Background: XAI in Digital Education

Research on developing explainability methods (e.g., visualization, text) for non-expert users of AI systems in the workplace and in educational institutions is expanding in recent years [15] aiming to tackle concerns about fairness, accountability, transparency and ethics of AI decisions and education interventions [5]. xAI approaches in digital education aim to deliver clear and transparent explanations for the AI-driven education decisions, enabling trust and accountability [8]. Thus, xAI solutions tackle the pitfalls associated with the use of AI-driven systems in e-learning, e.g., lack of transparency, misunderstanding of decisions and recommendations that generate mistrust, difficulty in adjustment to changing contexts [16].

Global xAI approaches (e.g., globally self-explaining, feature relevance, example-based), and local xAI approaches (e.g., locally self-explaining) are analyzed in [5]. Moreover, four dimensions of AI explanations for educational contexts are discussed in [17]: scope, depth (e.g., in relation to the level of selectiveness in explanations), alternatives, and flow (e.g., explanations as conditions or patterns).

Examples of xAI tools for education are RiPPLE [18] - an adaptive educational system with comparison, local, and example-based explanations approaches, FUMA – which assists learners in educational activities in open-ended learning environments [19], and AcaWriter [20] which supports writing, uses comparison and local explanations. Benefits of xAI systems in education include clarity to nurture comprehension, relevance about context, specificity concerning AI technology, traceability – which is relevant for accountability, and consistency [21]. Concurrently, several drawbacks exist, such as unnecessary use of complex models, inaccurate or incomplete explanations, misinterpretation, developing a false sense of understandability [5]. xAI solutions bring numerous privacy concerns, they require a high deployment cost, and convoluted technical implementations [21].

3 Related Work

Explanations of AI systems uphold transparency, interpretability, and trust [22, 23]. To foster learning, explanations must be pedagogically relevant and individualized to learners' cognitive needs, stimulating metacognition through reflection and planning [5]. Next to personalized learning and feedback, examples of xAI uses in education, as presented in [24], include ethical and regulatory frameworks development relevant to accreditation standards.

SHAP (SHapley Additive exPlanations) [25] and LIME (Local Interpretable Model-agnostic Explanations) [26] are xAI tools used in education. For example, in [27], SHAP is applied to explain the way extra trees model predicts learners' programming progress. The use of SHAP and LIME can indicate learners' academic risks, helping teachers construct interventions [28]. A framework using SHAP values to improve real-time learners' performance prediction in serious educational games is presented in [29].

Actual scientific works on xAI in education often target particular topics, such as pedagogy (e.g., [30]), system design (e.g., [31]), students' performance prediction [29, 32]. Most reviews provide an overview of opportunities, obstacles, and challenges of using xAI in education – see for example [8, 24, 33].

Frameworks for understanding xAI in E 4.0 are scarce. Based on insights from the fields of AI, human-computer interaction, cognitive and learning sciences, a framework for xAI in education is presented in [5]. It focuses on six aspects: stakeholders, pitfalls (e.g., inaccurate or incomplete explanations), benefits, approaches to present explanations, AI models, effective design of educational AI tools (e.g., using user experiences)

[5]. A deep-learning framework for games educational assessment is proposed in [34] which relies on Mamba State Space Model (see: [35]) and embeds an Episodic Memory Module to integrate human-understandable educational insights into the decision-making process, to apprehend key patterns used to predict learners' performance. This work is important for E4.0 because game-based assessment is increasingly used to assess STEM content, cognitive and soft skills [36]. An xAI conceptual framework for engineering education 5.0 and its integration in digital education ecosystems is presented in [37]; it comprises seven pillars: skills, knowledge, qualifications; teaching; learning; implementation; ICT Infrastructure; e-assessment; quality assurance.

The investigation of relevant scientific publications revealed that not many frameworks exist that capture the most relevant stakeholders of xAI in e-learning ecosystems for E4.0. The need to develop a unified framework for xAI in education that could supply a set of guidelines for the development and use of xAI in education is highlighted in [8]. Such an artefact would help stakeholders to sustain collaborative efforts among different organizations towards attaining the (enhanced) goals of education by making use of AI technologies [8]. This work tackles such aspects, as presented next.

4 XAI in DERE: Stakeholders, Use Scenarios, and Framework

To equip learners or engaged citizens with the knowledge and skills required by I4.0, educational institutions, research institutes, I4.0 enterprises, companies developing educational software, national and local authorities collaborate within educational ecosystems. DERE enable the integration of heterogenous e-learning systems, ICT infrastructures, and repositories that can be used by different stakeholders in e-learning ecosystems. Analyzing the characteristics of DERE for E4.0 (as in [4]) and for engineering education 5.0 (as in [37]) and the findings in [38] and [13], ten relevant stakeholders of xAI for DERE for E4.0 are identified and illustrated in Fig. 1. Differently from [38] and [13], Open Science Communities, Research and Technology Transfer institutes are here stakeholders. *Educational Institutions* (e.g., universities, professional schools, libraries) traditionally center on teaching, learning, and assessment activities. *Vocational and Employment Training Centers* (*VETCs*) are also important for E4.0 because they equip learners and engaged citizens with the knowledge and skills required by the economy as they rely on networks of stakeholders (e.g., trade unions, chambers), providing educational programs prior and after employment [39]. *Learners, Educators, and Engaged Citizens* enhance their knowledge and skills by having access to outcomes of *Research Institutes* and *Technology Transfer Institutes*, and educational activities offered by *Educational Institutions* and *VETCs*. *Open Science Communities* advocate to open up practices for the creation, evaluation, sharing, exploration and storing of scientific knowledge [40], which are crucial for the pursuit of further professional development and life-long-learning requirements of E4.0. *Policy Makers, National and Local Authorities* focus on defining policies, regulations and assess their compliance. This is especially important for the deployment of trustworthy AI-enabled educational systems [5]. *Funding Agencies* have a critical role in further advancing the areas of xAI for E4.0, for the development of the required technical infrastructure and research projects assessing the impact of integrating xAI methods in education. *AI and E-Learning Software Development Companies* are crucial for enhancing the performance of AI solutions in education, development of explainable outcomes, and continuous enrichment of their software solutions.

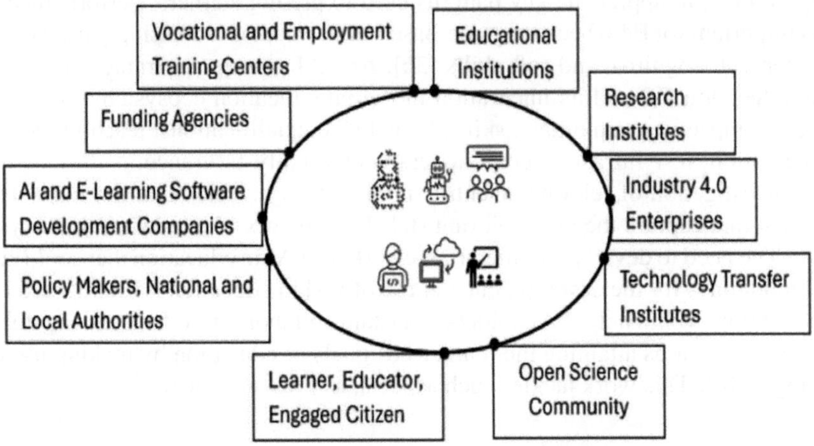

Fig. 1. xAI and DERE for E4.0: Main Stakeholders.

Figure 2 illustrates relationships among stakeholders, operations within the DERE, and where xAI can help. The arrows indicate the flow of information, which is bi-directional. E4.0 places students at the center of educational activities. Educators (e.g., human, robot, virtual tutor), Open Science Communities, Technology Transfer Institutes, Research Institutes, I4.0 enterprises access and contribute to the teaching/ learning resources (e.g., teaching and pedagogy methods, Open Educational Resources/OERs, games for education and assessment, resources for learning factories). The execution of these actions (marked with dash dot line) is made though the DERE ICT infrastructure, and specific rights are assigned to each stakeholder (e.g., by system administrators or owners). Learners access and use educational resources, participate in virtual learning events and group projects, execute individual and team projects, and xAI can help by displaying recommendations of additional learning resources with explanations, visual representations of the work progress, interventions, personalized feedback. By analyzing students' learning progress, educators can provide (with support from xAI systems) explanations on the personalized feedback and grades. The administrative employees of educational institutions receive insights about students' experience, risk of dropout, students' admission selection. Such activities are represented with light blue lines. xAI systems also help administrative employees to understand data privacy unwished issues through explanations of specialized studies (e.g., privacy-preserved algorithms, data leakage detection) when the number of devices connected to the DERE ICT infrastructure increases. Such insights enable them to take appropriate actions to enhance data privacy and improve infrastructure performance. Thus, xAI can help with ICT resources management. Explanations obtained by executing queries on the DERE ICT infrastructure are represented with dash lines. xAI is also important in the learning factories used in E4.0, e.g., to understand AI-enabled decisions concerning predictive maintenance, analysis of data collected from sensors.

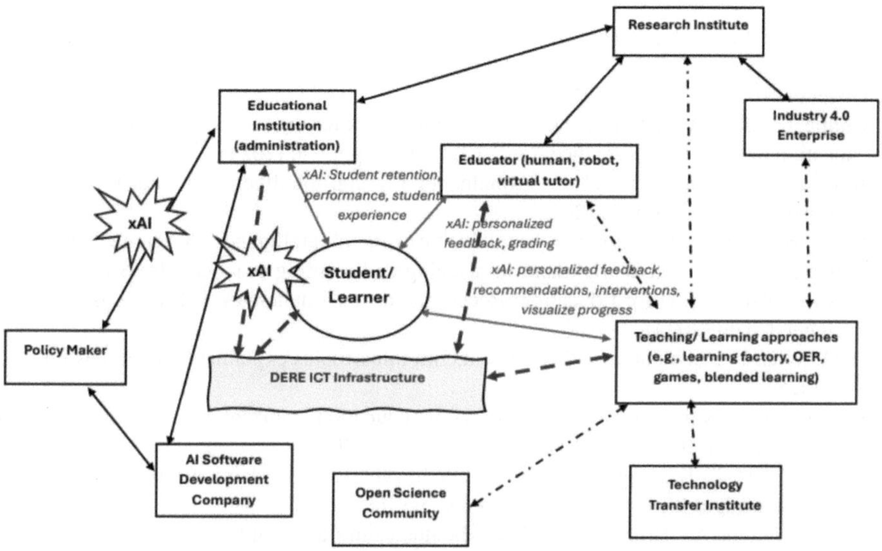

Fig. 2. Framework for xAI use scenarios

5 Conclusions and Future Work

xAI solutions in digital education provide clear and transparent explanations for the AI-driven education decisions, enabling trust and accountability [8]. This work explores the importance of integrating xAI methods in DERE for E4.0, presenting a framework for structuring the main stakeholders (educational institutions; research institutes; I4.0 enterprises; technology transfer institutes; open science communities; learners, educators, engaged citizens; policy makers, national and local authorities; AI and e-learning software development companies; funding agencies; vocational and training centers), and xAI use scenarios. xAI is useful not only in educational activities (e.g., to enhance trust), but also in the management of the ICT infrastructure of the DERE for E.4, quality assurance. Future work will focus on the further extension and validation of the proposed framework. It is indented to develop an electronic questionnaire and send it to relevant stakeholders in Germany.

6 Disclosure of Interests.

The authors have no competing interests to declare that are relevant to the content of this article.

References

1. Morales, E.B., Kipper, L.M. et al.: Integration of Industry 4.0 technologies with Education 4.0: advantages for improvements in learning. Inter. Technol. Smart Edu. 1741–5659 (2023)

2. Miranda, J., Navarrete C. et al.: The core components of education 4.0 in higher education: Three case studies in engineering education. Comput. Electr. Eng. **93**, 107278 (2021)
3. Oyetade K., Zuva T., Harmse A.: Integrating Industry 4.0 technologies into IT education. Cogent Edu. **12**(1), 2470195 (2025)
4. Chituc, C.-M.: A requirements engineering framework for digital ecosystems in research and education to enable open science. In: IEEE GECon, pp. 1–6 (2024)
5. Khosravi, H., Shum, S.B., et al.: Explainable artificial intelligence in education. Comput. Edu. Artif. Intell. **3**, 100074 (2022)
6. Singh, B., Kaunert, C.: Supremely explainable artificial intelligence (XAI) in education 5.0: Articulating constructive alignment in teaching and learning practices. In: Singh, T., et al. (eds.) Explainable AI for Education: Recent trends and challenges, ISEM 19, pp. 131–145. Springer, Cham (2024)
7. IBM: What is explainable AI? www.ibm.com/think/topics/explainable-ai. Accessed on 10 Feb 2026
8. Raccha, A., Seyam, M.: Explainable AI in education: Current trends, challenges, and opportunities. In: IEEE SoutheastCon, pp. 232–239 (2023)
9. Swamy, V., et al.: Trusting the explainers: teacher validation explainable artificial intelligence for course design. In: 13th LAK Conference, pp. 345–356 (2023)
10. Mu, T., Jetten, A., Brunskill E.: Towards suggesting actionable interventions for wheel-spinning students. In: EDM, pp. 183–193 (2020)
11. Hur, P., Lee, H., Bhat, S., Bosch, N.: Using machine learning explainability methods to personalize interventions for students. In: EDM, pp. 438–445 (2022)
12. Scheers, H., De Laet, T.: Interactive and explainable advising dashboard opens the black box of student success prediction. In: De Laet, T. et al. (eds.), Technology-Enhanced Learning for a Free, Safe, and Sustainable World, vol. 12884, pp. 52–66. Springer, Cham (2021)
13. Liu, Q., Pinto, J.D., Paquette L.: Applications of Explainable AI (XAI) in Education. In: Kourkoulou, D., et al. (eds.) Trust and Inclusion in AI-Mediated Education. Postdigital Science and Education,pp. 93–109. Springer, Cham (2024)
14. vom Brocke, J., et al.: Introduction to Design Science Research. In: vom Brocke, J., et al. (eds.) Design Science Research. Cases. Progress in IS, pp. 1–13. Springer, Cham (2020)
15. Long, D., Roberts, J., Magerko, B., Holstein, K., DiPaola, D., Martin, F.: AI literacy: finding common treads between, education, design, policy, and explainability. ACM CHI **329**, 1–6 (2023)
16. Samek, W., Montavon, G., Vedaldi, A., Hansen, L.M., Müller, K.R. (Eds.): Explainable AI: Interpreting, Explaining and Visualizing Deep Learning. LNAI, vol. 11700, Springer, Cham (2019)
17. Kesari, A., Sele, D., Ash, E., Bechtold, S.: Explaining eXplainable AI (2025). https://papers.ssrn.com/sol3/papers.cfm?abstract_id=4972085. https://doi.org/10.2139/ssrn.4972085. Accessed on 10 Nov 2025
18. Khosravi, H., Kitto, K., Joseph, W.: Ripple: a crowdsourced adaptive platform for recommendation of learning activities. J. Learn. Anal. **6**, 91–105 (2019)
19. Conati, C., Barral, O., Putnam, V., Rieger, L.: Toward personalized XAI: a case study in intelligent tutoring systems. Artif. Intell. **298**, 103503 (2021)
20. Knight, S., et al.: AcaWriter: a learning analytics tool for formative feedback on academic writing. J. Writing Res. **12**(1), 141–186 (2020)
21. Bellas, F., et al.: Explainable AI in education: Fostering human oversight and shared responsibility, European Digital Education Hub (2025). www.daadbrussels.eu/files/2025/06/EDEH_XAI-Report-1.pdf. Accessed on 10 Nov 2025
22. Herlocker, J.L., Konstan J.A., Riedl, J.: Explaining collaborative filtering recommendations. In: ACM CSCW, pp. 241–250 (2020)

23. Mathew, D.E., Ebem, D.U., Ikegwu A.C., Ukeoma, P.E., Dibiaezue, N.F.: Recent emerging techniques in explainable artificial intelligence to enhance the interpretable and understanding of AI models for human. Neural Processing Lett. **57**(16) (2025)
24. Chaushi, B.A. et al.: Explainable artificial intelligence in education: a comprehensive review. In: Longo, L. (ed.) Explainable Artificial Intelligence. xAI 2023. Communications in Computer and Information Science, vol. 1902, pp. 48–71. Springer, Cham (2023)
25. Lumberg, S.M., Lee, S.-I.: A unified approach to interpreting model predictions. In: NIPS, pp. 4768–4777 (2017)
26. Ribeiro, M.T., Singh, S., Guestrin, C.: "Why should I trust you?": Explaining the predictions of any classifier. In: ACM SIGKDD, pp. 1135–1144 (2016)
27. Choi, W.C., Lam, C.T., Mendes, A.J.: Analyzing the interpretability of machine learning prediction on student performance using shapley additive explanations. In: IEEE TALE, pp. 1–8 (2024)
28. Kumawat, P., Shaktawat, D.: The Role of Explainable AI (XAI) in enhancing transparency and trust in NLP- powered educational systems. Int. J. Sci. Res. Comput. Sci. Eng. Inf. Technol. **11**(8), 432–438 (2025)
29. Gomez, M.J., Sanchez, A.A., Albaladejo-Gonzalez, M., Garcia Clemente, F.J., Ruiperez-Valiente, J.A.: Utilising explainable Ai to enhance real-time student performance prediction in educational serious games. Expert Syst. **42**: e70008 (2025)
30. Umamaheswari, U., et al.: Enhancing engineering pedagogy through deep learning: Applications of explainable AI and neural networks. In: IEEE GIEST, pp. 1–6 (2024)
31. Leslie, D., Rincon, C., et al.: AI Explainability in Practice. The Alan Turing Institute (2024). www.turing.ac.uk/sites/default/files/2024-06/aieg-ati-7-explainabilityv1.2.pdf. Accessed 13 Nov 2025
32. Qiang, M., Liu, Z., Zhang, R.: Explainable AI in education: integrating educational domain knowledge into the deep learning model for improved student performance prediction. Sci. Rep. (2026)
33. Lopez-Pernas, O., Oliveira, E., Song, Y., Saqr, K.: AI, explainable AI and evaluative AI: Informed data-driven decision-making in education. In: Saqr, M., Lopez-Pernas, S. (eds.) Advanced Learning Analytics Methods, pp. 17–39. Springer, Cham (2026)
34. Zhang, F., Zhang, N., Zhang, X.: An explainable AI framework for game-based assessment: From model tuning to human insights. J. Comput. Assisted Learn. **42**, e70203 (2026)
35. Gu, A., Dao, T.: Mamba: linear-time sequence modeling with selective state spaces. ArXiv https://doi.org/10.48550/arXiv.2312.00752 (2024)
36. Gomez, M.J., Ruiperez-Valiente, J.A., Clemente, F.J.: A systematic literature review on games-based assessment studies: trends and challenges. IEEE Trans. Son Learn. Technol. **16**(4), 500–515 (2023)
37. Chituc, C.-M., Gómez, J.T., Haase, J.: Explainable artificial intelligence as an enabler for engineering education. In: 2026 IEEE Global Engineering Education Conference (EDUCON), Cairo, Egypt, 1–3 (2026). https://doi.org/10.1109/EDUCON67543.2026.11574416
38. Hoffman, R.R., Mueller, S.T., Klein, G., Jalaeian, M., Tate, C.: Explainable AI: roles and stakeholders, desirements and challenges. Front. Comput. Sci. **5**, 1117848 (2023)
39. European Commission, European Education Area: Vocational education and training initiatives. https://education.ec.europa.eu/education-levels/vocational-education-and-training/about-vocational-education-and-training. Accessed on 13 Mar 2026
40. UNESCO: Understanding Open Science (2022). https://unesdoc.unesco.org/ark:/48223/pf0000383323. Accessed on 13 Mar 2026

Comparison of the Runtime of Two Algorithms for the Linear Decomposition of ReLU Networks

Arn Dietz[1,3(✉)], Simon Lutz[2,3], Martin Brenzke[1], Thea Radüntz[1], and Emmanuel Müller[3]

[1] Federal Institute for Occupational Safety and Health (BAuA), Dortmund, Germany

[2] Research Center "Trustworthy Data Science and Security" of the University Alliance Ruhr, Dortmund, Germany

[3] TU-Dortmund University, Dortmund, Germany

dietz.arn@baua.bund.de

Abstract. Artificial neural networks are one of the key technologies in machine learning. In particular, networks using the ReLU-activation function are widely used in the community of formal verification and theoretical machine learning. Such networks can be represented by their linear decomposition, which consists of a set of convex polytopes together with associated linear functions that capture the network's behavior. This representation provides detailed insights into the learned structure of the model and enables the quantitative analysis of both linear and non-linear verification problems. However, obtaining the linear decomposition poses a computational challenge.

To the best of our knowledge, only two algorithms have been proposed for this task, yet a systematic and objective comparison between them is still missing. In this work, we implemented both approaches and conducted a comprehensive empirical evaluation of their runtime across a range of benchmark settings. Our results show that while one algorithm outperforms the other in many scenarios, both exhibit distinct strengths and weaknesses. Consequently, no single algorithm emerges as the clear winner, highlighting that performance is fundamentally shaped by the network's structural properties.

Keywords: ReLU-Network · Linear Decomposition · Benchmark

1 Introduction

Artificial **N**eural **N**etworks (NN) have emerged as one of the key technologies in machine learning over the past few decades. Among the various architectural design choices, the selection of the activation function plays a central

This work has been financially supported by Deutsche Forschungsgemeinschaft, DFG Project number 459419731, and the Research Center Trustworthy Data Science and Security (https://rc-trust.ai), one of the Research Alliance centers within the UA Ruhr (https://uaruhr.de).

D. Wolter and G. Schwalbe (Eds.): KI 2026, LNAI 16830, pp. 214–220, 2027.
https://doi.org/10.1007/978-3-032-32335-4_16

role. One of the most widely used activation functions in the community of formal verification is the **Re**ctified **L**inear **U**nit (ReLU), defined as follows: $\text{ReLU}(x) := x$ for $x > 0$, otherwise 0 [2,6]. In combination with the weights, a NN with ReLU activation function divides its input space into convex polytopes, upon which the graph of the NN is given as a linear function. We call the polytopes and corresponding functions, that represent the NN, the *linear decomposition* (LD). The LD offers a unique perspective on the NN that can be used to analyze and understand central aspects of machine learning. Researchers have used it to e.g. analyze the influence of different NN architectures on the partition of its input space [1], the impact of neurons on the behavior of the NN with respect to their depth in the architecture [4], or the global decision boundary in computer vision experiments [5].

Algorithms for obtaining a global LD are scarce, particularly for NN with input spaces of arbitrary dimension. To the best of our knowledge, there are two algorithms which we nickname the intersecting- [9] and the exploring-algorithm [8,10].

There is no benchmark available that compares the two algorithm types side by side. This is what we set out to do in this work. Since the runtime of both algorithms is dependent on the NN that is decomposed, it is hard to calculate how the runtime of the algorithm behaves with parameters like e.g., NN depth. In the first experiment we address this gap by measuring the runtime of the algorithms with respect to the depth and number of neurons of the decomposed NN. However, the NN in this first experiment are specifically designed to measure scalability and don't represent structures that are often encountered in praxis. Thus, in the second experiment, we measure the runtime of the two algorithms on structures that are frequently encountered in the literature.

2 Algorithms for Linear Decompositions

Our implementations of both algorithms[1] follow a common structure, with the LD computed in a layer-by-layer[2] fashion [9,10]. For a firm mathematical formulation of the underlying concepts, we refer to Ferlez et al. [3].

In general, each neuron's activation function in a given layer divides the input space into two half-spaces, separated by a hyperplane. The location of these hyperplanes is determined by all weights, biases, and activation functions that come before the corresponding neuron. Once the hyperplanes are computed, the next step is to obtain the partition of the *parent polytope* in the input space into *child polytopes* defined by these hyperplanes and the hyperplanes of the parent polytope. Both of our algorithms return a set of nonempty polytopes in their minimal representation. To check whether a hyperplane is necessary for representing a given polytope, a linear program of size #planes × input-space-dimension has to be solved. After the partition of the parent polytope induced by one layer is

[1] Code available at Zenodo.

[2] We speak of the combination of the ReLU with the linear weights before or, in case of the end of the NN behind it, as layer.

obtained, the same procedure can be applied recursively to each child polytope in the partition.

The intersecting algorithm [9] first considers all hyperplanes of the layer individually. The parent polytope is divided in two *split polytopes* by any hyperplane that intersects with it. To obtain a given child polytope, a set of one split polytope per hyperplane is considered. All polytopes in this set are intersected to obtain the final (possibly empty) child polytope. For k hyperplanes, splitting the parent polytope and the resulting $2k$ split polytopes, there are consequently 2^k ways to calculate intersections and find child polytopes. Each of these intersections has to be calculated to find the set of child polytopes.

As an alternative to the intersecting algorithm, which has to compute all possible intersections, Vincent et al. [8] and Xu et al. [10] introduced the exploring algorithm. The exploring algorithm starts with one point in the parent polytope. It then calculates the smallest polytope that can be formed by the newly introduced hyperplanes and the hyperplanes forming the parent polytope, around that specific point.

Each face of this polytope that is not shared with the parent polytope represents a boundary to a neighboring nonempty polytope. For each such neighbor, the algorithm checks whether it has already been explored and, if not, repeats the process. The procedure terminates once all identified polytopes have been explored and no new polytopes are found. This approach guarantees that each polytope is explored only once and considers only nonempty polytopes, making the runtime proportional to the actual number of child polytopes rather than the theoretical upper bound of 2^m. The trade-off is that all splitting hyperplanes and bounding planes of the polytope have to be taken into account at each step of polytope formation.

When comparing the two algorithms, the intersecting algorithm generally requires solving a larger number of linear programs, whereas the exploring algorithm deals with fewer but larger linear programs. Consequently, which algorithm is ultimately faster depends on the specific polytope structure generated by the NN, which in turn depends on the NN architecture and its weights. Due to these complex dependencies there is no known theoretical way to estimate how the runtime of the algorithm scales with parameters like NN input dimension or depth and how it behaves on common architectures.

3 Benchmarking Algorithms for Linear Decomposition

To address our two research objectives, namely scaling behavior and runtime on common NN structures, we conducted two experiments comparing the intersecting and exploring algorithms. Each experiment was dedicated to one of our two research questions.

3.1 General Setup

In both experiments, the NN's LD was calculated within a hypercube in the input space, centered at the origin and spanning an edge length of two.

The experiments were conducted on untrained NN that were initialized with random weights by means of PyTorch's [7] default procedure for random initialization. Both algorithms were implemented using a shared `C++` backend to gain greater control over the runtime behavior of the algorithms. All experiments were conducted using an "XMG PRO (E22) (XPR15E22)" laptop running an Intel Core i7-12700H CPU (14 Cores, microcode 1075) and 64 gigabytes of RAM on two 32 gigabyte banks clocked at 3200 MHz. No parallelization was used in the experiments to minimize the difference in runtime due to process scheduling and resource availability.

Not training the NN is motivated by two reasons. First, We don't want to introduce more parameters, like e.g., training algorithm and training task into the pipeline, since they can strongly differ from domain to domain. Secondly, preliminary tests indicated that training always seemed to reduce the number of polytopes, which in turn lowered the runtime. Consequently, untrained NN serve as "reasonable worst-case" scenario for empirical runtime evaluation. For each algorithm for the LD and each of the NN architectures featured in the experiments, we opted to calculate the decomposition 100 times, using different random initialization for the NN weights. We used a scheduling algorithm to distribute runtime evenly across all NN. We did not have enough resources to finish the computation of all 100 instances for all NN, resulting in fewer data points for the runtime intense configurations.

3.2 Experiment 1: Scaling Behavior

To investigate the scaling behavior of the runtime, we evaluated both algorithms on fully connected feed-forward NN that have the same number of neurons on each layer. We measured the runtime for NN with two to ten neurons per layer and depths varying from one to three layers.

The results can be seen in Fig. 1. Despite comprising at the most 30 neurons (Fig. 1a), the largest NN we decomposed required several hours to compute its LD. **NN with 3 layers:** The measured runtime for NN with three layers can be seen in Fig. 1a.

Comparing the runtime of the two algorithms across different numbers of neurons, we observe that both algorithms exhibit similar runtimes for small NN (two neurons per layer). However, as the number of neurons increases, the exploring algorithm begins to show a significantly better asymptotic runtime behavior. Moreover, the runtime of both algorithms appears to grow polynomial in these settings (in partial agreement with [3]).

NN with 1 Layer. In contrast to the experiments on multi-layer NN, an interesting phenomenon occurs when computing the LD of single-layer NN (Fig. 1b). While the exploring algorithm is faster for NN with three to eight neurons, it is outperformed by the intersecting algorithm as the number of neurons increases further. The experiments suggest an exponential growth in runtime.

As a side experiment, we also explored much deeper NN comprising several hundred layers. We found that the number of new polytopes introduced per layer

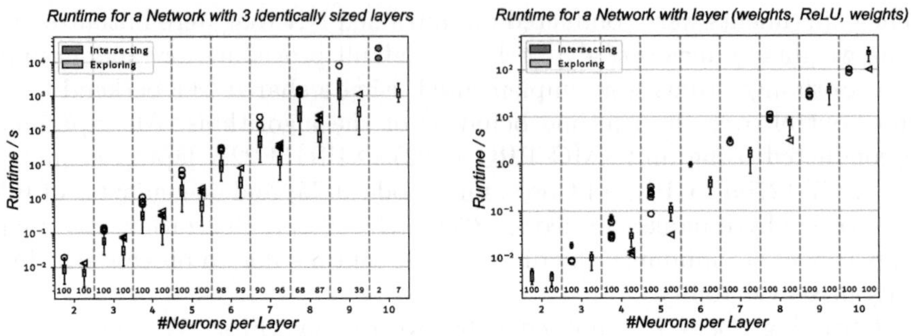

(a) (b)

Fig. 1. The left plot (a) displays the runtime for a NN consisting of three layers, each containing the same number of neurons. The right plot (b) displays the runtime for a NN consisting of a single layer. Numbers below the box plots denote the number of data points that were aggregated to the box plot.

drops drastically, so that after the fourth or fifth layer, virtually no additional polytopes are added to the decomposition.

3.3 Experiment 2: Runtime on Common Network Structures

To investigate the runtime of both algorithms on NN structures that are frequently encountered in applied scenarios, we tested them on fully connected encoder, decoder, and autoencoder architectures. Encoder NN have the highest number of neurons in the first layer, with progressively fewer neurons in subsequent layers, whereas decoder NN follow the opposite pattern. Autoencoder NN consist of a concatenation of an encoder and a decoder, with equal input and output dimension. The results of these practical tests are shown in Fig. 2. The exploring algorithm consistently outperforms the intersecting algorithm across all tested NN. Interestingly, decomposing the decoders is roughly an order of magnitude faster than decomposing the encoders. All decoders, except of one, have a two-dimensional input. However, the single decoder with the three-dimensional input exhibits the highest runtime among the decoders, even compared to NN with more than twice as many neurons. For autoencoders, the decomposition runtime is similar to that of encoders with the same input dimension.

3.4 Discussion

As discussed in Sect. 3.2, the runtime behavior of the intersecting algorithm is better than that of the intersecting algorithm, except when composing the first layer. One possible explanation for this observation is that, in the first layer of a NN, nearly all possible intersections of hyperplanes are nonempty. As a result, the number of polytopes processed by both algorithms, and consequently the

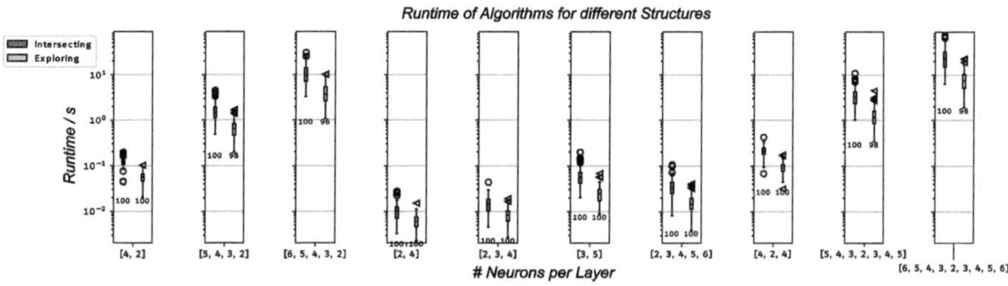

Fig. 2. Runtime of the intersecting and exploring algorithm on multiple NN structures. Numbers below the box plots denote the number of aggregated data points.

number of calls to a linear program solver, is almost identical. In such cases, the intersection algorithm can outperform the exploring algorithm because it considers fewer hyperplanes at each step, making each linear program faster to solve. This observation is in partial agreement with Hanin et al. [4], who also report that the first layers and the input dimension have the greatest impact on the total number of polytopes in the LD. In the second experiment, discussed in Sect. 3.3, there is a strong connection between measured runtime and the number of neurons on the first layer. This is consistent with the notion that most polytopes get introduced on that layer. Furthermore, the input dimension defines the row dimension of the linear problems that need to be solved during the calculation of the LD.

4 Conclusion and Outlook

We tested two algorithms for computing the LD of ReLU-NN across different NN structures. For multi-layer NN, both algorithms appear to scale polynomial. The exploring algorithm [8,10] is faster in almost all cases, except for the decomposition of the first layer, where the intersecting algorithm [9] performs better. Additionally, our results support the theory that the input dimension and input layer have the strongest influence on the number of polytopes in the LD.

The high runtime of both algorithms limited our analysis to relatively small NN, raising the question of whether these results generalize to larger architectures. Based on our findings, we identify three directions for future work. First, the algorithms could be accelerated through parallelization. Second, a more detailed analysis of the formation of linear regions would allow for a better theoretical runtime estimates. Third, following the direction of [4], the influence of training on the formation of linear regions should be investigated.

Finally, for practical applications, we recommend decomposing the first layer with the intersecting algorithm and all subsequent layers with the exploring algorithm to achieve the best runtime performance.

References

1. Berzins, A.: Polyhedral complex extraction from relu networks using edge subdivision. In: International Conference on Machine Learning, pp. 2234–2244. PMLR (2023)
2. Botoeva, E., Kouvaros, P., Kronqvist, J., Lomuscio, A., Misener, R.: Efficient verification of relu-based neural networks via dependency analysis. In: Proceedings of the AAAI Conference on Artificial Intelligence, vol. 34, no. (04), pp. 3291–3299 (2020)
3. Ferlez, J., Shoukry, Y.: Bounding the complexity of formally verifying neural networks: a geometric approach. In: 2021 60th IEEE Conference on Decision and Control (CDC), pp. 5104–5109. IEEE (2021)
4. Hanin, B., Rolnick, D.: Deep relu networks have surprisingly few activation patterns. Adv. Neural. Inf. Process. Syst. **32** (2019)
5. Humayun, A.I., Balestriero, R., Balakrishnan, G., Baraniuk, R.G.: Splinecam: Exact visualization and characterization of deep network geometry and decision boundaries. In: Proceedings of the IEEE/CVF Conference on Computer Vision and Pattern Recognition, pp. 3789–3798 (2023)
6. Kaulen, K., et al.: The 6th international verification of neural networks competition (vnn-comp 2025): Summary and results (2025). https://arxiv.org/abs/2512.19007
7. Paszke, A., et al.: Automatic differentiation in pytorch (2017)
8. Vincent, J.A., Schwager, M.: Reachable polyhedral marching (rpm): A safety verification algorithm for robotic systems with deep neural network components. In: 2021 IEEE International Conference on Robotics and Automation (ICRA), pp. 9029–9035. IEEE (2021)
9. Wang, Y.: Estimation and comparison of linear regions for relu networks. In: IJCAI. pp. 3544–3550 (2022)
10. Xu, S., Vaughan, J., Chen, J., Zhang, A., Sudjianto, A.: Traversing the local polytopes of relu neural networks: A unified approach for network verification (2021). arXiv preprint arXiv:2111.08922

Evaluating AI as Part of Social Mechanisms

Susanne Draheim[1], Ulrich Furbach[2(✉)], and Ralf Möller[3]

[1] Hamburg University of Applied Sciences, Hamburg, Germany
[2] University of Koblenz, Koblenz, Germany
uli@uni-koblenz.de
[3] University of Hamburg, Hamburg, Germany

Abstract. This article proposes a methodology for evaluating AI systems as components of social mechanisms rather than isolated artefacts. The research question we answer in the paper is: *How can an AI system's contribution to a human–agent mechanism be assessed with respect to collective outcomes, welfare, norms, and risks?* Combining mechanism design with analytical sociology, we propose the Star–Durkheim test as a diagnostic instrument for asking which collective goal is implemented, how welfare and fairness are affected, and which causal social dynamics may emerge. The test does not ask whether an AI appears human as done in the well-known Turing test, but investigates whether it contributes to, distorts, or endangers a socially situated mechanism. NotebookLM, Wikipedia, and autonomous vehicles illustrate the method; LLM prompting is treated as prototyping a Star-Durkheim test, not as full test automation.

Keywords: AI evaluation · social mechanisms · mechanism design · Star–Durkheim test · human-agent interaction

1 Introduction and Research Gap

Artificial intelligence is increasingly embedded in work, administration, education, knowledge production, and public infrastructure. Nevertheless, evaluation is still often framed as a comparison between a single AI system and a human benchmark. This framing is historically shaped by the Turing test [14] and continues in debates on human-level AI and anthropomorphism [6,16]. It helps measure task performance, but is too narrow when AI systems operate inside arrangements involving humans, institutions, norms, incentives, and other agents.

The gap addressed here is therefore not another benchmark for isolated model capability. The gap is a method for evaluating *AI-in-use*: AI systems that change the behavior of human participants, redistribute benefits and risks, and help generate collective outcomes. Related work exists in neighboring areas. Chatbot evaluation studies user satisfaction, trust, task success, and breakdowns

D. Wolter and G. Schwalbe (Eds.): KI 2026, LNAI 16830, pp. 221–227, 2027.
https://doi.org/10.1007/978-3-032-32335-4_17

[10,11]. Human–machine social systems emphasize mixed networks [13]. Mechanism design analyses outcomes, incentives, welfare, and fairness [9,15]. Our contribution is to integrate these strands into a compact diagnostic framework for social-mechanism evaluation rather than to present a new technical benchmark.

We call this framework the *Star–Durkheim test*. The name refers to Susan Leigh Star's proposal to shift attention from individual intelligence to the situated coordination work by which heterogeneous actors make collective action possible [12]. Furthermore, Durkheim's classic sociological concept of "social facts" is significant, as these facts exist outside the individual and constrain his or her actions. A useful AI system must therefore be evaluated by how it participates in rule-governed, normatively structured, and causally effective collective settings. This also explains why the Turing test is not rejected as historically irrelevant; it is rejected as insufficient for systems whose main effects arise in social deployment. A longer version of this paper is provided in [5].

2 Social Mechanisms

We use the term *social mechanism* for a social context in which humans and artificial agents interact to achieve a purpose under constraints relevant to humans, such as safety, fairness, accountability, and trust. An agentic AI system is then not merely a software component, but a participant in a mechanism. The object of evaluation is consequently neither the isolated model nor the whole of society. It is the contribution of a specific AI system, or a class of such systems, to a defined human–agent mechanism.

Mechanism design asks how rules can be designed so that individual actions lead to a desired collective outcome. Important concepts include the social choice function, social welfare, incentive compatibility, fairness, individual rationality, and budget balance [9,15]. In real human–agent settings, however, human behavior cannot be reduced to stable preferences or perfect rationality. Humans interpret rules, react to framing, have limited attention, and participate only if they trust the mechanism. A social mechanism must therefore be incentive-compatible for agents and behavior-compatible for humans.

Analytical sociology adds a complementary perspective: mechanisms explain how macro-level patterns emerge from micro-level actions [4,8]. It distinguishes causal explanation, micro-foundations, generativity, social dilemmas, homophily, and tipping points. In social practice, participants will understand and interpret mechanisms differently. Required is not perfect shared understanding, but sufficient visibility of rules, risks, and contestable outcomes for participants and regulators.

Thus, a social-mechanism perspective adds two questions to ordinary system evaluation. First, what is the mechanism in which the AI system becomes consequential? Second, how does the system change the relation between micro-actions and macro-outcomes? These questions make the evaluation object explicit and prevent the analysis from drifting between the agent, a multi-agent system, and an entire social situation.

3 The Star–Durkheim Test

The Star–Durkheim test is not a pass/fail imitation test. It is a diagnostic checklist with an explicit scoring convention. For a given AI system A, a mechanism M, and a participant group P, the test asks ten questions. Each item can be rated as *supported, partly supported, unsupported, or unclear.* A mechanism passes only for a stated evaluation purpose, for instance "deployment in a classroom", "public-traffic participation", or "knowledge-curation support". Passing does not require all answers to be positive. Rather, it requires that the intended collective goal is explicit, major harms are bounded, and unsupported or unclear items are treated as design or regulatory obligations.

1. **Social choice function.** What collective outcome is the mechanism supposed to produce?
2. **Social welfare.** Whose utilities, risks, and benefits count, and how are trade-offs justified?
3. **Incentives.** Can participants gain by manipulating inputs, rules, or other participants?
4. **Fairness.** Are risks and benefits distributed equitably across affected groups?
5. **Budget balance.** Are costs, data extraction, externalities, and infrastructure burdens internalized?
6. **Causal explanation.** Can relevant outcomes be traced to rules, inputs, decisions, and interactions?
7. **Micro-foundations.** Which local actions aggregate into macro-outcomes?
8. **Generativity.** Which repeated interaction patterns produce new norms or institutions?
9. **Social dynamics.** Which dilemmas, homophily effects, or strategic behaviors may arise?
10. **Tipping points.** Which thresholds could abruptly change behavior, norms, or risk?

The test is deliberately broader than a technical benchmark. It can incorporate technical evidence, empirical user studies, logging, legal analysis, stakeholder interviews, and simulation. Chatbot evaluation studies are relevant here, not as competitors, but as evidence sources for particular items such as trust, task success, user adaptation, and breakdowns in interaction [10,11]. The test therefore yields an audit trail: a table of ratings, the evidence used for each rating, and the resulting design or regulatory consequences.

4 Three Example Mechanisms

4.1 NotebookLM

NotebookLM is a document-grounded system in which a human uploads sources and receives summaries, answers, or audio overviews. The mechanism has a relatively narrow purpose: to help a user transform a document collection into usable secondary artefacts. We avoid the term "ground truth" here because many social mechanisms have multiple desirable outcomes and contested preferences. Instead, evaluation should compare the output with the uploaded sources, the user's stated purpose, and the expectations of the intended audience.

NotebookLM differs from a general chatbot because it is a retrieval-augmented system. Explanations of particular outputs should therefore rely primarily on source links, retrieved passages, and the transformation from source material to generated text, not merely on prompts or hidden model states. This makes causal explanation partly supported: the source basis may be inspectable, while the generation process remains only partly transparent. The mechanism is generative in the weaker sense that repeated interactions can produce new summaries, research notes, and teaching material. Claims about filter bubbles, homophily, or tipping points should be treated cautiously unless there are multiple users, shared corpora, or institutional adoption.

4.2 Wikipedia

Wikipedia is a large-scale knowledge-production mechanism in which humans and software agents jointly maintain articles. Bots revert vandalism, repair links, recommend tasks, and enforce procedural routines. A crucial distinction is that these bots are not the same as free LLM-based text generators. Wikipedia communities have developed strict rules for automated editing and increasingly cautious rules for LLM use, especially because unverifiable generated text can undermine sourcing norms. The social choice function is not "the true article", but a provisionally accepted article version produced under Wikipedia's norms of verifiability, neutrality, and community oversight. Fairness must also be treated as only partly supported. Formally, many users can edit; socially, participation is affected by expertise, time, conflict tolerance, and gendered participation patterns, a point emphasized in studies of Wikipedia's gender gap [7]. Causal explanation and micro-foundations are relatively strong because edits, reversions, talk-page discussions, bot actions, and policy references are archived. Generativity is strong: repeated editing produces not only articles but also norms, role structures, dispute procedures, and institutional memory.

4.3 Autonomous Vehicles

Autonomous vehicles in public traffic participate in a mechanism involving pedestrians, cyclists, human drivers, regulators, insurers, manufacturers, and infrastructure. The collective goal is not merely efficient mobility, but safe, lawful, predictable, and publicly legitimate mobility. Social welfare must include travel time, safety, environmental effects, accessibility, infrastructure costs, and the distribution of risks across vulnerable road users.

The trolley problem is commonly used as an example of a social dilemma. This is considered as misleading. As Coeckelbergh argues, trolley-style thought experiments often abstract from the social and subjective context in which real traffic decisions occur [3]. More relevant dilemmas include strategic yielding, congestion externalities, unequal deployment across neighborhoods, overreliance by human drivers, and conflicts between manufacturer optimization and public safety. Tipping points may arise when the share of autonomous vehicles changes traffic no rms or infrastructure de sign. Homophily may arise if vehicle-to-vehicle communication privileges autonomous vehicles over humans who cannot participate in that communication channel. The discussion of this section is summarized in Table 1.

Table 1. Illustrative Star–Durkheim ratings. "Partly" and "unclear" are not failures; they identify design and evidence needs.

Dimension	NotebookLM	Wikipedia	Autonomous vehicles
Social choice function	supported	supported	supported
Social welfare	partly	partly	partly
Incentives	supported	partly	partly
Fairness	supported	partly	partly
Budget balance	unclear	partly	partly
Causal explanation	partly	supported	partly
Micro-foundations	partly	supported	supported
Generativity	supported	supported	supported
Social dynamics	limited/unclear	partly	supported
Tipping points	unclear	supported	supported

5 From Prompting to Test Protocols

As part of our research process, we asked ChatGPT to apply the test to literature about autonomous vehicles. We now treat such prompting as a purely exploratory step. Asking an LLM to perform the Star–Durkheim test does not automate it.

It can summarize known arguments, reveal missing dimensions, or generate a first coding scheme, but it cannot observe the actual mechanism or verify the contribution of an AI system in practice. A credible research design would require four steps. First, define the mechanism, participants, institutional setting, and intended deployment purpose. Second, collect evidence: system documentation, logs, user studies, stakeholder interviews, simulations, and regulatory constraints. Third, rate each test item with justification and uncertainty. Fourth, translate unsupported or unclear items into design changes, deployment restrictions, or regulatory obligations. The LLM may assist in drafting hypotheses, but the test itself must be grounded in empirical and institutional evidence. This formulation also clarifies the role of the examples: they are not empirical validations, but worked illustrations of how the diagnostic vocabulary can structure later empirical work.

6 Economic and Regulatory Relevance

Brynjolfsson's "Turing trap" warns that human-like automation can concentrate wealth and power, whereas Agrawal, Gans and Goldfarb describe "Turing transformations" in which AI augments work by reorganizing tasks [1,2]. The difference is not only technical. It depends on the mechanism: who controls the AI, who benefits from productivity gains, who bears errors and externalities, and which counterfactual institutional arrangements are available.

This mechanism perspective also sharpens regulation. Risk-based frameworks such as the EU AI Act are necessary, but they mainly classify systems and obligations. A Star–Durkheim analysis asks an additional question: in which social mechanism is the AI embedded, and what does it do to welfare, fairness, incentives, explanation, and collective stability? This does not replace legal compliance; it connects technical evaluation, social-scientific explanation, and regulatory judgement. It is especially useful where technical compliance alone leaves open whether an AI system changes roles, incentives, or institutional dependencies in unacceptable ways.

7 Conclusion

The Star–Durkheim test reorients AI evaluation from human imitation to social contribution. It asks how a system participates in mechanisms that generate collective outcomes, distribute welfare, stabilize or destabilize norms, and affect human participants. The test framework remains conceptual, but it is formulated as a research design: it defines the object and pass condition of the test; it distinguishes LLM prompting from real test automation; and it qualifies speculative claims in the examples. It also defines the mechanism, gather evidence, rate the diagnostic items, and derive design or regulatory consequences. Thus, the test is not an alternative to benchmarks, user studies, or legal analysis. It connects them when AI systems become part of social mechanisms.

References

1. Agrawal, A., Gans, J., Goldfarb, A.: The Turing Transformation: Artificial Intelligence, Intelligence Augmentation, and Skill Premiums. NBER Working Paper (2023)
2. Brynjolfsson, E.: The turing trap: the promise and peril of human-like artificial intelligence. In: Augmented Education in the Global Age. Routledge (2023
3. Coeckelbergh, M.: AI Ethics. MIT Press, Cambridge (2020)
4. Demeulenaere, P.: What are mechanisms in social science? Eur. J. Soc. Theory **14**(1) (2011)
5. Draheim, S., Furbach, U., Möller, R.: Toward Testing AI: A Socio-Economic View (Technical Report) (2026). http://doi.org/10.25592/uhhfdm.18711
6. Floridi, L., Nobre, A.C.: Anthropomorphising machines and computerising minds. Mind. Mach. **34**(1) (2024)

7. Ford, H., Wajcman, J.: Anyone can edit, not everyone does: Wikipedia's infrastructure and the gender gap. Soc. Stud. Sci. **47**(4), 511–527 (2017)
8. Hedström, P., Ylikoski, P.: Analytical sociology and rational-choice theory. In: The Routledge Companion to Rational Choice. Routledge (2010)
9. Hurwicz, L., Reiter, S.: Designing Economic Mechanisms. Cambridge University Press (2006)
10. Luger, E., Sellen, A.: Like having a really bad PA: the gulf between user expectation and experience of conversational agents. CHI (2016)
11. Radlinski, F., Craswell, N.: A theoretical framework for conversational search. CHIIR (2017)
12. Star, S.L.: The structure of ill-structured solutions: boundary objects and heterogeneous distributed problem solving. In: Distributed Artificial Intelligence. Elsevier (1989)
13. Tsvetkova, M., Yasseri, T., Pescetelli, N., Werner, T.: Human-machine social systems. arXiv preprint (2024)
14. Turing, A.M.: Computing machinery and intelligence. Mind **59**(236), 433–460 (1950)
15. Vohra, R.V.: Mechanism Design: A Linear Programming Approach. Cambridge University Press (2011)
16. Wachter, W.T.: Computational brains and biological computers: AI, cognitive science, conceptual borrowing, and anthropomorphism. Master's thesis, Utrecht University (2024)

Safeguards for Speech2Speech LLM-Assistants: A Case Study in Automotive Applications

Gregor Endler[1(✉)], Sebastian Kraus[1], and Lukas Stappen[2]

[1] codemanufaktur GmbH, Erlangen, Germany
kontakt@codemanufaktur.com
[2] BMW Group, Munich, Germany

Abstract. Recent advances have introduced speech-to-speech (S2S) conversational assistants capable of producing natural-sounding interactions, including non-verbal cues like tonality and mood. In the automotive domain, this enables intuitive and humanlike in-car dialogue experiences. However, integrating these end-to-end assistants limits architectural options for programmable domain-specific safeguards. This paper discusses two implementation approaches for S2S guardrails: transcript-based and tool-based. Through an empirical evaluation, we demonstrate that both strategies are insufficient for industrial deployment in most cases due to prohibitive latency (delaying each answer by 0 to 1.4 s even for computationally cheap checks) and technical impediments (like potentially non-deterministic tool call behavior). Finally, we outline open challenges for S2S guardrails in the automotive context.

Keywords: LLM · Speech-to-Speech Assistants · LLM Guardrails · Responsible AI

1 Introduction

Voice interaction is a natural fit for automotive applications since it reduces manual and visual workload and allows eyes on road and hands on wheel. In contrast to traditional speech recognition systems, the use of Large Language Models (LLMs) in speech assistants enables free conversation flow instead of fixed keyword detection and a more natural understanding of user commands. However, this conversational freedom also enables novel attacks on the overall system. This is exacerbated with Speech2Speech (S2S) systems: While they offer new capabilities like producing and reacting to speech tonality, this comes at the cost of less control over the system's data flow: S2S systems allow less control over intermediate results than traditional text-based systems, i.e. more steps are handed off to the model itself or to a vendor's black box. Present safeguards do protect certain parts of such a system, but new attack surfaces also require new defenses. It remains an open question whether vendor blackbox guardrail

D. Wolter and G. Schwalbe (Eds.): KI 2026, LNAI 16830, pp. 228–235, 2027.
https://doi.org/10.1007/978-3-032-32335-4_18

approaches can fully capture application specific requirements, organizational constraints, and contextual threat models. Therefore, custom application-level guardrails are necessary to enforce concrete behavioral constraints beyond model intrinsic safeguards.

We explore two approaches for custom guardrails within implementation frameworks given by three major LLM vendors (Amazon, Google, and OpenAI): transcript-based and tool-based guardrails (see Sect. 3). To verify their fundamental applicability, we performed latency tests comparing a no-protections baseline against both guardrail variants. These experiments reveal that for two of the investigated APIs, guardrails introduce significant delays incompatible with fluid conversation, and that essential features for reliable guardrails integration are lacking. We discuss directions for future work and current shortcomings that need to be addressed for in-production use of custom made guardrails in S2S assistants.

2 Related Work

Many voice assistants rely on a chained architecture consisting of Speech Recognition, a text-based Large Language Model, and Text-to-Speech synthesis [7]. Recent Speech-to-Speech (S2S) architectures supersede this by processing and generating speech and audio directly without intermediate text [5,7,22]. This has the advantage of more natural conversation and may include non-verbal speech features like emotion and tonality. Multiple open- [8,9,16,25] and closed source solutions [1,11,19] exist.

Many approaches for LLM guardrails have been suggested [10]. Commercial providers offer configurable guardrails [3,12,18]. However, these are predominantly designed for text-based interactions and offer limited configurability for domain-specific requirements. Some frameworks [13,17] do provide programmable guardrails, but their integration with streaming S2S APIs introduces latency that may be unacceptable for real-time conversation.

Deploying speech assistants in vehicles introduces domain-specific requirements spanning technical resilience, safety, privacy, and fairness [21]. Resilient systems must defend against attacks that could trigger dangerous vehicle maneuvers. Privacy concerns arise when attackers extract sensitive information such as calendar entries or navigation history [26]. Circumventing safeguards to generate hate speech or discriminatory content violates fairness principles [24]. Automotive standards like TARA (ISO/SAE 21434 [14]) were developed for traditional cyber-physical systems with deterministic behavior, not for the probabilistic, adaptive, and linguistically unpredictable characteristics of generative AI. In addition, the automotive context imposes constraints including latency requirements for natural conversation (below approximately 0.4 s added delay [6,15,23]) and integration with safety-critical vehicle systems. These constraints make direct application of generic guardrail frameworks challenging.

3 S2S Guardrail Implementation Options

Based on the considerations above, we implemented two variants of S2S guardrails: Transcript-based and tool-based. Transcript-based guardrails denote functionality operating on transcripts handed back by the LLM. The transcripts may be constructed by the main LLM itself (as is the case for Gemini Flash [11] and Nova Sonic [4]) or by an auxiliary model (e.g. whisper-1 or gpt-4o-transcribe in case of GPT Realtime [20]). Figure 1 shows their data flow: (1) An arbitrator (e.g. a car's software backend) sends audio to the LLM. (2) In parallel, the LLM (a) creates a transcript that is passed to the input guardrails, and (b) creates an audio answer that is sent to the arbitrator and buffered there. (3) The input guardrails notify the arbitrator about their result based on the transcript. (4) The arbitrator sends the buffered audio to the output device if the guardrails were passed. Otherwise, the arbitrator instructs the model to react with previously defined refusal behavior.

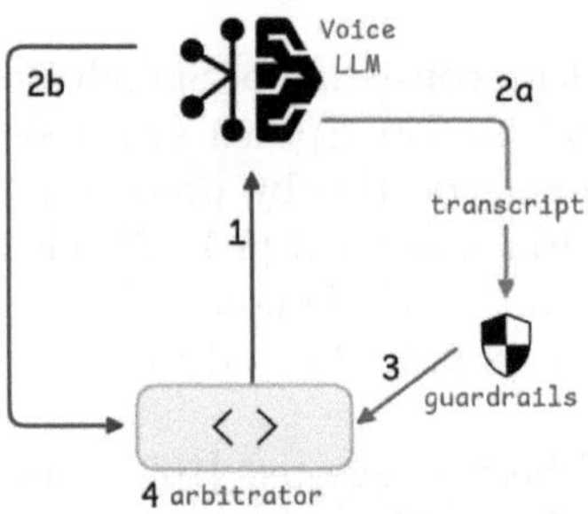

Fig. 1. Transcript-Based Guardrails.

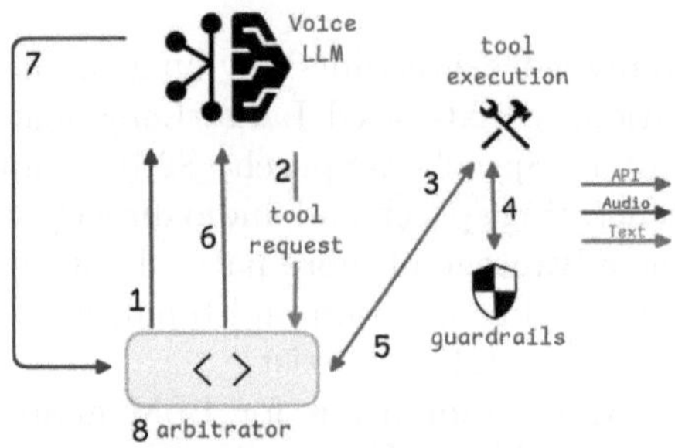

Fig. 2. Tool-Based Guardrails.

Tool-based guardrails denote separate functionality whose execution is requested by the LLM. Figure 2 shows the data flow: (1) The arbitrator sends audio to the LLM. (2) The LLM sends a tool request for the guardrails tool containing necessary parameters (like the transcript). (3) The arbitrator passes on the request and parameters to the guardrails tool. (4) The guardrails tool judges the input and passes back the result to tool execution. (5) Tool execution notifies the arbitrator about the result. (6) The arbitrator passes on the full tool result to the LLM. (7) The LLM decides between blocking and passing behavior based on the guardrails tool result, generates fitting audio, and sends the audio to the arbitrator. (8) The arbitrator sends the audio to the output device. Model providers may offer configurable guarantees about deterministic tool usage [2]. However, at the time of this writing no vendor offered comprehensive tool pipelining which may be necessary if guardrails require several tools, or if guardrails coexist with other mandatory tools.

Note that while transcript-based guardrails show fewer communications steps than tool-based guardrails between components in the architecture, the former's implementation requires a larger amount of custom code since it offloads fewer steps to the LLM.

4 Evaluation Setup

Detection accuracy or similar measures are not part of our analysis. We focus on the following non-functional requirements since they are a necessary precondition for industrial application: (R1) minimal added latency, (R2) deterministic model response when refusing user input, and (R3) safety first, i.e. guardrails must reliably be evaluated before every model answer. R2 and R3 are general requirements for guardrailed systems, while R1 specifically concerns the conversation flow benefits S2S systems deliver over chained systems: Adding delay as low as 0.4 s into conversations negatively impacts people's impression of their counterpart [23] and introduces confusion into the conversation [6]. Therefore, for S2S systems to be able to play to their strengths, guardrails introduced into the system should not significantly delay answer times.

Evaluation is broken up along the dimensions model (Google's Gemini Flash, Amazon's Nova Sonic, OpenAI's GPT Realtime), guardrails (none, tool-based, transcript-based), and input (malicious, non-malicious). Malicious input is defined as all text containing the specified trigger word "whale", a benign word that model vendors' own safety checks should not identify as problematic. This rules out conflicts between self-implemented and vendor-implemented guardrails. The three test dimensions' value sets yield $3 * 3 * 2 = 18$ distinct setups. Each test run was repeated 300 times, resulting in a total number of 5400 runs. To prevent temporary black box effects or time-related influences (like temporarily slow internet connectivity) from potentially overshadowing the effects of interest, the tests were repeated only after a single run along all test dimensions was completed, i.e. after each unique combinations of model, guardrails, and input.

5 Evaluation Results

As overall latency, we track the time that passes between the end of the user input (i.e. the time the user stops speaking) and the first audible response of the system. While the tool-based approach means no answer is generated until the mandatory guardrail result is returned, transcript-based guardrails need to interrupt running answer generation. At the time of this writing, not all vendors offered programmatic interruptions of a running session. To preserve comparability between vendors, interruption was performed by streaming a fixed audio message to the model asking for refusal. Duration of this audio message was subtracted from pertaining latencies to emulate an immediate interruption.

Figure 3 shows the results. The x-axis shows the delay between user speech end and start of the model's audio playback in milliseconds, the y-axis shows the density distribution of measurements, separated by whether the input was malicious or not. Each combination of model and guardrail type is shown in a separate plot. In addition to the density, the P50 quantiles for non-malicious and

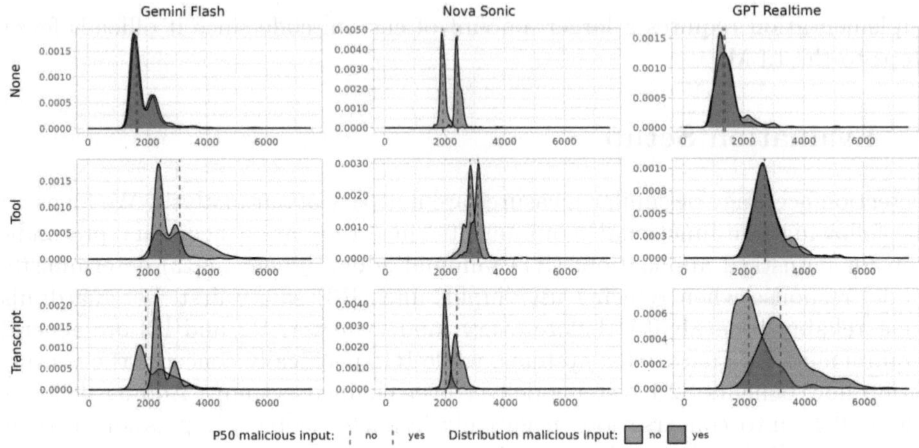

Fig. 3. Guardrails and Models Comparison.

Table 1. Latencies - Milliseconds non-malicious/malicious

model	guardrails	P50 n/m	P90 n/m	P99 n/m	mean n/m	SD n/m
Gemini	none	1616/1663	2278/2341	3598/3311	1828/1862	485/409
Gemini	tool	3096/2438	4109/3044	5009/3566	3149/2574	723/356
Gemini	transcript	1920/2339	3070/2960	4090/3421	2216/2477	602/313
Nova	none	1931/2431	2070/2591	2269/2876	1949/2457	127/155
Nova	tool	2841/3106	3018/3265	3478/3447	2825/3081	220/213
Nova	transcript	2004/2385	2153/2658	2333/2924	2022/2431	112/192
GPT	none	1391/1329	2112/1708	3035/2320	1488/1379	482/285
GPT	tool	2693/2697	3545/3586	4766/5040	2819/2841	556/646
GPT	transcript	2146/3199	3107/4591	4394/5811	2274/3377	627/866

malicious inputs are shown by dashed lines. Refer to Table 1 for the numeric values of P50, P90, and P99 quantiles, in addition to mean and standard deviation (truncated to full milliseconds).

For the "no guardrails" case, the difference between malicious and non-malicious input is expectedly negligible. Only Nova Sonic shows a slight difference, at a more narrow overall distribution than the other models. This difference is likely explained by the mildly different user inputs.

Tool guardrails delay answers for all models by roughly 0.6 to 1.4 s on average, with marginally larger delays for Gemini Flash and GPT Realtime compared to Nova Sonic. This impacts both malicious and non-malicious cases, as tool use always requires two model inferences (one to request the tool's result, another to use the tool's output) independent of the kind of input. Gemini Flash exposes a broader distribution in the non-malicious case, and a few outliers with longer

Table 2. Requirements Compliance

	Transcript-based			**Tool-based**		
	Gemini	**Nova**	**GPT**	**Gemini**	**Nova**	**GPT**
R1 non.	0.3s	0s	0.7s	1.4s	0.9s	1.3s
R1 mal.	0.6s	0s	1.8s	0.7s	0.6s	1.3s
R2	ok	ok	ok	ok	ok	ok
R3	ok	ok	limited	limited	ok	limited

durations occurred for Gemini Flash and GPT Realtime. Apart from these differences, and from the shift caused by added latency, the basic behavior of the models remain largely similar to the no guardrails case.

Transcript guardrails show slightly more varied distributions comparing malicious and non-malicious cases. Overall, they outperform tool-based guardrails in every case except for GPT Realtime and malicious input. The added latency in the non-malicious case is small enough for productive deployment for Gemini Flash and Nova Sonic. The latter shows added latency around 0 s for transcript guardrails in both cases. Note that the non-malicious case is less impacted for Gemini Flash and Nova Sonic than for GPT Realtime. This is likely due to the differing architecture of the corresponding inference systems, i.e. GPT Realtime's separate transcription model (see Sect. 3).

The overall compliance of the analyzed model and guardrail options with the requirements from Sect. 4 is shown in Table 2. Checking for deterministic refusal response (R2) did not expose any adverse behavior in our tests. Concerning safety, i.e. guardrails before answer (R3), transcript-based guardrails were well behaved with the (anecdotal) exception of some transcription errors for GPT Realtime, which could lead to guardrails erroneously passing. While we observed no errors for tool-based guardrails concerning R3, only Nova Sonic strictly guarantees tool execution before query answer. Concerning added latency (R1), all tool-based guardrails exceed the acceptable threshold with delays of 0.6–1.4 s for both benign and malicious input. Transcript-based guardrails violate this requirement for malicious input for Gemini Flash, and for both input types for GPT Realtime. Nova Sonic with transcript-based guardrails is the only combination that does not surpass the established 0.4 s threshold, with almost no added latency, and is therefore fully compliant with R1.

6 Future Work and Conclusion

Speech2Speech assistants offer compelling features like natural conversation flow. However, these come at a cost: the consolidation of speech processing into opaque, vendor-controlled models eliminates the intermediate text representations that conventional LLM guardrails depend upon. This case study examines two implementation options for regaining this control. The question it answers is "can customizable guardrails be integrated into S2S systems such that S2S benefits are preserved". We find that only one of the three vendor offerings investigated satisfies the corresponding requirements at the time of this writing. By consequence, productive use of S2S systems is currently dependent on external factors dictated by vendors, and thus is subject to change. As a next step, studies on the effectiveness of customizable guardrails according to their specific use cases are a necessity.

For vehicle assistants, this means the requirements for production-grade S2S guardrails cannot yet be fully guaranteed. Several developments could change this picture: vendor APIs exposing reliable and fast transcript streaming, mid-session refusal mechanisms, and novel approaches such as audio-native guardrails that bypass text intermediaries entirely. The automotive industry has long balanced innovation against safety. S2S technology is no exception: its benefits are evident, but so are the gaps between current capabilities and production requirements. Closing these gaps will require coordinated progress from model vendors, framework developers, and automotive integrators alike.

References

1. Amazon: Amazon Nova Sonic: Technical report and model card. https://www.amazon.science/publications/amazon-nova-sonic-technical-report-and-model-card. Accessed 31 Mar 2026
2. Amazon: Controlling how tools are chosen. https://docs.aws.amazon.com/nova/latest/userguide/speech-tools-choice.html. Accessed 31 Mar 2026
3. Amazon: How Amazon Bedrock Guardrails works. https://docs.aws.amazon.com/bedrock/latest/userguide/guardrails-how.html. Accessed 31 Mar 2026
4. Amazon: Introducing Amazon Nova Sonic: Human-like voice conversations for generative AI applications. https://aws.amazon.com/blogs/aws/introducing-amazon-nova-sonic-human-like-voice-conversations-for-generative-ai-applications/. Accessed 31 Mar 2026
5. Arora, S., et al.: On the landscape of spoken language models: a comprehensive survey. arXiv preprint arXiv:2504.08528 (2025)
6. Brady, P.T.: Effects of transmission delay on conversational behavior on echo-free telephone circuits. Bell Syst. Tech. J. **50**(1), 115–134 (1971)
7. Cui, W., et al.: Recent advances in speech language models: a survey. In: Proceedings of the 63rd Annual Meeting of the Association for Computational Linguistics (Volume 1: Long Papers), pp. 13943–13970. Association for Computational Linguistics (2025). https://doi.org/10.18653/v1/2025.acl-long.682
8. Défossez, A., et al.: Moshi: a speech-text foundation model for real-time dialogue. arXiv preprint arXiv:2410.00037 (2024)
9. Ding, D., et al.: Kimi-audio technical report. arXiv preprint arXiv:2504.18425 (2025)
10. Dong, Y., et al.: Building guardrails for large language models. arXiv preprint arXiv:2402.01822 (2024). https://doi.org/10.48550/ARXIV.2402.01822
11. Google: Gemini 2.5 Flash with Gemini Live API. https://cloud.google.com/vertex-ai/generative-ai/docs/models/gemini/2-5-flash-live-api. Accessed 31 Mar 2026
12. Google: Safety and content filters. https://cloud.google.com/vertex-ai/generative-ai/docs/multimodal/configure-safety-filters. Accessed 31 Mar 2026

13. Guardrails AI: The AI Reliability Platform. https://www.guardrailsai.com/. Accessed 31 Mar 2026
14. International Organization for Standardization: ISO/SAE 21434 Road vehicles – Cybersecurity engineering. https://www.iso.org/standard/70918.html. Accessed 31 Mar 2026
15. Krauss, R.M., Bricker, P.D.: Effects of transmission delay and access delay on the efficiency of verbal communication. J. Acoust. Soc. Am. **41**(2), 286–292 (1967)
16. Long, Z., et al.: Vita-audio: fast interleaved cross-modal token generation for efficient large speech-language model. arXiv preprint arXiv:2505.03739 (2025)
17. NVIDIA: NVIDIA NeMo Guardrails for Developers. https://developer.nvidia.com/nemo-guardrails. Accessed 31 Mar 2026
18. OpenAI: Moderation. https://platform.openai.com/docs/guides/moderation. Accessed 31 Mar 2026
19. OpenAI: Realtime API. https://platform.openai.com/docs/guides/realtime. Accessed 31 Mar 2026
20. OpenAI: Speech to text. https://platform.openai.com/docs/guides/speech-to-text. Accessed 31 Mar 2026
21. Papagiannidis, E., Mikalef, P., Conboy, K.: Responsible artificial intelligence governance: a review and research framework. J. Strateg. Inf. Syst. **34**(2), 101885 (2025). https://doi.org/10.1016/j.jsis.2024.101885
22. Peng, J., et al.: A survey on speech large language models for understanding. Authorea Preprints (2025)
23. Schoenenberg, K., Raake, A., Koeppe, J.: Why are you so slow? - misattribution of transmission delay to attributes of the conversation partner at the far-end. Int. J. Hum.-Comput. Stud. **72** (2014). https://doi.org/10.1016/j.ijhcs.2014.02.004
24. Strohmier, H., Dasri, Y., Murzello, D.: Exploring security vulnerabilities in chatgpt through multi-technique evaluation of resilience to jailbreak prompts and defensive measures. In: 2024 International Conference on Computer and Applications (ICCA), pp. 1–12. IEEE (2024). https://doi.org/10.1109/icca62237.2024.10928071
25. Xu, J., et al.: Qwen2. 5-omni technical report. arXiv preprint arXiv:2503.20215 (2025)
26. Yan, C., Ji, X., Wang, K., Jiang, Q., Jin, Z., Xu, W.: A survey on voice assistant security: attacks and countermeasures. ACM Comput. Surv. **55**(4), 1–36 (2022). https://doi.org/10.1145/3527153

From Large Language Model Predicates to Logic Tensor Networks: Neurosymbolic Offer Validation in Regulated Procurement

Cedric S. Haufe[1,2](✉) and Frieder Stolzenburg[1,3]

[1] Harz University of Applied Sciences, Wernigerode, Germany
{cedric+haufe,fstolzenburg}@hs-harz.de

[2] Merseburg University of Applied Sciences, Merseburg, Germany
cedric.haufe@hs-merseburg.de

[3] School of Computer Science and Engineering, University of New South Wales (UNSW), Sydney, Australia
f.stolzenburg@unsw.edu.au

Abstract. We present a neurosymbolic approach to validating offer documents in regulated public institutions. We employ a language model to extract information and then aggregate it with an LTN (Logic Tensor Network) to make an auditable decision. In regulated public institutions, decisions must be made in a manner that is both factually correct and legally verifiable. Our neurosymbolic approach allows existing domain-specific knowledge to be linked to the semantic text understanding of language models. The decisions resulting from our pipeline can be justified by predicate values, rule truth values, and corresponding text passages. Our experiments on a real corpus show that the proposed pipeline achieves performance comparable to existing models, but its key advantage lies in its interpretability, modular predicate extraction, and explicit support for XAI (Explainable AI).

Keywords: Neurosymbolic AI · Explainable AI (XAI) · Logic Tensor Networks (LTNs) · Offer Document Validation

1 Introduction

In regulated areas such as public academic institutions and their internal procurement systems, simple document classification, e.g., whether the document is an offer or an invoice or something different, is not sufficient. Decisions on the extent to which a document can be considered a valid offer must be traceable and legally sound. It must be clearly recognisable on the basis of which facts or characteristics a decision was made. Conventional document classification, for example based on purely statistical or neural network models does not provide any explanations directly linked to the original document [15]. Classic explainable rule-based systems, on the other hand, require that the decision-relevant

D. Wolter and G. Schwalbe (Eds.): KI 2026, LNAI 16830, pp. 236–243, 2027.
https://doi.org/10.1007/978-3-032-32335-4_19

properties of a document are already available in a structured form. Accordingly, these must first be extracted from the text, which decouples them from the original document [3]. This leads to a gap between powerful but difficult-to-explain text models [15] and precise but resource-intensive rule-based systems [7]. We bridge this gap with a neurosymbolic pipeline [3,7] which combines predicate extraction based on a Large Language Model (LLM) with a Logic Tensor Network (LTN) for aggregation and final decision-making [1,6,16]. Unlike alternative neural-symbolic systems like DeepProbLog [12] and NeurASP [17], our focus is evidence-preserving LLM predicate extraction for procurement documents. In the first step, an LLM evaluates the truth values of predefined domain-specific predicates for each potential offer [4]. An LTN aggregates these values together with coded assignment rules to make a decision about `IS_VALID_OFFER` and simultaneously provides predicate and rule truth values as an explanation. By storing the corresponding textual evidence in the predicate layer, it is thus possible to clearly identify which text passage has a high influence on the final decision.

2 Problem Definition and Data

2.1 Task Definition

Formally, let $\mathcal{D} = \{d_1, \ldots, d_N\}$ be the set of potential offers to be considered, where each $d_i \in \mathcal{D}$ represents the text extracted from a PDF, including any Optical Character Recognition (OCR) that may be required. For each document d_i, there is a binary ground truth label $y_i \in \{0, 1\}$ where $y_i = 1$ means that d_i can be accepted as a valid offer in the context described, and $y_i = 0$ means that it is not a valid offer (but rather, e.g., an invoice, delivery note, order confirmation, general price list, etc.) and therefore cannot be used for procurement. The primary task can thus be formulated as a binary classification task for documents: Given a document d, the corresponding label y has to be predicted. Accordingly, the decision must be based on explicit, domain-specific criteria and must be justifiable in the event of an audit or legal dispute [13,15]. We therefore model offer validation below as a binary classification task with additional requirements such as rule-based verifiability and explainability at the document level.

2.2 Predicate Space and Semantic Structure

Through manual pre-review of original offers submitted in the context of procurement and internal procurement guidelines, we identify a set of K domain-specific predicates that meaningfully characterise whether a document can be considered as an offer. In this context, $K = 8$ predicates were identified. First, we model a vector of these domain-specific predicates for each document d:

$$\mathbf{p}(d) = \big(p_1(d), \ldots, p_K(d)\big)$$

each of which describes a part of the central content-related properties of an offer. Each predicate $p_k(d)$ represents the degree to which a semantically clearly defined property is fulfilled and is later interpreted as a real truth value in $[0, 1]$: The value 0 corresponds to 'does not apply', values close to 1 correspond to 'clearly applies'. We use the following predicates:

OFFER_TITLE	Title or wording identifies the document as an offer.
OFFER_NUMBER	Offer number, reference or comparable identifier is present.
OFFER_VALIDITY	Validity period or validity scope is specified.
RESERVATION_CLAUSES	Legal reservations or restrictions are present.
PAYMENT_TERMS	Payment conditions are specified.
DELIVERY_TERMS	Delivery conditions or preconditions are specified.
SALES_CONTACT	A supplier or sales contact is given.
NOT_OFFER	Evidence indicates another document type, e.g. an invoice.

2.3 Data Set and Annotation

Our data set is based on a corpus of documents, which originate from actual procurements by a German public university. All documents are available in PDF format and include both digitally created content and scanned documents. The average length of a document is approximately two pages. The corpus is linguistically heterogeneous, with a focus on German-language documents. Each document d was manually assigned a binary label IS_VALID_OFFER(d) $\in \{0, 1\}$ which identifies the extent to which it is valid or invalid. A valid offer is marked with IS_VALID_OFFER $= 1$ and could be used in the real process. Documents that clearly serve a different purpose are marked with IS_VALID_OFFER(d) $= 0$. The annotation was carried out by the first author, partly in consultation with employees from internal specialist departments, in order to correctly interpret and reflect internal guidelines. This is taken as ground truth. The corpus considered here comprises a total of $N = 200$ documents, of which 35 % are annotated as valid offers. The documents contain personal data within the meaning of European data protection law.

3 Method: The Neurosymbolic Pipeline

3.1 Architecture Overview

The potential offers submitted in the course of a procurement process are first prepared. For this purpose, the text contained therein is extracted or, if necessary, OCR is performed. The locally deployed LLM is then used as a predicate layer to determine truth values for the domain-specific predicates (see Sect. 2.2). Since these potential offers usually contain several pages and numerous layout elements, the LLM does not work directly with the entire raw text. Instead, this raw text is divided into a series of meaningful text excerpts. For each predicate p_k, we then formulate a predicate-specific query and evaluate the chunks based on this. We use a multi-stage search module for this. First, a lexical ranking of the chunks is determined based on the Best Matching ranking algorithm (BM25)

[14]. This is followed by a semantic re-ranking, namely embedding similarity and an LLM-based cross-encoder. Only the chunks with the best evaluation are used to determine the truth values of the respective predicate [10,11]. After that, an LTN is used [1,6,16] to make a decision about the validity of the potential offers based on these truth values. The predicate values $\mathbf{p}(d)$ are used as continuous inputs to apply explicit domain-specific rules.

3.2 LLM-Based Predicate Extraction

The predicate layer determines a numerical value $p_k(d) \in [0, 1]$ for each potential offer d and each predicate p_k. The calculation is performed through structured interaction with an LLM, which uses selected chunks to make judgements and express confidence levels for each predicate. In all experiments, we primarily use a 14B instruction model from Qwen2.5 (`Qwen2.5-14B-Instruct`) [2] as the LLM within the predicate layer. For each predicate, we perform up to three calls to the 14B model to obtain syntactically valid and contextually usable JSON output. If this fails, a fallback call is made to a larger 32B LLM (Qwen2.5-32B-Instruct).

Our pipeline is based on the Multi-Class Self-Reflection approach (MCSR) [4]. For each predicate p_k, we use a three-level ordinal scale with the classes $c \in \{0, 1, 2\}$ (where 0 = not fulfilled, 1 = partially fulfilled or uncertain, 2 = clearly fulfilled or present). For a potential offer d and a predicate, the model receives a predicate-specific query describing the classes and their semantic meaning (e.g. 'no offer number recognisable', 'some clues are present but unclear', 'clearly marked as offer number'). In a single query ('evaluate – reflect – conclude'), the LLM first evaluates each class separately and outputs an initial confidence estimate together with evidence. This evaluation is then reflected upon and the class-related confidence values are revised on this basis. Finally, the class with the highest confidence is selected as the winning class [4]. The reflected confidence of this class is forwarded as a truth value to the decisive LTN layer. The resulting values $p_k(d) \in [0, 1]$ are used as fuzzy truth values in the LTN decision layer. Prompts and implementation details are available as repository (see https://github.com/cedricshaufe/From-Large-Language-Model-Predicates-to-Logic-Tensor-Networks and also [9]).

3.3 LTN-Based Decision Logic

The predicate layer described in Sect. 3.2 assigns a vector with continuous truth values to each potential offer d:

$$\mathbf{p}(d) \in [0, 1]^8$$

However, in our implementation, these eight predicates are mapped by 11 derived input channels. This allows clear evidence to be distinguished from vague/existing evidence for selected predicates, while still allowing them to be considered together. To aggregate these predicates, we use an LTN in the sense of Real Logic [1,6,16]. In Real Logic, predicates and formulas are assigned truth values in $[0, 1]$, and fuzzy logic operators are defined via differentiable T-norms, e.g. Gödel, Łukasiewicz, and Product [8]. Let $\wedge$, $\vee$ and $\neg$ be the fuzzy conjunction, disjunction and negation induced by the selected logic backend. In our pipeline, the influence of selected channels is mapped by learnable *smooth gates* $g_i = \sigma(\alpha_i) \in (0, 1)$ where σ denotes the sigmoid function, i.e. $\tilde{p}_i(d) = g_i\, p_i(d)$. *(NOT_OFFER)* is mapped as negative evidence by a separate learnable gate. Using the fuzzy operators of the selected backend, we first determine a core for the positive evidence PosCore(d) and then a core for the negative evidence NegCore(d) *(NOT_OFFER)*. The base offer value is defined as

$$O_{\text{base}}(d) \;=\; \text{PosCore}(d) \;\wedge\; \neg\, \text{NegCore}(d),$$

which yields $O_{\text{base}}(d) \in [0, 1]$. A series of fuzzy logic implications are formulated using predicates. This means that the final decision can also be supported by domain-specific rules. These rules describe when an offer is valid in this context. These implications are evaluated using a fuzzy implication function [8]. A truth value $R_k(d) \in [0, 1]$ is assigned to each rule. The LTN decision layer outputs a base evaluation $\mathrm{O}_{\text{base}}(d)$. This is calculated from the gated predicate channels using the selected fuzzy logic backend. `IS_VALID_OFFER` is decided by applying a threshold to the base score. The threshold to be used is determined on the training data of each fold by optimising the F_1-score of the positive class. The learnable gating parameters are trained in a supervised manner by minimising the binary cross-entropy (BCE) on the training split of each fold.

4 Experimental Setup

4.1 Model Variants

We evaluate **MCSR+LTN** as a combination of MCSR-based predicate estimation and LTN-based decision logic, **LTN** as a classic baseline, **BERT** as a purely neural baseline and **LLM (BM25+Semantic-CE)** as a direct LLM baseline. For the LTN-based variants, we examine several configurations of the logical backend (e.g. Łukasiewicz logic and product-based T-norms) to assess their influence [1,8,16].

4.2 Evaluation Report

Since the available data set is small and slightly unbalanced (see Sect. 2.3), we use stratified 5-fold cross-validation. This involves performing 5 repetitions, resulting in 25 folds with a similar class distribution. In each fold, four folds serve as the training data set and one fold serves as the test data set. The metrics obtained are averaged across the 25 test folds. The hyperparameters of the models are determined exclusively on the basis of the training data of one fold. The test data of one fold is only used for the final evaluation. Since `IS_VALID_OFFER` is a binary task with unbalanced class distribution (35 % positive class), we primarily specify the F_1-score of the positive class $\mathrm{F1}_{\text{pos}}$.

5 Empirical Results

5.1 Overall Comparison of Pipelines

Table 1 shows a post-hoc summary of the best F_1 results for each pipeline. The pure LTN variant achieves an average F_1 value of 0.899 for the positive class and accordingly serves as the neurosymbolic baseline.

Table 1. Post-hoc average test performance of the approaches considered over 25 test folds (5 stratified splits × 5-fold cross-validation, $N = 200$, 35 % valid offers).

Pipeline	Fuzzy-Logic	F_1 (pos.)
LTN	Łukasiewicz	0.899 ± 0.064
MCSR+LTN	Product	0.874 ± 0.043
BERT	–	0.859 ± 0.097
LLM (BM25+Semantic-CE)	–	0.843 ± 0.059

MCSR-based predicate recognition does not surpass the classic-LTN configuration on this corpus and achieves F_1=0.874. In comparison, the sole use of the same language model and retrieval with an F_1 value of 0.843 performs slightly worse than the MCSR approach. As a purely neural reference, we additionally use a BERT-based document classification (bert-base-german-cased [5]), which predicts `IS_VALID_OFFER` directly from the full texts. With an identical cross-validation protocol, BERT achieves a mean F_1 value of 0.859 ± 0.097 (Table 1).

6 Conclusion

In this article, we have presented a neurosymbolic pipeline for validating offers in a regulated context. This pipeline enables text evidence to be linked to logical predefined rules, making the decision taken explainable. Our experiments with a real corpus of potential offers in the described context show that the performance of the proposed pipeline is comparable to the described baseline models. The strength of the proposed pipeline lies in its interpretability and modular predicate extraction. However, the approach remains limited by several factors: The data set is relatively small, annotated by a single person and comes from a specific institutional and legal context, the rules are domain-specific and hand-coded, and the LLM-based predicate estimators are currently only tested for the German language. Therefore, we understand the results as proof of concept for explainable offer validation in regulated contexts.

Statement of the Authors. GPT-5.1 (OpenAI) was used to assist with wording, stylistic revision, code support, prompt design refinement used in the experiments (LLM queries) and the creation of preliminary summaries of external literature. A translation programme (DeepL) was used to assist with the translation from German into English for this text.

References

1. Badreddine, S., d'Avila Garcez, A., Serafini, L., Spranger, M.: Logic tensor networks. Artif. Intell. **303**, 103649 (2022). https://doi.org/10.1016/j.artint.2021.103649
2. Bai, J., et al.: Qwen technical report (2023). https://arxiv.org/pdf/2309.16609
3. Besold, T.R., et al.: Neural-symbolic learning and reasoning: a survey and interpretation. In: Hitzler, P., Sarker, M.K. (eds.) Neuro-Symbolic Artificial Intelligence: The State of the Art, chap. 1. Frontiers in Artificial Intelligence and Applications, IOS Press, Amsterdam and Berlin and Washington, DC (2022). https://doi.org/10.3233/FAIA210348
4. Bodhwani, U., Ling, Y., Dong, S., Feng, Y., Li, H., Goyal, A.: A calibrated reflection approach for enhancing confidence estimation in LLMs. In: Cao, T., et al. (eds.) Proceedings of the 5th Workshop on Trustworthy NLP (TrustNLP 2025), pp. 399–411. Association for Computational Linguistics, Stroudsburg, PA, USA (2025). https://doi.org/10.18653/v1/2025.trustnlp-main.26
5. Devlin, J., Chang, M.W., Lee, K., Toutanova, K.: Bert: pre-training of deep bidirectional transformers for language understanding. In: Burstein, J., Doran, C., Solorio, T. (eds.) Proceedings of the 2019 Conference of the North American Chapter of the Association for Computational Linguistics: Human Language Technologies, Volume 1 (Long and Short Papers), pp. 4171–4186. Association for Computational Linguistics, Minneapolis, Minnesota (2019). https://doi.org/10.18653/v1/N19-1423. https://aclanthology.org/N19-1423/
6. Donadello, I., Serafini, L., d'Avila Garcez, A.: Logic tensor networks for semantic image interpretation. In: Sierra, C. (ed.) International Joint Conferences on Artificial Intelligence (IJCAI 2017), pp. 1596–1602. Curran Associates Inc, Red Hook, NY (2017). https://doi.org/10.24963/ijcai.2017/221
7. Garcez, A.D., Lamb, L.C.: Neurosymbolic AI: the 3rd wave. Artif. Intell. Rev. **56**(11), 12387–12406 (2023). https://doi.org/10.1007/s10462-023-10448-w
8. Hájek, P.: Metamathematics of Fuzzy Logic, Trends in Logic, vol. 4. Kluwer Academic, Dordrecht (1998). https://doi.org/10.1007/978-94-011-5300-3
9. Haufe, C., Stolzenburg, F.: From large language model predicates to logic tensor networks: neurosymbolic offer validation in regulated procurement. CoRR – Computing Research Repository arXiv:2604.05539, Cornell University Library (2026). https://arxiv.org/abs/2604.05539
10. Lewis, P., et al.: Retrieval-augmented generation for knowledge-intensive NLP tasks. In: H. Larochelle, M. Ranzato, R. Hadsell, M.F. Balcan, H. Lin (eds.) Advances in Neural Information Processing Systems, vol. 33, pp. 9459–9474. Curran Associates, Inc (2020). https://dl.acm.org/doi/proceedings/10.5555/3495724
11. Lin, J., Nogueira, R., Yates, A.: Pretrained Transformers for Text Ranking: BERT and Beyond. Synthesis Lectures on Human Language Technologies, 1st edn. Springer, Cham (2022). https://doi.org/10.1007/978-3-031-02181-7
12. Manhaeve, R., Dumančić, S., Kimmig, A., Demeester, T., De Raedt, L.: Neural probabilistic logic programming in DeepProbLog. Artif. Intell. **298**, 103504 (2021). https://doi.org/10.1016/j.artint.2021.103504
13. Richmond, K.M., Muddamsetty, S.M., Gammeltoft-Hansen, T., Olsen, H.P., Moeslund, T.B.: Explainable AI and law: an evidential survey. Digit. Soc. **3**(1), 1 (2023). https://doi.org/10.1007/s44206-023-00081-z
14. Robertson, S., Zaragoza, H.: The probabilistic relevance framework: BM25 and beyond. Found. Trends® Inf. Retrieval **3**(4), 333–389 (2009). https://doi.org/10.1561/1500000019

15. Rudin, C.: Stop explaining black box machine learning models for high stakes decisions and use interpretable models instead. Nat. Mach. Intell. **1**(5), 206–215 (2019). https://doi.org/10.1038/s42256-019-0048-x
16. Serafini, L., d'Avila Garcez, A.S.: Learning and reasoning with logic tensor networks. In: Adorni, G., Cagnoni, S., Gori, M., Maratea, M. (eds.) AI*IA 2016. LNCS (LNAI), vol. 10037, pp. 334–348. Springer, Cham (2016). https://doi.org/10.1007/978-3-319-49130-1_25
17. Yang, Z., Ishay, A., Lee, J.: Neurasp: embracing neural networks into answer set programming. In: Proceedings of the Twenty-Ninth International Joint Conference on Artificial Intelligence, pp. 1755–1762 (2020). https://doi.org/10.24963/ijcai.2020/243

Quantum Temporal Convolution Network

Rihab Hoceini[1(✉)] and Ahmed Bouida[2]

[1] Naturwissenschaftlich-Technische Fakultät, Universität Siegen, 57068 Siegen, Germany
Rihab3.Hoceini@student.uni-siegen.de

[2] Laboratory of Information Processing and Telecommunication (LTIT), University TAHRI Mohamed, Bechar, Algeria

Abstract. A promising application for the potential revolutionization offered by quantum computing is the field of machine learning through the application of quantum machine learning. Yet a critical challenge remains: no definitive evidence demonstrating a systematic performance advantage of quantum machine learning models over their classical approaches. Researchers have attempted to address this uncertainty by employing focused benchmarking experiments that explore particular model architectures and particular computational tasks and datasets with different complexities. In this work, we conduct a systematic benchmarking of the quantum temporal convolutional network (QTCN) against its classical counterpart. To ensure a rigorous and controlled comparison, we implement a mirror quantum architecture that faithfully replicates the structural design of the classical TCN. Experimental results shows that the QTCN outperforms classical models only on complex, richly structured datasets like those from the music domain. Furthermore, by showing exactly how entanglement improves the model's performance in complex datasets, we provide a clear path for future improvements.

Keywords: Sequential Data · Entanglement · Benchmarking Quantum Models

1 Introduction

Sequential data mining has attracted considerable interest across domains including finance, medicine, and agriculture [9,10]. With the growing volume of stored data and the pressure to develop innovative machine learning methods, quantum computing has emerged as a promising avenue for enhancing classical techniques [12,17]. Quantum analogues of classical machine learning models have demonstrated theoretical speedups [6], yet clear evidence of practical quantum advantage remains limited. Systematic and fair benchmarking under identical experimental conditions is therefore essential. Our main contribution is the benchmarking of the quantum temporal convolutional network (QTCN) against its classical counterpart across varying levels of data complexity. To ensure a fair

D. Wolter and G. Schwalbe (Eds.): KI 2026, LNAI 16830, pp. 244–251, 2027.
https://doi.org/10.1007/978-3-032-32335-4_20

comparison, the QTCN is designed as a direct structural mirror of the classical TCN, preserving its architecture and causality constraints. To the best of our knowledge, this constitutes the first implementation that faithfully reproduces the exact structure of a classical TCN within a quantum framework.

2 Quantum Temporal Convolutional Network

The proposed quantum temporal convolutional network (QTCN) preserves the overall structure of standard temporal convolutional networks (TCNs) while introducing quantum processing modules. The general architecture using residual blocks, illustrated in Fig. 1, is composed of three main stages: an input layer, a stack of residual blocks with quantum dilated convolutions, and a fully connected output layer. Each input vector at time step $x_t \in \mathbb{R}^2$ is linearly projected into a higher-dimensional hidden space of size h as $z_t = W_{\text{input}} x_t + b_{\text{input}}$.

2.1 Residual Blocks with Quantum Dilated Convolutions

The TCN enforces the causal constraint through causal convolutions, where the output at time t depends only on elements up to and including time t. Dilated convolutions increase the receptive field without reducing resolution. Since the effectiveness of the TCN fundamentally relies on dilated convolution, it provides a natural foundation for quantum integration. In the QTCN, the dilated convolution is realized through an entanglement-based module.

The proposed model employs a two-layer encoding strategy. The first layer is a temporal phase encoding, mapping input x_i to a quantum state via:

$$U_{\text{phase}}(x_i) = e^{-ix_i\pi\frac{(2i+1)}{n}Z} \tag{1}$$

The second layer is a standard angle encoding: $U_{R_y}(x_i) = R_y(x_i\pi)$. Together, these layers jointly embed temporal order and amplitude information, making the representation more expressive and physically grounded. Entanglement is applied after encoding, realizing the dilated convolution through entangling gate translations over qubit distances [8]:

$$\prod_{i=0}^{n-d-1} (\text{CNOT}_{i,i+d} \cdot R_Z(w_i)_{i+d}) \tag{2}$$

where $\text{CNOT}_{i,i+d}$ entangles qubit i with qubit $i+d$, and $R_Z(w_i)$ are trainable rotations on the target qubits. For an n-qubit system with dilation rate d, CNOT operations are applied between qubits i and $i+d$ for even i, followed by R_Z rotations on the target qubits. The final feature representation is obtained by measuring Pauli-Z expectation values for all qubits.

The QTCN uses three residual blocks with exponentially growing dilation rates (2^n, yielding rates 1, 2, 4), with skip connections ensuring stable gradient flow:

$$f_{res}(x) = F(x) + x \tag{3}$$

where $F(x)$ is the output of the quantum-convolutional path and a 1×1 convolution is applied when needed to match dimensions. Temporal chomping preserves causal structure by removing future-looking artifacts introduced by dilation.

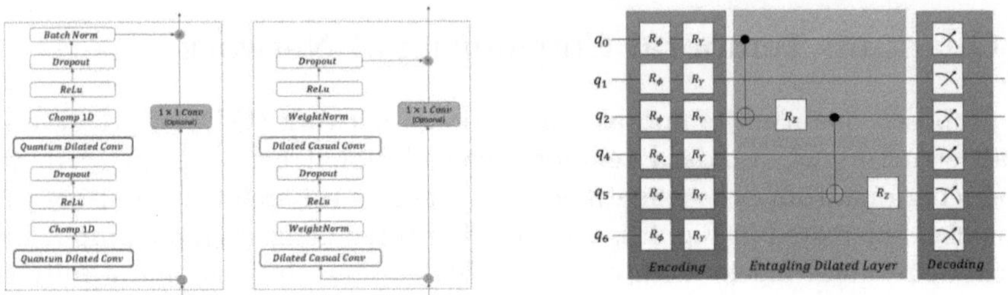

(a) (b)

Fig. 1. (a) Residual block structures in the QTCN (left) and the standard TCN (right). The two architectures are identical except that the classical dilated causal convolution is replaced by a quantum dilated convolution in QTCN (red blocks). (b) Example of a Quantum Dilated Convolutional Neural Network (QDCNN) circuit with dilation rate = 2. (Color figure online)

2.2 Modeling Sequence Data

For benchmarking, we selected datasets previously used in the original TCN evaluation [4], ordered from low to high complexity: Adding Problem [13], Sequential MNIST [14], and polyphonic music datasets (JSB Chorales and Nottingham) [2]. This ordering is critical for evaluating whether quantum advantage is data-complexity-dependent (Table 1).

Table 1. Benchmarking sequence tasks

Task	Input	Task	Complexity
Adding Problem	Sequence length n, depth 2	Sum of two marked values	Low
Sequential MNIST	784×1 pixel sequence	Classify digit	Moderate
JSB Chorales	88-bit piano vectors	Predict next notes	High
Nottingham	88-bit piano vectors	Predict next notes	Higher

3 Results and Discussion

We evaluate the QTCN on standard sequence modeling benchmarks relative to classical TCN, LSTM, GRU, RNN [4], and R-Transformer [22] under identical experimental conditions. All experiments use the PennyLane `default.qubit` simulator with PyTorch, the same datasets and splits as the classical TCN study, and identical optimizers, learning rates, epochs, and evaluation metrics. Simulations are run on a workstation with an AMD Ryzen 9 CPU, 64 GB RAM, and an NVIDIA Quadro A5000 GPU (16 GB VRAM) (Table 2).

Table 2. Hyperparameter configurations per dataset

Dataset	Qubits	LR	Batch	Epochs	Dropout
Adding Problem	6	4×10^{-3}	32	10	0
JSB Chorales	6	1×10^{-3}	–	100	0.2
Nottingham	6	1×10^{-3}	–	100	0.5
Sequential MNIST	6	2×10^{-3}	64	20	0

Table 3. Benchmark results on sequence modeling tasks.

Task (Metric)	LSTM	GRU	RNN	TCN	QTCN	R-Trans.
Seq. MNIST (accuracy)	87.2	96.2	21.5	99.0	50	**99.1**
Adding T=600 (loss)	0.164	5.3e-5	0.177	**5.8e-5**	0.139	–
JSB Chorales (loss)	8.45	8.43	8.91	8.10	**0.0026**	–
Nottingham (loss)	3.29	3.46	4.05	3.07	**3.9e-5**	2.37

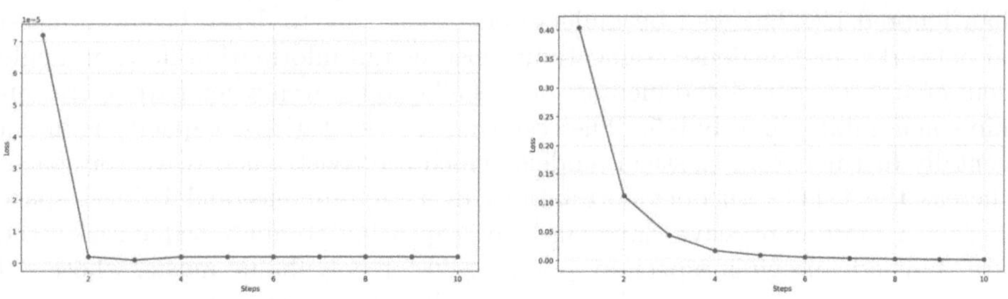

(a) (b)

Fig. 2. Test losses across epochs for the Nottingham (a) and JSB Chorales (b) datasets

The results reveal a strong performance differential across tasks. The QTCN excels on music modeling, outperforming all classical baselines by several orders of magnitude, while underperforming on lower-complexity tasks (Table 3).

- **Sequential MNIST.** The QTCN achieves an accuracy of 50.0, near chance level, well below the TCN (99.0) and R-Transformer (99.1). This task requires classifying pixel-level sequential patterns where classical models already perform at near-perfect levels, leaving limited room for any structural quantum benefit.
- **Adding Problem.** The QTCN loss (0.139) is comparable to the underperforming LSTM (0.164) and RNN (0.177), while GRU (5.3×10^{-5}) and TCN (5.8×10^{-5}) achieve several orders of magnitude lower values. The task is low-complexity and well-suited to classical architectures, providing insufficient structural richness for quantum operations to offer advantage.
- **Polyphonic Music.** The QTCN achieves remarkable performance on both music datasets. On JSB Chorales, the QTCN obtains a loss of 0.0026, compared to 8.10 for the TCN and 2.37 for the R-Transformer. On Nottingham, the QTCN yields a near-zero loss of 3.9×10^{-5}, while the TCN and R-Transformer achieve 3.07 and 2.37, respectively. As shown in Fig. 2, both music datasets exhibit stable, gradual convergence with training and validation curves closely aligned, indicating robust generalization without overfitting. Importantly, prior work [7,11,18] shows that quantum models can achieve high training accuracy while generalizing well from limited data, supporting the interpretation that the observed performance reflects genuine quantum learning.

The core mechanism enabling this advantage is the entanglement module within the QDCNN circuit. Unlike classical dilated convolutions, which skip intermediate positions and only indirectly aggregate their context [23], the quantum dilated convolution correlates these positions non-locally through entanglement, weaving intermediate data into the entangled quantum state. Entanglement entropy has been shown to rise as quantum CNNs learn finer features, confirming that intermediate "skipped" positions are actively encoded rather than ignored [3]. This can be understood by analogy to dense layers in classical networks: just as dense connectivity ensures full information flow, entanglement guarantees correlated memory across all qubits, even when gate operations skip some qubits directly [15]. The resulting representational capacity is fundamentally distinct from classical models, which are constrained to vector spaces, whereas the QTCN encodes correlations in a high-dimensional Hilbert space, offering a more expressive "language" for capturing complex sequential structure. This advantage is especially pronounced for polyphonic music, whose rich harmonic and rhythmic correlations naturally align with entanglement-based representations. Prior work [1,19] argues that musical relationships are intrinsically entanglement-like, and that classical sequence models such as RNNs and LSTMs compress musical history into a single hidden vector, limiting their capacity to represent inherent ambiguity. By contrast, the QTCN replaces the hidden state with a density matrix, enabling simultaneous representation of multiple musical interpretations, uncertainty, and coherence—properties that are crucial for modeling polyphonic structure and likely explain the substantial gains in NLL loss. Further support comes from studies linking music cognition to quantum-probabilistic frameworks [5,16], where expectation and meaning follow superposed and context-dependent states rather than classical logic.

3.1 Quantum and Classical TCN Comparison

Classical dilated convolutions expand the receptive field by skipping intermediate positions, which are not directly processed but only indirectly incorporated through context aggregation [20,21]. In the QDCNN, dilation is instead realized through entangling gate translations over increasing qubit distances, where a shift by i qubits corresponds to a dilation rate of 2^i. Rather than ignoring skipped positions, entanglement correlates them non-locally, ensuring they are woven into the joint quantum state.

Beyond the entanglement advantage, the QTCN offers several additional benefits over the classical TCN:

1. **Lower parameter count.** The QTCN requires substantially fewer parameters than fully classical TCNs. In all experimental settings, the QTCN contains no more than 45k parameters, as detailed in Table 4.

Table 4. Trainable parameter counts for QTCN and classical TCN

Dataset	QTCN Parameters	Classical TCN Parameters
Adding Problem ($T = 600$)	~38k	~70k
JSB Chorales	~38k	~300k
Nottingham	~38k	~1M
Sequential MNIST	~39k	~70k

2. **Enhanced feature representation.** Quantum data encoding maps classical inputs to a higher-dimensional quantum feature space, increasing representational expressiveness.
3. **More efficient long-range dependency capture.** QTCN's quantum dilated convolutions capture long-range dependencies with substantially fewer layers than classical TCNs, as demonstrated by superior performance on complex datasets even with a minimal QDCNN configuration.
4. **Quantum parallelism.** In addition to classical convolutional parallelism, the QTCN benefits from quantum parallelism, whereby quantum operations encode and manipulate multiple states simultaneously.

A current limitation of the QTCN is that the dilation rate is constrained by the number of qubits, which restricts its maximum achievable range.

4 Conclusion

We presented the QTCN, a quantum temporal convolutional network that mirrors the architecture and causality constraints of the classical TCN for principled quantum-classical benchmarking. Systematic evaluation across datasets of increasing complexity demonstrates that the QTCN provides significant improvements over the classical TCN on highly structured sequential data, while underperforming on simpler tasks. These findings indicate that quantum advantage is strongly data-dependent, and that meaningful quantum benefit in machine learning requires architectures carefully matched to problems exhibiting long-range dependencies and non-local correlations. Future work should target large language modeling tasks, where the high structural complexity of language data may further amplify the quantum advantage observed here.

Acknowledgments. The authors acknowledge support by the Deutsche Forschungsgemeinschaft (DFG, German Research Foundation), project number 534951134.

References

1. Abdyssagin, R.B., Coecke, B.: Quantum concept music score from quantum picturalism: musical incarnation of a bell-pair under measurements (2025). arXiv preprint arXiv:2510.05391
2. Allan, M., Williams, C.: Harmonising chorales by probabilistic inference. Adv. Neural. Inf. Process. Syst. **17** (2004)
3. Anagiannis, V., Cheng, M.C.: Entangled q-convolutional neural nets. Mach. Learn. Sci. Technol. **2**(4), 045026 (2021)
4. Bai, S., Kolter, J.Z., Koltun, V.: An empirical evaluation of generic convolutional and recurrent networks for sequence modeling (2018). arXiv preprint arXiv:1803.01271
5. Beim Graben, P., Blutner, R.: Quantum approaches to music cognition. J. Math. Psychol. **91**, 38–50 (2019)
6. Biamonte, J., Wittek, P., Pancotti, N., Rebentrost, P., Wiebe, N., Lloyd, S.: Quantum machine learning. Nature **549**(7671), 195–202 (2017)
7. Caro, M.C., et al.: Generalization in quantum machine learning from few training data. Nat. Commun. **13**(1), 4919 (2022)
8. Chen, Y.: QDCNN: quantum dilated convolutional neural network (2021). arXiv preprint arXiv:2110.15667
9. Esling, P., Agon, C.: Time-series data mining. ACM Comput. Surv. (CSUR) **45**(1), 1–34 (2012)
10. Fu, T.C.: A review on time series data mining. Eng. Appl. Artif. Intell. **24**(1), 164–181 (2011)
11. Gil-Fuster, E., Eisert, J., Bravo-Prieto, C.: Understanding quantum machine learning also requires rethinking generalization. Nat. Commun. **15**(1), 2277 (2024)
12. Hilbert, M.: Priscila lópez the world's technological capacity to store, communicate, and compute information. Science **60**, 65 (2017)
13. Hochreiter, S., Schmidhuber, J.: Long short-term memory. Neural Comput. **9**(8), 1735–1780 (1997)

14. LeCun, Y., Bottou, L., Bengio, Y., Haffner, P.: Gradient-based learning applied to document recognition. Proc. IEEE **86**(11), 2278–2324 (1998)
15. Levine, Y., Sharir, O., Cohen, N., Shashua, A.: Quantum entanglement in deep learning architectures. Phys. Rev. Lett. **122**(6), 065301 (2019)
16. Miranda, E.R.: Advances in Quantum Computer Music, vol. 6, World Scientific (2024)
17. Nielsen, M.A., Chuang, I.L.: Quantum computation and quantum information, Cambridge University Press (2010)
18. Peters, E., Schuld, M.: Generalization despite overfitting in quantum machine learning models. Quantum **7**, 1210 (2023)
19. Seo, J., Montiel, M.: Density matrix RNN (DM-RNN): a quantum information theoretic framework for modeling musical context and polyphony (2026). arXiv preprint arXiv:2601.04592
20. Wang, P., et al.: Understanding convolution for semantic segmentation. In: IEEE Winter Conference on Applications of Computer Vision (WACV), pp. 1451–1460. IEEE (2018)
21. Wang, Z., Ji, S.: Smoothed dilated convolutions for improved dense prediction. In: Proceedings of the 24th ACM SIGKDD International Conference on Knowledge Discovery & Data Mining, pp. 2486–2495 (2018)
22. Wang, Z., Ma, Y., Liu, Z., Tang, J.: R-transformer: recurrent neural network enhanced transformer (2019). arXiv preprint arXiv:1907.05572
23. Ziegler, T., Fritsche, M., Kuhn, L., Donhauser, K.: Efficient smoothing of dilated convolutions for image segmentation (2019). arXiv preprint arXiv:1903.07992

Constrained Entity Selection Under Partial Knowledge for LLM-Based Knowledge Graph QA

Emanuel Kitzelmann(✉)

Brandenburg University of Applied Sciences, Brandenburg a.d.H., Germany
emanuel.kitzelmann@th-brandenburg.de

Abstract. Large language models are increasingly used for knowledge graph question answering (KGQA), but can fail to correctly ground answers in the underlying graph. Current approaches to LLM-based KGQA either rely on full semantic parsing into executable queries such as SPARQL, which is brittle in practice due to complex schemas or incompleteness of real-world KGs, or on LLM-reasoning and answer generation over KGs, which can be more robust but lacks formal guarantees.

In this work, we study a complementary setting in which *candidate* answers are generated by an LLM-based system and subsequently verified using lightweight symbolic constraints derived from the question. We introduce *Constrained Entity Selection under Partial Knowledge (CES-PK)*, a problem formulation that focuses on eliminating invalid answers and providing symbolic support for valid ones without requiring construction of executable logical forms. To account for incomplete KGs, we employ a three-valued constraint semantics (*satisfied, violated, unknown*) that avoids incorrect rejections under open-world assumptions.

To demonstrate the effects of our method, we instantiate CES-PK over the Hetionet biomedical knowledge graph and evaluate both controlled and LLM-generated candidate sets. Experiments show that constraint-based verification improves precision while preserving recall and provides additional symbolic evidence for remaining candidates.

Keywords: Knowledge Graph Question Answering · Large Language Models · Constraint-Based Verification · Incomplete Knowledge Graphs

1 Introduction

Large language models (LLMs) are increasingly used for knowledge graph question answering (KGQA) [11], but may fail to correctly ground answers in the underlying graph and violate structural or semantic constraints.

Current LLM approaches to KGQA typically follow one of two paradigms. In semantic parsing [3,4], questions are translated into executable logical forms such as SPARQL queries. While this enables precise answers, generating correct

D. Wolter and G. Schwalbe (Eds.): KI 2026, LNAI 16830, pp. 252–259, 2027.
https://doi.org/10.1007/978-3-032-32335-4_21

queries remains challenging for complex schemas and incomplete KGs [5]. In contrast, retrieval-augmented or agentic approaches such as [12] use LLMs to reason over KGs. These methods are more flexible and robust to missing information but lack formal guarantees and may produce hallucinated answers.

In this work, we propose a complementary perspective that avoids both full semantic parsing and unconstrained LLM reasoning. Instead, we extract lightweight necessary constraints from the question to verify candidate answers produced by an upstream system (e.g., an agentic LLM pipeline). This verification layer filters invalid candidates, retains candidates that cannot be disproven under incomplete knowledge, and provides symbolic support for valid candidates.

We formalize this setting as *Constrained Entity Selection under Partial Knowledge (CES-PK)*. To account for the open-world nature of real-world KGs, we employ a three-valued constraint semantics that distinguishes between satisfied, violated, and unknown constraints. This allows us to reject candidates only in the presence of explicit violations, thereby avoiding false negatives caused by missing information.

We instantiate this framework for entity-centric queries over the Hetionet biomedical KG [7] and evaluate it on both controlled and LLM-generated candidate sets. We show that constraint-based verification improves precision while preserving recall and providing support for KG-grounded answers. Furthermore, we analyze the complementary roles of constraint types: exclusion constraints contribute to filtering, whereas positive relation constraints contribute to verification through support.

Contributions. This paper makes the following contributions:

- We introduce Constrained Entity Selection under Partial Knowledge (CES-PK), a problem formulation for post-hoc verification of KGQA answers without requiring full semantic parsing.
- We analyze the complementary roles of constraint types for filtering and verification with a three-valued constraint semantics for incomplete KGs.
- We provide an empirical study demonstrating that lightweight constraint-based verification improves precision while preserving recall and additionally provides support scores for retained answers.

2 Problem and Method

2.1 Problem Setting

We consider a KGQA setting where candidate answers are produced by an upstream component and may contain incorrect or unsupported entities.

Let $G = (V, E)$ be a knowledge graph [9] with entities V and typed relations $E \subseteq V \times R \times V$. Given a question q, we assume a candidate set $C(q) \subseteq V$ and an (unknown) set of correct answers $A(q) \subseteq V$. Rather than deriving $A(q)$ directly, we aim to identify candidates consistent with necessary conditions implied by the question.

Constrained Entity Selection under Partial Knowledge (CES-PK). Given $C(q)$ and a set of constraints $\mathcal{C}(q)$ derived from q, compute a subset $C^*(q) \subseteq C(q)$ such that no retained candidate violates any constraint under incomplete knowledge and associate remaining answers in $C^*(q)$ with support scores reflecting the degree of constraint satisfaction.

2.2 Assumptions on the Knowledge Graph

We assume that the KG is factually correct but may be incomplete, i.e., all represented triples are true, while some true facts may be missing (open-world assumption) [8]. All candidate entities are assumed to be present in the graph.

2.3 Constraints

We consider lightweight necessary constraints extracted from the question with respect to a known schema (this set of constraint types can be extended, e.g., to capture joins or cardinality constraints):

- Type constraints: $\text{type}(x, T)$
- Relation constraints: $R(x, y)$
- Exclusion constraints: $\neg R(x, y)$

2.4 Three-Valued Constraint Semantics

Due to incompleteness, constraints $c(x)$ for candidate answers x over graph G are evaluated under a three-valued semantics: $[\![c(x)]\!]_G \in \{\mathsf{sat}, \mathsf{viol}, \mathsf{unk}\}$.

Relation Constraints.

$$[\![R(x,y)]\!]_G = \begin{cases} \mathsf{sat} & \text{if } (x, R, y) \in E \\ \mathsf{unk} & \text{otherwise} \end{cases}$$

Exclusion Constraints.

$$[\![\neg R(x,y)]\!]_G = \begin{cases} \mathsf{viol} & \text{if } (x, R, y) \in E \\ \mathsf{unk} & \text{otherwise} \end{cases}$$

Type Constraints.

$$[\![\text{type}(x,T)]\!]_G = \begin{cases} \mathsf{sat} & \text{if } \text{type}(x) = T \\ \mathsf{viol} & \text{otherwise} \end{cases}$$

2.5 Constraint-Based Filtering and Support-Based Verification

We retain only candidates that do not violate any constraint:

$$C^*(q) = \{x \in C(q) \mid \forall c \in \mathcal{C}(q) : [\![c(x)]\!]_G \neq \mathsf{viol}\}.$$

This strategy relies solely on explicit violations and is therefore robust under incomplete knowledge.

Further, let

$$\mathcal{C}^+(q) = \{c \in \mathcal{C}(q) \mid \mathsf{sat} \in \mathrm{range}(c)\}$$

denote the subset of constraints that can provide positive evidence by being satisfied. The support of a candidate x is defined as the fraction of constraints in $\mathcal{C}^+(q)$ that evaluate to sat:

$$\mathrm{support}(x, q) = \frac{|\{c \in \mathcal{C}^+(q) \mid [\![c(x)]\!]_G = \mathsf{sat}\}|}{|\mathcal{C}^+(q)|}.$$

3 Experiments

3.1 Experimental Setup

We evaluate the proposed constraint-based verification approach on entity-centric KGQA tasks using the Hetionet[1] biomedical KG [7].[2]

The evaluation is designed as a controlled study to isolate the effect of constraint-based verification independently of upstream candidate generation. We simulate answer generation by sampling queries and gold answers from the Hetionet KG and then generate candidate answers from gold answers by systematically adding incorrect answers (false positives). For the controlled candidate sets, all gold answers are included by construction; since our method only removes candidates with explicit constraint violations, recall remains constant. In addition, we evaluate CES-PK with LLM-generated candidate sets, where GPT-4.1-mini selects candidate entities from closed answer pools based on natural-language query descriptions.

We consider two query types that fit our constraints (these can be extended by more complex forms including more complex constraint types):

- Q1: Which compounds treat disease D?
- Q2: Which compounds treat disease D but do not cause side effect S?

For each query type, we derive queries by sampling diseases and side effects from the KG and construct gold answer sets from the graph. We construct candidate sets that simulate LLM-generated answers by combining gold answers

[1] Hetionet (https://het.io/) is a typed KG and contains 47,031 nodes of 11 entity types and 2,250,197 edges (triples) across 24 typed relations. In the experiments, nodes of types *Compound*, *Disease* and *Side Effect* and triples of the relations *treats* (*Compound* to *Disease*) and *causes* (*Compound* to *Side Effect*) are used.

[2] Code and experimental artifacts: https://github.com/ekitzelmann/ces-pk.

with sampled distractors, including type-incorrect entities and candidates that violate the exclusion constraint (for Q2).

Constraints include type (C1), relation (C2), and exclusion (C3) constraints. Evaluation is based on precision before and after filtering and support scores after filtering. Since all gold answers are included in the candidate sets, recall remains constant at 1.0. In the present experiments, $\mathcal{C}^+(q)$ consists of the type and positive relation constraints, such that $|\mathcal{C}^+(q)| = 2$ for both Q1 and Q2.

3.2 Results

Table 1. Performance of constraint-based filtering and support-based verification.

Query	Prec.(before)	Prec.(after)	Δ	Recall	Supp.(gold)	Supp.(non-gold)
Q1	0.66	0.70	+0.04	1.00	1.00	0.42
Q2	0.17	0.62	+0.45	1.00	1.00	0.74

Table 2. Effect of simulated KG incompleteness (10% edge removal).

Query	Prec.(after)	Δ	Recall	Supp.(gold)	Supp.(non-gold)
Q1	0.70	+0.04	1.00	0.95	0.42
Q2	0.53	+0.37	1.00	0.95	0.69

Table 1 summarizes filtering performance and support-based verification evidence on the Hetionet KG. For Q1, constraint-based filtering yields a modest precision improvement (+0.04) due to removed type-inconsistent candidates. For Q2, we achieve a substantial precision increase from 0.17 to 0.62 (+0.45) due to exclusion constraints that eliminate candidates violating the negated condition. Overall, precision improves from 0.41 to 0.66 while recall remains unaffected.

The results show distinct roles of constraint types. Type constraints (C1) provide consistent filtering signals, while exclusion constraints (C3) are the primary driver of filtering in Q2. Relation constraints (C2) do not lead to violations under OWA but contribute to verification by providing support if satisfied.

Support scores provide additional discrimination between candidates. Gold answers achieve a mean support of 1.0 compared to 0.42 (Q1) and 0.74 (Q2) for non-gold candidates. This indicates that positive constraints contribute useful verification signals even when filtering is limited.

To further analyze the impact of KG incompleteness, we randomly removed 10% of the relevant *treats* and *causes* edges after constructing the gold answer sets. Results are shown in Table 2. Precision and support scores decrease, as missing edges reduce the number of detectable violations and positive confirmations, while the method continues to preserve recall.

We additionally evaluated CES-PK on candidate sets generated by GPT-4.1-mini from natural-language questions and closed candidate pools. The LLM achieved a recall of 0.44 and a precision of 0.17. CES-PK increased precision to 0.71 while preserving recall, demonstrating the complementary role of KG-based verification.

3.3 Discussion

The results show that lightweight constraints improve precision without requiring full semantic parsing. Negative constraints provide filtering signals when explicit violations are present, while positive constraints contribute evidence for verification. The three-valued semantics preserves recall under incomplete knowledge.

Limitations. The evaluation is based on controlled candidate sets and the assumption of constraints being perfectly extracted from natural language queries rather than capturing end-to-end KGQA performance. The KG is assumed to be factually correct, including correct and complete type information, but incomplete with respect to relation triples. In the presence of incorrect triples, missing entities, imperfect type information or other typical defects of real-world KGs, constraint evaluation may lead to false rejections or misleading support scores.

4 Related Work

KGQA with LLMs [1,12,14] is approached in different ways: In semantic parsing approaches [2], an LLM translates natural language questions into executable logical forms [4,6]. Such methods enable precise and verifiable answers, but remain brittle in practice as generating correct queries over complex schemas is challenging.

Another line of work uses LLMs for reasoning over knowledge graphs and generating answers. In [1], relevant triples are retrieved from the KG by entity linking which are then verbalized and injected as additional context into the prompt. Think-on-Graph [12] allows LLMs to iteratively explore graph neighborhoods and construct reasoning paths. These methods typically work without additional training and are more robust but can produce hallucinated or non-grounded answers. Moreover, incomplete KGs remain challenging. To address the issue of unreliable LLM-based reasoning, [10] introduce constraints constructed from the KG that guide the LLM decoding to generate well-formed reasoning chains. In contrast, the method proposed in this paper uses constraints to post-hoc verify answer candidates. In [5], integration of link prediction into LLM-based reasoning over KGs is suggested to address incomplete KGs.

Our work is also related to research on generation followed by verification [13], where it is shown that LLMs are effective at generating solution candidates but unreliable at verifying them.

5 Conclusions

We introduced Constrained Entity Selection under Partial Knowledge (CES-PK), a framework for post-hoc verification of candidate answers in knowledge graph question answering. Instead of relying on full semantic parsing or unconstrained neural generation, our approach uses lightweight necessary constraints together with a three-valued semantics to filter invalid candidates and provide symbolic support for valid ones under incomplete knowledge.

Our experimental results demonstrate that constraint-based verification can substantially improve precision while preserving recall in a controlled setting. In particular, we show that exclusion constraints provide strong negative signals for filtering, whereas positive relation constraints contribute to verification through support.

The proposed approach assumes that the underlying knowledge graph is factually correct but incomplete and that all candidate entities are present in the graph. Furthermore, our evaluation is based on controlled candidate sets and does not yet capture end-to-end KGQA performance under noisy knowledge graphs.

Future work includes integrating the proposed verification layer into full KGQA pipelines, studying robustness under incomplete and noisy graphs, LLM-based constraint extraction from natural language queries, and extending constraints to more complex query types and schemas.

References

1. Baek, J., Aji, A.F., Saffari, A.: Knowledge-augmented language model prompting for zero-shot knowledge graph question answering. In: Dalvi Mishra, B., Durrett, G., Jansen, P., Neves Ribeiro, D., Wei, J. (eds.) Proceedings of the 1st Workshop on Natural Language Reasoning and Structured Explanations (NLRSE), pp. 78–106. Association for Computational Linguistics, Toronto, Canada (2023). https://doi.org/10.18653/v1/2023.nlrse-1.7
2. Berant, J., et al.: Semantic parsing on freebase from question-answer pairs. In: Bethard, S. (ed.) Proceedings of the 2013 Conference on Empirical Methods in Natural Language Processing, pp. 1533–1544. Association for Computational Linguistics, Seattle, Washington, USA (2013)
3. Bhandiwad, D., et al.: Bridging language models and knowledge graphs with controlled natural languages. Knowl.-Based Syst. **337**, 115405 (2026). https://doi.org/10.1016/j.knosys.2026.115405
4. D'Abramo, J., Zugarini, A., Torroni, P.: Investigating large language models for Text-to-SPARQL generation. In: Shi, W., et al., (eds.) Proceedings of the 4th International Workshop on Knowledge-Augmented Methods for Natural Language Processing, pp. 66–80. Association for Computational Linguistics, Albuquerque, New Mexico, USA (2025). https://doi.org/10.18653/v1/2025.knowledgenlp-1.5
5. El Khatib, O.: Reasoning over incomplete knowledge graphs. In: Proceedings of the 34th ACM International Conference on Information and Knowledge Management, pp. 6785–6788. CIKM '25, Association for Computing Machinery, New York, NY, USA (2025). https://doi.org/10.1145/3746252.3761657

6. Feng, T., et al.: RGR-KBQA: generating logical forms for question answering using knowledge-graph-enhanced large language model. In: Schockaert, S. (ed.) Proceedings of the 31st International Conference on Computational Linguistics, pp. 3057–3070. Association for Computational Linguistics, Abu Dhabi, UAE (2025)
7. Himmelstein, D.S., et al.: Systematic integration of biomedical knowledge prioritizes drugs for repurposing. eLife **6**, e26726 (2017). https://doi.org/10.7554/eLife.26726
8. Hitzler, P., Krtzsch, M., Rudolph, S.: Foundations of Semantic Web Technologies, 1st edn. Chapman & Hall/CRC (2009)
9. Hogan, A., et al.: Knowledge graphs. ACM Comput. Surv. **54**(4), 71:1–71:37 (2021). https://doi.org/10.1145/3447772
10. Li, K., Zhang, T., Wu, X., Luo, H., Glass, J.R., Meng, H.M.: Decoding on graphs: faithful and sound reasoning on knowledge graphs through generation of well-formed chains. In: Che, W., Nabende, J., Shutova, E., Pilehvar, M.T. (eds.) Proceedings of the 63rd Annual Meeting of the Association for Computational Linguistics (Volume 1: Long Papers), pp. 24349–24364. Association for Computational Linguistics, Vienna, Austria (2025). https://doi.org/10.18653/v1/2025.acl-long.1186
11. Ma, C., Chen, Y., Wu, T., Khan, A., Wang, H.: Large language models meet knowledge graphs for question answering: synthesis and opportunities. In: Christodoulopoulos, C., Chakraborty, T., Rose, C., Peng, V. (eds.) Proceedings of the 2025 Conference on Empirical Methods in Natural Language Processing, pp. 24578–24597. Association for Computational Linguistics, Suzhou, China (2025). https://doi.org/10.18653/v1/2025.emnlp-main.1249
12. Sun, J., et al.: Think-on-graph: deep and responsible reasoning of large language model on knowledge graph. In: The Twelfth International Conference on Learning Representations (2023)
13. Valmeekam, K., Marquez, M., Sreedharan, S., Kambhampati, S.: On the planning abilities of large language models - a critical investigation. In: Advances in Neural Information Processing Systems, vol. 36, pp. 75993–76005 (2023)
14. Wagner, R., Kitzelmann, E., Boersch, I.: Mitigating hallucination by integrating knowledge graphs into LLM inference - a systematic literature review. In: Zhao, J., Wang, M., Liu, Z. (eds.) Proceedings of the 63rd Annual Meeting of the Association for Computational Linguistics (Volume 4: Student Research Workshop), pp. 795–805. Association for Computational Linguistics, Vienna, Austria (2025). https://doi.org/10.18653/v1/2025.acl-srw.53

Qualitative Comparison Between Marker-Based and Video-Based Human Pose Estimation in the Context of Imitation Learning

Max Lödige[1(✉)], Alexander Fabisch[2], and Lisa Gutzeit[1]

[1] Robotics Research Group, University of Bremen, Bremen, Germany
{loedige,Lisa.Gutzeit}@uni-bremen.de

[2] Robotics Innovation Center, German Research Center for Artificial Intelligence (DFKI GmbH), Bremen, Germany
Alexander.Fabisch@dfki.de

Abstract. Imitation learning from human demonstration often relies on marker-based motion capture, which restricts data recording to controlled environments. Video-based motion capture presents an alternative that reduces the recording effort. To compare both, we develop a novel evaluation framework using four categories of metrics, namely pose estimation quality, trajectory distance, behaviour separability, and grasp characterization, applied to three state-of-the-art video-based 3D pose estimation models in a pick-and-place scenario with parallel recording. Using this framework, we show that video-based pose estimation using a depth map captures actions and trajectories well enough for imitation learning, but high-fidelity movement such as grasping remains beyond the current capabilities of all evaluated video-based modalities.

1 Introduction and Related Work

As robots are increasingly used in highly dynamic environments, traditionally programmed behaviours reach their limit in adaptability and thus result in the development of more dynamic learning pipelines. Imitation learning is one approach for such a dynamic learning pipeline and is shown to work well in robotic learning paradigms due to its efficiency in teaching tasks that are hard to express as reward function in traditional reinforcement learning [7]. The subfield of imitation learning from human demonstration places a human in the role of the expert, in which a robot learns how to perform a task by observing the human. To gather such expert data, current approaches mainly rely on external tools such as marker-based motion capture or controllers [15]. These tools provide highly accurate data but restrict recording to controlled laboratory environments. A potential alternative is video-based human pose estimation, a field of computer vision that estimates human keypoint locations from RGB or RGBD data, often

M. Lödige—Research conducted while affiliated to University of Bremen.

D. Wolter and G. Schwalbe (Eds.): KI 2026, LNAI 16830, pp. 260–268, 2027.
https://doi.org/10.1007/978-3-032-32335-4_22

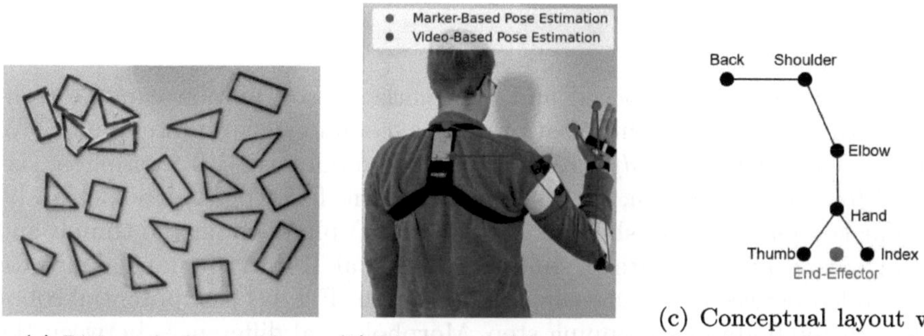

(a) Pick-and-place table. (b) Markers and keypoints. (c) Conceptual layout with virtual end-effector point.

Fig. 1. Experimental setup.

from a single camera. This drastically reduces the sensing requirements for a robotic system and enables imitation learning from human demonstration outside of carefully prepared laboratory settings, at the cost of reduced accuracy. This work's main contribution is the development of an evaluation framework designed to assess the quality of human pose estimation in the context of imitation learning. Traditional imitation learning evaluation measures the trained agent's behaviour (e.g., task success rate), which introduces confounding variables such as morphological differences or algorithmic bias. To evaluate the data quality independently from any single imitation learning technique, we introduce a novel framework comprising four metric categories: pose estimation quality, trajectory distance, behaviour separability, and grasp characterization. We utilize marker-based motion capture as the ground truth, as it is the recognised gold standard for imitation learning from human demonstration, and apply the framework to compare it against three distinct video-based motion capture approaches.

2 Study

Pick-and-place is a canonical manipulation primitive that underpins many household and assembly tasks, making it a representative testbed for imitation learning. The study design follows the diverse behaviours methodology of Jia et al. [13], applying the principles of diverse behaviour, multiple demonstrations, variable trajectory lengths, and task variations [13, Chapter 3.2]. The scenario consists of five uniquely shaped blocks, each sorted from one of three fixed starting positions to a fixed goal position (5 blocks, 15 starting and 5 release positions), with positions obtained from a previous calibration and marked on the table via printed outlines (Fig. 1a). The study was conducted with nine participants, each recording ten sets.

3 Modalities

We implement three video-based and one marker-based motion capture techniques, with temporal synchronisation and a common coordinate frame. We adopt the *COCO-WholeBody* layout [16] (133 landmarks). Targeting a six-degree-of-freedom robot arm, we track a single arm following Gutzeit et al. [9] using four keypoints (back, shoulder, elbow, wrist) plus two on the thumb and index finger to capture the grasp, similar to Ren et al. [21]. A virtual end-effector point is added between the index finger and thumb (Fig. 1c) as a potential robot target in the embodiment mapping step. Morphological differences between the marker setup and the keypoint locations (Fig. 1b) are taken into account in the evaluation.

3.1 Marker-Based Motion Capture

The marker-based motion capture uses the *Qualisys* product suite, which provides automatic human pose estimation from passive markers and serves as the ground truth due to its high accuracy. The video-based modalities are translated into the *Qualisys* coordinate frame via a static frame constructed from multiple markers attached to the depth camera.

3.2 Video-Based Motion Capture

All three video-based techniques use data captured via a *ZED stereo camera.*

Direct 3D Pose Estimation: End-to-end models map an image to 3D coordinates, avoiding erroneous intermediate steps but remaining susceptible to background and environmental variations, and the vast solution space makes sub-optimal solutions likely [20]. We use RTMW [14] with the RTMDet bounding-box detector [18], processing each frame independently.

Depth-Camera-Based 3D Pose Estimation: Mapping 2D keypoints to 3D via the per-pixel depth value is affected by occlusions, since the estimate is placed on the occluding object rather than on the body [5,6]. Even without occlusion, a small offset occurs as the estimate sits on the body surface. We implement the naive 2D-to-3D projection using the 2D version of RTMW [14] with RTMDet [18]. To our knowledge no pose-refinement model with the *COCO-WholeBody* layout exists, and the naive approach performs adequately for this study.

Pose-Lifter-Based Two-stage Pose Estimation: Pose-lifting lifts independent 2D keypoints to 3D without an external depth reference, extrapolating the depth axis from a single view. The 2-stage pipeline [12] builds on accurate 2D keypoint estimators. We adopt the *PAFUSE* model [22], which extends pose-lifting to the *COCO-WholeBody* dataset.

4 Data Collection

Data Synchronisation: The marker- and video-based pipelines are synchronized via nearest-neighbor down-sampling of the high-frequency marker timestamps to the low-frequency video timestamps, resulting in a negligible synchronisation error of $\Delta t_{sync} \approx 2.6 \pm 0.15$ ms.

Coordinate Transform: Pose estimation models output either person-centric or camera-centric coordinates. Most models without a depth reference are person-centric, but imitation learning requires a common coordinate system for pose and object. We bridge this gap with a Perspective-n-Point (PnP) projection from the estimated 2D image keypoints to the 3D object keypoints, yielding the camera pose relative to the person-centric output. PnP only needs RGB and a calibrated camera intrinsic K but is sensitive to calibration errors and 2D–3D mismatches. We therefore also implement a second approach that aligns the model output with the depth-map output via procrustes analysis [1,8], combining the advantages of both modalities since the model output handles occlusions better than the depth map.

5 Evaluation Metrics

The primary contribution of this work is a set of human pose estimation data quality metrics decoupled from any single imitation learning algorithm. Traditional metrics measure whether an agent has learned the intended behaviour [13,19], but they confound the algorithm and the record- and embodiment-mapping steps [3]. We instead evaluate the data on qualities that are generally important for imitation learning without committing to a particular technique.

Pose Estimation Quality: The most common metric, the *Mean Per Joint Position Error* (*MPJPE*), cannot be used here due to the morphology differences, but we include its derivatives *MPJVE* and *MPJAE* (velocity and acceleration). Since embodiment mapping (e.g., inverse kinematics) reduces the impact of keypoints other than root and end-effector, we additionally consider the velocity error of the virtual end-effector point and the coefficient of determination R^2_{speed} for the velocity difference [17]:

$$R^2_{speed} = 1 - \frac{\sum_i \|v_{marker}(i) - v_{video}(i)\|^2}{\sum_i \|v_{marker}(i) - \bar{v}_{marker}(i)\|^2} \tag{1}$$

where v_{marker} and v_{video} are the combined velocities in the x- and y-direction. Bone length deviation ΔL measures temporal consistency, as it should not vary across time. Due to the morphology differences we report the per-technique standard deviation and test whether the video-based deviation is significantly larger than the ground truth via a one-sided Wilcoxon signed rank test [25].

Trajectory Comparison: End-effector trajectories incorporate both path and velocity information. The static offset due to the morphology difference is removed via an initial spatial transform aligning the modalities at the first frame of each video [24]. The distance is measured both as the root mean square distance and as a normalized dynamic time warping [24], capturing the spatio-temporal and spatial relationships, respectively. We additionally compute the distance correlation $dCor$ [23] and the trajectory accuracy $R^2_{trajectory}$ [17]:

$$R^2_{trajectory} = 1 - \frac{\sum_i \|p_m(i) - p_v(i)\|^2}{\sum_i \|p_m(i) - \bar{p}_m(i)\|^2} \quad (2)$$

where p_m and p_v are the marker- and video-based end-effector positions. $R^2_{trajectory}$ captures both path and velocity differences, while $dCor$, due to its double normalization [23], captures only the path correlation.

Behaviour Separability: This metric quantifies how well an agent could distinguish different actions a_n [13]. Behaviour distinction is captured by the end-effector position at the moment of grasping a block. We fit a K-Means clustering on the per-participant 2D end-effector positions projected onto the table plane at the grasping frame, and compare the predicted cluster labels against the true block labels, with a confidence interval from the bootstrapping approach of Champagne et al. [4].

Grasp Characterization: We use three metrics. The first is the 2D-plane distance from the end-effector to the closest point on the relevant shape outline at the grasping frame, tested against the marker-based modality via a two-sided Wilcoxon signed rank test [25]. The second is the target position error $RMSE_{pos}$ [17], the $RMSE$ of the L^2-norm between marker- and video-based end-effector positions at the grasping frame. The third is the approach-vector angle error $\Delta\alpha$, where the approach vector is orthogonal to the index-thumb vector and directed from the wrist toward the end-effector.

6 Results and Discussion

Full results are in Table 1.

Pose Estimation Quality: The depth-based approach captures the ground truth best and is the only modality whose velocity and acceleration metrics would make it usable for imitation learning. The pose lifter has the smallest bone length deviation ΔL, likely due to soft-tissue artifacts on the marker side [2,10]. PnP projection markedly degrades the speed accuracy of the direct and pose lifter estimations, as it assumes a 2D-3D correspondence that does not hold here. Procrustes alignment improves the result mostly by averaging with the depth-map error.

Trajectory Distance: The $RMSE_{lsed}$ of the depth mapping is comparable to state-of-the-art MPJPE $\approx$ 5cm [11,14,22], while the two state-of-the-art models suffer from the coordinate system translation. $R^2_{trajectory}$ is adequate only for depth mapping. $dCor$ is satisfactory for all modalities except the projected

Table 1. Comprehensive experimental results for all modalities. Metrics marked n.a. are not applicable to the specific evaluation, while / indicates values exceeding the display range.

	Pose Estimation Quality						Behaviour Separability	
	Pose		End-Effector		Bone Var. (cm)			
Modality	MPJVE ($\frac{m}{s}$)	MPJAE ($\frac{m}{s^2}$)	Vel. Acc. ($\frac{m}{s}$)	Speed Acc.	ΔL (cm)	p-value	Mean Acc.	$CI_{95\%}$
Marker-based	n.a.	n.a.	n.a.	n.a.	0.28	n.a.	0.98	[0.89, 1.00]
Depth mapping	0.143 ± 0.049	1.089 ± 0.424	0.081 ± 0.045	0.75	0.45	0.027	0.94	[0.85, 1.00]
Pose Lifter (raw)	0.290 ± 0.048	1.472 ± 0.275	0.336 ± 0.143	0.26	0.19	0.844	0.67	[0.53, 0.82]
+ PnP projection	0.345 ± 0.119	2.556 ± 0.941	0.296 ± 0.232	−4.45	n.a.	n.a.	0.69	[0.56, 0.82]
+ procrustes analysis	0.164 ± 0.046	1.244 ± 0.407	0.116 ± 0.068	0.30	n.a.	n.a.	0.94	[0.82, 1.00]
Direct Est. (raw)	0.516 ± 0.274	3.924 ± 2.370	0.444 ± 0.385	−21.12	10.04	0.008	0.55	[0.44, 0.67]
+ PnP projection	/	/	2.261 ± 1.575	−554.69	n.a.	n.a.	0.57	[0.45, 0.68]
+ Procrustes analysis	/	/	0.552 ± 0.388	−20.67	n.a.	n.a.	0.71	[0.56, 0.89]

	Trajectory Dist.		Trajectory Similarity		Shape Proximity		Grasp Metric	
Modality	$RMSE_{lsed}$ (cm)	dtw_{norm} (cm)	R^2	$dCor$	Mean (m)	p-value	Distance (m)	Angle
Marker-based	n.a.	n.a.	n.a.	n.a.	0.007	n.a.	-	-
Depth mapping	4.26	1.06	0.879	0.933	0.032	0.0039	(0.064 ± 0.023)	35.61°
Pose Lifter (projection)	17.89	2.23	-1.165	0.956	0.367	0.0039	(0.442 ± 0.194)	34.76°
Pose Lifter (procrustes)	6.10	1.28	0.766	0.988	0.031	0.0039	(0.069 ± 0.023)	36.30°
Direct Est. (projection)	87.21	4.89	-56.653	0.752	0.661	0.0039	(0.754 ± 0.508)	53.49°
Direct Est. (procrustes)	13.08	1.86	-0.275	0.94	0.075	0.0039	(0.120 ± 0.067)	53.63°

direct estimation, and notably exceeds depth mapping for the pose lifter, indicating that the path is well described once offset and velocity inconsistencies are removed. An imitation learning agent could thus learn a close representation of the trajectories from depth mapping and aligned pose lifter outputs.

Behaviour Separability: Figure 2 shows that the marker-based and depth mapping approaches both score near the maximum, demonstrating that the end-effector estimation is accurate enough to distinguish actions a. The pose lifter and direct estimation reach satisfactory accuracy only when aligned with the depth map via procrustes analysis. Their raw and projected variants remain too noisy.

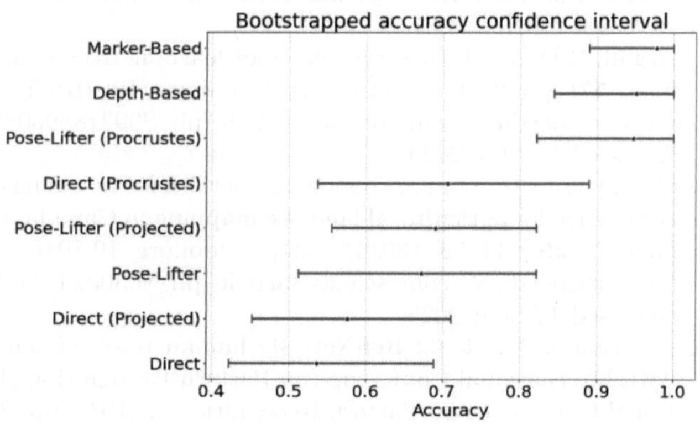

Fig. 2. Mean accuracy and 95% CI of bootstrapped K-Means clustering.

Grasp Characterization: The marker-based approach reaches a mean end-effector to shape distance of about 7 mm, against 3.2 cm for the depth mapping, in line with state-of-the-art MPJPE of $\approx$ 5 cm. The best end-effector position error is $\approx$ 6.5 cm with an angle error of $\sim$ 36°. Such an end-effector distance would likely prevent an imitation learning agent from properly grasping the objects.

Conclusion: Depth-based estimation is a viable alternative to marker-based capture for trajectory-heavy imitation, but the evaluated video-based modalities cannot yet represent fine-grained tasks. The limiting factor is not pose estimation accuracy alone but also coordinate system and temporal consistency. Future work should explore depth-aware pose lifters or hybrid imitation and reinforcement learning, and extend the framework beyond this controlled-lab scenario.

Acknowledgments. This research was partially financed by the German Federal Ministry of Research, Technology and Space (BMFTR) through the ActGPT project, grant number 01IW25002, and partially supported by the German Federal Ministry of Research, Technology and Space (BMFTR) under the Robotics Institute Germany (RIG).

Disclosure of Interests. The authors have no competing interests.

References

1. Akca, D.: Generalized Procrustes Analysis and Its Applications in Photogrammetry (2003)
2. Ancillao, A., Aertbeliën, E., De Schutter, J.: Effect of the soft tissue artifact on marker measurements and on the calculation of the helical axis of the knee during a squat movement: a study on the CAMS-knee dataset. Med. Eng. Phys. **110**, 103915 (2022). https://doi.org/10.1016/j.medengphy.2022.103915. https://www.sciencedirect.com/science/article/pii/S1350453322001631. ISSN: 1350–4533. Accessed 09 Nov 2025
3. Argall, B.D., et al.: A survey of robot learning from demonstration. Robot. Auton. Syst. **57**(5, 469–483 (2009). https://doi.org/10.1016/j.robot.2008.10.024. https://www.sciencedirect.com/science/article/pii/S0921889008001772. ISSN: 0921–8890. Accessed 15 May 2025
4. Champagne, C., et al.: A bootstrap method for assessing classification accuracy and confidence for agricultural land use mapping in Canada. Int. J. Appl. Earth Observ. Geoinf. **29**, 44–52 (2014). https://doi.org/10.1016/j.jag.2013.12.016. https://www.sciencedirect.com/science/article/pii/S0303243414000026. ISSN: 1569–8432. Accessed 17 Sept 2025
5. D'Eusanio, A., et al.: RefiNet: 3D human pose refinement with depth maps. In: 25th International Conference on Pattern Recognition (ICPR). 2020 25th International Conference on Pattern Recognition (ICPR), pp. 2320–2327 (2021). https://doi.org/10.1109/ICPR48806.2021.9412451. https://ieeexplore.ieee.org/document/9412451. Accessed 18 Sept 2025
6. Garg, M., Ghosh, D., Mohan Pradhan, P.: OccRobNet: occlusion robust network for accurate 3d interacting hand-object pose estimation. In: National Conference on Communications (NCC), pp. 1–6 (2025). https://doi.org/10.1109/NCC63735.2025.10983334
7. Gavenski, N., et al.: A survey of imitation learning methods, environments and metrics **30** (2024). https://doi.org/10.48550/arXiv.2404.19456. *[1085]FontCategoryNonProportional[cs arXiv: 2404.19456. http://arxiv.org/abs/2404.19456. Accessed 11 Mar 2025
8. Gower, J.C.: Generalized procrustes analysis. Psychometrika **40**(1), 33–51 (1975). https://doi.org/10.1007/BF02291478. ISSN: 1860–0980. Accessed 16 Sept 2025

9. Gutzeit, L., et al.: The BesMan learning platform for automated robot skill learning. Front. Robot. AI **5**, 43 (2018). https://doi.org/10.3389/frobt.2018.00043. https://www.frontiersin.org/article/10.3389/frobt.2018.00043/full. ISSN: 2296–9144. Accessed 15 May 2025
10. Herda, L., et al.: Using skeleton-based tracking to increase the reliability of optical motion capture. Hum. Move. Sci. **20**(3), 313–341 (2001). https://doi.org/10.1016/S0167-9457(01)00050-1. https://www.sciencedirect.com/science/article/pii/S0167945701000501. ISSN: 0167–9457. Accessed 11 Sept 2025
11. Holmquist, K., Wandt, B.: DiffPose: multi-hypothesis human pose estimation using diffusion models. In: Proceedings of the IEEE/CVF International Conference on Computer Vision (ICCV), pp. 15931–15941 (2023). https://doi.org/10.1109/ICCV51070.2023.01464
12. Hsu, C., Roger Jang, J.: Enhancing 3D human pose estimation with bone length adjustment. In: Computer Vision – ACCV 2024, pp. 242–257. Springer (2024). https://doi.org/10.1007/978-981-96-0885-0_14
13. Jia, X., et al.: towards diverse behaviors: a benchmark for imitation learning with human demonstrations (2023). https://openreview.net/forum?id=6pPYRXKPpw. Accessed 19 Mar 2025
14. Jiang, T., Xie, X., Li, Y.: RTMW: real-time multi-person 2d and 3d whole-body pose estimation (2024). https://doi.org/10.48550/arXiv.2407.08634. http://arxiv.org/abs/2407.08634. Accessed 11 Mar 2025
15. Jiang, X., et al.: A comprehensive user study on augmented reality-based data collection interfaces for robot learning. In: Proceedings of the 2024 ACM/IEEE International Conference on Human-Robot Interaction, pp. 333–342. HRI '24. New York, NY, USA: Association for Computing Machinery (2024). https://doi.org/10.1145/3610977.3634995. ISBN: 979-8-4007-0322-5. Accessed 17 Sept 2025
16. Jin, S., et al.: Whole-body human pose estimation in the wild. In: Vedaldi, A., et al., (ed.) Computer Vision – ECCV 2020, pp. 196–214. Cham: Springer International Publishing (2020). https://doi.org/10.1007/978-3-030-58545-7_12. ISBN: 978-3-030-58545-7
17. Lemme, A., et al.: Open-source benchmarking for learned reaching motion generation in robotics. Paladyn J. Behav. Robot. **6**(1), 2081–4836 (2015). https://doi.org/10.1515/pjbr-2015-0002. https://www.degruyterbrill.com/document/doi/10.1515/pjbr-2015-0002/html. Accessed 24 Sept 2025
18. Lyu, C., et al.: RTMDet: an empirical study of designing real-time object detectors (2022). https://doi.org/10.48550/arXiv.2212.07784. arXiv: 2212.07784. http://arxiv.org/abs/2212.07784. Accessed 20 Sept 2025
19. Mukherjee, D., et al.: A survey of robot learning strategies for human-robot collaboration in industrial settings. Robot. Comput. Integrated Manuf. **73**, 102231 (2022). . https://doi.org/10.1016/j.rcim.2021.102231. https://www.sciencedirect.com/science/article/pii/S0736584521001137. ISSN: 0736–5845. Accessed 27 Mar 2025
20. Neupane, R., Li, K., Boka, T.: A survey on deep 3d human pose estimation. Artif. Intell. Rev. **58** (2024). https://doi.org/10.1007/s10462-024-11019-3
21. Ren, J., et al.: Motion tracks: a unified representation for human-robot transfer in few-shot imitation learning. In: IEEE International Conference on Robotics and Automation (ICRA), pp. 8802–8810 (2025). https://doi.org/10.1109/ICRA55743.2025.11128834
22. Samet, N., et al.: PAFUSE: part-based diffusion for 3d whole-body pose estimation. In: Computer Vision – ECCV 2024 Workshops, pp. 151–169. Springer (2024). https://doi.org/10.1007/978-3-031-91575-8_10

23. Székely, G.J., Rizzo, M.L.: Brownian distance covariance. Ann. Appl. Stat. **3**(4) (2009). https://doi.org/10.1214/09-AOAS312. arXiv: 1010.0297. http://arxiv.org/abs/1010.0297. ISSN: 1932-6157. Accessed 25 Sept 2025
24. Tao, Y., et al.: A comparative analysis of trajectory similarity measures. GISci. Remote Sens. **58**(5), 643–669 (2021). https://doi.org/10.1080/15481603.2021.1908927. https://www.tandfonline.com/doi/full/10.1080/15481603.2021.1908927. ISSN: 1548-1603. Accessed 09 Sept 2025
25. Wilcoxon, F.: Individual comparisons by ranking methods. Biometric. Bull. **1**(6), 80–83 (1945). https://doi.org/10.2307/3001968

Multi-species Mixing for Weakly Supervised SED Under Domain Shift

Novruz Mammadli[1,2(✉)], Thiago S. Gouvêa[1,2], and Daniel Sonntag[1,2]

[1] German Research Center for Artificial Intelligence (DFKI), Oldenburg, Germany
{novruz.mammadli,thiago.gouvea,daniel.sonntag}@dfki.de
[2] University of Oldenburg, Oldenburg, Germany
{novruz.mammadli,thiago.gouvea,daniel.sonntag}@uni-oldenburg.de
https://iml.dfki.de/ , https://uol.de/aai

Abstract. Passive Acoustic Monitoring (PAM) is increasingly used for biodiversity monitoring, but training sound event detectors for PAM remains difficult because strong temporal annotations are expensive to obtain. Archival sound libraries provide weakly labelled focal recordings at scale, yet these recordings differ substantially from PAM soundscapes. Focal recordings typically contain one dominant species under relatively clean conditions, whereas PAM recordings often contain overlapping vocalisations from multiple species together with environmental noise. This mismatch limits the transferability of weakly supervised models trained on sound libraries.

This paper investigates whether synthetic multi-species training augmentation can reduce this transfer gap. We build on a weakly supervised sound event detection pipeline using BirdNET embeddings and a linear classifier, and augment the training data by synthetically mixing focal recordings into artificial multi-species soundscapes with randomized temporal overlap and mixture weights. The PAM evaluation data remain unchanged. Experiments on five anuran species show improvements in transfer performance. Compared with training on original focal recordings only, synthetic augmentation increases recall and F1-score at both bag and segment level, while causing a moderate reduction in precision. The best bag-level micro-F1 improves from 0.6792 to 0.7687, and the best segment-level micro-F1 improves from 0.5473 to 0.6120. These results indicate that simulating multi-species co-occurrence during training is a practical way to improve weakly supervised transfer from sound libraries to PAM data.

Keywords: Weakly Supervised Sound Event Detection · Multiple Instance Learning · Synthetic Data Augmentation · Transfer Learning · Passive Acoustic Monitoring

1 Introduction

Passive Acoustic Monitoring (PAM) has become an important method for large-scale biodiversity monitoring because it enables continuous and non-invasive

D. Wolter and G. Schwalbe (Eds.): KI 2026, LNAI 16830, pp. 269–276, 2027.
https://doi.org/10.1007/978-3-032-32335-4_23

observation of ecosystems over long time periods [10,11]. However, automatic analysis of these recordings remains challenging, as supervised sound event detection typically requires temporally precise annotations that are expensive to obtain and depend on expert knowledge [4–6,9].

To address this limitation, recent work has explored the use of archival sound libraries as training resources. Collections such as FNJV[1], the Macaulay Library[2], and Xeno-Canto[3] provide large numbers of recordings with weak file-level labels indicating species presence [12]. These recordings are abundant and taxonomically diverse, but they are typically focal recordings dominated by a single target species. In contrast, PAM recordings represent complex soundscapes containing overlapping vocalizations and environmental noise [1,8,9]. This structural mismatch limits transfer from sound-library training data to monitoring scenarios.

Weakly supervised sound event detection (WSSED) enables learning from file-level annotations while still producing temporally localized predictions. In particular, Multiple Instance Learning (MIL) supports instance-level inference from weak labels and has shown promising results for acoustic monitoring tasks [3,13,15]. Pretrained acoustic representations such as BirdNET embeddings further support efficient transfer to downstream PAM tasks when combined with lightweight classifiers [8,9]. However, weak supervision alone does not reliably resolve the mismatch between focal recordings and multi-species monitoring soundscapes.

In this paper, we investigate whether synthetic multi-species training augmentation can reduce this transfer gap. We generate artificial mixtures by combining recordings from multiple species to better reflect overlapping acoustic conditions in PAM soundscapes, while keeping the evaluation dataset unchanged. Experiments on five anuran species show that this strategy improves recall and F1-score at both bag and segment level, indicating that modelling multi-species co-occurrence during training improves weakly supervised transfer from sound libraries to PAM data without additional annotations.

2 Related Work

WSSED enables learning from clip-level annotations while still producing temporally localized predictions. A common formulation is MIL, where recordings are treated as bags of temporal instances and predictions are aggregated through pooling strategies [15]. Architectures such as TALNet and duration-robust extensions including CDur demonstrate that weak labels can support effective localization despite missing onset–offset annotations [3,15]. In ecoacoustic settings, weak supervision has further been shown to support multi-label classification and extraction of fine-grained information from PAM datasets [12,13].

---

[1] https://www2.ib.unicamp.br/fnjv/.
[2] https://www.macaulaylibrary.org/.
[3] https://xeno-canto.org/.

Transfer learning is widely used in PAM because strong annotations are scarce and expensive to obtain [5,16]. BirdNET provides transferable acoustic representations trained on large sound collections and generalizes effectively across taxa when combined with lightweight downstream classifiers [8,9]. However, archival sound libraries typically contain focal recordings dominated by single species, whereas PAM data consist of multi-species soundscapes with overlapping calls and environmental noise [1,8,9]. This mismatch limits direct transfer from weakly labelled collections to monitoring scenarios.

Data augmentation is commonly used to improve robustness in sound event detection through noise injection, spectral masking, waveform perturbations, and background mixing [8]. Synthetic soundscape generation has also been explored to compensate for limited annotations, typically by inserting isolated vocalizations into background recordings or applying mixture-based augmentation [9,14,16]. However, these approaches mainly address noise robustness or data scarcity rather than modelling ecological co-occurrence during training from focal recordings. Source separation applied to PAM recordings is a conceptually related alternative, but requires solving the unknown-source-count problem and imposes additional inference-time cost on datasets that are already large by design. Our approach instead narrows the domain gap at training time, leaving PAM inference unchanged.

Explicit simulation of multi-species overlap has been explored only in a limited number of bioacoustic studies, for example through synthetic polyphonic mixtures or domain-randomized soundscape generation [2,7]. Such approaches are rarely studied together with weak supervision or evaluated for improving transfer from sound libraries to PAM recordings. Modelling ecological co-occurrence during training from focal recordings therefore remains underexplored in weakly supervised pipelines targeting deployment on monitoring data.

3 Methods

3.1 Weakly Supervised Localisation with BirdNET Embeddings

This work follows a WSSED formulation in which recordings are annotated only at file level. Each recording is treated as a bag of 3-s long temporal segments and processed using a MIL framework that enables instance-level predictions from weak labels [3,15].

Instead of training an acoustic encoder from scratch, we use pretrained BirdNET embeddings as segment-level representations [8]. These embeddings provide transferable acoustic features that support downstream biodiversity monitoring tasks [9]. Segment-level embeddings are passed to a linear classifier trained with binary cross-entropy loss and aggregated through MIL pooling to obtain recording-level predictions. This enables joint classification and localisation from weak annotations and supports inference at both bag and segment level on PAM data.

3.2 Synthetic Multi-species Augmentation

To reduce the mismatch between focal recordings and monitoring soundscapes, we generate synthetic multi-species mixtures from sound-library recordings. The FNJV training subset used in this study contains 632 focal recordings across five target species (names abbreviated as in [1]), and synthetic mixtures are generated exclusively from this subset.

To analyse augmentation effects independently of dataset size, training sets are constructed with varying proportions of original and synthetic recordings while keeping the total number of training samples constant. We evaluate four ratios: 0.714/0.286, 0.6/0.4, 0.5/0.5, and 0.4/0.6 (original/synthetic). Synthetic mixtures contain varying numbers of overlapping species to approximate typical monitoring conditions. Specifically, 70% contain two species, 20% contain three species, and 10% contain four species. Synthetic mixtures are used only during training, while validation and test sets contain only real recordings.

3.3 Synthetic Mixture Generation Procedure

Synthetic mixtures are constructed by combining recordings from different species within a shared temporal canvas. All recordings are converted to 48 kHz mono before mixing. For each mixture, the longest recording defines the reference duration and shorter recordings are inserted at random temporal offsets to generate varying overlap patterns.

Each source signal is peak-normalised prior to mixing. Random mixing weights are sampled from the range 0.6 to 1.0 and normalised to sum to one before sample-wise summation. The resulting mixture is peak-normalised again and amplitude-limited to prevent clipping during storage.

4 Results and Discussion

We evaluate the effect of synthetic multi-species augmentation by varying the proportion of synthetic mixtures in the training set while keeping validation and test data unchanged (AnuraSet). Results are reported at both bag level and segment level using micro- and macro-averaged precision, recall, and F1-score.

Increasing the proportion of synthetic mixtures increases recall at both bag level and segment level while reducing precision. Bag-level micro F1 increases from 0.6792 with only original recordings to 0.7535 at a synthetic ratio of 0.286, and reaches 0.7687 at a 0.5 / 0.5 ratio. Segment-level micro F1 increases from 0.5473 without augmentation to 0.6011 at a 0.286 ratio and reaches 0.6120 at a 0.4 / 0.6 ratio. Macro-level F1 follows the same pattern, with bag-level macro F1 increasing from 0.3882 to 0.5507, and segment-level macro F1 increasing from 0.2670 to 0.3999 (see Fig. 1). These results show that modelling overlapping acoustic conditions during training reduces the mismatch between focal recordings and PAM soundscapes.

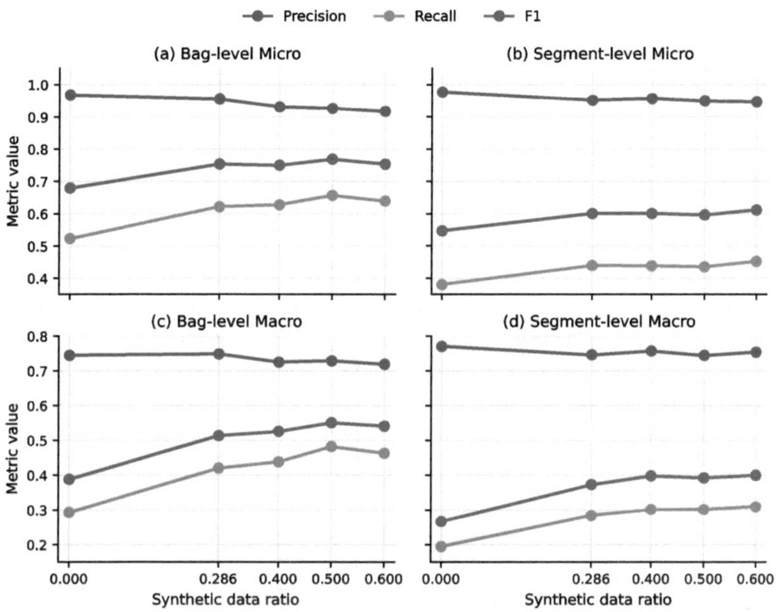

Fig. 1. Effect of the synthetic-data ratio on bag-level and segment-level performance. The x-axis shows the synthetic data ratio used in training, and the y-axis shows the metric value (see color code). Each subplot reports Precision, Recall, and F1-score for a different evaluation setting: (a) bag-level micro, (b) segment-level micro, (c) bag-level macro, and (d) segment-level macro.

Species-level results show that recall improvements are largest for BOARAN and LEPFUS. For BOARAN, segment-level recall increases from 0.0988 without augmentation to 0.5256 at a 0.4 / 0.6 ratio, and segment-level F1 increases from 0.1775 to 0.6395. For LEPFUS, recall increases from 0.1357 to 0.1996, with segment-level F1 increasing from 0.2390 to 0.3328. In contrast, DENMIN segment-level F1 changes from 0.7996 to 0.8071 across the same ratios (see Fig. 2). These differences indicate that synthetic mixtures improve detection performance for some species with low baseline transfer from focal recordings, particularly BOARAN and LEPFUS. Precision decreases as the proportion of synthetic mixtures increases, reflecting the expected sensitivity–specificity trade-off in weakly supervised detection. However, the increase in recall leads to higher F1-scores across nearly all configurations. Balanced mixtures of original and synthetic recordings produce the strongest bag-level performance, while segment-level performance reaches its highest value at a 0.4 / 0.6 ratio. SCIFUS remained undetected (recall = 0) across all configurations. This indicates that synthetic overlap alone cannot compensate for severe class imbalance or limited training data and suggests that additional recordings or complementary training strategies are required for such cases.

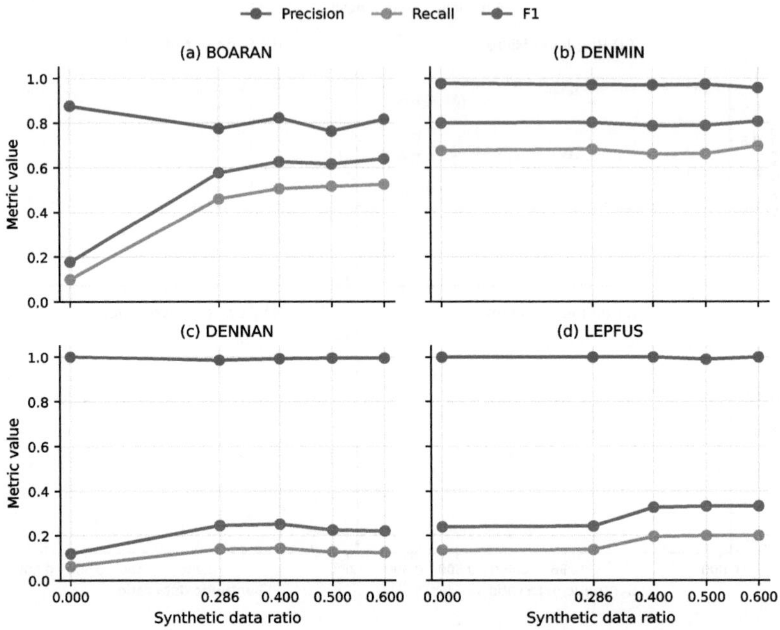

Fig. 2. Effect of the synthetic-data ratio on segment-level species-wise performance. The x-axis shows the synthetic data ratio used in training, and the y-axis shows the metric value. Each subplot reports Precision, Recall, and F1-score for a different species: (a) BOARAN, (b) DENMIN, (c) DENNAN, and (d) LEPFUS. SCIFUS is excluded as all metrics are zero across all configurations.

5 Conclusion

This paper investigated whether synthetic multi-species training augmentation improves weakly supervised transfer from sound-library recordings to PAM data using a Multiple Instance Learning pipeline with BirdNET embeddings. The results show that incorporating synthetic overlap during training improves transfer from focal recordings to monitoring soundscapes without requiring additional annotations. However, performance for SCIFUS remained unchanged across all configurations, indicating that synthetic augmentation alone cannot compensate for severe class imbalance. Future work will investigate alternative mixture construction strategies, including energy-based weighting and signal-to-noise ratio controlled mixing, as well as the individual effects of different overlap configurations. In particular, a systematic analysis of mixture complexity and PAM-like species co-occurrence structures may further improve weakly supervised transfer from sound libraries to monitoring data.

Acknowledgements. Focal recordings kindly provided by Simone Dena (FNJV). This research is part of the Computational Sustainability & Technology project area (https://cst.dfki.de/), and has been supported by the Lower Saxony Ministry of Science and Culture (MWK) in zukunft.niedersachsen program, the Federal Ministry of Research, Technology and Space (BMFTR) under grant number 16IW26002 (AMENABLE), and the Endowed Chair of AAI at the University of Oldenburg.

References

1. Cañas, J.S., et al.: A dataset for benchmarking Neotropical anuran calls identification in passive acoustic monitoring. Sci. Data **10**(1), 771 (2023). https://doi.org/10.1038/s41597-023-02666-2
2. Crous, M.: Polyphonic bird sound event detection with convolutional recurrent neural networks (2019). https://api.semanticscholar.org/CorpusID:208331581
3. Dinkel, H., Wu, M., Yu, K.: Towards duration robust weakly supervised sound event detection. CoRR **abs/2101.07687** (2021). https://arxiv.org/abs/2101.07687
4. Gibb, R., Browning, E., Glover-Kapfer, P., Jones, K.E.: Emerging opportunities and challenges for passive acoustics in ecological assessment and monitoring. Methods Ecol. Evol. **10**(2), 169–185 (2019)
5. Gouvêa, T.S., et al.: Interactive Machine Learning Solutions for Acoustic Monitoring of Animal Wildlife in Biosphere Reserves. In: Proceedings of the Thirty-Second International Joint Conference on Artificial Intelligence. pp. 6405–6413. International Joint Conferences on Artificial Intelligence Organization, Macau, SAR China (2023). https://doi.org/10.24963/ijcai.2023/711
6. Hartig, F., et al.: Novel community data in ecology-properties and prospects. Trends Ecol. Evolution **39**(3), 280–293 (2024)
7. Hoffman, B., et al.: Synthetic data enables context-aware bioacoustic sound event detection (2025). https://arxiv.org/abs/2503.00296
8. Kahl, S., Wood, C.M., Eibl, M., Klinck, H.: BirdNET: a deep learning solution for avian diversity monitoring. Ecological Informatics **61**, 101236 (2021). https://doi.org/10.1016/j.ecoinf.2021.101236
9. Kath, H., Serafini, P.P., Campos, I.B., Gouvêa, T.S., Sonntag, D.: Leveraging transfer learning and active learning for data annotation in passive acoustic monitoring of wildlife. Ecol. Inform. **82**, 102710 (2024). https://doi.org/10.1016/j.ecoinf.2024.102710
10. Shonfield, J., Bayne, E.M.: Autonomous recording units in avian ecological research: current use and future applications. Avian Conservation Ecol. **12**(1), 14 (2017)
11. Sugai, L.S.M., Silva, T.S.F., Ribeiro, J.W., Llusia, D.: Terrestrial passive acoustic monitoring: review and perspectives. Bioscience **69**(1), 15–25 (2019)
12. Troshani, I., Gouvêa, T.S., Sonntag, D.: Leveraging Sound Collections for Animal Species Classification with Weakly Supervised Learning. In: 3rd Annual AAAI Workshop on AI to Accelerate Science and Engineering (AI2ASE). Vancouver, Canada (2024). https://ai-2-ase.github.io/papers/19%5cCameraReady.pdf
13. Troshani, I., Gouvêa, T.S., Sonntag, D.: Leveraging Weakly Supervised and Multiple Instance Learning for Multi-label Classification of Passive Acoustic Monitoring Data. In: Hotho, A., Rudolph, S. (eds.) KI 2024: Advances in Artificial Intelligence, pp. 260–272. Springer Nature Switzerland, Cham (2024). https://doi.org/10.1007/978-3-031-70893-0_19

14. Turpault, N., Serizel, R., Parag Shah, A., Salamon, J.: Sound event detection in domestic environments with weakly labeled data and soundscape synthesis. In: Workshop on Detection and Classification of Acoustic Scenes and Events. New York City, United States (2019). https://inria.hal.science/hal-02160855
15. Wang, Y., Li, J., Metze, F.: A Comparison of Five Multiple Instance Learning Pooling Functions for Sound Event Detection with Weak Labeling. ICASSP 2019 - 2019 IEEE International Conference on Acoustics, Speech and Signal Processing (ICASSP), pp. 31–35 (2019). https://doi.org/10.1109/ICASSP.2019.8682847
16. Weldy, M.J., et al.: Simulated soundscapes and transfer learning boost the performance of acoustic classifiers under data scarcity. Methods Ecol. Evol. **17**(2), 322–338 (2026)

A Comparison of Repositioning and Scheduling Algorithms for the Ride-Hailing Problem

Lauren Paul[1,2], Sebastian Hübner[1], Christina Plump[1,2(✉)], Bernhard J. Berger[3], and Rolf Drechsler[1,2]

[1] Faculty of Mathematics and Computer Science, University of Bremen, Bremen, Germany
cplump@uni-bremen.de
[2] Cyber-Phyiscal Systems, German Research Center of Artificial Intelligence, Bremen, Germany
[3] Institute of Embedded Systems, Hamburg University of Technology, Hamburg, Germany

Abstract. The *Ride-Hailing Problem* is an online optimization challenge that coordinates a fleet of vehicles to serve requests revealed over time. The problem is NP-hard, and many solution approaches use stochastic or machine-learning based algorithms, which perform well but are difficult to interpret. We study the trade-offs between performance and explainability. Our results show that greedy assignment consistently outperforms more complex methods, indicating that explainability need not come at the cost of efficiency. We also find that the effectiveness of repositioning strategies strongly depends on demand patterns, highlighting the value of context-aware policies.

Keywords: ride-hailing problem · dynamic optimisation · repositioning · explainability · scheduling

1 Introduction

Online optimization is central to real-world logistical challenges such as resource allocation and scheduling, where information about incoming jobs is not known ahead of time [25]. The ride-hailing problem is one such online optimization problem with real-world applications. On-demand ride hailing services like Uber and Lyft must match dynamically arising customer requests to drivers in real-time [18,24]. One primary optimization goal is the maximization of profit; however, customer satisfaction also plays an important role, incentivizing reduced waiting times [4].

Due to the inherent complexity of the ride-hailing problem (RHP) [30], many existing solution approaches rely on stochastic metaheuristics [7,10,11,16,31] or machine-learning (ML) techniques to optimize scheduling and repositioning

D. Wolter and G. Schwalbe (Eds.): KI 2026, LNAI 16830, pp. 277–284, 2027.
https://doi.org/10.1007/978-3-032-32335-4_24

strategies [22,23,26,27,32]. While these methods achieve strong performance in practice, their decision-making processes are often difficult to explain and remain opaque to customers and operators alike. This has fueled growing interest in explainability as a research direction [17]. Explainable optimization algorithms provide justifications for their choices, thereby increasing trust and potentially improving user satisfaction [12,17].

In this work, we extend existing research on the RHP with a focus on explainability. Specifically, we address the following research questions: (RQ1) How do request frequency and distribution affect the performance of different repositioning strategies? (RQ2) Is there a trade-off between performance and explainability in the investigated RHP algorithms, and how does demand shape their performance?

To answer these questions, we evaluate a variety of approaches, including a transparent greedy heuristic, batching [1] and load-reduction-based approaches [2,9] adapted from scheduling literature, as well as Xu et al.'s LEARNING-PLANNING algorithm [28], which incorporates machine learning to optimize assignments. Our findings show that the simple greedy strategy consistently outperforms more complex approaches, highlighting that explainable algorithms can achieve strong performance even when compared to more sophisticated ML-approaches. Additionally, we observe that different repositioning strategies perform best under different demand conditions, suggesting that adaptively choosing repositioning strategies based on request patterns could yield additional benefits.

2 Methodology

In this section, we introduce the ride-hailing problem and describe the scheduling and repositioning algorithms developed and evaluated in the remainder of this paper.

2.1 Problem Description

An RHP instance is defined on a directed weighted graph $G = (V, E, w)$, where $w : V \times V \to \mathbb{R}_+$ denotes driving time, with a set $\mathcal{M}$ of m vehicles and a sequence $\mathcal{J}$ of n requests over time horizon $T \in \mathbb{N}_+$. Vehicle locations at time t are given by $\mathcal{X}_t = (x_1^t, \dots, x_m^t)$, with $\mathcal{X}_0$ specifying starting positions.

Each request $j = (r, s, d)$ has release time r, pick-up location $s \in V$, and drop-off location $d \in V$. A vehicle v serves j upon reaching s at some $t \geq r$ and traveling to d. The completion time of j, C_j, is $r + w(s, d)$. Pick-ups and drop-offs are assumed to be instantaneous.

A feasible solution assigns sequences of requests to vehicles such that no request is served before its release time and no vehicle serves two requests simultaneously.

Solutions are evaluated with respect to **customer satisfaction**, measured by the total *flow time*, i.e., $\sum_{j \in \mathcal{J}} (C_j - r_j)$ and **operating costs**, measured by the cumulative *driving time*, i.e., the total time vehicles spend driving rather than idle: $\sum_{i=1}^{T}\sum_{j=1}^{m} w(x_j^{i-1}, x_j^i)$.

2.2 Scheduling Algorithms

Scheduling algorithms define strategies of assigning requests to vehicles. The following algorithms are used and extended in our application.

Greedy. The GREEDY algorithm is an intuitive solution approach well described in the literature [14,15,20]. At any time t, let $J_t = \{j = (r', s, d) \mid r' \leq t \wedge j \text{ not yet served}\}$ denote the set of released but unserved requests. If a vehicle finishes its current request at time t and is located at d, it is assigned a request $j \in \arg\min_{j \in J_t} w(d, s_j)$, and $J_t \leftarrow J_t \setminus \{j\}$. If $J_t = \emptyset$, the vehicle stays idle until a request is released. This is repeated until all requests have been served.

Least-Expected-Load. The *load* of a vehicle v, denoted L_v, is defined as the time needed for v to serve all requests currently assigned to it. Let d_f^v denote the drop-off location of the final request assigned to v. Then, upon receiving a new request $j = (r, s, d)$, the LEAST-EXPECTED-LOAD algorithm assigns j to some $v \in \arg\min_{v \in \mathcal{V}}(L_v + w(d_f^v, s) + w(s, d))$, extending the greedy list-scheduling algorithm for load-balancing on related machines [2,9]. We also incorporate a background swap-based local search that periodically exchanges two jobs in a randomly selected vehicle's schedule until no improving swaps remain.

Batching. Batching is a well-studied paradigm in online matching [1]. This algorithm collects requests into a batch $\mathcal{J}_b$ and assigns them via a min-cost matching when any of the following conditions hold ($t_c :=$ current time point):

1) **Age:** $x.r + t_{max} \geq t_c$ for some $x \in \mathcal{J}_{t_c,b}$.
2) **Batch Size:** Number of requests $n_b = |\mathcal{J}_{t_c,b}|$ surpasses a given threshold l_g, i.e. $n_b > l_g$.
3) **Request Frequency:** In a certain time frame t_w the number of requests $n_{t_w} = |\{x | x \in \mathcal{J}_{t_c,b} \wedge x.r + \alpha_w \cdot t_w \geq t_c\}$ surpasses a given threshold l_t, i.e. $n_{t_w} > l_t$.

The threshold values l_g and l_t are chosen to be proportional to the number of vehicles m, such that $l_g = \alpha_g \cdot m$ and $l_t = \alpha_t \cdot m$, where α_g and α_t are configurable (we use $\alpha_g = 3.5$, $\alpha_t = 2.5$). The time frame t_w used in condition (3) is based on the average of all previous consecutive requests at time point t_c: $\frac{1}{|\mathcal{J}'|-1}\sum_{i=1}^{j} x_i.r - x_{i-1}.r$, with $\mathcal{J}' = \{x_0, ..., x_j\}$. The maximum waiting time for a request is then proportional to the obtained time frame, i.e. $t_{max} = \beta_{max} \cdot t_w$, where $\beta_{max} = 2$ is also configurable.

Repositioning is incorporated via the k-Centers algorithm (see Table 1). A vehicle is repositioned if sufficient time has passed since its last repositioning ($t_{rt} = \beta_{rt} \cdot t_w$, $\beta_{rt} = 4$) *and* it has served at least one request since then, provided no batched request is currently pending.

Learning-Planning. Following Xu et al. [28], this approach operates in two phases. In the offline phase, historical data is used to estimate spatio-temporal value patterns via incremental state-value updates. In the online phase, these learned values are combined with immediate rewards as edge weights in a bipartite matching, solved via the Hungarian algorithm [13,21,29]. We refer to [28] for full implementation details; our parameter choices are $R = 10D$ and $\gamma = 0.9$.

2.3 Repositioning Algorithms

Repositioning strategies find new locations for vehicles which are not currently serving any request. These locations should be selected to optimize a vehicle's ability to serve future requests, for example, by placing it closer to an area from which future requests are expected to arise. The repositioning strategies considered in this work are summarized in Table 1.

All strategies except the District strategy, which has fixed vehicle-district assignments, assign vehicles to districts or centroids or centers via a min-cost matching calculated via the Hungarian algorithm [13,21,29].

Table 1. Summary of repositioning strategies. For clustering-based strategies, centroids/centers are selected from received requests.

Algorithm	Zoning Strategy	Scheduling Algorithm(s)
District	Fixed-size districts.	Greedy
District-Swap	Fixed-size districts.	Greedy
k-Means [3,6]	k request centroids, arbitrary-sized clusters.	Greedy
Balanced k-Means [19]	k request centroids, prioritises evenly sized clusters.	Greedy
k-Centers [5,8]	k centers chosen to minimise the maximum distance between a request and a center.	Batching, Learning-Planning

3 Evaluation

Setup. For evaluation, eight test instances were generated, modeling multiple realistic scenarios. We varied three factors: request frequency (busy (HF) and slow hours (LF)), the presence (HS) or absence (U) of a *hot-spot* (an area with elevated request frequency, e.g., a stadium or airport), and service duration (6 or 12 h) which defines the time horizon of the instance. To provide a lower-bound on algorithm performance w.r.t. total flow-time, the offline optimum was computed using a MILP formulation, solved with CPLEX 22.1.2.0 on an Intel Core i7-10700 CPU.

Repositioning Strategies. In order to assess the impact of different repositioning strategies on algorithmic performance, we evaluated combinations of the Greedy algorithm with the repositioning strategies described in Sect. 2.3 across ten runs for each of the eight instances described above. Using Greedy without repositioning as a baseline, we compared combinations of the Greedy algorithm with k-MEANS (km), BALANCED k-MEANS (bkm), DISTRICT (Dist), and DISTRICT-SWAP (D-swap) repositioning strategies. Results are summarized in Tables 2 and 3, instances encode the used setup[1].

Table 2. Results for Total Flow Time (values divided by 10,000)

Instance	Gr.	km	bkm	Dist.	D-Swap
HFHS6	26.1	**25.8**	26.0	26.0	26.1
HFHS12	56.0	57.2	56.7	**55.9**	56.3
HFU6	18.7	18.0	18.7	**17.8**	17.8
HFU12	48.3	47.2	48.8	47.3	**47.2**
LFHS6	1.7	2.0	**1.7**	2.6	2.8
LFHS12	2.7	**2.6**	2.7	3.8	4.1
LFU6	5.6	**4.9**	5.6	5.2	5.3
LFU12	9.6	**8.2**	9.0	8.4	8.6

Table 3. Results for Sum of Driving Times (values divided by 1,000)

Instance	Gr.	km	bkm	Dist.	D-Swap
HFHS6	**107.7**	109.0	107.6	111.9	112.3
HFHS12	**217.5**	219.2	217.9	223.2	222.5
HFU6	**126.5**	132.8	126.8	135.0	132.9
HFU12	**231.1**	243.4	231.6	242.4	239.0
LFHS6	**14.1**	48.8	**14.1**	39.9	41.3
LFHS12	**22.7**	76.3	22.8	59.8	60.9
LFU6	**53.6**	91.0	53.8	76.5	71.2
LFU12	**91.4**	160.2	108.8	124.3	117.9

Assignment Strategies. We next compared ride-hailing algorithms that pursue strategies beyond the basic GREEDY approach. Some of these algorithms, including LEARNING-PLANNING and BATCHING, incorporate their own custom assignment and repositioning strategies to improve performance. Others, such as LEAST-EXPECTED-LOAD, do not exploit repositioning at all. For reference, we also included GREEDY as a baseline, as well as GREEDY with k-MEANS repositioning. Each algorithm was executed ten times on the eight instances described above. Figure 1 presents flow time and driving time for four selected instances, illustrating the relative differences across algorithms under different demand conditions.

GREEDY-based strategies consistently outperform all other algorithms across request frequencies and distributions for total flow time. In low-frequency instances, both BATCHING exhibits significantly higher flow times, whereas LEAST-EXPECTED-LOAD performs similarly to GREEDY without repositioning. For high-frequency instances, LEARNING-PLANNING and LEAST-EXPECTED-LOAD show the worst performance.

Results for Reseach Questions. For **RQ 1**, we investigate the effectiveness of repositioning strategies under different demand conditions. Our results indicate that district-based repositioning strategies which aim to evenly distribute vehicles across the service area outperform request-density based repositioning strategies. However, for non-uniform request distributions, district-based strategies increase total driving distance without reducing total flow-time. When request frequency is high, vehicles are frequently interrupted before completing repositioning, resulting in similar performance across all strategies.

[1] The necessary information for reproducing the results can be found with the following Zenodo package https://doi.org/10.5281/zenodo.20457001.

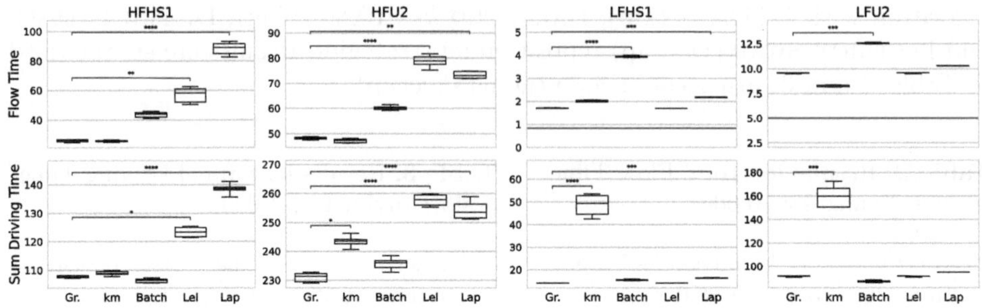

Fig. 1. Boxplots of total flow time (above) and total driving time (below) for selected instances and ride-hailing algorithms (Left to right: Greedy, Greedy + k-Means repositioning, Batching, Least Expected Load, Learning-Planning). The blue line in the low-frequency instances represents the optimal offline solution. Bars indicate significant difference from the greedy baseline, determined by KruskalWallis tests followed by post-hoc Dunn' (Color figure online)s tests (* $p < 0.05$, ** $p < 0.01$, *** $p < 0.001$, **** $p < 0.0001$).

RQ 2 investigates trade-offs between performance and explainability. Explainability decreases from Greedy (distance-based, fully transparent) through Least-Expected-Load (mostly interpretable) and Batching (opaque parameters) to Learning-Planning (learned rewards, difficult to explain in real-time). Yet Greedy and its variants consistently outperform all others in flow time and driving time, suggesting that *more complex algorithms do not necessarily yield better performance.* The best Greedy variants achieve flow times roughly double the offline optimal, with a smaller gap on uniform instances, indicating concentrated demand exposes a limitation of greedy assignment.

Limitations. This study has several limitations. First, explainability is assessed qualitatively based on the authors' judgment, without formal quantitative measures. Second, all experimental instances were synthetically generated, which may limit the external validity of the findings. Finally, several modeling simplifications were made, e.g., indefinitely waiting users.

4 Conclusion and Future Work

We compared the performance of scheduling and repositioning algorithms for the RHP based on total flow and driving time. We implemented extensions on existing algorithms as well as the ability to combine a scheduling algorithm with different repositioning strategies. Our results show that the greedy algorithm outperforms the more complex approaches and that repositioning can be beneficial. In future work, we want to extend the scenario with time windows and the ability to share a vehicle among customers. Future work could also benefit from the development of explainability metrics and/or user surveys. Finally, we plan to evaluate our algorithms on real datasets to adapt to real-world scenarios.

Acknowledgments. GenAI has been used to support with polishing the final texts and building scripts for generating figures. All output has been reviewed by the authors.

We thank the students of the ElO4Future project at the University of Bremen for supporting with providing the overall framework for evaluation. This work has been carried out within the project CAUSE, which has been funded by Deutsche Forschungsgemeinschaft (DFG) GRK 2972 - Project Number: 513623283.

References

1. Ackermann, C., Rieck, J.: A novel repositioning approach and analysis for dynamic ride-hailing problems. EURO J. Transp. Logistics **12**, 100109 (2023)
2. Aspnes, J., Azar, Y., Fiat, A., Plotkin, S., Waarts, O.: On-line routing of virtual circuits with applications to load balancing and machine scheduling. J. ACM **44**(3), 486–504 (1997)
3. Dehariya, V.K., Shrivastava, S.K., Jain, R.: Clustering of image data set using kmeans and fuzzy k-means algorithms. In: 2010 International Conference on Computational Intelligence and Communication Networks, pp. 386–391 (2010)
4. DIMACS: ride-hailing problem (2022)
5. Dyer, M., Frieze, A.: A simple heuristic for the p-centre problem. Oper. Res. Lett. **3**(6), 285–288 (1985)
6. El Morr, C., Jammal, M., Ali-Hassan, H., El-Hallak, W.: K-Means, pp. 361–384. Springer International Publishing, Cham (2022)
7. Furuhata, M., Dessouky, M., Ordóñez, F., Brunet, M.E., Wang, X., Koenig, S.: Ridesharing: the state-of-the-art and future directions. Trans. Res. Part B: Methodol. **57**, 28–46 (2013)
8. Gonzalez, T.F.: Clustering to minimize the maximum intercluster distance. Theoret. Comput. Sci. **38**, 293–306 (1985)
9. Graham, R.L.: Bounds for certain multiprocessing anomalies. Bell Syst. Tech. J. **45**(9), 1563–1581 (1966)
10. Herbawi, W., Weber, M.: The ridematching problem with time windows in dynamic ridesharing: a model and a genetic algorithm. In: 2012 IEEE Congress on Evolutionary Computation, pp. 1–8. IEEE (2012)
11. Jung, J., Jayakrishnan, R., Park, J.Y.: Dynamic shared-taxi dispatch algorithm with hybrid-simulated annealing. Comput.-Aided Civil Infrastructure Eng. **31**(4), 275–291 (2016)
12. Kamath, U., Liu, J.: Introduction to interpretability and explainability. In: Explainable artificial intelligence: an introduction to interpretable machine learning, pp. 1–26. Springer (2021)
13. Kuhn, H.W.: The Hungarian method for the assignment problem. Naval Res. Logistics Quarterly **2**(1–2), 83–97 (1955)
14. Lee, D.H., Wang, H., Cheu, R.L., Teo, S.H.: Taxi dispatch system based on current demands and real-time traffic conditions. Transp. Res. Rec. **1882**(1), 193–200 (2004)
15. Liao, Z.: Real-time taxi dispatching using global positioning systems. Commun. ACM **46**(5), 81–83 (2003)
16. Liu, Z., Zhou, C., Li, J., Wang, C., Zhang, P.: Improved genetic algorithm-based path planning for multi-vehicle pickup in smart transportation. Smart Cities **8**(4) (2025)

17. Lumbreras, S., Ciller, P.: Interpretable optimization: Why and how we should explain optimization models. Appl. Sci. **15**(10) (2025)
18. Lyft: 2024 sustainability & impact report (2024)
19. de Maeyer, R., Sieranoja, S., Fränti, P.: Balanced k-means revisited. Appl. Comput. Intell. **3**(2), 145–179 (2023)
20. Manasse, M., McGeoch, L., Sleator, D.: Competitive algorithms for on-line problems. In: Proceedings of the Twentieth Annual ACM Symposium on Theory of Computing, pp. 322–333. STOC '1988, Association for Computing Machinery, New York, NY, USA (1988)
21. Munkres, J.: Algorithms for the assignment and transportation problems. J. Soc. Ind. Appl. Math. **5**(1), 32–38 (1957)
22. Parimala, M., Lopez, D., Senthilkumar, N.: A survey on density based clustering algorithms for mining large spatial databases. Int. J. Adv. Sci. Technol. **31**(1), 59–66 (2011)
23. Qin, Z.T., Zhu, H., Ye, J.: Reinforcement learning for ridesharing: a survey. In: 2021 IEEE International Intelligent Transportation Systems Conference (ITSC), pp. 2447–2454. IEEE (2021)
24. TinuTinucci, R.: Update zur elektrifizierung von uber (2025)
25. Vaze, R.: Preface, pp. xiii–xviii. Cambridge University Press (2023)
26. Veres, M., Moussa, M.: Deep learning for intelligent transportation systems: a survey of emerging trends. IEEE Trans. Intell. Transp. Syst. **21**(8), 3152–3168 (2019)
27. Wen, D., Li, Y., Lau, F.C.M.: A survey of machine learning-based ride-hailing planning. IEEE Trans. Intell. Transp. Syst. **25**(6), 4734–4753 (2024)
28. Xu, Z., et al.: Large-scale order dispatch in on-demand ride-hailing platforms: a learning and planning approach. In: Proceedings of the 24th ACM SIGKDD International Conference on Knowledge Discovery & Data Mining, pp. 905–913. KDD '2018, Association for Computing Machinery, New York, NY, USA (2018)
29. Yadav, S.S., Lopes, P.A.C., Ilic, A., Patra, S.K.: Hungarian algorithm for subcarrier assignment problem using gpu and cuda. Int. J. Commun. Syst. **32**(4), e3884 dac.3884 (2019)
30. Yalaoui, F., Quy Nguyen, N.: Identical machine scheduling problem with sequence-dependent setup times: Milp formulations computational study **11**(1), 15–34 (2021)
31. Zhan, X., Szeto, W., Shui, C., Chen, X.M.: A modified artificial bee colony algorithm for the dynamic ride-hailing sharing problem. Transportation Research Part E: Logistics and Transportation Review 150 (2021)
32. Zheng, L., Chen, L., Ye, J.: Order dispatch in price-aware ridesharing. Proc. VLDB Endowment **11**(8), 853–865 (2018)

An Ontology-Grounded Representation for Defeasible Professional Ethics Analysis

Christopher B. Rauch(✉)

Drexel University, Philadelphia, PA 19104, USA
cr625@drexel.edu

Abstract. Professional ethics boards in fields such as engineering must identify applicable obligations when multiple provisions of the same ethical code generate competing requirements. In prior work we defined a nine-component case representation for professional ethics analysis. This paper presents the ontological implementation of that representation, grounded in the Basic Formal Ontology (BFO) and classified through the Information Artifact Ontology (IAO). Type-level disjointness is verified by the Pellet OWL-DL reasoner. Three object properties (`competesWith`, `prevailsOver`, `defeasibleUnder`) expose the competition structure between obligations as asserted, SPARQL-queryable relationships between typed individuals. OntServe, an ontology server, instantiates the representation as a knowledge graph of case ontologies extracted from a professional board of ethics archive.

Keywords: professional ethics · ontology · defeasible reasoning · case representation · OWL-DL · knowledge graph · BFO

1 Introduction

The evaluation of professional conduct often draws on multiple ethical traditions, including deontology, consequentialism, and virtue-based role ethics [17]. Automated case analysis must represent this normative content while also tracking the temporal sequences of actions and events. Professional ethics evaluation is bounded by established codes [7], defined roles, and the case record, where codes map to deontic structures, roles anchor obligation assignments, and the actions and events of a case introduce temporal ordering.

These three dimensions (deontic structure, role-based obligations, and temporal ordering) require formal, queryable components [17,18]. In prior work [13,14] we defined a nine-component case representation for professional ethics analysis. This paper presents the ontological implementation of that representation, grounded in the Basic Formal Ontology (BFO) [2], serialized in RDF/OWL, and served through OntServe,[1] a SPARQL-queryable ontology server. The implementation encodes temporal relations through Allen's [1] interval algebra via

[1] OntServe provides the knowledge layer for ProEthica (https://proethica.org), a deployed case-analysis system for professional ethics. Source https://github.com/cr625/OntServe, live endpoint https://ontserve.ontorealm.net.

D. Wolter and G. Schwalbe (Eds.): KI 2026, LNAI 16830, pp. 285–291, 2027.
https://doi.org/10.1007/978-3-032-32335-4_25

OWL-Time [5], and the Pellet OWL-DL reasoner [16] verifies type-level disjointness across entity classifications. Three object properties (`competesWith`, `prevailsOver`, `defeasibleUnder`) represent obligation competition as first-class graph relationships, so the defeasible patterns in professional ethics cases are queryable by SPARQL and available to external reasoning engines.

2 Background

Two surveys map the computational ethics field. Tolmeijer et al. [17] classify implementations across ethical theories, design choices, and technical properties, finding that about half draw on a single ethical theory and few incorporate professional domain codes. Zhong et al. [18] reframe the field around the decision-making process, organizing approaches by their source of ethical guidance, decision method, and evaluation criteria. Through this lens, professional ethics evaluation has a distinctive configuration. The source of guidance is an established domain code combined with precedent cases, and evaluation references expert-authored adjudications. Both surveys find the machine ethics field short of standardized benchmarks, with most systems evaluated only informally, if at all, and call for evaluation data grounded in expert judgment.

The National Society of Professional Engineers (NSPE) Board of Ethical Review (BER) has published over 650 advisory opinions applying the NSPE Code of Ethics to specific fact patterns, many citing prior board decisions [11]. Source and decision-method components of this configuration appear in prior work. Ashley and McLaren [3] developed case-based knowledge representations for practical ethics, and McLaren's [10] SIROCCO retrieves operationalized principles and relevant past cases as the source of guidance for new professional-ethics problems. Berreby et al.'s [4] modular framework, built on a modified Event Calculus, provides a decision method that composes obligations, actions, and events with explicit temporal semantics.

3 Defeasible Normative Representation

The D-tuple $D = (R, P, O, S, Rs, A, E, Ca, Cs)$ defines nine components that represent the structural elements involved in obligation competition within professional ethics cases. Three functional dimensions organize them [13]. Contextual Grounding components, namely Roles (R), States (S), and Resources (Rs), establish who acts under what conditions with what knowledge. Normative Structure components, namely Principles (P), Obligations (O), Capabilities (Ca), and Constraints (Cs), define what conduct is required, permitted, and prohibited. Temporal Dynamics components, namely Actions (A) and Events (E), record what occurred and in what order.

The BFO/IAO classification [2] grounds the component disjointness. States are specifically dependent continuants and Actions and Events are processes, so the continuant/occurrent boundary makes them disjoint. Principles, Obligations, and Constraints are directive information entities and Resources are descriptive information content entities, two kinds of information content entity that the ontology declares disjoint.

3.1 Defeasible Normative Structure

The dependency structure of the D-tuple represents the relationships along which obligations compete in professional ethics evaluation. Professional ethics is inherently defeasible [15]. Obligations derived from one Principle can be overridden by stronger Obligations derived from another when specific States obtain [8]. Defeasibility operates along these typed relationships. Representing the components as typed individuals with named edges between them makes the competition structure explicit and queryable. The three edges carry explicit OWL signatures. `competesWith` is symmetric and relates an Obligation to an Obligation, `prevailsOver` relates an Obligation to an Obligation and is declared asymmetric and irreflexive, and `defeasibleUnder` relates an Obligation to the State under which it is overridden. The extraction asserts these edges from the board's resolution text rather than deriving them by inference.

The dependency chain $R \to P \to O$ establishes the normative structure. A Role adheres to applicable Principles, which derive concrete Obligations. These dependencies are materialized in each case ontology as the object properties `adheresToPrinciple`, `hasObligation`, and `derivedFromPrinciple`, so the chain is traversable by SPARQL. This derivation follows Dennis et al. [6], who show that abstract principles require translation into context-dependent rules. Unlike their policy-and-order formalism for autonomous systems, the present contribution is a deployed representation that exposes obligation competition as queryable structure for external reasoners rather than a plan-selection procedure. The D-tuple does not resolve the resulting competitions. It makes them explicit as named, typed relationships that a human evaluator or external reasoning engine can query and adjudicate.

For example, an environmental engineer who performed wetland delineation for a client discovers, after the engagement has ended, that the client illegally filled the wetlands without permits [11]. The duty of confidentiality to the former client competes with the paramount duty to protect public welfare, and under the violation the confidentiality obligation is defeasible while the public-welfare duty prevails, discharged by reporting to the proper authority. The $R \to P \to O$ chain produces both obligations from the same Role, but the State determines which prevails. NSPE BER Case 04–8 (2004)[2] illustrates this with a concrete scenario. The extraction client (Sect. 4) produces typed OWL individuals from the case narrative. A separate edge-extraction pass then links competing Obligation and State individuals with the three defeasibility object properties, attaching to each edge a PROV-O derivation that records the verbatim source quote. Figure 1 shows three typed individuals extracted from this case and the defeasibility edges (`competesWith`, `prevailsOver`, `defeasibleUnder`) introduced in the core ontology to expose this pattern as first-class graph structure.

[2] https://www.nspe.org/career-growth/ethics/board-ethical-review-cases/public-welfare-client-action-following-engineers.

```
# State that activates the competition (from case 04-8 facts)
case86:State_WetlandViolation
    a proeth:UnpermittedWetlandFillViolationState ;
    rdfs:label "Client's unpermitted wetland fill; public safety at risk" .

# Obligation A: confidentiality to the former client (NSPE II.1.c)
case86:Obl_Confidentiality
    a proeth:ConfidentialityObligation ;
    proeth:sourcetext "shall not reveal facts ... without the prior
        consent of the client (NSPE II.1.c)" .

# Obligation B: hold public welfare paramount (NSPE I.1)
case86:Obl_PublicWelfare
    a proeth:SafetyObligation ;
    proeth:sourcetext "Hold paramount the safety, health, and welfare
        of the public (NSPE I.1)" .

# Defeasibility edges (core ontology)
case86:Obl_Confidentiality
    proeth-core:competesWith case86:Obl_PublicWelfare ;
    proeth-core:defeasibleUnder case86:State_WetlandViolation .

case86:Obl_PublicWelfare
    proeth-core:prevailsOver case86:Obl_Confidentiality .
```

Fig. 1. NSPE BER Case 04–8 (Public Welfare, Client Action Following Engineer's Services). An environmental engineer discovers, after services end, that a former client has illegally filled wetlands. Two obligations under the current NSPE Code compete, confidentiality to the client (II.1.c) and the paramount duty to public welfare (I.1, discharged by reporting to the proper authority). The State representing the unpermitted fill renders the confidentiality obligation defeasible, and the public-welfare obligation prevails. Type-level classification verified by the Pellet reasoner (Sect. 4). Prefixes denote the core ontology (`proeth-core:`), the engineering domain ontology (`proeth:`), and the case individual layer (`case86:`). Local names abbreviated. Provenance triples omitted.

3.2 Architectural Separation for Decidability

Representing defeasible normative reasoning in full generality exceeds the expressiveness of decidable description logics, and OWL-DL cannot natively express obligation override. The architecture separates concerns. The type-level ontology (component classifications, disjointness axioms, BFO alignments) remains within OWL-DL and benefits from sound and complete reasoning by Pellet [16], while the defeasible patterns are carried as the structured, SPARQL-queryable relationships described above, available to external engines that support non-monotonic inference, such as defeasible-rule systems with explicit priorities [8]. This is a deliberate boundary. The ontology captures the board's resolution as provenance-grounded structure, and external engines handle defeasible inference.

4 Implementation

The representation described in Sect. 3 requires an infrastructure that serves formally typed case ontologies, validates LLM-extracted classifications, and exposes the graph to SPARQL queries. OntServe implements this infrastructure as a three-layer ontology architecture.

The core layer declares the nine component classes with an `owl:AllDisjointClasses` assertion and the BFO/IAO alignments described in Sect. 3. A domain layer adds profession-specific subclasses. For engineering ethics, these include subclasses of Obligation for disclosure duties and public safety requirements, and subclasses of Resource for NSPE Code provisions and board precedents [11]. Each case then produces an individual layer: one OWL ontology per case that contains the typed individuals from that narrative and links to shared class definitions in the domain and core layers.

The repository currently holds 142 ontologies: 119 case ontologies, 11 external imports (including BFO, IAO, Relations Ontology, and PROV-O), and 12 ProEthica ontologies (core, intermediate, cases, provenance, four codes of ethics for NSPE/ASCE/ASME/IEEE, and four engineering domain ontologies). The full graph is served through a SPARQL endpoint.

OntServe exposes ontology definitions via the Model Context Protocol (MCP) for use by extraction clients. The current client is an LLM that proposes typed entities from case text without traversing the ontology or drawing inferences. The companion paper [13] documents this nine-component extraction in full. The defeasibility edges are added afterward by a separate pass, one call per case to Claude Sonnet 4.6 at temperature 0.1, with output constrained to the previously extracted individuals and each edge carrying a PROV-O derivation. Pellet (Sect. 3.2), implemented via owlready2 [9], verifies that each case ontology satisfies the core-layer disjointness assertion declared in Sect. 3. A State misclassified as an Action, for example, would violate this disjointness and produce an inconsistency.

5 Evaluation

The ontological infrastructure of Sects. 3 and 4 was evaluated for three properties of the knowledge graph, namely structural coverage, ontological consistency, and downstream retrieval performance.

The extraction client produced 119 case ontologies from NSPE Board of Ethical Review opinions spanning 1958 to 2025. Each case ontology contains typed individuals classified across the nine components, with coverage across all three functional dimensions in every case. Entity classes accumulate across cases, so the shared vocabulary grows without duplication. The defeasibility layer comprises 1,872 `competesWith`, 788 `prevailsOver`, and 2,177 `defeasibleUnder` edges, with at least one `prevailsOver` edge present in 118 of the 119 cases.

Ontological consistency follows from the formal structure. The `owl:AllDisjointClasses` assertion over all nine components means that the SPARQL endpoint can validate classification integrity without additional logic. A query checking for entities with two incompatible component types will return empty because the ontology makes such a classification incoherent at the schema level. Pellet confirms consistency for all 119 case ontologies. Its check is type-level, covering disjointness across the nine components together with the asymmetry and irreflexivity of `prevailsOver`. It does not validate extraction accuracy and does not perform defeasible inference.

The shared entity vocabulary also supports case retrieval: component-aware embeddings over the same 119-case pool recover cited precedents at three to eight times the random baseline [13].

The evaluation is limited in three respects. The case base covers a single professional domain. Expert evaluation of whether the typed classifications and defeasibility relationships match domain practitioners' judgment has not yet been conducted. The defeasibility edges are asserted by the extractor from each board opinion rather than derived by a reasoner.

6 Conclusion

The D-tuple provides a representation for professional ethics cases that unifies deontic dependency chains and formal ontological classification within a single deployed graph. Three defeasibility object properties expose the competition structure between obligations as queryable graph relationships.

OntServe instantiates this representation as a knowledge base with a SPARQL endpoint for cross-case queries and an MCP interface for extraction clients. A prior application of role-based ethics validation to military medical triage [12] shows the evaluation model operating in a professional domain through formal code resources, and argues the approach extends to other professional domains. Future work includes integrating a defeasible logic engine to formally resolve the obligation competitions that the current representation captures as structured data.

Data Availability Statement. The NSPE Board of Ethical Review cases used in this study are publicly available through the NSPE Ethics Resources website. The 119 case ontologies, supporting ontologies, and extraction pipeline are maintained in the OntServe repository (see Sect. 1). An archival copy is also available in a Zenodo repository.

Disclosure of Interests. The author has no competing interests to declare.

Declaration on Generative AI. During the preparation of this work, the author used Claude (Anthropic) to assist with manuscript editing, and subsequently reviewed and edited the content, taking full responsibility for this publication.

References

1. Allen, J.F.: Maintaining knowledge about temporal intervals. Commun. ACM **26**(11), 832–843 (1983). https://doi.org/10.1145/182.358434
2. Arp, R., Smith, B., Spear, A.D.: Building Ontologies with Basic Formal Ontology. MIT Press (2015)
3. Ashley, K.D., McLaren, B.M.: A CBR knowledge representation for practical ethics. In: Haton, J.-P., Keane, M., Manago, M. (eds.) EWCBR 1994. LNCS, vol. 984, pp. 180–197. Springer, Heidelberg (1995). https://doi.org/10.1007/3-540-60364-6_36

4. Berreby, F., Bourgne, G., Ganascia, J.G.: A declarative modular framework for representing and applying ethical principles. In: 16th Conference on Autonomous Agents and MultiAgent Systems, pp. 96–104 (2017)
5. Cox, S., Little, C.: OWL-Time: Time ontology in OWL. W3C Recommendation (2017). https://www.w3.org/TR/owl-time/
6. Dennis, L.A., Fisher, M., Slavkovik, M., Webster, M.: Formal verification of ethical choices in autonomous systems. Rob. Autonomous Syst. **77**, 1–14 (2016). https://doi.org/10.1016/j.robot.2015.11.012
7. Frankel, M.S.: Professional codes: why, how, and with what impact? J. Bus. Ethics **8**(2–3), 109–115 (1989). https://doi.org/10.1007/BF00382575
8. Horty, J.F.: Reasons and oughts. In: Reasons as Defaults. Oxford University Press (2012). https://doi.org/10.1093/acprof:oso/9780199744077.003.0003
9. Lamy, J.B.: Owlready: ontology-oriented programming in Python with automatic classification and high level constructs for biomedical ontologies. Artif. Intell. Med. **80**, 11–28 (2017). https://doi.org/10.1016/j.artmed.2017.07.002
10. McLaren, B.M.: Extensionally defining principles and cases in ethics: An AI model. Artif. Intell. **150**(1–2), 145–181 (2003). https://doi.org/10.1016/S0004-3702(03)00135-8
11. National Society of Professional Engineers: Board of ethical review cases (2025). https://www.nspe.org/resources/ethics/ethics-resources/board-ethical-review-cases
12. Rauch, C.B., Molineaux, M., Mainali, M., Sen, A., Floyd, M.W., Weber, R.O.: Role-based ethics for decision-maker alignment. In: 2025 IEEE Conference on Artificial Intelligence (CAI), pp. 1209–1212 (2025). https://doi.org/10.1109/CAI64502.2025.00209
13. Rauch, C.B., Weber, R.O.: Component-aware case retrieval for professional ethics with ontology-constrained LLM extraction. In: ICCBR 2026 (2026). To appear
14. Rauch, C.B., Weber, R.O.: ProEthica: a professional role based ethical analysis tool using LLM-orchestrated, ontology supported case based reasoning. In: Proceedings of the AAAI Conference on Artificial Intelligence. vol. 40, pp. 41673–41675 (2026). https://doi.org/10.1609/aaai.v40i48.42377
15. Ross, W.D.: The Right and the Good. Clarendon Press, Oxford (1930)
16. Sirin, E., Parsia, B., Grau, B.C., Kalyanpur, A., Katz, Y.: Pellet: a practical OWL-DL reasoner. J. Web Semantics **5**(2), 51–53 (2007). https://doi.org/10.1016/j.websem.2007.03.004
17. Tolmeijer, S., Kneer, M., Sarasua, C., Christen, M., Bernstein, A.: Implementations in machine ethics: a survey. ACM Comput. Surveys **53**(6), 132:1–132:38 (2020). https://doi.org/10.1145/3419633
18. Zhong, T., Song, Y., Limarga, R., Pagnucco, M.: Computational machine ethics: a survey. J. Artif. Intell. Res. **82**, 1581–1628 (2025). https://doi.org/10.1613/jair.1.16836

WaLo2D: Testbed for Multi-agent Warehouse Logistics Reinforcement Learning Experiments

Christoph Saad(✉) and Stefan Geißelsöder

University of Applied Sciences Ansbach, 91522 Ansbach, Germany
{christoph.saad,stefan.geisselsoeder}@hs-ansbach.de
https://www.hs-ansbach.de

Abstract. This paper introduces ***Wa****rehouse* ***Lo****gistics* ***2D*** (*WaLo2D*), an open-source environment designed for testing multi-agent reinforcement learning algorithms in automated warehouse logistics. *WaLo2D* is a configurable, low-compute simulation that models simple 2D warehouse tasks. This enables researchers and developers to quickly evaluate cooperative strategies for package storage, pick-up, and redistribution centre management. While more realistic 3D simulations are essential for final deployment, they often slow down early policy training due to the time-consuming manual crafting of details and high hardware requirements. In contrast, overly simplified models, such as discrete grid-based navigation, may not generalise well. *WaLo2D* bridges this gap by providing an accessible testbed that accelerates the initial evaluation of algorithms and tuning of reward functions, which is a critical advantage given the high number of repetitions required in multi-agent reinforcement learning experiments. It supports logistics scenarios, such as package routing, storage management and truck loading. The project is available at https://github.com/KIForAN/WaLo2D.

1 Introduction

In today's economy, warehouses and logistics centres have become essential for online shopping and industrial production. As demand grows, it is becoming progressively more challenging - and consequently more costly - to secure enough qualified personnel to operate equipment such as forklifts, handle packages and oversee the loading and unloading of delivery trucks. Consequently, the industry is shifting towards automated and autonomous solutions, including multi-robot and swarm systems. The coordination and task assignment of these robots can be achieved through classical algorithms or machine learning tools such as reinforcement learning (RL). Whilst classical methods have been demonstrated to be effective in addressing specific warehouse sub-problems, they are not well-suited to dynamic environments where policies must adapt to stochastic package arrivals, variable robot capabilities, and evolving storage layouts. RL provides a principled framework for the learning of adaptive strategies through interaction, a matter of increasing relevance as warehouses transition towards fully

D. Wolter and G. Schwalbe (Eds.): KI 2026, LNAI 16830, pp. 292–299, 2027.
https://doi.org/10.1007/978-3-032-32335-4_26

autonomous operations. Effective RL training depends on a suitable simulation environment. While several 3D-based warehouse-specific simulations exist, most require extensive manual configuration and setup, making them time-consuming and resource-intensive. Conversely, many research experiments rely on oversimplified models, such as grid-based systems, which fail to capture the nuances of real-world operations. To effectively train RL policies, reward functions must be carefully designed, and appropriate algorithms must be selected for each task, a challenge that remains an active area of research. To address these challenges, we introduce *WaLo2D*, a simulation environment that balances complexity, computational cost, and realism. Its design focuses on fast iterations and testing of various reward functions as well as RL policies. Solutions developed with an increased variation in simulations can more robustly be adapted to more complex simulations or real environments. Our goal is for *WaLo2D* to become a standardised RL testbed for diverse multi-robot warehouse logistics tasks.

2 Related Work

Training RL policies for warehouse-related tasks has been explored through various simulation environments. For instance, Cestero et al. [1] trained a single agent within a discrete grid-based environment to manage warehouse operations. Similarly, Baras et al. [2] employed a multi-robot grid-based system, where an algorithm was used to select the next robot for package pickup in conjunction with a classical path planner. While these environments allow for rapid experimentation, they lack the fidelity needed to capture the complexities of real-world warehouse dynamics, and can hinder the transfer of learned policies to physical systems. In contrast, other researchers focus on integrating more realistic simulations into their frameworks. Leon et al. [3] connected FlexSim, a powerful industrial manufacturing and warehouse simulation software, with Gym [4], allowing for the development of policies mimicking human decision-making. However, these high-fidelity simulations often require substantial computational resources and manual configuration, slowing down the crucial iterative development process for RL experimentation. Similarly, environments built with advanced simulation tools such as Gazebo [5] and ROS/ROS2 [6,7], combined with RL interfaces like that proposed by La et al. [8], provide realistic physics and sensor models, but introduce complexity in setup and tuning. For even greater visual fidelity, game engines such as Unreal Engine [9] can be combined with real ROS-capable robots [10] or physics engines like MuJoCo [11,12]. Additionally, Nvidia's Isaac simulator [13] offers a unified solution for both physics and visualization simulations. Salimpour et al. [14] further demonstrated the potential of combining Nvidia's Isaac simulator with Gazebo and real ROS-capable robots to enhance sim-to-real transfer. *WaLo2D* aims to offer a solution between these extremes. It provides a simulation environment that offers the needed balance between realism and computational efficiency, enabling faster iteration and reward function tuning than high-fidelity simulators while avoiding the limitations of simplified grid-based approaches. This 2D design, combined with simplified physics, supports rapid and accurate prototyping, which is especially beneficial for multi-agent reinforcement learning (MARL) in warehouse logistics.

3 Project Structure

3.1 Warehouse Simulation

The warehouse simulation is implemented in Python 3 and uses efficient linear algebra with `numpy` arrays [15]. For the rendering of the warehouse, robots, and other entities, we use the popular `pygame` [16] library for building 2D games. The simulation supports four primary entity types. **Mobile robots:** These are the agents which represent autonomous mobile robots (AMRs), operating within the warehouse. Modelled as simple rectangles with a position and rotation, they support omnidirectional driving using holonomic dynamics [17]. They can move in both the X and Y directions and rotate, similar to applications described in [18]. **Packages:** These represent various goods that require transportation and have designated goals such as trucks and storage spaces. **Storage spaces:** These static, rectangular locations serve as designated areas for storing packages. **Trucks:** Trucks are connected to a loading bay, and can load or unload one or more packages using a FIFO buffer. Each mobile robot has an optional goal state that can be set or modified at runtime. Robots also maintain an internal battery state with a simple energy consumption mechanism, each action, or waiting period consumes energy differently. Users can define multiple robot types, each characterised by its own size, maximum velocity, battery capacity, and energy consumption parameters. Currently, robots do not differentiate between package sizes and handle them uniformly. The simulation simplifies certain physical interactions for efficiency. Collision detection between robots is simplified: empty robots do not trigger collision responses during package pickup operations, while loaded robots maintain full collision awareness. This simplification reduces computational overhead without significantly affecting policy learning. The simulation uses a simplified loading and unloading mechanism. When a robot triggers a pick-up or drop-off action, it performs simple feasibility checks to determine whether a loading or unloading procedure can be initiated. These checks ensure that the robot is in the correct state (i.e. that it not already carrying a load and is within reach) before proceeding. In a real scenario, the user can then trigger their specific loading and unloading implementation based on the type of robot and package. After loading, the packages are attached to the robot and move with it during navigation. The simulation also considers these loaded packages when clipping the robot's position at the warehouse edge. Additionally, packages can be dropped off anywhere, including undesignated areas, enabling flexible task execution. In the simulation, trucks have defined arrival and departure times, which impose strict time windows during which robots must unload packages before the truck departs. Future developments will include delayed departures that trigger penalties within the reward functions. Looking ahead to features not yet in this release, we plan to integrate additional simulation elements such as charging stations for robots, static obstacles and walls, and sensors (e.g.

LiDAR). These enhancements will support longer logistics scenarios involving multiple charging cycles, realistic warehouse layouts and active obstacle avoidance. *WaLo2D* is designed to accommodate two main use cases shown in Fig. 1. **Storage Management:** Efficient storage of goods is critical within warehouses or factories. **Redistribution Centres:** These centres repeatedly handle incoming trucks delivering new packages that must be unloaded, regrouped, and then dispatched by different trucks. A combination of both use cases is also feasible.

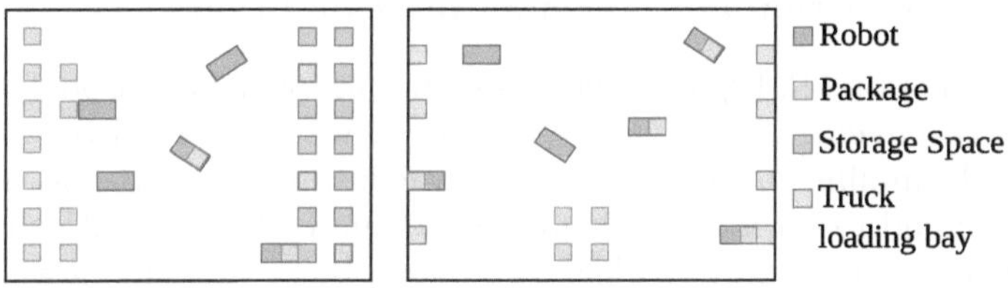

Fig. 1. Storage management (L) and redistribution centre (R) use case examples.

3.2 Reinforcement Learning Environment

To build proper benchmark, we selected an open interface that is compatible with a variety of MARL libraries. We opted for PettingZoo's Parallel API [19], which is based on Gymnasium [20], a maintained fork of the industry-standard Gym [4]. This API enables all robots to act simultaneously. The environment defines observation and action spaces for all agents. The common observation is a vector composed of the encoding of the type of each robot, its pose $P(x, y, \alpha)$, the pose of each package, the goal or destination pose of each package, and the number of steps remaining before their assigned truck departs. While this encoding covers the basic state, it isn't maximally efficient for increasing numbers of agents on limited hardware. The agent-specific observation is a vector that includes the robot's current pose, the goal pose set by the agent's action, a flag indicating whether a goal has been set, the loading state, the battery level, the distance and direction (in polar coordinates) to the nearest package, truck, or storage space, and a flag showing the available action capabilities (i.e., whether the robot can load or unload packages). Combining both observations results in a vector of length $4 \times N_R + 4 \times N_P + N_{P_t} + 17$, where N_R, N_P, and N_{P_t} are the number of robots, packages, and packages with a departure constraint respectively. All values normalised to $[0, 1]$ and binary flags encoded as 0 for `False` and 1 for `True`. The action space consists of a movement velocity vector, representing the linear velocities along each axis and the rotational speed. It also includes a new goal pose for the robot, a flag to indicate when this new goal has been set, and flags to indicate whether packages are being loaded or unloaded. This produces a nine-dimensional action vector, with velocities normalised to the interval $[-1, 1]$ and flags activated when their value exceeds 0.5. A provided action mask in the info dictionary indicates the valid actions for each agent at each timestep. Movement is permitted only if the battery level is above zero, while loading and unloading depend on whether a package is already loaded or within reach. Setting a new goal pose is always permitted. By design, the environment includes a configurable maximum timestep limit per episode, which can be adjusted as required. Users can manually configure all warehouse and robot parameters.

3.3 Reward Function and Terminating Condition

The reward function (R, Eq. 1) determines what agents learn through interaction with the environment. At the warehouse level, we aim to deliver all packages on time while minimising collective energy consumption. At the agent level, each robot should reach its goal, load/unload successfully, avoid collisions, and conserve energy individually. We balance these objectives using a weighted sum of common (r_c, Eq. 2) and individual (r_i, Eq. 3) components:

$$R = \omega_r \cdot r_c + (1 - \omega_r) \cdot r_i \tag{1}$$

$$r_c = \omega_{dp} \cdot r_{dp} + \omega_t \cdot r_{pt} + \omega_{ec} \cdot r_e \tag{2}$$

$$r_i = \omega_g \cdot r_g + \omega_{sl/u} \cdot \mathbf{S}_{sl/u} + \omega_c \cdot \mathbf{S}_c + \omega_{pd} \cdot \mathbf{S}_{pd} + \omega_{ei} \cdot r_{ei} \tag{3}$$

where $\omega_r \in [0, 1]$ controls the cooperation-individual effort trade-off. The reward function Eq. 1 components are summarized below. All terms are normalized to $[0, 1]$ preventing any single component from dominating the gradient during training. Each weight ω_x can be configured at initialization or updated at run-time for curriculum-based learning [21]. Common terms include package delivery progress $r_{dp} = N_{P_D}/N_P$ where N_{P_D} is the number of delivered packages, deadline reward $r_{pt} = \left(\sum_{N_{P_D}}^{p} \exp(-\omega_{ts} \cdot t_{dp})\right)/N_{P_D}$ with scaling factor ω_{ts} controlling sensitivity to deadlines, and global energy efficiency $r_e = 1/E$ where E is the global energy usage. Individual terms include goal proximity $r_g = 1 - e_{gi}$, load/unload success flags $\mathbf{S}_{sl/u}$, collision penalty $\mathbf{S}_c$, successful package delivery $\mathbf{S}_{pd}$ and individual energy efficiency $r_{ei} = 1/E_i$ where E_i the individual energy usage and $e_{gi} = (d_i/d_w) \cdot \omega_{dr} + (\alpha_i/2\pi) \cdot (1 - \omega_{dr})$ the position error, d_i the linear distance to the goal, α_i the angular error, ω_{dr} the weight ratio between them, and d_w the warehouse diagonal length used for normalization. An episode ends when a termination condition is reached. For example: all packages reach their destination, trucks depart before they are fully loaded, and when a robot collides or runs out of battery. Early termination occurs when the time limit for the environment is reached, or when another robot terminates.

4 Limitations and Future Development

WaLo2D provides a unified interface and configurable testbed for benchmarking various MARL algorithms in logistics scenarios. While the current version offers many useful features, there is opportunity to enhance its realism and scalability. Although *WaLo2D* is highly configurable, some aspects of the simulation could be improved. Currently, the loading and unloading actions rely on simple binary checks and collision handling is simplified to omit less critical cases. These simplifications are sufficient for initial experiments, but they present opportunities for more detailed modelling. Furthermore, it is not possible to define walls or additional collision objects; instead, warehouse edges are treated as boundaries where robot positions are clipped if they attempt to cross an edge. In addition, the simulation does not support sensors for detecting nearby objects, relying instead on a list of positions for nearby robots and packages. Incorporating sensor capabilities would enable more realistic interactions with the environment. Despite variations in size, all robots handle packages uniformly, meaning a smaller robot could carry a larger package. Since the simulation is two-dimensional by design, it cannot natively support 3D visual sensors or similar elements. While the robots have batteries with variable energy consumption, the ability to charge them is not yet implemented. This limits task complexity and duration, but this issue will be addressed in future iterations. As for now, the simulation backend lacks GPU acceleration or vectorisation, both of which could further improve performance. Finally, *WaLo2D* is still in development and still lacks experimental validation. Training scripts and comparison benchmarks using existing RL methods are in progress and will be made available. Future versions of *WaLo2D* will incorporate several enhancements to address these shortcomings. Charging stations will be added, enabling prolonged logistics tasks to be simulated with multiple charging cycles. Support will be added for walls and other static, collision-capable objects, allowing for more complex warehouse layouts and realistic scene divisions. Adding LiDAR sensors will allow detecting nearby obstacles, eliminating the need to maintain an exhaustive list of obstacle positions. We plan to support different robot, package, and cargo types, allowing for a more heterogeneous warehouse. Both the observation and action spaces should be refined by adding extra states and sensor inputs. Transitioning to a simulation backend that natively supports GPU acceleration and vectorisation, such as VMAS [22], will significantly improve performance and scalability. These planned developments will address current limitations and expand the applicability of *WaLo2D* as a robust testbed for MARL in logistics scenarios.

5 Conclusion

WaLo2D provides a configurable and accessible platform for advancing MARL in warehouse logistics. By integrating a configurable simulation environment with a bespoke RL interface, it facilitates the development and evaluation of policies for intricate logistics scenarios, such as package routing, storage management and truck loading. Its low-compute design enables rapid iteration and efficient reward function tuning, thereby accelerating the development cycle for researchers and practitioners. We believe that *WaLo2D* will be a valuable resource for the community, encouraging innovation and the adoption of more

RL-based and especially MARL-based solutions in automated warehouse environments. Future work will focus on incorporating sensor modelling, obstacles, and charging stations to further enhance realism and applicability.

References

1. Cestero, J., Quartulli, M., Metelli, A.M., Restelli, M.: Storehouse: a reinforcement learning environment for optimizing warehouse management. In: 2022 International Joint Conference on Neural Networks (IJCNN), pp. 1–9 (2022). https://doi.org/10.1109/ijcnn55064.2022.9891985
2. Baras, N., Chatzisavvas, A., Ziouzios, D., Dasygenis, M.: Improving automatic warehouse throughput by optimizing task allocation and validating the algorithm in a developed simulation tool. Automation **2**(3), 116–126 (2021). https://doi.org/10.3390/automation2030007
3. Leon, J.F., Li, Y., Martin, X.A., Calvet, L., Panadero, J., Juan, A.A.: A hybrid simulation and reinforcement learning algorithm for enhancing efficiency in warehouse operations. Algorithms **16**(9), 408 (2023). https://doi.org/10.3390/a16090408
4. Brockman, G., et al.: OpenAI Gym. arXiv preprint arXiv:1606.01540 (2016)
5. Koenig, N., Howard, A.: Design and use paradigms for gazebo, an open-source multi-robot simulator. In: 2004 IEEE/RSJ International Conference on Intelligent Robots and Systems (IROS) (IEEE Cat. No. 04CH37566), vol. 3, pp. 2149–2154 (2004). https://doi.org/10.1109/IROS.2004.1389727
6. Quigley, M., et al.: Ros: an open-source robot operating system. In: ICRA Workshop on Open Source Software, vol. 3 (2009)
7. Macenski, S., Foote, T., Gerkey, B., Lalancette, C., Woodall, W.: Robot operating system 2: design, architecture, and uses in the wild. Sci. Robot. **7**(66), eabm6074 (2022). https://doi.org/10.1126/scirobotics.abm6074
8. La, W.G., Kong, L., Muralidhara, S., Nichat, P.: DeepSim: A Reinforcement Learning Environment Build Toolkit for ROS and Gazebo. arXiv preprint arXiv:2205.08034 (2022)
9. Epic Games: Unreal Engine 5 (2019). https://www.unrealengine.com
10. Nesti, F., D'Amico, G., Marinoni, M., Buttazzo, G.: SimPRIVE: a simulation framework for physical robot interaction with virtual environments. In: 2025 IEEE 28th International Conference on Intelligent Transportation Systems (ITSC), pp. 907–913 (2025). https://doi.org/10.1109/ITSC60802.2025.11423662
11. Todorov, E., Erez, T., Tassa, Y.: Mujoco: a physics engine for model-based control. In: IEEE/RSJ International Conference on Intelligent Robots and Systems, pp. 5026–5033 (2012). https://doi.org/10.1109/IROS.2012.6386109
12. Embley-Riches, J., Liu, J., Julier, S., Kanoulas, D.: Unreal robotics lab: a high-fidelity robotics simulator with advanced physics and rendering. In: IEEE International Conference on Robotics and Automation (ICRA) (2026)
13. Mittal, M., et al.: Orbit: a unified simulation framework for interactive robot learning environments. IEEE Robot. Autom. Lett. **8**(6), 3740–3747 (2023). https://doi.org/10.1109/lra.2023.3270034
14. Salimpour, S., Peña-Queralta, J., Paez-Granados, D., Heikkonen, J., Westerlund, T.: Sim-to-Real Transfer for Mobile Robots with Reinforcement Learning: from NVIDIA Isaac Sim to Gazebo and Real ROS 2 Robots. arXiv preprint arXiv:2501.02902 (2025)

15. Harris, C.R., et al.: Array programming with NumPy. Nature **585**(7825), 357–362 (2020). https://doi.org/10.1038/s41586-020-2649-2
16. Shinners, P., et al.: Pygame (2012). https://www.pygame.org/
17. Muir, P.F., Neuman, C.P.: Kinematic modeling of wheeled mobile robots. J. Robot. Syst. **4**(2), 281–340 (1987). https://doi.org/10.1002/rob.4620040209
18. Patruno, C., Renò, V., Nitti, M., Mosca, N., Di Summa, M., Stella, E.: Vision-based omnidirectional indoor robots for autonomous navigation and localization in manufacturing industry. Heliyon **10**(4), e26042 (2024). https://doi.org/10.1016/j.heliyon.2024.e26042
19. Terry, J., et al.: Pettingzoo: Gym for multi-agent reinforcement learning. Adv. Neural. Inf. Process. Syst. **34**, 15032–15043 (2021)
20. Towers, M., et al.: Gymnasium: A Standard Interface for Reinforcement Learning Environments. arXiv preprint arXiv:2407.17032 (2024)
21. Li, Z., Xin, J., Li, N.: Autonomous exploration and mapping for mobile robots via cumulative curriculum reinforcement learning. In: 2023 IEEE/RSJ International Conference on Intelligent Robots and Systems (IROS), pp. 7495–7500 (2023). https://doi.org/10.1109/IROS55552.2023.10342066
22. Bettini, M., Kortvelesy, R., Blumenkamp, J., Prorok, A.: VMAS: a vectorized multi-agent simulator for collective robot learning. In: Springer Proceedings in Advanced Robotics, pp. 42–56 (2024). https://doi.org/10.1007/978-3-031-51497-5_4

PictSure: Pretraining Embeddings Matters for In-context Learning Image Classifiers

Lukas Schiesser[1(✉)], Cornelius Wolff[2], Sophie Haas[1], and Simon Pukrop[1]

[1] German Research Center for AI (DFKI), Hamburger Str. 24, 49084 Osnabrück, Germany
{lukas.schiesser,sophie.haas,simon.pukrop}@dfki.de

[2] Centrum Wiskunde & Informatica (CWI), Science Park 123, 1098 XG Amsterdam, The Netherlands
cornelius.wolff@cwi.nl

Abstract. Building image classification models remains cumbersome in data-scarce domains, where collecting large labeled datasets is impractical. In-context learning (ICL) is a promising paradigm for few-shot image classification (FSIC), but prior work has underexplored the relative importance of encoder pretraining versus fusion-layer training data. We present PictSure, a vision-only ICL family of models that demonstrates the potential of easy-to-use fusion transformer architectures, as well as the need for better embedding representations across a wider range of image domains. In both in-domain and out-of-domain evaluations, we find that representation quality induced by pretraining strongly correlates with downstream ICL performance. Crucially, varying the training dataset for the fusion transformer, from ImageNet alone to diverse multi-domain mixtures, provides limited additional performance gains under the evaluated settings, demonstrating that the fusion layer appears capable of adapting effectively once embeddings are sufficiently structured. These results show that the bottleneck in visual ICL is representation quality, not fusion-module training diversity. To facilitate adoption and reproducibility, we release all model weights as open-source artifacts and provide an MCP server that exposes PictSure as a callable tool for LLM-based agentic systems, enabling few-shot image classification to be invoked directly within AI pipelines without integration overhead. Code can be found at https://github.com/PictSure and models at https://huggingface.co/pictsure.

Keywords: In-Context Learning · Few-Shot Image Classification · Meta Learning · Domain Generalization

1 Introduction

Collecting large labeled datasets is impractical in many real-world domains such as medical imaging or agriculture, where expert annotation is costly and privacy constraints may apply [21,29,31,33]. Few-shot image classification (FSIC)

L. Schiesser and C. Wolff—These authors contributed equally to this work.

D. Wolter and G. Schwalbe (Eds.): KI 2026, LNAI 16830, pp. 300–308, 2027.
https://doi.org/10.1007/978-3-032-32335-4_27

addresses this by enabling models to recognize unseen classes from only a handful of examples [24]. In-context learning (ICL) is a particularly attractive paradigm for FSIC: a transformer is provided with labeled support image-label pairs alongside a query, and predicts the query label without any parameter updates at inference time [5,7]. This eliminates costly fine-tuning and supports immediate deployment across changing task definitions.

Existing visual ICL work, such as CAML [7] and SgVA-CLIP [16], rely on CLIP-based encoders whose language-grounded representations struggle with fine-grained or domain-shifted categories [17]. Prior work has largely overlooked a more fundamental question: *how much does the choice of encoder and its pretraining strategy determine ICL performance?* Evidence that a linear probe on strong embeddings can outperform sophisticated meta-learners [26] suggests representation quality may be the dominant factor.

We present **PictSure**, a set of vision-only ICL models designed to tackle this question. To isolate the effect of image encoding on the downstream ICL task, we keep the fusion architecture fixed and systematically vary the encoder and pretraining objective, comparing a supervised ResNet [8] pretrained on ImageNet-21k [19], a contrastive CLIP encoder [17], and a self-supervised DINOv2 [15]. Our central findings are twofold. First, the encoder and its pretraining matter far more than the training set of the ICL transformer itself: models without pretrained encoders fail to converge, while a well-pretrained encoder enables strong in-domain and out-of-domain transfer. Second, expanding the number and diversity of training datasets for the fusion transformer yields negligible gains. The fusion layer learns to read the embedding space from ImageNet alone, demonstrating how readily the ICL transformer adapts once representations are well-structured. This confirms that the bottleneck is not the fusion module's exposure to diverse tasks, but the quality of the embedding space, suggesting that better representations that improve class separability are a key lever for performance gains. The main contributions are: (1) PictSure, a transformer-based vision-only in-context learner requiring no fine-tuning or language supervision; (2) a systematic study showing encoder pretraining quality is the dominant performance driver in visual ICL; (3) competitive out-of-domain results on medical benchmarks (Brain Tumor, OrganCMNIST), demonstrating the advantage of purely visual embeddings for domain generalization; (4) a fully open-source baseline for future FSIC research, providing a clean, reproducible foundation for studying transformer-based fusion layers under varying encoder designs, including an MCP server that exposes PictSure as a tool for agentic systems to perform few-shot image classification directly within AI pipelines.

2 Background and Model

FSIC and ICL. An alternative paradigm is ICL which eliminates parameter updates by conditioning on a demonstration set $\mathscr{D} = \{(x_i, y_i)\}_{i=1}^{m}$ provided at inference time to predict the label of a query [5]:

$$F_\theta : (\mathscr{D}, x_q) \rightarrow \hat{y_q}$$

Prior work such as CAML [7] extends this paradigm to vision by leveraging CLIP-based encoders to perform ICL over images. However, these approaches inherit a key limitation of language-aligned representations: they often fail to preserve fine-grained visual distinctions and degrade under domain shift, as textual descriptions provide only weak supervision for subtle inter-class differences [7,17].

PictSure Architecture. Each support image x_i is encoded by a frozen visual encoder ϕ_{img} into $v_i \in \mathbb{R}^d$; its one-hot label y_i is projected by ϕ_{lbl} into $\ell_i \in \mathbb{R}^d$. These are concatenated into a joint token $t_i = [v_i; \ell_i]$; the query uses $t_q = [v_q; \mathbf{0}]$. The ICL transformer $\mathcal{T}$ then processes the full sequence under an asymmetric mask: support tokens attend to each other freely, the query attends to all support tokens, but support tokens cannot attend to the query—mirroring meta-inference without mutual contamination. The output query representation is classified via:

$$\hat{y_q} = f_{\text{cls}}(\mathcal{T}([t_1, \dots, t_m, t_q])) \in \mathbb{R}^n$$

The transformer uses four blocks, eight attention heads, and model dimension 1024. The broad architecture is illustrated in Fig. 1. Models are trained on 10-way 5-shot episodes sampled from ImageNet-21K [19] (10,000 episodes per epoch, images at 224×224).

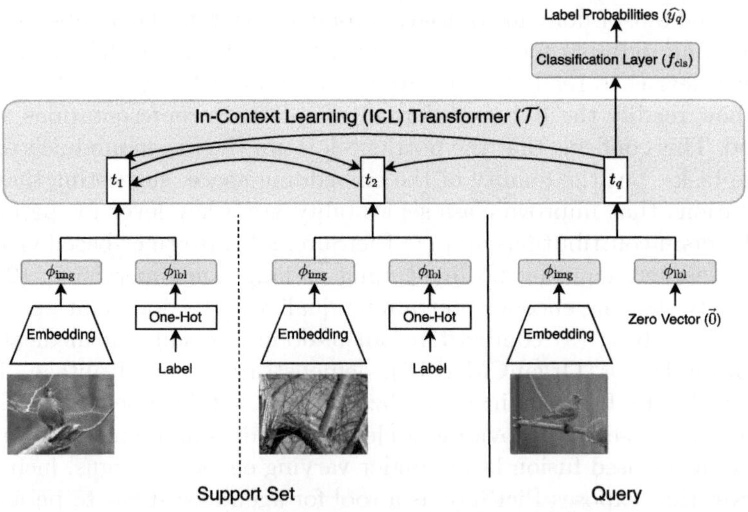

Fig. 1. Overview of the PictSure architecture.

3 Training

We evaluate three embedding backbones integrated into PictSure, varying only the encoder (with frozen weights) and projection while keeping the ICL transformer architecture the same. ResNet [8] is a supervised convolutional network trained on ImageNet1K using standard classification objectives. CLIP [17] is a Vision Transformer trained via contrastive alignment on 400 million image–text pairs, with its image encoder frozen during integration. DINOv2 [15] is a ViT trained through self-distillation and masked-image modeling on 142 million images without any labels. Across all settings, pretrained and frozen encoders prove necessary for consistent convergence and strong few-shot performance.

We study two fusion-transformer training configurations that vary only in the composition of the training data. The *ImageNet* setting trains exclusively on ImageNet-21K [19], the standard pretraining corpus used in prior work.

The *Default* setting replaces this with a multi-domain mixture of sixteen datasets spanning diverse visual categories: ILSVRC-2012 [20] (20%), Places365 [32] (10%), VGGFace2 [6] (10%), Products10K [3] (10%), LEGO Parts [12] (10%), Food-101 [4] (5%), SD-198 [25] (5%), ChestX [28] (5%), Cars196 [11] (5%), WildlifeReID-10K [1] (5%), EuroSAT [9] (4%), PlantVillage (2.5%), Fruits-360 [22] (2.5%), HAM10000 [27] (2%), Oxford Flowers [14] (2%), and KAU-BCMD [2] (2%). This mixture deliberately spans general, fine-grained, medical, agricultural, and remote-sensing imagery to test whether broader domain coverage during fusion training improves out-of-domain generalization.

4 Model Evaluation

We evaluated the performance of our PictSure model variations across a diverse range of visual domains. Both in-domain and out-of-domain datasets, comprising general, agricultural, and medical imagery were used for the evaluation, namely tieredImageNet [18], PlantDoc [23], Brain Tumor Classification (MRI) dataset [13], and OCTMNIST [30]. All evaluations use 5-way k-shot tasks with $k \in \{1, 5\}$, averaged over 2000 episodes per dataset and reported as mean accuracy $\pm$ standard error.

Baselines. We compare multiple variants of PictSure against several established baselines. First, we include the representation learning baseline of [26], consisting of a pretrained embedding network followed by a task-specific linear classifier trained on support embeddings (RFS). Second, we consider the method of [10], which combines large-scale pretraining, ProtoNet-based meta-training, and task-specific fine-tuning (PMF). We further include CAML [7], a CLIP-based approach to few-shot learning. In addition, we evaluate the multimodal model Qwen3.5 122B in a pure ICL setting, where the model receives m support imageâĂŞlabel pairs and a query (images resized to 224×224) without parameter updates. All methods are evaluated on 5-way 1-shot and 5-way 5-shot tasks. We report mean accuracy and standard error across episodes. Figure 2 summarizes the results. As a supervised baseline, we train a multilayer perceptron (MLP) directly on the pre-computed embeddings. The network consists of an input projection layer followed by four residual blocks, each comprising two fully-connected layers with batch normalization, ReLU activations, and dropout, with a linear output head. To match the evaluation protocol of our primary method, we repeatedly sample random subsets of 10 classes from each dataset (200 runs per dataset) and train a separate MLP on each subset. Models are optimized with AdamW using a linear learning rate decay schedule and early stopping.

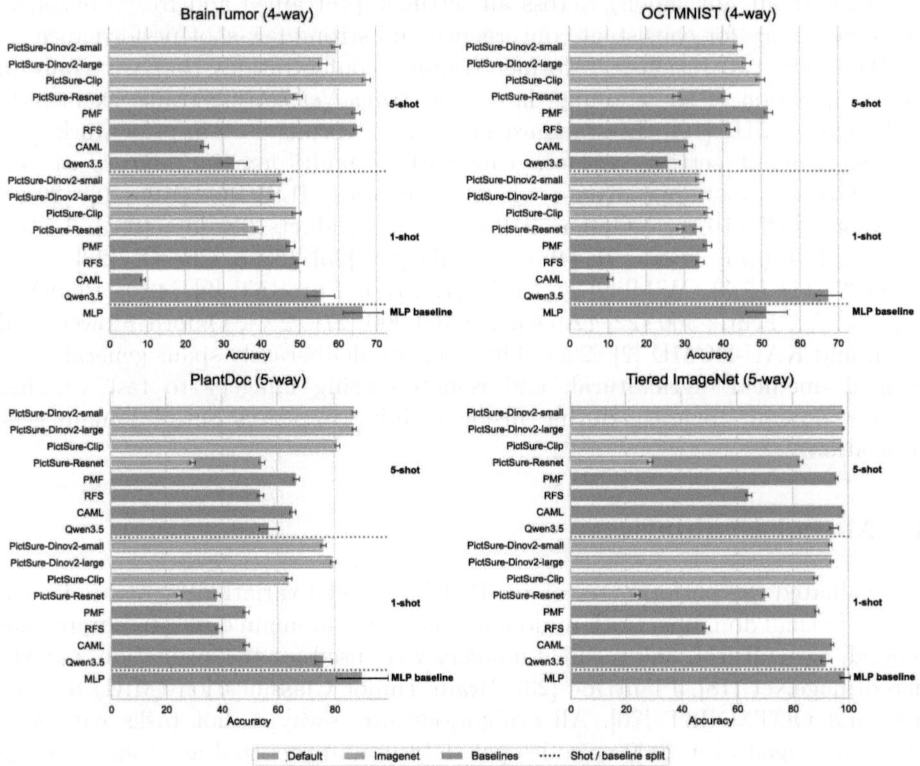

Fig. 2. Test results across all PictSure model variants compared to baselines.

5 Analysis

Encoder quality appears to be one of the strongest factors influencing PictSure's performance. DINOv2 and CLIP variants consistently outperform the ResNet-based variant across all benchmarks, most clearly on tieredImageNet and PlantDoc in both shot settings. These results support the hypothesis that strong representations may contribute more to performance than increased adaptation complexity in the evaluated setting. The fusion transformer showed limited sensitivity to training-data composition across the evaluated datasets. The *Default* and *Imagenet* settings yield nearly identical results in our experiments, suggesting ImageNet-21K-style supervision is sufficient for learning supportâĂŞquery interaction and that further gains are more strongly associated with representation quality than data diversity. The exception is ResNet-50, which shows a modest sensitivity to training data composition. We hypothesize that this is because ResNet's global-average-pooled representations carry less structural information than ViT patch tokens, leaving the fusion module with a less separable embedding space to work from; in that regime, exposure to more varied training tasks may partially compensate for the representational deficit, whereas with a strong encoder the fusion layer benefits less from additional diversity. PictSure's relative performance depends on the target domain. It is highly competitive on tiered-ImageNet and particularly strong on PlantDoc, where DINOv2 variants outperform RFS, PMF, and CAML. On OCTMNIST and Brain Tumor it remains competitive, though PMF, RFS, and Qwen3.5 can match or exceed it. PictSure demonstrates competitive cross-domain transfer performance, with its clearest advantages on natural-image benchmarks. With CLIP embeddings frozen, PictSure remains relatively consistent across domains, whereas CAML shows a clear drop on the medical datasets, despite using the same encoder models. Thus, the main difference between adaptation methods appears to be robustness to domain shift rather than absolute performance gains. The supervised MLP baseline reinforces this: its strong performance confirms that pretrained embeddings already contain substantial task-relevant information. Beyond accuracy, PictSure offers a favorable efficiency profile, substantially smaller than CAML and Qwen3.5 while remaining competitive across benchmarks, with advantages over RFS and PMF in transfer performance, lightweight fusion, and stable inference.

6 Outlook and Conclusion

Our results support an encoder-centric perspective on visual ICL design. The fusion transformer learns quickly and reliably once embeddings are well-structured, while changes in fusion complexity or training data provide only limited gains when representations are weak. Representation quality appears to be the limiting factor, not the transformer's ability to perform support-query fusion.

This points to a clear path forward: if ICL transformers already act as robust readers of embedding spaces, further gains are to be found in building better visual representations through stronger pretraining objectives, better encoder architectures, and improved encoder-task alignment under distribution shift.

To lower the barrier to adoption, we release an MCP server exposing PictSure as a callable tool for agentic systems, enabling few-shot image classification within AI pipelines without integration overhead. Future work should prioritize representation learning at scale while keeping the fusion module lightweight, including improved pretraining curricula, broader encoder families, and extended class coverage beyond the current 10-way setup.

References

1. Adam, L., Čermák, V., Papafitsoros, K., Picek, L.: WildlifeReID-10k: wildlife re-identification dataset with 10k individual animals (2025). https://doi.org/10.48550/arXiv.2406.09211. http://arxiv.org/abs/2406.09211. arXiv:2406.09211
2. Alsolami, A.S., Shalash, W., Alsaggaf, W., Ashoor, S., Refaat, H., Elmogy, M.: King abdulaziz university breast cancer mammogram dataset (KAU-BCMD). Data **6**(11), 111 (2021). ISSN 2306-5729. https://doi.org/10.3390/data6110111. https://www.mdpi.com/2306-5729/6/11/111
3. Bai, Y., Chen, Y., Yu, W., Wang, L., Zhang, W.: Products-10K: A Large-scale Product Recognition Dataset (2020). https://doi.org/10.48550/arXiv.2008.10545. http://arxiv.org/abs/2008.10545. arXiv:2008.10545
4. Bossard, L., Guillaumin, M., Van Gool, L.: Food-101 – mining discriminative components with random forests. In: Fleet, D., Pajdla, T., Schiele, B., Tuytelaars, T. (eds.) ECCV 2014. LNCS, vol. 8694, pp. 446–461. Springer, Cham (2014). https://doi.org/10.1007/978-3-319-10599-4_29
5. Brown, T., et al.: Language models are few-shot learners. In: Advances in Neural Information Processing Systems, vol. 33, pp. 1877–1901, Curran Associates, Inc. (2020). https://papers.nips.cc/paper/2020/hash/1457c0d6bfcb4967418bfb8ac142f64a-Abstract.html
6. Cao, Q., Shen, L., Xie, W., Parkhi, O.M., Zisserman, A.: VGGFace2: a dataset for recognising faces across pose and age (2018). https://doi.org/10.48550/arXiv.1710.08092. http://arxiv.org/abs/1710.08092. arXiv:1710.08092
7. Fifty, C., et al.: Context-aware meta-learning. In: The Twelfth International Conference on Learning Representations (2024). https://openreview.net/forum?id=lJYAkDVnRU
8. He, K., Zhang, X., Ren, S., Sun, J.: Deep residual learning for image recognition. In: 2016 IEEE Conference on Computer Vision and Pattern Recognition (CVPR), Las Vegas, NV, USA, pp. 770–778. IEEE (2016). ISBN 978-1-4673-8851-1. https://doi.org/10.1109/CVPR.2016.90. http://ieeexplore.ieee.org/document/7780459/
9. Helber, P., Bischke, B., Dengel, A., Borth, D.: EuroSAT: a novel dataset and deep learning benchmark for land use and land cover classification. IEEE J. Sel. Top. Appl. Earth Obs. Remote Sens. **12**(7), 2217–2226 (2019). ISSN 1939-1404, 2151-1535. https://doi.org/10.1109/JSTARS.2019.2918242. https://ieeexplore.ieee.org/document/8736785/
10. Hu, S.X., Li, D., Stuhmer, J., Kim, M., Hospedales, T.M.: Pushing the limits of simple pipelines for few-shot learning: external data and fine-tuning make a difference. In: 2022 IEEE/CVF Conference on Computer Vision and Pattern Recognition (CVPR), pp. 9058–9067. IEEE, New Orleans, LA, USA (2022). ISBN 978-1-6654-6946-3. https://doi.org/10.1109/CVPR52688.2022.00886. https://ieeexplore.ieee.org/document/9879354/
11. Krause, J., Stark, M., Deng, J., Fei-Fei, L.: 3D object representations for fine-grained categorization. In: Proceedings of the IEEE International Conference on Computer Vision Workshops (ICCVW), pp. 554–561, Sydney, Australia (2013). https://doi.org/10.1109/ICCVW.2013.77. https://ieeexplore.ieee.org/document/6755874
12. Lego: Lego Parts Classification Dataset - 2.4M Renders (2025). https://www.kaggle.com/datasets/mihahamyt/lego-parts-classification-dataset-2-4m-renders
13. Nickparvar, M.: Brain tumor MRI dataset (2026). https://doi.org/10.34740/KAGGLE/DSV/14832123. https://www.kaggle.com/dsv/14832123

14. Nilsback, M.E., Zisserman, A.: Automated flower classification over a large number of classes. In: 2008 Sixth Indian Conference on Computer Vision, Graphics & Image Processing, pp. 722–729. IEEE, Bhubaneswar, India (2008). https://doi.org/10.1109/ICVGIP.2008.47. http://ieeexplore.ieee.org/document/4756141/
15. Oquab, M., et al.: DINOv2: learning robust visual features without supervision. Trans. Mach. Learn. Res. (2024)
16. Peng, F., Yang, X., Xiao, L., Wang, Y., Xu, C.: SgVA-CLIP: semantic-guided visual adapting of vision-language models for few-shot image classification. IEEE Trans. Multimedia **26**, 3469–3480 (2024). ISSN 1520-9210, 1941-0077. https://doi.org/10.1109/TMM.2023.3311646. https://ieeexplore.ieee.org/document/10243119/
17. Radford, A., et al.: Learning transferable visual models from natural language supervision. In: International Conference on Machine Learning, pp. 8748–8763. PmLR (2021)
18. Ren, M., et al.: Meta-learning for semi-supervised few-shot classification. arXiv (2018)
19. Ridnik, T., Ben-Baruch, E., Noy, A., Zelnik, L.: ImageNet-21K pretraining for the masses. In: Vanschoren, J., Yeung, S. (eds.) Proceedings of the Neural Information Processing Systems Track on Datasets and Benchmarks, vol. 1 (2021). https://datasets-benchmarks-proceedings.neurips.cc/paper_files/paper/2021/file/98f13708210194c475687be6106a3b84-Paper-round1.pdf
20. Russakovsky, O., et al.: ImageNet large scale visual recognition challenge. Int. J. Comput. Vis. **115**(3), 211–252 (2015). ISSN 0920-5691, 1573-140. https://doi.org/10.1007/s11263-015-0816-y
21. Dharani Devi, G., Jeyalakshmi, J.: Privacy-preserving breast cancer classification: a federated transfer learning approach. J. Imaging Inform. Med. **37**(4), 1488–1504 (2024). ISSN 2948-2933. https://doi.org/10.1007/s10278-024-01035-8
22. Sa, I., Ge, Z., Dayoub, F., Upcroft, B., Perez, T., McCool, C.: Deepfruits: a fruit detection system using deep neural networks. Sensors **16**(8), 1222 (2016)
23. Singh, D., Jain, N., Jain, P., Kayal, P., Kumawat, S., Batra, N.: PlantDoc: a dataset for visual plant disease detection. In: Proceedings of the 7th ACM IKDD CoDS and 25th COMAD, pp. 249–253. ACM, Hyderabad India (2020). ISBN 978-1-4503-7738-6. https://doi.org/10.1145/3371158.3371196. https://dl.acm.org/doi/10.1145/3371158.3371196
24. Snell, J., Swersky, K., Zemel, R.: Prototypical networks for few-shot learning. In: Advances in Neural Information Processing Systems, p. 30 (2017)
25. Sun, X., Yang, J., Sun, M., Wang, K.: A benchmark for automatic visual classification of clinical skin disease images. In: Leibe, B., Matas, J., Sebe, N., Welling, M. (eds.) ECCV 2016. LNCS, vol. 9910, pp. 206–222. Springer, Cham (2016). https://doi.org/10.1007/978-3-319-46466-4_13
26. Tian, Y., Wang, Y., Krishnan, D., Tenenbaum, J.B., Isola, P.: Rethinking few-shot image classification: a good embedding is all you need? In: Vedaldi, A., Bischof, H., Brox, T., Frahm, J.-M. (eds.) ECCV 2020. LNCS, vol. 12359, pp. 266–282. Springer, Cham (2020). https://doi.org/10.1007/978-3-030-58568-6_16
27. Tschandl, P., Rosendahl, C., Kittler, H.: The HAM10000 dataset, a large collection of multi-source dermatoscopic images of common pigmented skin lesions. Sci. Data **5**(1), 180161 (2018). ISSN 2052-4463. https://doi.org/10.1038/sdata.2018.161. https://www.nature.com/articles/sdata2018161
28. Wang, X., Peng, Y., Lu, L., Lu, Z., Bagheri, M., Summers, R.M.: ChestX-ray8: hospital-scale chest X-ray database and benchmarks on weakly-supervised classification and localization of common thorax diseases. In: 2017 IEEE Conference on Computer Vision and Pattern Recognition (CVPR), pp. 3462–3471 (2017)

29. Yang, J., Guo, X., Li, Y., Marinello, F., Ercisli, S., Zhang, Z.: A survey of few-shot learning in smart agriculture: developments, applications, and challenges. Plant Methods **18**(1), 28 (2022)
30. Yang, J., et al.: MedMNIST v2 - a large-scale lightweight benchmark for 2D and 3D biomedical image classification. Sci. Data **10**(1), 41 (2023). ISSN 2052-4463. https://doi.org/10.1038/s41597-022-01721-8. https://www.nature.com/articles/s41597-022-01721-8
31. Zhang, S., Metaxas, D.: On the challenges and perspectives of foundation models for medical image analysis. Med. Image Anal. **91**, 102996 (2024)
32. Zhou, B., Lapedriza, A., Khosla, A., Oliva, A., Torralba, A.: Places: a 10 million image database for scene recognition. IEEE Trans. Pattern Anal. Mach. Intell. **40**(6), 1452–1464 (2018). ISSN 0162-8828, 2160-9292, 1939-3539. https://doi.org/10.1109/TPAMI.2017.2723009. https://ieeexplore.ieee.org/document/7968387/
33. Zhou, Y., Yan, H., Ding, K., Cai, T., Zhang, Y.: Few-shot image classification of crop diseases based on vision-language models. Sensors **24**(18), 6109 (2024)

Explainable-AI-Based Training for Relevance-Based Robust Reinforcement Learning

Benedikt Schlereth-Groh[1(✉)], Şakir Furkan Yöndem[1], Ramin Tavakoli Kolagari[1], and Ute Schmid[2]

[1] Technische Hochschule Nürnberg, Keßlerplatz 12, 90489 Nürnberg, Germany
{benedikt.schlereth-groh,sakirfurkan.yoendem, ramin.tavakolikolagari}@th-nuernberg.de

[2] Otto-Friedrich-Universität Bamberg, Kapuzinerstraße 16, 96047 Bamberg, Germany
ute.schmid@uni-bamberg.de

https://www.th-nuernberg.de/, https://www.uni-bamberg.de/

Abstract. Deep neural networks (DNNs) have been demonstrated to enable autonomous decision-making across a range of domains, including finance, industrial control, robotics and medicine. Nevertheless, the opaque nature of these systems renders it challenging to verify behaviour, anticipate edge cases, or define operational boundaries. To address this issue, we propose the use of explainability-based training methods for reinforcement learning (RL) agents, with the aim of improving both model performance and robustness. Using concept bottleneck models (CBMs), sparse autoencoders (SAEs) and the Remove and Retrain (ROAR) approach during training has been shown to improve model performance. Random and guided occlusion methods have been evaluated using models that make decisions based on visual input. The results show that xAI-based training improves agent behaviour in benign environments and enhances robustness in scenarios where key information is missing. We can therefore demonstrate the potential of xAI-based training as a practical pathway towards more robust and reliable autonomous systems.

Keywords: Reinforcement Learning · explainable AI · Concept Bottleneck · Sparse Autoencoder · Remove and Retrain · Robustness

1 Introduction

Remarkable results have been achieved using deep reinforcement learning across a wide range of sequential decision-making tasks, from mastering complex board games [26] to controlling agents in high-dimensional continuous environments

Code: https://github.com/BenSchlereth/Explainable-AI-Based-Training-for-Relevance-based-Robust-Reinforcement-Learning.

D. Wolter and G. Schwalbe (Eds.): KI 2026, LNAI 16830, pp. 309–316, 2027.
https://doi.org/10.1007/978-3-032-32335-4_28

[21]. One key factor behind these successes is the ability of deep neural networks to learn features from raw pixel observations [17,18]. However, despite these advances, this leads to opacity of the learned agent. It is rarely clear which aspects of the observation space influence a particular decision, why a policy fails in specific situations or whether the features exploited during training are relevant to the task or just correlated with the training reward [19]. This lack of interpretability raises scientific and practical concerns, given that RL agents are being considered for deployment in real-world domains where autonomous decisions must be accountable and auditable [6].

Explainable AI (XAI) is a broad research programme that aims to make the internal representations and decision processes of deep neural networks understandable to human observers [2]. Techniques for identifying important areas for classification tasks where the relationship between inputs and outputs is fixed have been well studied in the context of supervised training [2]. However, transferring these tools to the reinforcement learning setting introduces a distinct set of challenges.

To demonstrate how policies can be improved, we examine three mechanisms for incorporating XAI into deep RL training. We then evaluate the impact of these mechanisms on the performance, robustness and interpretability of policies trained using Proximal Policy Optimisation (PPO) in pixel-based environments. The first mechanism involves training a Concept Bottleneck Model using supervised concept annotations. This model directs all policy decisions through a human-defined vocabulary, thereby revealing the reasoning behind the agent's actions in terms of interpretable features. The second mechanism uses a sparse autoencoder pretrained on environment observations with a top-k sparsity constraint. Its frozen encoder is then used as a structured feature extractor during policy learning. The third mechanism is an iterative Remove and Retrain procedure driven by GradCAM attributions. This procedure identifies and masks the pixel regions on which the current best-performing model relies most frequently at regular intervals.

We propose a training framework that integrates GradCAM-based attribution with a remove-and-retrain procedure for iterative feature suppression in deep reinforcement learning (RL). We demonstrate the superiority of this approach in terms of reward and robustness compared to sparse autoencoder and concept bottleneck alternatives. We also provide a systematic comparison of all three eXplainable AI (XAI) integration strategies in terms of performance, robustness, and interpretability.

2 Background

To understand the used methodology, it is first necessary to review and compare existing literature.

2.1 Explainable AI for Reinforcement Learning

Interpreting the inner workings of Deep Neural Networks can be done using explainable AI (XAI). Sparse Autoencoders promise to disentangle features in neural networks to improve the understandability of deep neural networks for large language models [3]. Luo *et al.* demonstrated that SAE also works for the image classification task using convolutional neural networks [15]. The architecture of the autoencoder is also transferred to reinforcement learning in the form of interpretable deep Q-networks, as described by the work of Annasamy and Sycara [1] and DuPlessie [5]. Concept Bottlenecks on the other hand first are introduced to tackle object detection by using human specified concepts to learn new classes [14]. Later Koh *et al.* showed how concepts can be used for classification by deep neural networks to learn high-level concepts from which the correct class can be learned [13]. Successive Concept Bottleneck agents (SCoBots) have shown that concept bottlenecks can work with reinforcement learning [4] and LICORICE even tries to minimize the number of concepts [27]. Remove and Retrain (ROAR) is coined by Hooker *et al.* [10] and describe how important information can be removed to increase the performance of classification network.

2.2 Robustness Evaluations for Reinforcement Learning

To understand how robustness can be evaluated on decision-making process different existing approaches need to be compared. In Reinforcement learning either the average reward after a set number of training steps [1] or the reward over the training time are compared between different algorithms [9,24]. The work of Gu *et al.* introduces action and observation disruptions and shows how the reward can decrease if the environment is not as perfect as during the training [8]. Adversarial attacks can generate imperfect observations, leading to a degradation of the achievable score [11]. On the other hand, leveraging adversarial training can improve the learning process [20]. Changes to environmental parameters such as friction or gravity can also reduce the effectiveness of a neural network in performing a given task. Mankowitz *et al.* propose a learning approach to mitigate these parameter changes [16]. Besides adversarial attacks an attribution based method can be of interest as well. Other work shows robustness for object detection in the absence of the most important point which is also novel for Reinforcement Learning [23].

3 Methodology

Different Methods to improve the learning process are presented here. By leveraging x-AI Methods not only the opaque nature of neural networks can be lifted but also train a more robust decision-making robust.

Training is conducted using Proximal Policy Optimization (PPO). At each update step, the convolutional encoder extracts spatial features from the current observation, which are then passed through the linear layers to produce policy logits and a value estimate. The deep neural network for all experiments is similar to allow consistent comparisons between the different approaches. All environments provide a 84×84 greyscale image and four consecutive observations are stacked and fed into the neural network to provide a suitable action. While continuos actions are more applicable to real world examples like car racing [7,12] for better comparisons discrete actions, also popular with RL, are chosen to streamline the training and evaluation process with the different environments.

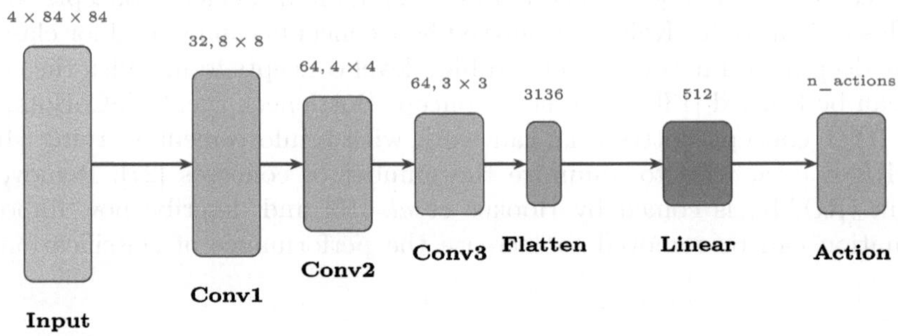

Fig. 1. Network architecture from Mnih *et al.* [18]

The convolution layers in Fig. 1 are used to extract features and the linear layers enable the network to make the correct decisions. The neural network architecture is the same as that provided by Mnih *et al.* [18] in Stable Baselines3 [22].

As training Methods we test and evaluate Concept Bottlenecks (CBMs), Sparse Autoencoders (SAE) and a Remove and Retrain (ROAR) procedure, introduced by Hooker *et al.* [10].

Concept Bottleneck Models (CBMs) address this limitation by grounding the agent's decision-making in a set of human-defined, semantically meaningful concepts. The policy is constrained to reason through a fixed vocabulary of concepts that are explicitly aligned with domain knowledge.

The Sparse Autoencoder (SAE) extracts a compact, disentangled representation of the observation space. The sparse structure of the learned encoding prompts the model to identify distinctive features that encapsulate the most significant aspects of the environment. These features can then guide and regularise the RL training process.

Remove and Retrains couples Gradient-weighted Class Activations Mapping (GradCAM) [25] and removes important input regions during the reinforcement learning process.

3.1 Robustness Evaluations

To assess robustness, all trained policies are evaluated under three controlled perturbation conditions that are applied at test time. The baseline condition provides each agent with the original, unmodified observation to establish a reference. In the noise masking condition, the observation is corrupted by randomly masking a subset of pixels to test whether the learned representations remain stable under low-level, task-unrelated perturbations. In the attribution masking condition, GradCAM is applied to identify the region with the highest attribution, which is then masked out. An agent whose performance deteriorates significantly under this condition has learned a brittle, spatially concentrated policy. In contrast, an agent whose performance remains stable has distributed its reliance across a broader feature set and is considered more robust.

4 Experiments

A series of experiments was conducted in different environments, using 84×84 greyscale outputs and four stacked frames. Discrete actions similar to pressing buttons in arcade games were selected for all test settings. The Atari games demonstrate the efficacy of various training methods for solving classic reinforcement learning problems. All games were trained with 10 million steps to ensure a high-performing model was found. To validate sufficient testing, evaluation was performed over 100 epochs.

4.1 Car Racing

Table 1. Carracing Evaluation

	Default Training	Concept Training	SAE Training	ROAR Training
Default Eval	792 ± 137	$\mathbf{859 \pm 94}$	845 ± 160	830 ± 114
Random	752 ± 165	$\mathbf{868 \pm 78}$	829 ± 153	859 ± 79
Guided Noise	752 ± 157	$\mathbf{839 \pm 99}$	809 ± 144	828 ± 130

The differences between the various training and evaluation methods are not significant in Table 1, but they all surpass the default training concept. Therefore, all training methods are valid solutions for improving the autonomous racing car's learning capabilities. Despite a slight decline and occasional increase in reward, all methods remain effective against random and guided occlusion.

Table 2. MsPacman Evaluation

	Default Training	Concept Training	SAE Training	ROAR Training
Default Eval	3142 ± 870	1373 ± 379	2032 ± 566	**4363 ± 1231**
Random	**1166 ± 561**	1035 ± 516	948 ± 442	1048 ± 467
Guided Noise	2345 ± 353	1043 ± 336	2093 ± 541	**2427 ± 959**

4.2 MsPacman

Table 2 compares the total rewards achieved by the different training methods on the different evaluation metrics. With unperturbed inputs, the Remove and Retrain method outperforms the others, but the steep decline in achievable reward with perturbed images indicates non-robust agents. Showcasing how the training process rewards focusing on only a small fraction of the input to make the decision and therefore lacking robustness for occlusions on small areas.

4.3 Pong

Table 3. Pong Evaluation

	Default Training	Concept Training	SAE Training	ROAR Training
Default Eval	−6 ± 5	−20 ± 1	−21 ± 0	**−5 ± 5**
Random	−21 ± 1	−21 ± 0	−21 ± 0	**−21 ± 1**
Guided Noise	−7 ± 5	−20 ± 1	−21 ± 0	**−5 ± 6**

Finally, the same testing procedure was used for the game Pong. As can be seen in Table 3, the training with CBMs and SAE fails as the minimum possible reward is −21 points. Although the ROAR training achieves a relatively successful policy, it does not reach the maximum available reward of 21. The random noise is detrimental to all policies as it is similar in size and colour to the actual ball.

5 Conclusion

This study examined the integration of explainable AI techniques into deep reinforcement learning. Three distinct methodological approaches (ROAR, Sparse Autoencoder, and Concept Bottleneck Model) were evaluated within a unified PPO training framework, assessing both policy performance and interpretability. Of these methods, ROAR achieved the highest cumulative rewards. It repeatedly challenged the policy to generalise beyond dominant visual shortcuts by iteratively suppressing the pixel regions most relied upon by the current best-performing model. However, this performance improvement comes at the cost of interpretability: the resulting policy remains opaque, with decisions that are difficult to trace. Although sparse autoencoders and concept bottlenecks provide a viable alternative for explaining features, they are not yet appropriate for all environments. Future work should examine the sensitivity of the ROAR procedure to masking strategy, attribution checkpoint frequency and sparsity level.

Acknowledgments. This work was accomplished within the project VAL, FKZ 53T20008TN, EBA Az. 8fd/003-1255#008-VAL, funded by the German Federal Ministry of Transport.

References

1. Annasamy, R.M., Sycara, K.P.: Towards better interpretability in deep Q-networks (2018). ArXiv:abs/1809.05630
2. Bennetot, A., et al.: A practical tutorial on explainable AI techniques. ACM Comput. Surv. **57**, 1–44 (2024)
3. Cunningham, H., Ewart, A., Smith, L.R., Huben, R., Sharkey, L.: Sparse autoencoders find highly interpretable features in language models (2023). ArXiv:abs/2309.08600
4. Delfosse, Q., Sztwiertnia, S., Stammer, W., Rothermel, M., Kersting, K.: Interpretable concept bottlenecks to align reinforcement learning agents (2024). ArXiv:abs/2401.05821
5. DuPlessie, C.: Dead feature counts in sparse autoencoders predict underlying deep q networks' effectiveness. In: Fumero, M., Domine, C., L"ahner, Z., Cannistraci, I., Zhao, B., Williams, A. (eds.) Proceedings of UniReps: the Third Edition of the Workshop on Unifying Representations in Neural Models. Proceedings of Machine Learning Research, vol. 322, pp. 385–397. PMLR (2026). https://proceedings.mlr.press/v322/duplessie26a.html
6. Glanois, C., et al.: A survey on interpretable reinforcement learning. Mach. Learn. **113**, 5847–5890 (2021)
7. Grooten, B., MacAlpine, P., Subramanian, K., Stone, P., Wurman, P.R.: Out-of-distribution generalization with a SPARC: racing 100 unseen vehicles with a single policy (2025). ArXiv:abs/2511.09737
8. Gu, S., et al.: Robust gymnasium: a unified modular benchmark for robust reinforcement learning (2025). ArXiv:abs/2502.19652
9. Hessel, M., et al.: Rainbow: combining improvements in deep reinforcement learning. In: AAAI Conference on Artificial Intelligence (2017)
10. Hooker, S., Erhan, D., Kindermans, P.J., Kim, B.: A benchmark for interpretability methods in deep neural networks. In: Neural Information Processing Systems (2018)
11. Huang, S., Papernot, N., Goodfellow, I., Duan, Y., Abbeel, P.: Adversarial attacks on neural network policies (2017). https://arxiv.org/abs/1702.02284
12. Kaufmann, E., Bauersfeld, L., Loquercio, A., Müller, M., Koltun, V., Scaramuzza, D.: Champion-level drone racing using deep reinforcement learning. Nature **620**, 982–987 (2023)
13. Koh, P.W., Nguyen, T., Tang, Y.S., Mussmann, S.O., Pierson, E., Kim, B., Liang, P.: Concept bottleneck models (2020). ArXiv:abs/2007.04612

14. Lampert, C.H., Nickisch, H., Harmeling, S.: Learning to detect unseen object classes by between-class attribute transfer. In: IEEE Conference on Computer Vision and Pattern Recognition, pp. 951–958 (2009)
15. Luo, W., Li, J., Yang, J., Xu, W., Zhang, J.: Convolutional sparse autoencoders for image classification. IEEE Trans. Neural Netw. Learn. Syst. **29**, 3289–3294 (2018)
16. Mankowitz, D.J., Mann, T.A., Bacon, P.L., Precup, D., Mannor, S.: Learning robust options (2018). https://arxiv.org/abs/1802.03236
17. Mnih, V., et al.: Playing Atari with deep reinforcement learning. ArXiv:abs/1312.5602 (2013)
18. Mnih, V., et al.: Human-level control through deep reinforcement learning. Nature **518**, 529–533 (2015)
19. Ocana, J.M.C., Capobianco, R., Nardi, D.: An overview of environmental features that impact deep reinforcement learning in sparse-reward domains. J. Artif. Intell. Res. **76**, 1181–1218 (2023)
20. Pattanaik, A., Tang, Z., Liu, S., Bommannan, G., Chowdhary, G.: Robust deep reinforcement learning with adversarial attacks. In: Proceedings of the 17th International Conference on Autonomous Agents and MultiAgent Systems, AAMAS '18, pp. 2040–2042. International Foundation for Autonomous Agents and Multiagent Systems, Richland (2018)
21. Pérez-Dattari, R., Celemin, C., Ruiz-del-Solar, J., Kober, J.: Continuous control for high-dimensional state spaces: an interactive learning approach. CoRR abs/1908.05256 (2019). http://arxiv.org/abs/1908.05256
22. Raffin, A., Hill, A., Gleave, A., Kanervisto, A., Ernestus, M., Dormann, N.: Stable-baselines3: reliable reinforcement learning implementations. J. Mach. Learn. Res. **22**(268), 1–8 (2021). http://jmlr.org/papers/v22/20-1364.html
23. Schlereth-Groh, B., Kolagari, R.T., Schmid, U.: XAIRob - an explainable-AI-based relative robustness measure for object detection. Deutsche Jahrestagung für Künstliche Intelligenz (2025)
24. Schulman, J., Wolski, F., Dhariwal, P., Radford, A., Klimov, O.: Proximal policy optimization algorithms (2017). ArXiv:abs/1707.06347
25. Selvaraju, R.R., Das, A., Vedantam, R., Cogswell, M., Parikh, D., Batra, D.: Grad-CAM: visual explanations from deep networks via gradient-based localization. Int. J. Comput. Vision **128**, 336–359 (2016)
26. Silver, D., et al.: Mastering the game of go without human knowledge. Nature **550**, 354–359 (2017)
27. Ye, Z., Milani, S., Gordon, G.J., Fang, F.: LICORICE: label-efficient concept-based interpretable reinforcement learning (2025). https://arxiv.org/abs/2407.15786

Can We Predict LLM Reasoning Failures? Structural Predictability of Modal and Conditional Inference Errors

Fatemeh Shahrokhshahi(✉) and Farzan Mohammadi

Department of Computer Engineering, Istanbul Aydin University, Istanbul, Turkey
fatemehshahrokhshahi@stu.aydin.edu.tr

Abstract. Large language models fail systematically on modal and conditional reasoning tasks, yet whether such failures are foreseeable remains unexplored. Selective prediction, the ability to abstain when a prediction is likely wrong, has been studied for factual NLP tasks but not for structured logical reasoning. We investigate whether LLM failures on seven modal and conditional inference patterns are predictable from the structural properties of reasoning problems, without relying on model outputs. Using 3,776 inference instances across nine models and three prompting strategies, we train an external classifier to predict per-instance failure from input-side features. Leave-one-pattern-out cross-validation reveals substantial variation in predictability: AUCROC ranges from 0.69 to 0.93, with patterns involving "must" operators being most predictable. We further show that targeted prompting (LogiCue), while reducing overall failures substantially, makes remaining failures structurally harder to predict. These findings suggest that input-side and output-side reliability mechanisms serve complementary roles in LLM reasoning pipelines.

Keywords: Selective prediction · Modal reasoning · LLM reliability · Learning with abstention · Logical inference · LLM reasoning · Modal logic · Uncertainty quantification · Failure prediction

1 Introduction

Large language models exhibit systematic failures on logical reasoning tasks involving modal operators such as "must" and "might" and conditional constructions [1]. Even frontier-scale models answer incorrectly on well-formed inference problems where the logically correct answer is unambiguous. This is not a fringe observation: recent surveys confirm that significant challenges remain in logical question answering and logical consistency, with conditional and modal reasoning explicitly identified as an important open frontier [12].

Recent work has proposed targeted prompting strategies, such as LogiCue [2,3], that substantially reduce these failures through pattern-specific metacognitive cues. However, improving average accuracy alone is insufficient

D. Wolter and G. Schwalbe (Eds.): KI 2026, LNAI 16830, pp. 317–323, 2027.
https://doi.org/10.1007/978-3-032-32335-4_29

for reliable deployment. In safety-critical applications, knowing *when* a model is likely to fail matters as much as improving how often it succeeds. Existing work on LLM self-assessment shows models are often poorly calibrated about their own confidence [10,11].

Selective prediction [5] addresses this by enabling systems to abstain when failure is likely. Recent work demonstrated effective selective prediction for factual NLP tasks [7,9] and visual question answering [8]. However, logical reasoning presents a fundamentally different challenge: failures are systematic, not random, and tied to specific inference types. This raises a natural question: can we predict which reasoning problems will cause failure *before* querying the model at all?

We investigate this question using a controlled dataset of modal and conditional inference instances. Our contributions are: (1) We demonstrate that LLM reasoning failures are structurally predictable, with AUCROC reaching 0.93 on the most predictable patterns. (2) We identify which patterns are most and least foreseeable, revealing a clear relationship between operator type and predictability. (3) We show that prompting method critically affects failure predictability: LogiCue reduces failures but makes remaining failures structurally harder to predict.

2 Background and Related Work

Modal and Conditional Reasoning. Holliday et al. [1] identified systematic failures on modal and conditional inference across a wide range of models, introducing a benchmark of seven challenging patterns. Shahrokhshahi et al. [2] extended this with the LogiCue framework, achieving 82.8% accuracy vs. 31.9% zero-shot across nine models. Chain-of-thought prompting [16] partially addresses reasoning failures but does not solve the underlying predictability problem. Broader surveys [12,13] confirm these failures are systematic rather than incidental.

Selective Prediction. The selective prediction paradigm [5,6] enables systems to withhold predictions when confidence is low. Traditional uncertainty quantification is computationally prohibitive for LLMs [14], motivating black-box approaches. Schönwälder et al. [7] train an external rejector on past LLM outputs using text embeddings, achieving AUCROC 0.67–0.71 on factual tasks. Xin et al. [9] first applied selective prediction to NLP tasks. Zhang and Wang [8] apply conformal prediction to visual question answering post-hoc.

Our work differs in two respects. First, we predict failure from *input structure alone*, before any model query, whereas Schönwäder et al. require past model outputs. Second, we study *logical reasoning* rather than factual retrieval: models fail not from lack of knowledge but from consistently applying incorrect inference rules. This consistency is precisely what makes structural prediction viable, and what makes the post-prompting breakdown of predictability surprising and worth studying.

3 Methodology

3.1 Dataset

We use the LogiCue dataset [2,3], comprising 3,776 instances across seven patterns originally identified by Holliday et al. [1]: Modus Tollens with "must" (MTmu) and "might" (MTmi), Disjunctive Syllogism with "must" (DSmu) and "might" (DSmi), Contraposition (CT), Antecedent Strengthening defeasible (ASd), and Complex Modus Ponens (CMP). Each pattern contains 20 instances evaluated across nine models (GPT-5, Claude Sonnet 4.5, Claude Haiku 4.5, DeepSeek Reasoner, Gemini 2.0 Flash, Gemma3 12B, LLaMA 3.2 3B, Phi-4, Qwen 2.5 7B) under three prompting strategies: zero-shot, chain-of-thought [16], and LogiCue. The correct answer is "no" for all seven patterns, reflecting logically invalid or defeasible inferences that models systematically tend to accept.

3.2 Feature Extraction

We extract 20 structural features from each problem text without accessing model outputs. Features cover: **modal operators** (counts of "must", "might", "could", "likely", "necessarily", negated modals); **negation** ("not", contracted forms, "no", "never"); **conditionals** ("if", "then", "unless", "only if", nested conditional indicator); **surface features** (word count, sentence count, disjunctive markers); and **question type** (binary indicators for "does it follow", "is it likely", "must it be", "can we infer"). We also include prompting method (0/1/2) and model scale (small/medium/large, 0/1/2).

To illustrate, consider this DSmu instance: *"From 'Either the book is on the shelf or it must be resting on the table' together with 'It's not the case that the book must be resting on the table', can we infer 'The book is on the shelf'?"* The correct answer is *no*, yet GPT-5 answers *yes* under zero-shot prompting. Key features: `modal_must`=2, `disj_count`=2, `neg_total`=1. The co-occurrence of double "must" with disjunctive markers is the structural signature the rejector learns, consistent with DSmu's AUCROC of 0.935.

3.3 Rejector Training and Evaluation

We train Logistic Regression, Random Forest (200 trees), Gradient Boosting (200 estimators), and SVM (RBF kernel) classifiers to predict binary correctness from the extracted features alone, across all nine models jointly. We evaluate with leave-one-pattern-out cross-validation: train on six patterns, test on the held-out seventh. This tests generalisation across reasoning types, a more demanding setup than standard k-fold. Following Schönwälder et al. [7], we report AUCROC as the threshold-agnostic primary metric. Table 1 (left) reports the best-performing classifier per pattern; the right side uses Random Forest consistently to enable fair cross-pattern comparison of prompting effects. Code and trained models are available at [4].

Table 1. Left: Per-pattern predictability (leave-one-pattern-out CV), sorted by AUCROC. Best classifier per pattern: LR = Logistic Regression, RF = Random Forest, SVM, GB = Gradient Boosting. Fail% = incorrect responses across all nine models. Right: failure AUCROC by prompting method (Random Forest, Random Forest); ZS = Zero-Shot, CoT = Chain-of-Thought. Values below 0.50 indicate below-random predictability.

Per-Pattern				Failure AUCROC by Prompting		
Pattern	Fail%	AUCROC	Clf	ZS	CoT	LogiCue
DSmu	69.6	0.935	LR	.76	.41	.43
MTmu	70.4	0.907	RF	.75	.62	.49
CT	78.2	0.840	LR	.41	.78	.16
MTmi	40.2	0.765	SVM	.58	.47	.12
DSmi	28.3	0.762	LR	.47	.48	.40
CMP	54.6	0.691	GB	.47	.57	.58
ASd	10.7	0.685	LR	.54	.65	.58

4 Results

4.1 Overall Predictability

Mean leave-one-pattern-out AUCROC scores are 0.78 (Logistic Regression), 0.77 (Gradient Boosting and Random Forest), and 0.74 (SVM), well above the random baseline of 0.50. These are competitive with Schönwälder et al. [7] (0.67–0.71 on factual tasks) despite our strictly more demanding cross-pattern evaluation and zero-query setup.

4.2 Per-Pattern Predictability

Table 1 (left) and Fig. 1 show per-pattern results. Patterns involving "must" operators (DSmu, MTmu) are most predictable (AUCROC > 0.90), consistent with LLMs systematically overgeneralising Boolean logic to modal contexts [1]: this flaw produces a highly consistent error signature across models and instances, detectable from input structure alone. CT, despite the highest failure rate (78.2%), is also well predictable (AUCROC 0.84) because contraposition errors arise from a single uniform confound, models consistently treat "If P then Q" as equivalent to "If Q then P", producing a structurally regular failure regardless of surface content. CMP and ASd show lower predictability for distinct reasons: CMP involves nested probabilistic reasoning that produces structurally irregular failures with no dominant feature, while ASd's 10.7% failure rate provides insufficient training signal for the rejector to learn a reliable decision boundary.

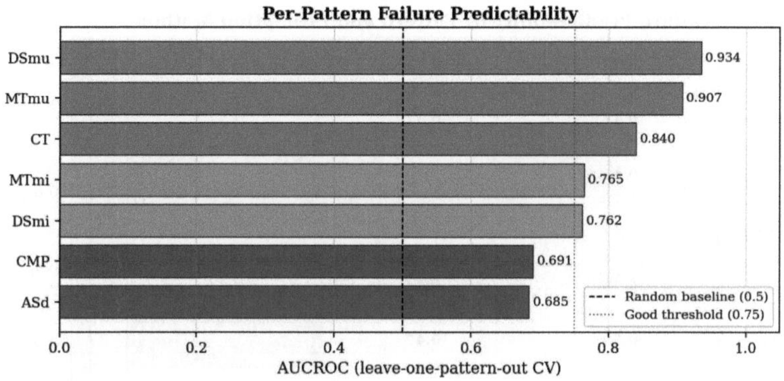

Fig. 1. Per-pattern AUCROC (leave-one-pattern-out CV). Green ≥0.80, orange 0.70–0.80, red <0.70. Dashed line: random baseline (0.50). (Color figure online)

4.3 Effect of Prompting Method

Table 1 (right) and Fig. 2 show AUCROC by pattern and prompting method. LogiCue substantially reduces failures (82.8% accuracy vs. 31.9% zero-shot) but makes remaining failures structurally harder to predict. For CT, AUCROC drops from 0.41 to 0.16; for MTmi, from 0.58 to 0.12. Values below 0.50 indicate that LogiCue failures are *anti-correlated* with structural features: the failures that survive targeted prompting do not follow the same structural patterns as baseline failures. A plausible interpretation is that LogiCue's pattern-specific cues suppress the most structurally regular failure modes, leaving only atypical edge cases that do not fit the learned rejection boundary. This suggests a complementary role for output-side abstention mechanisms to catch these unpredictable residual failures that structural features alone cannot anticipate.

4.4 Feature Importance

Prompting method dominates (importance 0.392), followed by word count (0.128) and model scale (0.122). Among text features, `modal_must` (0.036) and `neg_total` (0.034) contribute most. The dominance of prompting method confirms that *how* a model is prompted is more predictive of failure than structural problem content, reinforcing prompt selection as a first-order reliability lever in deployment.

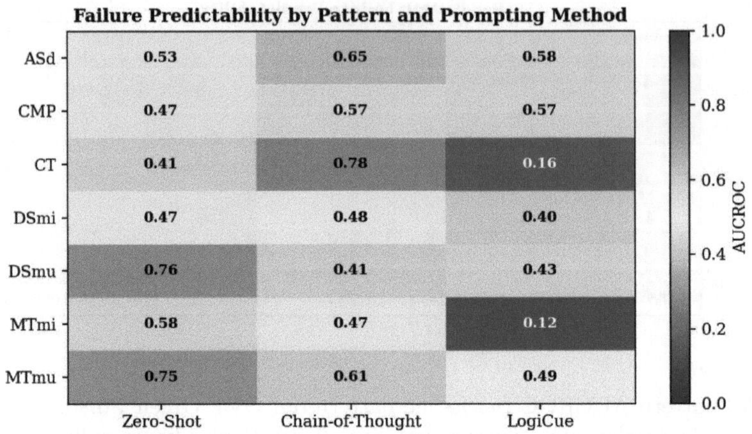

Fig. 2. Failure predictability by pattern and prompting method. Red cells reveal that LogiCue makes residual failures structurally harder to anticipate. (Color figure online)

5 Discussion and Conclusion

LLM reasoning failures on modal and conditional inference are not uniformly unpredictable. A simple logistic regression on structural features achieves mean AUCROC 0.78 across pattern types, matching or exceeding more complex selective prediction systems on factual tasks. Predictability is driven by structural regularity of the failure mode, not failure frequency: CT (78.2% failure rate, AUCROC 0.84) is more predictable than ASd (10.7%, AUCROC 0.69). Deployers cannot rely on failure rate alone to assess predictability; selective prediction systems should be evaluated per reasoning type rather than aggregated across tasks.

The most significant finding is the interaction between prompting and predictability. Recent work shows that high accuracy does not guarantee reliable uncertainty estimation in LLMs [15]. Our results extend this to structural predictability: LogiCue's effectiveness comes at the direct cost of predictability of residual errors. This motivates a **two-stage reliability framework**: *Stage 1* uses targeted prompting to eliminate structurally predictable failures; *Stage 2* applies output-side abstention [7] to handle the unpredictable residual that survives Stage 1. Prior work on LLM self-assessment confirms models cannot reliably signal these residual failures themselves [10, 11], reinforcing the need for external mechanisms at Stage 2.

Limitations. Our features rely on surface statistics; richer representations (parse trees, embeddings) may improve predictability for CMP and ASd. The non-textual features dominate, raising questions about deployment settings where method and model are fixed. Additionally, our dataset covers seven specific inference patterns; whether these findings generalise to other forms of logical reasoning such as syllogistic or counterfactual inference remains an open question.

Conclusion. Using leave-one-pattern-out cross-validation on 3,776 instances across nine models and three prompting strategies, we showed failure predictability varies from AUCROC 0.69 to 0.93, with "must"-involving patterns most foreseeable. Targeted prompting reduces failures but creates structurally unpredictable residuals, suggesting input-side and output-side reliability mechanisms serve complementary roles. Future work should explore richer features and integration of dual-stage selective prediction into safety-critical reasoning pipelines.

References

1. Holliday, W.H., Mandelkern, M., Zhang, C.E.: Conditional and modal reasoning in large language models. In: EMNLP, pp. 3800–3821 (2024)
2. Shahrokhshahi, F., Mohammadi, F., Sonmez, F.: LogiCue: targeted prompting for improved modal and conditional reasoning in LLMs. Procedia Comput. Sci. **275**, 484–492 (2026)
3. Shahrokhshahi, F.: LogiCue: code and dataset repository (2025). https://github.com/fatemeshahrokhshahi/LogiCue
4. Shahrokhshahi, F.: LLM failure prediction: code and models repository (2026). https://github.com/fatemeshahrokhshahi/LLM-Failure-Prediction
5. Geifman, Y., El-Yaniv, R.: Selective classification for deep neural networks. In: , vol. 30 (2017)
6. Hendrickx, K., et al.: Machine learning with a reject option: a survey. Mach. Learn. **113**, 3073–3110 (2024)
7. Schönwälder, E., Falkenberg, C., Hartmann, C., Lehner, W.: Abstention is all you need. In: IEEE DSAA 2025 (2025)
8. Zhang, L., Wang, C.: Selective prediction for VQA via conformal calibration. In: AIEA 2025 (2025)
9. Xin, J., Tang, R., Yu, Y., Lin, J.: The art of abstention: Selective prediction and error regularization for NLP. In: ACL, pp. 1040–1051 (2021)
10. Xiong, M., et al.: Can LLMs express their uncertainty? An empirical evaluation of confidence elicitation. In: ICLR (2024)
11. Kadavath, S.: Language models (mostly) know what they know (2022). arXiv:2207.05221
12. Cheng, F., et al.: Empowering LLMs with logical reasoning: a comprehensive survey. In: IJCAI-25 (2025)
13. Xu, F.: Are large language models really good logical reasoners? A comprehensive evaluation, (2023). arXiv:2306.09841
14. Liu, X.: Uncertainty quantification and calibration in LLMs: a survey. In: KDD (2025)
15. Tao, L.: Revisiting uncertainty estimation in large language models (2025). arXiv:2505.23854
16. Wei, J.: Chain-of-thought prompting elicits reasoning in LLMs. In: NeurIPS, vol. 35 (2022)

Neuro-Symbolic Verification of LLM Outputs for Data-Sensitive Domains

Paul Sigloch[1(✉)] and Christoph Benzmüller[1,2]

[1] University of Bamberg, Bamberg, Germany
paul.sigloch@uni-bamberg.de
[2] Free University of Berlin, Berlin, Germany
christoph.benzmueller@uni-bamberg.de

Abstract. LLMs deployed in high-stakes domains face fundamental reliability challenges: hallucinations and privacy vulnerabilities create unacceptable risks when errors carry legal, financial, or safety consequences. This paper presents a validated systems architecture that combines tableaux-based input verification, actor-based fault isolation, and type-aware post-generation verification, using deterministic symbolic checks for structured claims and neural semantic similarity for free-text claims. Validated through HAIMEDA, a locally deployed medical-device damage assessment system, the architecture detects 83% of hallucinated structured entities and 72% of semantic fabrications while reducing report creation time by 30%, demonstrating that neuro-symbolic architectures can provide principled safeguards for LLM deployment in data-sensitive domains.

Keywords: Neuro-symbolic AI · LLM verification · Formal verification · Trustworthy AI · Hybrid AI · Actor model · AI system architecture

1 Introduction

Large language models (LLMs) perform strongly across many tasks, yet their deployment in high-stakes domains remains challenging. Hallucinations, i.e., confidently generated but factually unsupported content, occur at rates of 3% to 10% even in state-of-the-art models [12,13]. In professional settings such as medical diagnosis, legal review, and regulatory affairs, where errors carry legal, financial, or safety consequences, such failure rates are unacceptable.

Beyond accuracy, many data-sensitive workflows cannot rely on cloud-based APIs due to regulatory, institutional, or externally imposed restrictions on data transmission [7,14]. Even when GDPR-compliant data processing agreements are available, confidentiality duties and contractual obligations arising from medical-legal expert practices may still preclude external transmission. Although retrieval-augmented generation (RAG) and chain-of-thought prompting improve reliability, they do not provide the guarantees required for high-stakes workflows. A more principled approach requires integrating complementary AI paradigms.

D. Wolter and G. Schwalbe (Eds.): KI 2026, LNAI 16830, pp. 324–331, 2027.
https://doi.org/10.1007/978-3-032-32335-4_30

Hybrid AI systems address this gap by combining neural methods, which excel at pattern recognition and natural language processing, with symbolic methods that provide explicit reasoning and verifiable guarantees [9]. Despite the growing recognition of this potential, there is still a lack of validated end-to-end verification architectures for locally deployed LLM systems in data-sensitive domains [3].

This paper makes two technical contributions for verifiable LLM deployment in data-sensitive domains. First, we propose a verification architecture for LLM-assisted generation in data-sensitive domains, combining tableaux-based input validation, actor-based fault isolation, and a type-aware post-generation verification method that uses deterministic symbolic checks for structured claims and semantic similarity scoring for free-text claims. Second, we validate this architecture through HAIMEDA, a locally deployed medical device assessment reporting system that demonstrates strong detection of unsupported content and measurable improvements to workflow. The full architectural details, complete validation procedure, and extended evaluation are available in the extended online version [22].

2 Related Work

Research relevant to hybrid verification of LLM-generated content builds on three areas: neuro-symbolic architectures, hallucination detection methods, and output verification systems.

Neuro-symbolic integration combines neural learning with symbolic reasoning [9]. Representative frameworks such as Logic Tensor Networks [2] and DeepProbLog [16] embed logic into differentiable or probabilistic pipelines, but they require architecture changes or joint training, making them less suitable as external verification layers for pretrained LLMs.

For hallucination detection, self-consistency methods [24] measure agreement across sampled responses, while retrieval-augmented verification [8] cross-references outputs against external knowledge. Both approaches can inherit distributional biases from the models they verify [12,13]. Runtime guardrails such as Guardrails AI [5] and NeMo Guardrails [19] enforce format and policy checks. Similarly, domain-specific systems such as TrustKG [4] demonstrate verification in specialized contexts. However, these approaches are typically point solutions rather than generalizable architectural patterns. Notably, none combines formal input verification with type-aware semantic post-processing into a complete architecture that can be deployed under strict data-sovereignty constraints.

3 Verification Architecture and Design Rationale

Deploying LLMs in data-sensitive domains raises verification challenges that guided the design of the proposed architecture. Input validation benefits from decidable guarantees before committing to costly inference. Output verification requires mechanisms for both symbolic and neural analysis, ideally with fault isolation to prevent cascading failures. Privacy considerations in regulated domains often necessitate local deployment rather than cloud-based APIs. Our architecture addresses these challenges by combining tableaux-based verification for input constraints, actor-model concurrency for fault-isolated parallel processing, and neuro-symbolic integration for output verification.

The architecture is guided by four design principles: local-first processing for data sovereignty [14], modular separation of symbolic and neural components [18], actor-based fault isolation with functional immutability for robustness [1,11], and type-aware claim verification, i.e., deterministic symbolic checks for structured claims and neural semantic checks for free-text claims [9].

3.1 Tableaux Logic for Input Verification

In workflows for report generation in data-sensitive domains, input validation is a consistency problem over interacting constraints. Report sections have different requirements: some are narrative, some follow a strict schema, and some carry legally consequential obligations. This variability requires a mechanism that can express cumulative obligations and alternative sufficiency paths within one declarative scheme.

Tableaux methods decompose formulas into conjunctive (α) obligations that must all hold, and disjunctive (β) branches that represent admissible alternatives. For propositional and decidable fragments, this yields terminating, sound and complete procedures [23]. The architecture encodes validation as a configurable hierarchy: *core conditions* $\mathcal{C}$ evaluate atomic predicates such as metadata presence or title quality; *meta conditions* express set-theoretic relationships over condition groups; and *aggregate conditions* compute statistics over condition attributes. Let $\mathcal{C}_{pos}$ collect conditions whose observed satisfaction state matches their expected state, and let $\mathcal{C}_{neg}$ collect the remaining polarity mismatches. A mandatory-consistency gate checks $(\mathcal{C}_{req} \cap \mathcal{C}_{eval}) \subseteq \mathcal{C}_{pos}$, i.e., all evaluated required conditions must match their expected state, while an aggregate rule bounds mismatch via $|\mathcal{C}_{neg}| \leq \tau$. Together, these condition types, dependency checks, and gating rules are combined into a single validation algorithm described in full in the extended online version [22].

Example: Context-Sufficiency Gate. As a concrete example from medical-device assessment, before generating the section that describes the damage, the system checks whether the input provides sufficient grounding to avoid hallucinated device specifics. A meta condition c_{ready} accepts two structurally distinct evidence combinations:

$$\varphi_{c_{\text{ready}}} \equiv \left(c_{\text{dev\_type}} \wedge c_{\text{serial}} \wedge c_{\text{category}}\right) \vee \left(c_{\text{category}} \wedge c_{\text{damage\_desc}} \wedge c_{\text{party}}\right),$$

where the left disjunct captures full technical identification and the right captures legally sufficient narrative grounding. The tableau opens one branch per disjunct. If the serial number is absent, the first branch fails, but the second can still satisfy c_{ready} if the narrative evidence is sufficient. Generation is blocked only if both branches fail. This avoids enumerating all admissible field combinations procedurally and illustrates how α/β-decomposition maps directly to set intersection and union over condition identifiers.

3.2 Type-Aware Post-Processing Verification

LLMs may produce text that satisfies formatting constraints while lacking source support [13]. Neural self-verification is unreliable because it can inherit the same distributional biases that produce hallucinations [12]. The architecture therefore applies a type-dependent strategy. Structured entities such as dates, identifiers, and numeric values undergo symbolic pattern matching for deterministic verification. Semantic content is assessed with a five-metric similarity scheme combining TF-IDF similarity, domain-specific semantic similarity, normalized Euclidean similarity, token overlap, and keyword overlap. Multilingual sentence embeddings [20] support the semantic component. Inter-metric agreement yields a confidence score. Bidirectional comparison detects two failure modes: *hallucinations* (output entities unsupported by input) and *missing content* (input entities absent from output). Detected discrepancies trigger interactive corrections.

For example, if the source contains `BF-1HTJ0` and `2024-11-03`, while the generated output contains `BF-1HTJO` and `03.11.2024`, symbolic matching accepts the date as format-equivalent but flags the identifier mismatch deterministically. Statement-level claims are evaluated using the five-metric scheme with unresolved cases forwarded for manual oversight.

4 HAIMEDA: System Instantiation

Medical device damage assessment combines PII, health-related data, and legally consequential documentation, making it a representative data-sensitive workflow. HAIMEDA (Hybrid AI for Medical Device Assessment) instantiates the proposed architecture in this setting. While cloud APIs can be made GDPR-compliant via data-processing agreements [7], this case is constrained more strictly. HAIMEDA was developed in collaboration with a domain expert who is a publicly appointed and sworn expert witness and a certified medical device engineer. This expert works under statutory and contractual confidentiality obligations. Requirements arising from the Medical Devices Regulation [6], its German implementing act [10], and contracts with commissioning authorities therefore make local-first processing a deployment requirement rather than a preference.

4.1 System Architecture

HAIMEDA is coordinated by a central orchestration layer that runs generation and verification in fault-isolated workers. The verification workflow centers on the interaction between two core modules. The *Report Authoring Module* (RAM) handles report generation through structured templates and incorporates verification feedback during revision. The *Information Integrity Verification Module* (IIVM) implements multi-stage verification through the symbolic pre-processor (Sect. 3.1) and the type-aware post-processor (Sect. 3.2). Additional modules support RAG-based information retrieval, feedback presentation, and dynamic interactive editing. Figure 1 illustrates module coordination during report creation.

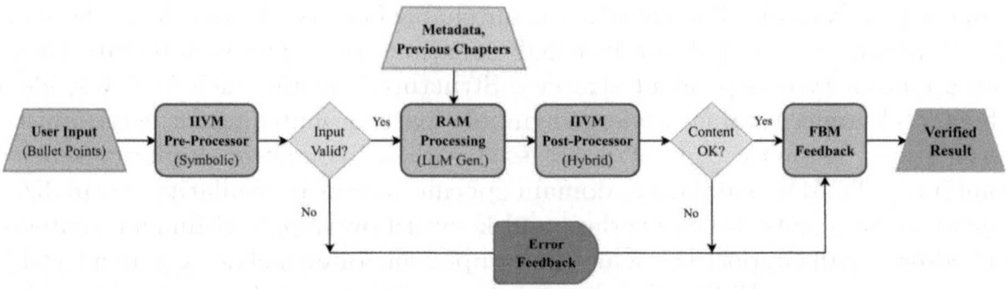

Fig. 1. HAIMEDA workflow. The symbolic pre-processor validates input, the orchestration layer gates or permits generation, the post-processor verifies output, and the Feedback Module (FBM) returns validation results to the user.

5 Evaluation

All experiments ran on consumer hardware representative of deployment conditions: AMD Ryzen 9 5900X with 64 GB of RAM, and an NVIDIA RTX 4090 with 24 GB of VRAM. Content generation used a fine-tuned `Llama3- DiscoLeo-Instruct- 8B` variant that was trained on 899 historical assessment reports, all on local hardware. The IIVM was evaluated over 100 runs per component using three test suite categories: correct statements serving as negative controls, deliberately hallucinated content with substituted entity values and plausible but incorrect statements, and versions with critical information removed. Ground truth was established through manual annotation against the source documents.

Practical utility was assessed together with the domain expert through a controlled task-timing comparison [21]: three standardized assessments were completed using HAIMEDA and three without it. Standardization was achieved by selecting comparable cases, which were evaluated using uniform assessment templates defined by the domain expert. The scope of the measurement included content writing, document-based research, and final review. Unaffected activities, such as on-site inspection and stakeholder communication, were excluded. The 30% reduction in total productive time reflects the mean across the six timed assessments. Content writing time decreased by 50%, document-based research by 33%, and final review time doubled. These findings align with previous studies demonstrating that generative AI can significantly enhance the productivity of writing-intensive tasks, while necessitating human verification and integration efforts to ensure professional-grade output [15,17].

5.1 Verification Effectiveness

Table 1 reports the component-wise detection rates for unsupported and missing content across the verification pipeline, highlighting the complementarity of symbolic and semantic methods. Here, "consensus similarity" refers to the multi-metric semantic verification scheme described in Sect. 3.2.

Table 1. IIVM verification performance across component types, showing detection rates for hallucinated and missing content based on 100 test runs per component.

Component	Method	Hallucinated	Missing
Preprocessing	Tableaux logic	—	100%
Entities	Regex patterns	83%	90%
Phrases	Semantic rules	76%	90%
Statements	Consensus similarity	72%	65%

Overall, the results support the type-aware design, whereby symbolic checks provide deterministic coverage when constraints are formalizable, while neural similarity extends verification to unconstrained text [12,13]. However, this broader semantic coverage comes at a latency cost: while symbolic preprocessing stays below 20 ms, statement verification averages 16.6 s for chapters of about 600 words. This discrepancy reflects the greater difficulty of verifying semantically unconstrained text. Structured entities are discrete and can often be matched exactly. In contrast, hallucinated statements may be paraphrased, appear plausible in context, or be only partially supported. Detecting omissions is even more difficult because the verifier must infer the absence of expected content from weak similarity rather than from an explicit contradiction.

The observed performance depends on domain-specific resources, regex patterns, and threshold calibration for statement-level scoring. Since no dedicated ablation study was conducted, the evaluation targets integrated system utility rather than the effects of isolated components. Nevertheless, the component-wise results support the usefulness of the type-aware split, as rule-only checks cannot reliably cover free-text statements, whereas embedding-only verification lacks the exactness guarantees required for structured fields such as identifiers and dates.

6 Conclusion

This paper presented a neuro-symbolic architecture with a type-aware verification approach for LLM-assisted generation in data-sensitive domains. The principled decomposition assigns symbolic methods to constraint checking and hybrid neuro-symbolic methods to semantically unconstrained content, enabling fault isolation and locally deployable quality control pipelines. The HAIMEDA instantiation demonstrates the practicality of this decomposition in a regulated professional workflow. It detects 83% of hallucinated structured entities and 72% of semantic hallucinations while reducing report creation time by 30%. Beyond detection rates, the architecture transforms verification signals into actionable feedback that facilitates interactive report revision.

Future work should evaluate its transferability to legal and financial settings, conduct ablation studies over alternative constraint engines and similarity backends, and assess whether larger, locally deployable models reduce the verification burden or if the need for guardrail architectures remains unchanged.

References

1. Armstrong, J.L.: Making reliable distributed systems in the presence of software errors. In: Ph.D. Thesis, Royal Institute of Technology, Stockholm, Sweden (2003). https://api.semanticscholar.org/CorpusID:28795665
2. Badreddine, S., d'Avila Garcez, A., Serafini, L., Spranger, M.: Logic tensor networks. Artif. Intell. **303**, 103649 (2022). https://doi.org/10.1016/j.artint.2021.103649
3. Besold, T.R., et al.: Neural-symbolic learning and reasoning: a survey and interpretation. In: Hitzler, P., Sarker, M.K. (eds.) Neuro-Symbolic Artificial Intelligence: The State of the Art, Frontiers in Artificial Intelligence and Applications, vol. 342, pp. 1–51. IOS Press (2021). https://doi.org/10.3233/FAIA210348
4. Chudasama, Y., Huang, H., Purohit, D., Vidal, M.E.: Toward interpretable hybrid ai: integrating knowledge graphs and symbolic reasoning in medicine. IEEE Access **13**, 39489–39509 (2025). https://doi.org/10.1109/ACCESS.2025.3529133
5. Dong, Y., et al.: Building guardrails for large language models (2024). https://arxiv.org/abs/2402.01822
6. European Parliament and Council of the European Union: Regulation (eu) 2017/745 of the european parliament and of the council of 5 april 2017 on medical devices, amending directive 2001/83/ec, regulation (ec) no 178/2002 and regulation (ec) no 1223/2009 and repealing council directives 90/385/eec and 93/42/eec (text with eea relevance) (2017). http://data.europa.eu/eli/reg/2017/745/2017-05-05, consolidated version
7. European Union: Regulation (EU) 2016/679 of the European Parliament and of the Council (General Data Protection Regulation) (2016). http://data.europa.eu/eli/reg/2016/679/oj, oJ L 119, 4.5.2016
8. Gao, L., et al.: RARR: researching and revising what language models say, using language models. In: Rogers, A., Boyd-Graber, J., Okazaki, N. (eds.) Proceedings of the 61st Annual Meeting of the Association for Computational Linguistics (Volume 1: Long Papers), pp. 16477–16508. Association for Computational Linguistics, Toronto, Canada (2023). https://doi.org/10.18653/v1/2023.acl-long.910
9. Garcez, A.D., Lamb, L.C.: Neurosymbolic AI: the 3rd wave. Artif. Intell. Rev. **56**(11), 12387–12406 (2023). https://doi.org/10.1007/s10462-023-10448-w
10. German Federal Parliament: Medizinprodukterecht-Durchführungsgesetz (mpdg) (2021). https://www.gesetze-im-internet.de/mpdg/, bGBl. I S. 833, as amended by Article 15 of the Act of 20 December 2023 (BGBl. 2023 I Nr. 408)

11. Hewitt, C., Bishop, P., Steiger, R.: A universal modular actor formalism for artificial intelligence. In: Proceedings of the 3rd International Joint Conference on Artificial Intelligence, pp. 235–245. IJCAI'73, Morgan Kaufmann Publishers Inc., San Francisco, CA, USA (1973)
12. Huang, J., et al.: Large language models cannot self-correct reasoning yet (2024)
13. Ji, Z., et al.: Survey of hallucination in natural language generation. ACM Comput. Surv. **55**(12) (2023). https://doi.org/10.1145/3571730
14. Kleppmann, M., Wiggins, A., van Hardenberg, P., McGranaghan, M.: Local-first software: you own your data, in spite of the cloud. In: Proceedings of the 2019 ACM SIGPLAN International Symposium on New Ideas, New Paradigms, and Reflections on Programming and Software, pp. 154–178. Onward! 2019, Association for Computing Machinery, New York, NY, USA (2019). https://doi.org/10.1145/3359591.3359737
15. Lee, H.P.H., et al.: The impact of generative ai on critical thinking: self-reported reductions in cognitive effort and confidence effects from a survey of knowledge workers. In: Proceedings of the 2025 CHI Conference on Human Factors in Computing Systems. CHI '25, Association for Computing Machinery, New York, NY, USA (2025). https://doi.org/10.1145/3706598.3713778
16. Manhaeve, R., Dumančić, S., Kimmig, A., Demeester, T., De Raedt, L.: Neural probabilistic logic programming in deepproblog. Artif. Intell. **298**, 103504 (2021). https://doi.org/10.1016/j.artint.2021.103504
17. Noy, S., Zhang, W.: Experimental evidence on the productivity effects of generative artificial intelligence. Science **381**(6654), 187–192 (2023). https://doi.org/10.1126/science.adh2586
18. Parnas, D.L.: On the criteria to be used in decomposing systems into modules. Commun. ACM **15**(12), 1053–1058 (1972). https://doi.org/10.1145/361598.361623
19. Rebedea, T., Dinu, R., Sreedhar, M.N., Parisien, C., Cohen, J.: NeMo guardrails: a toolkit for controllable and safe LLM applications with programmable rails. In: Feng, Y., Lefever, E. (eds.) Proceedings of the 2023 Conference on Empirical Methods in Natural Language Processing: System Demonstrations, pp. 431–445. Association for Computational Linguistics, Singapore (2023). https://doi.org/10.18653/v1/2023.emnlp-demo.40
20. Reimers, N., Gurevych, I., Inui, K., Jiang, J., Ng, V.: Proceedings of the 2019 Conference on Empirical Methods in Natural Language Processing and the 9th International Joint Conference on Natural Language Processing (EMNLP-IJCNLP) (2019). Presented at the. https://doi.org/10.18653/v1/D19-1410 Sentence-BERT: Sentence embeddings using Siamese BERT-networks
21. Sauro, J., Dumas, J.S.: Comparison of three one-question, post-task usability questionnaires. In: Proceedings of the SIGCHI Conference on Human Factors in Computing Systems, pp. 1599–1608. Association for Computing Machinery, New York, NY, USA (2009). https://doi.org/10.1145/1518701.1518946
22. Sigloch, P., Benzmüller, C.: Neuro-symbolic verification of LLM outputs for data-sensitive domains (extended preprint) (2026).https://doi.org/10.48550/arXiv.2605.26942, extended arXiv preprint with full architectural, algorithmic, and evaluation details
23. Smullyan, R.M.: First-Order Logic. Dover, 1 edn. (1995)
24. Wang, X., et al.: Self-consistency improves chain of thought reasoning in language models (2023). https://arxiv.org/abs/2203.11171

A Hybrid Approach for Generating Planning Models from Texts

Teodor Stoev(✉) and Kristina Yordanova

Institute of Data Science, University of Greifswald, Greifswald, Germany
{teodor.stoev,kristina.yordanova}@uni-greifswald.de

Abstract. AI planning is a central problem in Knowledge Representation (KR), as it requires expressive action theories, structured domain models, and formal reasoning mechanisms. With the increase of domain complexity, manually building planning models becomes a tedious and error-prone task, highlighting the need for methods that can learn symbolic knowledge from unstructured data while preserving formal semantics. Recent advances in language processing, especially large language models (LLMs), promise great potential for model extraction from text. They, however, are prone to hallucination and lack the ability to validate the extracted knowledge required for formal planning and reasoning. To address the above challenges, we introduce a novel methodology for automatic extraction of formal models expressed in the Planning Domain Definition Language (PDDL) from textual instructions. Our methodology combines linguistic, statistical, symbolic and LLM-based techniques within a knowledge-driven framework. In doing so, it enables the learning of symbolic abstractions such as action schemas, type hierarchies, preconditions, and effects, while also providing an explicit mechanism for explainability by making the derivation of the final formal representation transparent and traceable. As an intermediate representation, we construct a language-independent knowledge graph, called a Situation Model (SM), which captures relational dependencies and domain constraints in a structured and reusable form. We evaluate the proposed hybrid approach by investigating syntactic and semantic correctness via AI planning, as well as validation against manually created plans from everyday-life domains, demonstrating the benefits of integrating KR techniques with LLM-based extraction.

Keywords: PDDL generation · LLMs · knowledge representation

1 Introduction

Planning models typically incorporate knowledge as precondition-effect rules to enable plan generation. However, manual modelling is often time-consuming and error-prone [23]. Textual data, particularly instructional texts, is a promising source for model learning. Despite challenges like implicit knowledge and omitted steps [4], their concise, imperative structure is preferable to richer texts [36]. Learning a model from textual instructions requires ([3] and [34]): (1) extracting action semantics, (2) learning model semantics via language grounding, (3) translating these into a computational model for

D. Wolter and G. Schwalbe (Eds.): KI 2026, LNAI 16830, pp. 332–340, 2027.
https://doi.org/10.1007/978-3-032-32335-4_31

planning, and (4) building a situation model - a knowledge graph that provides situational context and facilitates mapping the extracted structure to various formalisms.

This work presents a hybrid methodology for the automatic extraction of Planning Domain Definition Language (PDDL) models from textual instructions by combining large language models (LLMs) with linguistic and statistical approaches. Additionally, it introduces an updated, publicly available dataset containing instructions and plans for everyday activities. Finally, the study evaluates the proposed approach by directly comparing it to pure LLM baselines.

2 Related Work

Classical approaches to model extraction rely on explicit causal relations, either through manual definitions [3] or grammatical patterns in complex texts [29], assuming that causal relations are expressed within individual sentences [32]. More recent approaches combine linguistic, statistical, and ML methods to extract model elements and causal relations [2, 16, 17, 36]. With the rise of LLMs, research has shifted toward direct model generation from natural language [16]. LLMs provide access to implicit domain knowledge and cross-sentence causal relations, but often produce inaccurate planning models [13]. To address this, recent work combines LLMs with validation, feedback, reinforcement learning, or prompt-engineering techniques [12, 21, 30]. An underexplored aspect is the use of intermediate semantic representations [21, 36]. Since LLMs have shown strong performance in knowledge graph construction and augmentation [11, 38, 39], situation models (SMs) could provide a structured, language-independent representation that supports mapping to multiple planning formalisms. In contrast, many recent approaches rely on direct natural-language-to-model generation. As evaluation metrics, most works focus on syntactic and semantic correctness [12, 20, 30] or plan generation success [9, 17, 36], while plan validation is used less frequently [9, 20]. Unlike our approach, prior LLM-based methods require additional structured inputs such as domain descriptions, action specifications, initial states, or object definitions [19, 33, 37].

3 Approach

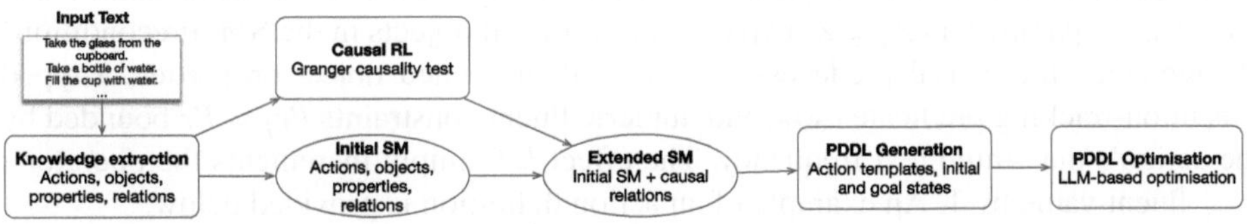

Fig. 1. Proposed methodology. RL: relation extraction; SM: situation model.

Figure 1 illustrates our PDDL generation approach. Linguistic analysis (co-reference resolution, POS tagging, and dependency parsing) is used to extract actions, objects, properties, and causal relations. These are integrated into an SM, a knowledge graph (KG) representing the domain context and enabling language-independent mapping to planning formalisms. The final PDDL model is then generated and refined using an LLM. Our pipeline first resolves text co-references, then extracts grammatical roles and syntactic relations via POS tagging and dependency parsing. Each sentence s consists of words $W_s = w_{1_s}, \ldots, w_{m_s}$. Verbs $v \in V \subset W$ correspond to actions $E \subset V$, represented in infinitive or present tense. Objects are extracted from nouns $n \in N \subset W$ and divided into direct (**DO**) and indirect (**IDO**) objects. The DO $d \in D$ are linked to actions through $dobj(e,d)$[1] and denote entities affected by the action. The IDO $i \in I$ provide spatial, directional, or instrumental information and are connected through prepositions $p(e, i_p)$. The complete object set is defined as $O := D \cup I$. Properties $c \in C$ are extracted via adjectival, nominal, or numerical modifiers and represented as $property(c,o)$.

Following the linguistic pipeline, we build the initial SM as a knowledge graph $G := (W, R)$ where nodes are words (W) and edges represent extracted relations (R). This unified graph integrates both object hierarchies and causal dependencies. First, we construct a context-aware object hierarchy to define PDDL types; we use a language taxonomy L and semantic embeddings to extract, disambiguate, and adaptively prune hypernym ("is-a") chains. Second, we include causal relations into the graph to serve as the building blocks for PDDL preconditions and effects. These include object-level property predicates (intrinsic states and indirect roles) and action-level implicit causal relations (predictive causality [7]). We identify implicit causality across five syntactic action structures (verbs with direct, indirect, mixed, multiple indirect, or no objects) by treating action sentence-frequency vectors as time series (following [35]), and applying the Granger causality test [8]. Explicit causal relations are also added using pattern matching (e.g., "if...then"). Algorithm 1 formalizes the process of SM construction.

In the next step we translate the SM into a complete planning model formalized as a tuple $M := (P, R_L, A, Z, s_0, g)$, which operationalizes directly into standard PDDL domain and problem files. The domain file captures the structural environment definitions: the predicate set P, the taxonomy hierarchy R_L (used for typing), and the set of action schemas A. The problem file specifies the concrete scenario instance: the global grounded arguments Z, the initial state s_0 (aggregating grounded property predicates and an artificial *isInit* predicate), and the goal configuration g (comprising grounded numeric execution predicates at their maximum text frequencies). Within this macro structure, the action set A is populated by individual operators derived from SM actions. Each operator is defined as a tuple $a := (e, Z_a, Pr, Ef) \in A$, where the action name e and its localized parameters $Z_a \subseteq Z$ map to relation-linked objects in the SM. Preconditions Pr aggregate the causal predecessor actions, their related object properties, a typed execution-tracking predicate e_{exec}, and numeric fluent constraints $Pr_f \subseteq Pr$ bounded by the action's maximum text frequency. The effect Ef simply increments the operator's e_{exec} fluent value by 1. An example of an action definition is provided below:

```
(:action putUtensilFurniture
  :parameters ( ?u - utensil ?f - furniture )
  :precondition
```

[1] This is the notation for a direct object relationship of the Dependency parser.

```
    (and ( >=(takeUtensil-executed ?u) 1) (isSharpUtensil ?u))
  :effect
    (and (increase (putUtensilFurniture-executed ?u ?f)1) (not (isInit))))
```

Next, a planner is used to search for a plan for the generated PDDL. If planning fails, an LLM-based optimization step iteratively corrects the domain and problem files using the planner's error logs until a valid plan emerges or an iteration limit is reached.

Algorithm 1 Construction of the situation model

Require: $L_1 := \emptyset, R_L := \emptyset, Q := \emptyset, W_1 := \emptyset, R_1 := \emptyset, G := (W_1, R_1)$ ▷ empty set of hyperonyms, isa relations, causal relations, all words, all relations and an empty situation model
Require: C, E, O, R ▷ sets of properties, actions, objects, and relations
Require: $L : (W_2, R_2)$ ▷ a language taxonomy, consisting of words and relations
$L_1, R_L \leftarrow \mathit{hypernyms}(O, L)$ ▷ the hypernyms and the hypernyms relations are extracted
for $o \in O$ **do** ▷ for each object get the isa relation
  for $r \in R_L$ **do**
    if $\exists l \in L_1$, such that $r = \mathit{isa}(o, l)$ **then**
      $R_1 \leftarrow R_1 \cup \mathit{isa}(o, l)$
    end if
  end for
end for
$W_1 \leftarrow L_1 \cup E \cup C \cup O$ ▷ the words in the SM consist of all hypernyms, actions, properties and objects
$Q \leftarrow \mathit{causal\text{-}relation}(E, O)$
$R_1 \leftarrow R_1 \cup R \cup Q$ ▷ the relations in the SM consist of the isa relation, the grammatical dependencies and the causal relations
$G \leftarrow \mathit{reduce\text{-}graph}(G)$
return G ▷ return the SM

4 Experimental Setup

We use a dataset [5] containing 83 everyday-life instructional texts from 12 domains, complete with ground-truth (GT) plans. We modified the dataset due to some inconsistencies in the annotation[2]. We excluded classical planning domains to eliminate LLM training data leakage biases. We compare against PDDL models generated by six LLMs (GPT-5.1 [31], GPT-5-mini [31], nemotron-3-nano-30b-a3b [6], qwen3.5-plus-02-15 [26], deepseek-chat-v3.1 [18], claude-sonnet-4.5 [1]) using a two-stage strategy: (1) an initial prompt dictating PDDL syntax, causal order, and formatting constraints to generate files for baseline evaluation; and (2) an iterative error-correction prompt for failing models. Successful baseline plans are then validated via CCBM (Fig. 2).

[2] The updated dataset is available on GitHub: https://github.com/DataScienceLab-HGW/A-Hybrid-Approach-for-Generating-Planning-Models-from-Texts.

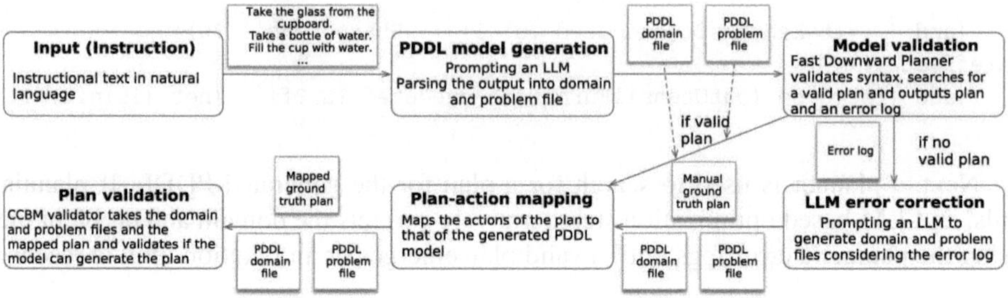

Fig. 2. Evaluation strategy for LLM-generated PDDL.

We evaluate the output across three distinct dimensions. (1) *Syntactic accuracy*: To map GT steps to successfully generated plans despite naming variations (e.g., `milk` vs. `milkBottle`), we use a fuzzy matching algorithm based on bidirectional substring containment which enforces strict one-to-one correspondence and equal object cardinality to ensure correct argument structures, yielding precision, recall, and F1-scores for actions, objects, and sequences. (2) *PDDL solvability rate*: We measure the ratio of generated models that successfully reach the goal. Our proposed approach is evaluated using the ENHSP planner[3] [28], while LLM baselines use Fast Downward (FD) [10][4] to leverage the detailed error logs required for iterative correction. (3) *Plan validation*: We analyze structural task execution using the CCBM plan validator [14,15]. Since naming variability prevents exact string matching, we use an LLM prompt[5] to automatically map and align GT steps to the newly grounded PDDL actions prior to running CCBM. Our proposed approach utilizes Stanza [25] for dependency/POS parsing, Fastcoref [24] for co-reference resolution, and WordNet [22] as *L*.

5 Results

Regarding **plan validation success** (Fig. 3), our unoptimized approach outperforms all standalone LLMs without correction step. Using iterative error correction drastically improves LLM performance, allowing Claude 4.5 to ultimately match our optimized hybrid model's peak success rate (74 validations). However, analyzing **plan lengths** against GT plans reveals that LLM baselines exhibit significant deviations (Fig. 4): shorter generated plans suggest under-specified domains (e.g., missing constraints), whereas longer ones imply missing efficient actions. Regarding **syntactic accuracy** (Fig. 5), while most LLMs match isolated actions adequately, they fail under strict sequence matching (action + objects). Baselines average $\mu = 0.14$, whereas our optimized method achieves 0.48, demonstrating superior structural alignment with GT definitions.

[3] The ENHSP planner can handle numeric fluents, and our approach is capable of generating both, such variables and the corresponding operators.

[4] Using the LAMA 2011 configuration [27].

[5] We enforce deterministic LLM decoding (`temperature: 0, top_p: 0, seed: 42`).

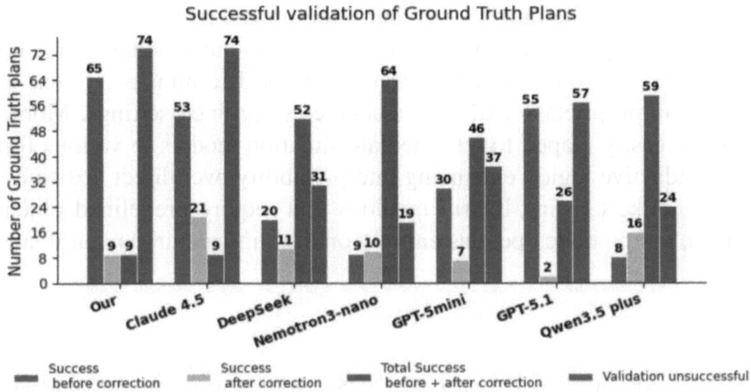

Fig. 3. Plan validation success.

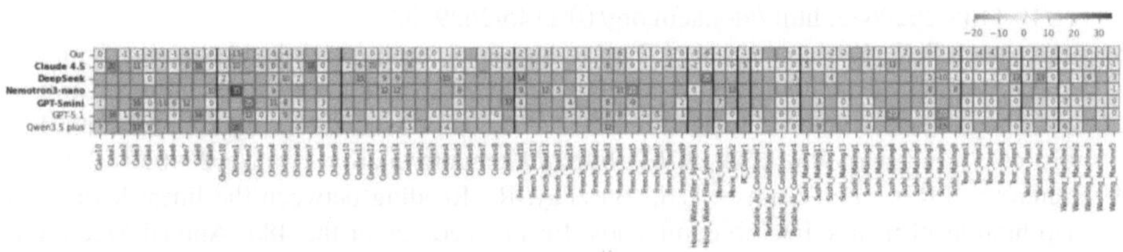

Fig. 4. Length differences: $length(\mathrm{GT}) - length(\mathrm{generated})$ for CCBM-validated models (grey: failed). Bold indicates significant deviations (Wilcoxon test, $\alpha = 0.05$).

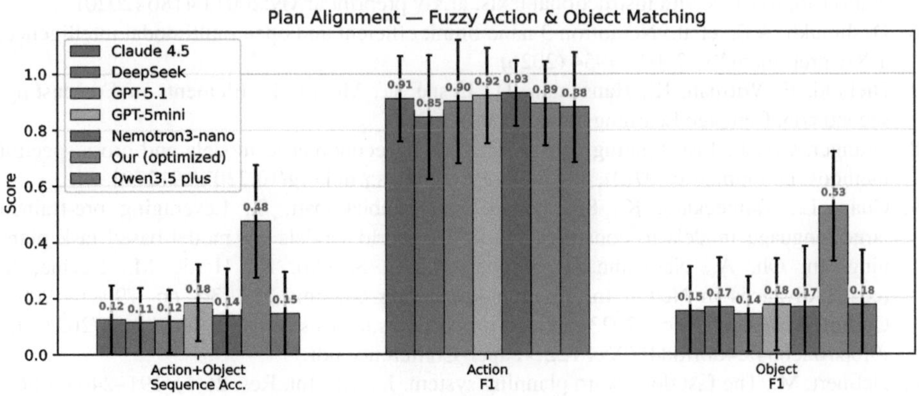

Fig. 5. Syntactic accuracy as F1-score.

6 Conclusion and Discussion

We proposed a hybrid approach combining linguistic, statistical, and LLM techniques to extract PDDL from instructions, outperforming pure LLMs in syntactic correctness.

For plan validation, Claude outperforms our unoptimized method only after a correction step; however, applying a correction mechanism to our pipeline yields equivalent performance. Crucially, our standalone framework is deterministic, faster, and more cost-effective than proprietary LLMs in resource-constrained settings. Moreover, our approach can be easily maped to intermediate situation models to various formalisms (e.g., CCBM, inductive logic), enhancing interpretability over direct text-to-code mappings. Finally, unlike existing hybrid methods that require predefined object sets or action schemas, our pipeline operates entirely on raw, unstructured natural language.

References

1. Anthropic: Introducing claude sonnet 4.5 (2025). https://www.anthropic.com/news/claude-sonnet-4-5
2. Benotti, L., Lau, T., Villalba, M.: Interpreting natural language instructions using language, vision, and behavior. ACM Trans. Interact. Intell. Syst. **4**(3), 13:1–13:22 (2014). https://doi.org/10.1145/2629632, http://doi.acm.org/10.1145/2629632
3. Branavan, S.R.K., Kushman, N., Lei, T., Barzilay, R.: Learning high-level planning from text. In: Proceedings of the 50th Annual Meeting of the Association for Computational Linguistics: Long Papers - Volume 1, pp. 126–135. ACL '12, Association for Computational Linguistics, Stroudsburg, PA, USA (2012). http://dl.acm.org/citation.cfm?id=2390524.2390543
4. Branavan, S.R.K., Zettlemoyer, L.S., Barzilay, R.: Reading between the lines: learning to map high-level instructions to commands. In: Proceedings of the 48th Annual Meeting of the Association for Computational Linguistics, pp. 1268–1277. ACL '10, Association for Computational Linguistics, Stroudsburg, PA, USA (2010). http://dl.acm.org/citation.cfm?id=1858681.1858810
5. Chowdhury, D.P., Biswas, A., Sosnowski, T., Yordanova, K.: Towards evaluating plan generation approaches with instructional texts. arXiv preprint arXiv:2001.04186 (2020)
6. Deshmukh, A.S., et al.: Nemotron 3 nano omni: efficient and open multimodal intelligence. arXiv preprint arXiv:2604.24954 (2026)
7. Diebold, F., Witman, K., Hanseman, D., Lysne, L., Moore, T.: Elements of Forecasting, second edn. Cengage Learning, USA (2000)
8. Granger, C.W.J.: Investigating causal relations by econometric models and cross-spectral methods. Econometrica **37**(3), 424–438 (1969). https://doi.org/10.2307/1912791
9. Guan, L., Valmeekam, K., Sreedharan, S., Kambhampati, S.: Leveraging pre-trained large language models to construct and utilize world models for model-based task planning. In: Oh, A., Naumann, T., Globerson, A., Saenko, K., Hardt, M., Levine, S. (eds.) Advances in Neural Information Processing Systems, vol. 36, pp. 79081–79094. Curran Associates, Inc. (2023). https://proceedings.neurips.cc/paper_files/paper/2023/file/f9f54762cbb4fe4dbffdd4f792c31221-Paper-Conference.pdf
10. Helmert, M.: The fast downward planning system. J. Artif. Int. Res. **26**(1), 191–246 (2006)
11. Jhajj, G., Zhang, X., Gustafson, J.R., Lin, F., Lin, M.P.C.: Educational knowledge graph creation and augmentation via llms. In: Sifaleras, A., Lin, F. (eds.) Generative Intelligence and Intelligent Tutoring Systems. ITS 2024. LNCS, vol. 14799, pp. 292–304. Springer, Cham (2024). https://doi.org/10.1007/978-3-031-63031-6_25
12. Kagitha, P.P., Zhu, A., Zhang, L.: Addressing the challenges of planning language generation. arXiv preprint arXiv:2505.14763 (2025)
13. Kambhampati, S.: Can large language models reason and plan? Ann. N. Y. Acad. Sci. **1534**(1), 15–18 (2024). https://doi.org/10.1111/nyas.15125

14. Kirste, T., Krüger, F.: CCBM-a tool for activity recognition using computational causal behavior models. Tech. Rep. CS-01-12, Universität Rostock, Rostock, Germany (2012)
15. Krüger, F., Nyolt, M., Yordanova, K., Hein, A., Kirste, T.: Computational state space models for activity and intention recognition. a feasibility study. PloS one **9**(11), e109381 (2014)
16. Li, R., Cui, L., Lin, S., Haslum, P.: Naruto: Automatically acquiring planning models from narrative texts. In: Proceedings of the AAAI Conference on Artificial Intelligence, vol. 38, no. 18, pp. 20194–20202 (2024). https://doi.org/10.1609/aaai.v38i18.29999
17. Lindsay, A., Read, J., Ferreira, J., Hayton, T., Porteous, J., Gregory, P.: Framer: planning models from natural language action descriptions. In: Proceedings of International Conference on Automated Planning and Scheduling (2017). https://aaai.org/ocs/index.php/ICAPS/ICAPS17/paper/view/15735
18. Liu, A., et al.: Deepseek-v3 technical report. arXiv preprint arXiv:2412.19437 (2024)
19. Liu, B., et al.: Llm+ p: empowering large language models with optimal planning proficiency. arXiv preprint arXiv:2304.11477 (2023)
20. Mahdavi, S., Aoki, R., Tang, K., Cao, Y.: Leveraging environment interaction for automated pddl translation and planning with large language models. In: Globerson, A., et al. (eds.) Advances in Neural Information Processing Systems, vol. 37, pp. 38960–39008. Curran Associates, Inc. (2024). https://proceedings.neurips.cc/paper_files/paper/2024/file/44af065477781e7f8a8589b14a62c489-Paper-Conference.pdf
21. Miglani, S., Yorke-Smith, N.: One-shot learning of pddl models from natural language process manuals. In: ICAPS'20 Workshop on Knowledge Engineering for Planning and Scheduling (2020). https://api.semanticscholar.org/CorpusID:231626460
22. Miller, G.A.: Wordnet: a lexical database for English. Commun. ACM **38**(11), 39–41 (1995)
23. Nguyen, T.A., Kambhampati, S., Do, M.: Synthesizing robust plans under incomplete domain models. In: Burges, C., Bottou, L., Welling, M., Ghahramani, Z., Weinberger, K. (eds.) Advances in Neural Information Processing Systems, vol. 26, pp. 2472–2480. Curran Associates, Inc. (2013). http://papers.nips.cc/paper/5120-synthesizing-robust-plans-under-incomplete-domain-models.pdf
24. Otmazgin, S., Cattan, A., Goldberg, Y.: F-coref: fast, accurate and easy to use coreference resolution. In: Buntine, W., Liakata, M. (eds.) Proceedings of the 2nd Conference of the Asia-Pacific Chapter of the Association for Computational Linguistics and the 12th International Joint Conference on Natural Language Processing: System Demonstrations, pp. 48–56. Association for Computational Linguistics, Taipei, Taiwan (2022). https://doi.org/10.18653/v1/2022.aacl-demo.6
25. Qi, P., Zhang, Y., Zhang, Y., Bolton, J., Manning, C.D.: Stanza: a python natural language processing toolkit for many human languages. In: Proceedings of the 58th Annual Meeting of the Association for Computational Linguistics: System Demonstrations, pp. 101–108 (2020)
26. Qwen Team: Qwen3.5: Towards native multimodal agents (2026). https://qwen.ai/blog?id=qwen3.5
27. Richter, S., Westphal, M., Helmert, M.: Lama 2008 and 2011. In: International Planning Competition, pp. 117–124. ICAPS Freiburg, Germany (2011)
28. Scala, E., Haslum, P., Thiébaux, S.: Heuristics for numeric planning via subgoaling (2016)
29. Sil, A., Yates, A.: Extracting strips representations of actions and events. In: Proceedings of the International Conference Recent Advances in Natural Language Processing 2011, pp. 1–8. RANLP 2011 Organising Committee, Hissar, Bulgaria (2011). http://aclweb.org/anthology/R11-1001
30. Silver, T., Dan, S., Srinivas, K., Tenenbaum, J.B., Kaelbling, L., Katz, M.: Generalized planning in pddl domains with pretrained large language models. In: Proceedings of the AAAI Conference on Artificial Intelligence, vol. 38, pp. 20256–20264 (2024)
31. Singh, A., et al.: Openai gpt-5 system card (2026). https://arxiv.org/abs/2601.03267

32. Tenorth, M., Nyga, D., Beetz, M.: Understanding and executing instructions for everyday manipulation tasks from the world wide web. In: IEEE International Conference on Robotics and Automation (ICRA), pp. 1486–1491 (2010). https://doi.org/10.1109/ROBOT.2010.5509955
33. Xie, Y., Yu, C., Zhu, T., Bai, J., Gong, Z., Soh, H.: Translating natural language to planning goals with large-language models. arXiv preprint arXiv:2302.05128 (2023)
34. Ye, J., Dobson, S., McKeever, S.: Review: situation identification techniques in pervasive computing: a review. Pervasive Mob. Comput. **8**(1), 36–66 (2012). https://doi.org/10.1016/j.pmcj.2011.01.004
35. Yordanova, K.: Discovering causal relations in textual instructions. In: Recent Advances in Natural Language Processing, pp. 714–720. RANLP 2015 Organising Committee, Hissar, Bulgaria (2015). http://www.aclweb.org/anthology/R15-1091
36. Yordanova, K.: Extracting planning operators from instructional texts for behaviour interpretation. In: German Conference on Artificial Intelligence, pp. 215–228. Berlin, Germany (2018). https://doi.org/10.1007/978-3-030-00111-7_19
37. Zhang, T., et al.: Proc2pddl: open-domain planning representations from texts. arXiv preprint arXiv:2403.00092 (2024)
38. Zhang, Y., Chen, Z., Guo, L., Xu, Y., Zhang, W., Chen, H.: Making large language models perform better in knowledge graph completion. In: Proceedings of the 32nd ACM International Conference on Multimedia, pp. 233–242. MM '24, Association for Computing Machinery, New York, NY, USA (2024). https://doi.org/10.1145/3664647.3681327
39. Zhu, Y., et al.: LLMs for knowledge graph construction and reasoning: recent capabilities and future opportunities. World Wide Web **27**(5), 58 (2024). https://doi.org/10.1007/s11280-024-01297-w

Extended Abstracts

Efficient Time-Series Approximation with Linear Recurrent Neural Networks

Frieder Stolzenburg[1,2(✉)], Sandra Litz[1], Olivia Michael[2], and Oliver Obst[2]

[1] Harz University of Applied Sciences, Wernigerode, Germany
fstolzenburg@hs-harz.de
[2] School of Computer Science and Engineering, University of New South Wales (UNSW), Sydney, NSW, Australia
{f.stolzenburg,o.obst}@unsw.edu.au

Abstract. Linear recurrent neural networks (LRNNs) provide a simple yet powerful framework for modeling time series. Unlike traditional recurrent neural networks, LRNNs use linear activation functions and can be trained without backpropagation by solving linear equation systems. This paper summarizes their theoretical properties, learning procedure, and ability to approximate arbitrary time-dependent functions. A key contribution is a method for reducing network size using eigenvalue analysis, enabling both efficient learning and architecture optimization, which is nowadays an important topic. We demonstrate the properties and advantages of LRNNs by several case studies, among them multiple superimposed oscillators (MSO), robotic soccer (RoboCup), and stock price prediction. LRNNs outperform the previous state-of-the-art for the MSO task with a minimal number of units.

1 Introduction

Time-series modeling is essential in many domains such as forecasting, signal processing, and control systems. Recurrent neural networks (RNNs), particularly variants of networks with long short-term memory (LSTM) [6], are widely used but often require complex training procedures. Research in time-series analysis and hence the modeling dynamics of complex systems has a long tradition and remains highly active due to its crucial role in many real-world applications [9]. Among other benefits, the analysis of time series enables data compression, i.e., compact representation of time series by a function $f(t)$, and prediction of future values.

Numerous studies address these topics using RNNs. Autoregressive frameworks [1] are also common in current machine-learning applications such as large language models (LLMs). Nevertheless, usually iterative methods like backpropagation are employed for neural network learning. This is not needed for *linear recurrent neural networks* (LRNNs), i.e., the class of RNNs with linear activation, which we discuss here. Despite their simplicity, LRNNs can approximate

This paper is an extended abstract of [13], published in *Neural Computing and Applications* **37**, 27027–27055 (2025), see also https://arxiv.org/abs/1802.03308.

D. Wolter and G. Schwalbe (Eds.): KI 2026, LNAI 16830, pp. 343–346, 2027.
https://doi.org/10.1007/978-3-032-32335-4_32

arbitrary time-dependent functions $f(t)$, can be trained efficiently using simple linear algebra, and allow direct architecture reduction via eigenvalue analysis.

2 Linear Recurrent Neural Networks

An LRNN consists of neurons and connections between them. They are annotated with *weights* which are compiled into the *transition matrix* W of size $N \times N$, containing input, output and reservoir weight submatrices. An entry w_{ij} in row i and column j denotes the weight of the edge from neuron j to neuron i. The network evolves as $f(t) = W^t \cdot s$ where s is the start state. Key properties of LRNNs are (1) linear activation, (2) random input and reservoir weights, (3) only output weights are learned, and (4) the spectral radius of the reservoir is normalized to 1.

Using eigendecomposition $W = V \cdot D \cdot V^{-1}$ with column eigenvectors $v_1, \ldots, v_N$ in V and corresponding eigenvalues $\lambda_1, \ldots, \lambda_N$, the system evolves as $f(t) = x_1 {\lambda_1}^t v_1 + \cdots + x_N {\lambda_N}^t v_N$ with $x = \begin{bmatrix} x_1 \cdots x_N \end{bmatrix}^\top$ such that $x = V^{-1} \cdot s$. This can be generalized to Jordan decomposition with Jordan matrix J and arbitrary start vectors y with all nonzero entries. It can be shown that always a matrix A exists such that $f(t) = A \cdot J^t \cdot y$.

This shows that network behavior is governed by eigenvalues, in particular the eigenvalue λ with maximal absolute value (defining the spectral radius). We have (1) contraction to a singularity for $|\lambda| < 1$, (2) oscillation for $|\lambda| = 1$, and (3) exponential growth for $|\lambda| > 1$. For large t, LRNN dynamics simplify drastically: Most components vanish, the remaining dynamics lie in at most two dimensions, and the output follows an ellipse trajectory. Thus, complex high-dimensional systems reduce to simple oscillatory behavior over time.

3 Learning Procedure and Network Size Reduction

Training is performed via linear regression instead of backpropagation. Given $X = \begin{bmatrix} S(0) \cdots S(n-1) \\ R(0) \cdots R(n-1) \end{bmatrix}$ and $Y = \begin{bmatrix} S(1) & \cdots & S(n) \end{bmatrix}$, where S and R are the possibly multi-dimensional input and reservoir time series, we simply solve $W_{\text{out}} = Y \cdot X^{-1}$ to compute the output weights. This is efficient and avoids gradient-based optimization. LRNNs satisfy an approximation theorem: *Any time-dependent function $f(t)$ can be approximated arbitrarily well and learned given sufficient reservoir size.*

A major contribution of this paper is reducing network size using eigenvalue analysis. The method works follows: After training, we (1) compute the eigenvalues of W, (2) rank the Jordan components of W by relevance, (3) remove those with minimal contribution, and (4) ensure that the error remains below some threshold. This yields significantly smaller networks with sparse structure, improved generalization of time series, and faster computation. Unlike pruning methods, network size reduction is performed in a single step here.

4 Properties, Insights, and Experimental Findings

The learning procedure, even with network size reduction, is computationally efficient in $O(N^3)$. No iterative optimization is required. Therefore, it is faster than traditional RNN training. LRNNs are related to autoregressive models [1] like current large language models (LLMs), echo state networks (ESNs) [7], and state-space models [5,12]. But LRNNs uniquely combine linear learning, exact approximation, and architecture reduction.

Experiments demonstrate that LRNNs achieve high accuracy on time-series prediction, outperform traditional methods on oscillatory tasks, and learn compact representations, e.g., minimal networks. As benchmarks, (1) multiple superimposed oscillators (MSO) [8], (2) number puzzles [4], (3) robot soccer simulation [11], and (4) predicting stock prices [10] are considered.

For instance, the MSO time series is generated by summing up K (pure) sinusoids. It requires only $2K$ neurons in LRNNs, where each frequency corresponds to one eigenvalue pair. LRNNs outperform the previous state of the art for the MSO task with this minimal number of units. All experiments are performed with a program written by the authors in Octave [3], available at http://github.com/OliverObst/decorating/.

5 Conclusion

LRNNs provide a powerful alternative to traditional RNNs. Despite their simplicity, they approximate complex time-dependent functions, enable efficient training without backpropagation, and support network size reduction. Their combination of theoretical elegance and practical efficiency makes them a valuable tool for time-series analysis and dynamic system modeling. Future work will focus on extending the procedure, in particular network size reduction, to RNNs augmented with nonlinear activation, see also [2], to make an even larger class of networks more efficient.

References

1. Akaike, H.: Fitting autoregressive models for prediction. Ann. Inst. Stat. Math. **21**(1), 243–247 (1969). https://doi.org/10.1007/BF02532251.pdf
2. Brunton, S.L., Proctor, J.L., Kutz, J.N.: Discovering governing equations from data by sparse identification of nonlinear dynamical systems. Proc. Natl. Acad. Sci. U.S.A. **113**(15), 3932–3937 (2016). https://doi.org/10.1073/pnas.1517384113
3. Eaton, J.W., Bateman, D., Hauberg, S., Wehbring, R.: GNU Octave – a High-Level Interactive Language for Numerical Computations (2017). http://www.octave.org/
4. Glüge, S., Wendemuth, A.: Solving number series with simple recurrent networks. In: Ferrández de Vicente, J.M., Álvarez Sánchez, J.R., de la Paz López, F., Toledo-Moreo, F.J. (eds.) Natural and Artificial Models in Computation and Biology – 5th International Work-Conference on the Interplay between Natural and Artificial Computation, IWINAC 2013. Proceedings, Part I, LNCS, vol. 7930, pp. 412–420. Springer, Berlin, Heidelberg (2013). https://doi.org/10.1007/978-3-642-38637-4_43

5. Gu, A., Goel, K., Ré, C.: Efficiently modeling long sequences with structured state spaces. In: The International Conference on Learning Representations (ICLR) (2022). http://arxiv.org/abs/2111.00396
6. Hochreiter, S., Schmidhuber, J.: Long short-term memory. Neural Comput. **9**(8), 1735–1780 (1997). https://doi.org/10.1162/neco.1997.9.8.1735
7. Jaeger, H., Haas, H.: Harnessing nonlinearity: predicting chaotic systems and saving energy in wireless communication. Science **2**(304), 78–80 (2004). https://doi.org/10.1126/science.1091277
8. Koryakin, D., Lohmann, J., Butz, M.V.: Balanced echo state networks. Neural Netw. **36**, 35–45 (2012). https://doi.org/10.1016/j.neunet.2012.08.008
9. Lipton, Z.C., Berkowitz, J., Elkan, C.: A critical review of recurrent neural networks for sequence learning. CoRR – Computing Research Repository abs/1506.00019, Cornell University Library (2015). http://arxiv.org/abs/1506.00019
10. Litz, S.: Predicting stock prices using recurrent neural networks. WAIT – Wernigeröder Automatisierungs- und Informatiktexte 01/2020, Harz University of Applied Sciences (2020). https://doi.org/10.25673/35875
11. Michael, O., Obst, O., Schmidsberger, F., Stolzenburg, F.: Analysing soccer games with clustering and conceptors. In: Akiyama, H., Obst, O., Sammut, C., Tonidandel, F. (eds.) RoboCup 2017: Robot World Cup XXI. RoboCup 2017. LNCS, vol. 11175, pp. 120–131. Springer, Cham (2018). https://doi.org/10.1007/978-3-030-00308-1_10
12. Orvieto, A., et al.: Resurrecting recurrent neural networks for long sequences. In: Proceedings of the 40th International Conference on Machine Learning, pp. 26670–26698. ICML'23, JMLR.org, Honolulu, HI, USA (2023). https://doi.org/10.5555/3618408.3619518
13. Stolzenburg, F., Litz, S., Michael, O., Obst, O.: Efficient time-series approximation with linear recurrent neural networks: architecture learning and predictive power. Neural Comput. Appl. **37**, 27027–27055 (2025). https://doi.org/10.1007/s00521-025-11655-y

Author Index

D. Wolter and G. Schwalbe (Eds.): KI 2026, LNAI 16830, pp. 347–348, 2027.
https://doi.org/10.1007/978-3-032-32335-4

MIX
Papier aus verantwortungsvollen Quellen
Paper from responsible sources
FSC® C105338

If you have any concerns about our products,
you can contact us on
ProductSafety@springernature.com

In case Publisher is established outside the EU,
the EU authorized representative is:
Springer Nature Customer Service Center GmbH
Europaplatz 3, 69115 Heidelberg, Germany

Printed by Libri Plureos GmbH
in Hamburg, Germany